CONSUMER BEHAVIOR

CONSUMER BEHAVIOR

EIGHTH EDITION

Leon G. Schiffman

J. Donald Kennedy Chair in E-Commerce

Peter J. Tobin College of Business

St. John's University, New York City

Leslie Lazar Kanuk

Emeritus Professor of Marketing

Graduate School and University Center

City University of New York

PEARSON

Prentice Hall

Upper Saddle River, NJ 07458

Senior Editor: Bruce Kaplan
VP/Editor-in-Chief: Jeff Shelstad
Assistant Editor: Melissa Pellerano
Editorial Assistant: Danielle Rose Serra
Media Project Manager: Anthony Palmiotto
Executive Marketing Manager: Michelle O'Brien
Marketing Assistant: Amanda Fisher
Managing Editor (Production): Judy Leale
Production Editor: Theresa Festa
Production Assistant: Joe DeProspero
Permissions Supervisor: Suzanne Grappi
Manufacturing Buyer: Diane Peirano
Design Manager: Maria Lange
Designer: Michael J. Fruhbeis
Interior Design: Michael J. Fruhbeis
Cover Design: Michael J. Fruhbeis
Manager, Print Production: Christy Mahon
Composition/Full-Service Project Management: Carlisle Communications, Ltd.
Printer/Binder: R.R. Donnelley

Credits and acknowledgments borrowed from other sources and reproduced, with permission, in this textbook appear on appropriate page within text.

Pearson Prentice Hall™ is a trademark of Pearson Education, Inc.
Pearson® is a registered trademark of Pearson plc
Prentice Hall® is a registered trademark of Pearson Education, Inc.

Pearson Education LTD.
Pearson Education Singapore, Pte. Ltd
Pearson Education, Canada, Ltd
Pearson Education–Japan

Pearson Education Australia PTY, Limited
Pearson Education North Asia Ltd
Pearson Educación de Mexico, S.A. de C.V.
Pearson Education Malaysia, Pte. Ltd

10 9 8 7 6 5 4 3 2 1
ISBN: 0-13-067335-8

To Jack, Jaqui, and Alan Kanuk; Randi and Van Dauler;
and Max and Sarah

and

To Elaine, Janet, and David Schiffman; Dana and Bradley;
Eileen and Alan, Melissa and Rob; and Allison, Noah, and Reid

Brief Contents

Contents

■ PART III
CONSUMERS IN THEIR SOCIAL AND
CULTURAL SETTINGS / 327

Preface

In this eighth edition of ***Consumer Behavior,*** we examine the full range of consumer behavior within the context of the expanding influence of the high-tech global environment in which we live. Indeed, the current edition represents our own transition in writing a book that has been researched almost entirely through electronic means from a vast array of global library sources and services. We have been greatly influenced in our thinking and writing by the impact that the Internet has had on consumer information, decision making, and purchasing options. This is reflected in the substantial increase in attention that we have given to consumers' behavior on the Internet, and the importance and power of the Internet as both a *channel of information* and a *channel of distribution.*

In this new edition, we have intensified our emphasis on marketing strategy, using both a theoretical and applications-oriented approach. Always true believers in the marketing concept, we have tried our best to meet the needs of our consumers—students, marketing practitioners, and professors of consumer behavior—by providing a text that is highly readable and that clearly explains the relevant and timely concepts on which the discipline of consumer behavior is based. We

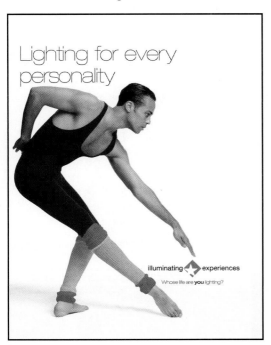

have supplemented this material with a great many real-world examples in order to demonstrate how consumer behavioral concepts are used by marketing practitioners to solve marketing problems and to develop and implement effective marketing strategies.

To make the eighth edition as useful as possible to both graduate and undergraduate students, we have sought to maintain an even balance of basic behavioral concepts, research findings, and applied marketing examples. We remain convinced that effective market segmentation provides the structure and direction for successful market practice; to this end, we have paid particular attention to revising and refining the discussion of market segmentation.

Overview of Major Changes

The text has been thoroughly updated and revised, yet substantially shortened to focus attention on critical consumer behavior concepts and to highlight the linkages between interrelated principles and processes. Some of the major changes include:

- A major focus on how the Internet has changed the way people obtain product and service information and make purchases almost anywhere in the world.

- The addition of thirty-two short cases, two per chapter, to help students learn by applying behavioral concepts to real-world business problems. These cases consider such things as product testing on the Internet, purchasing medicine online from another country, and customization.

- An enhanced global outlook that fosters a richer understanding of the dynamics of cultural differences and enhances students' appreciation of the universality of consumer behavior.

- Streamlined coverage through a slimmed-down edition designed to encourage and maintain student interest with a lively discussion of timely issues and current marketing applications.

- A comprehensive model, built on the simple model presented in the first chapter, highlighting the interrelationships between and among the concepts examined throughout the book and both simplifies and facilitates retention of the material covered.

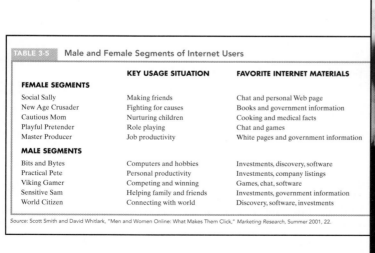

TABLE 3-5	Male and Female Segments of Internet Users	
	KEY USAGE SITUATION	**FAVORITE INTERNET MATERIALS**
FEMALE SEGMENTS		
Social Sally	Making friends	Chat and personal Web page
New Age Crusader	Fighting for causes	Books and government information
Cautious Mom	Nurturing children	Cooking and medical facts
Playful Pretender	Role playing	Chat and games
Master Producer	Job productivity	White pages and government information
MALE SEGMENTS		
Bits and Bytes	Computers and hobbies	Investments, discovery, software
Practical Pete	Personal productivity	Investments, company listings
Viking Gamer	Competing and winning	Games, chat, software
Sensitive Sam	Helping family and friends	Investments, government information
World Citizen	Connecting with world	Discovery, software, investments

Source: Scott Smith and David Whitlark, "Men and Women Online: What Makes Them Click," *Marketing Research*, Summer 2001, 22.

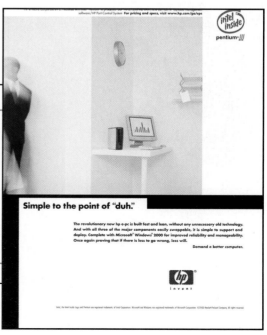

Organization of the Text

This eighth edition of *Consumer Behavior* is divided into four parts, consisting of 16 chapters. Part I provides the background and tools for a strong and comprehensive understanding of the consumer behavior principles examined throughout the rest of the book. Chapter 1, The Impact of the Digital Revolution on Consumer Behavior, sets the tone for the book. It introduces the reader to the study of consumer behavior, its diversity, its development, and the latest evolution of the marketing concept and examines how companies use past consumption behavior as the foundation for creating and keeping satisfied and profitable lifetime customers. The chapter also introduces a simple model of consumer decision making that provides a structural framework for understanding the interrelationships among the consumer behavior principles examined throughout the book. Chapter 2 provides readers with a detailed overview of the critical consumer research process and the techniques associated with consumer behavior research, including a discussion of positivist and interpretivist research methods. Chapter 3 presents a comprehensive examination of the newest insights into effective market segmentation.

Part II discusses the consumer as an individual. Chapter 4 presents an in-depth discussion of consumer needs and motivations, exploring both the rational and emotional bases of consumer actions. Chapter 5 discusses the impact of the full range of personality theories on consumer behavior and explores consumer materialism, fixated consumption, and compulsive consumption behavior. The chapter considers the related concepts of self and self-image and includes an

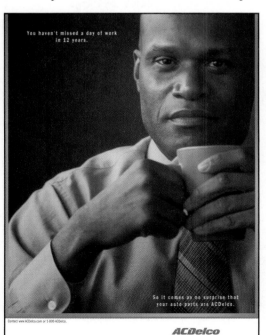

expanded discussion of virtual personality and self. Chapter 6 provides a comprehensive examination of the impact of consumer perception on marketing strategy and the importance of product positioning and repositioning. Chapter 7 examines how consumers learn and discusses behavioral and cognitive learning theories, limited and extensive information processing, and the applications of consumer involvement theory to marketing practice. Chapter 8 offers an in-depth examination of consumer attitudes. Chapter 9 demonstrates that communication is the bridge between individuals and the world and people around them, and includes a timely discussion of advertising, traditional and new media, and the effective use of persuasion.

Part III is concerned with the social and cultural dimensions of consumer behavior. It begins with a discussion of consumer reference groups (including virtual groups and virtual communities), family role orientations, and changing family lifestyles. Chapters 11 and 12 present consumers in their social and cultural milieus and discusses the emergence of the "techno class." Chapter 13 investigates the impact of societal and subcultural values, beliefs, and customs on consumer behavior. Chapter 14 concludes this part with an extensive discussion of cross-cultural marketing within an increasingly global marketplace.

Part IV explores various aspects of consumer decision making. Chapter 15 offers a comprehensive discussion of personal influence, opinion leadership, and the diffusion of innovations. Chapter 16 describes how consumers make product decisions, and expands on the increasingly important practice of relationship marketing. This section concludes with a deeper and more comprehensive model of consumer decision making, building on the simple model briefly introduced in Chapter 1, and ties together the psychological, social, and cultural concepts discussed throughout the book. It includes an extensive exploration of consumer gifting behavior and an examination of the expanding research focus on individual consumption behavior and the symbolic meanings of consumer possessions.

Supplements

The following state-of-the-art supplements package has been created to support the eighth edition of *Consumer Behavior*.

INSTRUCTOR'S RESOURCE MANUAL

This helpful teaching resource contains chapter objectives, lecture outlines, chapter summaries, answers to end-of-chapter questions and exercises, and more!

TEST ITEM FILE

Extensively revised for the eighth edition, the Test Item File contains more than 1,500 items, including multiple-choice, true-false, and essay questions that are graded for difficulty and page-referenced to the text. Also available is the new TestGen-EQ test generating software, a computerized package that allows instructors to custom design, save, and generate classroom tests. The test program permits instructors to edit, add, or delete questions from the test bank; analyze test results; and organize a database of tests and student results. This new software allows for greater flexibility and ease of use. It provides many options for organizing and displaying tests, along with a search and sort feature.

POWERPOINT SLIDES

A PowerPoint set containing more than 400 electronic slides covers key concepts and includes complete lecture notes with key figures and ads from the text. These files may be downloaded from the Prentice Hall Web site at **www.prenhall.com/ schiffman** and are also available on the Instructor's Resource CD-ROM.

INSTRUCTOR'S RESOURCE CD-ROM

One source for all supplement needs. This CD contains all the print and technology supplements on a single CD-ROM, providing the instructor with the freedom to transport the entire supplements package from office, to home, to classroom. The Instructor's Resource CD-ROM permits customization of any of the ancillaries, the printing of only the chapters or materials desired, and accessing any item from the package within the classroom.

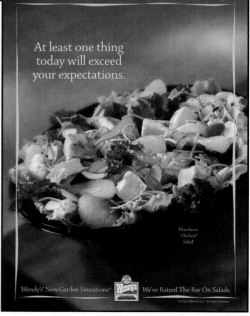

CONSUMER BEHAVIOR VIDEO LIBRARY

PH and BusinessNOW have partnered to create a completely new Consumer Behavior video library for the Eighth Edition. Using today's popular newsmagazine format, students are taken on location and behind closed doors. Each news story profiles a well-known or up-and-coming company leading the way in its industry. Teaching materials to accompany the video library are available on the companion website.

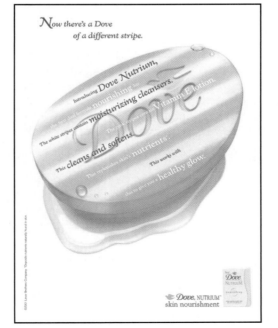

Suave® Ultimate Protection Anti-perspirant has a new look.
But still works just as well as Secret® Platinum. For less.

Suave. Don't you look smart.

Now there's a Dove
of a different stripe.

Introducing Dove Nutrium,
nourishing moisturizing cleansers.

The white stripes contain

Dove

This cleans and softens.

nutrients.

This works with

healthy glow.

Dove. NUTRIUM™
skin nourishment

WEB EXERCISES

The eighth edition also offers Web-based exercises for each chapter in the text. Located online at www.prenhall.com/schiffman, each Web question challenges students to use the Internet to resolve consumer behavior issues.

COMPANION WEBSITE:

www.prenhall.com/schiffman

Prentice Hall's acclaimed Web resource provides professors and students with a customized course Website that features a complete array of teaching and learning material. For instructors: downloadable versions of the Instructor's Resource Manual, Test Item File, and PowerPoint Slides, plus additional resources such as Internet exercises and cases. The syllabus builder enables professors to plan their own course! An interactive student Study Guide with quizzes is provided for students.

INNOVATIVE ONLINE COURSES

Standard Online Courses in WebCT, CourseCompass, and BlackBoard. No technical expertise needed! Teach a complete online course or a web-enhanced course. Professors are able to add their own course materials, take advantage of online testing and Gradebook opportunities, and utilize the bulletin board and discussion board functions. Free to students with purchase of the text.

Acknowledgments

Of the many people who have been enormously helpful in the preparation of this eighth edition of *Consumer Behavior*, we are especially grateful to our own consumers, the graduate and undergraduate students of consumer behavior and their professors, who have provided us with invaluable experiential feedback to our earlier editions.

We would also like to thank new colleagues and friends at the Tobin College of Business at St. John's University, in particular: Dean Peter Tobin and Associate Dean Nejdet Delener. Dr. Sreedhar Kavil and the St. John's Department of Marketing have provided a warm and friendly environment in which to write. Our thanks go, too, to our many friends and colleagues in the Department of Marketing at Baruch's Zicklin School of Business.

We especially would like to thank the following people who reviewed the seventh edition and offered many thoughtful comments and suggestions: Ronald J. Adams, University of North Florida; Peter Bloch, University of Missouri-Columbia; John E. Crawford, Lipscomb University; Eva M. Hyatt, Appalachian State University; Dongwook Kim, Michigan Technological University; Deanna R. D. Mader, Marshall University; Kay Palan, Iowa State University; and Stephen P. Ramocki, Rhode Island College. Fredrica Rudell of Iona College provided many useful comments about the seventh edition, and Nora Rifon of Michigan State University gave us useful advice about mind maps.

Over the years, we have received many thoughtful suggestions, insights, and highly constructive comments from the following professors: Benny Barak and Elaine Sherman, Hofstra University; Martin Topol, Pace University; Harold Kassarjian, UCLA; David Brinberg, Virginia Polytechnic Institute; Steve Gould, Baruch College; John Holmes, Simmons College; Joel Saegert, The University of Texas at San Antonio; Lewis Hershey, Eastern Missouri State College; William R. Dillon, Southern Methodist University; Havva J. Meric, East Carolina University; Ron Goldsmith, Florida State University; Richard Yalch, University of Washington; Mark Young, Winona State University; Michael Taylor, Marietta College; Daniel Johnson, Bradford University; Bob Settle, San Diego State University; Gerald Cavallo, Fairfield University; Kristina Cannon-Bonventre, Northeastern University; Kathy Petit, University of Idaho; Douglas W. Mellott, Jr., Radford University; Darvin R. Hoffman, Texas A&I; David Sheperd, University of Tennessee at Chattanooga; John T. Shaw, Providence College; Janet G. Hibbard, Eastern Kentucky University; Ron Lennon, Barry University; Jeanne Mueller, Cornell University; Charles Gulas, Wright State University; James W. Cagley, University of Tulsa; Kenneth R. Lord, Niagara University; Paul Chao, University of Northern Iowa; John H. Holmes, Skidmore College; Donna Fricke, Maine Maritime Academy; Sheri Zeigler, University of Hawaii; Christina Goulding, Wolverhampton University, United Kingdom; U. B. Bradley, London Guildhall University, United Kingdom; Adrienne Czerwin-Abbott, Dublin Institute of Technology, Ireland; and Bernard A. Delagneau, The University of Wales, Aberystwyth, United Kingdom.

Many other professors, students, and colleagues have made a contribution to our thinking; among these are Amit Srivastav, Shawn Fitzgerald, and Martha Cook of Baruch College; Mary Kay of Montclair State University; Mary Long of Pace University; and Charles McMellon of Hofstra University. Deborah Y. Cohn of Yeshiva University provided some original thinking and an interesting perspective on consumer gifting. Joyce Jenkins and Evie Reissman have provided us with unique insights into individual consumer behavior. Norma Bakke has given us important, on-site perspectives on global consumer behavior.

We would like to warmly acknowledge Alan Pollack, who has provided us with invaluable insights into legal issues on intellectual property and the marketing process. We also acknowledge Horace Phillimore of Gardmat Electronics; Ken Weinstein of First Alert Professional; Hank Edelman and Tana Edwards of Patek Philippe; Don Siebert an independent marketing consultant; Ross Copper of Arc Integrated Marketing; Lancy Herman of Mediamark Research; and Walter McCullough and Moya Amateau of Monroe Mendelsohn Research. We are grateful to the executives and staff of the following research firms for their continuous flow of interesting illustrative materials: Claritas Corporation, Simmons Marketing Research Bureau, Donnelley Marketing Information Services, and SRI International.

Our sincerest thanks go to the many people at Prentice Hall who aided and supported us in the editorial, design, and production processes of this eighth edition, specifically our editor, Bruce Kaplan, who has provided us with invaluable direction and encouragement; Theresa Festa, our ever-diligent and supportive production editor; Michelle O'Brien, our marketing manager, and her assistant, Amanda Fisher; and editorial assistant Danielle Rose Serra. We are very grateful to Melissa Pellerano, our Supplements editor; Michael Fruhbeis, our cover designer; Anthony Palmiotto, media project manager; and Donna Mulder, our copyeditor. We also want to acknowledge the careful work and detailed follow-up of the Permission Group (in particular Cheryl and Joe Besenjak, Stephanie Kwasigroch).

Finally, we would like to give very special recognition to Professor Stanley Garfunkel of CUNY and to Professor Joseph Wisenblit of Seton Hall University, for their untiring support, assistance, advice, encouragement, and, most of all, friendship.

PART ONE

Introduction

I

Chapter 1 introduces the reader to the study of consumer behavior, its diversity, its development, and the role of consumer research. It concludes with a detailed discussion of ethical considerations in marketing and consumer practices and introduces a simple model of consumer decision making. Chapter 2 provides a detailed overview of the critical research process and the techniques associated with consumer behavior research, including a discussion of positivist and interpretivist research methods. Chapter 3 presents a comprehensive examination of market segmentation and demonstrates how consumer behavior variables provide both the conceptual framework and the strategic direction for the practical segmentation of markets.

ABSOLUT LATEST.

Introduction: The Impact of the Digital Revolution on Consumer Behavior

In the futuristic thriller movie *Minority Report* that takes place in the year 2054, the hero, played by actor Tom Cruise, experiences the ultimate one-to-one marketing. As the hero passes by a billboard featuring the American Express card, the billboard becomes a hologram, presumably visible only to him, portraying his picture and personal data and urging him to use the card. He then enters a Gap store where customers are met by voices greeting them by name, asking them how they liked previous purchases, and suggesting items that they may like based on their past purchases. Indeed, as portrayed in this film, the year 2054 will be a marketer's paradise. But in many ways futuristic marketing is already here: Shoppers in many supermarkets receive, upon checkout, personalized coupons based on their purchases; many newspapers allow online readers to create personalized editions in which customized ads are featured; and consumers can now purchase highly personalized versions of many products. For example, at Nike's Web site, buyers can now choose among many models of sneakers in different price ranges, customize the chosen shoe using several colors and features (e.g., some models even allow buyers to choose the colors of the Nike Swoosh and the laces), put a personal ID on each shoe, pay for the product, and have it shipped directly to them.

As we marvel at these new marketing technologies, we must also put them in appropriate perspective. In principle, they are extensions of the salesperson in a local shoe store who recognizes customers by name and by preferences, or the neighborhood grocer who remembers the routine daily purchases of each customer and places them on the counter before the customer even asks for them, or the small-town jeweler who keeps track of customers' special occasions and prepares a selection of appropriate gifts for them to purchase as anniversaries and birthdays approach. All these businesspeople have engaged in one-to-one marketing long before the term was coined and many decades before personalized digital communications became available. And the objectives of the shoe salesperson, the grocer, and the jeweler were the same then as those of large companies today: to attain customers, retain good customers, sell them more products, and make a profit.

Today, the **digital revolution** of the marketplace allows much greater customization of products, services, and promotional messages than older marketing tools. By doing so, it enables marketers to build and maintain relationships with customers—just like the salesperson, grocer, and jeweler discussed earlier have done for many decades—but on a much greater and more efficient scale. Digital technologies also enable marketers to collect and analyze increasingly complex data on consumers' buying patterns and personal characteristics. On the other hand, the same technologies enable consumers to find more information about products and services, including prices, more easily, efficiently, and, for the most part, from the comfort of their own homes.

Over a period of a decade or so, the digital revolution has introduced several drastic changes into the business environment:

Consumers have more power than ever before. They can use "intelligent agents" to locate the best prices for products or services, bid on various marketing offerings, bypass distribution outlets and middlemen, and shop for goods around the globe and around the clock from the convenience of their homes.

Consumers have access to more information than ever before. They can easily find reviews for products they are considering buying that have been posted by previous buyers, click a button to compare the features of different product models at the sites of online retailers, and subscribe to "virtual communities" of persons who share the same interests they do.

Marketers can offer more services and products than ever before. The digitization of information enables sellers to *customize* the products and services they are selling and still sell them at reasonable prices. It also allows marketers to customize the promotional messages directed at many customers. For example, Amazon.com sends personalized e-mails to previous book purchasers announcing newly published books; these suggestions are based on a determination of the interests of the targeted consumers derived from their past purchases. Similarly, an online drugstore may vary the initial display returning buyers see when they revisit its Web site. Buyers whose past purchases indicate that they tend to buy national brands will see a display arranged by brand. Past purchasers who bought mostly products that were on sale or store brands will see a display categorized by price and discounted products.

The exchange between marketers and customers is increasingly interactive and instantaneous. Traditional advertising is a one-way street where the marketer pays a large sum of money to reach a large number of potential buyers via a mass medium, and then assesses whether or not the message was effective via future sales or market studies. On the other hand, digital communication enables a two-way interactive exchange in which consumers can instantly react to the marketer's message by, say, clicking on links within a given Web site or even by leaving the site. Thus, marketers can quickly gauge the effectiveness of their promotional messages rather than rely on delayed feedback through sales information that is collected after the fact.

Marketers can gather more information about consumers more quickly and easily. Marketers can track consumers' online behavior and also gather information by requiring visitors to Web sites to register and provide some information about themselves before they get access to the site's features. Thus, marketers can construct and update their consumer databases efficiently and inexpensively.

Impact reaches beyond the PC-based connection to the Web. Presently, most of the digital communication between consumers and marketers takes place via a PC connected to the Web through a phone line, a cable modem, or another high-speed connection. However, the digital revolution also gave us PDAs (personal digital assistants) that are rapidly becoming connected to the Web, often wirelessly. And it is likely that very soon our cell phones and PDAs will be combined into one product. In addition, many U.S. homes now have TV cable boxes that enable two-way communication with broadcasters and, as we switch to high-definition TV, all cable subscribers will have such boxes. Also, many experts predict that TV and the PC will merge into a single device that will provide households with hundreds of cable channels, interactive capabilities with broadcasters, and high-speed, wireless access to the Web. Supermarket scanners that keep track of households' purchases and instantly provide personalized coupons at the check-out counter and telephone devices that enable us to identify telemarketers automatically are two of the many additional products made possible by recently developed technologies.

The digital revolution of the marketplace and its impact on consumer behavior present many challenges for today's marketers. For example, the TiVo digital recorder allows viewers to control what they watch on TV, when they watch it, and whether or not to watch the commercials for which marketers spend billions of dollars per year. The TiVo recorder downloads programming information and allows users to record many hours of TV programming onto a hard drive without the hassle of videocassettes. Users can program the recorder by topic or keyword, easily play back selected segments, and, to the delight of many viewers, hit a single button for preprogrammed quick skips of strings of TV commercials. Since TiVo (and other similar devices) are shifting the power over viewing behavior from the broadcaster to the viewer, should broadcasters develop their own TiVo-like systems? Should they try to block the sales of such devices legally on the grounds that such devices contribute to copyright infringement? Or should they develop business models centered on viewers paying for content? These questions are no longer hypothetical and will have to be addressed relatively soon.[1]

- Should marketers begin reducing their advertising expenditures on the major networks' TV programs in anticipation of the growth of products such as TiVo? Should they insist that broadcasters develop new measurement systems? Or should they invest in technologies that embed electronic tags of ads visible only to digital video recorder users, as some advertisers are already doing?[2]

- Should companies that produce nondurable consumer goods, such as Nike, begin shifting resources away from building consumer demand via advertising for products carried by independently owned retailers and into direct distribution systems based on customized offerings?

- Should universities stop printing paper catalogs and should companies stop advertising job opportunities in newspapers in view of the fact that such information

can be distributed and updated less expensively and more efficiently online—
where more and more of the individuals interested in this information are looking
for it?

Some suggest that because virtual competition eliminates distance and location-
based benefits (such as a desirable store location) and because it is increasingly
dominated by intelligent merchant-brokerage agents that steer consumers toward
the lowest possible price for a chosen product, online competition is likely to resemble perfect competition. In such a marketplace, sellers will compete almost exclusively on the basis of price, and any other differentiation features—such as a strong
brand name and reputation—will not matter. Does this mean that branding and
competitive differentiation—two key features of modern marketing—will become
meaningless in the virtual marketplace?

The Definition and Scope of Consumer Behavior

The answers to the preceding questions are presently unknown but the source from
which they will evolve is clear. That source is **consumer behavior.** The term
consumer behavior is defined as the behavior that consumers display in *searching
for, purchasing, using, evaluating and disposing of products and services that they
expect will satisfy their needs.* Consumer behavior focuses on how individuals make
decisions to spend their available resources (time, money, effort) on consumption-
related items. That includes what they buy, why they buy it, when they buy it, where
they buy it, how often they buy it, how often they use it, how they evaluate it after
the purchase and the impact of such evaluations on future purchases, and how they
dispose of it.

One of the most important constants among all of us, despite our differences, is
that above all we are consumers. We use or consume on a regular basis food, clothing, shelter, transportation, education, equipment, vacations, necessities, luxuries,
services, and even ideas. As consumers, we play a vital role in the health of the
economy—local, national, and international. The purchase decisions we make
affect the demand for basic raw materials, for transportation, for production, for
banking; they affect the employment of workers and the deployment of resources,
the success of some industries and the failure of others. In order to succeed in any
business, and especially in today's dynamic and rapidly evolving marketplace, marketers need to know everything they can about consumers—what they want, what
they think, how they work, how they spend their leisure time. They need to understand the personal and group influences that affect consumer decisions and how
these decisions are made.

The term *consumer behavior* describes two different kinds of consuming entities: the personal consumer and the organizational consumer. The **personal consumer** buys goods and services for his or her own use, for the use of the household, or as a gift for a friend. In each of these contexts, the products are bought for final use by individuals, who are referred to as *end users* or ultimate consumers. The second category of consumer—the **organizational consumer**—includes profit and not-for-profit businesses, government agencies (local, state, and national), and institutions (e.g., schools, hospitals, and prisons), all of which must buy products, equipment, and services in order to run their organizations. Despite the importance of both categories of consumers—individuals and organizations—this book will focus on the individual consumer, who purchases for his or her own personal use or for household use. End-use consumption is perhaps the most pervasive of all types of consumer behavior, for it involves every individual, of every age and background, in the role of either buyer or user, or both.

Development of the Marketing Concept and the Discipline of Consumer Behavior

The field of consumer behavior is rooted in the **marketing concept,** a business orientation that evolved in the 1950s through several alternative approaches toward doing business referred to, respectively, as the *production concept,* the *product concept,* and the *selling concept.*

No single product has impacted Americans more than the personal automobile. And the business leader who gave us the affordable car and the business approach called the *production concept* was Henry Ford. Before the early 1900s, only wealthy consumers could afford automobiles because cars were assembled individually and it took considerable time and expense to produce each car. In the early 1900s, Henry Ford became consumed with the idea of producing cars that average Americans could afford. In 1908, Ford began selling the sturdy and reliable Model T for $850—an inexpensive price for that day. Soon he found out that he could not meet the overwhelming consumer demand for his cars and, in 1913, he introduced the assembly line. The new production method enabled Ford to produce good-quality cars more quickly and much less expensively. In 1916, Ford sold Model Ts for $360 and sold more than 100 times as many cars as he did in 1908.[3] In only eight years, Americans got the product that led to our nation's extensive system of highways and the emergence of suburbs and adjacent shopping malls—two key features of our lives and consumption patterns even today.

The production concept assumes that consumers are mostly interested in product availability at low prices; its implicit marketing objectives are cheap, efficient production and intensive distribution. This orientation makes sense when consumers are more interested in obtaining the product than they are in specific features and will buy what's available rather than wait for what they really want. Today using this orientation makes sense in developing countries or in other situations in which the main objective is to expand the market.

The *product concept* assumes that consumers will buy the product that offers them the highest quality, the best performance, and the most features. A product orientation leads the company to strive constantly to improve the quality of its product and to add new features that are technically feasible without finding out first whether or not consumers really want these features. A product orientation often leads to "marketing myopia," that is, a focus on the product rather than on the consumer needs it presumes to satisfy. Marketing myopia may cause a company to ignore crucial changes in the marketplace because it causes marketers to look in the mirror rather than through the window. Thus, American railroads today are a far less significant economic force than they were some 50 years ago because their management was convinced that travelers wanted trains and overlooked the competition for transportation from personal cars, airlines, busses, and trucks. These railroad executives focused on the product (i.e., trains) rather than the need that it satisfies (transportation).[4] Similarly, designers and engineers working on a new model of a personal digital assistant (PDA) must always remember that people do not buy PDAs—they buy ways to organize and retrieve data in a manner that will save them time and effort. If PDA designers and engineers forget this simple fact, they may improve the product far beyond its worth to the consumer.

A natural evolution from both the production concept and the product concept is the *selling concept,* in which a marketer's primary focus is selling the product(s) that it has unilaterally decided to produce. The assumption of the selling concept is that consumers are unlikely to buy the product unless they are aggressively persuaded to do so—mostly through the "hard sell" approach. The problem with this approach is that it fails to consider customer satisfaction. When consumers are induced to buy products they do not want or need, they will not buy them again. Also, they are likely to communicate any dissatisfaction with the product through negative word of mouth that serves to dissuade potential consumers from making similar purchases. Today the selling concept is typically utilized by marketers of unsought goods (such as life insurance), by political parties "selling" their candidates aggressively to apathetic voters, and by firms that have excess inventory.

THE MARKETING CONCEPT

The field of consumer behavior is rooted in a marketing strategy that evolved in the late 1950s, when some marketers began to realize that they could sell more goods, more easily, if they produced only those goods they had already determined that consumers would buy. Instead of trying to persuade customers to buy what the firm had already produced, marketing-oriented firms found that it was a lot easier to produce only products they had first confirmed, through research, that consumers wanted. Consumer needs and wants became the firm's primary focus. This consumer-oriented marketing philosophy came to be known as the *marketing concept.*

The key assumption underlying the marketing concept is that, to be successful, a company must determine the needs and wants of specific target markets and deliver the desired satisfactions better than the competition. The marketing concept is based on the premise that a marketer should make what it can sell, instead of trying to sell what it has made. Whereas the selling concept focuses on the needs of the *sellers* and on existing products, the marketing concept focuses on the needs of the *buyer.* The selling concept focuses on profits through sales volume; the marketing concept focuses on profits through customer satisfaction.

It is interesting to note that even before the evolution of the marketing concept, an intuitive understanding of consumer behavior was the key to the growth of companies that have remained highly successful, even today. Apparently, companies centered on understanding customers are the ones that continue to grow and remain leaders in their industries in spite of increased competition and changing business environments. Three anecdotes depicting three business leaders who led such companies are presented in Table 1-1.

TABLE 1-1	Three Business Leaders Who Understood Consumer Behavior Long Before the Development of the Marketing Concept

1. In 1923, as the automobile market was growing rapidly thanks to Henry Ford's mass production, *Alfred P. Sloan* became president and chairman of General Motors. He inherited a company that was built through takeovers of small car companies, and therefore produced many ill-sorted models unguided by clear business objectives. Sloan reorganized the company and in 1924 articulated the company's product strategy as "a car for every purse and purpose." While Ford continued to produce the Model T until 1927, GM offered a variety of affordable mass-produced models—from the aristocratic Cadillac to the proletarian Chevrolet—and took over a large portion of Ford's market share. About 30 years before the birth of the marketing concept, Alfred Sloan realized that all consumers are not alike and the importance of *market segmentation.*[a]

2. In the 1930s, *Colonel Sanders,* America's Chicken King, opened a roadside restaurant where he developed the recipes and cooking methods that are the key to KFC's successes even today. As the restaurant grew in popularity, Sanders enlarged it and also opened a roadside motel. At that time, motels had a bad reputation and "nice" people driving long distances generally stayed at downtown hotels. Sanders decided to try and overcome this image by putting a sample room of his clean and comfortable motel in the middle of his successful restaurant, and even put the entrance to the restaurant's ladies' room in that room. Sanders understood the importance of image and of turning an offering into a success by *repositioning,* long before this idea was articulated as a business objective. Later on, Sanders came up with the idea of franchising his cooking methods and chicken recipe, while keeping the ingredients of the recipe a secret, and founded KFC and a businees model that has since been adopted by many other fast-food chains.[b]

3. In the 1950s, *Ray Kroc* met the brothers McDonald who pioneered the idea of fast food as we know it today in a single outlet in California and became their partner. Ray Kroc envisioned thousands of McDonald's outlets across the country. Trying to pinpoint the best locations for the new restaurants, Kroc used to fly over towns and look for church steeples. He believed that where there were churches there were good American families—the kind of people he wanted as customers. Intuitively, Kroc understood and practiced *market targeting.* In 1961, Kroc opened Hamburger University as a training center for the company's franchisees and their employees, and pioneered the idea of centralized training as a key to delivering standardized products across a large number of geographically spread-out outlets.[c]

Sources: [a] www.gm.com/company/corp_info/history.
[b] *Colonel Sanders, America's Chicken King,* VHS Tape, A&E Television Networks, 1998.
[c] *Ray Kroc, Fast Food McMillionaire,* VHS Tape, A&E Television Networks, 1998.

IMPLEMENTING THE MARKETING CONCEPT

The widespread adoption of the marketing concept by American business provided the impetus for the study of consumer behavior. To identify unsatisfied consumer needs, companies had to engage in extensive marketing research. In so doing, they discovered that consumers were highly complex individuals, subject to a variety of psychological and social needs quite apart from their survival needs. They discovered that the needs and priorities of different consumer segments differed dramatically, and in order to design new products and marketing strategies that would fulfill consumer needs, they had to study consumers and their consumption behavior in depth. Thus, the marketing concept underscored the importance of consumer research and laid the groundwork for the application of consumer behavior principles to marketing strategy. The strategic tools that are used to implement the marketing concept include *segmentation, targeting, positioning* and the *marketing mix.*

THE ROLE OF CONSUMER RESEARCH

Consumer research describes the process and tools used to study consumer behavior. Broadly speaking, there are two theoretical perspectives that guide the development of consumer research methodology: the *positivist* approach and the *interpretivist* approach.

Positivists tend to be objective and empirical, to seek causes for behavior, and to conduct research studies that can be generalized to larger populations. Consumer research designed to provide data to be used for strategic managerial decisions falls into this category.

The research done by *interpretivists*, on the other hand, tends to be qualitative and based on small samples. Although they tend to view each consumption situation as unique and nonpredictable, interpretivists seek to find common patterns of operative values, meanings, and behavior across consumption situations. Chapter 2 explores the basic assumptions and methodology of each research approach in some detail.

SEGMENTATION, TARGETING, AND POSITIONING

The focus of the marketing concept is consumer needs. At the same time, recognizing the high degree of diversity among us, consumer researchers seek to identify the many similarities—or constants—that exist among the peoples of the world. For example, we all have the same kinds of biological needs, no matter where we are born—the needs for food, for nourishment, for water, for air, and for shelter from the elements. We also acquire needs after we are born. These needs are shaped by the environment and the culture in which we live, by our education, and by our experiences. The interesting thing about acquired needs is that there are usually many people who develop the same needs. This commonality of need or interest constitutes a market segment, which enabling the marketer to target consumers with specifically designed products and/or promotional appeals that satisfy the needs of that segment. The marketer must also adapt the image of its product (i.e., "position" it), so that each market segment perceives the product as better fulfilling its specific needs than competitive products. The three elements of this strategic framework are *market segmentation, targeting,* and *positioning.*

Market segmentation is the process of dividing a market into subsets of consumers with common needs or characteristics. The variables and methods used to form such subsets are detailed in Chapter 3. Because most companies have limited resources, few companies can pursue all of the market segments identified. Market **targeting** is selecting one or more of the segments identified for the company to pursue. The criteria for selecting target markets are detailed in Chapter 3.

Positioning is developing a distinct image for the product or service in the mind of the consumer, an image that will differentiate the offering from competing ones and squarely communicate to consumers that the particular product or service will fulfill their needs better than competing brands. Successful positioning centers around two key principles: first, communicating the *benefits* that the product will provide rather than the product's features. As one marketing sage pointed out: ". . . consumers do not buy drill bits—they buy ways to make holes." Second, because there are many similar products in almost any marketplace, an effective positioning strategy must develop and communicate a "unique selling proposition"—a distinct benefit or point of difference—for the product or service. In fact, most of the new products introduced by marketers (including new forms of existing products such as new flavors, sizes, etc.) fail to capture a significant market share and are discontinued because they are perceived by consumers as "me too" products lacking a unique image or benefit. In Chapter 6, the concepts and tools of positioning are explored further.

The Marketing Mix

The **marketing mix** consists of a company's service and/or product offerings to consumers and the methods and tools it selects to accomplish the exchange. The marketing mix consists of four elements: (1) the *product* or *service* (i.e., the fea-

TABLE 1-2	Rollerblade: Effective Implementation of the Marketing Concept

Less than two decades ago, in-line skates were an off-season training tool for hockey players. In the mid-1980s, Rollerblade developed marketing strategies that positioned in-line skating as a new sport. The company sold in-line skates to bicycle and conventional skate rental stores in two trend-setting places: Miami Beach, Florida, and Venice Beach, California, and a new form of recreational sport that appeals to many age groups and social classes was born. Backed by aggressive marketing and public relations, the popularity of the new sport soared and was quickly integrated into the mainstream. As competition appeared, Rollerblade continued to lead the market with such innovations as breathable shoe liners, buckle closure systems, and female-specific skates; today the company holds several hundred patented innovations.

The company's product line illustrates the utilization of segmentation, targeting, and positioning strategies. The company targets five segments and offers models that provide different benefits to the members of each segment: (1) *Men* can choose among models designed for expert, intermediate, or demanding skaters, and among such benefits as style, technological innovation, and performance. (2) *Women* are targeted with similar choices as men. (3) There are several models for *kids*. (4) *Street and park skaters* can choose among models focused on durability, performance, or attention to detail. (5) *Race skaters* are targeted with a model offering high-tech features and top performance. The models offered to men, women, and kids include brakes, whereas the models offered to street, park, and race skaters do not.

Rollerblade's entire marketing mix stems from its core product. In addition to the in-line skates, the company sells helmets, skate bags, and wrist, elbow, and knee protectors. The skates are priced along a range varying from very expensive models offered to aggressive skaters who look for maximum performance, to value-oriented skaters, to recreational skaters. The products are distributed in a variety of outlets—both domestic and overseas—in a way that reflects the market segments targeted and the skate models' prices. The company advertises its products in the mass media, issues frequent press releases as part of its public relations, and promotes its products through athletic and event sponsorships, as well as its "Skate School."

The company's Web site also includes features that encourage skaters to revisit, such as a list of places to skate (arranged by state), a dealer locator, skating tips, tips for people who wish to take up the sport, and suggestions on skating safety. These features show that Rollerblade has a thorough understanding of customer retention as well as social responsibility, concepts that are discussed later in this chapter.

Source: Developed from material available at www.rollerblade.com.

tures, designs, brands, and packaging offered, along with postpurchase benefits such as warranties and return policies); (2) the *price* (the list price, including discounts, allowances, and payment methods); (3) the *place* (the distribution of the product or service through specific store and nonstore outlets); (4) *promotion* (the advertising, sales promotion, public relations, and sales efforts designed to build awareness of and demand for the product or service). Table 1-2 depicts the implementation of the elements of the marketing concept by the Rollerblade company.

Customer Value, Satisfaction, and Retention

Since its emergence in the 1950s, many companies have very successfully adopted the marketing concept. The result has been more products, in more sizes, models, versions, and packages, offered to more precisely targeted (and often smaller) target markets. This has resulted in an increasingly competitive marketplace. And, in the 1990s, the digital revolution enabled many marketers to offer even more products and services and distribute them more widely, while reducing the costs and barriers of entering many industries. It has accelerated the rate at which new competitors enter markets and also has speeded up the rate at which successful segmentation, targeting, and positioning approaches must be updated or changed, as they are imitated or made obsolete by the offerings of new business rivals.

Savvy marketers today realize that in order to outperform competitors they must achieve the full profit potential from each and every customer. They must make the customer the core of the company's organizational culture, across all departments and functions, and ensure that each and every employee views any exchange with a customer as part of a *customer relationship,* not as a *transaction.* The three drivers of successful relationships between marketers and customers are *customer value,* high levels of *customer satisfaction,* and building a structure for *customer retention.*

PROVIDING CUSTOMER VALUE

Customer value is defined as the *ratio between the customer's perceived benefits (economic, functional and psychological) and the resources (monetary, time, effort, psychological) used to obtain those benefits.* Perceived value is relative and subjective. For example, diners at an exclusive French restaurant in Washington, D.C., where a meal with beverages may cost up to $250 per person, may expect unique and delicious food, immaculate service, and beautiful decor. Some diners may receive even more than they had expected and will leave the restaurant feeling that the experience was worth the money and other resources expended (such as a month-long wait for a reservation). Other diners may go with expectations so high that they leave the restaurant disappointed. On the other hand, many millions of customers each year visit thousands of McDonald's restaurants, in scores of countries around the globe, where they purchase standard, inexpensive meals from franchise owners and employees systematically trained by the McDonald's Corporation to deliver the company's four core standards: *quality, service, cleanliness,* and *value.* Customers flock to McDonald's outlets repeatedly because the restaurants are uniform, customers know what to expect, and they feel that they are getting value for the resources they expend.

Developing a *value proposition* (a term rapidly replacing the popular business phrase "unique selling proposition") is the core of successful positioning. For example, Lexus claims to deliver to its buyers *quality, zero defects in manufacturing,* and *superior* and *personal postpurchase service.* Dell's value proposition for personal computer users consists of *customized* PC systems *assembled speedily* and sold at *economical prices.* W Hotels is a relatively new but fast-growing chain of upscale boutique hotels. The company offers customers striking modern designs that seek a balance between form and substance. Each of the company's five New York City hotels (all opened since 1998) offers visitors a slightly unique experience centered on the history and "feel" of the neighborhood in which it is located and also stresses the comfort, functionality, and modern features of the rooms.[5] Measures of customers' expectations and evaluations of products and services are discussed in Chapter 2, and the strategic applications of perceived customer value are explored in Chapter 6.

CUSTOMER SATISFACTION

Customer satisfaction is the individual's perception of the performance of the product or service in relation to his or her expectations. As noted earlier, customers will have drastically different expectations of an expensive French restaurant and a

McDonald's, although both are part of the restaurant industry. The concept of customer satisfaction is a function of customer expectations. A customer whose experience falls below expectations (e.g., used dishes not cleared quickly enough at an expensive restaurant or cold fries served at a McDonald's) will be dissatisfied. Diners whose experiences match expectations will be satisfied. And customers whose expectations are exceeded (e.g., by small samples of delicious food "from the Chef" served between courses at the expensive restaurant, or a well-designed play area for children at a McDonald's outlet) will be very satisfied or delighted.

A widely quoted study that linked levels of customer satisfaction with customer behavior identified several types of customers: completely satisfied customers who are either *loyalists* who keep purchasing, or *apostles* whose experiences exceed their expectations and who provide very positive word of mouth about the company to others; "*defectors*" who feel neutral or merely satisfied and are likely to stop doing business with the company; consumer "*terrorists*" who have had negative experiences with the company and who spread negative word of mouth; "*hostages*" who are unhappy customers who stay with the company because of a monopolistic environment or low prices and who are difficult and costly to deal with because of their frequent complaints; and *mercenaries* who are very satisfied customers but who have no real loyalty to the company and may defect because of a lower price elsewhere or on impulse, defying the satisfaction–loyalty rationale. The researchers propose that companies should strive to create *apostles,* raise the satisfaction of *defectors* and turn them into *loyalists,* avoid having *terrorists* or *hostages,* and reduce the number of *mercenaries.*[6] Customer satisfaction measurement tools and techniques are discussed in Chapter 2.

CUSTOMER RETENTION

The overall objective of providing value to customers continuously and more effectively than the competition is to have highly satisfied (even delighted) customers; this strategy of **customer retention** makes it in the best interest of customers to stay with the company rather than switch to another firm. In almost all business situations, it is more expensive to win new customers than to keep existing ones. Studies have shown that small reductions in customer defections produce significant increases in profits because (1) loyal customers buy more products; (2) loyal customers are less price sensitive and pay less attention to competitors' advertising; (3) servicing existing customers, who are familiar with the firm's offerings and processes, is cheaper; and (4) loyal customers spread positive word of mouth and refer other customers. Furthermore, marketing efforts aimed at attracting new customers are expensive; indeed, in saturated markets, it may be impossible to find new customers. Today the Internet and digital marketer–consumer interactions are ideal tools for tailoring products and services to the specific needs of consumers (often termed *one-to-one marketing*), offering them more value through increased *customer intimacy* and keeping the customers returning to the company.[7]

Marketers who designate increasing customer retention rates as a strategic corporate goal must also recognize that all customers are not equal. Sophisticated marketers build *selective relationships* with customers, based on where customers rank in terms of profitability, rather than merely strive "to retain customers." A customer retention–savvy company closely monitors its customers' consumption volume and patterns, establishes tiers of customers according to their profitability levels, and develops distinct strategies toward each group of customers. For example, some stockbrokers program their phones to recognize the phone numbers of high-volume traders to ensure that their calls receive priority. Customers who have purchased and registered several of a company's products should receive extensive and expedited customer support. On the other hand, a bank's less profitable customers who, say, make little use of their credit cards or maintain the minimum balance needed to receive free checking should not have penalties waived for bounced checks or late payments. Some companies also identify customer groups that are unlikely to purchase more if pursued more aggressively; such customers are often discouraged from staying with the company or even "fired" as customers.

Classifying customers according to profitability levels goes beyond traditional segmentation methods that subdivide consumers on the basis of demographic, sociocultural, or behavioral characteristics. *Customer profitability-focused marketing* tracks costs and revenues of individual customers and then categorizes them into tiers based on consumption behaviors that are specific to the company's offerings. Such a strategy is probably the most effective way to utilize the knowledge of consumer behavior. For example, a recent study advocates using a "customer pyramid" where customers are grouped into four tiers: (1) The *platinum tier* includes heavy users who are not price sensitive and who are willing to try new offerings; (2) the *gold tier* consists of customers who are heavy users but not as profitable because they are more price sensitive than those in the higher tier, ask for more discounts, and are likely to buy from several providers; (3) the *iron tier* consists of customers whose spending volume and profitability do not merit special treatment from the company; (4) the *lead tier* includes customers who actually cost the company money because they claim more attention than is merited by their spending, tie up company resources, and spread negative word of mouth. The authors of the study urge companies to develop distinct marketing responses for each group.[8] Methods for collecting the customer data needed to develop the kind of retention systems discussed

---

TABLE 1-3   **The Sewell Automotive Company**

Carl Sewell owns and manages the Sewell Automotive Company—a chain of 12 car dealerships in Texas and Louisiana. The company sells many models and brands of new and preowned (not "used") cars. Carl Sewell's name has become synonymous with the phrase "customers for life," the title of a widely quoted book he co-authored in which he explains his business philosophy.

Sewell's objective is to create customers with lifetime value, not on making one sale based on price. Assuming that a car costs $25,000, a customer entering a Sewell dealership represents $300,000 in sales because Sewell figured that the customer is likely to buy 12 cars in a lifetime (plus $12,000 for parts and service). And if the customer has a great experience, he or she will tell a friend about it and that person represents another $312,000 in potential profit to the company because, as savvy marketers have long known, word of mouth is the best advertising.

Sewell's customers do not come to his dealerships because of low prices; they flock to Sewell because they receive value for their money. They are willing to pay a little more because they get a warm, enjoyable shopping experience, highly polite and competent staff, dealerships that have more convenient hours than others in the industry, access to free loaner cars delivered at the dealership or to the customer's home, and extraordinarily reliable service at reasonable prices.

The key drivers behind the operation are the multiple measures that the company uses to study customers' expectations and satisfaction. The company's Client Relations Department provides independent reporting of customers' levels of satisfaction. The unit consists of client relations representatives, and each one is assigned to one or more dealerships. The representatives solicit input from all customers who purchase a new or preowned car or had service repairs or body shop work done on their cars. The results of these surveys are tabulated, communicated to the dealerships, and used to identify areas in need of customer service improvement. In addition to these internal measures of customer satisfaction, the company uses J.D. Power and Associates, a highly reputable firm that monitors customer satisfaction in many industries, to collect additional data from Sewell's customers about their car purchase and service experiences.

Source: Carl Sewell and Paul B. Brown, *Customers for Life: How to Turn That One-Time Buyer into a Lifetime Customer,* New York: Doubleday, 1990; "A Look at the Client Relations Department," internal material, Sewell Automotive Company, 2002; Richard Urban, "Carl Sewell's Never-Ending Journey," *Business Dallas,* November/December 1998, 10–15.

here are described in Chapter 2. Table 1-3 portrays a company whose philosophy and success are rooted in the concept of customer retention.

A corporate philosophy centered on customer value, satisfaction, and retention evolves from the marketing concept and also unfolds new dimensions of marketing. Table 1-4 compares traditional marketing with perceived value and retention marketing. Applications of consumer behavior concepts to value and retention-focused marketing are discussed throughout the book.

| TABLE 1-4 | The Traditional Marketing Concept Versus Value- and Retention-Focused Marketing |

THE TRADITIONAL MARKETING CONCEPT	VALUE AND RETENTION-FOCUSED MARKETING
Make only what you can sell instead of trying to sell what you make.	Use technology that enables customers to customize what you make.
Do not focus on the product; focus on the need that it satisfies.	Focus on the product's perceived value, as well as the need that it satisfies.
Market products and services that match customers' needs better than competitors' offerings.	Utilize an understanding of customer needs to develop offerings that customers perceive as more valuable than competitors' offerings.
Research consumer needs and characteristics.	Research the levels of profit associated with various consumer needs and characteristics.
Understand the purchase behavior process and the influences on consumer behavior.	Understand consumer behavior in relation to the company's product.
Realize that each customer transaction is a discrete sale.	Make each customer transaction part of an ongoing relationship with the customer.
Segment the market based on customers' geographic, demographic, psychological, sociocultural, lifestyle, and product-usage related characteristics.	Use hybrid segmentation that combines the traditional segmentation bases with data on the customer's purchase levels and patterns of use of the company's products.
Target large groups of customers that share common characteristics with messages transmitted through mass media.	Invest in technologies that enable you to send one-to-one promotional messages via digital channels.
Use one-way promotions whose effectiveness is measured through sales data or marketing surveys.	Use interactive communications in which messages to customers are tailored according to their responses to previous communications.
Create loyalty programs based on the volume purchased.	Create customer tiers based on both volume and consumption patterns.
Encourage customers to stay with the company and buy more.	Make it very unattractive for your customers to switch to a competitor and encourage them to purchase "better"—in a manner that will raise the company's profitability levels.
Determine marketing budgets on the basis of the numbers of customers you are trying to reach.	Base your marketing budget on the "lifetime value" of typical customers in each of the targeted segments compared with the resources needed to acquire them as customers.
Conduct customer satisfaction surveys and present the results to management.	Conduct customer satisfaction surveys that include a component which studies the customer's word of mouth about the company, and use the results immediately to enhance customer relationships.
Create customer trust and loyalty to the company and high levels of customer satisfaction.	Create customer intimacy and bonds with completely satisfied, "delighted" customers.

Source: Joseph Wisenblit, "Beyond the Marketing Concept: From 'Make Only What You Can Sell' to 'Let Customers Customize What You Make'," Working Paper, May 2002, The Stillman School of Business, Seton Hall University, South Orange, NJ.

Marketing Ethics and Social Responsibility

The marketing concept as we know it—fulfilling the needs of target audiences—is sometimes inappropriate. This is particularly true in situations in which the means for need satisfaction, the product or service provided to fulfill customer "needs," can be harmful to the individual or to society (e.g., drugs, tobacco) or cause environmental deterioration. Given the fact that all companies prosper when society prospers, many people believe that all of us, companies as well as individuals, would be better off if social responsibility were an integral component of every marketing decision. A reassessment of the traditional marketing concept suggests that a more appropriate conceptualization for the times in which we live would balance the needs of society with the needs of the individual and the organization. The **societal marketing concept** requires that all marketers adhere to principles of social responsibility in the marketing of their goods and services; that is, they should endeavor to satisfy the needs and wants of their target markets in ways that preserve and enhance the well-being of consumers and society as a whole. Thus, a restructured definition of the marketing concept calls on marketers to *fulfill the needs of the target audience in ways that improve society as a whole, while fulfilling the objectives of the organization.* According to the societal marketing concept, fast-food restaurants should develop foods that contain less fat and starch and more nutrients, and marketers should not advertise alcoholic beverages or cigarettes to young people, or use young models or professional athletes in liquor or tobacco advertisements, because celebrities so often serve as role models for the young.

A serious deterrent to widespread implementation of the societal marketing concept is the short-term orientation embraced by most business executives in their drive for increased market share and quick profits. This short-term orientation derives from the fact that managerial performance usually is evaluated on the basis of short-term results. Thus, a young and ambitious advertising executive may create a striking advertising campaign using unreasonably slim females with pale faces and withdrawn expressions in order to dramatically increase the sales of the advertised product, without considering the negative impact of the campaign, such as an increase in eating disorders among young women or the implicit approval of drug-taking reflected in the models' appearances. The societal marketing concept, however, advocates a long-term perspective. It recognizes that all companies would be better off in a stronger, healthier society, and that companies that incorporate ethical behavior and social responsibility in all of their business dealings attract and maintain loyal consumer support over the long term.

The primary purpose for studying consumer behavior as part of a marketing curriculum is to understand why and how consumers make their purchase decisions. These insights enable marketers to design more effective marketing strategies, especially today when advanced technologies enable marketers to collect more data about consumers and target them more precisely. Some critics are concerned that an in-depth understanding of consumer behavior makes it possible for unethical marketers to exploit human vulnerabilities in the marketplace and engage in other unethical marketing practices in order to achieve individual business objectives. As a result, many trade associations have developed industry-wide *codes of ethics,* because they recognize that industry-wide self-regulation is in every member's best interests in that it deters government from imposing its own regulations on the industry. A number of companies have incorporated specific social goals into their mission statements and include programs in support of these goals as integral components of their strategic planning. They believe that **marketing ethics** and social responsibility are important components of organizational effectiveness. Most companies recognize that socially responsible activities improve their image among consumers, stockholders, the financial community, and other relevant publics. They have found that ethical and socially responsible practices are simply good business, resulting not only in a favorable image, but ultimately in increased sales. The converse is also true: Perceptions of a company's lack of social responsibility or unethical marketing strategies negatively affect consumer purchase decisions. Applicable marketing ethics and social responsibility issues are discussed throughout the book.

Consumer Behavior and Decision Making Are Interdisciplinary

Consumer behavior was a relatively new field of study in the mid- to late 1960s. Because it had no history or body of research of its own, marketing theorists borrowed heavily from concepts developed in other scientific disciplines, such as *psychology* (the study of the individual), *sociology* (the study of groups), *social psychology* (the study of how an individual operates in groups), *anthropology* (the influence of society on the individual), and *economics* to form the basis of this new marketing discipline. Many early theories concerning consumer behavior were based on economic theory on the notion that individuals act rationally to maximize their benefits (satisfactions) in the purchase of goods and services. Later research discovered that consumers are just as likely to purchase impulsively and to be influenced not only by family and friends, by advertisers and role models, but also by mood, situation, and emotion. All of these factors combine to form a comprehensive model of consumer behavior that reflects both the cognitive and emotional aspects of consumer decision making.

A SIMPLIFIED MODEL OF CONSUMER DECISION MAKING

The process of **consumer decision making** can be viewed as three distinct but interlocking stages: the **input** stage, the **process** stage, and the **output** stage. These stages are depicted in the simplified model of consumer decision making in Figure 1-1.

The *input* stage influences the consumer's recognition of a product need and consists of two major sources of information: the firm's marketing efforts (the product itself, its price, its promotion, and where it is sold) and the external sociological influences on the consumer (family, friends, neighbors, other informal and noncommercial sources, social class, and cultural and subcultural memberships). The cumulative impact of each firm's marketing efforts, the influence of family, friends, and neighbors, and society's existing code of behavior, are all inputs that are likely to affect what consumers purchase and how they use what they buy.

The *process* stage of the model focuses on how consumers make decisions. The psychological factors inherent in each individual (motivation, perception, learning, personality, and attitudes) affect how the external inputs from the input stage influence the consumer's recognition of a need, prepurchase search for information, and evaluation of alternatives. The experience gained through evaluation of alternatives, in turn, affects the consumer's existing psychological attributes.

The *output* stage of the consumer decision-making model consists of two closely related postdecision activities: purchase behavior and postpurchase evaluation. Purchase behavior for a low-cost, nondurable product (e.g., a new shampoo) may be influenced by a manufacturer's coupon and may actually be a trial purchase; if the consumer is satisfied, he or she may repeat the purchase. The trial is the exploratory phase of purchase behavior in which the consumer evaluates the product through

FIGURE 1-1

A Simple Model of
Consumer Decision
Making

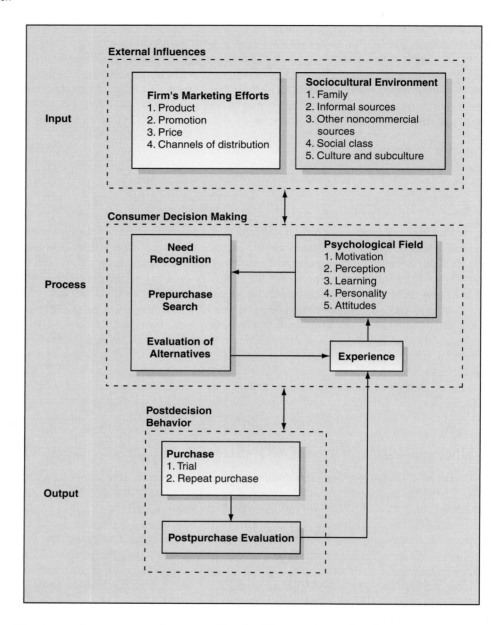

direct use. A repeat purchase usually signifies product adoption. For a relatively durable product such as a laptop ("relatively" durable because of the rapid rate of obsolescence), the purchase is more likely to signify adoption.

The consumer decision-making model is examined in greater depth in Chapter 16, where it ties together in great detail the psychological and sociocultural concepts explored throughout the book.

The Plan of This Book

In an effort to build a useful conceptual framework that both enhances understanding and permits practical application of consumer behavior principles to marketing strategy, this book is divided into four parts: Part 1 gives an introduction to the study of consumer behavior, Part 2 discusses the consumer as an individual, Part 3 examines consumers in their social and cultural settings, and Part 4 synthesizes all of the variables discussed earlier into the consumer decision-making process.

Chapter 1 introduced the reader to the study of consumer behavior as an interdisciplinary science that investigates the consumption-related activities of individuals. It described the reasons for the development of consumer behavior as an academic discipline and as an applied science, and introduced a simplified model of consumer decision making that links together all of the personal and group influences that affect consumption decisions. Chapter 2 examines the methodology of consumer research, including the assumptions underlying qualitative and quantitative research approaches. Chapter 3 discusses the process of market segmentation, including the demographic, sociocultural, and psychographic bases for segmenting markets.

Part 2 focuses on the psychological characteristics of the consumer. Chapter 4 discusses how individuals are motivated, Chapter 5 examines the impact of individual personality characteristics on consumer behavior, Chapter 6 explores consumer perception, Chapter 7 examines how consumers learn, Chapter 8 discusses consumer attitudes, and Chapter 9 concludes Part 2 with an examination of the communications process and consumer persuasion.

Part 3 focuses on consumers as members of society, subject to varying external influences on their buying behavior, such as their group and family memberships (Chapter 10), social class (Chapter 11), and the broad cultural and specific subcultural groups to which they belong (Chapters 12 and 13). The importance of cross-cultural consumer research to international marketing is explored in Chapter 14.

Part 4 examines the consumer decision-making process. Chapter 15 discusses the consumer's reactions to innovation and change and describes the process by which new products are adopted and become diffused throughout society. The book concludes with Chapter 16, an in-depth discussion of consumer decision making that shows how all the psychological and sociocultural variables discussed in Parts 2 and 3 influence the consumer's decision-making process.

Summary

The study of consumer behavior enables marketers to understand and predict consumer behavior in the marketplace; it is concerned not only with what consumers buy but also with why, when, where, how, and how often they buy it. Consumer research is the methodology used to study consumer behavior; it takes place at every phase of the consumption process: before, during, and after the purchase.

Consumer behavior is interdisciplinary; that is, it is based on concepts and theories about people that have been developed by scientists in such diverse disciplines as psychology, sociology, social psychology, cultural anthropology, and economics.

Consumer behavior has become an integral part of strategic market planning. The belief that ethics and social responsibility should also be integral components of every marketing decision is embodied in a revised marketing concept—the societal marketing concept—that calls on marketers to fulfill the needs of their target markets in ways that improve society as a whole.

Discussion Questions

1. Describe the impact of the digital revolution on marketing and on consumer behavior.

2. Describe the interrelationship between the consumer behavior discipline and the marketing concept.

3. Describe the interrelationship between consumer research, market segmentation and targeting, and the development of the marketing mix.

4. Discuss the role of social and behavioral sciences in developing the consumer decision-making model.

5. Apply each of the two models depicted in Table 1-4 (i.e., traditional marketing and value and retention marketing) to the marketing of cellular phone services. You may want to incorporate into your answer your own and your peers' experiences in selecting cellular communications providers.

Exercises

1. You are the marketing manager of Citibank's Online Banking Division. How would you apply the concepts of providing value and customer satisfaction and retention to designing and marketing effective online banking?

2. Locate two examples (e.g., advertisements, articles, etc.) depicting practices that are consistent

with the societal marketing concept and two examples of business practices that contradict this concept. Explain your choices.

3. Apply each of the concepts featured in the section describing the development of the marketing concept to manufacturing and marketing automobiles.

Key Terms

- Consumer behavior
- Consumer decision making
- Consumer research
- Customer retention
- Customer satisfaction
- Customer value

- Digital revolution
- Marketing concept
- Marketing ethics
- Marketing mix
- Market segmentation

- Organizational consumer
- Personal consumer
- Positioning
- Societal marketing concept
- Targeting

Notes

1. Amy Harmon, "Digital Video Recorders Give Advertisers Pause," *New York Times,* May 23, 2002.
2. Ibid.
3. Davis Hounshell, *From the American System to Mass Production 1800–1932* (Baltimore/London: John Hopkins University Press, 1984), 224.
4. Theodore Levitt, "Marketing Myopia," *Harvard Business Review,* July–August 1960, 45–56.
5. www.starwood.com/whotels.
6. Thomas O. Jones and W. Earl Sasser, Jr., "Why Satisfied Customers Defect," *Harvard Business Review,* November–December 1995, 88–99.
7. Frederick F. Reichheld and W. Earl Sasser, Jr., "Zero Defections: Quality Comes to Services," *Harvard Business Review,* September–October 1990, 105–111; Michael Treacy and Fred Wiersema, "Customer Intimacy and Other Value Disciplines," *Harvard Business Review,* January–February 1993, 84–93; Bob Mueller, "Keeping Your Customers from Defecting," *Beyond Computing,* April 1999, 30–31.
8. Valerie A. Zeithaml, Roland T. Rust, and Katherine N. Lemon, "The Customer Pyramid: Creating and Serving Profitable Customers," *California Management Review,* Summer 2001, 118–142.

Consumer Research

The field of consumer research developed as an extension of the field of marketing research. Just as the findings of marketing research were used to improve managerial decision making, so too were the findings of consumer research. Studying consumer behavior enables marketers to predict how consumers will react to promotional messages and to understand why they make the purchase decisions they do. Marketers realize that if they know more about the consumer decision-making process, they can design marketing strategies and promotional messages that will influence consumers more effectively. Recently marketers began to realize that customer research is a unique subset of marketing research, which merits the utilization of specialized research methods that collect customer data and also enhance the company's relationship with its customers. Table 2-1 details comparisons between customer research and marketing research.

TABLE 2-1	Comparisons Between Customer Research and Marketing Research

	CUSTOMER RESEARCH	**MARKETING RESEARCH**
Study purpose	Data collection and, potentially, strengthening the relationship between the customers and the company. Contacted customers are told the identity of the survey's sponsor.	Data collection only. Respondents are not told the research sponsor's identity. Respondents cooperate because they are asked and sometimes paid.
Respondents' level of involvement and expectations	Increase respondents' involvement by indicating that the data collected will be used to improve the company's offerings. Respondents who tell the researcher about problems expect corrective action.	The respondents' level of involvement is generally low.
The sample size and the researcher's attitude toward the respondents	Since the survey is an opportunity to build relationships with customers, as many as possible are contacted. Respondents expect the researcher to know their usage habits concerning the company's offerings.	A sufficient number of respondents are contacted to achieve statistical validity at a given confidence level. When approached, respondents do not expect the researcher to know anything about them.
How the data are collected and analyzed	The data collected can be linked to specific respondents and analyzed at the respondent level.	The data are collected anonymously and aggregated. Typically, comparisons among sample averages are used in the analysis.
End result	Appropriate data are identified to fix product and service problems and to correct individual participant's problems.	Product and service problems are identified.
Follow-up surveys	Follow-up is encouraged. Customers who report problems expect some feedback. The follow-up may be linked to information collected previously from the same respondent.	Linking data collected to specific respondents and using the data in follow-up contacts is considered unethical.

Source: Douglas R. Pruden and Terry G. Vavra, "Customer Research, Not Marketing Research," *Marketing Research*, Summer 2000, 14–19.

Consumer Research Paradigms

The early consumer researchers gave little thought to the impact of mood, emotion, or situation on consumer decisions. They believed that marketing was simply applied economics, and that consumers were rational decision makers who objectively evaluated the goods and services available to them and selected those that gave them the highest utility (satisfaction) at the lowest cost.

Despite their assumptions that consumers were logical problem solvers who engaged in careful thought processing (i.e., information processing) to arrive at their consumption decisions, researchers soon realized that consumers were not always consciously aware of why they made the decisions they did. Even when they were aware of their basic motivations, consumers were not always willing to reveal those reasons. In 1939, a Viennese psychoanalyst named Ernest Dichter began to use Freudian psychoanalytic techniques to uncover the hidden motivations of consumers. By the late 1950s, his research methodology (called **motivational research**), which was essentially qualitative in approach, was widely adopted by consumer researchers. As a result of Dichter's work and subsequent research designed to search deep within the consumer's psyche, consumer researchers today use two different types of research methodology to study consumer behavior—**quantitative research** and **qualitative research.**

QUANTITATIVE RESEARCH

Quantitative research is descriptive in nature and is used by researchers to understand the effects of various promotional inputs on the consumer, thus enabling marketers to "predict" consumer behavior. This research approach is known as **positivism,** and consumer researchers primarily concerned with predicting consumer behavior are known as *positivists*. The research methods used in positivist research are borrowed primarily from the natural sciences and consist of experiments, survey techniques, and observation. The findings are descriptive, empirical, and, if collected randomly (i.e., using a probability sample), can be generalized to larger populations. Because the data collected are quantitative, they lend themselves to sophisticated statistical analysis.

QUALITATIVE RESEARCH

Qualitative research methods consist of depth interviews, focus groups, metaphor analysis, collage research, and projective techniques (discussed later in the chapter). These techniques are administered by a highly trained interviewer-analyst who also analyzes the findings; thus, the findings tend to be somewhat subjective. Because sample sizes are necessarily small, findings cannot be generalized to larger populations. They are primarily used to obtain new ideas for promotional campaigns and products that can be tested more thoroughly in larger, more comprehensive studies.

A number of academicians from the field of consumer behavior, as well as from related social science disciplines, have become more interested in the act of *consumption* rather than in the act of *buying* (i.e., decision making). They view consumer behavior as a subset of human behavior, and increased understanding as a key to reducing negative aspects of consumer behavior (the so-called "dark side" of consumer behavior), such as drug addiction, shoplifting, alcoholism, and compulsive buying. Interest in understanding consumer experiences has led to the term **interpretivism,** and the researchers who adopt this paradigm are known as *interpretivists*.

Interpretivists engage in qualitative research. Among the research methodologies they use are depth interviews, projective techniques, and other methods borrowed from cultural anthropology to study the meanings of cultural practices and symbols. Broadly speaking, the findings of qualitative research cannot be generalized to large populations but, as discussed in the following section, qualitative research nevertheless has an important role in managerial decision making. Table 2-2 compares the purposes and assumptions of positivist research and interpretivist research.

COMBINING QUALITATIVE AND QUANTITATIVE RESEARCH FINDINGS

Marketers often use a combination of quantitative and qualitative research to help make strategic marketing decisions. For example, they use qualitative research findings to discover new ideas and to develop promotional strategy, and quantitative

TABLE 2-2	Comparisons Between Positivism and Interpretivism

	POSITIVISM	INTERPRETIVISM
Purpose	Prediction of consumer actions	Understanding consumption practices
Other descriptive terms	Positivism is also known as modernism, logical empiricism, operationalism, and objectivism	Interpretivists are also known as experientialists and postmodernists; interpretivism is also known as naturalism, humanism, and postpositivism
Methodology and research tools	*Quantitative* research: surveys, experiments, and observations	*Qualitative research:* depth interviews and projective techniques *Ethnography:* a technique borrowed from cultural anthropology in which the researchers place themselves (participate) in the society under study in an effort to absorb the meaning of various cultural practices *Semiotics:* the study of symbols and the meanings they convey
Assumptions	• Rationality: consumers make decisions after weighing alternatives • The causes and effects of behavior can be identified and isolated • Individuals are problem solvers who engage in information processing • A single reality exists • Events can be objectively measured • Causes of behavior can be identified; by manipulating causes (i.e., inputs), the marketer can influence behavior (i.e., outcomes) • Findings can be generalized to larger populations	• There is no single objective truth • Reality is subjective • Cause and effect cannot be isolated • Each consumption experience is unique • Researcher–respondent interactions affect research findings • Often findings are not generalizable to larger populations

Not all researchers agree that interpretive research enhances traditional quantitative and qualitative market research. There is also disagreement regarding the alternative terms used to describe each research approach. The following sources illustrate the various conceptualizations of positivism and interpretivism.

Sources: Richard Lutz, "Positivism, Naturalism, and Pluralism in Consumer Research: Paradigms in Paradise," *Advances in Consumer Research,* 16 (Provo, UT: Association for Consumer Research, 1989), 17; John Sherry, "Postmodern Alternatives: The Interpretive Turn in Consumer Research," in *Handbook of Consumer Behavior,* eds. H. Kassarjian and T. Robertson (Upper Saddle River, NJ: Prentice Hall, 1991); Morris B. Holbrook and John O'Shaughnessy, "On the Scientific Status of Consumer Research and the Need for an Interpretive Approach to Studying Consumption Behavior," *Journal of Consumer Research,* 15, December 1988, 398–402; and Morris Holbrook and Elizabeth C. Hirschman, "The Experimental Aspects of Consumption: Consumer Fantasies, Feelings, and Fun," *Journal of Consumer Research,* 9, 2 (1982): 132–134.

research findings to predict consumer reactions to various promotional inputs. Frequently, ideas stemming from qualitative research are tested empirically and become the basis for the design of quantitative studies.

Marketers have discovered that these two research paradigms are really complementary in nature. The prediction made possible by quantitative (positivist) research and the understanding provided by qualitative (interpretivist) research together produce a richer and more robust profile of consumer behavior than either research approach used alone. The combined findings enable marketers to design more meaningful and effective marketing strategies.

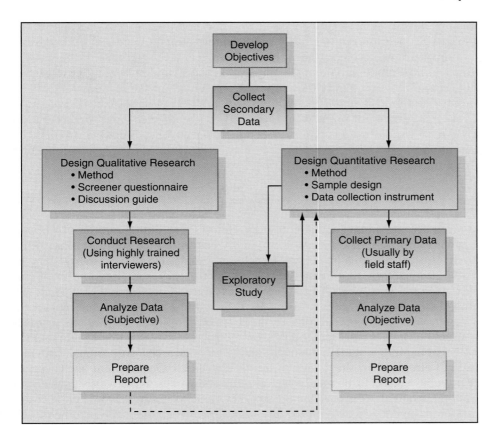

FIGURE 2-1

The Consumer
Research Process

The Consumer Research Process

The major steps in the consumer research process include (1) defining the objectives of the research, (2) collecting and evaluating secondary data, (3) designing a primary research study, (4) collecting primary data, (5) analyzing the data, and (6) preparing a report on the findings. Figure 2-1 depicts a model of the consumer research process.

DEVELOPING RESEARCH OBJECTIVES

The first step in the consumer research process is to carefully define the **objectives** of the study. Is it to segment the market for plasma television sets? To find out consumer attitudes about online shopping? To determine what percentage of households use e-mail? It is important for the marketing manager and the researcher to agree at the outset on the purposes and objectives of the study to ensure that the research design is appropriate. A carefully thought-out statement of objectives helps to define the type and level of information needed.

For example, if the purpose of the study is to come up with new ideas for products or promotional campaigns, then a qualitative study is usually undertaken, in which respondents spend a significant amount of time face-to-face with a highly trained professional interviewer-analyst who also does the analysis. Because of the high costs of each interview, a fairly small sample of respondents is studied; thus, the findings are not projectable to the marketplace. If the purpose of the study is to find out how many people in the population (i.e., what percentage) use certain products and how frequently they use them, then a quantitative study that can be computer analyzed is undertaken. Sometimes, in designing a quantitative study, the researcher may not know what questions to ask. In such cases, before undertaking a full-scale study, the researcher is likely to conduct a small-scale **exploratory study** to identify the critical issues to include in the data collection instrument (e.g., questionnaire).

COLLECTING SECONDARY DATA

A search for **secondary data** generally follows the statement of objectives. Secondary information is any data originally generated for some purpose other than the present research objectives. It includes findings based on research done by outside organizations, data generated in-house for earlier studies, and even customer information collected by the firm's sales or credit departments. Locating secondary data is called **secondary research.** (Original research performed by individual researchers or organizations to meet specific objectives is called **primary research.**) Secondary research findings sometimes provide sufficient insight into the problem at hand to eliminate the need for primary research. Most often, it provides clues and direction for the design of primary research. Government agencies, private population data firms, marketing research companies, and advertising agencies are all important sources of secondary market data. For example, the United States Census Bureau collects data on the age, education, occupation, and income of U.S. residents by state and region and also provides projections on the future growth or decline of various demographic segments. Additional information on rents, places of work, automobile ownership, and patterns of migration is provided by the government in studies of census tracts within major metropolitan areas. Mediamark Research provides information about the reader profiles and circulation figures of newspapers and magazines. The Claritas organization provides demographic and lifestyle profiles of the consumers residing in each U.S. zip code. Any firm operating globally may find key statistics about any country in the world in the CIA's electronic *World Factbook* published on the Web. Table 2-3 lists some major sources of secondary data.

If more detailed information on purchasing patterns or product usage is needed or if psychological or sociocultural consumer information is sought, then primary data must be collected. Research to secure such information is more costly and more time consuming than secondary research but is likely to yield a more accurate picture than studies based on secondary data alone.

Syndicated Data

Because it is often very costly to collect primary data, many companies routinely purchase syndicated data on consumption patterns. Syndicated data are data of interest to a large number of users that are collected periodically and compiled and analyzed according to a standard procedure; then sold to interested buyers. For example, Nielsen Media Research compiles reports on the *numbers of U.S. households* tuned to national TV broadcasts (via computerized boxes with modems connected to each set in the households sampled), on *who is watching* national TV programs (by using "people meters," devices that enable members of the sampled

TABLE 2-3	Secondary Data Sources

A. INTERNAL SOURCES

Company profit and loss statements, balance sheets, sales figures, sales-call reports, invoices, inventory records, and prior research reports.

B. GOVERNMENT PUBLICATIONS

- *Statistical Abstract of the United States*
- *Country and City Data Book*
- *Industrial Outlook*
- *Marketing Information Guide*
- Other government publications include the *Annual Survey of Manufacturers; Business Statistics; Census of Manufacturers; Census of Population; Census of Retail Trade, Wholesale Trade, and Selected Service Industries; Census of Transportation; Federal Reserve Bulletin; Monthly Labor Review; Survey of Current Business;* and *Vital Statistics Report.*

C. PERIODICALS AND BOOKS

- *Business Periodicals Index*
- *Standard and Poor's Industry*
- *Moody's Manuals*
- *Encyclopedia of Associations*
- Marketing journals include the *Journal of Marketing, Journal of Marketing Research,* and *Journal of Consumer Research.*
- Useful trade magazines include *Advertising Age, Chain Store Age, Progressive Grocer, Sales & Marketing Management,* and *Stores.*
- Useful general business magazines include *Business Week, Fortune, Forbes, The Economist,* and *Harvard Business Review.*

D. COMMERCIAL DATA

- *Nielsen Company:* Data on products and brands sold through retail outlets (Retail Index Services), supermarket scanner data (Scantrack), data on television audiences (Media Research Services), magazine circulation data (Neodata Services, Inc.), and others.
- *MRCA Information Services:* Data on weekly family purchases of consumer products (National Consumer Panel) and data on home food consumption (National Menu Census).
- *Information Resources, Inc.:* Supermarket scanner data (InfoScan) and data on the impact of supermarket promotions (PromotioScan).
- *SAMI/Burke:* Reports on warehouse withdrawals to food stores in selected market areas (SAMI reports) and supermarket scanner data (Samscam).
- *Simmons Market Research Bureau (MRB Group):* Annual reports covering television markets, sporting goods, and proprietary drugs, with demographic data by sex, income, age, and brand preferences (selective markets and media reaching them).
- Other commercial research houses selling data to subscribers include the Audit Bureau of Circulation; Arbitron, Audits and Surveys; Dun & Bradstreet's; National Family Opinion; Standard Rate & Data Service; and Starch.

households to record their individual viewing patterns), and on the viewing of *local TV programs* (by using diaries in which samples of viewers record the programs they watched). These reports are sold to companies and advertising agencies and are used as "currency"; the more audience the program delivers, the more the commercial time within that program is worth to advertisers.

Customer Profitability and Lifetime Value Data

The widely cited so-called "80/20 rule" states that, generally, a relatively small percentage of all customers (e.g., 20 percent) accounts for a disproportionately large portion of the company's sales and profits (e.g., 80 percent). With the increased focus on building and maintaining long-term relationships with customers, many companies are now developing systems that will identify highly profitable customers as quickly as possible and target these customers with special offers to buy even more of the company's products and services. Such systems stem from the collection and analysis of *internal* secondary data, such as past customer transactions, letters from customers, sales-call reports, warranty cards, and data on the frequency and duration of customer interactions. Based on these data, savvy marketers compute **customer lifetime value** (CLV) profiles for various customer segments. The CLV can be computed from customer acquisition costs (the resources needed to establish a relationship with the customer), the profits generated from individual sales to each customer, the costs of handling customers and their orders (some customers may place more complex and variable orders that cost more to handle), and the expected duration of the relationship. A model depicting the linkage of internal data to customer profitability is shown in Figure 2-2.

DESIGNING PRIMARY RESEARCH

The design of a research study is based on the purposes of the study. If descriptive information is needed, then a quantitative study is likely to be undertaken; if the purpose is to get new ideas (e.g., for repositioning a product), then a qualitative study is undertaken. Because the approach for each type of research differs in terms of method of data collection, sample design, and type of data collection instrument used, each research approach is discussed separately below.

Quantitative Research Designs

A quantitative research study consists of a research design, the data collection methods and instruments to be used, and the sample design. Three basic designs are used in quantitative research: observation, experimentation (in a laboratory or in the field, such as in a retail store), or survey (i.e., by questioning people).

Observational Research Observational research is an important method of consumer research because marketers recognize that the best way to gain an in-depth understanding of the relationship between people and products is by watching them in the process of buying and using products. Many large corporations and advertising agencies use trained researchers/observers to watch, note, and sometimes videotape consumers in stores, malls, or their own homes. For example, in studying responses to a new mint-flavored Listerine, the Warner Lambert Company hired a research firm that paid 37 New York City families to let it install cameras in their bathrooms to videotape mouthwash usage. The study found that consumers who used Scope gave the product a swish and spit it out. On the other hand, users of the new Listerine kept the mouthwash in their mouths for much longer (one subject even held the mouthwash in his mouth as he left home and got into the car, and only spit it out after driving a couple of blocks).[1] By watching people interact with products, observational researchers gain a better understanding of what the product symbolizes to a consumer and greater insight into the bond between people and products that is the essence of brand loyalty.

Mechanical observation uses a mechanical or electronic device to record customer behavior or response to a particular marketing stimulus. For example, a retailer may use a traffic counter to determine the business viability of a new store

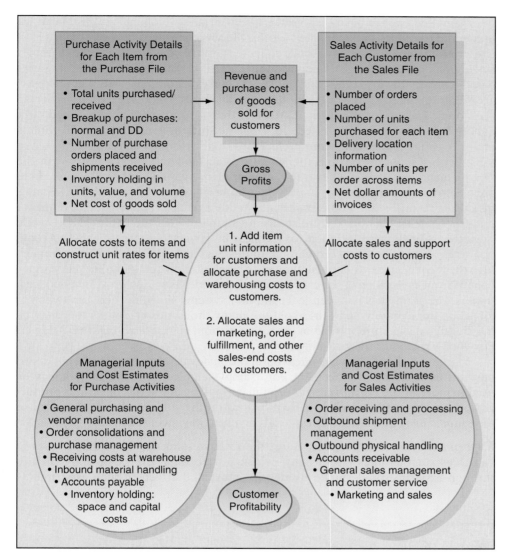

FIGURE 2-2

Linking Information
Sources to Arrive at
Customer Profitability
Source: Rakesh Niraj,
Mahendra Gupta, and
Chakravarthi Narasimhan,
"Customer Profitability in a
Supply Chain," *Journal of
Marketing,* July 2001.

location, government planners may use data collected from electronic EZ Pass devices in passenger cars to decide which roads should be expanded, and banks can use security cameras to observe problems customers may have in using ATMs.

Consumers use more and more technological devices to buy because such instruments generally reduce reliance on cash or sales assistance and often provide rewards for using them. For example, consumers who use supermarket frequency shopping cards often receive offers for promotional discounts tailored specifically for them at checkout counters. Moviegoers who order tickets online can pick them up at ATM-like devices at movie theaters and avoid waiting in line at the box office. Of course, as consumers use more and more highly convenient technologies, such as credit and ATM cards, EZ Passes, frequency cards, automated phone systems, and online shopping, there are more and more electronic records of their consumption patterns. These records are not anonymous, and savvy marketers are beginning to collect these data and use them, sometimes almost instantly, to influence consumption behavior. The ethical and privacy issues stemming from collecting data that are not anonymous via technological devices are receiving more and more public debates.

Gambling casinos have been in the forefront of developing systems that track individual customer data collected during the various stages of a customer's visit and cross-matching them with data collected on previous visits of that customer (including spending usage). They use this data to classify visitors into categories based on their "loyalty levels" and implement corresponding rewards that are delivered almost immediately. For example, normally about 50,000 people a day visit the Foxwood's Casino in Connecticut. Most of them use magnetic cards called "frequent player cards." Sophisticated electronic network systems monitor the gaming patterns, eating habits, and room preferences of all visitors. When a player sits at a table, within seconds, the casino's manager can read the guest's history on the screen, including alcoholic beverages preferred and gaming habits. Because there are electronic tags in the chips issued to each player, when a player leaves the table, his or her record is updated instantly and made available at any contact point for that customer throughout the entire casino complex. Thus, the casino can instantly reward customers who are good for business by giving them free meals and room upgrades and inviting them to gamble in designated VIP lounges. The customers love the frequency cards because they keep track of their spending, and the casinos benefit from each swipe of the card because it provides more information about customers. The casino has two identical computer systems and, if needed, can switch to a backup immediately and thus avoid the many thousands of dollars that may be lost during an even brief period of operating without computers.[2] Figure 2-3 depicts Foxwood's customer tracking system.

Marketers also use physiological observation devices that monitor respondents' patterns of information processing. For example, an electronic eye camera may be used to monitor the *eye movements* of subjects looking at a series of various product advertisements, and electronic sensors placed on the subjects' heads can monitor the *brain activity* and attentiveness levels involved in viewing each ad.

Experimentation It is possible to test the relative sales appeal of many types of variables such as package designs, prices, promotional offers, or copy themes through experiments designed to identify cause and effect. In such experiments

FIGURE 2-3

Foxwood's Casino Customer Tracking System
Courtesy of Kim S. Nash, "Casinos Hit Jackpot with Customer Data," *Computer World*, July 2, 2001, 17.

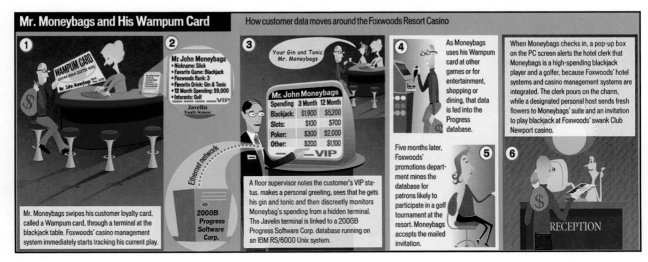

(called *causal research*), only some variables are manipulated (the *independent variables*), while all other elements are kept constant. A **controlled experiment** of this type ensures that any difference in the outcome (the *dependent variable*) is due to different treatments of the variable under study and not to extraneous factors. For example, one study tested the effectiveness of using an attractive versus unattractive endorser in promoting two types of products: products that are used to enhance one's attractiveness (e.g., a men's cologne) and products that are not (e.g., a pen). The endorser used was a fictitious character named Phil Johnson who was described as a member of the U.S. Olympic water polo team. The photograph depicting the attractive endorser was a scanned image of an attractive athletic man, whereas the picture depicting the unattractive endorser was the same image graphically modified to reduce attractiveness. The subjects viewed each endorser-product combination for 15 seconds (simulating the viewing of an actual print ad) and then filled out a questionnaire that measured their attitudes and purchase intentions toward the products advertised. In this study, the combinations of the product (i.e., used/not used to enhance one's attractiveness) and the endorser's attractiveness (i.e., attractive/nonattractive endorser) were the *manipulated treatments* (i.e., the independent variables) and the combination of the attitudes and purchase intentions toward the product was the *dependent variable*. The study discovered that the attractive endorser was more effective in promoting both types of products.[3]

A major application of causal research is **test marketing** in which, prior to launching a new product, elements such as package, price, and promotion are manipulated in a controlled setting in order to predict sales or gauge the possible responses to the product. Today some researchers employ *virtual reality methods*. For example, in a market test, respondents can view supermarket shelves stocked with many products, including different versions of the same product, on computer screens, "pick up" an item by touching the image, examine it by rotating the image with a track ball, and place it in a shopping cart if they decide to buy it. The researchers observe how long the respondents spend in looking at the product, the time spent in examining each side of the package, the products purchased, and the order of the purchases.[4]

Surveys If researchers wish to ask consumers about their purchase preferences and consumption experiences they can do so in person, by mail, by telephone, or online. Each of these survey methods has certain advantages and certain disadvantages that the researcher must weigh when selecting the method of contact (see Table 2-4).

Personal interview surveys most often take place in the home or in retail shopping areas. The latter, referred to as *mall intercepts*, are used more frequently than

TABLE 2-4 Comparative Advantages and Disadvantages of Mail, Telephone, Personal Interview, and Online Surveys

	MAIL	**TELEPHONE**	**PERSONAL INTERVIEW**	**ONLINE**
Cost	Low	Moderate	High	Low
Speed	Slow	Immediate	Slow	Fast
Response rate	Low	Moderate	High	Self-selected
Geographic flexibility	Excellent	Good	Difficult	Excellent
Interviewer bias	N/A	Moderate	Problematic	N/A
Interviewer supervision	N/A	Easy	Difficult	N/A
Quality of response	Limited	Limited	Excellent	Excellent

home interviews because of the high incidence of not-at-home working women and the reluctance of many people today to allow a stranger into their home.

Telephone surveys are also used to collect consumer data; however, evenings and weekends are often the only times to reach telephone respondents, who tend to be less responsive—even hostile—to calls that interrupt dinner, television viewing, or general relaxation. The difficulties of reaching people with unlisted telephone numbers have been solved through random-digit dialing, and the costs of a wide-spread telephone survey are often minimized by using toll-free telephone lines. Other problems arise, however, from the increased use of answering machines and caller ID to screen calls. Some market research companies have tried to automate telephone surveys, but many respondents are even less willing to interact with an electronic voice than with a live interviewer.

Mail surveys are conducted by sending questionnaires directly to individuals at their home. One of the major problems of mail questionnaires is a low response rate, but researchers have developed a number of techniques to increase returns, such as enclosing a stamped, self-addressed envelope, using a provocative questionnaire, and sending prenotification letters as well as follow-up letters. A number of commercial research firms that specialize in consumer surveys have set up panels of consumers who, for a token fee, agree to complete the research company's mail questionnaires on a regular basis. Sometimes panel members are also asked to keep diaries of their purchases.

Online surveys are sometimes conducted on the Internet. Respondents are directed to the marketer's (or researcher's) Web site by computer ads or home pages; thus, the samples are self-selected and the results, therefore, cannot be projected to the larger population. Most computer polls ask respondents to complete a profile consisting of demographic questions that enable the researchers to classify the responses to the substantive product or service questions.

Researchers who conduct computer polling believe that the anonymity of the Internet encourages respondents to be more forthright and honest than they would be if asked the same questions in person or by mail; others believe that the data collected may be suspect because some respondents may create new online personalities that do not reflect their own beliefs or behavior. Some survey organizations cite the inherent advantages of wide reach and affordability in online polling.

Quantitative Research Data Collection Instruments

Data collection instruments are developed as part of a study's total research design to systematize the collection of data and to ensure that all respondents are asked the same questions in the same order. Data collection instruments include questionnaires, personal inventories, attitude scales, and, for qualitative data, discussion guides. Data collection instruments are usually pretested and "debugged" to assure the validity and reliability of the research study. A study is said to have **validity** if it does, in fact, collect the appropriate data needed to answer the questions or objectives stated in the first (objectives) stage of the research process. A study is said to have **reliability** if the same questions, asked of a similar sample, produce the same findings. Often a sample is systematically divided in two, and each half is given the same questionnaire to complete. If the results from each half are similar, the questionnaire is said to have *split-half reliability.*

Questionnaires For quantitative research, the primary data collection instrument is the questionnaire, which can be sent through the mail to selected respondents for self-administration or can be administered by field interviewers in person or by telephone. In order to motivate respondents to take the time to respond to surveys, researchers have found that questionnaires must be interesting, objective, unambiguous, easy to complete, and generally not burdensome. To enhance the analysis and facilitate the classification of responses into meaningful categories, question- naires include both substantive questions that are relevant to the purposes of the study and pertinent demographic questions.

The questionnaire itself can be *disguised* or *undisguised* as to its true purpose; a disguised questionnaire sometimes yields more truthful answers and avoids responses that respondents may think are expected or sought. Questions can be *open-ended* (requiring answers in the respondent's own words) or *closed-ended* (the respondent merely checks the appropriate answer from a list of options). Open-ended questions yield more insightful information but are more difficult to code and to analyze; closed-ended questions are relatively simple to tabulate and analyze, but the answers are limited to the alternative responses provided (i.e., to the existing insights of the questionnaire designer). Great care must be taken in wording each question to avoid biasing the responses. The sequence of questions is also important: The opening questions must be interesting enough to "draw" the respondent into participating, they must proceed in a logical order, and demo- graphic (classification) questions should be placed at the end, where they are more likely to be answered. The format of the questionnaire and the wording and sequence of the questions affect the validity of the responses and, in the case of mail questionnaires, the number (rate) of responses received. Questionnaires usu- ally offer respondents confidentiality or anonymity to dispel any reluctance about self-disclosure.

Attitude Scales Researchers often present respondents with a list of products or product attributes for which they are asked to indicate their relative feelings or eval- uations. The instruments most frequently used to capture this evaluative data are called **attitude scales.** The most frequently used attitude scales are Likert scales, semantic differential scales, behavior intention scales, and rank-order scales.

The *Likert scale* is the most popular form of attitude scale because it is easy for researchers to prepare and to interpret, and simple for consumers to answer. They check or write the number corresponding to their level of "agreement" or "dis- agreement" with each of a series of statements that describes the attitude object under investigation. The scale consists of an equal number of agreement/disagreement choices on either side of a neutral choice. A principal benefit of the Likert scale is that it gives the researcher the option of considering the responses to each state- ment separately or of combining the responses to produce an overall score.

The *semantic differential scale,* like the Likert scale, is relatively easy to con- struct and administer. The scale typically consists of a series of bipolar adjectives (such as good/bad, hot/cold, like/dislike, or expensive/inexpensive) anchored at the ends of an odd-numbered (e.g., five- or seven-point) continuum. Respondents are asked to evaluate a concept (or a product or company) on the basis of each attribute by checking the point on the continuum that best reflects their feelings or beliefs. Care must be taken to vary the location of positive and negative terms from the left side of the continuum to the right side to avoid consumer response bias. Sometimes an even-numbered scale is used to eliminate the option of a neutral answer. An important feature of the semantic differential scale is that it can be used to develop graphic consumer profiles of the concept under study. Semantic differential profiles are also used to compare consumer perceptions of competitive products and to indi- cate areas for product improvement when perceptions of the existing product are measured against perceptions of the "ideal" product.

The *behavior intention scale* measures the likelihood that consumers will act in a certain way in the future, such as buying the product again or recommending it to a friend. These scales are easy to construct, and consumers are asked to make subjective judgments regarding their future behavior.

With *rank-order scales,* subjects are asked to rank items such as products (or retail stores or Web sites) in order of preference in terms of some criterion, such as overall quality or value for the money. Rank-order scaling procedures provide important competitive information and enable marketers to identify needed areas of improvement in product design and product positioning. Figure 2-4 provides examples of the attitude scales that are frequently utilized in consumer research.

Qualitative Research Designs and Data Collection Methods

In selecting the appropriate research format for a qualitative study, the researcher has to take into consideration the purpose of the study and the types of data needed. Although the research methods used may differ in composition, they all have roots in psychoanalytic and clinical aspects of psychology, and they stress open-ended and free-response types of questions to stimulate respondents to reveal their innermost thoughts and beliefs.

The key data collection techniques for qualitative studies are depth interviews, focus groups, projective techniques, and metaphor analysis. These techniques are regularly used in the early stages of attitude research to pinpoint relevant product-related beliefs or attributes and to develop an initial picture of consumer attitudes (especially the beliefs and attributes they associate with particular products and services).

Depth Interviews A **depth interview** is a lengthy (generally 30 minutes to an hour), nonstructured interview between a respondent and a highly trained interviewer, who minimizes his or her own participation in the discussion after establishing the general subject to be discussed. (However, as noted earlier, interpretative researchers often take a more active role in the discussion.) Respondents are encouraged to talk freely about their activities, attitudes, and interests in addition to the product category or brand under study. Transcripts, videotapes, or audiotape recordings of interviews are then carefully studied, together with reports of respondents' moods and any gestures or "body language" they may have used to convey attitudes or motives. Such studies provide marketers with valuable ideas about product design or redesign and provide insights for positioning or repositioning the product. For purposes of copytesting, respondents might be asked to describe in depth various ads they are shown. Other techniques include *autodriving* in which researchers show respondents photos, videos, and audiotapes of their own shopping behavior and ask them to explicitly comment on their consumption actions.[5]

Focus Groups A **focus group** consists of 8 to 10 respondents who meet with a moderator-analyst for a group discussion "focused" on a particular product or product category (or any other subject of research interest). Respondents are encouraged to discuss their interests, attitudes, reactions, motives, lifestyles, feelings about the product or product category, usage experience, and so forth.

Because a focus group takes about 2 hours to complete, a researcher can easily conduct two or three focus groups (with a total of 30 respondents) in one day, while it might take that same researcher five or six days to conduct 30 individual depth interviews. Analysis of responses in both depth interviews and focus groups requires a great deal of skill on the part of the researcher. Focus group sessions are invariably taped, and sometimes videotaped, to assist in the analysis. Interviews are usually held in specially designed conference rooms with one-way mirrors that enable marketers and advertising agency staff to observe the sessions without disrupting or inhibiting the responses.

Respondents are recruited on the basis of a carefully drawn consumer profile (called a screener questionnaire) based on specifications defined by marketing

FIGURE 2-4

Attitude Scales

LIKERT SCALE

For each of the following statements, please check the response that best describes the extent to which you agree or disagree with each statement.

	Strongly Agree	Somewhat Agree	Neither Agree nor Disagree	Somewhat Disagree	Strongly Disagree
It's fun to shop online.					
I am afraid to give my credit card number online.					

Two widely used applications of the Likert Scale to measure consumer attitudes are:

SATISFACTION MEASURES

Over all, how satisfied are you with Bank X's online banking?

Very Satisfied	Somewhat Satisfied	Neither Satisfied nor Dissatisfied	Somewhat Dissatisfied	Very Dissatisfied

IMPORTANCE SCALES

The following list of features are associated with shopping on the Internet. For each feature, please check the one alternative that best expresses how important or unimportant that feature is to you.

	Extremely Important	Somewhat Important	Neither Important nor Unimportant	Somewhat Unimportant	Not at All Important
Speed of downloading the order form					
Being able to register with the site					

SEMANTIC DIFFERENTIAL SCALE

For each of the following features, please check one alternative that best expresses your impression of how that feature applies to **online banking:**

Competitive rates ├──┼──┼──┼──┼──┼──┤ Noncompetitive rates

Reliable ├──┼──┼──┼──┼──┼──┤ Unreliable

Note: The same semantic differential scale can be applied to two competitive offerings, such as online banking and regular banking, and a graphic representation of the profiles of the two alternatives, along with the bipolar adjectives included in the scale, can be easily constructed.

BEHAVIOR INTENTION SCALES

How likely are you to continue using Bank X's online banking for the next six months?

Definitely Will Continue	Probably Will Continue	Might or Might Not Continue	Probably Will Not Continue	Definitely Will Not Continue

How likely are you to recommend Bank X's online banking to a friend?

Definitely Will Recommend	Probably Will Recommend	Might or Might Not Recommend	Probably Will Not Recommend	Definitely Will Not Recommend

RANK ORDER SCALE

We would like to find out about your preferences regarding banking methods. Please rank the following banking methods by placing a "1" in front of the method that you prefer most, a "2" next to your second preference, and continuing until you have ranked all of the methods.

_____ Inside the bank   _____ Online banking   _____ Banking by telephone

_____ ATM   _____ Banking by mail

FIGURE 2-5

Selected Portions of a
Discussion Guide

> 1. Why did you decide to use your current cellular company? (Probe)
> 2. How long have you used your current cellular company? (Probe)
> 3. Have you ever switched services? When? What caused the change? (Probe)
> 4. What do you think of the overall quality of your current service? (Probe)
> 5. What are the important criteria in selecting a cellular service? (Probe)
>
> Examples of Probe questions:
>   a. Tell me more about that . . .
>   b. Share your thinking on this . . .
>   c. Does anyone see it differently . . .

management and usually are paid a fee for their participation. Sometimes users of the company's brands are clustered in one or more groups, and their responses are compared to those of nonusers interviewed in other groups.

Some marketers prefer focus groups to individual depth interviews because it takes less time over all to complete the study, and they feel that the freewheeling group discussions and group dynamics tend to yield a greater number of new ideas and insights than depth interviews. Other marketers prefer individual depth interviews because they feel that respondents are free of group pressure and thus are less likely to give socially acceptable (and not necessarily truthful) responses, are more likely to remain attentive during the entire interview, and—because of the greater personal attention received—are more likely to reveal private thoughts. Figure 2-5 presents a portion of a discussion guide that might be used in a focus-group session to gain insights into the attitudes of consumers toward various cellular service providers. The findings would be equally relevant to the positioning of a new cellular service provider or the repositioning of an existing provider.

Projective Techniques Projective techniques are designed to tap the underlying motives of individuals despite their unconscious rationalizations or efforts at conscious concealment. They consist of a variety of disguised "tests" that contain ambiguous stimuli, such as incomplete sentences, untitled pictures or cartoons, ink blots, word-association tests, and other-person characterizations. Projective techniques are sometimes administered as part of a focus group but more often are used during depth interviews. Because projective methods are closely associated with researching consumer needs and motivation, they are more fully discussed in Chapter 4.

Metaphor Analysis In the 1990s, a stream of consumer research emerged suggesting that most communication is nonverbal and that people do not think in words but in images. If consumers' thought processes consist of series of images, or pictures in their mind, then it is likely that many respondents cannot adequately convey their feelings and attitudes about the research subject (such as a product or brand) through the use of words alone. Therefore, it is important to enable consumers to represent their images in an alternate, nonverbal form—through the use, say, of sounds, music, drawings, or pictures. The use of one form of expression to describe or represent feelings about another is called a *metaphor*. A number of consumer theorists have come to believe that people use metaphors as the most basic method of thought and communication.

The Zaltman Metaphor Elicitation Technique (ZMET)—the first patented marketing research tool in the United States—relies on visual images to assess consumers' deep and subconscious thoughts about products, services, and marketing strategies. In one study about consumer perceptions of advertising, prescreened respondents were asked to bring in to a depth interview pictures that illustrated their perceptions of the value of advertising. They were asked to bring pictures from magazines, newspapers, artwork, photos they took especially for the study or from existing collections, but not actual print advertisements. Each respondent participated in a two-hour videotaped interview (on average, each respondent brought in 13 images representing his or her impressions of the value of advertising). The interview used several methods that are part of the ZMET technique to elicit key metaphors and the interrelationships among them from the respondents. The interviews were then analyzed by qualified researchers according to the ZMET criteria. The findings revealed that the *ambivalent* respondents had both favorable (e.g., information and entertainment values) and unfavorable (e.g., misrepresentation of reality) impressions of advertising; *skeptics* had mostly negative, but some positive impressions of advertising; and *hostile* respondents viewed advertising as an all-negative force.[6] Another application of ZMET is using the instrument to get consumers' reactions to movie scripts.[7]

Customer Satisfaction Measurement

Gauging the level of customer satisfaction and its determinants is critical for every company. Marketers can use such data to retain customers, sell more products and services, improve the quality and value of their offerings, and operate more effectively and efficiently. **Customer satisfaction measurement** includes quantitative and qualitative measures, as well as a variety of contact methods with customers. These methods and instruments and examples of their application to business situations are detailed in Table 2-5.

TABLE 2-5	Customer Satisfaction Data Collection Instruments
Customer satisfaction surveys	Generally, customer satisfaction surveys use 5-point semantic differential scales ranging from "very dissatisfied" to "very satisfied." These surveys measure how satisfied the customers are along relevant attributes of the product or service and the relative importance of the attributes (using an importance scale). Research shows that customers who indicate they are "very satisfied" (typically a score of 5 on the satisfaction scale) are much more profitable and loyal than customers who indicate that they are "satisfied" (a score of 4). Therefore, companies that merely strive to have "satisfied" customers are making a crucial error.[a]
Customers' expectations versus their perceptions of the product or service delivered	This approach states that customers' satisfaction or dissatisfaction is a function of the difference between what they had *expected* to get from the product or service purchased and their perceptions of what they *received*. A group of researchers developed a scale that measures the performance of the service received against two expectations levels: *adequate* service and *desired* service, and also measures the customers' future intentions regarding purchasing the service.[b] This approach is more sophisticated than standard customer satisfaction surveys and more likely to yield results that can be used to develop corrective measures for products and services that fall short of customers' expectations.
Mystery shoppers	This method consists of employing professional observers, posing as customers, to survey and provide an unbiased evaluation of the operation's service against the company's service standards in order to identify opportunities for improving productivity and efficiency. For example, one bank used mystery shoppers who, while dealing with a bank employee on another matter, dropped hints about buying a house or seeking to borrow college funds. Employees were scored on how quickly and effectively they provided information about the bank's pertinent product or service.[c] The *Wall Street Journal* employed a Dallas firm to dispatch mystery shoppers to 25 McDonald's outlets in the New York, Chicago, Dallas, and Los Angeles regions. The reports indicated that only 64% of the employees encountered by the mystery shoppers greeted customers with a smile, only 52% repeated the order for accuracy, and only 36% mentioned food promotions or larger-size products.[d]

(continued on next page)

TABLE 2-5	(Continued)
Critical incident method	This method consists of asking customers to think back and describe interactions that they had with employees in a particular industry, such as hotels or airlines, that they recall as particularly satisfying or dissatisfying. This qualitative tool can yield important insights that can be used to train employees better. One study discovered that, somewhat surprisingly, many experiences cited as particularly satisfying were incidents where the service provided initially failed but, because it was "recovered" well by the service employee, the customer remembered it as a particularly satisfactory experience.[e] Some argue that this method, if used by itself, is insufficient, but should only be used in the context of additional data on the customer–marketer relationship.[f]
Analyzing customer complaints	Research indicates that only a few unsatisfied customers actually complain. Most unsatisfied customers say nothing but switch to competitors. A good complaint analysis system should: 1. Encourage customers to complain and provide suggestions for improvements by having adequate forms (with sufficient space to write comments) and mechanisms beyond the routine "how was everything?" questions. A good approach is to include examples on the suggestions and complaint forms of how past customer input helped improve service. 2. Establish "listening posts" where specially designated employees either listen to customers' comments or actively solicit input from them (e.g., in a hotel lobby or on checkout lines). 3. Each complaint, by itself, provides little information. The company must have a system in which complaints are categorized and then analyzed. 4. Use software to speed up complaint analysis and handling. eBay uses software on its Web site to track customers' opinions, capture complaints, and follow up on them very quickly. The company says it has reduced customer dissatisfaction by nearly 30% after one year of using this tool.[g]
Analyzing customer defections	Because high customer loyalty rates are an important competitive advantage, and because it is generally much cheaper to retain customers than to get new ones, companies must find out *why* customers leave (e.g., through exit interviews) and also *intervene* when customers' behaviors show that they may be considering leaving. For example, one bank that was losing about 20% of its customers every year discovered that segmenting defecting customers along demographic and family life cycle characteristics was ineffective in reducing defection rates. The bank then compared 500 transaction records of loyal customers with 500 transaction records of defectors, along such dimensions as number of transactions, frequency of transactions, and fluctuations in average balances. The bank then identified transaction patterns that may indicate future defection and started targeting potential defectors and encouraging them to stay.[h]

[a]Thomas O. Jones and W. Earl Sasser, Jr., "Why Satisfied Customers Defect," *Harvard Business Review,* November–December 1995, 88–99.
[b]A. Parasuraman, Valarie A. Zeithaml, and Leonard L. Berry, "Moving Forward in Service Quality Research: Measuring Different Customer-Expectation Levels, Comparing Alternative Scales, and Examining the Performance-Behavioral Intentions Link," Report No. 94–114, Marketing Science Institute, 1994.
[c]Cynthia Vinarsky, "Mystery Shoppers Monitor Warren, Ohio, Credit Union's Customer Service," *Knight Ridder Business News,* March 19, 2002, 1.
[d]Shirley Leung, "McDonald's Asks Mystery Shoppers What Ails Sales—Undercover Customers to Rate Service and Food Quality; Our Own Give It a 81.9%," *Wall Street Journal,* December 17, 2001, B1.
[e]Mary Jo Bitner and Bernard H. Booms, "The Service Encounter: Diagnosing Favorable and Unfavorable Incidents," *Journal of Marketing,* January 1990, 71–84.
[f]Bo Edvardsson and Tore Strandvik, "Is a Critical Incident Critical for a Customer Relationship?" *Managing Service Quality,* 2000, 82–91.
[g]L. Biff Motley, "Speeding Up Handling of Satisfaction Problems" *Bank Marketing,* September 2001, 35.
[h]Michael M. Pearson and Guy H. Gessner "Transactional Segmentation to Slow Customer Defections," *Marketing Management,* Summer 1999, 16–23.

Sampling and Data Collection

An integral component of a research design is the sampling plan. Specifically, the sampling plan addresses three questions: whom to survey (the sampling unit), how many to survey (the sample size), and how to select them (the sampling procedure). Deciding whom to survey requires explicit definition of the *universe* or boundaries of the market from which data are sought so that an appropriate sample can be selected (such as

TABLE 2-6	Sampling

PROBABILITY SAMPLE

Simple random sample	Every member of the population has a known and equal chance of being selected.
Systematic random sample	A member of the population is selected at random and then every "*n*th" person is selected.
Stratified random sample	The population is divided into mutually exclusive groups (such as age groups), and random samples are drawn from each group.
Cluster (area) sample	The population is divided into mutually exclusive groups (such as blocks), and the researcher draws a sample of the groups to interview.

NONPROBABILITY SAMPLE

Convenience sample	The researcher selects the most accessible population members from whom to obtain information (e.g., students in a classroom).
Judgment sample	The researcher uses his or her judgment to select population members who are good sources for accurate information (e.g., experts in the relevant field of study).
Quota sample	The researcher interviews a prescribed number of people in each of several categories (e.g., 50 men and 50 women).

working mothers). Interviewing the correct target market or potential target market is basic to the validity of the study.

The size of the sample is dependent both on the size of the budget and on the degree of confidence that the marketer wants to place in the findings. The larger the sample, the more likely the responses will reflect the total universe under study. It is interesting to note, however, that a small sample can often provide highly reliable findings, depending on the sampling procedure adopted. (The exact number needed to achieve a specific level of confidence in the accuracy of the findings can be computed with a mathematical formula that is beyond the scope of this discussion.)

If the researcher wants the findings to be projectable to the total population, then a **probability sample** should be chosen; if it is sufficient to have the findings "representative" of the population, then a **nonprobability sample** can be selected. Table 2-6 summarizes the features of various types of probability and nonprobability designs.

As indicated earlier, qualitative studies usually require highly trained social scientists to collect data. A quantitative study generally uses a field staff that is either recruited and trained directly by the researcher or contracted from a company that specializes in conducting field interviews. In either case, it is often necessary to verify whether the interviews have, in fact, taken place. This is sometimes done by a postcard mailing to respondents asking them to verify that they participated in an interview on the date recorded on the questionnaire form. Completed questionnaires are reviewed on a regular basis as the research study progresses to ensure that the recorded responses are clear, complete, and legible.

In qualitative research, the moderator or test administrator usually analyzes the responses received. In quantitative research, the researcher supervises the analysis. Open-ended responses are first coded and quantified (i.e., converted into numerical scores); then all of the responses are tabulated and analyzed using sophisticated analytical programs that correlate the data by selected variables and cluster the data by selected demographic characteristics.

In both qualitative and quantitative research, the research report includes a brief executive summary of the findings. Depending on the assignment from marketing management, the research report may or may not include recommendations for marketing action. The body of the report includes a full description of the methodology used and, for quantitative research, also includes tables and graphics to support the findings. A sample of the questionnaire is usually included in the appendix to enable management to evaluate the objectivity of the findings.

CONDUCTING A RESEARCH STUDY

In designing a research study, researchers adapt the research process described in the previous sections to the special needs of the study. For example, if a researcher is told that the purpose of the study is to develop a segmentation strategy for a new online dating service, he or she would first collect secondary data, such as population statistics (e.g., the number of men and women online in selected metropolitan areas within a certain age range, their marital status, and occupations). Then, together with the marketing manager, the researcher would specify the parameters (i.e., define the sampling unit) of the population to be studied (e.g., single, college-educated men and women between the ages of 18 and 45 who live or work within the Boston metropolitan area). A qualitative study (e.g., focus groups) might be undertaken first to gather information about the target population's attitudes and concerns about meeting people online, their special interests, and the specific services and precautions they would like an online dating service to provide. This phase of the research should result in tentative generalizations about the specific age group(s) to target and the services to offer.

The marketing manager then might instruct the researcher to conduct a quantitative study to confirm and attach "hard" numbers (percentages) to the findings that emerged from the focus groups. The first-phase study should have provided sufficient insights to develop a research design and to launch directly into a large-scale survey. If, however, there is still doubt about any element of the research design, such as question wording or format, they might decide first to do a small-scale exploratory study. Then, after refining the questionnaire and any other needed elements of the research design, they would launch a full-scale quantitative survey, using a probability sample that would allow them to project the findings to the total population of singles (as originally defined). The analysis should cluster prospective consumers of the online dating service into segments based on relevant sociocultural or lifestyle characteristics and on media habits, attitudes, perceptions, and geodemographic characteristics.

Summary

The field of consumer research developed as an extension of the field of marketing research to enable marketers to predict how consumers would react in the marketplace and to understand the reasons they made the purchase decisions they did. Consumer research undertaken from a managerial perspective to improve strategic marketing decisions is known as positivism. Positivist research is quantitative and empirical and tries to identify cause-and-effect relationships in buying situations. It is often supplemented with qualitative research.

Qualitative research is concerned with probing deep within the consumer's psyche to understand the motivations, feelings, and emotions that drive consumer behavior. Qualitative research findings cannot be projected to larger populations but are used primarily to provide new ideas and insights for the development of positioning strategies. Interpretivism, a qualitative research perspective, is generally more concerned with understanding the act of consuming rather than the act of buying (consumer decision making). Interpretivists view consumer behavior as a subset of human behavior, and increased understanding as a key to eliminating some of the ills associated with destructive consumer behavior.

Each theoretical research perspective is based on its own specific assumptions and uses its own research techniques. Positivists typically use probability studies that can be generalized to larger populations. Interpretivists tend to view consumption experiences as unique situations that occur at specific moments in time; therefore, they cannot be generalized to larger populations. The two theoretical research orientations are highly complementary and, when used together, provide a deeper and more insightful understanding of consumer behavior than either approach used alone.

The consumer research process—whether quantitative or qualitative in approach—generally consists of six steps: defining objectives, collecting secondary data, developing a research design, collecting primary data, analyzing the data, and preparing a report of the findings. The researcher must make every effort to ensure that the research findings are reliable (that a replication of the study would provide the same results) and valid (that they answer the specific questions for which the study was originally undertaken).

Discussion Questions

1. Have you ever been selected as a respondent in a marketing research survey? If yes, how were you contacted? Why do you think you, in particular, were selected? Did you know or could you guess the purpose of the survey? Do you know the name of the company or brand involved in the survey?

2. Identify a purchase you have made that was motivated primarily by your desire to obtain a special "feeling" or an "experience." Would the positivist or interpretivist research paradigm be a more appropriate way to study your consumption behavior? Explain your answer.

3. What is the difference between primary and secondary research? Under what circumstances might the availability of secondary data make primary research unnecessary? What are some major sources of secondary data?

4. Visit the Web sites of A.C. Nielsen Research. Which of Nielsen's syndicated data services would you use to develop a *customer lifetime value and profitability analysis* for a product or service of your choice?

5. A manufacturer of powdered fruit drinks would like to investigate the effects of food

color and label information on consumers' perceptions of flavor and product preferences. Would you advise the manufacturer to use observational research, experimentation, or a survey? Explain your choice.

6. Why might a researcher prefer to use focus groups rather than depth interviews? When might depth interviews be preferable?

7. Compare the advantages and disadvantages of mail, telephone, personal, and online surveys.

8. How would the interpretation of survey results change if the researcher used a probability sample rather than a nonprobability sample? Explain your answer.

9. Why is customer satisfaction measurement an important part of marketing research? Apply one of the methods in Table 2-5 to measure your fellow students' satisfaction with the services provided by the registrar at your university.

Exercises

1. Neutrogena is a manufacturer of personal care products for young adults. The company would like to extend its facial cleansers product line. Design a (1) qualitative and (2) quantitative research design for the company focused on this objective.

2. A real-life customer tracking model is featured in Figure 2-3. Develop a similar model for tracking customers' visits to one of Disney's theme parks.

3. Develop a questionnaire to measure students' attitudes toward the instructor in this course.

    a. Prepare five statements measuring students' attitudes via a Likert scale.

    b. Prepare five semantic differential scales to measure student attitudes. Can the same dimensions be measured by using either scaling technique? Explain your answer.

Key Terms

- **Attitude scales**
- **Controlled experiment**
- **Customer lifetime value**
- **Customer satisfaction measurement**
- **Depth interview**
- **Exploratory study**
- **Focus group**

- **Interpretivism**
- **Motivational research**
- **Nonprobability sample**
- **Objectives**
- **Positivism**
- **Primary research**
- **Probability sample**

- **Qualitative research**
- **Quantitative research**
- **Reliability**
- **Secondary data**
- **Secondary research**
- **Test marketing**
- **Validity**

Notes

1. Leslie Kaufman, "Enough Talk," *Newsweek,* August 19, 1997, 48–49.

2. Kim S. Nash, "Casinos Hit Jackpot with Customer Data," *Computer World,* July 2, 2001, 16–17; *Modern Marvels: Casino Technology,* VHS Tape, 1999, A&E Television Networks.

3. Brian D. Till and Michael Busler, "The Match-Up Hypothesis: Physical Attractiveness, Expertise, and the Role of Fit on Brand Attitude, Purchase Intent and Brand Beliefs," *Journal of Advertising,* Fall 2000, 1–13.

4. Joseph F. Hair, Robert P. Bush, and David J. Ortinau, *Marketing Research,* 2nd ed. (New York: McGraw Hill Irwin, 2003), Chapter 10.

5. Deborah D. Heisley and Sidney J. Levy, "Autodriving: A Photoelicitation Technique," *Journal of Consumer Research,* December 1991, 257–272.

6. Robin A. Coutler, Gerald Zaltman, and Keith S. Coutler, "Interpreting Consumer Perceptions of Advertising: An Application of the Zaltman Metaphor Elicitation Technique," *Journal of Advertising,* Winter 2001, 1–21.

7. Emily Eakin, "Penetrating the Mind by Metaphor," *New York Times,* February 23, 2002, B9, B11.

You're working out instead of eating out.
Because there aren't enough hours in the day.

You're doing more, being smarter, and constantly performing
at your best. It's a demanding life that uses up essential nutrients.
And you don't always eat the way you know you should
to replenish them. That's why there's New Centrum® Performance.™
It starts as a complete* Centrum® multi, then we add higher levels
of energy essential nutrients, including key B vitamins and antioxidants,
plus ginkgo and ginseng to help energize your mind and body.†
Here's a new kind of multi, specially designed for today's demanding life.

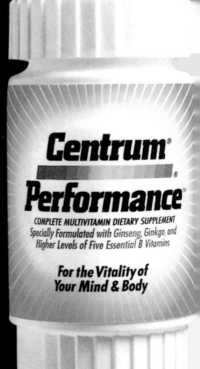

Centrum®
Performance™
COMPLETE MULTIVITAMIN DIETARY SUPPLEMENT
Specially Formulated with Ginseng, Ginkgo, and
Higher Levels of Five Essential B Vitamins

**For the Vitality of
Your Mind & Body**

New Centrum® Performance™
Life Demands It.™

www.centrum.com

Use as a part of a healthy lifestyle. *Contains all nutrients with an RDI.
†These statements have not been evaluated by the Food & Drug Administration.
This product is not intended to diagnose, treat, cure, or prevent any disease.

Market Segmentation

Market segmentation and diversity are complementary concepts. Without a diverse marketplace composed of many different peoples with different backgrounds, countries of origin, interests, needs and wants, and perceptions, there would be little reason to segment markets. Diversity in the global marketplace makes market segmentation an attractive, viable, and potentially highly profitable strategy. The necessary conditions for successful segmentation of any market are a large enough population with sufficient money to spend (general affluence) and sufficient diversity to lend itself to partitioning the market into sizable segments on the basis of demographic, psychological, or other strategic variables. The presence of these conditions in the United States, Canada, Western Europe, Japan, Australia, and other industrialized nations makes these marketplaces extremely attractive to global marketers.

When marketers provide a range of product or service choices to meet diverse consumer interests, consumers are better satisfied, and their overall happiness, satisfaction, and quality of life are ultimately enhanced. Thus, market segmentation is a positive force for both consumers and marketers alike.

What Is Market Segmentation?

Market segmentation can be defined as the process of dividing a market into distinct subsets of consumers with common needs or characteristics and selecting one or more segments to target with a distinct marketing mix. Before the widespread acceptance of market segmentation, the prevailing way of doing business with consumers was through **mass marketing**—that is, offering the same product and marketing mix to all consumers. The essence of this strategy was summed up by the entrepreneur Henry Ford, who offered the Model T automobile to the public "in any color they wanted, as long as it was black."

If all consumers were alike—if they all had the same needs, wants, and desires, and the same background, education, and experience—mass (undifferentiated) marketing would be a logical strategy. Its primary advantage is that it costs less: Only one advertising campaign is needed, only one marketing strategy is developed, and usually only one standardized product is offered. Some companies, primarily those that deal in agricultural products or very basic manufactured goods, successfully follow a mass-marketing strategy. Other marketers, however, see major drawbacks in an undifferentiated marketing approach. When trying to sell the same product to every prospective customer with a single advertising campaign, the marketer must portray its product as a means for satisfying a common or generic need and, therefore, often ends up appealing to no one. A hot water heater may fulfill a widespread need to provide the home with hot water for bathing, dishwashing, and washing clothes, but a standard-size hot water heater may be too big for a grandmother who lives alone and too small for a family of six. Without market differentiation, both the grandmother and the family of six would have to make do with the very same model, and, as we all know, "making do" is a far cry from being satisfied.

The strategy of segmentation allows producers to avoid head-on competition in the marketplace by differentiating their offerings, not only on the basis of price but also through styling, packaging, promotional appeal, method of distribution, and superior service. Marketers have found that the costs of consumer segmentation research, shorter production runs, and differentiated promotional campaigns are usually more than offset by increased sales. In most cases, consumers readily accept the passed-through cost increases for products that more closely satisfy their specific needs.

Market segmentation is just the first step in a three-phase marketing strategy. After segmenting the market into homogeneous clusters, the marketer then must select one or more segments to target. To accomplish this, the marketer must decide on a specific marketing mix—that is, a specific product, price, channel, and/or promotional appeal for each distinct segment. The third step is **positioning** the product so that it is perceived by the consumers in each target segment as satisfying their needs better than other competitive offerings.

WHO USES MARKET SEGMENTATION?

Because the strategy of market segmentation benefits both the consumer *and* the marketer, marketers of consumer goods are eager practitioners. For example, Toyota (www.toyota.com) targets its Celica automobile with its sporty styling, minimal rear seat, and small trunk to young singles; it targets its Avalon, a much larger vehicle, at the family car buyer needing a roomier vehicle. Another example is the market segmentation frequently carried out by food service companies operating

TABLE 3-1	Campus Dining

STAR GAZERS SEGMENT	FUN EXPRESS SEGMENT
Light and healthy foods	Variety, taste, and nutrition
Breakfast: bagel, muffin, cereal	Breakfast: Belgian waffles, omelets, fruit
Lunch: Italian, deli, wraps, expensive options	Lunch: Italian, Mexican, meat/potato/ veggie, grilled/fried chicken sandwich
Late night: frozen yogurt, ice cream	Late night: bakery, cereal, fruit
Price insensitive	Price conscious, like to buy on sale
Brand conscious, follow fashion	Like counterculture brands that change
Work full-time over summer	Work part-time over summer
Active, outgoing, social	Value leisure time
Parents' household income: $100,000+	Parents' household income: $30,000–$60,000
Impulsive shopper	

on college campuses. To illustrate, Sodexho (www.sodexho.com) has developed a segmentation program called LifeSTYLING that allows the company to segment the student body into six segments, each with its own lifestyle characteristics that determine the type of menu items various students prefer, the brands they prefer, the times they prefer to eat, and how to effectively reach them.[1] Table 3-1 presents a closer look at two of these six segments.

Market segmentation also has been adopted by retailers. A great example is Gap, Inc. Gap (www.gap.com) targets different age, income, and lifestyle segments in a diversity of retail outlets. Gap and Super Gap stores are designed to attract a wide age range of consumers who seek a casual and relaxed style of dress. Gap targets upscale consumers through its Banana Republic stores (www.bananarepublic.com) and somewhat downscale customers with its Old Navy Clothing Company stores (www.oldnavy.com). It targets young parents (who are also likely to be Gap or Banana Republic shoppers) with its Baby Gap and Gap Kids stores.[2] Gap is mindful of catering to the needs of specific market components and acknowledging their unique or particular buying patterns.

Hotels also segment their markets and target different chains to different market segments. For example, Marriott (www.marriott.com) operates some 13 "lodging brands." A few examples of its lodging options and the prime target segments Mariott is aiming at include *Fairfield Inns* (for those interested in price-conscious short stays), *SpringHill Suites* (for guests desiring modestly priced suites), *Residence Inns* (for those seeking apartment-like accommodations for extended stays), *Courtyard* (for price-conscious businesspeople), *Marriott Hotels* (for full-service business travelers), and *Marriott Resorts* (for those desiring leisure or vacation accommodations).

Industrial firms also segment their markets, as do not-for-profit organizations and the media. For example, Peterbilt Motors Company (www.peterbilt.com) produces different models of trucks to meet the needs of long-haul truckers, construction projects, refuse collection companies, logging firms, and so on. The company's Web site offers a listing of its various vehicles by segment type. Charities such as the American Cancer Society (www.cancer.org) and UNICEF (www.unicef.org) frequently focus their fund-raising efforts on "heavy givers." Some performing arts centers segment their subscribers on the basis of *benefits sought* and have succeeded in increasing attendance through specialized promotional appeals.

More and more businesses today are using database marketing programs to find out who their best customers are, and these firms will then divide their customer base into segments. It has been suggested that a firm's customer base can be grouped into at least four major segments: (1) *LoLows* (low current share, low-consumption customers), (2) *HiLows* (high current share, low-consumption customers), (3) *LowHighs* (low current share, high-consumption customers), and (4) *HiHighs* (high current share, high-consumption customers). The firm, according to this segmentation, can "starve" the *LoLows,* "tickle" the *HiLows,* "chase" the *LowHighs,* and "stroke" the *HiHighs.*[3]

HOW MARKET SEGMENTATION OPERATES

Segmentation studies are designed to discover the needs and wants of specific groups of consumers, so that specialized goods and services can be developed and promoted to satisfy each group's needs. Many new products have been developed to fill gaps in the marketplace revealed by segmentation research. For instance, Centrum (**www.centrum.com**) has developed a variety of Focused Formula vitamin products that are designed to appeal directly to individuals with specific health issues (e.g., Centrum Prostate, Centrum Heart, Centrum Bone Health, Centrum Energy, Centrum Stress, and Centrum Mental Clarity).

Segmentation studies also are used to guide the redesign or **repositioning** of a product or the addition of a new market segment. For example, Nintendo (**www.nintendo.com**) has expanded its vision for its electronic games to include adult users (promising adult game players "kid-like" fun), and Wolverine, perhaps best known as a manufacturer of men's work boots, now markets a work boot especially designed for women's feet. Similarly, Tootsie Roll, an ever popular marketer of lollipops, is offering yogurt-flavored fruit-smoothie lollipops to adults.[4]

In addition to filling product gaps, segmentation research is regularly used by marketers to identify the most appropriate media in which to place advertisements. Almost all media vehicles—from TV and radio stations to newspapers and magazines—use segmentation research to determine the characteristics of their audience and to publicize their findings in order to attract advertisers seeking a similar audience.

In some cases if segments of customers are large enough and can attract enough advertising, the media will spin off separate programs or publications targeted to the specific segments. For example, *People* (**www.people.com**) has created a separate magazine for teenagers titled *Teen People* (**www.teenpeople.com**). In a somewhat similar fashion, *TIME* (**www.time.com**) targets different segments with special editions of its magazine. Not only does an advertiser have the choice of placing an ad in geographically based editions (e.g., international, U.S., regional, state, and spot market versions of each issue), but also some of the other editions offered by the magazine include a "Gold" edition for upscale mature adults, an "Inside Business" edition for top, middle, and technical management, and a "Women's" edition for affluent professional women. The magazine's Web site indicates that "there are more than 400 ways to buy advertising in *TIME.*" New magazines, TV stations, and radio stations are constantly being created to meet the unfulfilled needs of specific market segments. For example, TeleFutura, a new Spanish-language television network which is available on over 40 stations and hundreds of cable systems, is accessible to over 75 percent of the U.S. Hispanic population.[5]

Bases for Segmentation

The first step in developing a segmentation strategy is to select the most appropriate base(s) on which to segment the market. Nine major categories of consumer characteristics provide the most popular bases for market segmentation. They include geographic factors, demographic factors, psychological factors, psychographic (lifestyle) characteristics, sociocultural variables, use-related characteristics, use-situation factors, benefits sought, and forms of **hybrid segmentation**—such as demographic-psychographic profiles, geodemographic factors, and values and lifestyles. Hybrid segmentation formats each use a combination of several segmentation bases to create rich and comprehensive profiles of particular consumer segments (e.g., a combination of a specific age range, income range, lifestyle, and profession). For example, the Bump Fighter Shaving System, manufactured by the American Safety Razor Company (**www.asrco.com**), is a replaceable-blade razor designed specifically for African American males. The product line has been expanded to now include shaving gel, skin conditioner, a disposable version of the razor, and a treatment mask (to be applied prior to sleeping). Table 3-2 lists the nine segmentation bases, divided into specific variables with examples of each. The following section discusses each of the nine segmentation bases. (Various psychological and sociocultural segmentation variables are examined in greater depth in later chapters.)

GEOGRAPHIC SEGMENTATION

In **geographic segmentation,** the market is divided by location. The theory behind this strategy is that people who live in the same area share some similar needs and wants and that these needs and wants differ from those of people living in other areas. For example, certain food products and/or varieties sell better in one region than in others. More specifically, salsa outsells ketchup in the Southwest, whereas coffee-bean grinders are a "must" in kitchens of people living in the Northwest.[6]

Geographic preferences may also extend to brands, with the East and West Coasts preferring Skippy peanut butter (**www.peanutbutter.com**), the Midwest preferring Jif (**www.jif.com**), and the South buying more Peter Pan (**www.conagra.com**).[7] Consider the growth of Starbucks Coffee (**www.starbucks.com**), whose first store opened in Seattle in 1971. Nearly 20 years later, after a rapid expansion into the eastern states during the 1990s, Starbucks decided to introduce the Milder Dimensions® line of coffees in 1998 to better satisfy its East Coast consumers who tend to prefer a milder coffee than their West Coast counterparts.

Some marketing scholars have argued that direct-mail merchandise catalogs, national toll-free telephone numbers, satellite television transmission, global communication networks, and especially the Internet have erased all regional boundaries and that geographic segmentation should be replaced by a single global marketing strategy. Clearly, any company that decides to put its catalog on the Internet makes it easy for individuals all over the world to browse and become customers. For example, vintage wristwatch dealers in New York, Boston, or Dallas (primarily selling 1940s–1970s high-end wristwatches to collectors) have posted their catalogs on the Web, advertise their Web addresses in *International Wristwatch* and other similar magazines, and gladly accept orders from both U.S. and overseas customers. For the consumers who shop on the Internet, it often makes little difference if online retailers are around the corner or halfway around the world—the only factor that differs is the shipping charge.

TABLE 3-2   Market Segmentation Categories and Selected Variables

SEGMENTATION BASE	SELECTED SEGMENTATION VARIABLES
GEOGRAPHIC SEGMENTATION	
Region	Southwest, Mountain states, Alaska, Hawaii
City size	Major metropolitan areas, small cities, towns
Density of area	Urban, suburban, exurban, rural
Climate	Temperate, hot, humid, rainy
DEMOGRAPHIC SEGMENTATION	
Age	Under 12, 12–17, 18–34, 35–49, 50–64, 65–74, 75–99, 100+
Sex	Male, female
Marital status	Single, married, divorced, living together, widowed
Income	Under $25,000, $25,000–$34,999, $35,000–$49,999, $50,000–$74,999, $75,000–$99,999, $100,000 and over
Education	Some high school, high school graduate, some college, college graduate, postgraduate
Occupation	Professional, blue-collar, white-collar, agricultural, military
PSYCHOLOGICAL SEGMENTATION	
Needs-motivation	Shelter, safety, security, affection, sense of self-worth
Personality	Extroverts, novelty seekers, aggressives, low dogmatics
Perception	Low-risk, moderate-risk, high-risk
Learning-involvement	Low-involvement, high-involvement
Attitudes	Positive attitude, negative attitude
PSYCHOGRAPHIC	
(Lifestyle) Segmentation	Economy-minded, couch potatoes, outdoors enthusiasts, status seekers
SOCIOCULTURAL SEGMENTATION	
Cultures	American, Italian, Chinese, Mexican, French, Pakistani
Religion	Catholic, Protestant, Jewish, Moslem, other
Subcultures (race/ethnic)	African American, Caucasian, Asian, Hispanic
Social class	Lower, middle, upper
Family life cycle	Bachelors, young marrieds, full nesters, empty nesters
USE-RELATED SEGMENTATION	
Usage rate	Heavy users, medium users, light users, nonusers
Awareness status	Unaware, aware, interested, enthusiastic
Brand loyalty	None, some, strong
USE-SITUATION SEGMENTATION	
Time	Leisure, work, rush, morning, night
Objective	Personal, gift, snack, fun, achievement
Location	Home, work, friend's home, in-store
Person	Self, family members, friends, boss, peer
BENEFIT SEGMENTATION	Convenience, social acceptance, long lasting, economy, value-for-the-money
HYBRID SEGMENTATION	
Demographic/psychographic	Combination of demographic and psychographic profiles of consumer segments profiles
Geodemographics	"Money and Brains," "Black Enterprise," "Old Yankee Rows," "Downtown Dixie Style"
SRI VALS™	Actualizer, Fulfilled, Believer, Achiever, Striver, Experiencer, Maker, Struggler

VALS™ is an example of a demographic/psychographic profile. PRIZM is an example of a geodemographic profile.

Other marketers have, for a number of years, been moving in the opposite direction and developing highly regionalized marketing strategies. For example, Campbell's Soup (www.campbellsoup.com) segments its domestic market into more than 20 regions, each with its own advertising and promotion budget. Within each region, Campbell's sales managers have the authority to develop specific advertising and promotional campaigns geared to local market needs and conditions, using local media ranging from newspapers to church bulletins. They work closely with local retailers on displays and promotions and report that their **micromarketing** strategies have won strong consumer support.

Marketers have observed divergent consumer purchasing patterns among urban, suburban, and rural areas. Throughout the United States, more furs and expensive jewelry are sold in cities than in small towns. Even within a large metropolitan area, different types of household furnishings and leisure products are sold in the central city and in the suburbs. Convertible sofas and small appliances are more likely to be bought by city apartment dwellers; suburban homeowners are better prospects for lawn mowers and barbecue grills. Probably the best example of successful segmentation based on geographic density is the giant Wal-Mart operation (www.walmart.com). Historically, Wal-Mart's basic marketing strategy was to locate discount stores in small towns (often in rural areas) that other major retail chain operations were ignoring at the time.

In summary, geographic segmentation is a useful strategy for many marketers. It is relatively easy to find geographically based differences for many products. In addition, geographic segments can be easily reached through the local media, including newspapers, TV and radio, and regional editions of magazines.

DEMOGRAPHIC SEGMENTATION

Demographic characteristics, such as age, sex, marital status, income, occupation, and education, are most often used as the basis for market segmentation. Demography refers to the vital and measurable statistics of a population. Demographics help to *locate* a target market, whereas psychological and sociocultural characteristics help to *describe* how its members *think* and how they *feel*. Demographic information is often the most accessible and cost-effective way to identify a target market. Indeed, most secondary data, including census data, are expressed in demographic terms. Demographics are easier to measure than other segmentation variables; they are invariably included in psychographic and sociocultural studies because they add meaning to the findings. *American Demographics* (www.demographics.com) publishes each month research dealing with demographic issues, and a number of its articles relate demographic variables to other segmentation bases.

Demographic variables reveal ongoing trends that signal business opportunities, such as shifts in age, gender, and income distribution. For example, demographic studies consistently show that the "mature-adult market" (the 50+ market) has a much greater proportion of disposable income than its younger counterparts. This factor alone makes consumers over age 50 a critical market segment for products and services that they buy for themselves, for their adult children, and for their grandchildren.

Age

Product needs and interests often vary with consumers' age. For instance, investors younger than 55 years of age have been found to base their investment decisions on long-term gain and consider current income and intermediate gain less important, whereas investors over 55 years of age tend to be more cautious and place more importance on the intermediate gain and current income of a potential investment.[8] Because of such age-motivated differences, marketers have found age to be a particularly useful demographic variable for market segmentation. Many marketers have carved themselves a niche in the marketplace by concentrating on a specific age segment. For example, although children often consume boxed juice drinks, Minute Maid Company (**www.minutemaid.com**) offers single-serve drinks in pouches, rather than boxes, in order to better appeal to the "tween" market.[9] And one of the reasons why Heinz introduced EZ Squirt ketchup (which includes one version that is green in color) was to better appeal to tweens.[10] Still further, in seeking to cater to consumers under 25 years of age, Pepsi (**www.pepsi.com**) understood that the Internet represented the primary medium of choice and, therefore, increased its effort to create online programs directed at this audience.[11]

The best way to reach a consumer with an advertising message can also be a function of age. For example, approximately 95 percent of U.S. teenagers listen to FM radio, and they average more than 10 hours weekly of such listening. Because radio is a highly selective medium, it can be efficiently employed to reach different segments of teenagers, based on gender, ethnic, and/or geographic dimensions.[12]

Age, especially chronological age, implies a number of underlying forces. In particular, demographers have drawn an important distinction between *age effects* (occurrences due to chronological age) and *cohort effects* (occurrences due to growing up during a specific time period). Examples of the *age effect* are the heightened interest in leisure travel that often occurs for people (single and married) during middle age (particularly in their late fifties or early sixties) and the interest in learning to play golf. Although people of all ages learn to play golf, it is particularly prevalent among people in their fifties. These two trends are examples of age effects because they especially seem to happen as people reach a particular age category.[13] Table 3-3 presents a series of life development stages related to age effects.

TABLE 3-3	Segmentation by Seven Life Development Stages

MAJOR PHASE NAME	AGE	LIFE DEVELOPMENT STAGE (AGE)	MAJOR STAGE TASK
Provisional Adulthood	18–29	Pulling Up Roots	Detaching from family, searching for identity, choosing a career
First Adulthood	30–49	Reaching Out (30–35)	Selecting a mate, working on career
		Questions/Questions (36–44)	Searching for personal values, reevaluating relationships
		Midlife Explosion (45–49)	Searching for meaning, reassessing marriage, relating to teenage children with depression being common in this stage
Second Adulthood	50–85+	Settling Down (50–55)	Adjusting to realities of work, adjusting to an empty nest, being active in community
		Mellowing (56–64)	Adjusting to health problems, approaching retirement
		Retirement (65+)	Adjusting to retirement, reassessing finances, being concerned with health

Source: Adapted from Linda Morton, "Segmenting Publics by Life Development Stages," *Public Relations Quarterly,* Spring 1999, 46; as based on Gail Sheehy, *New Passages: Mapping Your Life Across Time* (New York: Ballantine Books), 1995.

In contrast, the nature of *cohort effects* is captured by the idea that people hold onto the interests they grew up to appreciate. If 10 years from today it is determined that many rock-and-roll fans are over 55, it would not be because older people have suddenly altered their musical tastes but because the baby boomers who grew up with rock and roll have become older. As Bill Whitehead, CEO of the advertising agency Bates North America, noted: "When baby boomers are 70, they'll still eat pizza and still listen to the [Rolling] Stones."[14] It is important for marketers to be aware of the distinction between age effects and cohort effects: One stresses the impact of aging, whereas the second stresses the influence of the period when a person is born and shared experiences with others of the same age (i.e., experienced the same general history—music, TV shows, and emerging technology).

We must remember that cohort effects are lifelong. Table 3-4 identifies and distinguishes among six different age cohort groups.[15]

Sex

Gender is quite frequently a distinguishing segmentation variable. Women have traditionally been the main users of such products as hair coloring and cosmetics, and men have been the main users of tools and shaving preparations. However, sex roles have blurred, and gender is no longer an accurate way to distinguish consumers in some product categories. For example, women are buying household repair tools, and men have become significant users of skin care and hair products. It is becoming increasingly common to see magazine ads and TV commercials that depict men and women in roles traditionally occupied by the opposite sex. For example, many ads reflect the expanded child-nurturing roles of young fathers in today's society.

Much of the change in sex roles has occurred because of the continued impact of dual-income households. One consequence for marketers is that women are not so readily accessible through traditional media as they once were. Because working women do not have much time to watch TV or listen to the radio, many advertisers now emphasize magazines in their media schedules, especially those specifically aimed at working women (e.g., *Working Woman* and *Working Mother*). Direct marketers also have been targeting time-pressured working women who use merchandise catalogs, convenient 800 numbers, and Internet sites as ways of shopping for personal clothing and accessories, as well as many household and family needs.

Recent research has shown that men and women differ in terms of the way they look at their Internet usage. Specifically, men tend to "click on" a Web site because they are "information hungry," whereas women click because "they expect communications media to entertain and educate."[16] Table 3-5 presents additional male and female differences when it comes to using the Internet and compares some key usage situations and favorite Internet materials for men versus women.

Marital Status

Traditionally, the family has been the focus of most marketing efforts, and for many products and services, the household continues to be the relevant consuming unit. Marketers are interested in the number and kinds of households that buy and/or own certain products. They also are interested in determining the demographic and media profiles of household decision makers (the persons involved in the actual selection of the product) to develop appropriate marketing strategies.

Marketers have discovered the benefits of targeting specific marital status groupings, such as singles, divorced individuals, single parents, and dual-income married couples. For instance, singles, especially one-person households with incomes greater than $50,000, comprise a market segment that tends to be above

TABLE 3-4   Six American Adult Cohorts

NAME	BIRTH DATES	CHARACTERISTICS	MARKETING EXAMPLE
Depression Cohort	1912–1921	Defined by the Great Depression. Greatly concerned with financial security, values economic security and frugality.	A West Coast savings and loan association used Groucho Marx's *You Bet Your Life* TV sidekick to assure potential depositors that their money was "safe."
World War II Cohort	1922–1927	Defined by World War II. Faced a common enemy, left loved ones behind, deferred marriage, children, and careers.	A cable TV provider increased subscriptions via a direct-marketing campaign that stated "If you remember V-J Day, we've got some new programs you're going to love."
Postwar Cohort	1928–1945	Benefited from a long period of economic growth and social calm. Act conservative and prefer the familiar, the secure, and the comfortable.	The Vermont Country Store, a marketer of nostalgic products, includes pictures from the 1950s and cohort-appropriate copy in its catalogs.
Boomers I Cohort	1946–1954	Came of age during the Vietnam era. Influenced by the assassinations of President Kennedy, Martin Luther King, Jr., and Robert Kennedy. Value individualism, self-indulgence, and stimulation. Grew up in economic good times and spend heavily because they expect the good times to continue. Very cause oriented.	Baby Boomers' parents, not Baby Boomers, relate to prunes, but research by the California Prune Board found that prunes contain ingredients that allow aging Baby Boomers to hold onto their sexual vitality.
Boomers II Cohort	1956–1965	Came of age as Vietnam War ended, Watergate was over, and the Arab oil embargo halted economic gains. Have little faith in institutions but have a narcissistic preoccupation that leads to self-help activities and self-deprecation. Spend like Boomers I but because they feel they can always get a loan, a second mortgage, or another credit card.	A finance company advertises to Boomers II by stating in its radio commercial that "Everyone else has a BMW, or a new set of golf clubs, and they're not any better than you are."
Generation X Cohort	1966–1976	Often called "slackers" "whiners," and/or "a generation of aging Bart Simpsons." Have little to hang on to and are often the children of divorce and day care. Feel alienated and believe that they have little hope of being able to have their parents' lifestyle. This cohort has no "defining moment."	Can be reached with irreverent, rebellious, self-mocking portrayals, such as the *Simpsons, South Park,* and *Married with Children* TV programs.

Source: Adapted from Charles Schewe, Geoffrey Meredith, and Stephanie Noble, "Defining Moments: Segmenting by Cohorts," *MM*, Fall 2000, 48–53.

TABLE 3-5	Male and Female Segments of Internet Users	
	KEY USAGE SITUATION	**FAVORITE INTERNET MATERIALS**
FEMALE SEGMENTS		
Social Sally	Making friends	Chat and personal Web page
New Age Crusader	Fighting for causes	Books and government information
Cautious Mom	Nurturing children	Cooking and medical facts
Playful Pretender	Role playing	Chat and games
Master Producer	Job productivity	White pages and government information
MALE SEGMENTS		
Bits and Bytes	Computers and hobbies	Investments, discovery, software
Practical Pete	Personal productivity	Investments, company listings
Viking Gamer	Competing and winning	Games, chat, software
Sensitive Sam	Helping family and friends	Investments, government information
World Citizen	Connecting with world	Discovery, software, investments

Source: Scott Smith and David Whitlark, "Men and Women Online: What Makes Them Click," *Marketing Research*, Summer 2001, 22.

average in the usage of products not traditionally associated with supermarkets (e.g., cognac, books, loose tea) and below average in their consumption of traditional supermarket products (e.g., catsup, peanut butter, mayonnaise). Such insights can be particularly useful to a supermarket manager operating in a neighborhood of one-person households when deciding on the merchandise mix for the store. Some marketers target one-person households with single-serving prepared foods (e.g., Maxwell House Coffee Singles, Campbell's Soup To Go!) and others with mini-appliances such as small microwave ovens and two-cup coffee makers. (The family as a consuming unit is discussed in greater detail in Chapter 10.)

Income, Education, and Occupation

Income has long been an important variable for distinguishing between market segments. Marketers commonly segment markets on the basis of income because they feel that it is a strong indicator of the ability (or inability) to pay for a product or a specific model of the product. For instance, initially marketers of home computers under $1,000 felt that such products would be particularly attractive to homes with modest family incomes. However, these low-priced PCs also proved to be quite popular with higher-income families who wanted additional computers for younger family members.

Income is often combined with other demographic variables to more accurately define target markets. To illustrate, high income has been combined with age to identify the important *affluent elderly* segment. It also has been combined with both age and occupational status to produce the so-called *yuppie* segment, a sought-after subgroup of the baby boomer market.

Education, occupation, and income tend to be closely correlated in almost a cause-and-effect relationship. High-level occupations that produce high incomes usually require advanced educational training. Individuals with little education rarely qualify for high-level jobs. Insights on Internet usage preferences tend to support the close relationship among income, occupation, and education. Research reveals that consumers with lower incomes, lower education, and blue-collar occupations tend to spend more time online at home than those with higher income, higher education, and white-collar occupations.[17] One possible reason for this difference is that those in blue-collar jobs often do not have access to the Internet during the course of the workday.

PSYCHOLOGICAL SEGMENTATION

Psychological characteristics refer to the inner or intrinsic qualities of the individual consumer. Consumer segmentation strategies are often based on specific psychological variables. For instance, consumers may be segmented in terms of their *motivations, personality, perceptions, learning,* and *attitudes.* (Part 2 examines in detail the wide range of psychological variables that influence consumer decision making and consumption behavior.)

PSYCHOGRAPHIC SEGMENTATION

Marketing practitioners have heartily embraced psychographic research, which is closely aligned with psychological research, especially personality and attitude measurement. This form of applied consumer research (commonly referred to as lifestyle analysis) has proven to be a valuable marketing tool that helps identify promising consumer segments that are likely to be responsive to specific marketing messages.

The psychographic profile of a consumer segment can be thought of as a composite of consumers' measured activities, interests, and opinions (**AIOs**). As an approach to constructing consumer psychographic profiles, AIO research seeks consumers' responses to a large number of statements that measure activities (how the consumer or family spends time, e.g., golfing, volunteering at a local blood bank, gardening), interests (the consumer's or family's preferences and priorities, e.g., home, fashion, food), and opinions (how the consumer feels about a wide variety of events and political issues, social issues, the state of the economy, ecology). In their most common form, AIO-psychographic studies use a battery of statements (a **psychographic inventory**) designed to identify relevant aspects of a consumer's personality, buying motives, interests, attitudes, beliefs, and values. Table 3-6 presents a portion

---

TABLE 3-6 A Portion of an AIO Inventory Used to Identify Techno-Road-Warriors

Instructions: *Please read each statement and place an "x" in the box that **best** indicates how strongly you **"agree"** or **"disagree"** with the statement.*

	AGREE COMPLETELY						DISAGREE COMPLETELY
I feel that my life is moving faster and faster, sometimes just too fast.	[1]	[2]	[3]	[4]	[5]	[6]	[7]
If I could consider the "pluses" and "minuses," technology has been good for me.	[1]	[2]	[3]	[4]	[5]	[6]	[7]
I find that I have to pull myself away from e-mail.	[1]	[2]	[3]	[4]	[5]	[6]	[7]
Given my lifestyle, I have more of a shortage of time than money.	[1]	[2]	[3]	[4]	[5]	[6]	[7]
I like the benefits of the Internet, but I often don't have the time to take advantage of them.	[1]	[2]	[3]	[4]	[5]	[6]	[7]
I am generally open to considering new practices and new technology.	[1]	[2]	[3]	[4]	[5]	[6]	[7]

TABLE 3-7	A Hypothetical Psychographic Profile of the Techno-Road-Warrior

- *Goes on the Internet more than six times a week*
- *Sends and/or receives 15 or more e-mail messages a week*
- *Regularly visits Web sites to gather information and/or to comparison shop*
- *Often buys personal items via 800 numbers and/or over the Internet*
- *May trade stocks and/or make travel reservations over the Internet*
- *Earns $100,000 or more a year*
- *Belongs to several rewards programs (e.g., frequent flyer programs, hotel programs, rent-a-car programs)*

of a psychographic inventory designed to gauge "techno-road-warriors," business-people who spend a high percentage of their workweek on the road, equipped with laptop computers, pagers, cellular telephones, and electronic organizers. Table 3-7 presents a hypothetical psychographic profile of a techno-road-warrior. The appeal of psychographic research lies in the frequently vivid and practical profiles of con-sumer segments that it can produce (which will be illustrated later in this chapter).

The results of psychographic segmentation efforts are frequently reflected in firms' marketing messages. For instance, Centrum Performance vitamins (see Figure 3-1) are targeted to individuals who would prefer to spend their lunch hour working out rather than eating out (**www.centrum.com**). Psychographic segmenta-tion is further discussed later in the chapter, where we consider hybrid segmentation strategies that combine psychographic and demographic variables to create rich descriptive profiles of consumer segments.

SOCIOCULTURAL SEGMENTATION

Sociological (group) and *anthropological* (cultural) variables—that is, **sociocultural variables**—provide further bases for market segmentation. For example, consumer markets have been successfully subdivided into segments on the basis of stage in the family life cycle, social class, core cultural values, subcultural memberships, and cross-cultural affiliation.

Family Life Cycle

Family life cycle segmentation is based on the premise that many families pass through similar phases in their formation, growth, and final dissolution. At each phase, the family unit needs different products and services. Young single people, for example, need basic furniture for their first apartment, whereas their parents, finally free of child rearing, often refurnish their homes with more elaborate pieces. Family life cycle is a composite variable based explicitly on *marital* and *family status* but implicitly reflects *relative age, income,* and *employment status.* Each of the stages in the traditional family life cycle (*bachelorhood, honeymooners, parenthood, postpar-enthood,* and *dissolution*) represents an important target segment to a variety of marketers. For example, the financial services industry segments customers in terms of family life cycle stages because it has been found that families' financial needs tend to shift as they progress through the various stages of life.[18] (Chapter 10 dis-cusses the family life cycle in greater depth and shows how marketers cater to the needs and wishes of consumers in each stage of the life cycle.)

FIGURE 3-1

Centrum Performance Vitamins Targets a "Working Out" Lifestyle

Copyright © Wyeth and used with permission.

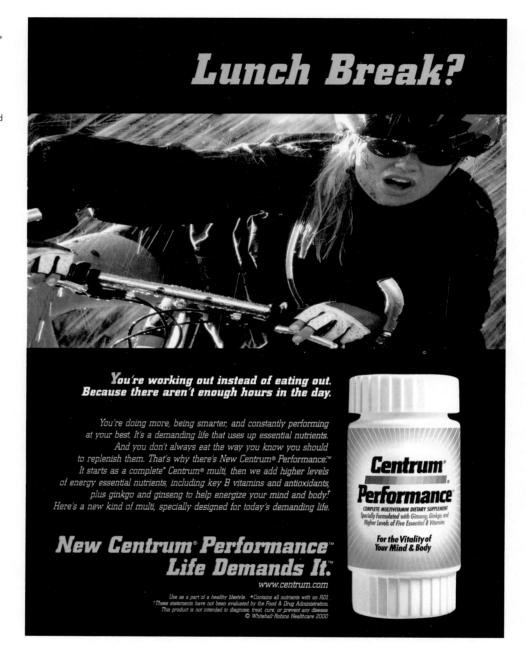

Social Class

Social class (or relative status in the community) can be used as a base for market segmentation and is usually measured by a weighted index of several demographic variables, such as education, occupation, and income. The concept of *social class* implies a hierarchy in which individuals in the same class generally have the same degree of status, whereas members of other classes have either higher or lower status. Studies have shown that consumers in different social classes vary in terms of values, product preferences, and buying habits. Many major banks and investment companies, for example, offer a variety of different levels of service to people of different social classes (e.g., private banking services to the upper classes). For example some investment companies appeal to upper-class customers with offering them options that correspond to their wealthy status. In contrast, a financial program targeted to a lower social class might talk instead about savings accounts or certificates of deposit. Chapter 11 discusses in depth the use of social class as a segmentation variable.

Culture and Subculture

Some marketers have found it useful to segment their markets on the basis of cultural heritage because members of the same culture tend to share the same values, beliefs, and customs. Marketers who use cultural segmentation stress specific, widely held cultural values with which they hope consumers will identify (e.g., for American consumers, *youthfulness* and *fitness and health*). Cultural segmentation is particularly successful in international marketing, but it is important for the marketer to understand fully the target country's beliefs, values, and customs (the cross-cultural context).

Within the larger culture, distinct subgroups (subcultures) often are united by certain experiences, values, or beliefs that make effective market segments. These groupings could be based on a specific demographic characteristic (such as race, religion, ethnicity, or age) or lifestyle characteristic (teachers, joggers). In the United States, African Americans, Hispanic Americans, Asian Americans, and the elderly are important subcultural market segments. Research on subcultural differences, which will be discussed more fully in Chapter 13, tends to reveal that consumers are more responsive to promotional messages that they perceive relate to their own ethnicity (e.g., African American consumers tend to respond favorably to recognize and positively account for their specific interests and background).[19]

Culturally distinct segments can be prospects for the same product but often are targeted more efficiently with different promotional appeals. For example, a bicycle might be promoted as an efficient means of transportation in Asia and as a health-and-fitness product in the United States. Similarly, a fishing rod or shotgun could be advertised in many parts of the world as a way to put food on the dinner table but might be promoted in the United States as leisure-time sporting equipment. A recent study that divided China's urban consumers into four segments ("working poor," "salary class," "little rich," and "yuppies") found that for all four groups television was the most popular medium of entertainment and information. However, the working poor spend the most time listening to radio, while yuppies and the little rich spend the most time reading newspapers and magazines.[20] (Chapters 12, 13, and 14 examine cultural, subcultural, and cross-cultural bases of market segmentation in greater detail.)

Cross-Cultural or Global Marketing Segmentation

As the world has gotten smaller and smaller, a true global marketplace has developed. For example, as you read this you may be sitting on an IKEA chair or sofa (Sweden), drinking Earl Grey tea (England), wearing a Swatch watch (Switzerland), Nike sneakers (China), a Polo golf shirt (Mexico), and Dockers pants (Dominican Republic). Some global market segments, such as teenagers, appear to want the same types of products, regardless of which nation they call home—products that are trendy, entertaining, and image oriented. This global "sameness" allowed Reebok, for example, to launch its Instapump line of sneakers using the same global advertising campaign in approximately 140 countries.[21] (The issue of global or international marketing segmentation will be more fully discussed in Chapter 14.)

USE-RELATED SEGMENTATION

An extremely popular and effective form of segmentation categorizes consumers in terms of product, service, or brand usage characteristics, such as level of usage, level of awareness, and degree of brand loyalty.

Rate of usage segmentation differentiates among heavy users, medium users, light users, and nonusers of a specific product, service, or brand. For example, research has consistently indicated that between 25 and 35 percent of beer drinkers account for more than 70 percent of all beer consumed. For this reason, most marketers prefer to target their advertising campaigns to heavy users rather than spend considerably more money trying to attract light users. This also explains the successful targeting of light beer to heavy drinkers on the basis that it is less filling (and, thus, can be consumed in greater quantities) than regular beer. Recent studies have found that heavy soup users were more socially active, creative, optimistic, witty, and less stubborn than light users and nonusers, and they were also less likely to read entertainment and sports magazines and more likely to read family and home magazines. Likewise, heavy users of travel agents in Singapore were more involved with and more enthusiastic about vacation travel, more innovative with regard to their selection of vacation travel products, more likely to travel for pleasure, and more widely exposed to travel information from the mass media.[22]

Marketers of a host of other products have also found that a relatively small group of heavy users accounts for a disproportionately large percentage of product usage; targeting these heavy users has become the basis of their marketing strategies. Other marketers take note of the gaps in market coverage for light and medium users and profitably target those segments.

Awareness status encompasses the notion of consumer awareness of the product, interest level in the product, readiness to buy the product, or whether consumers need to be informed about the product. Figure 3-2 presents an ad for Campbell's Tomato soup that is designed to create both awareness and interest among consumers who are interested in reducing their risk of cancer (and who wouldn't be?).

Sometimes *brand loyalty* is used as the basis for segmentation. Marketers often try to identify the characteristics of their brand-loyal consumers so that they can direct their promotional efforts to people with similar characteristics in the larger population. Other marketers target consumers who show no brand loyalty ("brand switchers") in the belief that such people represent greater market potential than consumers who are loyal to competing brands. Also, almost by definition, consumer innovators—often a prime target for new products—tend *not* to be brand loyal. (Chapter 15 discusses the characteristics of consumer innovators.)

Increasingly, marketers stimulate and reward brand loyalty by offering special benefits to consistent or frequent customers. Such frequent usage or relationship programs often take the form of a membership club (e.g., Hertz Number 1 Club Gold, American Airlines Platinum Level, or Marriott's Rewards). Relationship programs tend to provide special accommodations and services, as well as free extras, to keep these frequent customers loyal and happy. Figure 3-3 informs consumers how easy it is to earn free travel and other perks as a member of the Radisson Gold Reward™ program (**www.radisson.com**).

USAGE-SITUATION SEGMENTATION

Marketers recognize that the occasion or situation often determines what consumers will purchase or consume. For this reason, they sometimes focus on the **usage situation** as a segmentation variable.

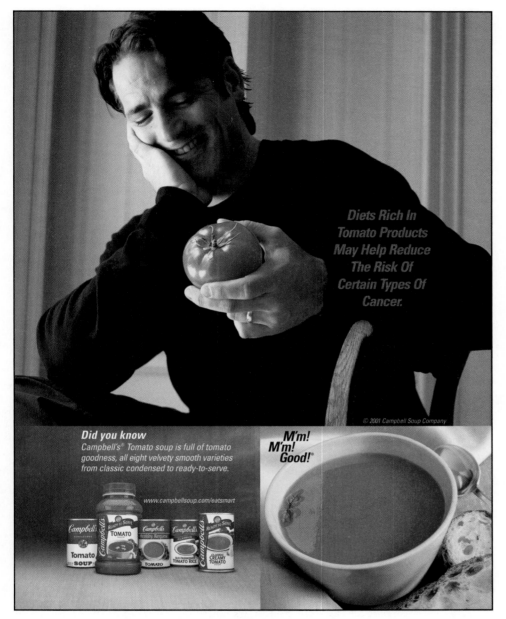

FIGURE 3-2

Campbell's Seeks to Create Awareness and Interest
Courtesy of Campbell Soup Company.

The following three statements reveal the potential of situation segmentation: "Whenever our daughter Jamie gets a raise or a promotion, we always take her out to dinner"; "When I'm away on business for a week or more, I try to stay at a Suites hotel"; "I always buy my wife flowers on Valentine's Day." Under other circumstances, in other situations, and on other occasions, the same consumer might make other choices. Some situational factors that might influence a purchase or consumption choice include whether it is a weekday or weekend (e.g., going to a movie); whether there is sufficient time (e.g., use of regular mail or express mail); whether it is a gift for a girlfriend, a parent, or a self-gift (a reward to one's self).

FIGURE 3-3

Ad Designed to Spell
Out the Rewards of
Customer Loyalty

Courtesy of Carlson Consumer
Group and American Express.

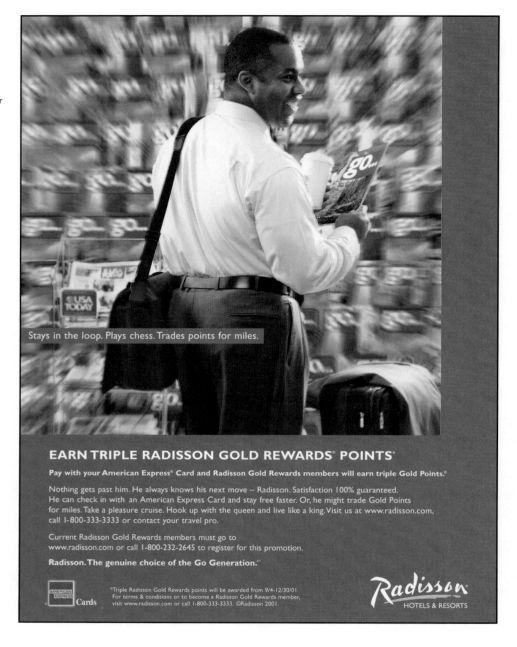

Many products are promoted for special usage occasions. The greeting card industry, for example, stresses special cards for a variety of occasions that seem to be increasing almost daily (Grandparents' Day, Secretaries' Day, etc.). The florist and candy industries promote their products for Valentine's Day and Mother's Day, the diamond industry promotes diamond rings as an engagement symbol, and the wristwatch industry promotes its products as graduation gifts. The Godiva chocolate ad in Figure 3-4 (www.godiva.com) is an example of situational, special usage segmentation. It appeared in magazines a week prior to Valentine's Day and suggests that a box of Godiva chocolate "will make her heart skip a beat."

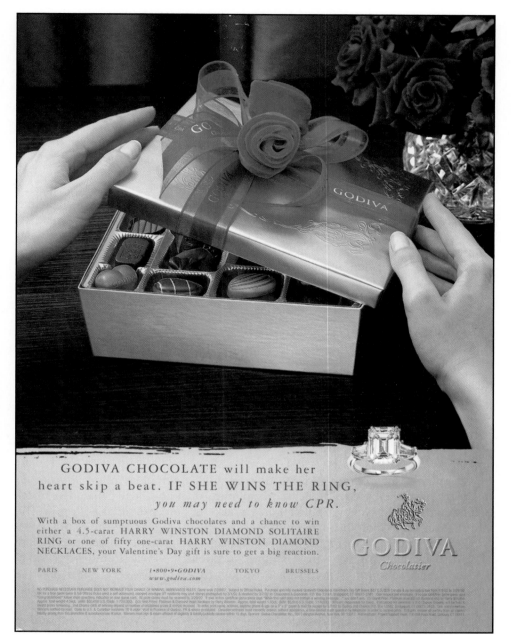

FIGURE 3-4

A Godiva Chocolate
Occasion-Specific Ad
for Valentine's Day

Courtesy of Margeotes|Fertitta
+ Partners and Godiva. Image
© Kenro Izu.

BENEFIT SEGMENTATION

Marketing and advertising executives constantly attempt to identify the one most important benefit of their product or service that will be most meaningful to consumers. Examples of benefits that are commonly used include *financial security* (Prudential Financial), *data protection* (iomega), *good health* (Wheaties), *fresh breath* (Eclipse gum), and *peace of mind* (Hefty One Zip bags).

In a recent article dealing with brand strategies in India, the point is made that "nothing is as effective as segmentation based on the benefits a group of customers seek from your brand." To illustrate, the article points out that in India Dettol soap is targeted to the hygiene-conscious consumer—the individual seeking protection from germs and contamination—rather than the consumer looking for beauty, fragrance, freshness, or economy.[23]

Changing lifestyles also play a major role in determining the product benefits that are important to consumers and provide marketers with opportunities for new products and services. For example, the microwave oven was the perfect solution to the needs of dual-income households, where neither the husband nor the wife has the time for lengthy meal preparation. Food marketers offer busy families the *benefit* of breakfast products that require only seconds to prepare.

Benefit segmentation can be used to position various brands within the same product category.[24] The classic case of successful benefit segmentation is the market for toothpaste, and a recent article suggested that if consumers are socially active, they want a toothpaste that can deliver white teeth and fresh breath; if they smoke, they want a toothpaste to fight stains; if disease prevention is their major focus, then they want a toothpaste that will fight germs; and if they have children, they want to lower their dental bills.[25] Figure 3-5 suggests that the primary benefits derived from using Crest Whitening Plus Scope toothpaste (www.crest.com) are whiter teeth and fresh breath.

HYBRID SEGMENTATION APPROACHES

Marketers commonly segment markets by combining several segmentation variables rather than relying on a single segmentation base. This section examines three hybrid segmentation approaches that provide marketers with richer and more accurately defined consumer segments than can be derived from using a single segmentation variable. These include psychographic-demographic profiles, geodemographics, VALS, and Yankelovich's Mindbase Segmentation.

Psychographic-Demographic Profiles

Psychographic and demographic profiles are highly complementary approaches that work best when used together. By combining the knowledge gained from both demographic and psychographic studies, marketers are provided with powerful information about their target markets.

Demographic-psychographic profiling has been widely used in the development of advertising campaigns to answer three questions: "Whom should we target?" "What should we say?" "Where should we say it?" To help advertisers answer the third question, many advertising media vehicles sponsor demographic-psychographic research on which they base very detailed *audience profiles*. Table 3-8 presents a selected demographic and psychographic profile of a *Newsweek* subscriber (www.newsweek.com). By offering media buyers such carefully defined dual profiles of their audiences, mass media publishers and broadcasters make it possible for advertisers to select media whose audiences most closely resemble their target markets.

A number of different research organizations have devised their own schemes to segment Internet users. Table 3-9 presents a segmentation system developed by Harris Interactive that defines six Internet shopper segments and is intended to provide e-tailers with a peek at the rich combination of spending habits and motivational factors underlying specific segments of Internet buyers.[26]

Finally, advertisers are increasingly designing ads that depict in words and/or pictures the essence of a particular target-market lifestyle or segment that they want to reach. In this spirit, Aqua Cat Cruises appeals to specific active and outdoor lifestyles (see Figure 3-6).

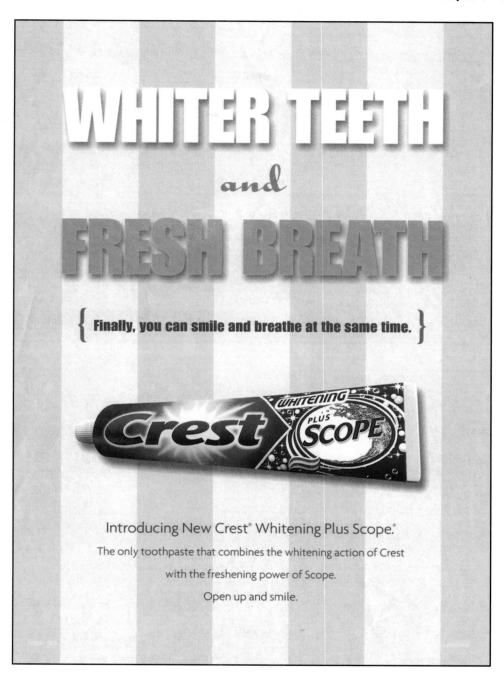

Geodemographic Segmentation

This type of hybrid segmentation scheme is based on the notion that people who live close to one another are likely to have similar financial means, tastes, preferences, lifestyles, and consumption habits (similar to the old adage, "Birds of a feather flock together"). This segmentation approach uses computers to generate geodemographic market clusters of like consumers. Specifically, computer software clusters the nation's 250,000+ neighborhoods into lifestyle groupings based on postal zip codes. Clusters are created based on consumer lifestyles, and a specific cluster includes zip codes that

TABLE 3-8 Selected Demographic-Psychographic Profile of *Newsweek*, National Edition

TOTAL ADULT READERS, 19,593,000	PERCENT 100.0	INDEX 100
Men	55.9	117
Professionals/managers	35.3	174
Age 35 to 49 (median age 44.8 years)	36.5	114
At least a college graduate	43.1	187
Household income of $100,000-plus	25.1	172
Married	62.4	109
Own home	74.7	106
Make business purchase decision of $50,000-plus in past year	10.8	185
Own securities valued at $100,000-plus	9.4	179
Have Internet access at work or at home	72.5	129
Own a laptop/notebook PC	12.0	150
Spent $3,000 on any vacation in past	12.3	164
Rented a car 2-plus times for personal use in the past year	9.1	158
Own/lease sports utility vehicle (SUV) bought new	13.2	138

Source: www.newsweekmediakit.com/us/reader_national.html

TABLE 3-9 Six Internet Shopping Types

E-BIVALENT NEWBIES—Representing just 5 percent of the online shopping population, this group is the newest to the Internet, is somewhat older, likes shopping online the least, and spends the least online.

TIME-SENSITIVE MATERIALISTS—At 17 percent of all cybershoppers, these individuals are most interested in convenience and saving time, less likely to read product reviews, compare prices, or use coupons.

CLICKS & MORTAR—At 23 percent of the e-commerce community, this group tends to shop online but prefers to buy off-line, is more likely to be female homemakers, has privacy and security concerns about buying online, and visits brick-and-mortar shopping malls the most often.

HOOKED, ONLINE & SINGLE—Representing 16 percent of the online shopping population, these individuals are more likely to be young, single males with high incomes, have been on the Internet the longest, play games, download software, bank, invest, and shop online the most often.

HUNTER-GATHERERS—At 20 percent of the cybershopping set, members of this group are typically age 30–49 with two children, and most often go to sites that provide analysis and comparison of products and prices.

BRAND LOYALISTS—With 19 percent of the online purchasing community, these individuals are the most likely to go directly to the site address of a merchant they know, are the most satisfied with shopping online, and spend the most online.

Source: www.harrisinteractive.com

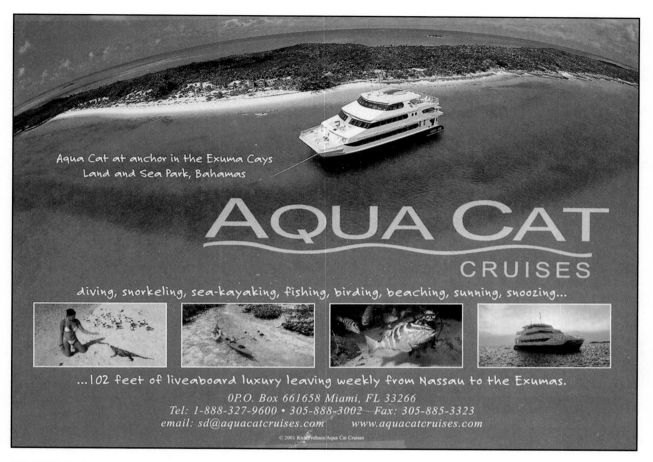

FIGURE 3-6

Aqua Cat Cruises Ad Targets an Active Outdoor Lifestyle

are composed of people with similar lifestyles widely scattered throughout the country. Marketers use the cluster data for direct-mail campaigns, to select retail sites and appropriate merchandise mixes, to locate banks and restaurants, and to design marketing strategies for specific market segments. For example, Eddie Bauer (www.eddiebauer.com) has employed Claritas demographics (www.claritas.com) to evaluate new retail store locations and is PRIZM coding current customers, and Duke Energy Corporation (www.duke-energy.com) has profiled its residential and small business customers with Claritas's databases as part of its customer retention program.[27] Table 3-10 presents five examples of geodemographic clusters.

Over the past 25 years, as the firm that started the clustering phenomenon, Claritas has increased the number of segments in American society from the 40 segments used in the 1970s and 1980s to the 62 segments it uses today. The Claritas search engine will pick the top five lifestyle clusters for each zip code; you can find out about your zip code by visiting www.yawyl.claritas.com.

Geodemographic segmentation is most useful when an advertiser's or marketer's best prospects (in terms of consumer personalities, goals, and interests) can be isolated in terms of where they live. However, for products and services used by a broad cross section of the American public, other segmentation schemes may be more productive.

TABLE 3-10 Sample Geodemographic Clusters

BLUE BLOOD ESTATES

- *0.8% of United States households*
- *Predominant employment: Professional*
- *Elite superrich families*
- *Key education level: College grads*
- *Adult age range: 35–44, 45–54, 55–64*

CHARACTERISTICS: America's wealthiest suburbs are populated by established executives, professionals, and heirs to "old money." These people are accustomed to privilege and live in luxury, often surrounded by servants. A tenth of this group are multimillionaires. The next level of affluence is a sharp drop from this pinnacle. Blue blood estate people belong to a country club, own mutual funds ($10,000+), purchase a car phone, watch TV golf, and read business magazines.

MIDCITY MIX

- *1.3% of United States households*
- *Predominant employment: Service, white collar*
- *African American singles and families*
- *Key educational level: High school, some college*
- *Adult age range: 35–54*

CHARACTERISTICS: These individuals and families are geographically centered in the Northeast and Great Lakes regions. They are ethnically diverse and a mix of white- and blue-collar employment. These rowhouse neighborhoods on the urban fringe are two-thirds black and have a high incidence of college enrollment. They go to pro basketball games, have veterans life insurance, eat canned hashes, listen to religious/gospel music, and read fashion/sports magazines.

GRAY COLLARS

- *2.1% of United States households*
- *Adult age range: 55–64, 65+*
- *Median household income: $31,400*
- *Aging couples in inner suburbs*

CHARACTERISTICS: For nearly two decades, we read about the decline of the Great Lakes industrial "Rust Belt." Decimated by foreign takeovers in the steel and automobile industries, the area lost a million jobs. Although most of the kids left, their highly skilled parents stayed and are now benefitting from a major U.S. industrial resurgence. They buy 1950s nostalgia, own CDs, eat canned cooked hams, listen to radio football, and read health/fitness magazines.

YOUNG INFLUENTIALS

- *1.1% of United States households*
- *Predominant employment: Professional, white collar*
- *Upwardly mobile singles and couples*
- *Key education level: College grads*
- *Adult age range: Under 24, 25–34*

CHARACTERISTICS: This cluster is dubbed the "Young Urban Professional." Before getting married they were the educated, high-tech, metropolitan sophisticates, the "swingers" and childless live-in couples, whose double incomes bought the good life in Boomtown U.S.A. They are the last of the yuppies. They go to college basketball games, have an American Express card, often drink imported beer, listen to progressive rock radio, and read style/fashion magazines.

SHOTGUNS AND PICKUPS

- *1.6% of United States households*
- *Predominant employment: Blue collar, farm*
- *Rural blue-collar workers and families*
- *Key education level: High school, grade school*
- *Adult age range: 35–44, 45–54*

CHARACTERISTICS: The least affluent of the "Country Families" clusters, members of this group are found in the Northeast, the Southeast, in the Great Lakes and Piedmont industrial regions. They lead the "Country Families" group in blue-collar jobs; the majority are married with school-age children. They are church-goers who also enjoy bowling, hunting, sewing, and attending auto races, smoke pipe tobacco, have medical loss of income insurance, drink Canadian whisky, listen to country radio, and read hunting/car and truck magazines.

SRI Consulting's Values and Lifestyle System (VALS™)

Drawing on Maslow's need hierarchy (see Chapter 4) and the concept of social character, in the late 1970s researchers at SRI Consulting (**www.sri.com**) developed a generalized segmentation scheme of the American population known as the values and lifestyle (**VALS**) system. This original system was designed to explain the dynamics of societal change and was quickly adapted as a marketing tool.

In 1989 SRIC revised the VALS system to focus more explicitly on explaining consumer purchase behavior. The current VALS typology classifies the American population into eight distinctive subgroups (segments) based on consumer responses to 35 attitudinal and four demographic questions.[28] Figure 3-7 depicts the VALS classification scheme and offers a brief profile of the consumer traits of each of the

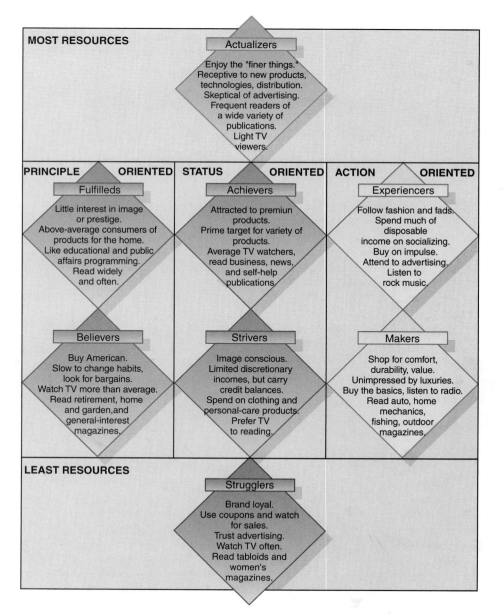

FIGURE 3-7

SRI VALS™ Segments
Source: Reprinted with permission of SRI Consulting Business Intelligence.

VALS segments. The major groupings (from left to right in Figure 3-7) are defined in terms of three major *self-orientations* and (from top to bottom) a new definition of resources: the *principle oriented* (consumers whose choices are motivated by their beliefs rather than by desires for approval), the *status oriented* (consumers whose choices are guided by the actions, approval, and opinions of others), and the *action oriented* (consumers who are motivated by a desire for social or physical activity, variety, and risk taking). Each of these three major self-orientations represents distinct attitudes, lifestyles, and decision-making styles. Resources (from most to least) include the range of psychological, physical, demographic, and material means and capacities consumers have to draw upon, including education, income, self-confidence, health, eagerness to buy, and energy level. Figure 3-8 presents information on the percentage of individuals in each of the eight VALS segments who participated in

FIGURE 3-8

VALS™ 2 Segments and Participation in Selected Sports

Source: Rebecca Piirto Heath, "You Can Buy a Thrill: Chasing the Ultimate Rush," *American Demographics,* June 1997, p. 48. **www.demographics.com**. © 1997 PRIMEDIA-Interec, Stamford, CT. Reprinted with permission.

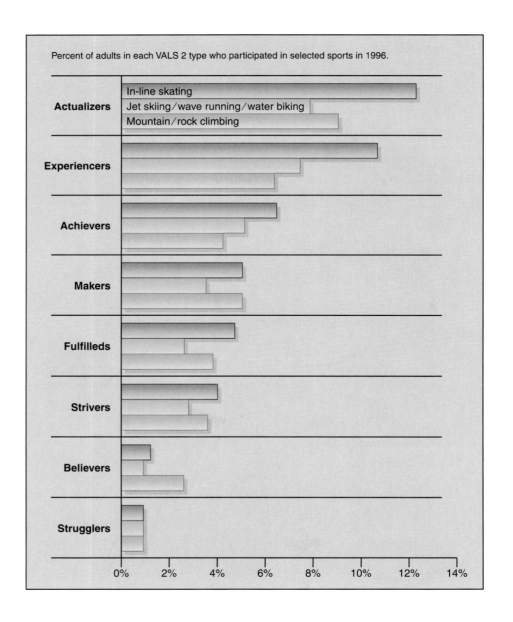

Percent of adults in each VALS 2 type who participated in selected sports in 1996.

TABLE 3-11 The Size of Each VALS™ Segment as Percent
of the United States Population

VALS™ SEGMENT	PERCENT OF POPULATION
Actualizer	11.7%
Fulfilled	10.5
Believer	17.0
Achiever	14.7
Striver	11.8
Experiencer	12.9
Maker	12.0
Struggler	9.5

Source: VALS™/Simmons.

selected sports in a recent year. For instance, the findings reveal that *Actualizers,
Experiencers,* and *Achievers* are more likely to participate in thrill-oriented sports
than other segments. Table 3-11 shows the size of each of the eight VALS segments as
a percentage of the population (also see **www.future.sri.com**).

In terms of consumer characteristics, the eight VALS segments differ in some
important ways. For instance, *Believers* tend to buy American-made products and
are slow to alter their consumption-related habits, whereas *Actualizers* are drawn to
top-of-the-line and new products, especially innovative technologies. Therefore, it is
not surprising that marketers of intelligent in-vehicle technologies (e.g., global positioning devices) must first target *Actualizers,* because they are early adopters of new
products.[29]

Yankelovich Mindbase Segmentation

A new segmentation methodology, Monitor Mindbase, was recently developed to
focus on households. Yankelovich researchers used their annual Monitor Survey of
American Values and Attitudes to identify the eight major groups and 32 subsegments that serve as the basis for Mindbase. As an example, a household in the "New
Traditionalist" segment views saving for a son's or daughter's college education as a
reward for having a successful child, whereas those in the "Family Limited" segment
consider it to be an obligation.[30] Table 3-12 presents the eight major Mindbase segments, and Table 3-13 provides some examples of the consumer behavior differences among the segments.

Criteria for Effective Targeting of Market Segments

The previous sections have described various bases on which consumers can be clustered into homogeneous market segments. The next challenge for the marketer is to
select one or more segments to target with an appropriate marketing mix. To be an
effective target, a market segment should be (1) identifiable, (2) sufficient (in terms
of size), (3) stable or growing, and (4) accessible (reachable) in terms of both media
and cost.

TABLE 3-12	The Eight Major Mindbase Segments
Up and Comers **16% of Adult** **Population**	Generation X. Young, single, no children. Average incomes. Ambitious, optimistic, and social. Receptive to new technology. Socially conscious, style conscious, and novelty seeking. Perceive themselves as intelligent, creative, attractive, and funny. Do not view themselves as neighborly or old-fashioned. Ideal targets for products and services that offer something new.
Young Materialists **8% of Adult** **Population**	Generation X. Young, single, no children. Average incomes. More men than women. Believe money and success equal happiness. Low level of social consciousness, highly self-focused, don't enjoy socializing. Perceive themselves as adventurous and attractive, not practical, spiritual, or open to new ideas. Highly stressed and style conscious. Enjoy shopping. Prime targets for products and services that make them feel important and successful, as well as fun and stylish.
Stressed by Life **12% of Adult** **Population**	Generation X. Young, mostly female, often unmarried, parents with lower incomes. Have a strong desire for novelty to help escape stress of daily life. Enjoy spending time with family and friends, watching movies, and playing games. Receptive to new technology but cynical about changes it brings. Perceive themselves as family oriented, funny, and attractive but not practical or old-fashioned. Good targets for products and services that offer to reduce stress and escape from reality.
New Traditionalists **14% of Adult** **Population**	Boomers. Married, with high incomes but low levels of materialism. Conservative, family and community oriented. High levels of social consciousness and low levels of cynicism. Enjoy nesting, reading, crafts, and gardening. Perceive themselves as old-fashioned, neighborly, and responsible. Receptive to new technology and comfortable with high levels of media consumption. Excellent target for products and services that help them maintain control of their well-ordered lives.
Family Limited **14% of Adult** **Population**	Boomers. Married with children. High incomes. Intense focus on family life, which impedes their social and community consciousness, as well as independent activities. Do not like novelty or technology and are disinterested in style. Cynical. Do not perceive themselves as ambitious, creative, adventurous, or attractive. Can be reached in messages with a family focus, in mediums such as family programming and children's cartoons.
Detached Introverts **9% of Adult** **Population**	Boomers. Usually male, with no children. Average incomes. Inactive, not social, do not care about style. Not socially conscious or novelty seeking. Neither community oriented nor focused on self. Have very few interests. Do not perceive themselves as self-confident, creative, spiritual, or funny. Somewhat cynical. Are considered a less desirable consumer group.
Renaissance Elders **15% of Adult** **Population**	Older, with average incomes but financially comfortable. Active seniors for whom family and community are very important. Socially conscious and old-fashioned. Open to new technology; many outside interests. Perceive themselves as spiritual, neighborly, self-confident, and open to new ideas. Not materialistic but somewhat style conscious. Ideal target for products and services that help them maintain their health, financial security, and family ties.
Retired from Life **12% of Adult** **Population**	Older. Not attracted to novelty and highly cynical about modern life. Care little for style or material goods. Perceive themselves as neighborly and old-fashioned but not intelligent, creative, spiritual, or funny. They are overwhelmed by information. Enjoy gardening and game shows. Hold little appeal to marketers as a target.

IDENTIFICATION

To divide the market into separate segments on the basis of a series of *common* or *shared* needs or characteristics that are relevant to the product or service, a marketer must be able to identify these relevant characteristics. Some segmentation variables, such as *geography* (location) or *demographics* (age, gender, occupation, race), are relatively easy to identify or are even observable. Others, such as

| TABLE 3-13 | Consumer Behavior of Mindbase Segments |

Index Values   Average for all Adults = 100

	CURRENTLY USE THE INTERNET	NO. OF OVERNIGHT TRIPS	HAVE A CAR LOAN	NO. OF ANN. STOCK TRANS.	CONTR. THIS YEAR TO 401K ACCT.
Up and Comers	126	131	89	106	78
Young Materialists	109	92	61	236	26
Stressed by Life	84	91	100	77	72
New Traditionalists	129	100	145	91	194
Family Limited	112	81	137	140	133
Detached Introverts	123	97	108	140	117
Renaissance Elders	95	121	89	70	94
Retired from Life	40	68	54	66	45

For example, Up and Comers take 31 percent more overnight trips than the average adult.

Source: From "Head Trips—A new way to understand consumer psychology," by David J. Lipke, *American Demographics,* October 2000. Copyright © 2000 Media Central Inc., a Primedia Company. All rights reserved. Reprinted by permission.

education, income, or *marital status,* can be determined through questionnaires. However, other characteristics, such as *benefits sought* or *lifestyle,* are more difficult to identify. A knowledge of consumer behavior is especially useful to marketers who use such intangible consumer characteristics as the basis for market segmentation.

SUFFICIENCY

For a market segment to be a worthwhile target, it must consist of a sufficient number of people to warrant tailoring a product or promotional campaign to its specific needs or interests. To estimate the size of each segment under consideration, marketers often use secondary demographic data, such as that provided by the United States Census Bureau (available at many libraries and online via the Internet), or they undertake a probability survey whose findings can be projected to the total market. (Consumer research methodology was described in Chapter 2.)

STABILITY

Most marketers prefer to target consumer segments that are relatively stable in terms of demographic and psychological factors and needs and that are likely to grow larger over time. They prefer to avoid "fickle" segments that are unpredictable in embracing fads. For example, teens are a sizable and easily identifiable market segment, eager to buy, able to spend, and easily reached. Yet, by the time a marketer produces merchandise for a popular teenage fad, interest in it may have waned.

ACCESSIBILITY

A fourth requirement for effective targeting is accessibility, which means that marketers must be able to reach the market segments they want to target in an economical way. Despite the wide availability of special-interest magazines and cable TV programs, marketers are constantly looking for new media that will enable them to reach their target markets with minimum waste of circulation and competition. One way this can be accomplished is via the Internet. Upon the request of the consumer, a growing number of Web sites periodically send e-mail messages concerning a subject of special interest to the computer user. For example, a resident of Houston, Texas, who likes to take short vacation trips, might have Continental Airlines e-mail her the coming weekend's special airfare, hotel, and rent-a-car deals.

Implementing Segmentation Strategies

Firms that use market segmentation can pursue a *concentrated* marketing strategy or a *differentiated* marketing strategy. In certain instances, they might use a **countersegmentation** strategy.

CONCENTRATED VERSUS DIFFERENTIATED MARKETING

Once an organization has identified its most promising market segments, it must decide whether to target one segment or several segments. The premise behind market segmentation is that each targeted segment receives a specially designed marketing mix, that is, a specially tailored product, price, distribution network, and/or promotional campaign. Targeting several segments using individual marketing mixes is called **differentiated marketing;** targeting just one segment with a unique marketing mix is called **concentrated marketing.**

Differentiated marketing is a highly appropriate segmentation strategy for financially strong companies that are well established in a product category and competitive with other firms that also are strong in the category (e.g., soft drinks, automobiles, or detergents). However, if a company is small or new to the field, concentrated marketing is probably a better bet. A company can survive and prosper by filling a niche not occupied by stronger companies. For example, Viadent toothpaste has become a leader in the small but increasingly important submarket of the overall tooth care market that focuses on products that fight gingivitis and other gum diseases.

COUNTERSEGMENTATION

Sometimes companies find that they must reconsider the extent to which they are segmenting their markets. They might find that some segments have contracted over time to the point that they do not warrant an individually designed marketing program. In such cases, the company seeks to discover a more generic need or consumer characteristic that would apply to the members of two or more segments and recombine those segments into a larger single segment that could be targeted with an individually tailored product or promotional campaign. This is called a *countersegmentation* strategy. Some business schools with wide course offerings in each department were forced to adopt a countersegmentation strategy when they discovered that students simply did not have enough available credits to take a full spectrum of in-depth courses in their major area of study. As a result, some courses had to be canceled each semester because of inadequate registration. For some schools, a countersegmentation strategy effectively solved the problem (e.g., by combining *advertising, publicity, sales promotion,* and *personal selling* courses into a single course called Promotion).

Summary

Market segmentation and diversity are complementary concepts. Without a diverse marketplace, composed of many different peoples with different backgrounds, countries of origin, interests, needs, and wants, there really would be little reason to segment markets.

Before the widespread adoption of the marketing concept, mass marketing (offering the same product or marketing mix to everyone) was the marketing strategy most widely used. Market segmentation followed as a more logical way to meet consumer needs. Segmentation is defined as the process of dividing a potential market into distinct subsets of consumers with a common need or characteristic and selecting one or more segments to target with a specially designed marketing mix. Besides aiding in the development of new products, segmentation studies assist in the redesign and repositioning of existing products, in the creation of promotional appeals, and the selection of advertising media.

Because segmentation strategies benefit both marketers and consumers, they have received wide support from both sides of the marketplace. Market segmentation is now widely used by manufacturers, retailers, and the nonprofit sector.

Nine major classes of consumer characteristics serve as the most common bases for market segmentation. These include geographic factors, demographic factors, psychological factors, psychographic characteristics, sociocultural variables, use-related characteristics, use-situation factors, benefits sought, and hybrid forms of segmentation (e.g., psychographic-demographic profiles, such as VALS™, and geodemographic factors, such as PRIZM™). Important criteria for segmenting markets include identification, sufficiency, stability, and accessibility. Once an organization has identified promising target markets, it must decide whether to target several segments (differentiated marketing) or just one segment (concentrated marketing). It then develops a positioning strategy for each targeted segment. In certain instances, a company might decide to follow a countersegmentation strategy and recombine two or more segments into one larger segment.

Discussion Questions

1. What is market segmentation? How is the practice of market segmentation related to the marketing concept?

2. How are market segmentation, targeting, and positioning interrelated? Illustrate how these three concepts can be used to develop a marketing strategy for a product of your choice.

3. Discuss the advantages and disadvantages of using demographics as a basis for segmentation. Can demographics and psychographics be used together to segment markets? Illustrate your answer with a specific example.

4. Many marketers have found that a relatively small group of heavy users accounts for a disproportionately large amount of the total product consumed. What are the advantages and disadvantages of targeting these heavy users?

5. Under which circumstances and for what types of products should a marketer segment the market on the basis of (a) awareness status, (b) brand loyalty, and (c) usage situation?

6. Some marketers consider benefit segmentation as the segmentation approach most consistent with the marketing concept. Do you agree or disagree with this view? Why?

7. Club Med is a prominent company in the vacation and travel industry. Describe how the company can use demographics and psychographics to identify TV shows and magazines in which to place its advertisements.

8. How can a marketer for a chain of health clubs use the VALS™ segmentation profiles to develop an advertising campaign? Which segments should be targeted? How should the health club be positioned to each of these segments?

9. For each of the following products, identify the segmentation base that you consider best for targeting consumers: (a) coffee, (b) soups, (c) home exercise equipment, (d) portable telephones, and (e) nonfat frozen yogurt. Explain your choices.

10. Apply the criteria for effective segmentation to marketing a product of your choice to college students.

Exercises

1. Select a product and brand that you use frequently and list the benefits you receive from using it. Without disclosing your list, ask a fellow student who uses a different brand in this product category (preferably, a friend of the opposite sex) to make a similar list for his or her brand. Compare the two lists and identify the implications for using benefit segmentation to market the two brands.

2. Does your lifestyle differ significantly from your parents' lifestyle? If so, how are the two lifestyles different? What factors cause these differences?

3. Do you anticipate any major changes in your lifestyle in the next five years? If so, into which VALS segment are you likely to belong five years from now? Explain.

4. The owners of a local health-food restaurant have asked you to prepare a psychographic profile of families living in the community surrounding the restaurant's location. Construct a 10-question psychographic inventory appropriate for segmenting families on the basis of their dining-out preferences.

5. Find three print advertisements that you believe are targeted at a particular psychographic segment. How effective do you think each ad is in terms of achieving its objective? Why?

Key Terms

-   **AIOs (activities, interests, opinions)**
-   **Benefit segmentation**
-   **Concentrated marketing**
-   **Countersegmentation**
-   **Demographic characteristics**
-   **Demographic segmentation**
-   **Differentiated marketing**

-   **Geographic segmentation**
-   **Hybrid segmentation**
-   **Mass marketing**
-   **Market segmentation**
-   **Micromarketing**
-   **Positioning**
-   **Psychographic inventory**

-   **Psychographic segmentation**
-   **Psychological segmentation**
-   **Repositioning**
-   **Sociocultural variables**
-   **Use-related segmentation**
-   **Usage situation**
-   **VALS**

Notes

1. David J. Lipke, "You Are What You Eat," *American Demographics,* October 2000, 42–46.
2. Nina Munk, "Gap Gets It," *Fortune,* August 3, 1998, 68–82.
3. Richard G. Barlow, "How to Court Various Target Markets," *Marketing News,* October 9, 2000, 22.
4. Sydney B. Leavens, "Seeking Boader Market, Candy Makers Aim New Lollipops at Adults," *Wall Street Journal,* August 24, 2001, B1.
5. Bernard Stamler, "Advertising," *New York Times,* January 16, 2002, C4.
6. "Parallel Universe," *American Demographics,* October 1999, 58–63.

7. Florence Fabricant, "The Geography of Taste," *New York Times Magazine,* March 10, 1996, 40–41.

8. Linda P. Morton, "Segmenting to Target Investors," *Public Relations Quarterly,* Summer 2000, 45–46.

9. Stephanie Thompson, "Minute Maid Line Takes Cooler Tack to Attract Tweens," *Advertising Age,* August 14, 2000, 43.

10. "Superstars of Spending," *Advertising Age,* February 12, 2001, S1, S10.

11. Ellen Neuborne, "Pepsi's Aim Is True," *Business Week E. Biz,* January 22, 2001, EB 52.

12. "Not Quite the TV Generation," *American Demographics,* May 1999, 35–36.

13. Linda Morton, "Segmenting Publics by Life Development Stages," *Public Relations Quarterly,* Spring 1999, 46.

14. Geoffrey Meredith and Charles Schewe, "The Power of Cohorts," *American Demographics,* December 1994, 22–31; Michael M. Phillips, "Selling by Evoking What Defines a Generation," *Wall Street Journal,* August 13, 1996, B1.

15. Charles Schewe, Geoffrey Meredith, and Stephanie Noble, "Defining Moments: Segmenting by Cohorts," *MM,* Fall 2000, 48–53.

16. Scott Smith and David Whitlark, "Men and Women Online: What Makes Them Click?" *Marketing Research,* Summer 2001, 20–25.

17. "Less Well-To-Do Web Surfers Spend More Time Online Than More Affluent People, According to Nielsen//NetRatings," *Business Wire,* September 21, 2000, 1.

18. Patrick Dalton, "Pick Your Targets," *Bankers News,* March 9, 1999, 1, 3.

19. Mark R. Forehand and Rohit Deshpandè, "What We See Makes Us Who We Are: Priming Ethnic Self-Awareness and Advertising Response," *Journal of Marketing Research,* 38, August 2001, 336–348.

20. Geng Cui and Quiming Liu, "Emerging Market Segments in a Transitional Economy: A Study of Urban Consumers in China," *Journal of International Marketing,* 9, 1, 2001, 84–106.

21. V. Kumar and Anish Nagpal, "Segmenting Global Markets: Look Before You Leap," *Marketing Research,* Spring 2001, 8–13.

22. Brian Wansink and Sea Bum Park, "Methods and Measures That Profile Heavy Users," *Journal of Advertising Research,* July–August 2000, 61–72; Ronald E. Goldsmith and Stephen W. Litvin, "Heavy Users of Travel Agents: A Segmentation Analysis of Vacation Travelers," *Journal of Travel Research,* November 1999, 127–133.

23. "India: Mantras to Work Brand Magic," *Businessline,* April 26, 2001, 1–4.

24. Russell Haley, "Benefit Segmentation: A Decision-Oriented Research Tool," *Marketing Management,* 4, Summer 1995, 59–62; Dianne Cermak, Karen Maru File, and Russ Alan Prince, "A Benefit Segmentation of the Major Donor Market," *Journal of Business Research,* February 1994, 121–130; Elisabeth Kastenholz, Duane Davis, and Gordon Paul, "Segmenting Tourism in Rural Areas: The Case of North and Central Portugal," *Journal of Travel Research,* 37, May 1999, 353–363.

25. William Trombetta, "A Strategic Overview," *Pharmaceutical Executive Supplement,* May 2001, 8–16.

26. Michael J. Weiss, "Online America," *American Demographics,* March 2001, 53–60.

27. www. claritas. com; Patricia Lloyd Williams, "Energy Marketing: What Do Customers Want?" *Fortnightly's Energy Customer Management,* Fall 2000, 36–41.

28. "Mediamark Research Inc. Enhances Data with Segmentation Analysis from VALS(TM) and Forrester," *PR Newswire,* August 22, 2001, 1; Linda P. Morton, "Segmenting Publics by Lifestyles," *Public Relations Quarterly,* Fall 1999, 46–47.

29. "Who Will Buy Intelligent In-Vehicle Products? New Report Assesses Consumer Perceptions and Acceptance of Intelligent Transportation Systems Products," *Business Wire,* November 2, 1999, 1.

30. David J. Lipke, "Head Trips—A New Way to Understand Consumer Psychology," *American Demographics,* October 2000, 38–40; "Yankelovich Launches Revolutionary New Marketing Tool," *Business Wire,* August 1, 2000, 1.

The Consumer as an Individual

PART 2 DISCUSSES THE CONSUMER AS AN INDIVIDUAL.

Chapters 4 through 8 provide the reader with a comprehensive picture of consumer psychology. These chapters explain the basic psychological concepts that account for individual behavior and demonstrate how these concepts influence the individual's consumption-related behavior. Chapter 9 shows how communication links consumers as individuals to the world and people around them.

Lighting for every
personality

illuminating ⬥ experiences

Whose life are **you** lighting?

CHAPTER FOUR

Consumer Motivation

Human needs—consumer needs—are the basis of all modern marketing. Needs are the essence of the marketing concept. The key to a company's survival, profitability, and growth in a highly competitive marketplace is its ability to identify and satisfy unfulfilled consumer needs better and sooner than the competition.

Marketers do not create needs, though in some instances they may make consumers more keenly aware of unfelt needs. Successful marketers define their markets in terms of the needs they presume to satisfy, not in terms of the products they sell. This is a market-oriented, rather than a production-oriented, approach to marketing. A marketing orientation focuses on the needs of the buyer; a production orientation focuses on the needs of the seller. The marketing concept implies that the manufacturer will make only what it knows people will buy; a production orientation implies that the manufacturer will try to sell whatever it decides to make.

The philosophy and marketing strategy of Charles Revson, the builder of the Revlon cosmetics empire, depict an insightful understanding of consumer needs. Charles Revson started by manufacturing nail polish, but he defined nail polish as a fashion accessory and not merely a nail covering. His strategy was designed to induce women to use different shades of nail polish to match different outfits, moods, and occasions. This approach vastly broadened the market for the product, because it persuaded women to buy and use many different colors of nail polish in the same season rather than wait to finish one bottle before buying another one. And Revson ensured that women would buy more and more bottles of nail polish by introducing new nail color fashions every season. Emulating GM's strategy of planned obsolescence (i.e., introducing new automobile models every year), Revlon would introduce new nail colors every fall and spring and, through heavy and effective advertising, would persuade women that buying the new colors would satisfy their need to appear fashionable and attractive.[1]

Similar to GM's segmentation strategy, Revson developed separate cosmetic lines targeting different consumer segments, such as the popularly priced *Revlon* (which Revson equated with the positioning of the Pontiac), *Natural Wonder* (targeting the youth market), and *Marcella Borghese* (positioned as the high-class line with international "flavor"). Most importantly, Revson understood that he was not selling women the physical product (e.g., nail laquer to cover their nails) but the fantasy that the nail polish would attract attention and bestow class and glamour on the user. Thus, Revson did not sell deep red polish; he sold *Fire and Ice*. He did not sell dark red polish; he sold *Berry Bon Bon*. Charles Revson summed up his philosophy by saying "In the factory, we make cosmetics; in the store, we sell hope." And selling hope, rather than the physical product known as cosmetics, allowed Revson to charge much more for his products. Rather than compete with other manufacturers on the basis of price, Revson competed on the basis of perceived quality and greater satisfaction of women's needs for fantasy and attention.[2]

Savvy companies define their missions in terms of the consumer needs they satisfy rather than the products they produce and sell. Because consumers' basic needs do not change but the products that satisfy them do, a corporate focus on making products that will satisfy consumers' needs ensures that the company stays in the forefront of the search for new and effective solutions. By doing so, such companies are likely to survive and grow despite strong competition or adverse economic conditions. On the other hand, companies that define themselves in terms of the products they make may suffer or even go out of business when their products are replaced by competitive offerings that better satisfy the same need. Table 4-1 includes examples of companies that define themselves as need–rather than product–oriented.

This chapter discusses basic needs that operate in most people to motivate behavior. It explores the influence that such needs have on consumption behavior. Later chapters in Part 2 explain why and how these basic human needs, or motives, are expressed in so many diverse ways.

Motivation as a Psychological Force

Motivation is the *driving force within individuals that impels them to action.* This driving force is produced by a state of tension, which exists as the result of an unfulfilled need. Individuals strive both consciously and subconsciously to reduce this tension through behavior that they anticipate will fulfill their needs and thus relieve them of the stress they feel. The specific goals they select and the patterns of action they undertake to achieve their goals are the results of individual thinking and learning. Figure 4-1 presents a model of the motivational process. It portrays motivation as a state of need-induced tension that "drives" the individual to engage in behavior that he or she believes will satisfy the need and thus reduce the tension. Whether gratification is actually achieved depends on the course of action pursued. The specific goals that consumers wish to achieve and the courses of action they take to attain these goals are selected on the basis of their thinking processes (cognition) and previous learning. Therefore, marketers must view motivation as the force that induces consumption and, through consumption experiences, the process of consumer learning (discussed in Chapter 7).

NEEDS

Every individual has needs: some are innate, others are acquired. **Innate needs** are physiological (i.e., *biogenic*); they include the needs for food, water, air, clothing,

TABLE 4-1	Product-Oriented Versus Need-Oriented Definitions	
	PRODUCT-ORIENTED	**CONSUMER NEED-ORIENTED DEFINITIONS**
Pfizer	We make pharmaceuticals.	"Pfizer Inc. is a research-based, global pharmaceutical company. We discover and develop innovative, value-added products that improve the quality of life of people around the world and help them enjoy longer, healthier, and more productive lives."[a]
Logitech	We make cameras and PC tracking devices.	"We provide innovative personal interface products that help people work, play, and communicate in the digital world."[b]
Ritz-Carlton	We rent rooms and provide facilities for meetings and events.	The company's credo stresses the genuine care and comfort of the guests, the finest personal service and facilities, a warm yet refined ambience, and an experience that fulfills even the unexpressed needs and wishes of the guests.[c]
Sony	We make electronics, movies, and recorded CDs.	Sony is adopting a new marketing concept called "segment solutions." Accordingly, Sony will no longer offer products for the mass market, but will offer consumers in different lifestyle segments a variety of solutions that meet virtually every lifestyle need. For example, Sony's Walkman and S-2 lines target "active lifestyle enthusiasts" by offering them the benefits of water and impact resistance, active control, and high visibility. The new products include features that allow users to carry, listen to, and manipulate many forms of recorded sounds.[d]

Sources: [a] www.pfizer.com; [b] www.logitech.com; [c] www.ritzcarlton.com; [d] Tobi Elkin, "Sony Marketing Aims at Lifestyle Segments," *Advertising Age*, March 18, 2002, 3, 72.

FIGURE 4-1

Model of the
Motivation Process
Source: From Jeffrey F.
Dugree et al. "Observations:
Translating Values into Product
Wants," *Journal of Advertising
Research, 36*, 6, (November
1996). Reprinted by permission of the Journal of the
American Marketing
Association.

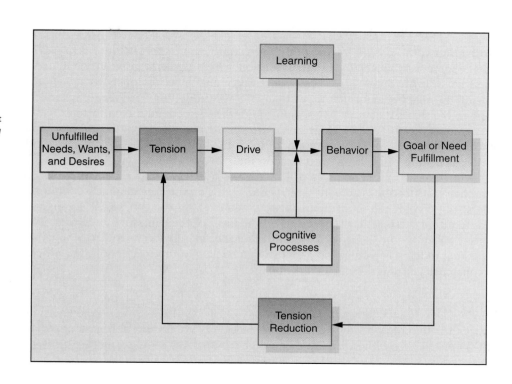

shelter, and sex. Because they are needed to sustain biological life, the biogenic needs are considered **primary needs** or motives.

Acquired needs are needs that we learn in response to our culture or environment. These may include needs for self-esteem, prestige, affection, power, and learning. Because acquired needs are generally psychological (i.e., *psychogenic*), they are considered **secondary needs** or motives. They result from the individual's subjective psychological state and from relationships with others. For example, all individuals need shelter from the elements; thus, finding a place to live fulfills an important primary need for a newly transferred executive. However, the kind of home she rents or buys may be the result of secondary needs. She may seek a place in which she and her husband can entertain large groups of people (and fulfill social needs); she may want to live in an exclusive community to impress her friends and family (and fulfill ego needs). The place where an individual ultimately chooses to live thus may serve to fulfill both primary and secondary needs.

GOALS

Goals are the sought-after results of motivated behavior. As Figure 4-1 indicated, all behavior is goal oriented. Our discussion of motivation in this chapter is in part concerned with **generic goals,** that is, the general classes or categories of goals that consumers see as a way to fulfill their needs. If a person tells his parents that he wants to get a graduate degree, he has stated a generic goal. If he says he wants to get an M.B.A. degree in marketing from the Kellogg School of Management of Northwestern University, he has expressed a product-specific goal. Marketers are particularly concerned with **product-specific goals,** that is, the specifically branded products and services that consumers select for goal fulfillment.

Individuals set goals on the basis of their personal values, and they select means (or behaviors) that they believe will help them achieve their desired goals. Figures 4-2 A, B, and C depict a framework of the goal structure behind losing weight and maintaining weight loss and the results of a study based on this model. Figure 4-2A depicts an overall framework for pursuing consumption-related goals. Figure 4-2B depicts the interrelationship among the needs driving the goal of losing weight (e.g., increased self-confidence, looking and feeling better, and living longer) and the behaviors required to achieve the goal (i.e., exercising and/or dieting). Figure 4-2C depicts the complex nature of goal setting based on subjects' responses to questions regarding their reasons for selecting weight loss as a goal, providing justification for each reason, and explaining each justification.[3] The three diagrams together depict the complexity of goal setting and the difficulties in understanding this process through a set theoretical model. Figure 4-3 depicts an ad that portrays subscribing to a health magazine as a means to achieve several physical appearance–related goals.

The Selection of Goals

For any given need, there are many different and appropriate goals. The goals selected by individuals depend on their personal experiences, physical capacity, prevailing cultural norms and values, and the goal's accessibility in the physical and social environment. For example, a young woman may wish to get a deep and even tan and may envision spending time in the sun as a way to achieve her goal. However, if her dermatologist advises her to avoid direct exposure to the sun, she may settle for a self-tanning product instead. The goal object has to be both socially acceptable and physically accessible. If cosmetic companies did not offer effective alternatives to tanning in the sun, our young woman would have to either ignore the

FIGURE 4-2

The Needs and Goals
Behind Losing or
Maintaining Body
Weight
Source: From "Goal Setting
and Goal Pursuit in the
Regulation of Body Weight,"
by Richard Bagozzi and
Elizabeth Edwards originally
published in *Psychology and
Health, 13,* 1998. Reprinted by
permission of Taylor & Francis
Ltd., **www.tandf.co.uk/journals**.

(A)

(B)

(C)

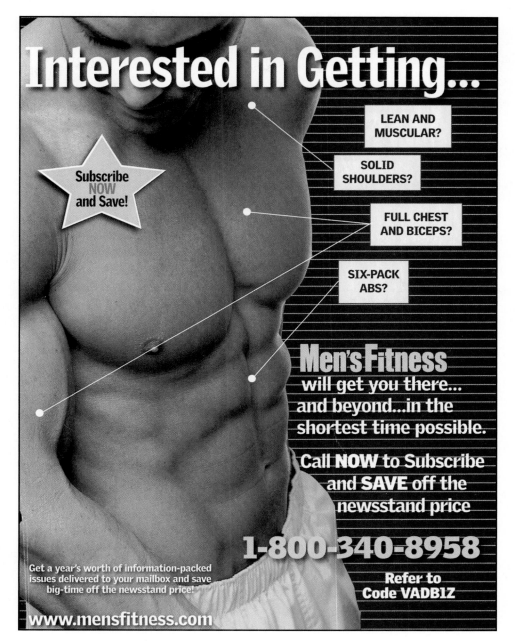

FIGURE 4-3

Achieving Goals by
Subscribing to a
Magazine

advice of her dermatologist or select a substitute goal, such as untanned (but undamaged) youthful-looking skin.

An individual's own perception of himself or herself also serves to influence the specific goals selected. The products a person owns, would like to own, or would not like to own are often perceived in terms of how closely they reflect that person's self-image. A product that is perceived as matching a consumer's self-image has a greater probability of being selected than one that is not.

Figure 4-4 presents a series of advertisements for Illuminating Experiences, a lighting fixture manufacturer that recognizes that individuals with different needs and interests still have the same need for appropriate lighting. Each ad in the series

FIGURE 4-4

Different Appeals for Same Goal Object

Courtesy of Illuminating Experiences. Agency is BrandStreet Advertising LLC. Copy by Ed Shankman, art by Dave Frank and design by Joe Gwgliuzza.

symbolically reflects a specific personality and self image with which viewers can identify, while providing an effective goal object to satisfy the universal need for good lighting.

Interdependence of Needs and Goals

Needs and goals are interdependent; neither exists without the other. However, people are often not as aware of their needs as they are of their goals. For example, a teenager may not consciously be aware of his social needs but may join a photography club to meet new friends. A local politician may not consciously be aware of a power need but may regularly run for public office. A college student may not consciously recognize her need for achievement but may strive to attain a straight A grade point average.

Individuals are usually somewhat more aware of their *physiological* needs than they are of their *psychological* needs. Most people know when they are hungry, thirsty, or cold, and they take appropriate steps to satisfy these needs. The same people may not consciously be aware of their needs for acceptance, self-esteem, or status. They may, however, subconsciously engage in behavior that satisfies their psychological (acquired) needs.

POSITIVE AND NEGATIVE MOTIVATION

Motivation can be **positive** or **negative** in direction. We may feel a driving force *toward* some object or condition or a driving force *away* from some object or condition. For example, a person may be impelled toward a restaurant to fulfill a hunger need, and away from motorcycle transportation to fulfill a safety need.

Some psychologists refer to positive drives as needs, wants, or desires and to negative drives as fears or aversions. However, although positive and negative motivational forces seem to differ dramatically in terms of physical (and sometimes emotional) activity, they are basically similar in that both serve to initiate and sustain human behavior. For this reason, researchers often refer to both kinds of drives or motives as *needs, wants,* and *desires.* Some theorists distinguish wants from needs by defining wants as product-specific needs. Others differentiate between desires, on the one hand, and needs and wants on the other. Thus, there is no uniformly accepted distinction among needs, wants, and desires.

Needs, wants, or desires may create goals that can be positive or negative. A positive goal is one toward which behavior is directed; thus, it is often referred to as an **approach object.** A negative goal is one from which behavior is directed away and is referred to as an **avoidance object.** Because both approach and avoidance goals are the results of motivated behavior, most researchers refer to both simply as *goals*. Consider this example: A middle-aged woman may have a positive goal of fitness and joins a health club to work out regularly. Her husband may view getting fat as a negative goal, and so he starts exercising as well. In the former case, the wife's actions are designed to achieve the positive goal of health and fitness; in the latter case, her husband's actions are designed to avoid a negative goal—a flabby physique. The product featured in Figure 4-5A offers users a positive goal and approach object, whereas the ad in Figure 4-5B depicts an avoidance object.

Sometimes people become motivationally aroused by a threat to or elimination of a behavioral freedom, such as the freedom to make a product choice. This motivational state is called **psychological reactance.** A classic example occurred in 1985 when the Coca-Cola Company changed its traditional formula and introduced "New Coke." Many people reacted negatively to the notion that their "freedom to choose" had been taken away, and they refused to buy New Coke. Company management responded to this unexpected psychological reaction by reintroducing the original formula as Classic Coke and gradually developing additional versions of Coke.

RATIONAL VERSUS EMOTIONAL MOTIVES

Some consumer behaviorists distinguish between so-called **rational motives** and **emotional motives.** They use the term *rationality* in the traditional economic sense, which assumes that consumers behave rationally by carefully considering all alternatives and choosing those that give them the greatest utility. In a marketing context, the term *rationality* implies that consumers select goals based on totally objective criteria,

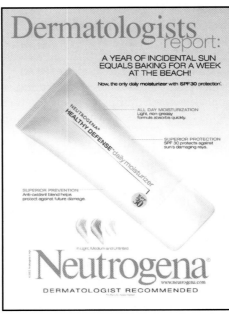

FIGURE 4-5

Positive Versus
Negative Motivation

such as size, weight, price, or miles per gallon. Emotional motives imply the selection of goals according to personal or subjective criteria (e.g., pride, fear, affection, or status).

The assumption underlying this distinction is that subjective or emotional criteria do not maximize utility or satisfaction. However, it is reasonable to assume that consumers always attempt to select alternatives that, in their view, serve to maximize their satisfaction. Obviously, the assessment of satisfaction is a very personal process, based on the individual's own need structure, as well as on past behavioral and social (or learned) experiences. What may appear irrational to an outside observer may be perfectly rational in the context of the consumer's own psychological field. For example, a person who pursues extensive plastic facial surgery in order to appear younger is using significant economic resources, such as the surgical fees, time lost in recovery, inconvenience, and the risk that something may go wrong. To that person, the pursuit of the goal of looking younger and utilization of the resources involved are perfectly rational choices. However, to many other persons within the same culture who are less concerned with aging, and certainly to persons from other cultures that are not as preoccupied with personal appearance as Westerners are, these choices appear completely irrational.

Consumer researchers who subscribe to the *positivist* research perspective tend to view all consumer behavior as rationally motivated, and they try to isolate the causes of such behavior so that they can predict and, thus, influence future behavior. *Experientialists* are often interested in studying the hedonistic pleasures that certain consumption behaviors provide, such as fun, or fantasy, or sensuality. They study consumers in order to gain insights and understanding of the behaviors consumers display in various unique circumstances.

The Dynamics of Motivation

Motivation is a highly dynamic construct that is constantly changing in reaction to life experiences. Needs and goals change and grow in response to an individual's physical condition, environment, interactions with others, and experiences. As individuals attain their goals, they develop new ones. If they do not attain their goals, they continue to strive for old goals or they develop substitute goals. Some of the reasons why need-driven human activity never ceases include the following: (1) Many needs are never fully satisfied; they continually impel actions designed to attain or maintain satisfaction. (2) As needs become satisfied, new and higher-order needs emerge that cause tension and induce activity. (3) People who achieve their goals set new and higher goals for themselves. The appeal of the ad in Figure 4-6 stems from the need to achieve and satisfy new and higher goals.

NEEDS ARE NEVER FULLY SATISFIED

Most human needs are never fully or permanently satisfied. For example, at fairly regular intervals throughout the day individuals experience hunger needs that must be satisfied. Most people regularly seek companionship and approval from others to satisfy their social needs. Even more complex psychological needs are rarely fully satisfied. For example, a person may partially satisfy a power need by working as administrative assistant to a local politician, but this vicarious taste of power may not sufficiently satisfy her need; thus, she may strive to work for a state legislator or even to run for political office herself. In this instance, temporary goal achievement does not adequately satisfy the need for power, and the individual strives harder in an effort to satisfy her need more fully.

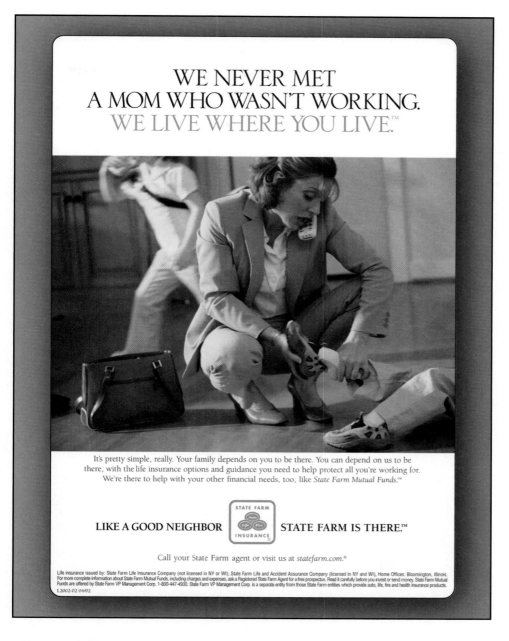

FIGURE 4-6

New and Higher Goals
Motivate Behavior
Courtesy of State Farm
Insurance.

NEW NEEDS EMERGE AS OLD NEEDS ARE SATISFIED

Some motivational theorists believe that a hierarchy of needs exists and that new, higher-order needs emerge as lower-order needs are fulfilled.[4] For example, a man who has largely satisfied his basic physiological needs (e.g., food, housing, etc.) may turn his efforts to achieving acceptance among his new neighbors by joining their political clubs and supporting their candidates. Once he is confident that he has achieved acceptance, he then may seek recognition by giving lavish parties or building a larger house.

Marketers must be attuned to changing needs. For example, the Mercedes-Benz ad shown in Figure 4-7 portrays three different car models corresponding to an individual's needs as he or she matures.

Product Alternatives for
Changing Consumer
Needs
Courtesy of Mercedes-Benz.
Image © Jake Chessum.

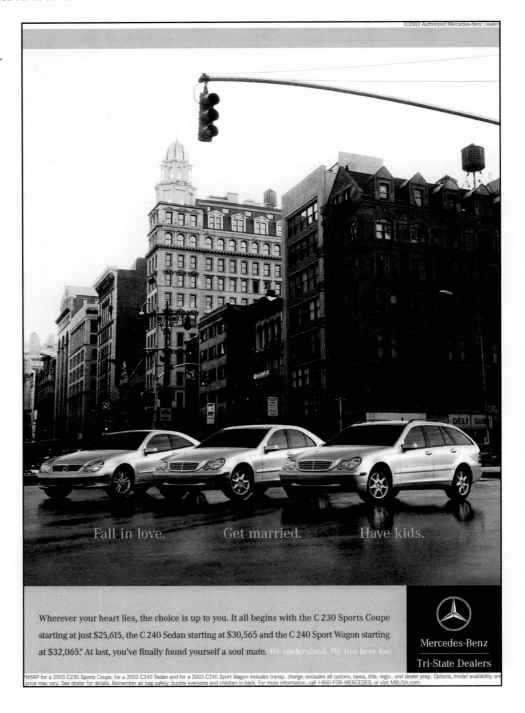

SUCCESS AND FAILURE INFLUENCE GOALS

A number of researchers have explored the nature of the goals that individuals set for
themselves. Broadly speaking, they have concluded that individuals who successfully
achieve their goals usually set new and higher goals; that is, they raise their **level of
aspiration.** This may be due to the fact that their success in reaching lower goals makes
them more confident of their ability to reach higher goals. Conversely, those who do

not reach their goals sometimes lower their levels of aspiration.[5] Thus, goal selection is often a function of success and failure. For example, a college senior who is not accepted into medical school may try instead to become a dentist or a podiatrist.

The nature and persistence of an individual's behavior are often influenced by expectations of success or failure in reaching certain goals. Those expectations, in turn, are often based on past experience. A person who takes good snapshots with an inexpensive camera may be motivated to buy a more sophisticated camera in the belief that it will enable her to take even better photographs. In this way, she eventually may upgrade her camera by several hundred dollars. On the other hand, a person who has not been able to take good photographs is just as likely to keep the same camera or even to lose all interest in photography.

These effects of success and failure on goal selection have strategy implications for marketers. Goals should be reasonably attainable. Advertisements should not promise more than the product will deliver. Products and services are often evaluated by the size and direction of the gap between consumer expectations and objective performance. Thus, even a good product will not be repurchased if it fails to live up to unrealistic expectations created by ads that "overpromise." Similarly, a consumer is likely to regard a mediocre product with greater satisfaction than it warrants if its performance exceeds her expectations.

SUBSTITUTE GOALS

When an individual cannot attain a specific goal or type of goal that he or she anticipates will satisfy certain needs, behavior may be directed to a **substitute goal.** Although the substitute goal may not be as satisfactory as the primary goal, it may be sufficient to dispel uncomfortable tension. Continued deprivation of a primary goal may result in the substitute goal assuming primary-goal status. For example, a woman who has stopped drinking whole milk because she is dieting may actually begin to prefer skim milk. A man who cannot afford a BMW may convince himself that a Mazda Miata has an image he clearly prefers.

FRUSTRATION

Failure to achieve a goal often results in feelings of frustration. At one time or another, everyone has experienced the frustration that comes from the inability to attain a goal. The barrier that prevents attainment of a goal may be personal to the individual (e.g., limited physical or financial resources) or an obstacle in the physical or social environment (e.g., a storm that causes the postponement of a long-awaited vacation). Regardless of the cause, individuals react differently to frustrating situations. Some people manage to cope by finding their way around the obstacle or, if that fails, by selecting a substitute goal. Others are less adaptive and may regard their inability to achieve a goal as a personal failure. Such people are likely to adopt a defense mechanism to protect their egos from feelings of inadequacy.

Defense Mechanisms

People who cannot cope with frustration often mentally redefine their frustrating situations in order to protect their self-images and defend their self-esteem. For example, a young woman may yearn for a European vacation she cannot afford. The coping individual may select a less expensive vacation trip to Disneyland or to a national park. The person who cannot cope may react with anger toward her boss for not paying her enough money to afford the vacation she prefers, or she may persuade herself that Europe is unseasonably warm this year. These last two possibilities are examples,

TABLE 4-2	Defense Mechanisms

DEFENSE MECHANISM	DESCRIPTION AND ILLUSTRATIONS
Aggression	In response to frustration, individuals may resort to aggressive behavior in attempting to protect their self-esteem. The tennis pro who slams his tennis racket to the ground when disappointed with his game or the baseball player who physically intimidates an empire for his call are examples of such conduct. So are consumer boycotts of companies or stores.
Rationalization	People sometimes resolve frustration by inventing plausible reasons for being unable to attain their goals (e.g., not having enough time to practice) or deciding that the goal is not really worth pursuing (e.g., how important is it to achieve a high bowling score?).
Regression	An individual may react to a frustrating situation with childish or immature behavior. A shopper attending a bargain sale, for example, may fight over merchandise and even rip a garment that another shopper will not relinquish rather than allow the other person to have it.
Withdrawal	Frustration may be resolved by simply withdrawing from the situation. For instance, a person who has difficulty achieving officer status in an organization may decide he can use his time more constructively in other activities and simply quit that organization.
Projection	An individual may redefine a frustrating situation by projecting blame for his or her own failures and inabilities on other objects or persons. Thus, the golfer who misses a stroke may blame his golf clubs or his caddy.
Autism	Autistic thinking is thinking dominated by needs and emotions, with little effort made to relate to reality. Such daydreaming, or fantasizing, enables the individual to attain imaginary gratification of unfulfilled needs. A person who is shy and lonely, for example, may daydream about a romantic love affair.
Identification	People resolve feelings of frustration by subconsciously identifying with other persons or situations that they consider relevant. For example, slice-of-life commercials often portray a stereotypical situation in which an individual experiences a frustration and then overcomes the problem by using the advertised product. If the viewer can identify with the frustrating situation, he or she may very likely adopt the proposed solution and buy the product advertised.
Repression	Another way that individuals avoid the tension arising from frustration is by repressing the unsatisfied need. Thus, individuals may "force" the need out of their conscious awareness. Sometimes repressed needs manifest themselves indirectly. The wife who is unable to bear children may teach school or work in a library; her husband may do volunteer work in a boys' club. The manifestation of repressed needs in a socially acceptable form is called *sublimation*, another type of defense mechanism.

respectively, of aggression and rationalization, **defense mechanisms** that people sometimes adopt to protect their egos from feelings of failure when they do not attain their goals. Other defense mechanisms include regression, withdrawal, projection, autism, identification, and repression. These defense mechanisms are described in Table 4-2. This listing of defense mechanisms is far from exhaustive, because individuals tend to develop their own ways of redefining frustrating situations to protect their self-esteem from the anxieties that result from experiencing failure. Marketers often consider this fact in their selection of advertising appeals and construct advertisements that portray a person resolving a particular frustration through the use of the advertised product.

MULTIPLICITY OF NEEDS

A consumer's behavior often fulfills more than one need. In fact, it is likely that specific goals are selected because they fulfill several needs. We buy clothing for protection and for a certain degree of modesty; in addition, our clothing fulfills a wide range of personal and social needs, such as acceptance or ego needs. Usually, however, there is one overriding (prepotent) need that initiates behavior. For example, a young woman may consider joining a health club because she has nothing special to do most evenings, she wants to wear midriff-baring clothes, and she wants to meet men outside a bar setting. If the cumulative amount of tension produced by each of these three reasons is sufficiently strong, she will probably join a health club. However, just one of the reasons (e.g., the desire to meet new men) may serve as the triggering mechanism; that would be the **prepotent need.**

Needs and Goals Vary Among Individuals

One cannot accurately infer motives from behavior. People with different needs may seek fulfillment through selection of the same goal; people with the same needs may seek fulfillment through different goals. Consider the following examples. Five people who are active in a consumer advocacy organization may each belong for a different reason. The first may be genuinely concerned with protecting consumer interests; the second may be concerned about an increase in counterfeit merchandise; the third may seek social contacts from organizational meetings; the fourth may enjoy the power of directing a large group; and the fifth may enjoy the status provided by membership in an attention-getting organization.

Similarly, five people may be driven by the same need (e.g., an ego need) to seek fulfillment in different ways. The first may seek advancement and recognition through a professional career; the second may become active in a political organization; the third may run in regional marathons; the fourth may take professional dance lessons; and the fifth may seek attention by monopolizing classroom discussions.

AROUSAL OF MOTIVES

Most of an individual's specific needs are dormant much of the time. The arousal of any particular set of needs at a specific moment in time may be caused by internal stimuli found in the individual's physiological condition, by emotional or cognitive processes, or by stimuli in the outside environment.

Physiological Arousal

Bodily needs at any one specific moment in time are based on the individual's physiological condition at that moment. A drop in blood sugar level or stomach contractions will trigger awareness of a hunger need. Secretion of sex hormones will awaken the sex need. A decrease in body temperature will induce shivering, which makes the individual aware of the need for warmth. Most of these physiological cues are involuntary; however, they arouse related needs that cause uncomfortable tensions until they are satisfied. For example, a person who is cold may turn up the heat in his bedroom and also make a mental note to buy a warm cardigan sweater to wear around the house.

Emotional Arousal

Sometimes daydreaming results in the arousal or stimulation of latent needs. People who are bored or who are frustrated in trying to achieve their goals often engage in daydreaming (autistic thinking), in which they imagine themselves in all sorts of desirable situations. These thoughts tend to arouse dormant needs, which may produce uncomfortable tensions that drive them into goal-oriented behavior. A young woman who daydreams of a torrid romance may spend her free time in Internet single chat rooms; a young man who dreams of being a famous novelist may enroll in a writing workshop.

Cognitive Arousal

Sometimes random thoughts can lead to a cognitive awareness of needs. An advertisement that provides reminders of home might trigger instant yearning to speak with one's parents. This is the basis for many long-distance telephone company campaigns that stress the low cost of international long-distance rates. Figure 4-8 depicts an ad directed at cognitive arousal of the need for a digital camera.

FIGURE 4-8

Cognitive Need Arousal
Courtesy of Canon.

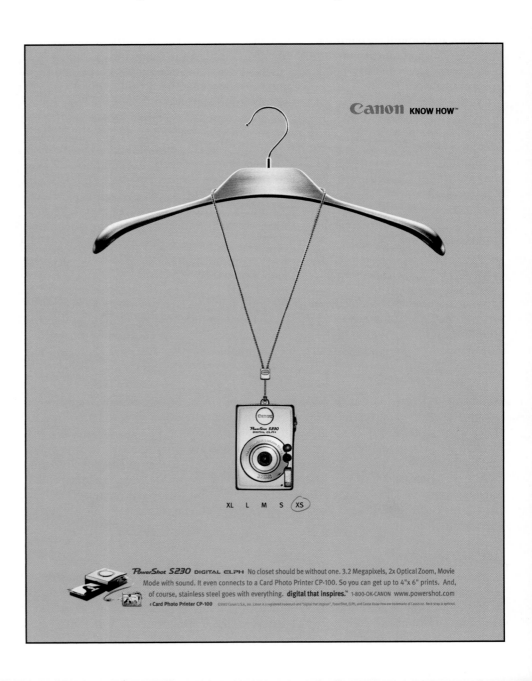

Environmental Arousal

The set of needs an individual experiences at a particular time are often activated by specific cues in the environment. Without these cues, the needs might remain dormant. For example, the 6 o'clock news, the sight or smell of bakery goods, fast-food commercials on television, the end of the school day—all of these may arouse the "need" for food. In such cases, modification of the environment may be necessary to reduce the arousal of hunger.

A most potent form of situational cue is the goal object itself. A woman may experience an overwhelming need for a new television set when she sees her neighbor's new high-definition home theater; a man may suddenly experience a "need" for a new car when passing a dealer's display window. Sometimes an advertisement or other environmental cue produces a psychological imbalance in the viewer's mind. For example, a young college student who constantly uses his cell phone may see a new, slick-looking cell phone model with more features displayed in a store window. The exposure may make him unhappy with his old cell phone and cause him to experience tension that will be reduced only when he buys himself the new cell phone model.

When people live in a complex and highly varied environment, they experience many opportunities for need arousal. Conversely, when their environment is poor or deprived, fewer needs are activated. This explains why television has had such a mixed effect on the lives of people in underdeveloped countries. It exposes them to various lifestyles and expensive products that they would not otherwise see, and it awakens wants and desires that they have little opportunity or even hope of satisfying. Thus, while television enriches many lives, it also serves to frustrate people with little money or education or hope, and may result in the adoption of such aggressive defense mechanisms as robbery, boycotts, or even revolts.

There are two opposing philosophies concerned with the arousal of human motives. The *behaviorist* school considers motivation to be a mechanical process; behavior is seen as the response to a stimulus, and elements of conscious thought are ignored. An extreme example of the *stimulus–response* theory of motivation is the impulse buyer who reacts largely to external stimuli in the buying situation. According to this theory, the consumer's cognitive control is limited; he or she does not act but reacts to stimuli in the marketplace. The *cognitive* school believes that all behavior is directed at goal achievement. Needs and past experiences are reasoned, categorized, and transformed into attitudes and beliefs that act as predispositions to behavior. These predispositions are focused on helping the individual satisfy needs, and they determine the actions that he or she takes to achieve this satisfaction.

Types and Systems of Needs

For many years, psychologists and others interested in human behavior have attempted to develop exhaustive lists of human needs. Most lists of human needs tend to be diverse in content as well as in length. Although there is little disagreement about specific physiological needs, there is considerable disagreement about specific psychological (i.e., psychogenic) needs.

In 1938, the psychologist Henry Murray prepared a detailed list of 28 psychogenic needs. This research was probably the first systematic approach to the understanding of nonbiological human needs. Murray believed that everyone has the same basic set of needs but that individuals differ in their priority ranking of these needs. Murray's basic needs include many motives that are assumed to play an important role in consumer behavior, such as acquisition, achievement, recognition, and exhibition (see Table 4-3).

TABLE 4-3	Murray's List of Psychogenic Needs

NEEDS ASSOCIATED WITH INANIMATE OBJECTS

Acquisition
Conservancy
Order
Retention
Construction

NEEDS THAT REFLECT AMBITION, POWER, ACCOMPLISHMENT, AND PRESTIGE

Superiority
Achievement
Recognition
Exhibition
Inviolacy (inviolate attitude)
Infavoidance (to avoid shame, failure, humiliation, ridicule)
Defendance (defensive attitude)
Counteraction (counteractive attitude)

NEEDS CONCERNED WITH HUMAN POWER

Dominance
Deference
Similance (suggestible attitude)
Autonomy
Contrariance (to act differently from others)

SADOMASOCHISTIC NEEDS

Aggression
Abasement

NEEDS CONCERNED WITH AFFECTION BETWEEN PEOPLE

Affiliation
Rejection
Nurturance (to nourish, aid, or protect the helpless)
Succorance (to seek aid, protection, or sympathy)
Play

NEEDS CONCERNED WITH SOCIAL INTERCOURSE (THE NEEDS TO ASK AND TELL)

Cognizance (inquiring attitude)
Exposition (expositive attitude)

Source: Adapted from Henry A. Murray, "Types of Human Needs," in David C. McClelland, *Studies in Motivation* (New York: Appleton-Century-Crofts, 1955), 63–66. Reprinted by permission of Irvington Publishers, Inc.

HIERARCHY OF NEEDS

Dr. Abraham Maslow, a clinical psychologist, formulated a widely accepted theory of human motivation based on the notion of a universal hierarchy of human needs.[6] Maslow's theory identifies five basic levels of human needs, which rank in order of importance from lower-level (biogenic) needs to higher-level (psychogenic) needs.

The theory postulates that individuals seek to satisfy lower-level needs before higher-level needs emerge. The lowest level of chronically unsatisfied need that an individual experiences serves to motivate his or her behavior. When that need is "fairly well" satisfied, a new (and higher) need emerges that the individual is motivated to fulfill. When this need is satisfied, a new (and still higher) need emerges, and so on. Of course, if a lower-level need experiences some renewed deprivation (e.g., thirst), it may temporarily become dominant again.

Figure 4-9 presents a diagram of **Maslow's hierarchy of needs.** For clarity, each level is depicted as mutually exclusive. According to the theory, however, there is some overlap between each level, as no need is ever completely satisfied. For this reason, although all levels of need below the level that is currently dominant continue to motivate behavior to some extent, the prime motivator—the major driving force within the individual—is the lowest level of need that remains largely unsatisfied.

Physiological Needs

In the hierarchy-of-needs theory, physiological needs are the first and most basic level of human needs. These needs, which are required to sustain biological life, include food, water, air, shelter, clothing, sex—all the biogenic needs, in fact, that were listed as primary needs earlier.

According to Maslow, physiological needs are dominant when they are chronically unsatisfied: "For the man who is extremely and dangerously hungry, no other interest exists but food. He dreams food, he remembers food, he thinks about food, he emotes only about food, he perceives only food, and he wants only food."[7] For many people in this country, the biogenic needs are generally satisfied, and higher-level needs are dominant. Unfortunately, however, the lives of the many homeless people in major cities and in physically devastated areas are focused almost entirely on satisfying their biogenic needs, such as the needs for food, clothing, and shelter. The many ads for products and services that promote physical health illustrate appeals to this level of the need hierarchy.

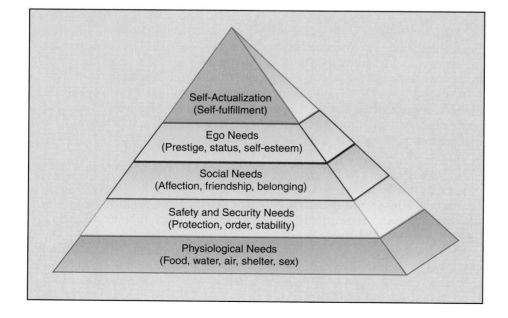

FIGURE 4-9

Maslow's Hierarchy of Needs

Safety Needs

After the first level of need is satisfied, safety and security needs become the driving force behind an individual's behavior. These needs are concerned not only with physical safety but also include order, stability, routine, familiarity, and control over one's life and environment. Health and the availability of health care are important safety concerns. Savings accounts, insurance policies, education, and vocational training are all means by which individuals satisfy the need for security.

Social Needs

The third level of Maslow's hierarchy includes such needs as love, affection, belonging, and acceptance. People seek warm and satisfying human relationships with other people and are motivated by love for their families. Because of the importance of social motives in our society, advertisers of many product categories emphasize this appeal in their advertisements.

Egoistic Needs

When social needs are more or less satisfied, the fourth level of Maslow's hierarchy becomes operative. This level is concerned with egoistic needs. These needs can take either an inward or an outward orientation, or both. Inwardly–directed ego needs reflect an individual's need for self-acceptance, self-esteem, success, independence, and personal satisfaction with a job well done. Outwardly–directed ego needs include the needs for prestige, reputation, status, and recognition from others. The presumed desire to "show off" one's success and achievement through material possessions is a reflection of an outwardly–oriented ego need. (See Figure 4-10.)

Need for Self-Actualization

According to Maslow, most people do not satisfy their ego needs sufficiently to ever move to the fifth level—the need for self-actualization (self-fulfillment). This need refers to an individual's desire to fulfill his or her potential—to become everything he or she is capable of becoming. In Maslow's words, "What a man can be, he must be."[8] This need is expressed in different ways by different people. A young man may desire to be an Olympic star and work single-mindedly for years to become the best in his sport. An artist may need to express herself on canvas; a research scientist may strive to find a new drug that eradicates cancer. Maslow noted that the self-actualization need is not necessarily a creative urge but that it is likely to take that form in people with some capacity for creativity. Some of our largest companies use motivation-based promotion to encourage their highly paid employees to look beyond their paychecks to find gratification and self-fulfillment in the workplace—to view their jobs as the way to become "all they can be." Figure 4-11 shows an ad for athletic shoes based on a self-actualization appeal (note that the shoes themselves are not featured in the ad).

An Evaluation of the Need Hierarchy and Marketing Applications

Maslow's hierarchy-of-needs theory postulates a five-level hierarchy of prepotent human needs. Higher-order needs become the driving force behind human behavior as lower-level needs are satisfied. The theory says, in effect, that dissatisfaction, not satisfaction, motivates behavior.

The need hierarchy has received wide acceptance in many social disciplines because it appears to reflect the assumed or inferred motivations of many people in our society. The five levels of need postulated by the hierarchy are sufficiently generic to encompass most lists of individual needs. The major problem with the

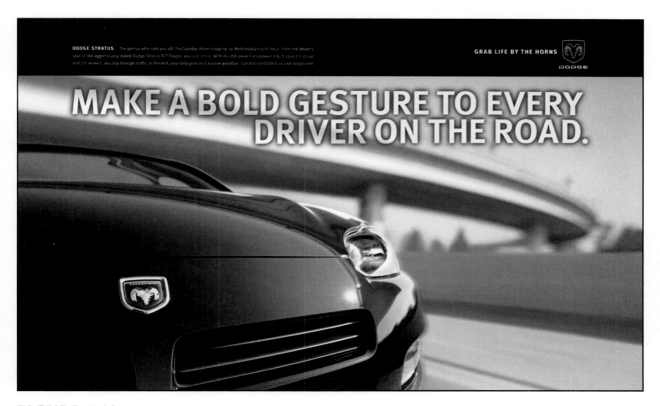

FIGURE 4-10

Appeal to Egoistic Needs
Courtesy of DaimlerChrysler.

theory is that it cannot be tested empirically; there is no way to measure precisely how satisfied one level of need must be before the next higher need becomes operative. The need hierarchy also appears to be very closely bound to our contemporary American culture (i.e., it appears to be both culture– and time–bound).

Despite these limitations, the hierarchy offers a highly useful framework for marketers trying to develop appropriate advertising appeals for their products. It is adaptable in two ways: First, it enables marketers to focus their advertising appeals on a need level that is likely to be shared by a large segment of the target audience; second, it facilitates product positioning or repositioning.

SEGMENTATION AND PROMOTIONAL APPLICATIONS

Maslow's need hierarchy is readily adaptable to market segmentation and the development of advertising appeals because there are consumer goods designed to satisfy each of the need levels and because most needs are shared by large segments of consumers. For example, individuals buy health foods, medicines, and low-fat and diet products to satisfy physiological needs. They buy insurance, preventive medical services, and home security systems to satisfy safety and security needs. Almost all personal care and grooming products (e.g., cosmetics, mouthwash, shaving cream), as well as most clothes, are bought to satisfy social needs. High-tech products such as computers or sound systems and luxury products such as furs, big cars, or expensive furniture are often bought to fulfill ego and esteem needs. Postgraduate college

FIGURE 4-11

Appeal to Self-
Actualization
Courtesy of Converse.

shine.

converse.com
© 2002 CONVERSE INC. ALL RIGHTS RESERVED.
SHINE IS A TRADEMARK OF CONVERSE INC.

education, hobby-related products, exotic and physically challenging adventure trips are sold as ways of achieving self-fulfillment.

The need hierarchy is often used as the basis for market segmentation with specific advertising appeals directed to one or more need-segment levels. For example, the Ford Taurus has been designed and advertised as a family car (a social appeal). The Mustang's ads stress power (egoistic) needs, as does the car ad shown in Figure 4-10, which suggests that driving the car advertised will impress other drivers. An ad for a very expensive sports car may use a self-actualization appeal such as "you deserve the very best." Volvo, on the other hand, targets more traditional buyers and its ads stress the safety appeal.

POSITIONING APPLICATIONS

Advertisers may use the need hierarchy for *positioning* products—that is, deciding how the product should be perceived by prospective consumers. The key to positioning is to find a niche—an unsatisfied need—that is not occupied by a competing product or brand. The need hierarchy is a very versatile tool for developing positioning strategies because different appeals for the same product can be based on different needs included in this framework. For example, many ads for soft drinks stress social appeal by showing a group of young people enjoying themselves and the advertised product. Other ads for nutritional drinks stress refreshment (a physiological need); still others may focus on low caloric content (thus indirectly appealing to the ego need).

A TRIO OF NEEDS

Some psychologists believe in the existence of a trio of basic needs: the needs for power, for affiliation, and for achievement. These needs can each be subsumed within Maslow's need hierarchy; considered individually, however, each has a unique relevance to consumer motivation.

Power

The power need relates to an individual's desire to control his or her environment. It includes the need to control other persons and various objects. This need appears to be closely related to the ego need, in that many individuals experience increased self-esteem when they exercise power over objects or people. An example of an appeal to the power need is shown in Figure 4-12.

Affiliation

Affiliation is a well-known and well-researched social motive that has far-reaching influence on consumer behavior. The affiliation need suggests that behavior is strongly influenced by the desire for friendship, for acceptance, for belonging. People with high affiliation needs tend to be socially dependent on others. They often select goods they feel will meet with the approval of friends. Teenagers who hang out at malls or techies who congregate at computer shows often do so more for the satisfaction of being with others than for making a purchase. An appeal to the affiliation needs of young adults is shown in Figure 4-13. The affiliation need is very similar to Maslow's social need.

Achievement

A considerable number of research studies have focused on the achievement need.[9] Individuals with a strong need for achievement often regard personal accomplishment as an end in itself. The achievement need is closely related to both the egoistic need and the self-actualization need. People with a high need for achievement tend to be more self-confident, enjoy taking calculated risks, actively research their environments, and value feedback. Monetary rewards provide an important type of feedback as to how they are doing. People with high achievement needs prefer situations in which they can take personal responsibility for finding solutions. High achievement is a useful promotional strategy for many products and services targeted to educated and affluent consumers. Figure 4-14 depicts a car ad appealing to female high achievers.

In summary, individuals with specific psychological needs tend to be receptive to advertising appeals directed at those needs. They also tend to be receptive to certain

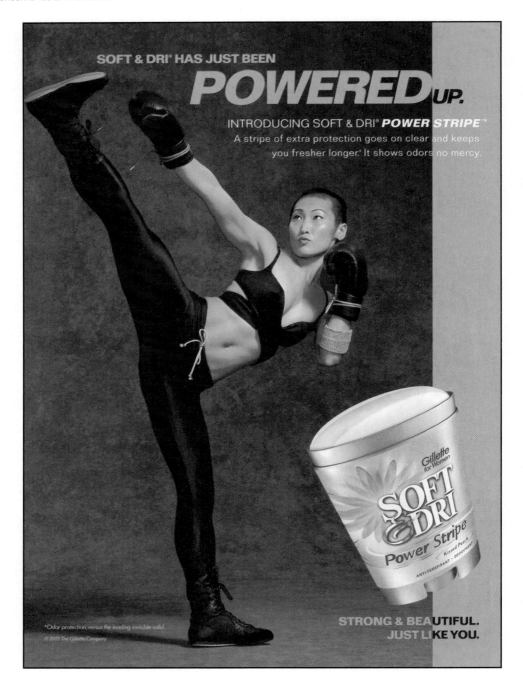

kinds of products. Thus, a knowledge of motivational theory provides marketers with key bases for segmenting markets and developing promotional strategies.

The Measurement of Motives

How are motives identified? How are they measured? How do researchers know which motives are responsible for certain kinds of behavior? These are difficult

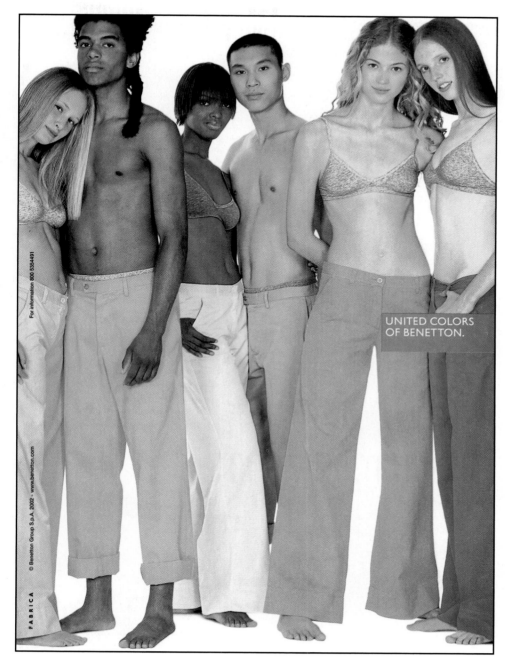

For information 800 5354491

© Benetton Group S.p.A. 2002 · www.benetton.com

FABRICA

UNITED COLORS
OF BENETTON.

FIGURE 4-13

Appeal to the Affiliation
Need
Photograph by James
Mollison. Courtesy of United
Colors of Benetton.

questions to answer because motives are hypothetical constructs—that is, they cannot be seen or touched, handled, smelled, or otherwise tangibly observed. For this reason, no single measurement method can be considered a reliable index. Instead, researchers usually rely on a combination of various qualitative research techniques to try to establish the presence and/or the strength of various motives.

Some psychologists are concerned that many measurement techniques do not meet the crucial test criteria of *validity* and *reliability.* (Remember, validity ensures

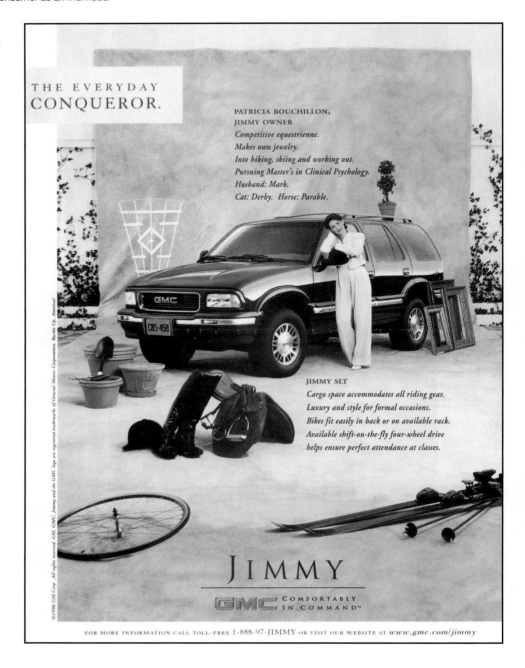

that the test measures what it purports to measure; reliability refers to the consistency with which the test measures what it does measure.) Constructing a scale that measures a specific need, while meeting both criteria, can be complex. For example, a recent research project employed six different studies to develop and validate a seemingly simply five-item scale to measure status consumption (defined as the tendency to purchase goods and services for the prestige that owning them bestows).

Respondents are asked to indicate their level of agreement or disagreement (a Likert scale) on the following five items:[10]

1. *I would buy a product just because it has status.*
2. *I am interested in new products with status.*
3. *I would pay more for a product if it had status.*
4. *The status of the product is irrelevant to me.*
5. *A product is more valuable to me if it has some snob appeal.*

As discussed in Chapter 2, the findings of qualitative research methods are highly dependent on the analyst; they focus not only on the data themselves but also on what the analyst thinks they imply. By using a combination of assessments (called *triangulation*) based on behavioral data (observation), subjective data (self-reports), and qualitative data (projective tests, collage research, etc.), many consumer researchers feel confident that they are achieving more valid insights into consumer motivations than they would by using any one technique alone. Though some marketers are concerned that qualitative research does not produce hard numbers that objectively "prove" the point under investigation, others are convinced that qualitative studies are more revealing than quantitative studies. However, there is a clear need for improved methodological procedures for measuring human motives.

MOTIVATIONAL RESEARCH

The term **motivational research,** which should logically include all types of research into human motives, has become a "term of art" used to refer to qualitative research designed to uncover the consumer's subconscious or hidden motivations. Based on the premise that consumers are not always aware of the reasons for their actions, motivational research attempts to discover underlying feelings, attitudes, and emotions concerning product, service, or brand use.

The Development of Motivational Research

Sigmund Freud's psychoanalytic theory of personality (discussed in Chapter 5) provided the foundation for the development of motivational research. This theory was built on the premise that unconscious needs or drives—especially biological and sexual drives—are at the heart of human motivation and personality. Freud constructed his theory from patients' recollections of early childhood experiences, analysis of their dreams, and the specific nature of their mental and physical adjustment problems.

Dr. Ernest Dichter, formerly a psychoanalyst in Vienna, adapted Freud's psychoanalytical techniques to the study of consumer buying habits. Up to this time, marketing research had focused on what consumers did (i.e., quantitative, descriptive studies). Dichter used qualitative research methods to find out *why* they did it. Marketers were quickly fascinated by the glib, entertaining, and usually surprising explanations offered for consumer behavior, especially since many of these explanations were grounded in sex. For example, marketers were told that cigarettes and Lifesaver candies were bought because of their sexual symbolism, that men regarded convertible cars as surrogate mistresses, and that women baked cakes to fulfill their reproductive yearnings. Before long, almost every major advertising agency in the country had a psychologist on staff to conduct motivational research studies. Four product profiles developed by Dichter and their applications to contemporary products are presented in Table 4-4.

TABLE 4-4 Dichter's Research: Selected Product Personality Profiles and Current Applications

BAKING

Dichter described *baking* as an expression of femininity and motherhood, evoking nostalgic memories of delicious odors pervading the house when the mother was baking. He said that when baking a cake, a woman is subconsciously and symbolically going through the act of giving birth, and the most fertile moment occurs when the baked product is pulled from the oven. Dichter also maintained that when a woman bakes a cake for a man, she is offering him a symbol of fertility.[a] The Betty Crocker image was based on this profile.

AUTOMOBILES

According to Dichter, the car allows consumers to convert their subconscious urges to destroy and their fear of death—two key forces in the human psyche—into reality. For example, the expression "step on it" stems from the desire to feel power, and the phrase "I just missed that car by inches" reflects the desire to play with danger. Based on this view, Dichter advised Esso (now Exxon) to tap into consumers' aggressive motives for driving cars in promoting the superiority of its gasoline product. The slogan "Put a tiger in your tank" was developed as a result of his advice.[b]

Dichter also maintained that cars have personalities, and that people become attached to their cars and view them as companions rather than objects. This notion stands behind his views that a man views a convertible as a mistress and a sedan as his wife.

DOLLS

Dolls play an important part in the socialization of children and are universally accepted as an essential toy for girls. Parents choose dolls that have the kind of characteristics they want their children to have, and the doll is an object for both the parents and the children to enjoy. When Mattel introduced Barbie in 1959, the company hired Dichter as a consultant. His research indicated that while girls liked the doll, their mothers detested the doll's perfect bodily proportions and Teutonic appearance. Dichter advised Mattel to market the doll as a teenage fashion model, reflecting the mother's desire for a daughter's proper and fashionable appearance. The advertising themes used subtly told mothers that it is better for their daughters to appear attractive to men rather than nondescript.[c]

ICE CREAM

Dichter described ice cream as an effortless food that does not have to be chewed and that melts in your mouth, a sign of abundance, an almost orgiastic kind of food that people eat as if they want it to run down their chins. Accordingly, he recommended that ice cream packaging should be round, with illustrations that run around the box panel, suggesting unlimited quantity.

Sources: [a]Ernest Dichter, *Handbook of Consumer Motivations* (New York: McGraw-Hill Book Company, 1964); Jack Hitt, "Does the Smell of Coffee Brewing Remind You of Your Mother?" *New York Times Magazine,* May 7, 2000, 6, 71. [b]Phil Patton, "Car Shrinks," *Fortune,* March 18, 2002, 6. [c]Barbara Lippert, "B-Ball Barbie," *Adweek,* November 9, 1998, 39.

By the early 1960s, however, marketers realized that motivational research had a number of drawbacks. Because of the intensive nature of qualitative research, samples necessarily were small; thus, there was concern about generalizing findings to the total market. Also, marketers soon realized that the analysis of projective tests and depth interviews was highly subjective. The same data given to three different analysts could produce three different reports, each offering its own explanation of the consumer behavior examined. Critics noted that many of the projective tests that were used had originally been developed for clinical purposes rather than for studies of marketing or consumer behavior. (One of the basic criteria for test development is that the test be developed and validated for the specific purpose and on the specific audience profile from which information is desired.)

Other consumer theorists noted additional inconsistencies in applying Freudian theory to the study of consumer behavior. First, psychoanalytic theory was structured specifically for use with disturbed people, whereas consumer behaviorists were interested in explaining the behavior of "typical" consumers. Second, Freudian theory was developed in an entirely different social context (nineteenth-century Vienna), whereas motivational research was introduced in the 1950s in postwar America. Finally, too many motivational researchers imputed highly exotic (usually sexual) reasons to rather prosaic consumer purchases. Marketers began to question their recommendations (e.g., Is it better to sell a man a pair of suspenders as a means of holding up his pants or as a "reaction to castration anxiety"? Is it easier to persuade a woman to buy a garden hose to water her lawn or as a symbol of "genital competition with males"?).

Though they are not usually identified as motivational research techniques, there are a number of associated qualitative research techniques that are used to delve into the consumer's unconscious or hidden motivations. These include collage research, metaphor analysis, means-end analysis, and laddering (see Chapter 2). In addition, Table 4-5 describes some frequently used projective techniques used to tap into consumers' hidden motivations. All of these qualitative research techniques provide invaluable insights to marketers who want to understand the motives underlying consumer behavior.

EVALUATION OF MOTIVATIONAL RESEARCH

Despite its criticisms, motivational research is still regarded as an important tool by marketers who want to gain deeper insights into the *whys* of consumer behavior than conventional marketing research techniques can yield. Since motivational research often reveals unsuspected consumer motivations concerning product or brand usage, its principal use today is in the development of new ideas for promotional campaigns, ideas that can penetrate the consumer's conscious awareness by appealing to unrecognized needs. For example, in trying to discover why women bought traditional roach sprays rather than a brand packaged in little plastic trays, researchers asked women to draw pictures of roaches and write stories about their sketches. They found that, for many of their respondents, roaches symbolized men who had left them feeling poor and powerless. The women reported that spraying the roaches and "watching them squirm and die" allowed them to express their hostility toward men and gave them feelings of greater control.[11]

Motivational research also provides marketers with a basic orientation for new product categories and enables them to explore consumer reactions to ideas and advertising copy at an early stage to avoid costly errors. Furthermore, as with all qualitative research techniques, motivational research findings provide consumer researchers with basic insights that enable them to design structured, quantitative marketing research studies to be conducted on larger, more representative samples of consumers.

Despite the drawbacks of motivational research, there is new and compelling evidence that the unconscious is the site of a far larger portion of mental life than even Freud envisioned. Research studies show that the unconscious mind may understand and respond to nonverbal symbols, form emotional responses, and guide actions largely independent of conscious awareness.[12]

TABLE 4-5   Projective Techniques Used in Motivational Research

METAPHOR ANALYSIS

This method, including the tool termed *ZMET*, was discussed in detail in Chapter 2. A recent study of European consumers' feelings about Coca-Cola used the ZMET technique to analyze collages of pictures composed by the respondents and their stated reasons for selecting these images. Contrary to the images of invigoration and sociability that are commonly portrayed in the product's ads, the study found that Coke invoked feelings of calm, solitude, and relaxation. (One of the respondents selected an image of a Buddhist monk meditating in a crowded soccer field to depict his feelings about the product.) Clearly, this finding calls for the integration of these perceptions into Coke's European advertising.

When DuPont used metaphor analysis to study women's emotions regarding pantyhose, women revealed that they evoked feelings of sensuality and being sexy and attractive to men. The implication of these findings is that pantyhose ads must appeal less to women's executive personas and more to their sexy and sensual feelings.[a]

STORYTELLING

This method consists of having customers tell real-life stories regarding their use of the product under study. By using this method to study parents' perceptions of diapers, Kimberly-Clark discovered that parents viewed diapers as clothing related to a particular stage in the child's development. Thus, if their children wore diapers too long, parents became distressed and embarrassed because they viewed it as their failure to toilet train their children. Using these data, the company introduced its highly successful Huggies Pull-Ups training pants—a product that established a new category in the U.S. diaper industry.[b]

A variation of storytelling is the "photo and tale" method in which consumers create pictures and stories about the product. The manufacturer of Combat, an insecticide in the form of plastic trays that kills roaches quickly and neatly, used the photo and tale method to study why its product was selling much less than Raid, a messier insecticide in the form of a can spray, in the southern part of the United States.

DRAWING PICTURES, CREATING PHOTO COLLAGES AND PHOTO-SORTS

Visual images are often used to study consumers' perceptions of various brands and to develop new advertising strategies.[c] For example, when respondents were asked to draw pictures of the typical Pillsbury cake-mix user, their drawings depicted old-fashioned, chubby females wearing frilly aprons. When asked to draw pictures of the Duncan Hines cake-mix user, their drawings showed slim, "with it" women wearing heels and miniskirts. These findings provided important input to Pillsbury concerning the need to reposition its product.

The advertising agency of Playtex (a manufacturer of bras) asked respondents to create collages from magazines that depict the typical user of the product. The collages they created depicted full-breasted, overweight, old-fashioned women. Then, using the technique "photo-sorts," the respondents were given stacks of photos and were asked to select pictures portraying their own self-images. Although many of the respondents were overweight, full-breasted, and old-fashioned in appearance, they selected photos showing physically fit, well-dressed, and independent women. The advertising agency advised Playtex to stop stressing the comfort of its bras in its ads and designed a new campaign showing sexy, thin, and big-bosomed women under the slogan "The fit that makes the fashion."

The Thematic Aperception Test, developed by Henry A. Murray, consists of showing pictures to individual respondents and asking them to tell a story about each picture. For example, research conducted for Clearasil employed an image of a female looking into a mirror under the caption "Here is a teenager looking into the mirror and seeing pimples." The researchers discovered that teenagers view their lives as fast-paced and socially active and that the discovery of a pimple abruptly disturbs the swiftness of their lives. The resulting advertising depicted a teenage male walking briskly down the street and spotting a pimple on his face in a store window. All motion around him stops. He applies Clearasil, the pimple disappears, and life resumes its pace.

In the word association method, respondents are presented with words, one at a time, and asked to utter or list the first word that comes to mind after they hear each word. This method is highly applicable to studying consumers' associations with existing brand names and those under development.

In sentence completion, respondents are asked to complete a sentence upon hearing the opening phrase (e.g., "People who drive convertibles. . .").

The third-person technique requires subjects to tell a story about someone else. For example, the researcher may present the respondents with a list of Internet sites visited during a given period and ask them to describe the person whose Web surfing this pattern reflects. Another application of this technique is to encourage the respondent to project his or her own feelings on an imaginary third person, thus avoiding personal embarrassment. For example, persons who are afraid to fly may feel embarrassed to elaborate on the reasons for that fear when asked directly. However, if asked to describe the reasons why an individual would be afraid to fly, subjects are likely to ascribe their own fears to another person. In doing so, they "project" their own apprehensions and anxieties regarding flying onto this third person.

Sources: [a]Emily Eakin, "Penetrating the Mind by Metaphor," *New York Times*, February 23, 2002, B9, B11. [b] Ronald B. Leiber, "Storytelling: A New Way to Get Close to Your Customer," *Fortune*, February 3, 1997. [c] Bernice Kramer, "Mind Games," *New York*, May 8, 1989, 33–40.

Summary

Motivation is the driving force within individuals that impels them to action. This driving force is produced by a state of uncomfortable tension, which exists as the result of an unsatisfied need. All individuals have needs, wants, and desires. The individual's subconscious drive to reduce need-induced tension results in behavior that he or she anticipates will satisfy needs and thus bring about a more comfortable internal state.

All behavior is goal oriented. Goals are the sought-after results of motivated behavior. The form or direction that behavior takes—the goal that is selected—is a result of thinking processes (cognition) and previous learning. There are two types of goals: generic goals and product-specific goals. A generic goal is a general category of goal that may fulfill a certain need; a product-specific goal is a specifically branded or labeled product that the individual sees as a way to fulfill a need. Product-specific needs are sometimes referred to as wants.

Innate needs—those an individual is born with—are physiological (biogenic) in nature; they include all the factors required to sustain physical life (e.g., food, water, clothing, shelter, sex, and physical safety). Acquired needs—those an individual develops after birth—are primarily psychological (psychogenic); they include love, acceptance, esteem, and self-fulfillment. For any given need, there are many different and appropriate goals. The specific goal selected depends on the individual's experiences, physical capacity, prevailing cultural norms and values, and the goal's accessibility in the physical and social environment.

Needs and goals are interdependent and change in response to the individual's physical condition, environment, interaction with other people, and experiences. As needs become satisfied, new, higher-order needs emerge that must be fulfilled.

Failure to achieve a goal often results in feelings of frustration. Individuals react to frustration in two ways: "fight" or "flight." They may cope by finding a way around the obstacle that prohibits goal attainment or by adopting a substitute goal (fight); or they may adopt a defense mechanism that enables them to protect their self-esteem (flight). Defense mechanisms include aggression, regression, rationalization, withdrawal, projection, autism, identification, and repression.

Motives cannot easily be inferred from consumer behavior. People with different needs may seek fulfillment through selection of the same goals; people with the same needs may seek fulfillment through different goals. Although some psychologists have suggested that individuals have different need priorities, others believe that most human beings experience the same basic needs, to which they assign a similar priority ranking. Maslow's hierarchy-of-needs theory proposes five levels of prepotent human needs: physiological needs, safety needs, social needs, egoistic needs, and self-actualization needs. Other needs widely integrated into consumer advertising include the needs for power, affiliation, and achievement.

There are three commonly used methods for identifying and "measuring" human motives: observation and inference, subjective reports, and qualitative research (including projective techniques). None of these methods is completely reliable by itself. Therefore, researchers often use a combination of two or three techniques in tandem to assess the presence or strength of consumer motives. Motivational research is qualitative research designed to delve below the consumer's level of conscious awareness. Despite some shortcomings, motivational research has proved to be of great value to marketers concerned with developing new ideas and new copy appeals.

Discussion Questions

1. a. "Marketers don't create needs; needs preexist marketers." Discuss this statement.

   b. Can marketing efforts change consumers' needs? Why or why not?

2. Consumers have both innate and acquired needs. Give examples of each kind of need and show how the same purchase can serve to fulfill either or both kinds of needs.

3. Specify both innate and acquired needs that would be useful bases for developing promotional strategies for
   a. global positioning systems
   b. Harley-Davidson motorcycles
   c. recruiting college seniors to work in public services

4. Why are consumers' needs and goals constantly changing? What factors influence the formation of new goals?

5. How can marketers use consumers' failures at achieving goals in developing promotional appeals for specific products and services? Give examples.

6. Most human needs are dormant much of the time. What factors cause their arousal? Give examples of ads for audio/video equipment that are designed to arouse latent consumer needs.

7. For each of the situations listed in question 3, select one level from Maslow's hierarchy of human needs that can be used to segment the market and position the product (or the organization). Explain your choices. What are the advantages and disadvantages of using Maslow's need hierarchy for segmentation and positioning applications?

8. a. How do researchers identify and measure human motives? Give examples.
   b. Does motivational research differ from qualitative research? Discuss.
   c. What are the strengths and weaknesses of motivational research?

Exercises

1. You are a member of an advertising team assembled to develop a promotional campaign for a new digital camera. Develop three headlines for this campaign, each based on one of the levels in Maslow's need hierarchy.

2. Find an advertisement that depicts a defense mechanism. Present it in class and discuss its effectiveness.

3. Explain briefly the needs for power, affiliation, and achievement. Find three advertisements that are designed to appeal to these needs.

Key Terms

- **Acquired needs**
- **Approach object**
- **Avoidance object**
- **Defense mechanisms**
- **Emotional motives**
- **Generic goals**
- **Innate needs**

- **Level of aspiration**
- **Maslow's hierarchy of needs**
- **Motivation**
- **Motivational research**
- **Positive versus negative motivation**
- **Prepotent need**

- **Primary needs**
- **Product-specific goals**
- **Psychological reactance**
- **Rational motives**
- **Secondary needs**
- **Substitute goal**

Notes

1. Andrew Tobias, *Fire and Ice* (New York: William Morrow and Company, 1976), Chapter 8.
2. Ibid.
3. Richard P. Bagozzi and Utpal Dholakia, "Goal Setting and Goal Striving in Consumer Behavior," *Journal of Marketing* (1999): 19–32.
4. See Abraham H. Maslow, "A Theory of Human Motivation," *Psychological Review,* 50 (1943): 370–396; Abraham H. Maslow, *Motivation and Personality* (New York: Harper & Row, 1954); and Abraham H. Maslow, *Toward a Psychology of Being* (New York: Van Nostrand Reinhold, 1968), 189–215.

5. A number of studies have focused on human levels of aspiration. See, for example, Kurt Lewin et al., "Level of Aspiration," in *Personality and Behavior Disorders,* ed. J. McV. Hunt (New York: Ronald Press, 1944); Howard Garland, "Goal Levels and Task Performance, a Compelling Replication of Some Compelling Results," *Journal of Applied Psychology,* 67, (1982), 245–248; Edwin A. Locke, Elizabeth Frederick, Cynthia Lee, and Philip Bobko, "Effect of Self Efficacy, Goals and Task Strategies on Task Performance," *Journal of Applied Psychology,* 69, 2, (1984): 241–251; Edwin A. Locke, Elizabeth Frederick, Elizabeth Buckner, and Philip Bobko, "Effect of Previously Assigned Goals on Self Set Goals and Performance," *Journal of Applied Psychology,* 72, 2 (1987): 204–211; and John R. Hollenbeck and Howard J. Klein, "Goal Commitment and the Goal Setting Process: Problems, Prospects and Proposals for Future Research," *Journal of Applied Psychology,* 2 (1987): 212–220.

6. Maslow, "A Theory of Human Motivation," 380.

7. Ibid.

8. Ibid.

9. See, for example, David C. McClelland, *Studies in Motivation* (New York: Appleton Century Crofts, 1955); David C. McClelland, "Business Drive and National Achievement," *Harvard Business Review,* July–August 1962; "Achievement Motivation Can Be Developed," *Harvard Business Review,* 5, 24, November–December 1965; and Abraham K. Korman, *The Psychology of Motivation* (Upper Saddle River, NJ: Prentice Hall, 1974).

10. Jacqueline K. Eastman, Ronald E. Goldsmith, and Lisa Reinecke Flynn, "Status Consumption in Consumer Behavior: Scale Development and Validation," *Journal of Marketing Theory and Practice,* Summer 1999, 41–52.

11. Daniel Goleman, "New View of Mind Gives Unconscious an Expanded Role," *New York Times,* February 7, 1984, C1-2.

12. Ronald Alsop, "Agencies Scrutinize Their Ads for Psychological Symbolism," *Wall Street Journal,* June 11, 1987, 27. See also David Mick, "Consumer Research and Semiotics: Exploring the Morphology of Signs, Symbols and Significance," *Journal of Consumer Research,* 13, September 1986, 196–213.

5

Personality and Consumer Behavior

Marketers have long tried to appeal to consumers in terms of their personality characteristics. They have intuitively felt that what consumers purchase, and when and how they consume, are likely to be influenced by personality factors. For this reason, advertising and marketing people have frequently depicted (or incorporated) specific personality traits or characteristics in their marketing and advertising messages. Some recent examples are an appeal to *individuality* for the Indian motorcycle (headline: "Take your own road"— www.indianmotorcycle.com), an appeal to *being challenged* by the golf courses at a Hyatt resort (headline: "What time would you like to lose your dignity, sir?"— www.hyatt.com), an appeal to *status and/or snobbery* for the Ford Thunderbird (headline: "Eliminates the need to know the guy working the door"— www.fordvehicles.com/cars/thunderbird), and an appeal by Mutual of Omaha to policyholders' *sense of self-assurance* (headline: "What gives you confidence?"— www.mutualofomaha.com).

This chapter is designed to provide the reader with an understanding of how *personality* and *self-concept* are related to various aspects of consumer behavior. It examines what personality is, reviews several major personality theories, and describes how these theories have stimulated marketing interest in the study of consumer personality. The chapter considers the important topics of *brand personality,* how the related concepts of *self* and *self-image* influence consumer attitudes and behavior, and concludes with an exploration of *virtual personality or self.*

What Is Personality?

The study of **personality** has been approached by theorists in a variety of ways. Some have emphasized the dual influence of heredity and early childhood experiences on personality development; others have stressed broader social and environmental influences and the fact that personalities develop continuously over time. Some theorists prefer to view personality as a unified whole; others focus on specific traits. The wide variation in viewpoints makes it difficult to arrive at a single definition. However, we propose that personality be defined as *those inner psychological characteristics that both determine and reflect how a person responds to his or her environment.*

The emphasis in this definition is on *inner characteristics*—those specific qualities, attributes, traits, factors, and mannerisms that distinguish one individual from other individuals. As discussed later in the chapter, the deeply ingrained characteristics that we call personality are likely to influence the individual's product choices: They affect the way consumers respond to marketers' promotional efforts, and when, where, and how they consume particular products or services. Therefore, the identification of specific personality characteristics associated with consumer behavior has proven to be highly useful in the development of a firm's market segmentation strategies.

THE NATURE OF PERSONALITY

In the study of personality, three distinct properties are of central importance: (1) *Personality reflects individual differences;* (2) *personality is consistent and enduring;* and (3) *personality can change.*

Personality Reflects Individual Differences

Because the inner characteristics that constitute an individual's personality are a unique combination of factors, no two individuals are exactly alike. Nevertheless, many individuals may be similar in terms of a single personality characteristic but not in terms of others. For instance, some people can be described as "high" in *venturesomeness* (e.g., willing to accept the risk of doing something new or different, such as skydiving or mountain climbing), whereas others can be described as "low" in *venturesomeness* (e.g., afraid to buy a really new product). Personality is a useful concept because it enables us to categorize consumers into different groups on the basis of one or even several traits. If each person were different in terms of all personality traits, it would be impossible to group consumers into segments, and there would be little reason for marketers to develop products and promotional campaigns targeted to particular segments.

Personality Is Consistent and Enduring

An individual's personality tends to be both consistent and enduring. Indeed, the mother who comments that her child "has been impulsive from the day he was born" is supporting the contention that personality has both consistency and endurance. Both qualities are essential if marketers are to explain or predict consumer behavior in terms of personality.

Although marketers cannot change consumers' personalities to conform to their products, if they know which personality characteristics influence specific consumer responses, they can attempt to appeal to the relevant traits inherent in their target group of consumers.

Even though consumers' personalities may be consistent, their consumption behavior often varies considerably because of the various psychological, sociocultural, environmental, and situational factors that affect behavior. For instance, although an individual's personality may be relatively stable, specific needs or motives, attitudes, reactions to group pressures, and even responses to newly available brands may cause a change in the person's behavior. Personality is only one of a combination of factors that influence how a consumer behaves.

Personality Can Change

Under certain circumstances personalities change. For instance, an individual's personality may be altered by major life events, such as the birth of a child, the death of a loved one, a divorce, or a significant career promotion. An individual's personality changes not only in response to abrupt events but also as part of a gradual maturing process—"He's growing up, he is much calmer," says an aunt after not seeing her nephew for five years.

There is also evidence that personality stereotypes may change over time. More specifically, although it is felt that men's personality has generally remained relatively constant over the past 50 years, women's personality has seemed to become increasingly more masculine and should continue to do so over the next 50 years. This prediction indicates a *convergence* in the personality characteristics of men and women.[1] The reason for this shift is that women have been moving into occupations that have traditionally been dominated by men and, therefore, have been associated with masculine personality attributes.

Theories of Personality

This section briefly reviews three major theories of personality: (1) **Freudian theory,** (2) **neo-Freudian theory,** and (3) **trait theory.** These theories have been chosen for discussion from among many theories of personality because each has played a prominent role in the study of the relationship between consumer behavior and personality.

FREUDIAN THEORY

Sigmund Freud's **psychoanalytic theory of personality** is a cornerstone of modern psychology. This theory was built on the premise that *unconscious needs or drives,* especially sexual and other biological drives, are at the heart of human motivation and personality. Freud constructed his theory on the basis of patients' recollections of early childhood experiences, analysis of their dreams, and the specific nature of their mental and physical adjustment problems.

Id, Superego, and Ego

Based on his analyses, Freud proposed that the human personality consists of three interacting systems: the *id*, the *superego*, and the *ego*. The id was conceptualized as a "warehouse" of primitive and impulsive drives—basic physiological needs such as thirst, hunger, and sex—for which the individual seeks immediate satisfaction without concern for the specific means of satisfaction. The ad for Mistic™ juice drinks (see Figure 5-1) captures the exciting "forces" associated with the primitive drives of the *id* when it declares "Give in to the juice." The positioning and appearance of the models add to this sense of excitement.

FIGURE 5-1

Ad Portraying the "Forces" of the Id
Courtesy of MISTIC, a registered trademark of Mistic Brands, Inc. Reprinted by permission.

Give in to the juice.

Go Bold

Mistic
PREMIUM JUICE DRINK
ORANGE CARROT

Mistic
www.mistic.com

© 2002 Mistic Brands, Inc. Mistic is a registered trademark of Mistic Brands, Inc.

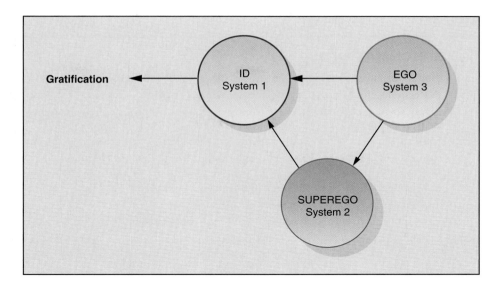

FIGURE 5-2

A Representation of the Interrelationships Among the Id, Ego, and Superego

In contrast to the id, the *superego* is conceptualized as the individual's internal expression of society's moral and ethical codes of conduct. The superego's role is to see that the individual satisfies needs in a socially acceptable fashion. Thus, the superego is a kind of "brake" that restrains or inhibits the impulsive forces of the id.

Finally, the *ego* is the individual's conscious control. It functions as an internal monitor that attempts to balance the impulsive demands of the id and the sociocultural constraints of the superego. Figure 5-2 represents the interrelationships among the three interacting systems. In addition to specifying a structure for personality, Freud emphasized that an individual's personality is formed as he or she passes through a number of distinct stages of infant and childhood development. These are the *oral, anal, phallic, latent,* and *genital* stages. Freud labeled four of these stages of development to conform to the area of the body on which he believed the child's sexual instincts are focused at the time.

According to Freudian theory, an adult's personality is determined by how well he or she deals with the crises that are experienced while passing through each of these stages (particularly the first three). For instance, if a child's oral needs are not adequately satisfied at the first stage of development, the person may become fixated at this stage and as an adult display a personality that includes such traits as dependence and excessive oral activity (e.g., gum chewing and smoking). When an individual is fixated at the anal stage, the adult personality may display other traits, such as an excessive need for neatness.

Freudian Theory and "Product Personality"

Researchers who apply Freud's psychoanalytic theory to the study of consumer personality believe that human drives are largely *unconscious* and that consumers are primarily unaware of their true reasons for buying what they buy. These researchers tend to see consumer purchases and/or consumption situations as a reflection and an extension of the consumer's own personality. In other words, they consider the consumer's appearance and possessions—grooming, clothing, jewelry, and so forth—as reflections of the individual's personality. Table 5-1 presents the results of a study of 19,000 consumers that examines the link between snack food perceptions and selected personality traits.[2] The findings of the research, for example, reveal that potato chips are associated with being ambitious, successful, and a high achiever and

TABLE 5-1	Snack Foods and Personality Traits

SNACK FOOD	PERSONALITY TRAITS
Potato chips	Ambitious, successful, high achiever, impatient with less than the best.
Tortilla chips	Perfectionist, high expectations, punctual, conservative, responsible.
Pretzels	Lively, easily bored with same old routine, flirtatious, intuitive, may overcommit to projects.
Snack crackers	Rational, logical, contemplative, shy, prefers time alone.
Cheese curls	Conscientious, principled, proper, fair, may appear rigid but has great integrity, plans ahead, loves order.
Nuts	Easygoing, empathetic, understanding, calm, even-tempered.
Popcorn	Takes charge, pitches in often, modest, self-confident but not a show-off.
Meat snacks	Gregarious, generous, trustworthy, tends to be overly trusting.

Source: From *What Flavor is Your Personality? Discover Who You Are by Looking at What You Eat,* by Alan Hirsch, MD., Naperville, Il, Sourcebooks, 2001.

impatient with less than the best, whereas popcorn seems to be related to a personality that takes charge, pitches in often, is modest and self-confident but not a show-off. (The related topics of *brand personality,* and the self and *self-images* are considered later in the chapter.)

NEO-FREUDIAN PERSONALITY THEORY

Several of Freud's colleagues disagreed with his contention that personality is primarily instinctual and sexual in nature. Instead, these neo-Freudians believed that *social relationships* are fundamental to the formation and development of personality. For instance, Alfred Adler viewed human beings as seeking to attain various rational goals, which he called *style of life.* He also placed much emphasis on the individual's efforts to overcome *feelings of inferiority* (i.e., by striving for superiority).

Harry Stack Sullivan, another neo-Freudian, stressed that people continuously attempt to establish significant and rewarding relationships with others. He was particularly concerned with the individual's efforts to reduce tensions, such as anxiety.

Like Sullivan, Karen Horney was also interested in *anxiety.* She focused on the impact of child–parent relationships and the individual's desire to conquer feelings of anxiety. Horney proposed that individuals be classified into three personality groups: *compliant, aggressive,* and *detached.*[3]

1. *Compliant individuals are those who move toward others (they desire to be loved, wanted, and appreciated).*
2. *Aggressive individuals are those who move against others (they desire to excel and win admiration).*
3. *Detached individuals are those who move away from others (they desire independence, self-reliance, self-sufficiency, and individualism or freedom from obligations).*

A personality test based on Horney's theory (the CAD) has been developed and tested within the context of consumer behavior.[4] The initial CAD research uncovered a number of tentative relationships between college students' scores and their product and brand usage patterns. For example, highly *compliant* students were found to prefer name-brand products such as Bayer aspirin (**www.bayer.com**); students classified as *aggressive* showed a preference for Old Spice deodorant (**www.oldspice.com**) over other brands (seemingly because of its masculine appeal); and highly *detached* students proved to be heavy tea drinkers (possibly reflecting their desire not to conform). More recent research has found that children who scored high in self-reliance—who preferred to do things independently of others (i.e., *detached* personalities)—were *less* likely to be brand loyal and were *more* likely to try different brands.[5]

Many marketers use some of these neo-Freudian theories intuitively. For example, marketers who position their products or services as providing an opportunity to belong or to be appreciated by others in a group or social setting would seem to be guided by Horney's characterization of the *detached* individual. Figure 5-3 shows

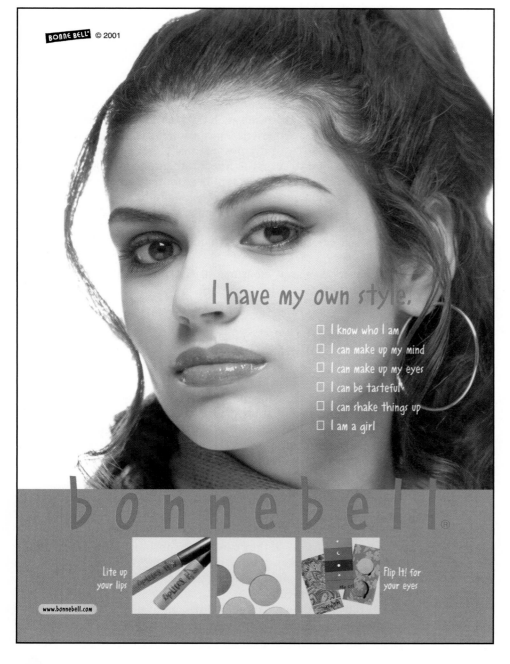

FIGURE 5-3

Ad Applying Horney's
Detached Personality
Courtesy of Bonne Bell.

an ad for Bonne Bell cosmetics that captures a positive image of the detached person. Its headline declares: "I have my own style." Then it includes a short (and cute) checklist of the underlying characteristics of "my own style."

TRAIT THEORY

Trait theory constitutes a major departure from the *qualitative* measures that typify the Freudian and neo-Freudian movements (e.g., personal observation, self-reported experiences, dream analysis, projective techniques).

The orientation of trait theory is primarily quantitative or empirical; it focuses on the measurement of personality in terms of specific psychological characteristics, called traits. A *trait* is defined as "any distinguishing, relatively enduring way in which one individual differs from another."[6] Trait theorists are concerned with the construction of personality tests (or inventories) that enable them to pinpoint individual differences in terms of specific traits.

Selected *single-trait personality* tests (which measure just one trait, such as self-confidence) are often developed specifically for use in consumer behavior studies. These tailor-made personality tests measure such traits as **consumer innovativeness** (how receptive a person is to new experiences), **consumer materialism** (the degree of the consumer's attachment to "worldly possessions"), and **consumer ethnocentrism** (the consumer's likelihood to accept or reject foreign-made products).

Trait researchers have found that it is generally more realistic to expect personality to be linked to how consumers *make their choices* and to the purchase or consumption of *a broad product category* rather than a specific brand. For example, there is more likely to be a relationship between a personality trait and whether or not an individual owns a convertible sports car than between a personality trait and the brand of convertible sports car purchased.

The next section shows how trait measures of personality are used to expand our understanding of consumer behavior.

Personality and Understanding Consumer Diversity

Marketers are interested in understanding how personality influences consumption behavior because such knowledge enables them to better understand consumers and to segment and target those consumers who are likely to respond positively to their product or service communications. Several specific personality traits that provide insights about consumer behavior are examined next.

CONSUMER INNOVATIVENESS AND RELATED PERSONALITY TRAITS

Marketing practitioners try to learn all they can about **consumer innovators**—those who are likely to be the first to try new products, services, or practices—for the market response of such innovators is often a critical indication of the eventual success or failure of a new product or service.

Personality traits that have been useful in differentiating between consumer innovators and noninnovators include *consumer innovativeness, dogmatism, social character, need for uniqueness, optimum stimulation level, sensation seeking,* and

TABLE 5-2	A Consumer Innovativeness Scale

In general, I am among the last in my circle of friends to buy a new (rock album[a]) when it appears.[b]

If I heard that a (new rock album) was available in the store, I would be interested enough to buy it.

Compared to my friends, I own few (rock albums).[b]

In general, I am the last in my circle of friends to know the (titles of the latest rock albums).[b]

I will buy a new (rock album), even if I haven't heard it yet.

I know the names of (new rock acts) before other people do.

Note: Measured on a 5-point "agreement" scale.
[a]The product category and related wording are altered to fit the purpose of the researcher.
[b]Items with a ([b]) are negatively worded and are scored inversely.
Source: Ronald E. Goldsmith and Charles F. Hofacker, "Measuring Consumer Innovativeness," *Journal of the Academy of Marketing Science*, 19 (1991), 212. Copyright © 1991 Academy of Marketing Science. Reprinted by permission.

variety-novelty seeking. (Chapter 15 examines nonpersonality characteristics that distinguish between consumer innovators and noninnovators.)

Consumer Innovativeness

Consumer researchers have endeavored to develop measurement instruments to gauge the level of consumer innovativeness, because such personality trait measures provide important insights into the nature and boundaries of a consumer's willingness to innovate.[7] Table 5-2 presents a six-item measure of consumer innovativeness that has been designed to have flexible boundaries in terms of the domain being studied; that is, the scale can be used to study a broad product category (e.g., personal computers), a subproduct category (e.g., notebook computers), or a product type (e.g., three-pound mini-notebook computers).

Recent consumer research indicates a positive relationship between innovative use of the Internet and buying online.[8] Still further, other research exploring the association between personality traits and innovative Internet behavior has reported that Internet shoppers tend to see themselves as being able to control their own future, using the Internet to seek out information, enjoying change, and not being afraid of uncertainty.[9]

Dogmatism

Consumer responses to distinctively unfamiliar products or product features (i.e., level of dogmatism—a personality-linked behavior) is of keen interest to many marketers, especially marketers of technologically rich products. **Dogmatism** is a personality trait that measures the degree of rigidity (versus openness) that individuals display toward the unfamiliar and toward information that is contrary to their own established beliefs.[10] A person who is *high dogmatic* approaches the unfamiliar defensively and with considerable discomfort and uncertainty. At the other end of the spectrum, a person who is *low dogmatic* will readily consider unfamiliar or opposing beliefs.

Consumers who are low in dogmatism (*open-minded*) are more likely to prefer innovative products to established or traditional alternatives. In contrast, highly dogmatic (*closed-minded*) consumers are more likely to choose established, rather than innovative, product alternatives.

Highly dogmatic consumers tend to be more receptive to ads for new products or services that contain an appeal from an authoritative figure. To this end, marketers have used celebrities and experts in their new-product advertising to make it easier for potentially reluctant consumers (noninnovators) to accept the innovation (see Figure 5-4). In contrast, low-dogmatic consumers (who are frequently high in innovativeness) seem to be more receptive to messages that stress factual differences, product benefits, and other forms of product-usage information.

Social Character

The personality trait known as *social character* has its origins in sociological research, which focuses on the identification and classification of individuals into distinct sociocultural types. As used in consumer psychology, social character is a personality trait that ranges on a continuum from **inner-directedness** to **other-directedness.** Inner-directed consumers tend to rely on their own inner values or standards in evaluating new products and are likely to be consumer innovators. Conversely, other-directed consumers tend to look to others for direction on what is right or wrong; thus, they are *less* likely to be consumer innovators.

Inner- and other-directed consumers are attracted to different types of promotional messages. Inner-directed people seem to prefer ads that stress product features and personal benefits (enabling them to use their own values and standards in evaluating products), whereas other-directed people prefer ads that feature an approving social environment or social acceptance (in keeping with their tendency to look to others for direction). Thus, other-directed individuals may be more easily influenced because of their natural inclination to go beyond the content of an ad and think in terms of likely social approval of a potential purchase.

Need for Uniqueness

We all know people who seek to be unique. For these people conformity to others' expectations or standards, either in appearance or in their possessions, is something to be avoided. Moreover, we would expect that it is easier to express or act uniquely if one does not have to pay a price in the form of others' criticism. Supporting this perspective, a recent study of consumers' need for uniqueness (NFU) explored the circumstances under which high NFU individuals do (and do not) make unconventional (i.e., unique) choices. The research revealed that when consumers are asked to explain their choices, but are not concerned about being criticized by others, they are more receptive to making unique choices.[11] Seeing the importance of NFU, other consumer researchers have developed an inventory to measure the trait within the context of consumer behavior. Table 5-3 presents a sample of items drawn from the inventory.

Optimum Stimulation Level

Some people seem to prefer a simple, uncluttered, and calm existence, whereas others prefer an environment crammed with novel, complex, and unusual experiences.

TABLE 5-3	Sample Items from a Consumers' Need for Uniqueness Scale[a]

I collect unusual products as a way of telling people I'm different.

When dressing, I have sometimes dared to be different in ways that others are likely to disapprove.

When products or brands I like become extremely popular, I lose interest in them.

As far as I'm concerned, when it comes to the products I buy and the situations in which I use them, customs and rules are made to be broken.

I have sometimes purchased unusual products or brands as a way to create a more distinctive personal image.

I sometimes look for one-of-a-kind products or brands so that I create a style that is all my own.

I avoid products or brands that have already been accepted and purchased by the average consumer.

[a]This inventory is measured on a 5-point Likert scale ranging from "strongly agree" to "strongly disagree."
Source: Kelly Tepper Tian, William O. Bearden, and Gary L. Hunter, "Consumers' Need for Uniqueness: Scale Development and Validation," *Journal of Consumer Research,* 28, June 2001, 50–66.

Consumer research has examined how such variations in individual needs for stimulation may be related to consumer behavior. Research has found that high **optimum stimulation levels** (OSLs) are linked with greater willingness to take risks, to try new products, to be innovative, to seek purchase-related information, and to accept new retail facilities than low OSLs.

OSL scores also seem to reflect a person's desired level of lifestyle stimulation.[12] For instance, consumers whose actual lifestyles are equivalent to their OSL scores appear to be *quite satisfied,* whereas those whose lifestyles are understimulated (i.e., their OSL scores are greater than the lifestyle they are currently living) are likely to be *bored.* Those whose lifestyles are overstimulated (i.e., their OSLs are lower than current reality) are likely to seek *rest* or *relief.* This suggests that the relationship between consumers' lifestyles and their OSLs is likely to influence their choices of products or services and how they manage and spend their time. For instance, a person who feels bored (an understimulated consumer) is likely to be attracted to a vacation that offers a great deal of activity and excitement. In contrast, a person who feels overwhelmed (an overstimulated consumer) is likely to seek a quiet, isolated, relaxing, and rejuvenating vacation.

Sensation Seeking

Closely related to the OSL concept is **sensation seeking** (SS), which has been defined as "a trait characterized by the need for varied, novel, and complex sensations and experience, and the willingness to take physical and social risks for the sake of such experience." Research evidence shows that teenage males with higher SS scores are more likely than other teenagers to prefer listening to heavy metal music and to engage in reckless or even dangerous behavior.[13]

Variety-Novelty Seeking

Still another personality-driven trait quite similar to and related to OSL is **variety** or **novelty seeking.**[14] There appear to be many different types of consumer variety seeking: *exploratory purchase behavior* (e.g., switching brands to experience new and possibly better alternatives), *vicarious exploration* (e.g., securing information about a new or different alternative and then contemplating or even daydreaming about the option), and *use innovativeness* (using an already adopted product in a new or novel way).[15] The use innovativeness trait is particularly relevant to technological products (such as home electronics products), in which some models offer an abundance of features and functions, whereas others contain just a few essential features or functions. For example, a consumer with a high variety-seeking score might purchase a stereo system with more features than a consumer with a lower variety-seeking score. Consumers with high variety-seeking scores are also more likely to be attracted to brands that claim to have novel features or multiple uses or applications.

Marketers, up to a point, benefit by offering additional options to consumers seeking more product variety because consumers with a high need for variety tend to search for marketers that provide a diverse product line (offering much choice).[16] However, a point may be reached where a marketer might offer too many products with too many features. In such a case, the consumer may be turned off and avoid a product line with too much variety. Ultimately, in searching for the "just right," marketers must walk the fine line between offering consumers too little and too much choice.

The stream of research examined here indicates that the consumer innovator differs from the noninnovator in terms of personality orientation. A knowledge of such personality differences should help marketers select target segments for new products and then to design distinctive promotional strategies for specific segments.

COGNITIVE PERSONALITY FACTORS

Consumer researchers have been increasingly interested in how **cognitive personality** factors influence various aspects of consumer behavior. In particular, two cognitive personality traits—**need for cognition** and **visualizers versus verbalizers**—have been useful in understanding selected aspects of consumer behavior.

Need for Cognition

A promising cognitive personality characteristic is need for cognition (NC). It measures a person's craving for or enjoyment of *thinking*. Available research indicates that consumers who are *high* in NC are more likely to be responsive to the part of an ad that is rich in product-related information or description; consumers who are relatively *low* in NC are more likely to be attracted to the background or peripheral aspects of an ad, such as an attractive model or well-known celebrity.[17] Related research among adolescents compared the effectiveness of a cartoon message and a written message. As expected, for low-NC subjects, the cartoon message was more effective in changing attitudes and subjective norms, whereas the written message was more effective for high-NC adolescents.[18] In still another study, it was found that message framing (e.g., positively emphasizing a brand's advantages) has more impact on low-NC individuals than it has on high-NC individuals.[19] Still further, research suggests that consumers who are high in NC are likely to spend more time processing print advertisements, which results in superior brand and ad claim recall.[20]

Need for cognition seems to play a role in an individual's use of the Internet. More precisely, NC has been positively related to Internet usage for product information, current events and news, and learning and education—all activities that incorporate a cognitive element.[21] Such research insights provide advertisers with valuable guidelines for creating advertising messages (including supporting art) that appeal to a particular target audience grouping's *need for cognition*.

Visualizers Versus Verbalizers

It is fairly well established that some people seem to be more open to and prefer the written word as a way of securing information, whereas others are more likely to respond to and prefer visual images or messages as sources of information. Consistent with such individual differences, cognitive personality research classifies consumers into two groups: *visualizers* (consumers who prefer visual information and products that stress the visual, such as membership in a videotape club) or *verbalizers* (consumers who prefer written or verbal information and products, such as membership in book clubs or audiotape clubs). Some marketers stress strong visual dimensions in order to attract visualizers (see Figure 5-5); others raise a question and provide the answer, or feature a detailed description or point-by-point explanation to attract verbalizers (see Figure 5-6).

FIGURE 5-5

Waterpik Ad Targets
Visualizers
Courtesy of Waterpik.

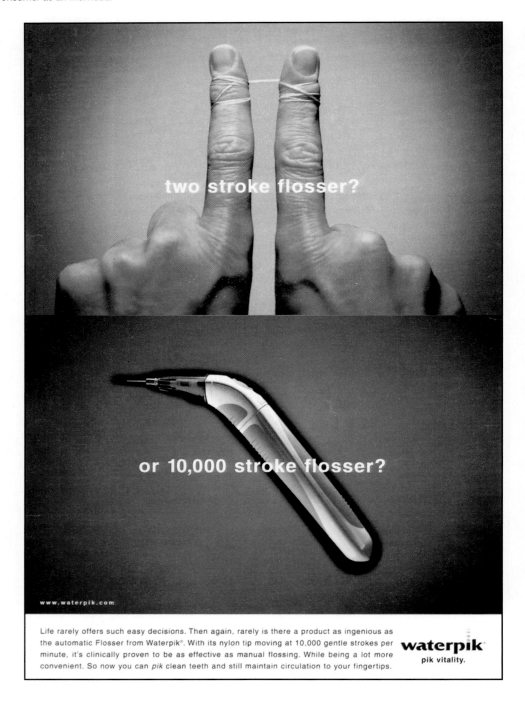

FROM CONSUMER MATERIALISM
TO COMPULSIVE CONSUMPTION

Consumer researchers have become increasingly interested in exploring various
consumption and possession traits. These traits range from *consumer materialism* to
fixated consumption behavior to *consumer compulsive behavior.*

FIGURE 5-6

Listerine Essential Care™ Targets Verbalizers
Courtesy of Pfizer Consumer Group, Pfizer Inc.

Consumer Materialism

Materialism (the extent to which a person is considered materialistic) is a topic frequently discussed in newspapers, in magazines, and on TV (e.g., "Americans are very materialistic") and in everyday conversations between friends ("He's so materialistic!"). Materialism, as a personality-like trait, distinguishes between individuals who regard possessions as essential to their identities and their lives and those for whom

TABLE 5-4	Sample Items from a Materialism Scale

SUCCESS

The things I own say a lot about how well I'm doing in life.

I don't place much emphasis on the amount of material objects people own as a sign of success.[a]

I like to own things that impress people.

CENTRALITY

I enjoy spending money on things that aren't practical.

I try to keep my life simple, as far as possessions are concerned.[a]

Buying things gives me a lot of pleasure.

HAPPINESS

I'd be happier if I could afford to buy more things.

I have all the things I really need to enjoy life.[a]

It sometimes bothers me quite a bit that I can't afford to buy all the things I'd like.

Note: Measured on a 5-point "agreement" scale.
[a]Items with an ([a]) are negatively worded and are scored inversely.
Source: From Marsha L. Richins and Scott Dawson, "A Consumer Values Orientation for Materialism and Its Measurement: Scale Development and Validation," *Journal of Consumer Research,* 19 (December 1992), 310. Reprinted by permission of The University of Chicago Press as publisher.

possessions are secondary.[22] Researchers have found some general support for the following characteristics of materialistic people: (1) They especially value acquiring and showing off possessions; (2) they are particularly self-centered and selfish; (3) they seek lifestyles full of possessions (e.g., they desire to have lots of "things," rather than a simple, uncluttered lifestyle); and (4) their many possessions do not give them greater personal satisfaction (i.e., their possessions do not lead to greater happiness).[23] Table 5-4 presents sample items from a materialism scale.

Materialism has often been linked to advertising, and researchers have suggested that in the United States there has been an increasing emphasis on materialism in the print media. It is important to remember, though, that the extent of consumer materialism can vary from country to country (e.g., consumer materialism is less developed in Mexico than in the United States) and, therefore, marketers must be careful when trying to export a successful U.S. marketing mix to another country.[24]

Fixated Consumption Behavior

Somewhere between materialism and compulsion, with respect to buying or possessing objects, is the notion of being *fixated* with regard to consuming or possessing. Like materialism, *fixated consumption behavior* is in the realm of normal and socially acceptable behavior. Fixated consumers do not keep their objects or purchases of interest a secret; rather, they frequently display them, and their involvement is openly shared with others who have a similar interest. In the world of serious collectors (Barbie dolls, Beanie Babies, rare antique quilts, or almost anything else that has drawn collectors), there are countless millions of *fixated consumers* pursuing their interests and trying to add to their collections. Take the case of *Star Trek* (**www.startrek.com**), which has been called the most successful and lucrative cult phenomenon in television history. Fans of the program are said to range from mainstream TV viewers to members of an alternative subculture and have purchased billions of dollars of licensed merchandise.[25]

Fixated consumers typically possess the following characteristics: (1) a deep (possibly passionate) interest in a particular object or product category, (2) a willingness to go to considerable lengths to secure additional examples of the object or product category of interest, and (3) the dedication of a considerable amount of discretionary time and money to searching out the object or product.[26] This profile of the fixated consumer describes many collectors or hobbyists (e.g., collectors of coins, stamps, antiques, vintage wristwatches, or fountain pens). Research exploring the dynamics of the fixated consumer (in this case, coin collectors) revealed that, for fixated consumers, there is not only an enduring involvement in the object category itself but also a considerable amount of involvement in the process of acquiring the object (sometimes referred to as the "hunt").[27]

Compulsive Consumption Behavior

Unlike materialism and fixated consumption, **compulsive consumption** is in the realm of abnormal behavior—an example of the dark side of consumption. Consumers who are compulsive have an *addiction;* in some respects they are out of control, and their actions may have damaging consequences to them and to those around them. Examples of compulsive consumption problems are uncontrollable shopping, gambling, drug addiction, alcoholism, and various food and eating disorders.[28] For instance, there are many women and a small number of men who are *chocoholics*—they have an intense craving (also termed an addiction) for chocolate.[29] From a marketing and consumer behavior perspective, *compulsive buying* can also be included in any list of compulsive activities. To control or possibly eliminate such compulsive problems generally requires some type of therapy or clinical treatment.

There have been some research efforts to develop a screener inventory to pinpoint compulsive buying behavior. Table 5-5 presents sample questions from several of these scales. Evidence suggests that some consumers use self-gifting, impulse buying, and compulsive buying as a way to influence or manage their moods; that is, the

---

TABLE 5-5 **Sample Items from Scales to Measure Compulsive Buying**

VALENCE, D'ASTOUS, AND FORTIER COMPULSIVE BUYING SCALE

1. When I have money, I cannot help but spend part or the whole of it.
2. I am often impulsive in my buying behavior.
3. As soon as I enter a shopping center, I have an irresistible urge to go into a shop to buy something.
4. I am one of those people who often responds to direct-mail offers (e.g., books or compact discs).
5. I have often bought a product that I did not need, while knowing I had very little money left.

FABER AND O'GUINN COMPULSIVE BUYING SCALE

1. If I have any money left at the end of the pay period, I just have to spend it.
2. I felt others would be horrified if they knew my spending habits.
3. I have bought things even though I couldn't afford them.
4. I wrote a check when I knew I didn't have enough money in the bank to cover it.
5. I bought something in order to make myself feel better.

Source: Gilles Valence, Alain d'Astous, and Louis Fortier, "Compulsive Buying: Concept and Measurement," *Journal of Consumer Policy,* 11 (1988), 419–433; Ronald J. Faber and Thomas C. O'Guinn, "A Clinical Screener for Compulsive Buying," *Journal of Consumer Research,* 19, December 1992, 459–469; and Leslie Cole and Dan Sherrell, "Comparing Scales to Measure Compulsive Buying: An Exploration of Their Dimensionality," in *Advances in Consumer Research,* 22, ed. Frank R. Kardes and Mita Sujan (Provo, UT: Association for Consumer Research, 1995): 419–427.

act of purchasing may convert a negative mood to a more positive one ("I'm depressed, I'll go out shopping and I'll feel better").[30]

CONSUMER ETHNOCENTRISM: RESPONSES TO FOREIGN-MADE PRODUCTS

In an effort to distinguish between consumer segments that are likely to be receptive to foreign-made products and those that are not, researchers have developed and tested the *consumer ethnocentrism* scale, called CETSCALE (see Table 5-6).[31] The CETSCALE has been successful in identifying consumers with a predisposition to accept (or reject) foreign-made products. Consumers who are highly ethnocentric are likely to feel that it is inappropriate or wrong to purchase foreign-made products because of the resulting economic impact on the domestic economy, whereas nonethnocentric consumers tend to evaluate foreign-made products—ostensibly more objectively—for their extrinsic characteristics (e.g., "how good are they?"). A portion of the consumers who would score low on an ethnocentric scale are actually likely to be quite receptive to products made in foreign countries.

Ethnocentrism has been found to vary by country and product. Mexican consumers, for example, are more ethnocentric than their French and American counterparts; and Malaysian consumers, while preferring to purchase slacks, shirts, undergarments, and belts that are locally manufactured, want to buy imported sunglasses and watches.[32] A recent article also suggests that some older American consumers, in remembrance of World War II, still refuse to purchase German- and/or Japanese-made products, whereas some German and Japanese consumers may feel similarly about American-made products.[33]

TABLE 5-6	The Consumer Ethnocentrism Scale—CETSCALE

1. American people should always buy American-made products instead of imports.
2. Only those products that are unavailable in the United States should be imported.
3. Buy American-made products. Keep America working.
4. American products, first, last, and foremost.
5. Purchasing foreign-made products is un-American.
6. It is not right to purchase foreign products, because it puts Americans out of jobs.
7. A real American should always buy American-made products.
8. We should purchase products manufactured in America instead of letting other countries get rich off us.
9. It is always best to purchase American products.
10. There should be very little trading or purchasing of goods from other countries unless out of necessity.
11. Americans should not buy foreign products, because this hurts American business and causes unemployment.
12. Curbs should be put on all imports.
13. It may cost me in the long run but I prefer to support American products.
14. Foreigners should not be allowed to put their products on our markets.
15. Foreign products should be taxed heavily to reduce their entry into the United States.
16. We should buy from foreign countries only those products that we cannot obtain within our own country.
17. American consumers who purchase products made in other countries are responsible for putting their fellow Americans out of work.

Notes: Response format is a 7-point Likert-type scale (strongly agree = 7, strongly disagree = 1). Range of scores is from 17 to 119. Calculated from confirmatory factor analysis of data from 4-area study.
Source: Terence A. Shimp and Subhash Sharma, "Consumer Ethnocentrism: Construction and Validation of the CETSCALE," *Journal of Marketing Research*, 24, August 1987, 282. Reprinted by permission.

TABLE 5-7	Strategies for Managing Country-of-Origin Effects		

	Country Image		
MARKETING MIX	**POSITIVE**	**NEGATIVE**	
Product	Emphasize "Made In"	Emphasize Brand Name	
Price	Premium Price	Low Price to Attract Value Conscious	
Place (Channel of Distribution)	Exclusive Locations	Establish Supply Chain Partners	
Promotion	Country Image Nation Sponsored	Brand Image Manufacturer Sponsored	

Source: Osman Mohamad, Zafar U. Ahmed, Earl D. Honeycutt, Jr., and Taizoon Hyder Tyebkhan, "Does 'Made In. . .' Matter to Consumers? A Malaysian Study of Country of Origin Effect," *Multinational Business Review*, Fall 2000, 73.

Marketers successfully target ethnocentric consumers in any national market by stressing a nationalistic theme in their promotional appeals (e.g., "Made in America" or "Made in France") because this segment is predisposed to buy products made in their native land. Honda, the Japanese auto maker, in an indirect appeal to ethnocentric Americans, had advertised that its Accord wagon is "Exported from America" to other markets (reinforcing that some of its automobiles are made in the United States). Table 5-7 presents a marketing mix strategy that can be used to manage country-of-origin effects. Specifically, if marketers determine that the potential customers in a particular country possess a *positive* image of products made in the country in which their products originate, the marketers may be able to create a marketing mix strategy that follows options in the *Positive* column. In contrast, if marketers assess that the potential customers in a particular country possess a *negative* image of products made in the country in which their products originate, the marketers might be wise to elect a marketing mix strategy that follows options in the *Negative* column of Table 5-7.

Brand Personality

Early in this chapter, as part of our discussion of Freudian theory, we introduced the notion of *product personality.* Consumers also subscribe to the notion of *brand personality;* that is, they attribute various descriptive personality-like traits or characteristics to different brands in a wide variety of product categories. For instance, with some help from frequent advertising, consumers tend to see Volvo (**www.volvo.com**) as representing safety, Perdue (chickens) as representing freshness (**www.perdue.com**), Nike as the athlete in all of us (**www.nike.com**), and BMW as performance driven (**www.bmw.com**).[34] In a similar fashion, the brand personality for Levi's 501 jeans (**www.levi.com**) is "dependable and rugged," "real and authentic," and "American and Western." Such personality-like images of brands reflect consumers' visions of the inner core of many strong brands of consumer products. As these examples reveal, a brand's personality can either be functional ("provides safety") or symbolic ("the athlete in all of us").[35] There is common sense and research evidence to conclude that any brand personality, as long as it is *strong* and *favorable,* will strengthen a brand.[36] However, it is not clear, for example, how many consumers would be willing to pay a 10 to 15 percent premium for a brand-name diamond.[37]

Two of the fast-food chains that many readers of this textbook may patronize with some frequency, Wendy's (www.wendys.com) and McDonald's (www.mcdonalds.com), are examples of companies that have built distinctive brand personalities for themselves. The Wendy's brand personality has been built around Dave Thomas, the chain's recently deceased founder, who represented the "clumsy guy next door in search of good fast food." In contrast, the McDonald's brand personality, through Ronald McDonald and other cartoon characters, has always been associated with fun.[38]

In other cases, marketers have provided an instant personality or heritage for a new product by employing a symbolic or fictional historical branding strategy. For example, when Brown Forman (www.brown-forman.com) entered the microbrewed beer market in 1996, it used the brand name "1886" for its new beer, which is the year that one of its other products, Jack Daniel's bourbon, was first distilled.[39]

BRAND PERSONIFICATION

Some marketers find it useful to create a **brand personification,** which tries to recast consumers' perception of the attributes of a product or service into a human-like character. For instance, in focus group research, well-known brands of dishwashing liquid have been likened to "demanding task masters" or "high-energy people." Many consumers express their inner feelings about products or brands in terms of their association with known personalities. Identifying consumers' current brand–personality links and creating personality links for new products are important marketing tasks.

The M&M "people" are a current "fun" example of brand personification (www.m-ms.com). It is based on the line of questioning that could ask the following: "If an M&M (or a chocolate-coated peanut variety) was a person, what kind of person would it be?" Additional questioning would be likely to explore how the color of the coating impacts consumers' perceived personality for the "M&M people."

To personify and humanize its model consumer, Celestial Seasonings, Inc. (www.celestialseasonings.com), the leading specialty tea maker in the United States, refers in its advertising to "Tracy Jones." And just who is Tracy Jones? According to Celestial Seasonings, she is "female, upscale, well educated, and highly involved in life in every way."[40] In a similar fashion, Mr. Coffee (www.mrcoffee.com), a popular brand of automatic-drip coffee makers, unexpectedly found in its focus group research that consumers were referring to Mr. Coffee as if the product were a person (e.g., "he makes good coffee" and "he's got a lot of different models and prices").[41] After careful consideration, the marketers decided to explore the possibility of creating a *brand personification.* Initial consumer research indicated that Mr. Coffee was seen as being "dependable," "friendly," "efficient," "intelligent," and "smart."

Figure 5-7 presents a *brand personality framework* that reflects extensive consumer research designed to pinpoint the structure and nature of a brand's personality. The framework suggests that there are five defining *dimensions* of a brand's personality ("sincerity," "excitement," "competence," "sophistication," and "ruggedness"), and 15 *facets* of personality that flow from the five dimensions (i.e., "down-to-earth," "daring," "reliable," "upper class," and "outdoors").[42] If we carefully review these brand personality dimensions and facets, it appears that this framework tends to accommodate the brand personalities pursued by many consumer products.

PRODUCT PERSONALITY AND GENDER

A product personality, or persona, frequently endows the product or brand with a gender. For instance, Celestial Seasonings' Tracy Jones was given a feminine per-

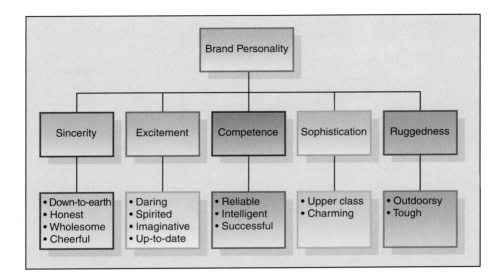

FIGURE 5-7

A Brand Personality
Framework
Source: Jennifer L. Aaker,
"Dimension of Brand
Personality," *Journal of
Marketing Research,* 35,
August 1997, 352. Reprinted
by permission of the American
Marketing Association.

sona, whereas Mr. Coffee was given a masculine personality. The assigning of gender as part of a product's personality description is fully consistent with the marketplace reality that products and services, in general, are viewed by consumers as having gender. A study that asked Chinese consumers to categorize various products in terms of gender, found that they perceived coffee and toothpaste to be masculine products, whereas bath soap and shampoo were seen as feminine products.[43]

Armed with knowledge of the perceived gender of a product or a specific brand, marketers are in a better position to select visuals and text copy for various marketing messages.

PRODUCT PERSONALITY AND GEOGRAPHY

Marketers learned long ago that certain products, in the minds of consumers, possess a strong geographical association (e.g., a New York bagel). Consequently, by employing geography in the product's name, the product's manufacturer creates a geographic personality for the product. Such a geographic personality can lead to geographic equity for the brand, meaning that in the consumer's memory, the knowledge of the brand reflects a strong geographic association.

Interestingly, geographic brand names can be either familiar or unfamiliar (or fictitious). For example, take "Philadelphia cream cheese." In fact, it is manufactured in Illinois, even though it uses the name of one of the largest cities in the United States. Still further, although we all know that Arizona is a state, Arizona ice tea is brewed and bottled in the state of New York. Fictitious geographic product names include Hidden Valley salad dressings and Bear Creek soups.[44]

But more important than whether the name is real or fictitious is whether the location and its image add to the product's brand equity.[45] Although Texas' Best Barbecue Sauce may be made in New Jersey, many Americans associate barbecue with Texas. Similarly, the Old El Paso brand of salsa capitalizes on the Mexican influence in the Southwest. The product may be made in Minneapolis, but a brand of salsa named Twin Cities Salsa (e.g., Minneapolis/St. Paul) just doesn't have the same cachet. Table 5-8 provides a list of familiar and not-so-familiar geographic brand names.

| TABLE 5-8 | Examples of Geographic Brand Names |

GEOGRAPHIC ORIENTATION	BRAND NAME	PRODUCT	LOCALE
Familiar/Actual	K.C. Masterpiece	BBQ Sauce	Oakland, CA
	London Pub	Vinegar	Bloomfield, NJ
	Old El Paso	Salsa	Minneapolis, MN
	Old Milwaukee	Beer	Detroit, MI
	Philadelphia	Cream Cheese	Glenview, IL
	San Francisco Intl	Buns/Rolls	Totowa, NJ
	Arizona Iced Tea	Iced Tea	Like Success, NY
Unfamiliar/Fictitious	Bear Creek	Soup	Harbor City, UT
	Green Forest	Paper Towels	Mexico
	Hidden Valley	Salad Dressing	Oakland, CA
	Italian Village	Ravioli	Secaucus, NJ
	Pepperwood Grove	Wine	Oakville, CA
	Sorrel Ridge	Jam	Port Reading, NJ

Source: K. Damon Aiken, Eric C. Koch, and Robert Mandrigal, "What's in a Name? Explorations in Geographic Equity and Geographic Personality," *American Marketing Association*, Winter 2000, 302.

PERSONALITY AND COLOR

Consumers not only ascribe personality traits to products and services, but they also tend to associate personality factors with specific colors. For instance, Coca-Cola (www.cocacola.com) is associated with red, which connotes excitement. Blue bottles are often used to sell wine because the color blue appeals particularly to female consumers, and they buy the majority of wine.[46] Yellow is associated with novelty, and black frequently connotes sophistication.[47] For this reason, brands wishing to create a sophisticated persona (such as Minute Maid juices or Pasta LaBella) or an upscale or premium image (e.g., Miller Beers' Miller Reserve) use labeling or packaging that is primarily black. A combination of black and white communicates that a product is carefully engineered, high tech, and sophisticated in design. IBM (www.ibm.com) has consistently used an all-black case with a few selected red buttons and bars to house its very successful line of Thinkpad laptops. Nike has used black, white, and a touch of red for selected models of its sport shoes. This color combination seems to imply advanced-performance sports shoes. Recently, M&M/Mars (www.mmmars.com) has exploited the folklore that its green M&Ms are aphrodisiacs by creating a green female M&M character that it has featured in some of its ads.[48] And although we all know that ketchup is red, Heinz (www.heinz.com) developed its green ketchup after doing research with more than 1,000 kids, who helped decide on the product's green color and its packaging (e.g., the bottle is designed to fit smaller hands).[49] A recent print and outdoor advertising campaign for LifeSavers, based on consumer flavor and color research, characterizes *cherry* as "Ms. Popularity," *lime* as "The Outsider," and *sour apple and cherry* (targeted to teens) as "The Troublemaker."[50]

Many fast-food restaurants use combinations of bright colors, like red, yellow, and blue, for their roadside signs and interior designs. These colors have come to be associated with fast service and inexpensive food. In contrast, fine dining restaurants tend to use sophisticated colors like gray, white, shades of tan, or other soft, pale, or muted colors to reflect the feeling of fine, leisurely service. Consumer

TABLE 5-9	The Personality-like Associations of Selected Colors

COLOR	PERSONALITY LINK	MARKETING INSIGHTS
Blue	Commands respect, authority	• America's favored color • IBM holds the title to blue • Associated with club soda • Men seek products packaged in blue • Houses painted blue are avoided • Low-calorie, skim milk • Coffee in a blue can perceived as "mild"
Yellow	Caution, novelty, temporary, warmth	• Eyes register it fastest • Coffee in yellow can tasted "weak" • Stops traffic • Sells a house
Green	Secure, natural, relaxed or easygoing, living things	• Good work environment • Associated with vegetables and chewing gum • Canada Dry ginger ale sales increased when it changed sugar-free package from red to green and white
Red	Human, exciting, hot, passionate, strong	• Makes food "smell" better • Coffee in a red can perceived as "rich" • Women have a preference for bluish red • Men have a preference for yellowish red • Coca-Cola "owns" red
Orange	Powerful, affordable, informal	• Draws attention quickly
Brown	Informal and relaxed, masculine, nature	• Coffee in a dark-brown can was "too strong" • Men seek products packaged in brown
White	Goodness, purity, chastity, cleanliness, delicacy, refinement, formality	• Suggests reduced calories • Pure and wholesome food • Clean, bath products, feminine
Black	Sophistication, power, authority, mystery	• Powerful clothing • High-tech electronics
Silver, Gold, Platinum	Regal, wealthy, stately	• Suggests premium price

Source: From Bernice Kanner, "Color Schemes," *New York* magazine, April 3, 1989, 22–23. Copyright 1996, New York Magazine. Distributed by Los Angeles Times. Reprinted by permission.

research sponsored by a marketer of popularly priced casual wear found that dark colors, such as gray, dark blue, and black, were preferred to pastel colors in wintry northeastern and midwestern markets. However, when the multimarket study reached sunny Phoenix, Arizona, a reversal occurred—the darker colors fell into disfavor, and rose, pinks, yellows, and turquoise became the preferred colors. Further research revealed that many people seek to contrast the somber backdrop of the desert with multicolor pastel clothing and home furnishings. Table 5-9 presents a list of various colors, their personality-like meanings, and associated marketing insights.

TABLE 5-10 A Cross-National Study of Color Ratings (measured on a 7-point scale)

Austria		Brazil		Canada		Colombia	
COLOR	**MEAN**	**COLOR**	**MEAN**	**COLOR**	**MEAN**	**COLOR**	**MEAN**
Blue	6.59	White	6.34	Black	5.52	Blue	6.23
Green	5.86	Blue	6.12	Blue	5.48	White	5.54
White	5.52	Green	5.35	White	5.41	Green	5.38
Black	5.21	Black	5.23	Red	5.24	Red	5.10
Red	4.34	Red	5.00	Green	5.21	Black	5.02
Orange	4.34	Brown	4.50	Purple	4.03	Purple	3.83
Brown	3.97	Yellow	4.31	Yellow	3.79	Yellow	3.63
Yellow	3.59	Purple	4.27	Orange	3.55	Gold	3.52
Purple	3.24	Gold	3.77	Gold	3.55	Brown	3.21
Gold	3.17	Orange	3.58	Brown	3.03	Orange	2.90

Hong Kong		PRC		Taiwan		United States	
COLOR	**MEAN**	**COLOR**	**MEAN**	**COLOR**	**MEAN**	**COLOR**	**MEAN**
White	5.84	Blue	5.81	Blue	6.27	Blue	5.90
Blue	5.37	White	5.65	White	6.23	Green	5.63
Black	5.21	Black	5.26	Purple	5.18	Black	5.31
Red	5.21	Red	5.16	Black	4.82	White	5.29
Yellow	5.05	Green	5.13	Green	4.82	Red	5.14
Purple	5.00	Gold	4.55	Yellow	4.64	Gold	3.94
Gold	4.84	Yellow	4.16	Brown	4.59	Purple	3.90
Green	4.58	Orange	4.13	Orange	4.36	Brown	3.80
Brown	4.11	Purple	3.87	Red	4.32	Orange	3.27
Orange	3.89	Brown	3.48	Gold	4.31	Yellow	3.26

Source: Thomas J. Madden, Kelly Hewett, and Martin S. Roth, "Managing Images in Different Cultures: A Cross-National Study of Color Meanings and Preferences," *Journal of International Marketing*, 8, 4, 2000, 95.

It is also important to point out that consumers' liking and disliking of specific colors can vary from one country to another. A recent study asked individuals in eight countries to rate each of 10 colors on a 7-point scale, and Table 5-10 presents these results.[51] To discover such insights, researchers use a variety of qualitative measurement techniques, such as *observation, focus groups, depth interviews,* and *projective techniques* (discussed in Chapter 2).

Self and Self-Image

Consumers have a variety of enduring images of themselves. These self-images, or perceptions of self, are very closely associated with personality in that individuals tend to buy products and services and patronize retailers whose images or personalities relate in some meaningful way to their own self-images. In essence, consumers seek to depict themselves in their brand choices—they tend to approach products with images that could enhance their self-concept and avoid those products that do not.[52] In this final section, we examine the issue of *one* or *multiple* selves, explore the makeup of the self-image, the notion of **extended self,** and the possibilities or options of *altering the self-image.*

ONE OR MULTIPLE SELVES

Historically, individuals have been thought to have a single self-image and to be interested, as consumers, in products and services that satisfy that single self. However, it is more accurate to think of consumers as having **multiple selves.**[53] This change in thinking reflects the understanding that a single consumer is likely to act quite differently with different people and in different situations. For instance, a person is likely to behave in different ways with parents, at school, at work, at a museum opening, or with friends at a nightclub. The healthy or normal person is likely to display a somewhat different personality in each of these different situations or social **roles.** In fact, acting exactly the same in all situations or roles and not adapting to the situation at hand may be considered a sign of an abnormal or unhealthy person.

In terms of consumer behavior, the idea that an individual embodies a number of different "selves" (i.e., has multiple self-images) suggests that marketers should target their products and services to consumers *within the context of a particular "self,"* and in certain cases, a choice of different products for different *selves.* (The notion of a consumer having multiple selves or playing multiple roles supports the application of usage situation as a segmentation base discussed in Chapter 3.)

THE MAKEUP OF THE SELF-IMAGE

Consistent with the idea of multiple self-images, each individual has an image of himself or herself as a certain kind of person, with certain traits, skills, habits, possessions, relationships, and ways of behaving. As with other types of images and personality, the individual's self-image is unique, the outgrowth of that person's background and experience. Individuals develop their self-images through interactions with other people—initially their parents, and then other individuals or groups with whom they relate over the years.

Products and brands have symbolic value for individuals, who evaluate them on the basis of their consistency (congruence) with their personal pictures or images of themselves. Some products seem to match one or more of an individual's self-images; others seem totally alien. It is generally believed that consumers attempt to preserve or enhance their self-images by selecting products and brands with "images" or "personalities" that they believe are congruent with their own self-images and avoiding products that are not.[54] This seems to be especially true for women; research reveals that more women than men (77 percent versus 64 percent) feel that the brands that they select reflect their personalities.[55]

Given this relationship between brand preference and consumers' self-images, it is natural that consumers use brands to help them in their task of defining themselves. Research indicates that consumers who have strong links to particular brands—a positive self-brand connection—see such brands *as representing an aspect of themselves.* For marketers, such *connections* are certainly an important step in the formation of consumer loyalty and a positive relationship with consumers.[56] Consider the two charts presented in Figure 5-8, which show purchase intent to be strongest when there is a good fit between brand image and self-image.[57]

A variety of different self-images have been recognized in the consumer behavior literature for a long time. In particular, many researchers have depicted some or all of the following kinds of self-image: (1) **actual self-image** (how consumers in fact

FIGURE 5-8

Self-Image, Brand Image, and Purchase Intent. (a) Fragrance Commerical: Self-Image and Brand-Image Convergence Among Respondents with Strong Purchase Intent.
(b) Fragrance Commercial: Self-Image and Brand-Image Convergence Among Respondents with Weak Purchase Intent.

Source: Abhilasha Mehta, "Using Self-Concept to Assess Advertising Effectiveness," *Journal of Advertising Research*, February 1999, 87.

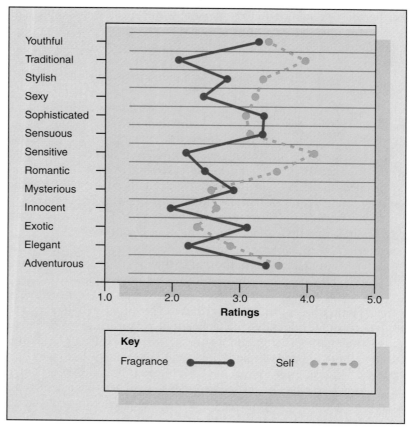

see themselves), (2) **ideal self-image** (how consumers would like to see themselves), (3) **social self-image** (how consumers feel others see them), and (4) **ideal social self-image** (how consumers would like others to see them).

It also seems useful to think in terms of two other types of self-images — **expected self** and the **"ought-to" self.** The *expected self-image* (how consumers expect to see themselves at some specified future time) is somewhere between the *actual* and *ideal* self-images. It is a future-oriented combination of what is (the actual self-image) and what consumers would like to be (the ideal self-image). As another interesting type of self-image — the *"ought-to" self* — consists of traits or characteristics that an individual believes it is his or her duty or obligation to possess.[58] Examples of this form of self-image might be the striving to achieve a deeper religious understanding or the seeking of a fair and just solution to a challenging ethical problem. Because the expected self and the ought-to self provide consumers with a realistic opportunity to change the self, they are both likely to be more valuable to marketers than the actual or ideal self-image as a guide for designing and promoting products.

In different contexts (i.e., in different situations and/or with respect to different products), consumers might select a different self-image to guide their attitudes or behavior. For instance, with some everyday household products, consumers might be guided by their actual self-image, whereas for some socially enhancing or socially conspicuous products, they might be guided by their social self-image. When it comes to a so-called fantasy product, they might be guided by either their ideal self-images or ideal social self-images. Figure 5-9 presents an ad for a relatively new model Patek Philippe ladies' wristwatch model that challenges the reader to contemplate for a moment what self-image she would project in the next 24 hours.

The concept of self-image has strategic implications for marketers. For example, marketers can segment their markets on the basis of relevant consumer self-images and then position their products or services as symbols of such self-images. Such a strategy is fully consistent with the marketing concept in that the marketer first assesses the needs of a consumer segment (with respect to both the product category and to an appropriate symbol of self-image) and then proceeds to develop and market a product or service that meets both criteria. The importance of marketing cannot be overstated, as brand equity theory (which focuses on the value inherent in a brand name) postulates that the power of a brand resides in the consumer's mind from both lived (purchase and usage) and mediated (advertising and promotion) experiences.[59]

THE EXTENDED SELF

The interrelationship between consumers' self-images and their possessions (i.e., objects they call their own) is an exciting topic. Specifically, consumers' possessions can be seen to confirm or extend their self-images. For instance, acquiring a desired or sought-after pair of "vintage" Nike sneakers might serve to expand or enrich a Japanese teenager's image of self. The teenager might now see herself as being more desirable, more fashionable, and more successful because she has a pair of the sought-after "vintage sneakers" (often one of the previous year's hard-to-get styles). In a similar manner, if the bracelet that a college student (let's call her Eleanor) received as a gift from her aunt was stolen, Eleanor is likely to feel diminished in some way. Indeed, the loss of a prized possession may lead Eleanor to "grieve" and to experience a variety of emotions, such as frustration, loss of control, the feeling of being violated, even the loss of magical protection.

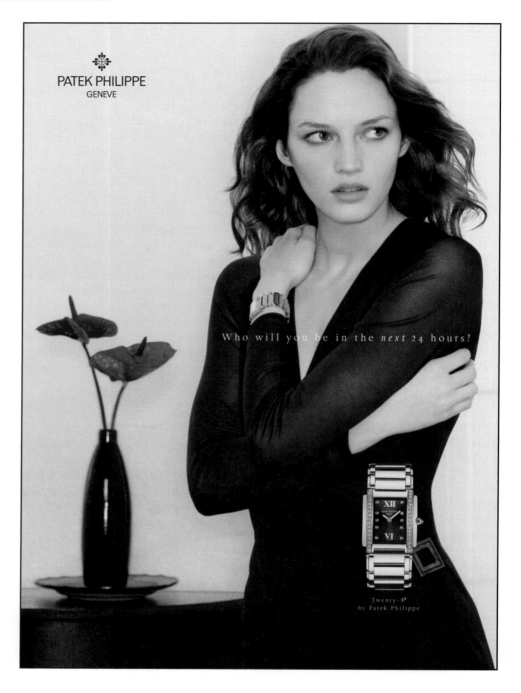

Table 5-11 presents sample items from a measurement instrument designed to reflect how particular possessions (e.g., a mountain bike) might become part of one's extended self.

The previous examples suggest that much human emotion can be connected to valued possessions. In such cases, possessions are considered extensions of the self. It has been proposed that possessions can extend the self in a number of ways: (1) *actually,* by allowing the person to do things that otherwise would be very difficult or impossible to accomplish (e.g., problem solving by using a computer);

TABLE 5-11	Sample Items from an Extended Self-Survey[a]

My _____ holds a special place in my life.

My _____ is central to my identity.

I feel emotionally attached to my _____ .

My _____ helps me narrow the gap between what I am and try to be.

If my _____ was stolen from me, I would feel as if part of me is missing.

I would be a different person without my _____ .

I take good care of my _____ .

I trust my _____ .

[a]A 6-point agree–disagree scale was used.
Source: Kimberly J. Dodson, "Peak Experiences and Mountain Biking: Incorporating the Bike in the Extended Self," *Advances in Consumer Research,* 1996. Reprinted by permission.

(2) *symbolically,* by making the person feel better or "bigger" (receiving an employee award for excellence); (3) by *conferring status or rank* (e.g., among collectors of rare works of art because of the ownership of a particular masterpiece); (4) by *bestowing feelings of immortality* by leaving valued possessions to young family members (this also has the potential of extending the recipients' selves); and (5) by *endowing with magical powers* (e.g., a pocket watch inherited from one's grandfather might be perceived as a magic amulet bestowing good luck when it is worn).[60]

ALTERING THE SELF

Sometimes consumers wish to change themselves to become a different or improved self. Clothing, grooming aids or cosmetics, and all kinds of accessories (such as sunglasses, jewelry, tattoos, or even colored contact lenses) offer consumers the opportunity to modify their appearances (to create a "makeover") and thereby to alter their "selves." In using *self-altering products,* consumers are frequently attempting to express their individualism or uniqueness by creating a new self, maintaining the existing self (or preventing the loss of self), and extending the self (modifying or changing the self). Sometimes consumers use self-altering products or services to conform to or take on the appearance of a particular type of person (such as a military person, a physician, a business executive, or a college professor).

Closely related to both self-image and altering the self is the idea of *personal vanity.* As a descriptor of people, vanity is often associated with acting self-important, self-interested, or admiring one's own appearance or achievements. Using a "vanity scale" (Table 5-12), researchers have investigated both *physical vanity* (an excessive concern for and/or a positive—or inflated—view of one's physical appearance) and *achievement vanity* (an excessive concern for and/or a positive or inflated view of one's personal achievements). They have found both these ideas are related to materialism, use of cosmetics, concern with clothing, and country club membership.[61]

There is also research evidence to suggest that self-monitoring may serve as a moderating variable when it comes to how well a person is guided by situational cues regarding social appropriateness. Low self-monitors are individuals who are typically guided by their inner feelings, whereas high self-monitors claim that they act differently in different situations and with different people.[62] Consequently, high self-monitors might be more prone to employ a self-altering product in order to enhance their ideal social self-image.

TABLE 5-12 Sample Items from a Vanity Scale

PHYSICAL-CONCERN ITEMS

1. The way I look is extremely important to me.
2. I am very concerned with my appearance.
3. It is important that I always look good.

PHYSICAL-VIEW ITEMS

1. People notice how attractive I am.
2. People are envious of my good looks.
3. My body is sexually appealing.

ACHIEVEMENT-CONCERN ITEMS

1. Professional achievements are an obsession with me.
2. Achieving greater success than my peers is important to me.
3. I want my achievements to be recognized by others.

ACHIEVEMENT-VIEW ITEMS

1. My achievements are highly regarded by others.
2. I am a good example of professional success.
3. Others wish they were as successful as me.

Source: Richard G. Netemeyer, Scot Burton, and Donald R. Lichtenstein, "Trait Aspects of Vanity: Measurement and Relevance to Consumer Behavior," *Journal of Consumer Research*, 21, March 1995, 624. Reprinted by permission of The University of Chicago Press as publisher.

Altering one's self, particularly one's appearance or body parts, can be accomplished by cosmetics, hair restyling or coloring, getting a tattoo, switching from eyeglasses to contact lenses (or the reverse), or undergoing cosmetic surgery (see Figure 5-10).

Virtual Personality or Self

With the widespread interest in using the Internet as a form of entertainment and as a social vehicle to meet new people with similar interests, there has been a tremendous growth in the use of online chat rooms. People who visit chat rooms are able to carry on real-time conversations about themselves and topics of mutual interest with people from all over the globe. Because at the present time most chats are actually text conversations rather than live video broadcasts, the participants usually never get to see each other. This creates an opportunity for chat room participants to try out new identities or to change their identities while online. For instance, one can change from male to female (known as "gender swapping"), from old to young, or from married to single; from white-collar professional to blue-collar worker, or from grossly overweight to svelte. In terms of personality, one can change from mild-mannered to aggressive, or from introvert to extrovert.

The notion of a **virtual personality** or **virtual self** provides an individual with the opportunity to try on different personalities or different identities, much like going to the mall and trying on different outfits in a department or specialty store. If the identity fits, or the personality can be enhanced, the individual may decide to keep

FIGURE 5-10

Ad Suggesting that the
Consumer Alter Herself
Courtesy of Unilever.

the new personality in favor of his or her old personality. From a consumer behavior point of view, it is likely that such opportunities to try out a new personality or alter the self may result in changes in selected forms of purchase behavior. This may in turn offer marketers new opportunities to target various "online selves."

Want to find out about your personality online? One Web site, **www.emode. com**, offers Internet users an online exam called "The Ultimate Personality Test," which takes perhaps 10 minutes to finish and categorizes the test taker into one of 13 personality types. Give it a try.[63]

Summary

Personality can be described as the psychological characteristics that both determine and reflect how a person responds to his or her environment. Although personality tends to be consistent and enduring, it may change abruptly in response to major life events, as well as gradually over time.

Three theories of personality are prominent in the study of consumer behavior: psychoanalytic theory, neo-Freudian theory, and trait theory. Freud's psychoanalytic theory provides the foundation for the study of motivational research, which operates on the premise that human drives are largely unconscious in nature and serve to motivate many consumer actions. Neo-Freudian theory tends to emphasize the fundamental role of social relationships in the formation and development of personality. Alfred Adler viewed human beings as seeking to overcome feelings of inferiority. Harry Stack Sullivan believed that people attempt to establish significant and rewarding relationships with others. Karen Horney saw individuals as trying to overcome feelings of anxiety and categorized them as compliant, aggressive, or detached.

Trait theory is a major departure from the qualitative (or subjective) approach to personality measurement. It postulates that individuals possess innate psychological traits (e.g., innovativeness, novelty seeking, need for cognition, materialism) to a greater or lesser degree, and that these traits can be measured by specially designed scales or inventories. Because they are simple to use and to score and can be self-administered, personality inventories are the preferred method for many researchers in the assessment of consumer personality. Product and brand personalities represent real opportunities for marketers to take advantage of consumers' connections to various brands they offer. Brands often have personalities—some include "humanlike" traits and even gender. These brand personalities help shape consumer responses, preferences, and loyalties.

Each individual has a perceived self-image (or multiple self-images) as a certain kind of person with certain traits, habits, possessions, relationships, and ways of behaving. Consumers frequently attempt to preserve, enhance, alter, or extend their self-images by purchasing products or services and shopping at stores they perceive as consistent with their relevant self-image(s) and by avoiding products and stores they perceive are not. With the growth of the Internet, there appear to be emerging virtual selves or virtual personalities. Consumer experiences with chat rooms sometimes provide an opportunity to explore new or alternative identities.

Discussion Questions

1. How would you explain the fact that, although no two individuals have identical personalities, personality is sometimes used in consumer research to identify distinct and sizable market segments?

2. Contrast the major characteristics of the following personality theories: (a) Freudian theory, (b) neo-Freudian theory, and (c) trait theory. In your answer, illustrate how each theory is applied to the understanding of consumer behavior.

3. Describe personality trait theory. Give five examples of how personality traits can be used in consumer research.

4. How can a marketer of cameras use research findings that indicate a target market consists primarily of inner-directed or other-directed consumers? Of consumers who are high (or low) on innovativeness?

5. Describe the type of promotional message that would be most suitable for each of the following personality market segments and give an example of each: (a) highly dogmatic consumers, (b) inner-directed consumers, (c) consumers with high optimum stimulation levels, (d) consumers with a high need for recognition, and (e) consumers who are visualizers versus consumers who are verbalizers.

6. Is there likely to be a difference in personality traits between individuals who readily purchase foreign-made products and those who prefer American-made products? How can marketers use the consumer ethnocentrism scale to segment consumers?

7. A marketer of health foods is attempting to segment a certain market on the basis of consumer self-image. Describe the four types of consumer self-image and discuss which one(s) would be most effective for the stated purpose.

Exercises

1. How do your clothing preferences differ from those of your friends? What personality traits might explain why your preferences are different from those of other people?

2. Find three print advertisements based on Freudian personality theory. Discuss how Freudian concepts are used in these ads. Do any of the ads personify a brand? If so, how?

3. Administer the nine items from the materialism scale (listed in Table 5-4) to two of your friends. In your view, are their consumption behaviors consistent with their scores on the scale? Why or why not?

Key Terms

- Actual self-image
- Brand personification
- Cognitive personality
- Compulsive consumption
- Consumer ethnocentrism
- Consumer innovativeness
- Consumer innovators
- Consumer materialism
- Dogmatism
- Expected self
- Extended self
- Freudian theory
- Ideal self-image
- Ideal social self-image
- Inner-directedness
- Multiple selves
- Need for cognition
- Neo-Freudian theory
- Optimum stimulation levels
- Other-directedness
- "Ought-to" self
- Personality
- Psychoanalytic theory of personality
- Roles
- Sensation seeking
- Social self-image
- Trait theory
- Variety- or novelty-seeking
- Virtual personality or self
- Visualizers versus verbalizers

Notes

1. Amanda B. Diekman and Alice H. Eagly, "Stereotypes as Dynamic Constructs: Women and Men of the Past, Present, and Future," *Personality and Social Psychology Bulletin,* 26, no. 10, October 2000, 1171–1188.

2. Ellen Creager, "Do Snack Foods Such as Nuts and Popcorn Affect Romance?" *The Patriot-News,* Harrisburg, PA, February 14, 2001, E11.

3. For example, see Karen Horney, *The Neurotic Personality of Our Time* (New York: Norton, 1937).

4. Joel B. Cohen, "An Interpersonal Orientation to the Study of Consumer Behavior," *Journal of Marketing Research,* 6, August 1967, 270–278; Arch G. Woodside and Ruth Andress, "CAD Eight Years Later," *Journal of the Academy of Marketing Science,* 3, Summer–Fall 1975, 309–313; see also Jon P. Noerager, "An Assessment of CAD: A Personality Instrument Developed Specifically for Marketing Research," *Journal of Marketing Research,* 16, February 1979, 53–59; and Pradeep K. Tyagi, "Validation of the CAD Instrument: A Replication," in *Advances in Consumer Research,* 10, eds. Richard P. Bogazzio and Alice M. Tybout (Ann Arbor, MI: Association for Consumer Research, 1983), 112–114.

5. Morton I. Jaffe, "Brand-Loyalty/Variety-Seeking and the Consumer's Personality: Comparing Children and Young Adults," in *Proceedings of the Society for Consumer Psychology,* eds. Scott B. MacKenzie and Douglas M. Stayman (La Jolla, CA: American Psychological Association, 1995), 144–151.

6. J. P. Guilford, *Personality* (New York: McGraw-Hill, 1959), 6.

7. Ronald E. Goldsmith and Charles F. Hofacker, "Measuring Consumer Innovativeness," *Journal of the Academy of Marketing Science,* 19 (1991): 209–221; Suresh Subramanian and Robert A. Mittelstaedt, "Conceptualizing Innovativeness as a Consumer Trait: Consequences and Alternatives," in *1991 AMA Educators' Proceedings,* eds. Mary C. Gilly and F. Robert Dwyer et al. (Chicago: American Marketing Association, 1991), 352–360; and "Reconceptualizing and Measuring Consumer Innovativeness," in *1992 AMA Educators' Proceedings,* eds. Robert P. Leone and V. Kumor, et al. (Chicago: American Marketing Association, 1992), 300–307.

8. Alka Varma Citrin, David E. Sprott, Steven N. Silverman, and Donald E. Stem, Jr., "From Internet Use to Internet Adoption: Is General Innovativeness Enough?," in *1999 AMA Winter Educators' Conference,* 10, eds. Anil Menon and Arun Sharma (Chicago: American Marketing Association, 1999), 232–233.

9. Angela D'Auria Stanton and Wilbur W. Stanton, "To Click or Not to Click: Personality Characteristics of Internet Versus Non-Internet Purchasers," in *2001 AMA Winter Educators' Conference,* 12, eds. Ram Krishnan and Madhu Viswanathan (Chicago: American Marketing Association, 2001), 161–162.

10. Milton Rokeach, *The Open and Closed Mind* (New York: Basic Books, 1960).

11. Itamar Simonson and Stephen M. Nowlis, "The Role of Explanations and Need for Uniqueness in Consumer Decision Making: Unconventional Choices Based on Reasons," *Journal of Consumer Research,* 27, June 2000, 49–68.

12. P. S. Raju, "Optimum Stimulation Level: Its Relationship to Personality, Demographics, and Exploratory Behavior," *Journal of Consumer Research,* 7, December 1980, 272–282; Leigh McAlister and Edgar Pessemier, "Variety Seeking Behavior: An Interdisciplinary Review," *Journal of Consumer Research,* 9, December 1982, 311–322; Jan-Benedict, E. M. Steenkamp and Hans Baumgartner, "The Role of Optimum Stimulation Level in Exploratory Consumer Behavior," *Journal of Consumer Research,* 19, December 1992, 434; Russell G. Wahlers and Michael J. Etzel, "A Consumer Response to Incongruity between Optimal Stimulation and Life Style Satisfaction," in *Advances in Consumer Research,* 12, eds. Elizabeth C. Hirschman and Morris B. Holbrook (Provo, UT: Association for Consumer Research, 1985), 97–101; and Jan-Benedict, E. M. Steenkamp, Frenkel ter Hofstede, and Michael Wedel, "A Cross-National Investigation into the Individual and National Cultural Antecedents of Consumer Innovativeness," *Journal of Marketing,* 62, April 1999, 55–69.

13. Linda McNamara and Mary E. Ballard, "Resting Arousal, Sensation Seeking, and Music Preference," *Genetic, Social, and General Psychology Monographs,* 1999, 125 (3), 229–250.

14. Satya Menon and Barbara E. Kahn, "The Impact of Context on Variety Seeking in Product Choices," *Journal of Consumer Research,* 22, December 1995, 285–295.

15. Elizabeth C. Hirschman, "Innovativeness, Novelty Seeking and Consumer Creativity," *Journal of Consumer Research,* 7, 1980, 283–295; Wayne Hoyer and Nancy M. Ridgway, "Variety Seeking as an Explanation for Exploratory Purchase Behavior: A Theoretical Model," in *Advances in Consumer Research,* 17, ed. Thomas C. Kinnear (Provo, UT: Association for Consumer Research, 1984), 114–119; and Minakshi Trivedi, "Using Variety-Seeking-Based Segmentation to Study Promotional Response," *Journal of the Academy of Marketing Science,* 27, no. 1, 37–49.

16. Barbara E. Kahn, "Dynamic Relationships with Customers: High-Variety Strategies," *Journal of the Academy of Marketing Science,* 26, Winter 1998, 47–53. Also see J. Jeffrey Inman, "The Role of Sensory-Specific Satiety in Attribute-Level Variety Seeking," *Journal of Consumer Research,* 28, June 2001, 105–120.

17. Richard Petty et al., "Personality and Ad Effectiveness: Exploring the Utility of Need for Cognition," in *Advances in Consumer Research,*

15, ed. Michael Houston (Ann Arbor, MI: Association for Consumer Research, 1988), 209–212; and Susan Powell Mantel and Frank R. Kardes, "The Role of Direction of Comparison, Attribute-Based Processing, and Attitude-Based Processing in Consumer Preference," *Journal of Consumer Research,* 25, March 1999, 335–352.

18. Arnold B. Bakker, "Persuasive Communication About AIDS Prevention: Need for Cognition Determines the Impact of Message Format," *AIDS Education and Prevention,* 11(2), 1999, 150–162.

19. Yong Zhang and Richard Buda, "Moderating Effects of Need for Cognition on Responses to Positively versus Negatively Framed Advertising Messages," *Journal of Advertising,* 28, no. 2, Summer 1999, 1–15.

20. Ayn E. Crowley and Wayne D. Hoyer, "The Relationship Between Need for Cognition and Other Individual Difference Variables: A Two-Dimensional Framework," in *Advances in Consumer Research,* 16, ed. Thomas K. Srull (Provo, UT: Association for Consumer Research, 1989), 37–43; and James W. Peltier and John A. Schibrowsky, "Need for Cognition, Advertisement Viewing Time and Memory for Advertising Stimuli," *Advances in Consumer Research,* 21 (1994): 244–250.

21. Tracy L. Tuten and Michael Bosnjak, "Understanding Differences in Web Usage: The Role of Need for Cognition and the Five Factor Model of Personality," *Social Behavior and Personality,* 29 (4), 2001, 391–398.

22. Russell W. Belk, "Three Scales to Measure Constructs Related to Materialism" and "Materialism: Trait Aspects of Living in the Material World," *Journal of Consumer Research,* 12, December 1985, 265–280.

23. Marsha L. Richins and Scott Dawson, "A Consumer Values Orientation for Materialism and Its Measurement: Scale Development and Validation," *Journal of Consumer Research,* 19, December 1992, 303–316; and Jeff Tanner and Jim Roberts, "Materialism Cometh," *Baylor Business Review,* Fall 2000, 8–9.

24. Reto Felix, Roberto Hernandez, and Wolfgang Hinck, "An Empirical Investigation of Materialism in Mexico," in *2000 AMA Educators' Proceedings,* 11, eds. Gregory T. Gundlach and Patrick E. Murphy (Chicago: American Marketing Association, 2000), 279–286.

25. Robert V. Kozinets, "Utopian Enterprise: Articulating the Meanings of *Star Trek's* Culture of Consumption," *Journal of Consumer Research,* 28, June 2001, 67–88.

26. Ronald J. Faber and Thomas C. O'Guinn, "A Clinical Screener for Compulsive Buying," *Journal of Consumer Research,* 19, December 1992, 459–469.

27. Ibid. Also see Stacey Menzel Baker and Robert A. Mittelstaedt, "The Meaning of the Search, Evaluation, and Selection of 'Yesterday's Cast-Offs': A Phenomenological Study into the Acquisition of the Collection," in *1995 AMA Educators' Proceedings,* eds. Barbara B. Stern and George M. Zinkan (Chicago: American Marketing Association, 1995), 152.

28. Elizabeth C. Hirschman, "The Consciousness of Addiction: Toward a General Theory of Compulsive Consumption," *Journal of Consumer Research,* 19, September 1992, 155–179; and Seung-Hee Lee, Sharron J. Lennon, and Nancy A. Rudd, "Compulsive Consumption Tendencies Among Television Shoppers," *Family and Consumer Sciences Research Journal,* 28, no. 4, June 2000, 463–488, and Booth Moore, "Shopping for a Defense—Consumer-Driven Culture Spills over into the Courtroom," *Houston Chronicle,* July 11, 2001, 8.

29. Kristen Bruinsma and Douglas L. Taren, "Chocolate: Food or Drug?" *Journal of the American Dietetic Association,* 99, no. 10, October 1999, 1249–1256.

30. Ronald J. Faber and Gary A. Christenson, "Can You Buy Happiness?: A Comparison of the Antecedent and Concurrent Moods Associated with the Shopping of Compulsive and Non-Compulsive Buyers," in *1995 Winter Educator's Conference,* 6, eds. David W. Stewart and Naufel J. Vilcassin (Chicago: American Marketing Association, 1995), 378–379.

31. Terence A. Shimp and Subhash Sharma, "Consumer Ethnocentrism: Construction and Validation of the CETSCALE," *Journal of Marketing Research,* 24, August 1987, 280–289; Richard G. Netemeyer, Srinivas Durvaula, and Donald R. Lichtenstein, "A Cross-National Assessment of the Reliability and Validity of the CETSCALE," *Journal of Marketing Research,* 28, August 1991, 320–327.

32. Osman Mohamad, Zafar U. Ahmed, Earl D. Honeycutt, Jr., and Taizoon Hyder Tyebkhan, "Does 'Made In...' Matter to Consumers? A Malaysian Study of Country of Origin Effect," *Multinational Business Review,* Fall 2000, 69–73; and Irvin Clarke, Mahesh N. Shankarmahesh, and John B. Ford, "Consumer Ethnocentrism, Materialism and Values: A Four Country Study," in *2000 AMA Winter Educators' Conference,* 11, eds., John P. Workman and William D. Perreault (Chicago: American Marketing Association, 2000), 102–103.

33. Subhash Sharma, Terence A. Shimp, and Jeongshin Shin, "Consumer Ethnocentrism: A Test of Antecedents and Moderators," *Journal of the Academy of Marketing Science,* 23 (1995), 27.

34. David Martin, "Branding: Finding That 'One Thing,'" *Brandweek,* February 16, 1998, 18.

35. Subodh Bhat and Srinivas K. Reddy, "Symbolic and Functional Positioning of Brands," *Journal of Consumer Marketing,* 15 (1998), 32–43.

36. Traci L. Haigood, "The Brand Personality Effect: An Empirical Investigation," in *1999 AMA Winter Educators' Conference,* 10, eds. Anil Menon and Arun Sharma (Chicago: American Marketing Association, 1999), 149–150; and Traci L. Haigood, "Deconstructing Brand Personality," in *2001 AMA Educators' Proceedings,* 12, eds. Greg W. Marshall and Stephen J. Grove (Chicago: American Marketing Association, 2001), 327–328.

37. Lauren Weber, "The Diamond Game, Shedding Its Mystery," *New York Times,* April 8, 2001, P1.

38. Judy A. Siguaw, Anna Mattila, and Jon R. Austin, "The Brand-Personality Scale," *Hotel and Restaurant Administration Quarterly,* June 1999, 48–55.

39. Janice S. Griffiths, Mary Zimmer, and Sheniqua K. Little, "The Effect of Reality Engineering on Consumers' Brand Perceptions Using a Fictional Historical Branding Strategy," *American Marketing Association,* Winter 1999, 250–258.

40. Tim Triplett, "When Tracy Speaks, Celestial Listens," *Marketing News,* October 24, 1994, 14.

41. David M. Morawski and Lacey J. Zachary, "Making Mr. Coffee," *Quirk's Marketing Research Review,* 6, March 1992, 6–7, 29–33.

42. Jennifer L. Aaker, "Dimension of Brand Personality," *Journal of Marketing Research,* 35, August 1997, 351–352.

43. Laura M. Milner and Dale Fodness, "Product Gender Perception: The Case of China," in *1995 Winter Educators' Conference,* 6, eds. David W. Stewart and Naufel J. Vilcassin (Chicago: American Marketing Association, 1995), 331–336.

44. K. Damon Aiken, Eric C. Koch, and Robert Mandrigal, "What's In a Name? Explorations in Geographic Equity and Geographic Personality," in *2000 AMA Winter Educators' Conference,* 11, eds., John P. Workman and William D. Perreault (Chicago: American Marketing Association, 2000), 301–308.

45. Max Blackston, "Observations: Building Brand Equity by Managing the Brand's Relationships," *Journal of Advertising Research,* November/December 2000, 101–105.

46. Elizabeth Jensen, "Blue Bottles, Gimmicky Labels Sell Wine," *Wall Street Journal,* July 7, 1997, B1.

47. Pamela S. Schindler, "Color and Contrast in Magazine Advertising," *Psychology & Marketing,* 3 (1986), 69–78.

48. Sally Goll Beatty, "Mars Inc. Dips into Sex to Lure Consumers into Arms of M&Ms," *Wall Street Journal,* January 23, 1997, 9.

49. "Heinz EZ Squirt™ Hits Store Shelves; Industry Watches Unusual Food Phenomenon Unfold," *PR Newswire,* October 17, 2000, 1.

50. Stephanie Thompson, "LifeSavers Effort Gets Personality," *Advertising Age,* January 21, 2002, 42. Also see Lawrence L. Garber, Jr., Eva M. Hyatt, and Richard G. Starr, Jr., "The Effects of Food Color on Perceived Flavor," *Journal of Marketing Theory and Practice,* Fall 2000, 59–72.

51. Thomas J. Madden, Kelly Hewett, and Martin S. Roth, "Managing Images in Different Cultures: A Cross-National Study of Color Meanings and Preferences," *Journal of International Marketing,* 8, no. 4, 2000, 90–107.

52. Kiran Karande, George M. Zinkhan, and Alyssa Baird Lum, "Brand Personality and Self Concept: A Replication and Extension," *AMA Summer 1997 Conference,* 165–171.

53. Hazel Markus and Paula Nurius, "Possible Selves," *American Psychologist* (1986), 954–969.

54. For a detailed discussion of self-images and congruence, see M. Joseph Sirgy, "Self-Concept in Consumer Behavior: A Critical Review," *Journal of Consumer Research,* 9, December 1992, 287–300; C. B. Claiborne and M. Joseph Sirgy, "Self-Image Congruence as a Model of Consumer Attitude Formation and Behavior: A Conceptual Review and Guide for Future Research," in *Developments in Marketing Science,* 13, ed. B. J. Dunlap (Cullowhee, NC: Academy of Marketing Science, 1990), 1–7; and J. S. Johar and M. Joseph Sirgy, "Value-Expressive versus Utilitarian Advertising Appeals: When and Why to Use Which Appeal," *Journal of Advertising,* 20, September 1991, 23–33.

55. "Sex Appeal," *Brandweek,* April 20, 1998, 26.

56. Susan Fournier, "Consumers and Their Brands: Developing Relationship Theory in Consumer Research," *Journal of Consumer Research,* 24, March 1998; and Kimberly J. Dodson, "Peak Experiences and Mountain Biking: Incorporating the Bike in the Extended Self," in *Advances in Consumer Research,* incomplete vol. 23, eds. Kim P. Cofman and John G. Lynch, Jr. (Provo, UT: Association for Consumer Research 1996), 317–322.

57. Abhilasha Mehta, "Using Self-Concept to Assess Advertising Effectiveness," *Journal of Advertising Research,* February 1999, 81–89.

58. Marlene M. Moretti and E. Tory Higgens, "Internal Representations of Others in Self-Regulation: A New Look at a Classic Issue," *Social Cognition,* 17, no. 2, 1999, 186–208.

59. Robert Underwood, Edward Bond, and Robert Baer, "Building Service Brands via Social Identity:

Lessons from the Sports Marketplace," *Journal of Marketing Theory and Practice,* Winter 2001, 1–13.

60. Russell W. Belk, "Possessions and the Extended Self," *Journal of Consumer Research,* 15, September 1988, 139–168; and Amy J. Morgan, "The Evolving Self in Consumer Behavior: Exploring Possible Selves," in *Advances in Consumer Research,* 20, eds. Leigh McAlister and Michael L. Rothschild (Provo, UT: Association for Consumer Research, 1992), 429–432.

61. Richard G. Netemeyer, Scot Burton, and Donald R. Lichtenstein, "Trait Aspects of Vanity: Measurement and Relevance to Consumer Behavior," *Journal of Consumer Research,* 21, March 1995, 613.

62. Jennifer L. Aaker, "The Malleable Self: The Role of Self-Expression in Persuasion," *Journal of Marketing Research,* XXXVI, February 1999, 45–57.

63. "Finding Out About Yourself Has Never Been This Fun! Emode's New Ultimate Personalty Test Connects People Online," *PR Newswire,* October 24, 2000, 1.

6

Consumer Perception

In 1967, Gablinger's beer was introduced as a "low-calorie" beer. It was promoted as a diet beer with the proposition that heavy beer drinkers (who buy most of the beer sold) would gain less weight drinking this product than they would drinking regular beer. The product failed. Five years later, Miller Lite was introduced as "less filling" under the slogan "everything you want in a beer . . . and less." The product was a great success and paved the way for many other brands of light beer.[1] Miller Lite succeeded because the company's promotion suggested beer drinkers could drink more beer than they already did without feeling full. Gablinger's failed because it told beer drinkers that they would gain less weight while drinking beer (though heavy beer drinkers are usually not concerned with their weight). In reality, in terms of physical product attributes, Gablinger's and Miller Lite were practically identical. It's how the two offerings were perceived by the target audience—how they were "positioned"—that made the difference. Whereas Gablinger's offered consumers a product *attribute* (i.e., less calories), Miller Lite offered them a product *benefit*—a less filling beer that allowed them to drink more beer.

Individuals act and react on the basis of their perceptions, not on the basis of objective reality. For each individual, *reality* is a totally personal phenomenon, based on that person's needs, wants, values, and personal experiences. Thus, to the marketer, consumers' perceptions are much more important than their knowledge of objective reality. For if one thinks about it, it's not what actually is so, but what consumers *think* is so, that affects their actions, their buying habits, their leisure habits, and so forth. And, because individuals make decisions and take actions based on what they perceive to be reality, it is important that marketers understand the whole notion of perception and its related concepts to more readily determine what factors influence consumers to buy. Before the introduction of low-calorie beer, consumers had no preconceived view of the product. Because Miller understood the behavior of beer drinkers, it provided the company with a way to interpret the new offering in a manner congruent with their needs, which Gablinger's failed to do earlier for the same product.

This chapter examines the psychological and physiological bases of human perception and discusses the principles that influence our perception and interpretation of the world we see. Knowledge of these principles enables astute marketers to develop advertisements that have a better-than-average chance of being seen and remembered by their target consumers.

Elements of Perception

Perception is defined as *the process by which an individual selects, organizes, and interprets stimuli into a meaningful and coherent picture of the world.* It can be described as "how we see the world around us." Two individuals may be exposed to the same stimuli under the same apparent conditions, but how each person recognizes, selects, organizes, and interprets these stimuli is a highly individual process based on each person's own needs, values, and expectations. The influence that each of these variables has on the perceptual process and its relevance to marketing will be explored later in the chapter. First, however, we will examine some of the basic concepts that underlie the perceptual process. These will be discussed within the framework of consumer behavior.

SENSATION

Sensation is the immediate and direct response of the sensory organs to stimuli. A *stimulus* is any unit of input to any of the senses. Examples of stimuli (i.e., sensory input) include products, packages, brand names, advertisements, and commercials. **Sensory receptors** are the human organs (the eyes, ears, nose, mouth, and skin) that receive sensory inputs. Their sensory functions are to see, hear, smell, taste, and feel. All of these functions are called into play, either singly or in combination, in the evaluation and use of most consumer products. Human sensitivity refers to the experience of sensation. Sensitivity to stimuli varies with the quality of an individual's sensory receptors (e.g., eyesight or hearing) and the amount (or *intensity*) of the stimuli to which he or she is exposed. For example, a blind person may have a more highly developed sense of hearing than the average sighted person and may be able to hear sounds that the average person cannot.

Sensation itself depends on energy change within the environment where the perception occurs (i.e., on differentiation of input). A perfectly bland or unchanging environment, regardless of the strength of the sensory input, provides little or no sensation at all. Thus, a person who lives on a busy street in midtown Manhattan would probably receive little or no sensation from the inputs of such noisy stimuli as horns honking, tires screeching, and fire engines clanging, because such sounds are so commonplace in New York City. In situations in which there is a great deal of sensory input, the senses do not detect small changes or differences in input. Thus, one honking horn more or less would never be noticed on a street with heavy traffic.

As sensory input *decreases,* however, our ability to detect changes in input or intensity *increases,* to the point that we attain maximum sensitivity under conditions of minimal stimulation. This accounts for the statement, "It was so quiet I could hear a pin drop." The ability of the human organism to accommodate itself to varying levels of sensitivity as external conditions vary not only provides more sensitivity when it is needed but also serves to protect us from damaging, disruptive, or irrelevant bombardment when the input level is high.

THE ABSOLUTE THRESHOLD

The lowest level at which an individual can experience a sensation is called the **absolute threshold.** The point at which a person can detect a difference between "something" and "nothing" is that person's absolute threshold for that stimulus. To illustrate, the distance at which a driver can note a specific billboard on a highway is that individual's absolute threshold. Two people riding together may first spot the billboard at different times (i.e., at different distances); thus, they appear to have different absolute thresholds. Under conditions of constant stimulation, such as driving through a "corridor" of billboards, the absolute threshold increases (i.e., the senses tend to become increasingly dulled). After an hour of driving through billboards, it is doubtful that any one billboard will make an impression. Hence, we often speak of "getting used to" a hot bath, a cold shower, or the bright sun. As our exposure to the stimulus increases, we notice it less. In the field of perception, the term *adaptation* refers specifically to "getting used to" certain sensations; that is, becoming accommodated to a certain level of stimulation.

Sensory adaptation is a problem that concerns many national advertisers, which is why they try to change their advertising campaigns regularly. They are concerned that consumers will get so used to their current print ads and TV commercials that they will no longer "see" them; that is, the ads will no longer provide sufficient sensory input to be noted.

In an effort to cut through the advertising clutter and ensure that consumers note their ads, some marketers try to *increase* sensory input. For example, Apple Computer once bought all the advertising space in an issue of *Newsweek* magazine to ensure that readers would note its ads. From time to time, various advertisers have taken all of the bus cards on certain bus routes to advertise their products, ensuring that wherever a rider sits, he or she will be exposed to the ad. Other advertisers try to attract attention by *decreasing* sensory input. For example, some print ads include a lot of empty space in order to accentuate the brand name or product illustration, and some TV ads use silence, the absence of audio sound, to generate attention. Figure 6-1 depicts the use of increased sensory input to support the product's advertising claim.

Some marketers seek unusual or technological media in which to place their advertisements in an effort to gain attention. Examples of such media include small monitors attached to shopping carts that feature actual brands in TV shows and in movies, individual TV screens (placed in the back of the seat ahead) on airplanes, and monitors integrated into the above-the-door floor indicators on elevators. Fragrance marketers often include fragrance samples in their direct-mail and magazine advertisements through sealed perfume inserts. Researchers have reported that the use of an ambient scent in a retail environment enhances the shopping experience for consumers and makes the time they spend examining merchandise, waiting in line, and waiting for help seem shorter than it actually is.[2] Some marketers have invested in the development of specially engineered scents to enhance their products and entice consumers to buy. Package designers try to determine consumers' absolute thresholds to make sure that their new-product designs will stand out from competitors' packages on retailers' shelves.

THE DIFFERENTIAL THRESHOLD

The minimal difference that can be detected between two similar stimuli is called the **differential threshold,** or the **just noticeable difference** (the j.n.d.). A nineteenth-century German scientist named Ernst Weber discovered that the j.n.d. between two stimuli was not an absolute amount, but an amount relative to the intensity of the first stimulus. **Weber's law,** as it has come to be known, states that the stronger the initial stimulus, the greater the additional intensity needed for the second stimulus to be perceived as different. For example, if the price of a large container of premium, freshly squeezed orange juice is $5.50, most consumers will probably not notice an increase of 25 cents (i.e., the increment would fall below the j.n.d.), and it may take an increase of 50 cents or more before a differential in price would be noticed. However, a similar 25-cent increase in the price of gasoline would be noticed very quickly by consumers because it is a significant percentage of the initial (base) cost of the gasoline.

According to Weber's law, an additional level of stimulus equivalent to the j.n.d. must be added for the majority of people to perceive a difference between the resulting stimulus and the initial stimulus. Let us say that Goddard's, a 130-year-old manufacturer of fine polishes, wants to improve its silver polish sufficiently to claim that it retards tarnish longer than the leading competitive brand. In a series of experiments, the company determines that the j.n.d. for its present polish (which now gives a shine that lasts about 20 days) is 5 days, or one-fourth longer. That means that the shine given by the improved silver polish must last at least 25 days (or one-fourth) longer if the new polish is to be perceived by the majority of users as, in fact, improved. By finding this j.n.d. of 5 days, the company has isolated the minimum amount of time necessary to make its claim of "lasts longer" believable to

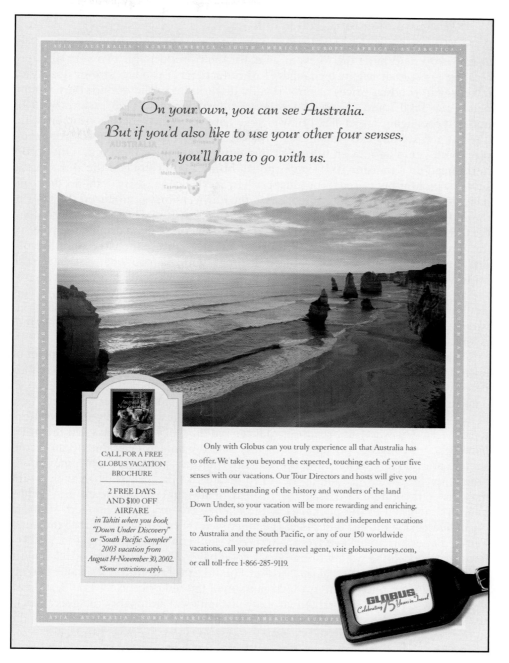

FIGURE 6-1

Increased Sensory Input
Courtesy of Globus.

the majority of consumers. If it had decided to make the polish effective for 23 days (just 3 extra days of product life), its claim of "lasts longer" would not be perceived as true by most consumers and, from the marketer's point of view, would be "wasted." On the other hand, if the company had decided to make the silver polish effective for 40 days, it would have sacrificed a good deal of repeat purchase frequency. Making the product improvement just equal to the j.n.d. thus becomes the most efficient decision that management can make.

Marketing Applications of the J.N.D.

Weber's law has important applications in marketing. Manufacturers and marketers endeavor to determine the relevant j.n.d. for their products for two very different reasons: (1) so that negative changes (e.g., reductions in product size or quality, or increases in product price) are not readily discernible to the public (they remain below the j.n.d.) and (2) so that product improvements (such as improved or updated packaging, larger size, or lower price) are very apparent to consumers without being wastefully extravagant (i.e., they are at or just above the j.n.d.). For example, some years ago, in an apparent misunderstanding of the j.n.d., Goddard's introduced an extension of its silver polish brand that prolonged the shine of the silver by months but raised its product price by merely pennies. By doing so, the company decreased its sales revenue because the new version cannibalized the sales of the old product and, at the same time, was purchased much less frequently than the old version. One marketing expert advised the company to double the price of the new product rather than make it just slightly more expensive than the old one.[3] However, for a nondurable consumer good, a product that has been improved dramatically but is doubled in price is inconsistent with the concept of the j.n.d. A better strategy would have been to introduce several successive versions of the polish; each version with a shine that lasts longer than the previous version (and at or above the j.n.d.) and offered at a higher price (but a price that is lower than the j.n.d.).

When it comes to product improvements, marketers very much want to meet or exceed the consumer's differential threshold; that is, they want consumers to readily perceive any improvements made in the original product. Marketers use the j.n.d. to determine the amount of improvement they should make in their products. Less than the j.n.d. is wasted effort because the improvement will not be perceived; more than the j.n.d. is wasteful because it reduces the level of repeat sales. On the other hand, when it comes to price increases, less than the j.n.d. is desirable because consumers are unlikely to notice it. Since many routinely purchased consumer goods are rather inexpensive, companies are reluctant to raise prices when their profit margins on these items are declining. Instead, many marketers decrease the product *quantity* included in the packages, while leaving the prices unchanged—thus, in effect, increasing the per unit price. The manufacturer of Huggies reduced the number of diapers in a package from 240 to 228 (and continued pricing it at $31.99); PepsiCo reduced the weight of one snack food bag from 14.5 ounces to 13.5 ounces (and maintained the price at $3.29), and Poland Spring reduced its water-cooler-sized bottle from 6 to 5 gallons (and maintained the old price at $9.25).[4] The packages for these products remained virtually unchanged. Presumably, the decreases in the number of items or weight of these products reflect j.n.d.-focused research; the reductions in quantity were below most consumers' j.n.d. for these products.

Marketers often want to update their existing package designs without losing the ready recognition of consumers who have been exposed to years of cumulative advertising impact. In such cases, they usually make a number of small changes, each carefully designed to fall below the j.n.d., so that consumers will perceive minimal difference between succeeding versions. For example, Betty Crocker, the General Mills symbol, has been updated seven times from 1936 to 1996 (see Figure 6-2).

When Lexmark International Inc. bought the office supplies and equipment line from IBM in March 1991, it agreed to relinquish the IBM name by 1996. Recognizing the need to build a brand image for Lexmark while moving away from the well-known IBM name, Lexmark officials conducted a four-stage campaign for

FIGURE 6-2

Sequential Changes in
the Betty Crocker
Symbol Fall Below the
j.n.d.

phasing in the Lexmark name on products. As Figure 6-3 indicates, Stage 1 carried only the IBM name, Stage 2 featured the IBM name and downplayed Lexmark, Stage 3 featured the Lexmark name and downplayed IBM, and Stage 4 features only the Lexmark name. Figure 6-4 shows a Lexmark ad with the transition complete.

Another interesting example is Ivory soap, which was introduced in 1879. The subtle packaging changes Ivory introduced over the years were each small enough to avoid notice, but the package managed to retain a contemporary look. The latest Ivory package is considerably different from the original, but the changes made at each step of the way were designed so skillfully that the transition has been hardly noticeable to consumers.

SUBLIMINAL PERCEPTION

In Chapter 4 we spoke of people being *motivated* below their level of conscious awareness. People are also *stimulated* below their level of conscious awareness; that is, they can perceive stimuli without being consciously aware that they are doing so. Stimuli that are too weak or too brief to be consciously seen or heard may nevertheless be strong enough to be perceived by one or more receptor cells. This process is called **subliminal perception** because the stimulus is beneath the threshold, or "limen," of conscious awareness, though obviously not beneath the absolute threshold of the receptors involved. (Perception of stimuli that are above the level of conscious awareness technically is called *supraliminal perception,* though it is usually referred to simply as perception.)

Since the 1950s, there have been sporadic reports of marketers using subliminal messages in their efforts to influence consumption behavior. At times, it has been difficult to separate truth from fiction regarding such alleged manipulations. When some of the subliminal methods were tested methodically using scientific research procedures, the research results did not support the notion that subliminal messages can persuade

FIGURE 6-3

Gradual Changes in Brand Name Below the j.n.d.

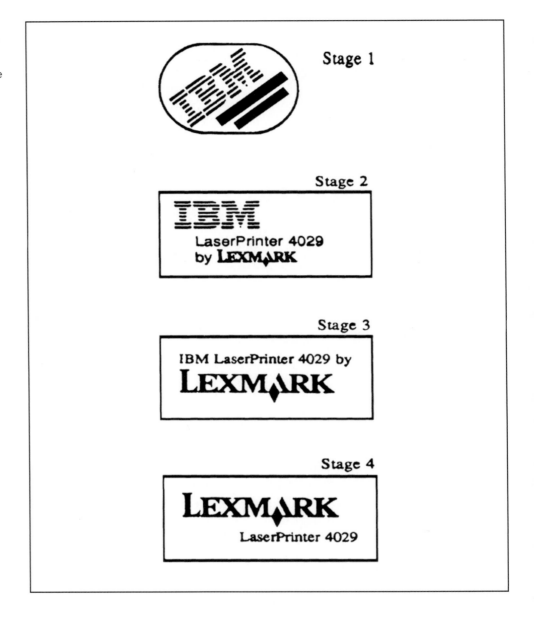

consumers to act in a given manner. The most widely publicized uses (or alleged uses) of subliminal messages and the corresponding research findings are described in Table 6-1.

Evaluating the Effectiveness of Subliminal Persuasion

Despite the many studies undertaken by academicians and researchers since the 1950s, there is no evidence that subliminal advertising persuades people to buy goods or services. A review of the literature indicates that subliminal perception research has been based on two theoretical approaches. According to the first theory, constant repetition of very weak (i.e., subthreshold) stimuli has an incremental effect that enables such stimuli to build response strength over many presentations. This would be the operative theory when weak stimuli are flashed repeatedly on a movie screen or played on a soundtrack or audiocassette. The second approach is based on the theory that subliminal sexual stimuli arouse unconscious sexual moti-

FIGURE 6-4

Transition Complete:
Lexmark Stands Alone

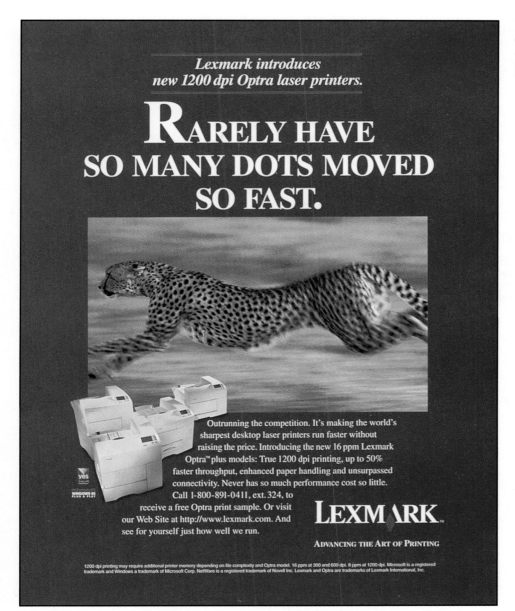

vations. This is the theory behind the use of sexual embeds in print advertising. But no studies have yet indicated that either of these theoretical approaches have been effectively used by advertisers to increase sales. However, there is some indication that subliminal advertising may provide new opportunities for modifying antisocial behavior through public awareness campaigns that call for individuals to make generalized responses to suggestions that enhance their personal performance or improve their attitudes.[5] There is also some (though not definitive) evidence that subliminal methods can indirectly influence attitudes and feelings toward brands.[6]

In summary, although there is some evidence that subliminal stimuli may influence affective reactions, there is no evidence that subliminal stimulation can influence consumption motives or actions. There continues to be a big gap between perception and persuasion. A recent review of the evidence on subliminal persuasion indicates

TABLE 6-1	Subliminal Perception: History and Research Findings

A DRIVE-IN MOVIE THEATER IN NEW JERSEY (1957)

The effectiveness of so-called subliminal advertising was reportedly tested at a drive-in movie in New Jersey in 1957, where the words "Eat popcorn" and "Drink Coca-Cola" were flashed on the screen during the movie. Exposure times were so short that viewers were unaware of seeing a message. It was reported that during the six-week test period, popcorn sales increased 58 percent and Coca-Cola sales increased 18 percent.[a] The public frenzy was further fueled by the publication of a book on motivational research entitled *The Hidden Persuaders,* which examined and further pursued the same kind of unconscious motives that were outlined in Dichter's research (see Chapter 4).[b] A series of highly imaginative laboratory experiments gave some support to the notion that individuals could perceive below the level of their conscious awareness but found no evidence that they could be persuaded to act in response to such subliminal stimulation. For example, one researcher found that although the simple subliminal stimulus COKE served to arouse thirst in subjects, the subliminal command DRINK COKE did not have a greater effect, nor did it have any behavioral consequences.[c]

THE PUBLICATION OF *SUBLIMINAL SEDUCTION* (1974)

Public indignation at the possibility of subliminal manipulation surfaced again in 1974 following the publication of a book entitled *Subliminal Seduction.*[d] The book charged that advertisers were using subliminal embeds in their print ads to persuade consumers to buy their advertised brands. It was alleged, for example, that liquor advertisers were trying to increase the subconscious appeal of their products by embedding sexually suggestive symbols in ice cubes floating in a pictured drink. As consumers increasingly complained about alleged subliminal messages on TV, even the Federal Communications Commission (FCC) studied the subject.[a] Research findings indicate that sexually oriented embeds do not influence consumer preferences.[e] Several experiments into the effectiveness of subliminal messages in television commercials concluded that it would be very difficult to use the technique on television, but that even if subliminal messages were to have "some influence," they would be much less effective than overt advertising messages and would likely interfere with consumers' memory for brand names.[f]

THE ALLEGATIONS AGAINST DISNEY (1990s)

There have been a number of allegations made about movies and videos produced by the Walt Disney Studios. For example:

1. *Aladdin:* Allegations that the hero whispers "good teenagers, take off your clothes" in a sub-audible voice.
2. *The Little Mermaid:* Allegations that one of the castle's spires on the video's cover resembles a penis; also that the minister officiating at a wedding ceremony in the movie displays an erection.
3. *The Lion King:* The letters "S-E-X" are formed in a cloud of dust.
4. *The Rescuers:* A very speedy image of a topless female appears in one scene.

As a result of these allegations, which Disney denied, Disney's products were boycotted by some consumer groups. However, it was later discovered that the nude image that appeared in the movie *The Rescuers* was apparently inserted as a prank in the movie's master in 1997, and Disney recalled copies of the movie in 1999.[g]

Sources: [a] sbe.d.umn.edu/subliminal/index.html. [b] Vance Packard, *The Hidden Persuaders* (New York: Pocket Books, 1957). [c] Sharon E. Beatty and Del I. Hawkins, "Subliminal Stimulation: Some New Data and Interpretation," *Journal of Advertising*, 18, 1989, 4–8. [d] Wilson Bryan Key, *Subliminal Seduction* (New York: New American Library, 1973). [e] Myron Gable, Henry T. Wilkens, Lynn Harris, and Richard Feinberg, "An Evaluation of Subliminally Embedded Sexual Stimuli in Graphics," *Journal of Advertising*, 16, 1, 1987, 26–31. [f] Kirk H. Smith and Martha Rogers, "Effectiveness of Subliminal Messages in Television Commercials: Two Experiments," *Journal of Applied Psychology*, 19, 6, 1994, 866–874. [g] Lisa Bannon, "How a Rumor Spread About Subliminal Sex in Disney's *Aladdin*," *Wall Street Journal*, October 24, 1995, A-1; Bruce Orwall, "Disney Recalls *The Rescuers* Video Containing Images of Topless Woman," *Wall Street Journal Interactive Edition*, January 11, 1999.

that the only way for subliminal techniques to have a significant persuasive effect would be through long-term repeated exposure under a limited set of circumstances, which would not be economically feasible or practical within an advertising context.[7]

As to sexual embeds, most researchers are of the opinion that "what you see is what you get"; that is, a vivid imagination can see whatever it wants to see in just about any situation. And that pretty much sums up the whole notion of perception: Individuals see what they want to see (e.g., what they are motivated to see) and what they expect to see. Several studies concerned with public beliefs about subliminal

PEOPLE HAVE BEEN TRYING TO FIND THE BREASTS IN THESE ICE CUBES SINCE 1957.

The advertising industry is sometimes charged with sneaking seductive little pictures into ads.

Supposedly, these pictures can get you to buy a product without your even seeing them.

Consider the photograph above. According to some people, there's a pair of female breasts hidden in the patterns of light refracted by the ice cubes.

Well, if you really searched you probably *could* see the breasts. For that matter, you could also see Millard Fillmore, a stuffed pork chop and a 1946 Dodge.

The point is that so-called "subliminal advertising" simply doesn't exist. Overactive imaginations, however, most certainly do.

So if anyone claims to see breasts in that drink up there, they aren't in the ice cubes.

They're in the eye of the beholder.

ADVERTISING
ANOTHER WORD FOR FREEDOM OF CHOICE.
American Association of Advertising Agencies

advertising found that a large percentage of Americans know what subliminal advertising is, they believe it is used by advertisers, and that it is effective in persuading consumers to buy.[8] To correct any misperceptions among the public that subliminal advertising does, in fact, exist, the advertising community occasionally sponsors ads like the one depicted in Figure 6-5, which ridicule the notion that subliminal techniques are effective or that they are used in advertising applications.

The Federal Communications Commission has adopted the position that subliminal messages, whether effective or not, are intended to deceive consumers and, therefore, contradict the public interest. However, because of the absence of any evidence that subliminal persuasion really works, no state or federal laws have been enacted to restrict the use of subliminal advertising.

Dynamics of Perception

The preceding section explained how the individual receives sensations from stimuli in the outside environment and how the human organism adapts to the level and intensity of sensory input. We now come to one of the major principles of perception: Raw sensory input by itself does not produce or explain the coherent picture of the world that most adults possess. Indeed, the study of perception is largely the study of what we subconsciously add to or subtract from raw sensory inputs to produce our own private picture of the world.

Human beings are constantly bombarded with stimuli during every minute and every hour of every day. The sensory world is made up of an almost infinite number of discrete sensations that are constantly and subtly changing. According to the principles of sensation, intensive stimulation "bounces off" most individuals, who subconsciously block (i.e., adapt to) the receipt of a heavy bombardment of stimuli. Otherwise, the billions of different stimuli to which we are constantly exposed might serve to confuse us totally and keep us perpetually disoriented in a constantly changing environment. However, neither of these consequences tends to occur, because perception is not a function of sensory input alone. Rather, perception is the result of two different kinds of inputs that interact to form the personal pictures—the perceptions—that each individual experiences.

One type of input is *physical stimuli* from the outside environment; the other type of input is provided by individuals themselves in the form of certain predispositions (expectations, motives, and learning) based on *previous experience*. The combination of these two very different kinds of inputs produces for each of us a very private, very personal picture of the world. Because each person is a unique individual, with unique experiences, needs, wants, desires, and expectations, it follows that each individual's perceptions are also unique. This explains why no two people see the world in precisely the same way.

Individuals are very selective as to which stimuli they "recognize"; they subconsciously organize the stimuli they do recognize according to widely held psychological principles, and they interpret such stimuli (they give meaning to them) subjectively in accordance with their personal needs, expectations, and experiences. Let us examine in some detail each of these three aspects of perception: the **selection, organization,** and **interpretation of stimuli.**

PERCEPTUAL SELECTION

Consumers subconsciously exercise a great deal of selectivity as to which aspects of the environment (which stimuli) they perceive. An individual may look at some things, ignore others, and turn away from still others. In actuality, people receive (i.e., perceive) only a small fraction of the stimuli to which they are exposed. Consider, for example, a woman in a supermarket. She may be exposed to over 20,000 products of different colors, sizes, and shapes; to perhaps 100 people (looking, walking, searching, talking); to smells (from fruit, meat, disinfectant, people); to sounds within the store (cash registers ringing, shopping carts rolling, air conditioners humming, and clerks sweeping, mopping aisles, stocking shelves); and to sounds from outside the store (planes passing, cars honking, tires screeching, children shouting, car doors slamming). Yet she manages on a regular basis to visit her local supermarket, select the items she needs, pay for them, and leave, all within a relatively brief period of time, without losing her sanity or her personal orientation to the world around her. This is because she exercises *selectivity* in perception.

Which stimuli get selected depends on two major factors in addition to the nature of the stimulus itself: (1) consumers' *previous experience* as it affects their *expectations* (what they are prepared, or "set," to see) and (2) their *motives* at the time (their needs, desires, interests, and so on). Each of these factors can serve to increase or decrease the probability that a stimulus will be perceived.

Nature of the Stimulus

Marketing stimuli include an enormous number of variables that affect the consumer's perception, such as the *nature* of the product, its *physical attributes,* the *package* design, the *brand* name, the *advertisements* and commercials (including copy claims, choice and sex of model, positioning of model, size of ad, typography), the *position* of a print ad or a commercial, and the *editorial* environment.

In general, *contrast* is one of the most attention-compelling attributes of a stimulus. Advertisers often use extreme attention-getting devices to achieve maximum contrast and, thus, penetrate the consumer's perceptual "screen." For example, a number of magazines and newspapers carry ads that readers can unfold to reveal oversized, posterlike advertisements for products ranging from cosmetics to automobiles, because of the "stopping power" of giant ads among more traditional sizes. However, advertising does not have to be unique to achieve a high degree of differentiation; it simply has to contrast with the environment in which it is run. The use of a dramatic image of the product against a white background with little copy in a print advertisement, the absence of sound in a commercial's opening scene, a 60-second commercial within a string of 20-second spots—all offer sufficient contrast from their environments to achieve differentiation and merit the consumer's attention. Figure 6-6 illustrates the attention-getting nature of a dramatic image of a product in an advertisement. In an effort to achieve contrast, advertisers are also using splashes of color in black-and-white print ads to highlight the advertised product.

With respect to packaging, astute marketers usually try to differentiate their packages to ensure rapid consumer perception. Since the average package on the supermarket shelf has about 1/10th of a second to make an impression on the consumer, it is important that every aspect of the package—the name, shape, color, label, and copy—provide sufficient sensory stimulation to be noted and remembered.

Sometimes advertisers capitalize on the lack of contrast (e.g., by positioning a TV commercial so close to the storyline of a program that viewers are unaware they are watching an advertisement until they are well into it). In the case of children's programming, the Federal Trade Commission has strictly limited the use of this technique. TV stars or cartoon characters are prohibited from promoting products during the children's shows in which they appear. In print advertising, some advertisers run print ads (called *advertorials*) that closely resemble editorial matter, making it increasingly difficult for readers to tell them apart. Also, advertisers are producing 30-minute commercials (called *infomercials*) that appear to the average viewer as documentaries and, thus, command more attentive viewing than obvious commercials would receive.

Expectations

People usually see what they expect to see, and what they expect to see is usually based on familiarity, previous experience, or preconditioned set (**expectations**). In a marketing context, people tend to perceive products and product attributes according to their own expectations. A student who has been told by his friends that a particular professor is

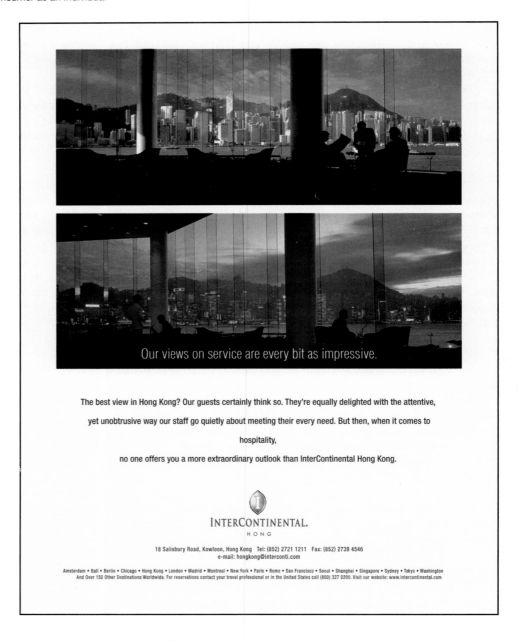

interesting and dynamic will probably perceive the professor in that manner when the class begins; a teenager who attends a horror movie that has been billed as terrifying will probably find it so. On the other hand, stimuli that conflict sharply with expectations often receive more attention than those that conform to expectations (see Figure 6-7).

For years, certain advertisers have used blatant sexuality in advertisements for products to which sex was not relevant, in the belief that such advertisements would attract a high degree of attention. However, ads with irrelevant sexuality often defeat the marketer's objectives because readers tend to remember the sexual aspects of the ad (e.g., the innuendo or the model), not the product or brand advertised. Nevertheless, some advertisers continue to use erotic appeals in promoting a wide variety of products, from office furniture to jeans. (The use of sex in advertising is discussed in Chapter 9.)

FIGURE 6-7

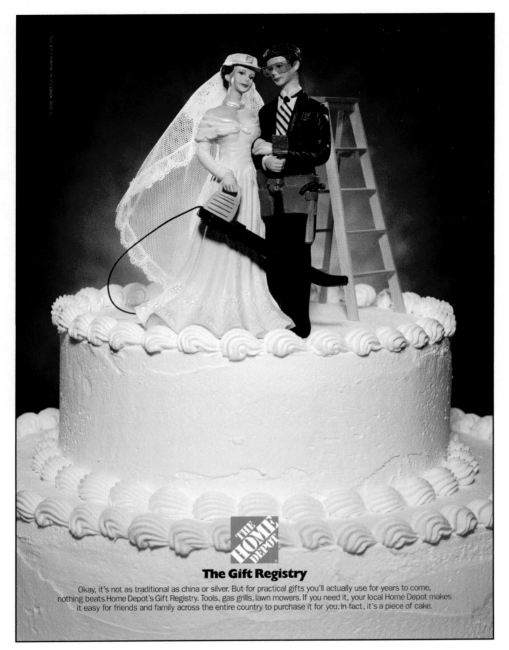

The Unexpected
Attracts Attention
Courtesy of The Home Depot.

Motives

People tend to perceive the things they need or want: The stronger the need, the greater the tendency to ignore unrelated stimuli in the environment. A student who is looking for a new cell phone provider is more likely to notice and read carefully ads for deals and special offers regarding such services than his roommate, who may be satisfied with his present cellular service. In general, there is a heightened awareness of stimuli that are relevant to one's needs and interests and a decreased awareness of stimuli that are irrelevant to those needs. An individual's perceptual process simply attunes itself more closely to those elements in the environment that are important to that person. Someone who is hungry is more likely to notice ads for food; a sexually repressed person may perceive sexual symbolism where none exists.

Marketing managers recognize the efficiency of targeting their products to the perceived needs of consumers. For example, a marketer can determine through marketing research what consumers consider to be the ideal attributes of the product category or what consumers perceive their needs to be in relation to the product category. The marketer can then segment the market on the basis of those needs and vary the product advertising so that consumers in each segment will perceive the product as meeting their own special needs, wants, and interests.

Selective Perception

As the preceding discussion illustrates, the consumer's "selection" of stimuli from the environment is based on the interaction of expectations and motives with the stimulus itself. These factors give rise to four important concepts concerning perception.

Selective Exposure   Consumers actively seek out messages that they find pleasant or with which they are sympathetic, and they actively avoid painful or threatening ones. They also selectively expose themselves to advertisements that reassure them of the wisdom of their purchase decisions.

Selective Attention   Consumers exercise a great deal of selectivity in terms of the attention they give to commercial stimuli. They have a heightened awareness of stimuli that meet their needs or interests and minimal awareness of stimuli irrelevant to their needs. Thus, consumers are likely to note ads for products that would satisfy their needs and disregard those in which they have no interest. People also vary in terms of the kinds of information in which they are interested and the form of message and type of medium they prefer. Some people are more interested in price, some in appearance, and some in social acceptability. Some people like complex, sophisticated messages; others like simple graphics.

Perceptual Defense   Consumers subconsciously screen out stimuli that they find psychologically threatening, even though exposure has already taken place. Thus, threatening or otherwise damaging stimuli are less likely to be consciously perceived than are neutral stimuli at the same level of exposure. Furthermore, individuals sometimes unconsciously distort information that is not consistent with their needs, values, and beliefs. One way to combat *perceptual defense* is to vary and increase the amount of sensory input. For example, since most smokers no longer pay attention to the written warning labels on cigarette packs, Canada now requires tobacco firms to feature graphic health warnings on cigarette packs; one such warning shows a damaged brain and warns about strokes, and another shows a limp cigarette and states that tobacco can cause impotence. [9]

Perceptual Blocking   Consumers protect themselves from being bombarded with stimuli by simply "tuning out"—blocking such stimuli from conscious awareness. They do so out of self-protection because of the visually overwhelming nature of the world in which we live. The popularity of such devices as *TiVo* and *ReplayTV,* which enable viewers to skip over TV commercials with great ease, is, in part, a result of *perceptual blocking.*

PERCEPTUAL ORGANIZATION

People do not experience the numerous stimuli they select from the environment as separate and discrete sensations; rather, they tend to organize them into groups and perceive them as unified wholes. Thus, the perceived characteristics of even the simplest stimulus are viewed as a function of the whole to which the stimulus appears to belong. This method of perceptual organization simplifies life considerably for the individual.

The specific principles underlying perceptual organization are often referred to by the name given the school of psychology that first developed it: **Gestalt psychology.** (*Gestalt,* in German, means pattern or configuration.) Three of the most basic principles of perceptual organization are *figure and ground, grouping,* and *closure.*

Figure and Ground

As was noted earlier, stimuli that contrast with their environment are more likely to be noticed. A sound must be louder or softer, a color brighter or paler. The simplest visual illustration consists of a figure on a ground (i.e., background). The figure is perceived more clearly because, in contrast to its ground, it appears to be well defined, solid, and in the forefront. The ground is usually perceived as indefinite, hazy, and continuous. The common line that separates the figure and the ground is generally attributed to the figure rather than to the ground, which helps give the figure greater definition. Consider the stimulus of music. People can either "bathe" in music or listen to music. In the first case, music is simply background to other activities; in the second, it is figure. Figure is more clearly perceived because it appears to be dominant; in contrast, ground appears to be subordinate and, therefore, less important.

People have a tendency to organize their perceptions into **figure-and-ground** relationships. How a figure–ground pattern is perceived can be influenced by prior pleasant or painful associations with one or the other element in isolation. For example, a short time following the destruction of the World Trade Center on September 11, 2001 by airplanes hijacked by terrorists, a professor in New Jersey came across an ad for Lufthansa (Germany's national airline) that featured a flying jet, photographed from the ground up, between two glass high-rise buildings. Rather than focusing on the brand and the jet (i.e., the "figure"), all the viewer could think about was the two tall glass towers in the background (i.e., the "ground"), and the possibility of the jet crashing into them. When the professor presented the ad to his students, many expressed the same thoughts. Clearly, this figure–ground reversal was the outcome of the painful events that occurred in September 2001.

Advertisers have to plan their advertisements carefully to make sure that the stimulus they want noted is seen as figure and not as ground. The musical background must not overwhelm the jingle; the background of an advertisement must not detract from the product. Print advertisers often silhouette their products against a nondistinct background to make sure that the features they want noted are clearly perceived. We are all familiar with figure-ground patterns, such as the picture of the woman in Figure 6-8. How old would you say she is? Look again very carefully. Depending on how you perceived figure and how you perceived ground, she can be either in her early twenties or her late seventies.

Marketers sometimes run advertisements that confuse the consumer because there is no clear indication of which is figure and which is ground. Of course, in some cases, the blurring of figure and ground is deliberate. The well-known Absolut Vodka campaign, started over 25 years ago, often runs print ads in which the figure (the shape of the Absolut bottle) is poorly delineated against its ground, challenging readers to search for the bottle; the resulting audience "participation" produces more intense ad scrutiny.

Grouping

Individuals tend to group stimuli so that they form a unified picture or impression. The perception of stimuli as groups or chunks of information, rather than as discrete bits of information, facilitates their memory and recall. **Grouping** can be used

FIGURE 6-8

Figure-and-Ground
Reversal

advantageously by marketers to imply certain desired meanings in connection with their products. For example, an advertisement for tea may show a young man and woman sipping tea in a beautifully appointed room before a blazing hearth. The overall mood implied by the grouping of stimuli leads the consumer to associate the drinking of tea with romance, fine living, and winter warmth.

Most of us can remember and repeat our Social Security numbers because we automatically group them into three *"chunks,"* rather than try to remember nine separate numbers. Similarly, we recall and repeat our phone number in three segments—the area code, first three digits, and the last four digits. Also, for decades, Americans had five-digit zip codes grouped as a single chunk; as four digits are being added to our zip codes, the U.S. Postal Service faces a challenge in getting Americans to recall the extra digits and add a chunk to their recollection of zip codes.

Closure

Individuals have a need for **closure.** They express this need by organizing their perceptions so that they form a complete picture. If the pattern of stimuli to which they are exposed is incomplete, they tend to perceive it, nevertheless, as complete; that is, they consciously or subconsciously fill in the missing pieces. Thus, a circle with a section of its periphery missing is invariably perceived as a circle, not an arc.

Incomplete messages or tasks are better remembered than completed ones. One explanation for this phenomenon is that a person who hears the beginning of a message or who begins a task develops a need to complete it. If he or she is prevented from doing so, a state of tension is created that manifests itself in improved memory for the incomplete task. For example, hearing the beginning of a message leads to the need to hear the rest of it—like waiting for the second shoe to drop.

The need for closure has interesting implications for marketers. Promotional messages in which viewers are required to "fill in" information beg for completion by consumers, and the very act of completion serves to involve them more deeply in the message (see Figure 6-9). In a related vein, advertisers have discovered that they can achieve excellent results by using the soundtrack of a frequently viewed television commercial on radio. Consumers who are familiar with the TV commercial

FIGURE 6-9

Using the Need for Closure to Increase Attention

perceive the audio track alone as incomplete; in their need for completion, they mentally play back the visual content from memory.

In summary, it is clear that perceptions are not equivalent to the raw sensory input of discrete stimuli, nor to the sum total of discrete stimuli. Rather, people tend to add to or subtract from stimuli to which they are exposed on the basis of their expectations and motives, using generalized principles of organization based on Gestalt theory.

PERCEPTUAL INTERPRETATION

The preceding discussion has emphasized that perception is a personal phenomenon. People exercise selectivity as to which stimuli they perceive, and they organize these stimuli on the basis of certain psychological principles. The interpretation of stimuli is also uniquely individual, because it is based on what individuals expect to see in light of their previous experience, on the number of plausible explanations they can envision, and on their motives and interests at the time of perception.

Stimuli are often highly ambiguous. Some stimuli are weak because of such factors as poor visibility, brief exposure, high noise level, or constant fluctuation. Even stimuli that are strong tend to fluctuate dramatically because of such factors as different angles of viewing, varying distances, and changing levels of illumination. Consumers usually attribute the sensory input they receive to sources they consider most likely to have caused the specific pattern of stimuli. Past experiences and social interactions help to form certain expectations that provide categories (or alternative explanations) that individuals use in interpreting stimuli. The narrower the individual's experience, the more limited the access to alternative categories.

When stimuli are highly ambiguous, an individual will usually interpret them in such a way that they serve to fulfill personal needs, wishes, interests, and so on. It is this principle that provides the rationale for the projective tests discussed in Chapter 4. Such tests provide ambiguous stimuli (such as incomplete sentences, unclear pictures, untitled cartoons, or ink blots) to respondents who are asked to interpret them. How a person describes a vague illustration, or what meaning the individual ascribes to an ink blot, is a reflection not of the stimulus itself, but of the subject's own needs, wants, and desires. Through the interpretation of ambiguous stimuli, respondents reveal a great deal about themselves.

How close a person's interpretations are to reality, then, depends on the clarity of the stimulus, the past experiences of the perceiver, and his or her motives and interests at the time of perception.

Perceptual Distortion

Individuals are subject to a number of influences that tend to distort their perceptions; some of these are discussed next.

Physical Appearances People tend to attribute the qualities they associate with certain people to others who may resemble them, whether or not they consciously recognize the similarity. For this reason, the selection of models for print advertisements and for television commercials can be a key element in their ultimate persuasiveness. Studies have found that attractive models are more persuasive and have a more positive influence on consumer attitudes and behavior than average-looking models; attractive men are perceived as more successful businessmen than average-looking men. Some research suggests that models influence consumers perceptions of physical attractiveness, and through comparisons, their own self-perceptions.[10] Recent research indicates that merely choosing a highly attractive model may not increase message effectiveness. One study revealed that highly attractive models are perceived as having more expertise regarding enhancing products (e.g., jewelry, lipstick, perfume) but not regarding problem-solving products (e.g., products that correct beauty flaws such as acne or dandruff).[11] Therefore, advertisers must ensure that there is a rational match between the product advertised and the physical attributes of the model used to promote it.

Stereotypes Individuals tend to carry pictures in their minds of the meanings of various kinds of stimuli. These stereotypes serve as expectations of what specific situations, people, or events will be like, and they are important determinants of how such stimuli are subsequently perceived. For example, an ad for Benetton featuring two men—one black and one white—handcuffed together, which was part of the "united colors of Benetton" campaign promoting racial harmony, produced a public outcry because people perceived it as depicting a white man arresting a black man.[12] Clearly, this perception was the result of stereotypes, since there was nothing in the ad to indicate that the white person was arresting the black person rather than the other way around. The ad for Akteo watches shown in Figure 6-10 is based on the notion that a man's watch reflects his individuality.

First Impressions First impressions tend to be lasting; yet, in forming such impressions, the perceiver does not yet know which stimuli are relevant, important, or predictive of later behavior. A shampoo commercial effectively used the line, "You'll never have a second chance to make a first impression." Since first impressions are often lasting, introducing a new product before it has been perfected may prove fatal to its ultimate success; subsequent information about its advantages, even if true, will often be negated by the memory of its early performance.

Jumping to Conclusions Many people tend to jump to conclusions before examining all the relevant evidence. For example, the consumer may hear just the beginning of a commercial message and draw conclusions regarding the product or service being advertised. For this reason, some copywriters are careful to give their most persuasive arguments first. In a recent study, a series of laboratory experiments tried to determine how the shape of food packaging affected consumers' perceptions of content volume. The study found that most consumers do not read the volume information on food labels, and they purchase packages that they believe contain greater volume, whether or not this is actually so. For example, consumers perceived elongated packaging to contain more volume than round packaging.[13] The studies also found a positive correlation between perceived product volume and consumption. Thus, the products inside packages that were perceived to hold more volume when purchased were also consumed faster after the purchase. Clearly, these findings have important implications for package design, advertising, and pricing.

Halo Effect Historically, the halo effect has been used to describe situations in which the evaluation of a single object or person on a multitude of dimensions is based on the evaluation of just one or a few dimensions (e.g., a man is trustworthy, fine, and noble because he looks you in the eye when he speaks). Consumer behaviorists broaden the notion of the halo effect to include the evaluation of multiple objects (e.g., a product line) on the basis of the evaluation of just one dimension (a brand name or a spokesperson). Using this broader definition, marketers take advantage of the halo effect when they extend a brand name associated with one line of products to another. The lucrative field of *licensing* is based on the halo effect. Manufacturers and retailers hope to acquire instant recognition and status for their products by associating them with a well-known name. (Chapter 7 discusses licensing in greater detail.)

Tampering with the perceived halo effect of a product or brand can have disastrous consequences. For example, in an attempt to enhance the image of JW Marriott, the Marriott hotel chain's upscale brand, Marriott took over the Righa Royal Hotel, an upscale hotel in New York City, and renamed it the JW Marriott New York. When the new name signs went up, the company discovered that scores of regular, upscale customers who always stayed at the Righa when visiting New York City canceled their reservations because they did not want to tell colleagues to contact them at the Marriott. The company restored the Righa Hotel name, with the JW Marriott name included in smaller print.[14]

Despite the many subjective influences on perceptual interpretation, individuals usually resolve stimulus ambiguity somewhat "realistically" on the basis of their previous experiences. Only in situations of unusual or changing stimulus conditions do expectations lead to wrong interpretations.

Consumer Imagery

Consumers have a number of enduring perceptions, or images, that are particularly relevant to the study of consumer behavior. Products and brands have symbolic value for individuals, who evaluate them on the basis of their consistency (congruence) with their personal pictures of themselves. Chapter 5 discussed consumer self-images and how consumers attempt to preserve or enhance their self-images by buying products and patronizing services that they believe are congruent with their self-images and by avoiding those that are not. The following section examines consumers' perceived images of products, brands, services, prices, product quality, retail stores, and manufacturers.

PRODUCT POSITIONING

The essence of successful marketing is the image that a product has in the mind of the consumer—that is, its **positioning.** Positioning is more important to the ultimate success of a product than are its actual characteristics, although products that are poorly made will not succeed in the long run on the basis of image alone. The core of effective positioning is a unique position that the product occupies in the mind of the consumer. Most new products fail because they are perceived as "me too" offerings that do not offer potential consumers any advantages or unique benefits over competitive products.

Marketers of different brands in the same category can effectively differentiate their offerings only if they stress the *benefits* that their brands provide rather than their products' physical features. The benefits featured in a product's positioning must reflect attributes that are important to and congruent with the perceptions of the targeted consumer segment. For example, the two energy bars, NutriGrain and Balance, are probably quite similar in terms of their nutritional composition and their physical characteristics; however, each one of the two brands is clearly positioned to offer a distinct benefit. NutriGrain is positioned as an alternative to unhealthy snack foods in the morning and Balance is positioned as an energy-providing product for the late afternoon.

Positioning strategy is the essence of the marketing mix; it complements the company's definition of the competition, its segmentation strategy, and its selection of target markets. For example, in its positioning as a breakfast food NutriGrain competes with other breakfast foods. Through research, the manufacturer has determined the characteristics of persons who are concerned about their health and appearance (yet eat unhealthy breakfast foods such as donuts) and the media that they read, listen to, and watch. (The marketers of Balance, must determine the characteristics of those who need a "pick-me-up" in the late afternoon and their media habits and develop a marketing plan that reflects all these elements.)

Positioning conveys the concept, or meaning, of the product or service in terms of how it fulfills a consumer need. A good positioning strategy should have a two-pronged meaning: one that is congruent with the consumer's needs while, at the same time, featuring the brand against its competition. For example, the classic 7-Up slogan "The Un-Cola" was designed to appeal to consumers' desire for an alternative to the most popular soft drink (by using the prefix *un*), while also elevating the product by placing it in the same league with its giant competitor (by using the word *cola*). Similarly, Avis's slogan "We are number 2, we try harder" reflects America's long history of supporting the underdog and, equally important, it sets Avis above its other competitors in the car rental industry (most people know that Hertz is number 1). Also, as demonstrated by 7-Up's change in positioning strategy to "Caffeine—never had it, never will" to depict its core benefit, the same product (or service) can be positioned differently to different market segments or can be repositioned to the same audience, without being physically changed.

The result of successful positioning strategy is a distinctive brand image on which consumers rely in making product choices. A positive brand image also leads to consumer loyalty, positive beliefs about brand value, and a willingness to search for the brand. A positive brand image also promotes consumer interest in future brand promotions and *inoculates* consumers against competitors' marketing activities. Furthermore, research suggests that an advertiser's positioning strategy affects consumer beliefs about its brand's attributes and the prices consumers are willing to pay.[15]

In today's highly competitive environment, a distinctive product image is most important, but also very difficult to create and maintain. As products become more complex and the marketplace more crowded, consumers rely more on the product's image and claimed benefits than on its actual attributes in making purchase decisions. The major positioning strategies are discussed in the following five sections.

Umbrella Positioning

This strategy entails creating an overall image of the company around which a lot of products can be featured individually. This strategy is appropriate for very large corporations with diversified product lines. For example, McDonald's positioning approaches over the years include "You deserve a break today at McDonald's," "Nobody can do it like McDonald's can," and "Good times, great taste."

Positioning Against the Competition

One of the most memorable TV commercials ever made is the 1984 ad introducing Apple's Macintosh. This very somber and futuristic commercial depicted IBM, without ever naming the company, as an oppressive giant resembling "Big Brother," an evil character featured in George Orwell's classic book *1984*. In a reference to Orwell's book, the ad concludes by stating that "On January 24, Apple Computer will introduce the Macintosh. And you'll see why 1984 won't be like '1984'." Decades later, Apple still uses "Be Different," a spin-off of the 1984 theme, to position its products. Another classic example is Wendy's "Where's the beef?" that was used to differentiate the smaller food chain from much larger competitors. Visa's past slogan "We make American Express green with envy" is another good example of this strategy. A Sunkist ad featured a lemon, in the form of a salt shaker, with the caption "Salternative." The Hertz car rental company has run TV ads depicting other car rental companies as lacking in features that Hertz's outlets generally possess, such as proximity to passenger terminals at airports (e.g., "Hertz? Not exactly").

Positioning Based on a Specific Benefit

FedEx created its highly reliable service image with the slogan "When it absolutely, positively has to be there overnight." Maxwell House Coffee is "good to the last drop." Bounty is "the quicker picker upper." These are examples of slogans that smartly and precisely depict key benefits of the brands they promote and have effectively positioned these brands in the minds of consumers. There are also many examples of products that failed because they were positioned to deliver a benefit that consumers either did not want or did not believe. For example, Gillette's "For Oily Hair Only" shampoo failed because most consumers do not acknowledge that they have oily hair. Pepsi's 1992 "Pepsi Crystal" was a clear, "natural" Pepsi that took away all the qualities, including the taste, that consumers liked about Pepsi's drink.[16] Effective depictions of a core benefit often include memorable imagery (e.g., the old lady featured in Wendy's classic "Where's the beef?" ad). Figure 6-11 uses the symbolism of a widely recognized landmark, the Leaning Tower of Pisa, as a negative goal, to promote the benefits of a calcium supplement.

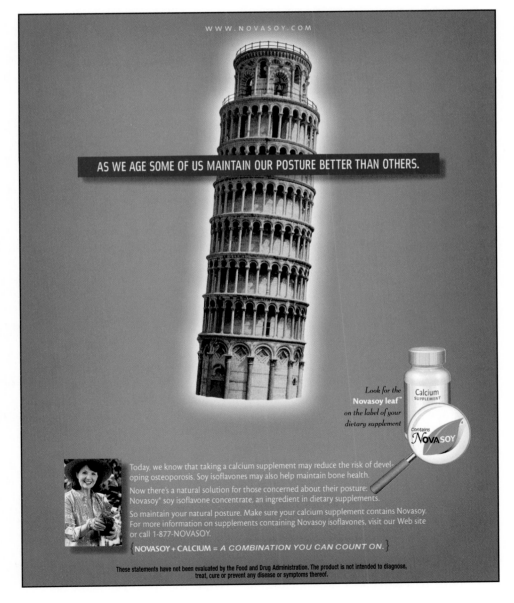

FIGURE 6-11

Using Imagery to Convey a Product Benefit
Courtesy of ADM Health.

Finding an "Unowned" Position

In highly competitive markets, finding a niche unfilled by other companies is challenging but not impossible. For example, Long Island's *Newsday,* in a reference to two competitive daily newspapers published in New York City (*The Daily News* and the *New York Times*), is positioned as "On top of the news and ahead of the times." In the crowded and commodity-like toothpaste market, where virtually every benefit associated with teeth care has been claimed by one or another well-established brand (e.g., social appeal, cavity prevention, specially made for children, etc.), Topol became a success because it was positioned as the smokers' toothpaste; successful introductions include products that fight tartar and gum disease. A very clever approach in finding (or even creating) an "unowned" position was Palmolive's claim to ". . . soften your hands as you do the dishes"; today, even though many people no longer wash dishes by hand, Palmolive positions its dishwashing liquid as "tough on grease, soft on hands."

Filling Several Positions

Because unfilled gaps or "unowned" perceptual positions present opportunities for competitors, sophisticated marketers create several distinct offerings, often in the form of different brands, to fill several identified niches. For example, among Anheuser-Busch's three major brands, Michelob is positioned as the "superpremium beer," Budweiser as the largest-selling "king of beers," and Busch as the "subpremium" brew; the prices of the three brands reflect their images. Tylenol's adult versions include a number of products for arthritis relief, such as Tylenol, Extra Strength Tylenol, Tylenol Arthritis Pain, Tylenol PM, and Aflexa. Procter & Gamble, the world's largest producer of laundry detergents (which are actually commodity-like products, since the physical makeup of almost all detergents is largely identical) offers consumers such brands as Bold (softens fabrics and removes fuzz), Cheer (protects against fading and fabric wear), Era (with proprietary technology that suspends soils), and several other detergents.[17] It would be difficult for a manufacturer to penetrate the detergent market with a product that offers a benefit that is not already provided by a P&G brand.

PRODUCT REPOSITIONING

Regardless of how well positioned a product appears to be, the marketer may be forced to reposition it in response to market events, such as a competitor cutting into the brand's market share or too many competitors stressing the same attribute. For example, rather than trying to meet the lower prices of high-quality private-label competition, some premium brand marketers have repositioned their brands to justify their higher prices, playing up brand attributes that had previously been ignored.

Another reason to reposition a product or service is to satisfy changing consumer preferences. For example, when health-oriented consumers began to avoid high-fat foods, many fast-food chains acted swiftly to reposition their images by offering salad bars and other health-oriented foods. Kentucky Fried Chicken changed its well-known corporate name to KFC in order to omit the dreaded word "fried" from its advertising. Weight Watchers repositioned its line of frozen foods from "dietetic" to "healthy," maintaining its diet-thin imagery while responding to a perceived shift in consumer values. The Avon Company decided to reposition its image from that of a company with legions of women selling their products door-to-door with self-deprecation and irony: A recent campaign showed pictures of accomplished women celebrities with the tag line, "Just another Avon lady." As birthrates declined and consumers' preferences for more gentle and pure products emerged, Johnson & Johnson repositioned its baby lotion, powder, and shampoo as products for grown-ups. One of the most successful product repositionings is the promotion of Arm & Hammer as America's standard for cleanliness and purity by showing it used as a trash can deodorizer, to remove wax from fresh produce, to remove the residue of hair styling products, and as a facial scrub.[18] In the renewed emphasis on home and hearth that followed the terrorist attacks on September 11, 2001, Berkshire repositioned its blankets as a cosy nesting place (see Figure 6-12).

FIGURE 6-12

Repositioning a Blanket as a Cosy Nest

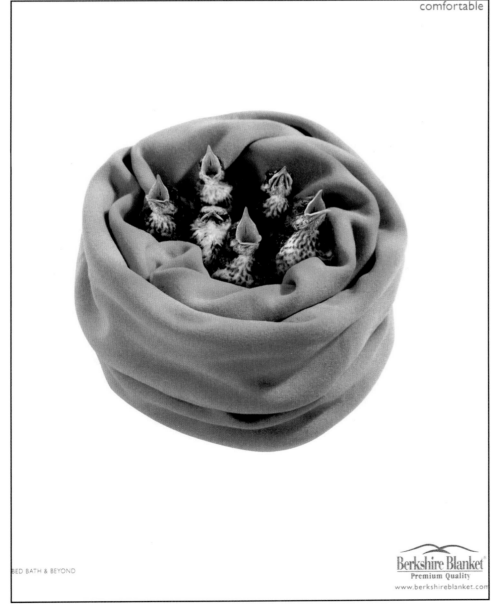

FIGURE 6-13

Perceptual Map of
Competitors Facilitates
Magazine
Repositioning

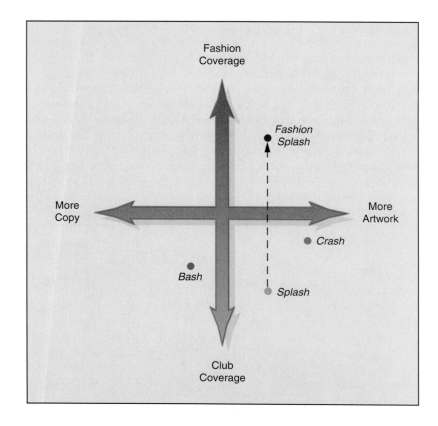

Perceptual Mapping

The technique of **perceptual mapping** helps marketers to determine just how their products or services appear to consumers in relation to competitive brands on one or more relevant characteristics. It enables them to see gaps in the positioning of all brands in the product or service class and to identify areas in which consumer needs are not being adequately met. For example, if a magazine publisher wants to introduce a new magazine to Generation Y, he may use perceptual mapping to uncover a niche of consumers with a special set of interests that are not being adequately or equally addressed by other magazines targeted to the same demographic segment. This insight allows him to position the new magazine as specifically focused on these interests. Or, a publisher may discover through perceptual mapping that consumers perceive its magazine (let's call it *Splash*) to be very similar in editorial content and format to its closest competitors, *Bash* and *Crash*. By changing the focus of its editorial features to appeal to a new market niche, the publisher can reposition the magazine (e.g., from *Splash* to *Fashion Splash*). Figure 6-13 presents this example in a perceptual map.

POSITIONING OF SERVICES

Compared with manufacturing firms, service marketers face several unique problems in positioning and promoting their offerings. Because services are intangible, image becomes a key factor in differentiating a service from its competition. Thus, the marketing objective is to enable the consumer to link a specific image with a specific brand name. Many service marketers have developed strategies to provide customers with visual images and tangible reminders of their service offerings. These include delivery vehicles painted in distinct colors, restaurant matchbooks, packaged hotel soaps and shampoos, and a variety of other specialty items. Many service companies feature real service employees in their ads (as tangible cues) and some use people-focused themes to differentiate themselves. For example, Harrah's Casino positions itself as "the people's place"; the Ritz-Carlton promotes its "guest experience" with the corporate motto "We are ladies and gentlemen serving ladies and gentlemen."

Many service companies market several versions of their service to different market segments by using a differentiated positioning strategy. However, they must be careful to avoid perceptual confusion among their customers. For example, Hilton Hotels recently purchased the Doubletree, Embassy Suites, and Hampton Inn chains. In spite of the shared ownership, the company must keep these brands separate and distinct from one another since each of these hotel brands targets a different segment—each with its own expectations regarding the service delivered.[19] Although distinct brand names are important to all products or services, they are particularly crucial in marketing services due to the abstract and intangible nature of many services. For example, names such as Federal Express (later abbreviated to FedEx) and Humana (a provider of health services) are excellent names because they are distinctive, memorable, and relevant to the services they feature. On the other hand, Allegis—a short-lived brand name aimed at creating a business travel concept by combining United Airlines, Hertz, Hilton and Westin Hotels under one umbrella—failed because it told consumers nothing about the type of services it offered.[20]

The design of the service environment is an important aspect of service positioning strategy and sharply influences consumer impressions and consumer and employee behavior. The physical environment is particularly important in creating a favorable impression for such services as banks, retail stores, and professional offices, because there are so few objective criteria by which consumers can judge the quality of the services they receive. The service environment conveys the image of the service provider with whom the service is so closely linked. Thus, the Polo Ralph Lauren store in its renovated 1895 mansion on New York's Upper East Side is the embodiment of the image Lauren wants to create for his clothes: traditionalism and Old World values. All the trappings of what one imagines to be the high-class and well-heeled ways of the very, very rich are here, from the baronial, hand-carved staircase lined with "family" portraits to the plush sitting rooms with working fireplaces. The Polo store image artfully extends the image of the clothing it sells and projects an Old World quality of living and shopping that its upscale target market finds appealing.

One study of service environments identified five environmental variables most important to bank customers: (1) privacy (both visually and verbally, with enclosed offices, transaction privacy, etc.); (2) efficiency/convenience (e.g., transaction areas that are easy to find, directional signs); (3) ambient background conditions (temperature, lighting, noise, music); (4) social conditions (the physical appearance of other people in the bank environment, such as bank customers and bank personnel); and (5) aesthetics (e.g., color, style, use of materials, and artwork).[21]

PERCEIVED PRICE

How a consumer perceives a price—as high, as low, as fair—has a strong influence on both purchase intentions and purchase satisfaction. Consider the perception of price fairness, for example. There is some evidence that customers do pay attention to the prices paid by other customers (such as senior citizens, frequent flyers, affinity club members), and that the differential pricing strategies used by some marketers are perceived as unfair by customers not eligible for the special prices. No one is happy knowing he or she paid twice as much for an airline ticket or a theater ticket as the person in the next seat. Perceptions of price unfairness affect consumers' perceptions of product value and, ultimately, their willingness to patronize a store or a service. One study, focused on the special challenges of service industries in pricing intangible products, proposed three types of pricing strategies based on the customer's perception of the value provided by the purchase (see Table 6-2).

Reference Prices

Products advertised as "on sale" tend to create enhanced customer perceptions of savings and value. Different formats used in sales advertisements have differing impacts, based on consumer **reference prices.** A reference price is *any price that a consumer uses as a basis for comparison in judging another price.* Reference prices can be external or internal. An advertiser generally uses a higher *external reference price* ("sold elsewhere at . . .") in an ad offering a lower sales price, to persuade the consumer that the product advertised is a really good buy. *Internal reference prices* are those prices (or price ranges) retrieved by the consumer from memory. Internal reference points are thought to play a major role in consumers' evaluations and perceptions of value of an advertised (external) price deal, as well as in the believability of any advertised reference price. Advertised prices (both reference and sales prices) are likely to affect consumers' internal reference prices (e.g., higher advertised prices lead to higher internal reference prices).[22]

TABLE 6-2	Three Pricing Strategies Focused on Perceived Value

PRICING STRATEGY	PROVIDES VALUE BY . . .	IMPLEMENTED AS . . .
Satisfaction-based pricing	Recognizing and reducing customers' perceptions of uncertainty, which the intangible nature of services magnifies.	Service guarantees. Benefit-driven pricing. Flat-rate pricing.
Relationship pricing	Encouraging long-term relationships with the company that customers view as beneficial.	Long-term contracts. Price bundling.
Efficiency pricing	Sharing with customers the cost savings that the company has achieved by understanding, managing, and reducing the costs of providing the service.	Cost-leader pricing.

Source: Leonard L. Berry and Yadav S. Manjit, "Capture and Communicate Value in the Pricing of Services," *Sloan Management Review,* Summer 1996, 41–51.

According to **acquisition-transaction utility** theory, two types of utility are associated with consumer purchases. *Acquisition utility* represents the consumer's perceived economic gain or loss associated with a purchase and is a function of product utility and purchase price. *Transaction utility* concerns the perceived pleasure or displeasure associated with the financial aspect of the purchase and is determined by the difference between the internal reference price and the purchase price.[23] For example, if a consumer wants to purchase a television set for which her internal reference price is approximately $500, and she buys a set that is sale-priced at $500, she receives no transaction utility. However, if either her internal reference price is increased or the sales price of the set is decreased, she will receive positive transaction utility, which increases the total utility she experiences with the purchase. Research findings indicate that transaction utility is significant only when the consumer is certain about consistency of quality.[24]

Several studies have investigated the effects on consumer price perceptions of three types of advertised reference prices: plausible low, plausible high, and implausible high. *Plausible low* prices are well within the range of acceptable market prices; *plausible high* are near the outer limits of the range but not beyond the realm of believability, and *implausible high* are well above the consumer's perceived range of acceptable market prices. As long as an advertised reference price is within a given consumer's acceptable price range, it is considered plausible and is assimilated. (See *assimilation-contrast theory* in Chapter 8.) If the advertised reference point is outside the range of acceptable prices (i.e., implausible), it will be *contrasted* and thus will not be perceived as a valid reference point. This will adversely affect both consumer evaluations and the advertiser's image of credibility.[25]

Tensile and Objective Price Claims

The semantic cues (i.e., specific wording) of the phrase used to communicate the price-related information may affect consumers' price perceptions. **Tensile price claims** (e.g., "save 10 to 40%," "save up to 60%," "save 20% or more") are used to promote a range of price discounts for a product line, an entire department, or sometimes an entire store. In contrast to tensile cues, **objective price claims** provide a single discount level (such as "save 25%"). Because of the broader range of sale merchandise that is covered by both tensile and objective price claims, they are likely to generate more store traffic and sales than reference price advertisements promoting individual products. Generally, ads that state a maximum discount level ("save up to 40%") are more effective than ads stating the minimum discount level ("save 10% or more") and ads stating a discount range ("save 10 to 40%").[26]

Consumer reactions to tensile price claims are affected by the *width* of the discount range. Several studies examined the effects of the three forms of tensile price claims (advertising a minimum, a maximum, or a range of savings) on consumers' price perceptions and their search and shopping intentions. The studies found that, for *broader* discount ranges, tensile claims stating the maximum level of savings have more positive effects than those stating the minimum level or the entire savings range. For more *narrow* discount ranges, tensile claims stating the maximum level of savings appear to be no more effective than claims stating the minimum level or the entire savings range.[27]

An experiment examining the effects of a "bundle price" (the marketing of two or more products or services in a single package for a special price) on consumer price perceptions found that additional savings offered directly on the bundle have a greater relative impact on buyers' perceptions of transaction value than savings offered on the bundle's individual items.[28] Consumers are less sensitive to price when using credit cards than when they use cash. Similarly, a recent study reported that consumers tend to be less sensitive to price when they shop online than when they shop in stores.[29]

PERCEIVED QUALITY

Consumers often judge the quality of a product or service on the basis of a variety of informational cues that they associate with the product. Some of these cues are **intrinsic** to the product or service, whereas others are **extrinsic.** Either singly or in composite, such cues provide the basis for perceptions of product and service quality.

Perceived Quality of Products

Cues that are *intrinsic* concern physical characteristics of the product itself, such as size, color, flavor, or aroma. In some cases, consumers use physical characteristics (e.g., the flavor of ice cream or cake) to judge product quality. Consumers like to believe that they base their evaluations of product quality on intrinsic cues, because that enables them to justify their product decisions (either positive or negative) as being "rational" or "objective" product choices. More often than not, however, they use extrinsic characteristics to judge quality. For example, though many consumers claim they buy a brand because of its superior taste, they are often unable to identify that brand in blind taste tests. One study discovered that the color of a powdered fruit drink product is a more important determinant than the label and the actual taste in determining the consumer's ability to identify the flavor correctly. The study's subjects perceived the purple or grape-colored versions of the powdered product "tart" in flavor and the orange-colored version as "flavorful, sweet, and refreshing."[30] *Consumer Reports* found that consumers often cannot differentiate among various cola beverages and that they base their preferences on such *extrinsic cues* as packaging, pricing, advertising, and even peer pressure.[31] In the absence of actual experience with a product, consumers often evaluate quality on the basis of cues that are external to the product itself, such as price, brand image, manufacturer's image, retail store image, or even the country of origin.

Many consumers use *country-of-origin* stereotypes to evaluate products (e.g., "German engineering is excellent" or "Japanese cars are reliable"). Many consumers believe that a "Made in the U.S.A." label means a product is "superior" or "very good." Yet for food products, a foreign image is often more enticing. For example, Haagen-Dazs, an American-made ice cream, has been incredibly successful with its made-up (and meaningless) Scandinavian-sounding name. The success of Smirnoff vodka, made in Connecticut, can be related to its so-called Russian derivation. Sorbet has become a very popular and chic dessert, now that it is no longer called sherbet. There are many other examples that support the notion that American consumers are much more impressed with foreign foods than they are with domestic foods.

Perceived Quality of Services

It is more difficult for consumers to evaluate the quality of services than the quality of products. This is true because of certain distinctive characteristics of services: They are intangible, they are variable, they are perishable, and they are simultaneously produced and consumed. To overcome the fact that consumers are unable to compare competing services side-by-side as they do with competing products, consumers rely on surrogate cues (i.e., extrinsic cues) to evaluate service quality. In evaluating a doctor's services, for example, they note the quality of the office and examining room furnishings, the number (and source) of framed degrees on the wall, the pleasantness of the receptionist and the professionalism of the nurse; all contribute to the consumer's overall evaluation of the quality of a doctor's services.

Because the actual quality of services can vary from day to day, from service employee to service employee, and from customer to customer (e.g., in food, in waitperson service, in haircuts, even in classes taught by the same professor), marketers try to standardize their services in order to provide consistency of quality. The downside of service standardization is the loss of customized services, which many consumers value.

Unlike products, which are first produced, then sold, and then consumed, most services are first sold and then produced and consumed simultaneously. Whereas a defective product is likely to be detected by factory quality control inspectors before it ever reaches the consumer, an inferior service is consumed as it is being produced; thus, there is little opportunity to correct it. For example, a defective haircut is difficult to correct, just as the negative impression caused by an abrupt or careless waiter is difficult to correct.

During peak demand hours, the interactive quality of services often declines, because both the customer and the service provider are hurried and under stress. Without special effort by the service provider to ensure consistency of services during peak hours, service image is likely to decline. Some marketers try to change demand patterns in order to distribute the service more equally over time. Long-distance telephone services, for instance, traditionally have offered a discount on telephone calls placed during off-peak hours (e.g., after 11:00 P.M. or on weekends); some restaurants offer a significantly less expensive "early bird" dinner for consumers who come in before 7:00 P.M. Research suggests that service providers can reduce the perceived waiting time and consequent negative service evaluation by filling the consumer's time. Diners may be invited to study the menu while waiting for a table; patients can view informative videos in the doctor's waiting room.[32]

The most widely accepted framework for researching service quality stems from the premise that a consumer's evaluation of service quality is a function of the magnitude and direction of the gap between the customer's *expectations of service* and the customer's *assessment (perception) of the service actually delivered*.[33] For example, a brand-new graduate student enrolled in an introductory marketing course at a highly reputable university has certain expectations about the intellectual abilities of her classmates, the richness of classroom discussions, and the professor's knowledge and communication skills. At the end of the term, her assessment of the course's quality is based on the differences between her expectations at the start of the term and her perceptions of the course at the end of the semester. If the course falls below her expectations, she will view it as a service of poor quality. If her expectations are exceeded, she will view the course as a high-quality educational experience. Of course, the expectations of a given service vary widely among different consumers of the same service. These expectations stem from word-of-mouth the consumer has heard about the service, her past experience, the promises made about the service in its ads and by its salespersons, the purchase alternatives available, and other situational factors.[34] Based on these factors, the sum total of a consumer's expectations of a service *before* receiving it is termed *predicted service;* services whose quality, as evaluated by the customer at the *end* of the service, significantly exceeds the predicted service are perceived as offerings of high quality and generate more customer satisfaction, increased probability of repeat purchase, and favorable word-of-mouth.[35]

The SERVQUAL scale was designed to measure the gap between customers' expectations of services and their perceptions of the actual service delivered, based on the following five dimensions: reliability, responsiveness, assurance, empathy, and tangibility.[36] These dimensions are divided into two groups: the *outcome* dimension (which focuses on the reliable delivery of the core service) and the *process* dimension (which focuses on how the core service is delivered, that is, the employees' responsiveness, assurance, and empathy in handling customers and the service's tangible aspects).[37] The process dimension offers the service provider a significant opportunity to exceed customer expectations. For example, although Federal Express provides the same core service as other couriers (the *outcome* dimension), it provides a superior *process* dimension through its advanced tracking system, which can provide customers with instant information about the status of their packages at any time between pickup and delivery; it also provides call centers with knowledgeable, well-trained, and polite employees who can readily answer customers' questions and handle problems. Thus, FedEx uses the process dimension as a method to exceed customers' expectations and has acquired the image of a company that has an important, customer-focused competitive advantage among the many companies providing the same core service. Figure 6-14 shows an ad centered around customer expectations; it also makes the service experience more tangible by depicting the warm interaction between the customer and service employee in a pleasant "homelike" service environment.

Since its development, the SERVQUAL scale has been used in numerous studies, though not all of its empirical findings correspond precisely to the five dimensions that the scale is designed to measure.[38] The scale has also been modified and its most recent version is featured in Table 6-3.

Researchers have tried to integrate the concepts of product quality and service quality into an overall *transaction satisfaction index,* on the basis that all product (i.e., tangible) purchases contain some element of service beyond the core tangible offering. For example, satisfaction with a retail purchase would include evaluation of the helpfulness and efficiency of the salesperson and the pleasantness of the surroundings. One research model suggests that the consumer's overall satisfaction with the transaction is based on the evaluation of three components: service quality, product quality, and price.[39]

Perceptions of high service quality and high customer satisfaction lead to higher levels of purchase intentions and repeat buying. One model depicting this relationship states that service quality and consumer behavioral intentions are related, and that service quality is a determinant of whether the consumer ultimately remains with the company or defects to a competitor. When service quality evaluations are high, customers' behavioral intentions tend to be favorable to the company, and they are likely to remain customers. When service evaluations are low, customer relationships are more likely to weaken, resulting in defection to a competitor. Figure 6-15 portrays this model and depicts the behavioral service quality as it affects the retention or defection of customers and the financial consequences of

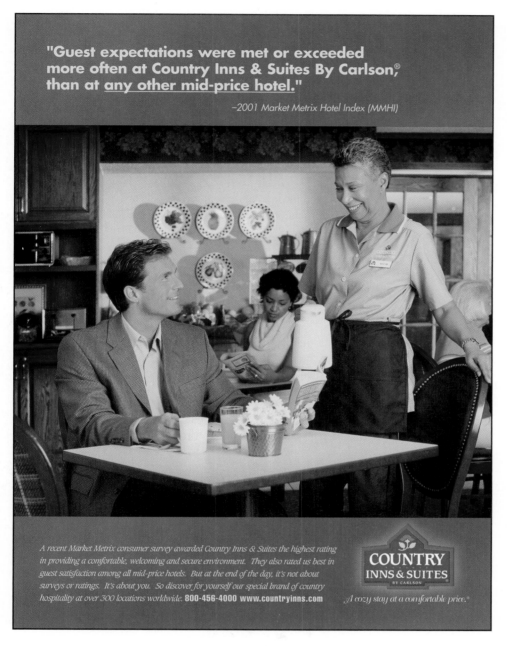

FIGURE 6-14

Tangible Cues Fulfilling
Customer Expectations
in a Service Ad
Courtesy of Country Inns
& Suites.

such customer behaviors for the company. Although there are many studies of customer evaluations of service quality, few studies have examined the relationship between such perceptions and future buying intentions, and even fewer studies have related customer evaluations to customer retention levels and, most importantly, to profitability. A recent study identified numerous aspects of the relationship between perceived service quality and profitability; these are yet to be explored.[40] Such research is very important to marketers because it will enable them to implement those service improvements that make customers more satisfied and at the same time increase company profits.

TABLE 6-3	SERVQUAL Dimensions for Measuring Service Quality
Reliability	Providing the service as promised, at the promised time and doing it right the first time; handling customer problems in a dependable manner and keeping customers informed.
Responsiveness	Prompt service, willingness to help customers, and readiness to respond to customer requests.
Assurance	Instilling confidence in customers and making them feel safe in their transactions; consistently courteous employees with the knowledge to answer customers' questions.
Empathy	Employees who deal with customers in a caring fashion and understand their needs; giving customers individual attention and having their best interests at heart.
Tangibility	Modern equipment, visually appealing facilities and materials related to the service, employees with professional appearance, and convenient operating hours.

Source: From "Moving Forward in Service Quality Research: Measuring Different Customer-Expectation Levels, Comparing Alternative Scales, and Examining the Performance-Behavioral Intentions Link," by A. Parasuraman, Valarie A. Zeithaml, and Leonard L. Berry, *Report No. 94–114,* Marketing Science Institute, 1994.

Today many services are delivered over the phone or the Internet, without direct visual contact between the customer and the service employee. Under these conditions, it is more difficult to research the factors that determine the customer's perception of service quality. Because more and more companies, including the manufacturers of many tangible products, use service-focused selling points to promote and differentiate their offerings, such consumer studies are crucial. Call centers are a key point for customer access to the company and also an important

FIGURE 6-15

Conceptual Model of the Behavioral and Financial Consequences of Service Quality
Source: Valarie A. Zeithaml, Leonard L. Berry, and A. Parasuraman, "The Behavioral Consequences of Service Quality," *Journal of Marketing, 60,* April 1996, 33. Reprinted by permission of the American Marketing Association.

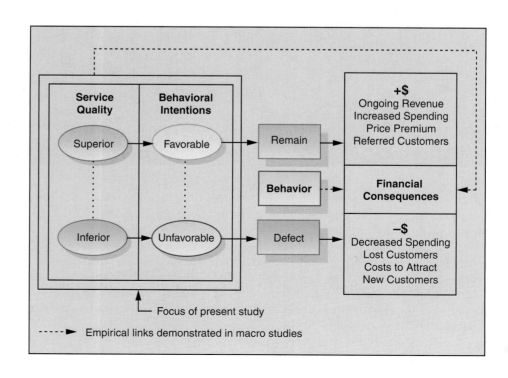

source of customer information. One study analyzed voice-to-voice encounters among customers and call-center employees, and developed a scale that measures customers' perceptions of such service experiences and their future intentions regarding the company represented by the call center contacted (see Table 6-4).

PRICE/QUALITY RELATIONSHIP

Perceived product value has been described as a trade-off between the product's perceived benefits (or quality) and the perceived sacrifice—both monetary and

---

TABLE 6-4 A Scale Measuring Customers' Perceptions of Call-Center Employees

ATTENTIVENESS

1. The agent did not make an attentive impression.*
2. The agent used short, affirmative words and sounds to indicate that (s)he was really listening.

PERCEPTIVENESS

1. The agent asked for more details and extra information during the conversation.
2. The agent continually attempted to understand what I was saying.
3. The agent paraphrased what had been said adequately.

RESPONSIVENESS

1. The agent offered relevant information to the questions I asked.
2. The agent used full sentences in his or her answers instead of just saying yes or no.
3. The agent did not recognize what information I needed.*

TRUST

1. I believe that this company takes customer calls seriously.
2. I feel that this company does not respond to customer problems with understanding.*
3. This company is ready and willing to offer support to customers.
4. I can count on this company to be sincere.

SATISFACTION

1. I am satisfied with the level of service the agent provided.
2. I am satisfied with the way I was spoken to by the agent.
3. I am satisfied with the information I got from the agent.
4. The telephone call with this agent was a satisfying experience.

CALL INTENTION

1. I will very likely contact this company again.
2. Next time I have any questions I will not hesitate to call again.
3. I would not be willing to discuss problems I have with this company over the phone.*

*Negatively phrased item.
Source: Ko de Ruyter and Martin G. M. Wetzels, *Journal of Service Research*, "The Impact of Perceived Listening Behavior in Voice-to-Voice Service Encounters," February 2000, pp. 276–284, copyright © 2000 by Sage Publications Ltd. Reprinted by permission of the publisher.

nonmonetary—necessary to acquire it. A number of research studies have found that consumers rely on price as an indicator of product quality, that consumers attribute different qualities to identical products that carry different price tags, and that such consumer characteristics as age and income affect the perception of value.[41] One study suggested that consumers using a **price/quality relationship** are actually relying on a well-known (and, hence, more expensive) brand name as an indicator of quality without actually relying directly on price per se.[42] A later study found out that consumers use price and brand to evaluate the prestige of the product but do not generally use these cues when they evaluate the product's performance.[43] Because price is so often considered an indicator of quality, some product advertisements deliberately emphasize a high price to underscore the marketers' claims of quality. Marketers understand that, at times, products with lower prices may be interpreted as reduced quality. At the same time, when consumers evaluate more concrete attributes of a product, such as performance and durability, they rely less on the price and brand name as indicators of quality than when they evaluate the product's prestige and symbolic value.[44] For these reasons, marketers must understand all the attributes that customers use to evaluate a given product and include all applicable information in order to counter any perceptions of negative quality associated with a lower price.

In most consumption situations, in addition to price, consumers also use such cues as the brand and the store in which the product is bought to evaluate its quality. Figure 6-16 presents a conceptual model of the effects of price, brand name, and store name on perceived product quality. In summary, consumers use price as a surrogate indicator of quality if they have little information to go on, or if they have little confidence in their own ability to make the product or service choice on other grounds. When the consumer is familiar with a brand name or has experience with a product (or service) or the store where it is purchased, price declines as a determining factor in product evaluation and purchase.

RETAIL STORE IMAGE

Retail stores have images of their own that serve to influence the perceived quality of products they carry and the decisions of consumers as to where to shop. These images stem from their design and physical environment, their pricing strategies, and product assortments. A study that examined the effects of specific store environmental factors on quality inferences found that consumer perceptions were more heavily influenced by ambient factors (such as the number, type, and behavior of other customers within the store and the sales personnel) than by store design features.[45]

A study of retail store image based on comparative *pricing strategies* found that consumers tend to perceive stores that offer a small discount on a large number of items (i.e., *frequency of price advantage*) as having lower prices over all than competing stores that offer larger discounts on a smaller number of products (i.e., *magnitude of price advantage*). Thus, frequent advertising that presents large numbers of price specials reinforces consumer beliefs about the competitiveness of a store's prices.[46] This finding has important implications for retailers' *positioning strategies.* In times of heavy competition, when it is tempting to hold frequent, large sales, covering many items, such strategies may result in an unwanted change in store image. Lord & Taylor's in New York, formerly positioned as an upscale, high-class department store, advertises sales so frequently and fills its aisles with sales racks proclaiming bargain prices, so that its upscale image has been tarnished, and its customer mix has changed.

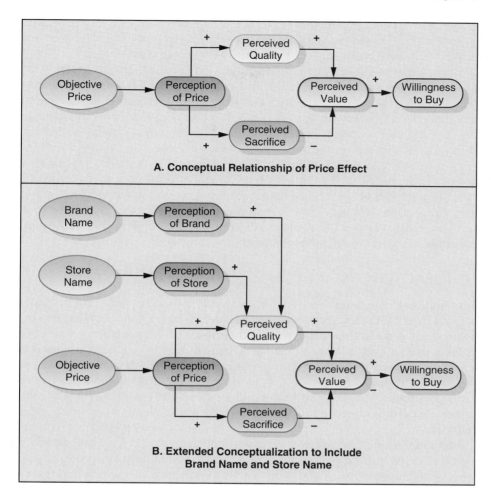

A. Conceptual Relationship of Price Effect

B. Extended Conceptualization to Include Brand Name and Store Name

FIGURE 6-16

Conceptual Model of the Effects of Price, Brand Name, and Store Name on Perceived Value
Source: W. B. Dodds, K. B. Monroe, and Dhruv Grewal, "Effects of Price, Brand and Store Information on Buyers' Product Evaluations," *Journal of Marketing Research*, 28, August 1991, 308. Reprinted by permission.

The width of product assortment also affects retail store image. Grocery retailers, for example, are often reluctant to reduce the number of products they carry out of concern that perceptions of a smaller assortment will reduce the likelihood that consumers will shop in their stores.[47] On the other hand, Whole Foods Markets—a relatively small supermarket chain—has carved itself a profitable niche by carrying a much smaller but highly selective range of products in comparison to conventional supermarkets. Whole Foods stores carry organic (perceived as healthier) products, many of which are bought from mom-and-pop producers; all food products carried are screened for artificial ingredients; and the chain is phasing out all products with hydrogenated fats. The chain has been much more profitable than conventional supermarkets in spite of its limited product assortment.[48] Clearly, the unique benefit that a store provides is more important than the number of items it carries in forming a favorable store image in consumers' minds.

The type of product the consumer wishes to buy influences his or her selection of a retail outlet; conversely, the consumer's evaluation of a product often is influenced by the knowledge of where it was bought. A consumer wishing to buy an elegant dress for a special occasion may go to a store with an elegant, high-fashion image, such as Saks Fifth Avenue. Regardless of what she actually pays for the dress she selects (regular price or marked-down price), she will probably perceive its quality to be high. However, she may perceive the quality of the identical dress to be much lower if she buys it in an off-price store with a low-price image.

Most studies of the effects of extrinsic cues on perceived product quality have focused on just one variable—either price *or* store image. However, when a second extrinsic cue is available (such as price *and* store image), perceived quality is sometimes a function of the interaction of both cues on the consumer. For example, when brand and retailer images become associated, the less favorable image becomes enhanced at the expense of the more favorable image. Thus, when a low-priced store carries a brand with a high-priced image, the image of the store will improve, whereas the image of the brand will be adversely affected. For that reason, marketers of prestigious designer goods often attempt to control the outlets where these products are sold. Also, when upscale stores sell left-over expensive items to discount stores, they remove the designer labels from these goods as part of the agreements they have with the manufacturers of these products.

MANUFACTURERS' IMAGE

Consumer imagery extends beyond perceived price and store image to the producers themselves. Manufacturers who enjoy a favorable image generally find that their new products are accepted more readily than those of manufacturers who have a less favorable or even a "neutral" image. Researchers have found that consumers generally have favorable perceptions of pioneer brands (the first in a product category), even after follower brands become available. They also found a positive correlation between *pioneer brand image* and an individual's *ideal self-image,* which suggests that positive perceptions toward pioneer brands lead to positive purchase intentions.[49]

Some major marketers introduce new products under the guise of supposedly smaller, pioneering (and presumably more forward-thinking) companies. The goal of this so-called *stealth* (or faux) *parentage* is to persuade consumers that the new brands are produced by independent, nonconformist free spirits, rather than by giant corporate entities. Companies sometimes use stealth parentage when they enter a product category totally unrelated to the one with which their corporate name has become synonymous. For example, when Disney Studios—a company with a wholesome, family-focused image—produces films that include violence and sex, it does so under the name Touchstone Pictures.

Today companies are using advertising, exhibits, and sponsorship of community events to enhance their images. Although some marketers argue that product and service advertising do more to boost the corporate image than *institutional* (image) advertising does, others see both types of advertising—product and institutional—as integral and complementary components of a total corporate communications program.

PERCEIVED RISK

Consumers must constantly make decisions regarding what products or services to buy and where to buy them. Because the outcomes (or consequences) of such decisions are often uncertain, the consumer perceives some degree of "risk" in making a purchase decision. **Perceived risk** is defined as *the uncertainty that consumers face when they cannot foresee the consequences of their purchase decisions.* This definition highlights two relevant dimensions of perceived risk: uncertainty and consequences.

TABLE 6-5	Types of Perceived Risk

Functional risk is the risk that the product will not perform as expected. ("Can the new PDA operate a full week without needing to be recharged?")

Physical risk is the risk to self and others that the product may pose. ("Is a cellular phone really safe, or does it emit harmful radiation?")

Financial risk is the risk that the product will not be worth its cost. ("Will a new and cheaper model of a Plasma TV monitor become available six months from now?")

Social risk is the risk that a poor product choice may result in social embarrassment. ("Will my classmates laugh at my purple mohawk haircut?")

Psychological risk is the risk that a poor product choice will bruise the consumer's ego. ("Will I be embarrassed when I invite friends to listen to music on my five-year-old stereo?")

Time risk is the risk that the time spent in product search may be wasted if the product does not perform as expected. ("Will I have to go through the shopping effort all over again?")

The degree of risk that consumers perceive and their own tolerance for risk taking are factors that influence their purchase strategies. It should be stressed that consumers are influenced by risks that they perceive, whether or not such risks actually exist. Risk that is not perceived—no matter how real or how dangerous—will not influence consumer behavior. The major types of risks that consumers perceive when making product decisions include *functional risk, physical risk, financial risk, social risk, psychological risk,* and *time risk* (see Table 6-5).

Perception of Risk Varies

Consumer perception of risk varies, depending on the person, the product, the situation, and the culture. The amount of risk perceived depends on the specific consumer. Some consumers tend to perceive high degrees of risk in various consumption situations; others tend to perceive little risk. For example, studies of risk perception among adolescents have found that adolescents who engage in high-risk consumption activities (such as smoking or drug use) have lower perceived risk than those who do not engage in high-risk activities.[50] *High-risk perceivers* are often described as **narrow categorizers** because they limit their choices (e.g., product choices) to a few safe alternatives. They would rather exclude some perfectly good alternatives than chance a poor selection. *Low-risk perceivers* have been described as **broad categorizers** because they tend to make their choices from a much wider range of alternatives. They would rather risk a poor selection than limit the number of alternatives from which they can choose. One study concluded that risk preference may be a stable personality trait, with experience a mediating factor in risk perception.[51]

An individual's perception of risk varies with product categories. For example, consumers are likely to perceive a higher degree of risk (e.g., functional risk, financial risk, time risk) in the purchase of a plasma television set than in the purchase of an automobile. In addition to *product-category* perceived risk, researchers have identified *product-specific* perceived risk.[52] One study found that consumers perceive service decisions to be riskier than product decisions, particularly in terms of social risk, physical risk, and psychological risk.[53]

The degree of risk perceived by a consumer is also affected by the shopping situation (e.g., a traditional retail store, online, catalog or direct-mail solicitations, or door-to-door sales). The sharp increase in mail-order catalog sales in recent years suggests that on the basis of positive experiences and word-of-mouth, consumers now tend to perceive less risk in mail-order shopping than they once did, despite their inability to physically inspect the merchandise before ordering. High-risk perceivers are unlikely to purchase items online despite the geometric expansion of online retailing. However, as they gain experience in online purchasing, it is likely that their levels of perceived risk regarding electronic buying will decline.

How Consumers Handle Risk

Consumers characteristically develop their own strategies for reducing perceived risk. These risk-reduction strategies enable them to act with increased confidence when making product decisions, even though the consequences of such decisions remain somewhat uncertain. Some of the more common risk-reduction strategies are discussed in the following sections.

Consumers Seek Information Consumers seek information about the product and product category through word-of-mouth communication (from friends and family and from other people whose opinions they value), from salespeople, and from the general media. They spend more time thinking about their choice and search for more information about the product alternatives when they associate a high degree of risk with the purchase. This strategy is straightforward and logical because the more information the consumer has about the product and the product category, the more predictable the probable consequences and, thus, the lower the perceived risk.

Consumers Are Brand Loyal Consumers avoid risk by remaining loyal to a brand with which they have been satisfied instead of purchasing new or untried brands. High-risk perceivers, for example, are more likely to be loyal to their old brands and less likely to purchase newly introduced products.

Consumers Select by Brand Image When consumers have had no experience with a product, they tend to "trust" a favored or well-known brand name. Consumers often think well-known brands are better and are worth buying for the implied assurance of quality, dependability, performance, and service. Marketers' promotional efforts supplement the perceived quality of their products by helping to build and sustain a favorable brand image.

Consumers Rely on Store Image If consumers have no other information about a product, they often trust the judgment of the merchandise buyers of a reputable store and depend on them to have made careful decisions in selecting products for resale. Store image also imparts the implication of product testing and the assurance of service, return privileges, and adjustment in case of dissatisfaction.

Consumers Buy the Most Expensive Model When in doubt, consumers often feel that the most expensive model is probably the best in terms of quality; that is, they equate price with quality. (The price/quality relationship was discussed earlier in this chapter.)

Consumers Seek Reassurance Consumers who are uncertain about the wisdom of a product choice seek reassurance through money-back guarantees, government and private laboratory test results, warranties, and prepurchase trial. For example, it is unlikely that anyone would buy a new model car without a test drive. Products that do not easily lend themselves to free or limited trial (such as a refrigerator) present a challenge to marketers.

The concept of perceived risk has major implications for the introduction of new products. Because high-risk perceivers are less likely to purchase new or innovative products than low-risk perceivers, it is important for marketers to provide such consumers with persuasive risk-reduction strategies, such as a well-known brand name (sometimes achieved through licensing), distribution through reputable retail outlets, informative advertising, publicity stories in the media, impartial test results, free samples, and money-back guarantees. Also, most stores that carry a number of different brands and models of the same product, as well as manufacturers of such diverse model lines, now offer online consumers quick and easy ways to generate side-by-side comparisons with detailed charts of the features of all the available models. It is likely that computer software will play an increasingly important part in reducing the information-seeking burden of perceived risk.

Summary

Perception is the process by which individuals select, organize, and interpret stimuli into a meaningful and coherent picture of the world. Perception has strategy implications for marketers because consumers make decisions based on what they perceive rather than on the basis of objective reality.

The lowest level at which an individual can perceive a specific stimulus is that person's absolute threshold. The minimal difference that can be perceived between two stimuli is called the differential threshold or just noticeable difference (j.n.d.). Most stimuli are perceived by consumers above the level of their conscious awareness; however, weak stimuli can be perceived below the level of conscious awareness (i.e., subliminally). Research refutes the notion that subliminal stimuli influence consumer buying decisions.

Consumers' selection of stimuli from the environment is based on the interaction of their expectations and motives with the stimulus itself. The principles of selective perception include the following concepts: selective exposure, selective attention, perceptual defense, and perceptual blocking. People usually perceive things they need or want and block the perception of unnecessary, unfavorable, or painful stimuli.

Consumers organize their perceptions into unified wholes according to the principles of Gestalt psychology: figure and ground, grouping, and closure. The interpretation of stimuli is highly subjective and is based on what the consumer expects to see in light of previous experience, on the number of plausible explanations he or she can envision, on motives and interests at the time of perception, and on the clarity of the stimulus itself. Influences that tend to distort objective interpretation include physical appearances, stereotypes, halo effects, irrelevant cues, first impressions, and the tendency to jump to conclusions.

Just as individuals have perceived images of themselves, they also have perceived images of products and brands. The perceived image of a product or service (how it is positioned) is probably more important to its ultimate success than are its actual physical characteristics. Products and services that are perceived distinctly and favorably have a much better chance of being purchased than products or services with unclear or unfavorable images.

Compared with manufacturing firms, service marketers face several unique problems in positioning and promoting their offerings because services are intangible, inherently variable, perishable, and are simultaneously produced and consumed. Regardless of how well positioned a product or service appears to be, the marketer may be forced to reposition it in response to market events, such as new competitor strategies or changing consumer preferences.

Consumers often judge the quality of a product or service on the basis of a variety of informational cues; some are intrinsic to the product (such as color, size, flavor, and aroma), while others are extrinsic (e.g., price, store image, brand image, and service environment). In the absence of direct experience or other information, consumers often rely on price as an indicator of quality. How a consumer perceives a price—as high, low, or fair—has a strong influence on purchase intentions and satisfaction. Consumers rely on both internal and external reference prices when assessing the fairness of a price.

Consumer imagery also includes perceived images of retail stores that influence the perceived quality of products they carry, as well as decisions as to where to shop. Manufacturers who enjoy a favorable image generally find that their new products are accepted more readily than those of manufacturers with less favorable or even neutral images.

Consumers often perceive risk in making product selections because of uncertainty as to the consequences of their product decisions. The most frequent types of risk that consumers perceive are functional risk, physical risk, financial risk, social risk, psychological risk, and time risk. Consumer strategies for reducing perceived risk include increased information search, brand loyalty, buying a well-known brand, buying from a reputable retailer, buying the most expensive brand, and seeking reassurance in the form of money-back guarantees, warranties, and prepurchase trial. The concept of perceived risk has important implications for marketers, who can facilitate the acceptance of new products by incorporating risk-reduction strategies in their new-product promotional campaigns.

Discussion Questions

1. How does sensory adaptation affect advertising effectiveness? How can marketers overcome sensory adaptation?

2. Discuss the differences between the absolute threshold and the differential threshold. Which one is more important to marketers? Explain your answer.

3. For each of these products—energy bars and expensive face moisturizers—describe how marketers can apply their knowledge of the differential threshold to packaging, pricing, and promotional claims during periods of (a) rising ingredient and materials costs and (b) increasing competition.

4. Does subliminal advertising work? Support your view.

5. How do advertisers use contrast to make sure that their ads are noticed? Would the lack of contrast between the ad and the medium in which it appears help or hinder the effectiveness of the ad? What are the ethical considerations in employing such strategies?

6. What are the implications of figure–ground relationships for print ads and for online ads? How can the figure–ground construct help or interfere with the communication of advertising messages?

7. Find two ads depicting two different types of perceptual distortions. Discuss your choices.

8. Why are marketers sometimes "forced" to reposition their products or services? Illustrate your answers with examples.

9. a. Why is it more difficult for consumers to evaluate the quality of services than the quality of products?

   b. Apply two of the concepts used to explain consumers' evaluations of service quality to your evaluation of this course up to this point in the semester.

10. Discuss the roles of extrinsic cues and intrinsic cues in the perceived quality of:

    a. wines.

    b. restaurants.

    c. plasma TV monitors.

    d. graduate education.

Exercises

1. Find three examples of print advertisements that use some of the stimulus factors discussed in this chapter to gain attention. For each example, evaluate the effectiveness of the stimulus factors used.

2. Define selective perception. Thinking back, relate one or two elements of this concept to your own attention patterns in viewing print advertisements and TV commercials.

3. Find an ad or example in another form (e.g., an article) illustrating two of the positioning approaches discussed in this chapter. Evaluate the effectiveness of each ad or example selected.

4. Select a company that produces several versions of the same product under the same or different brands (one that is not discussed in this chapter). Visit the firm's Web site and prepare a list of the product items and the positioning strategy for each of the products. (You may use the chapter's discussions of Anheuser-Busch, Tylenol, and Procter & Gamble as a guide to the type of company to choose.)

5. Construct a two-dimensional perceptual map of your college using the two attributes that were most influential in your selection. Then mark the position of your school on the diagram relative to that of another school you considered. Discuss the implications of this perceptual map for the student recruitment function of the university that you did not choose.

Key Terms

- **Absolute threshold**
- **Acquisition-transaction utility**
- **Broad versus narrow categorizers**
- **Closure**
- **Consumer imagery**
- **Differential threshold (j.n.d.)**
- **Expectations**
- **Figure and ground**
- **Gestalt psychology**
- **Grouping**
- **Intrinsic versus extrinsic cues**

- **Just noticeable difference (j.n.d.)**
- **Objective price claims**
- **Perceived price**
- **Perceived quality**
- **Perceived risk**
- **Perception**
- **Perceptual blocking**
- **Perceptual distortion**
- **Perceptual mapping**
- **Positioning**
- **Product positioning and repositioning**

- **Price/quality relationship**
- **Reference prices**
- **Selection, organization, and interpretation of stimuli**
- **Selective perception**
- **Sensation**
- **Sensory adaptation**
- **Sensory receptors**
- **Subliminal perception**
- **Tensile price claims**
- **Weber's law**

Notes

1. Robert McMath and Thomas Forbes, *What Were They Thinking?* (New York: Time Business, Random House, 1998), 13–14.
2. Eric R. Spangenberg, Ayn E. Crowley, and Pamela W. Henderson, "Improving the Store Environment: Do Olfactory Cues Affect Evaluations and Behaviors?" *Journal of Marketing,* 60, April 1996, 67–80.
3. Robert McMath and Thomas Forbes, *What Were They Thinking?* 66.
4. Greg Winter, "What Keeps a Bottom Line Healthy? Weight Loss," *New York Times,* January 2, 2001, 1.
5. Kathryn T. Theus, "Subliminal Advertising and the Psychology of Processing Unconscious Stimuli: A Review of Research," *Psychology and Marketing,* 11, 3, May–June 1994, 271–290. See also Dennis L.

Rosen and Surenra N. Singh, "An Investigation of Subliminal Embed Effect on Multiple Measures of Advertising Effectiveness," *Psychology and Marketing,* 9, 2, March–April 1992, 157–173.
6. For example, Andrew B. Aylesworth, Ronald C. Goodstein, and Ajay Kalra, "Effects of Archetypal Embeds of Feelings: An Indirect Route to Affecting Attitudes?" *Journal of Advertising,* Fall 1999, 73–81; Nicholas Epley, Kenneth Savitsky, and Robert A. Kachelski, "What Every Skeptic Should Know About Subliminal Persuasion," *Skeptical Inquirer,* September/October 1999, 4–58.
7. Carl L. Witte, Madhavan Parthasarathy, and James W. Gentry, "Subliminal Perception Versus Subliminal Persuasion: A Re-Examination of the Basic

Issues," *American Marketing Association,* Summer 1995, 133–138. See also Jack Haberstroh, *Ice Cube Sex: The Truth about Subliminal Advertising* (Notre Dame, IN: Cross Cultural Publications, 1994).

8. Martha Rogers and Christine A. Seiler, "The Answer Is No: A National Survey of Advertising Practitioners and Their Clients about Whether They Use Subliminal Advertising," *Journal of Advertising Research,* March–April 1994, 36–45; Martha Rogers and Kirk H. Smith, "Public Perceptions of Subliminal Advertising: Why Practitioners Shouldn't Ignore This Issue," *Journal of Advertising Research,* March–April 1993, 10–18. See also Nicolas E. Synodinos, "Subliminal Stimulation: What Does the Public Think about It?" in *Current Issues and Research in Advertising,* 11 (1 and 2), eds. James H. Leigh and Claude R. Martin Jr., 1988, 157–187.

9. Keith Naughton, "Gross Out, Smoke Out," *Newsweek,* March 25, 2002, 9.

10. Marsha L. Richins, "Social Comparison and the Idealized Images of Advertising," *Journal of Consumer Research,* 18, June 1991, 71–83. See also Mary C. Martin and James W. Gentry, "Stuck in the Model Trap: The Effects of Beautiful Models in Ads on Female Pre–Adolescents and Adolescents," *Journal of Advertising,* 26, 2, Summer 1997, 19–33.

11. Amanda B. Bower and Stacy Landreth, "Is Beauty Best? Highs Versus Normally Attractive Models in Advertising," *Journal of Advertising,* 30, 1, Spring 2001, 1–12.

12. Kim Foltz, "Campaign on Harmony Backfires on Benetton," *New York Times,* November 20, 1989, D8.

13. Priya Raghubir and Aradhna Krishna, "Vital Dimensions in Volume Perception: Can the Eye Fool the Stomach?" *JMR, Journal of Marketing Research,* August 1999, 313–326.

14. Joe Sharkey, "Hotels Learn the Importance of Expectations Built into a Brand Name," *New York Times,* June 18, 2002, C12.

15. Ajay Kalra and Ronald C. Goodstein, "The Impact of Advertising Positioning Strategies on Consumer Price Sensitivity," *Journal of Marketing Research,* 35, May 1998, 210–224.

16. Robert McMath and Thomas Forbes, *What Were They Thinking?* 28, 70.

17. The information about these companies was derived from their Web sites: www.anheuserbusch.com/overview, www.tylenol.com/products/adult, and www.pg.com/products.

18. www.armandhammer.com/FrontPorch/fs.htm.

19. Sharkey, "Hotels Learn the Importance of Expectations Built into a Brand Name."

20. Leonard L. Berry, Edwin F. Lefkowith, and Terry Clark, "In Services, What's in a Name?" *Harvard Business Review,* September–October 1988, 28–30.

21. Julie Baker, Leonard L. Berry, and A. Parasuraman, "The Marketing Impact of Branch Facility Design," *Journal of Retail Banking,* 10, 2, Summer 1988, 33–42.

22. Dhruv Grewal et al., "The Effects of Price Comparison Advertising on Buyers' Perceptions of Acquisition Value, Transaction Value, and Behavioral Intentions," *Journal of Marketing,* 62, April 1998, 46–59.

23. Katherine Fraccastoro, Scot Burton, and Abhijit Biswas, "Effective Use of Advertisements Promoting Sales Prices," *Journal of Consumer Marketing,* 10, 1, 1993, 61–79.

24. Joel E. Urbany et al., "Transaction Utility Effects: When Quality Is Uncertain," *Journal of the Academy of Marketing Science,* 25, 1, Winter 1997, 45–55.

25. Fraccastoro, "Effective Use of Advertisements," 61–79.

26. Ibid.

27. Abhijit Biswas and Scot Burton, "Consumer Perceptions of Tensile Price Claims in Advertisements: An Assessment of Claim Types Across Different Discount Levels," *Journal of the Academy of Marketing Science,* 21, 3, 1993, 217–229.

28. Manjit S. Yadav and Kent B. Monroe, "How Buyers Perceive Savings in a Bundle Price: An Examination of a Bundle's Transaction Value," *Journal of Marketing Research,* 30, August 1993, 350–358.

29. Robert D. Hershey Jr., "Information Age? Maybe Not, When It Comes to Prices," *New York Times,* August 23, 1998, D10.

30. Lawrence L. Garber Jr., Eva M. Hyatt, and Richard G. Starr Jr., "The Effects of Food Color on Perceived Flavor," *Journal of Marketing Theory and Practice,* Fall 2000, 59–72.

31. Michael J. McCarthy, "Forget the Ads: Cola Is Cola, Magazine Finds," *Wall Street Journal,* February 24, 1991, B1.

32. Shirley Taylor, "Waiting for Service: The Relationship Between Delay and Evaluations of Service," *Journal of Marketing,* 58, April 1994, 56–69. See also Michael K. Hui and David K. Tse, "What to Tell Consumers in Waits of Different Lengths: An Integrative Model of Service Evaluation," *Journal of Marketing,* 60, April 1996, 81–90.

33. Valarie A. Zeithaml, A. Parasuraman, and Leonard L. Berry, *Delivering Quality Service: Balancing Customer Perceptions and Expectations* (New York: The Free Press, 1990).

34. Valarie A. Zeithaml, Leonard L. Berry and A. Parasuraman, "The Nature and Determinants of Customer Expectation of Service," *Journal of the Academy of Marketing Science,* Winter 1993, 1–12.

35. Ibid.

36. A. Parasuraman, Leonard L. Berry, and Valerie A. Zeithaml, "Refinement and Reassessment of the

SERVQUAL Scale," *Journal of Retailing,* 67, 4, Winter 1991, 420–450.

37. A. Parasuraman, Leonard L. Berry, and Valerie A. Zeithaml, "Understanding Customer Expectations of Service," *Sloan Management Review,* Spring 1991, 39–48.

38. James M. Carman, "Consumer Perceptions of Service Quality: An Assessment of the SERVQUAL Dimensions," *Journal of Retailing,* 66, 1, Spring 1990, 33–55.

39. A. Parasuraman, Valarie A. Zeithaml, and Leonard L. Berry, "Reassessment of Expectations as a Comparison Standard in Measuring Service Quality: Implications for Further Research," *Journal of Marketing,* 58, January 1994, 111–124.

40. Valarie A. Zeithaml, "Service Quality, Profitability, and the Economic Worth of Customers: What We Know and What We Need to Learn," *Journal of the Academy of Marketing Science,* Winter 2000, 67–85.

41. For example, Kent Monroe, *Pricing: Making Profitable Decisions,* 2d ed. (New York: McGraw Hill, 1990); William Dodds, Kent Monroe, and Dhruv Grewal, "Effects of Price, Brand, and Store Information on Buyers' Product Evaluations," *Journal of Marketing Research,* 28, August 1991, 307–319; Tung Zong Chang and Albert R. Wildt, "Price, Product Information, and Purchase Intention: An Empirical Study," *Journal of the Academy of Marketing Science,* 22, 1, 1994, 16–27; Indrajit Sinha and Wayne S. DeSasrbo, "An Integrated Approach toward the Spatial Model of Perceived Customer Value," *Journal of Marketing Research,* 35, May 1998, 236–249.

42. Donald R. Liechtenstein, Nancy M. Ridgway, and Richard G. Nitemeyer, "Price Perception and Consumer Shopping Behavior: A Field Study," *Journal of Marketing Research,* 30, May 1993, 242.

43. Merrie Brucks and Valarie A. Zeithaml, "Price and Brand Name as Indicators of Quality Dimensions for Consumer Durables," *Journal of the Academy of Marketing Science,* Summer 2000, 359–374.

44. Ibid.

45. Julie Baker, Dhruv Grewal, and A. Parasuraman, "The Influence of Store Environment on Quality Inferences and Store Image," *Journal of the Academy of Marketing Science,* 22, 4, 1994, 328–339.

46. Joseph W. Alba, Susan M. Broniarczyk, Terence A. Shimp, and Joel E. Urbany, "The Influence of Prior Beliefs, Frequency Cues, and Magnitude Cues on Consumers' Perceptions of Comparative Price Data," *Journal of Consumer Research,* 21, September 1994, 219–235.

47. Susan M. Broniarczyk et al., "Consumers' Perceptions of the Assortment Carried in a Grocery Category: The Impact of Item Reduction," *Journal of Marketing Research,* 35, May 1998, 166–176.

48. Daren Fonda, "Organic Growth," *Time Bonus Section Inside Business,* August 2002, Y1–Y4.

49. Frank H. Alpert and Michael A. Kamins, "An Empirical Investigation of Consumer Memory, Attitude and Perceptions Toward Pioneer and Follower Brands," *Journal of Marketing,* 59, October 1995, 34–45.

50. Herbert H. Severson, Paul Slovic, and Sarah Hampson, "Adolescents' Perception of Risk: Understanding and Preventing High Risk Behavior," *Advances in Consumer Research,* 20, 1993, 177–182.

51. Elke U. Weber and Richard A. Milliman, "Perceived Risk Attitudes: Relating Risk Perception to Risky Choice," *Management Science,* 43, 2, February 1997, 123–144.

52. Grahame R. Dowling and Richard Staelin, "A Model of Perceived Risk and Intended Risk Handling Activity," *Journal of Consumer Research,* 21, June 1994, 119–134.

53. Keith B. Murray and John L. Schlacter, "The Impact of Services versus Goods on Consumers' Assessment of Perceived Risk and Variability," *Journal of the Academy of Marketing Sciences,* 18, Winter 1990, 51–65.

7

Consumer Learning

Listerine mouthwash has been on the market for many decades. Originally noted for its medicinal taste, Listerine mouthwash is now available in four flavors. The company has also introduced the hugely successful and highly publicized CoolMint Listerine PocketPaks—a product line extension in the form of thin, mintlike squares that melt in the mouth and eliminate bad breath. However, years ago, when the company first marketed Listerine toothpaste, consumers did not buy it. Even when the manufacturer repackaged the product, reintroduced it, advertised it, and included free samples with its mouthwash products, Listerine toothpaste did not gain a significant market share, probably because consumers continued to associate the brand name they had learned so well with the medicinal-smelling, sharp-tasting Listerine mouthwash.

Most consumers associate the name Ben-Gay with a topical cream that relieves muscle and joint pain when rubbed on the skin. But Ben-Gay aspirin flopped. Consumers were not prepared to take internally a product associated with a topical cream they had learned was for external use only. Nabisco's Oreo Little Fudgies were smaller versions of its Oreo cookie, with an external chocolate coating. The originally Oreo cookie inspired generations of consumers to pull both halves of the cookie apart and lick out the creamy filling. But consumers found that pulling apart a chocolate-coated Oreo was very messy, and so the product did not sell.[1]

Listerine toothpaste, Ben-Gay aspirin, and Nabisco's Oreo Little Fudgies were product extensions to successful products made by well-known and popular companies. They did not succeed because they required consumers to *learn* new consumption habits that *contradicted* previously learned and well-established product usage patterns of behavior.

How individuals learn is a matter of great interest and importance to academicians, to psychologists, to consumer researchers, and to marketers. The reason that marketers are concerned with how individuals learn is that they are vitally interested in teaching them, in their roles as consumers, about products, product attributes and their potential benefits: where to buy them, how to use them, how to maintain them, and even how to dispose of them. They are also vitally interested in how effectively they have taught consumers to prefer their brands and to differentiate their products from competitive offerings. Marketing strategies are based on communicating with the consumer—directly, through advertisements, and indirectly, through product appearance, packaging, price, and distribution channels. Marketers want their communications to be noted, believed, remembered, and recalled. For these reasons, they are interested in every aspect of the learning process.

However, despite the fact that learning is all-pervasive in our lives, there is no single, universal theory of how people learn. Instead, there are two major schools of thought concerning the learning process: One consists of *behavioral theories,* the other of *cognitive theories.* Cognitive theorists view learning as a function of purely mental processes, whereas behavioral theorists focus almost exclusively on observable behaviors (responses) that occur as the result of exposure to stimuli.

In this chapter, we examine the two general categories of learning theory:

behavioral learning theory and **cognitive learning theory.** Although these theories

differ markedly in a number of essentials, each theory offers insights to marketers

on how to shape their messages to consumers to bring about desired purchase

behavior. We also discuss how consumers store, retain, and retrieve information, and

how learning is measured. The chapter concludes with a discussion of how mar-

keters use learning theories in their marketing strategies.

The Elements of Consumer Learning

Because not all learning theorists agree on how learning takes place, it is difficult to come up with a generally accepted definition of learning. From a marketing per-spective, however, consumer learning can be thought of as *the process by which indi-viduals acquire the purchase and consumption knowledge and experience that they apply to future related behavior.* Several points in this definition are worth noting.

First, consumer learning is a *process;* that is, it continually evolves and changes as a result of newly acquired *knowledge* (which may be gained from reading, from discussions, from observation, from thinking) or from actual *experience.* Both newly acquired knowledge and personal experience serve as *feedback* to the individual and provide the basis for *future behavior* in similar situations.

The role of *experience* in learning does not mean that all learning is deliberately sought. Though much learning is *intentional* (i.e., it is acquired as the result of a care-ful search for information), a great deal of learning is also *incidental,* acquired by accident or without much effort. For example, some ads may induce learning (e.g., of brand names), even though the consumer's attention is elsewhere (on a magazine article rather than the advertisement on the facing page). Other ads are sought out and carefully read by consumers contemplating a major purchase decision.

The term **learning** encompasses the total range of learning, from simple, almost reflexive responses to the learning of abstract concepts and complex problem solv-ing. Most learning theorists recognize the existence of different types of learning and explain the differences through the use of distinctive models of learning.

Despite their different viewpoints, learning theorists in general agree that in order for learning to occur, certain basic elements must be present. The elements included in most learning theories are motivation, cues, response, and reinforce-ment. These concepts are discussed first because they tend to recur in the theories discussed later in this chapter.

MOTIVATION

The concept of **motivation** is important to learning theory. Remember, motivation is based on needs and goals. Motivation acts as a spur to learning. For example, men and women who want to become good tennis players are motivated to learn all they can about tennis and to practice whenever they can. They may seek information concerning the prices, quality, and characteristics of tennis racquets if they "learn" that a good racquet is instrumental to playing a good game. Conversely, individuals who are not interested in tennis are likely to ignore all information related to the game. The goal object (proficiency in tennis) simply has no relevance for them. The degree of relevance, or *involvement,* determines the consumer's level of motivation to search for knowledge or information about a product or service. (Involvement theory, as it has come to be known, will be discussed later in the chapter.) Uncovering consumer motives is one of the prime tasks of marketers, who then try to teach motivated consumer segments why and how their products will fulfill the consumer's needs.

CUES

If motives serve to stimulate learning, **cues** are the stimuli that give direction to these motives. An advertisement for a tennis camp may serve as a cue for tennis buffs, who may suddenly "recognize" that attending tennis camp is a concentrated way to improve their game while taking a vacation. The ad is the cue, or *stimulus,* that suggests a specific way to satisfy a salient motive. In the marketplace, price, styling, packaging, advertising, and store displays all serve as cues to help consumers fulfill their needs in product-specific ways.

Cues serve to direct consumer drives when they are consistent with consumer expectations. Marketers must be careful to provide cues that do not upset those expectations. For example, consumers expect designer clothes to be expensive and to be sold in upscale retail stores. Thus, a high-fashion designer should sell his or her clothes only through exclusive stores and advertise only in upscale fashion magazines. Each aspect of the marketing mix must reinforce the others if cues are to serve as the stimuli that guide consumer actions in the direction desired by the marketer.

RESPONSE

How individuals react to a drive or cue—how they behave—constitutes their **response.** Learning can occur even when responses are not overt. The automobile manufacturer that provides consistent cues to a consumer may not always succeed in stimulating a purchase. However, if the manufacturer succeeds in forming a favorable image of a particular automobile model in the consumer's mind, when the consumer is ready to buy, it is likely that he or she will consider that make or model.

A response is not tied to a need in a one-to-one fashion. Indeed, as was discussed in Chapter 4, a need or motive may evoke a whole variety of responses. For example, there are many ways to respond to the need for physical exercise besides playing tennis. Cues provide some direction, but there are many cues competing for the consumer's attention. Which response the consumer makes depends heavily on previous learning; that, in turn, depends on how related responses were reinforced previously.

REINFORCEMENT

Reinforcement increases the likelihood that a specific response will occur in the future as the result of particular cues or stimuli. For example, Figure 7-1 presents a three-step process for facial skin care based on three products (i.e., cues). This ad is instructional and designed to generate consumer learning. If a college student finds that the cleansing routine based on the three products featured in this ad relieve his acne problem, he is likely to continue buying and using these products. Through positive reinforcement, learning has taken place, since the facial cleansing system lived up to expectations. On the other hand, if the products had not provided relief from the problem when first used, the student would have no reason to associate the

FIGURE 7-1

Product Usage Leads to
Reinforcement
Courtesy of Neutrogena
Corporation.

brand with acne relief in the future. Because of the absence of reinforcement, it is
unlikely that he would buy that brand again.

With these basic principles established, we can now discuss some well-known
theories or models of how learning occurs.

Behavioral Learning Theories

Behavioral learning theories are sometimes referred to as **stimulus-response theories** because they are based on the premise that observable responses to specific
external stimuli signal that learning has taken place. When a person acts (responds)

in a predictable way to a known stimulus, he or she is said to have "learned." Behavioral theories are not so much concerned with the *process* of learning as they are with the *inputs* and *outcomes* of learning; that is, in the stimuli that consumers select from the environment and the observable behaviors that result. Two behavioral theories with great relevance to marketing are **classical conditioning** and **instrumental** (or **operant) conditioning.**

CLASSICAL CONDITIONING

Early classical conditioning theorists regarded all organisms (both animal and human) as relatively passive entities that could be taught certain behaviors through repetition (or "conditioning"). In everyday speech, the word *conditioning* has come to mean a kind of "knee-jerk" (or automatic) response to a situation built up through repeated exposure. If you get a headache every time you think of visiting your Aunt Gertrude, your reaction may be conditioned from years of boring visits with her.

Ivan Pavlov, a Russian physiologist, was the first to describe conditioning and to propose it as a general model of how learning occurs. According to Pavlovian theory, conditioned learning results when a stimulus that is paired with another stimulus that elicits a known response serves to produce the same response when used alone.

Pavlov demonstrated what he meant by **conditioned learning** in his studies with dogs. The dogs were hungry and highly motivated to eat. In his experiments, Pavlov sounded a bell and then immediately applied a meat paste to the dogs' tongues, which caused them to salivate. Learning (conditioning) occurred when, after a sufficient number of repetitions of the bell sound followed almost immediately by the food, the bell sound alone caused the dogs to salivate. The dogs associated the bell sound (the conditioned stimulus) with the meat paste (the unconditioned stimulus) and, after a number of pairings, gave the same unconditioned response (salivation) to the bell alone as they did to the meat paste. The unconditioned response to the meat paste became the conditioned response to the bell. Figure 7-2A models this relationship. An analogous situation would be one in which the smells of dinner cooking would cause your mouth to water. If you usually listen to the 6 o'clock news while waiting for dinner to be served, you would tend to associate the 6 o'clock news with dinner, so that eventually the sounds of the 6 o'clock news alone might cause your mouth to water, even if dinner was not being prepared and even if you were not hungry. Figure 7-2B diagrams this basic relationship.

In a consumer behavior context, an **unconditioned stimulus** might consist of a well-known brand symbol (such as the Neutrogena name) that implies dermatologists' endorsement and pure (chemically free) products (i.e., containing few potentially irritating ingredients, such as perfume scents commonly added to personal cleansing products). This previously acquired consumer perception of Neutrogena is the *unconditioned response.* **Conditioned stimuli** might consist of new products bearing the well-known symbol (such as the items depicted in Figure 7-1), and the *conditioned response* would be trying these products because of the belief that they embody the same attributes with which the Neutrogena name is associated. In the example given at the opening of the chapter, the brand name Listerine was the unconditioned stimulus associated with a medicinal taste, and avoiding Listerine brand toothpaste was the consumer's conditioned response.

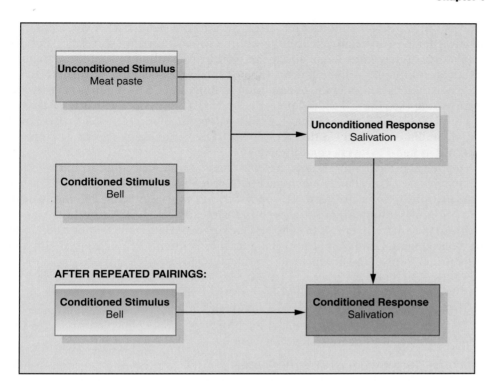

FIGURE 7-2A

Pavlovian Model of
Classical Conditioning

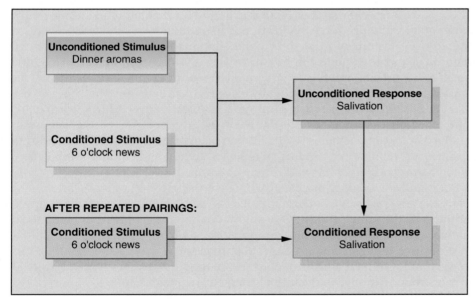

FIGURE 7-2B

Analogous Model of
Classical Conditioning

Cognitive Associative Learning

Contemporary behavioral scientists view classical conditioning as the learning of
associations among events that allows the organism to anticipate and "represent"
its environment. According to this view, the relationship (or contiguity) between
the conditioned stimulus and the unconditioned stimulus (the bell and the meat
paste) influenced the dogs' expectations, which in turn influenced their behavior

(salivation). Classical conditioning, then, rather than being a reflexive action, is seen as **cognitive associative learning**—not the acquisition of new reflexes, but the acquisition of new knowledge about the world.[2] According to some researchers, optimal conditioning—that is, the creation of a strong association between the conditioned stimulus (CS) and the unconditioned stimulus (US)—requires (1) forward conditioning (i.e., the CS should precede the US); (2) repeated pairings of the CS and the US; (3) a CS and US that logically belong together; (4) a CS that is novel and unfamiliar; and (5) a US that is biologically or symbolically salient. This model is known as **neo-Pavlovian conditioning.**[3]

Under neo-Pavlovian theory, the consumer can be viewed as an information seeker who uses logical and perceptual relations among events, along with his or her own preconceptions, to form a sophisticated representation of the world. Conditioning is the learning that results from exposure to relationships among events in the environment; such exposure creates expectations as to the structure of the environment. Conditioning also generates more attention to subsequent ads and other promotions of the product.[4]

Strategic Applications of Classical Conditioning

Three basic concepts derive from classical conditioning: *repetition, stimulus generalization,* and *stimulus discrimination.* Each of these concepts is important to the strategic applications of consumer behavior.

Repetition **Repetition** increases the strength of the association between a conditioned stimulus and an unconditioned stimulus and slows the process of forgetting. However, research suggests that there is a limit to the amount of repetition that will aid retention. Although some overlearning (i.e., repetition beyond what is necessary for learning) aids retention, at some point an individual can become satiated with numerous exposures, and both attention and retention will decline. This effect, known as **advertising wearout,** can be moderated by varying the advertising message. Some marketers avoid wearout by using *cosmetic variations* in their ads (using different backgrounds, different print types, different advertising spokespersons) while repeating the same advertising theme. For example, the classic, decades-old Absolut Vodka campaign has used the same theme with highly creative and varied backgrounds, relating the product to holidays, trends, and cultural symbols in the United States and across the world (e.g., see Figure 7-3).

Substantive variations are changes in advertising content across different versions of an advertisement. For example, the two ads in Figure 7-4 stress two different attributes of the same product. One study found that individuals exposed to substantively varied ads process more information about product attributes and have more positive thoughts about the product than those exposed to cosmetic variations. Attitudes formed as a result of exposure to substantively varied ads were also more resistant to change in the face of competitive attack.[5]

Although the principle of repetition is well established among advertisers, not everyone agrees on how much repetition is enough. Some marketing scholars believe that just three exposures to an advertisement are needed: one to make consumers aware of the product, a second to show consumers the relevance of the product, and a third to remind them of its benefits. Others think it may take 11 to 12 repetitions to increase the likelihood that consumers will actually receive the three exposures basic to the so-called *three-hit theory.*

The effectiveness of repetition is somewhat dependent upon the amount of competitive advertising to which the consumer is exposed. The higher the level of competitive ads, the greater the likelihood that *interference* will occur, causing consumers to forget previous learning that resulted from repetition.

Stimulus Generalization According to classical conditioning theorists, learning depends not only on repetition but also on the ability of individuals to generalize. Pavlov found, for example, that a dog could learn to salivate not only to the sound of a bell but also to the somewhat similar sound of jangling keys. If we were not

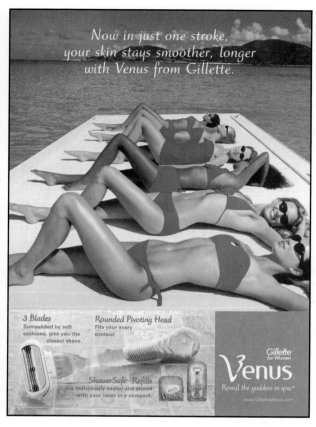

FIGURE 7-4

Substantive Variations in Two Ads for the Same Product
Courtesy of Gillette.

capable of **stimulus generalization**—that is, of making the same response to slightly different stimuli—not much learning would take place.

Stimulus generalization explains why some imitative "me-too" products succeed in the marketplace: Consumers confuse them with the original product they have seen advertised. It also explains why manufacturers of private-label brands try to make their packaging closely resemble the national brand leaders. They are hoping that consumers will confuse their packages with the leading brand and buy their product rather than the leading brand. Similarly packaged competitive products result in millions of lost sales for well-positioned and extensively advertised brands.

Product Line, Form, and Category Extensions The principle of stimulus generalization is applied by marketers to product line, form, and category extensions. In **product line extensions,** the marketer adds related products to an already established brand, knowing that the new product is more likely to be adopted when it is associated with a known and trusted brand name (see Figure 7-5).

Marketers also offer **product form extensions,** such as Crest Toothpaste to Crest Whitestrips, Listerine mouthwash to ListerinePaks (see Figure 7-6), and Ivory bath soap to Ivory liquid soap to Ivory shower gel. Marketers also offer **product category extensions** that generally target new market segments. (See Figure 7-7.)

The success of product extensions depends on a number of factors. If the image of the parent brand is one of quality and the new item is logically linked to the brand, consumers are more likely to bring positive associations to the new offerings introduced as product line, form, or category extensions. For example, Tylenol—a

FIGURE 7-6

Product Form
Extensions

highly trusted brand—initially introduced line extensions by making its products available in a number of different forms (tablets, capsules, gelcaps), strengths (regular, extra strength, and children's), and package sizes. It then extended its brand name to a wide range of related remedies for colds, flu, sinus congestion, and allergies, further segmenting the line for adults, children, and infants. The number of different products affiliated with a brand strengthens the brand name, as long as the company maintains a quality image across all brand extensions. Failure to do so, in the long run, is likely to negatively affect consumer confidence and evaluations of all the brand's offerings.

Family Branding Family branding—the practice of marketing a whole line of company products under the same brand name—is another strategy that capitalizes on the consumer's ability to generalize favorable brand associations from one product to others. The Campbell's Soup Company, for example, continues to add new food products to its product line under the Campbell's brand name, achieving ready acceptance for the new products from satisfied consumers of other Campbell's food products. Kraft Foods sells salad dressings, cheeses, snacks, and toppings under the Kraft brand name. The Ralph Lauren designer label on men's and women's clothing helps to achieve ready acceptance for these products in the upscale sportswear market.

On the other hand, Procter & Gamble (P&G) was built on the strength of its many individual brands in the same product category. For example, the company offers 11 brands of laundry products (mostly detergents, but also other fabric-care products), three brands of antiperspirants, and several brands of shampoo. Although offering many brands of the same product is expensive, the combined weight of its brands has always provided Procter & Gamble with great power in negotiating with advertising media and securing desirable shelf space for its products in the United States and around the world. It also enables the company to effectively combat any competitors who may try to introduce products in markets dominated by P&G. Nevertheless, in recent years and in an effort to cut costs, the company has consoli-

FIGURE 7-7

Product Category
Extensions
Courtesy of Neutrogena
Corporation.

dated its product lines under the umbrella P&G brand, sold off marginal and second-tier brands, standardized product formulas, and simplified its product offerings.

Retail private branding often achieves the same effect as family branding. For example, Wal-Mart used to advertise that its stores carried only "brands you trust." Now, the name Wal-Mart itself has become a "brand" that consumers have confidence in, and the name confers brand value on Wal-Mart's store brands.

Licensing Licensing—allowing a well-known brand name to be affixed to products of another manufacturer—is a marketing strategy that operates on the principle of *stimulus generalization*. The names of designers, manufacturers, celebrities,

FIGURE 7-8

Shoe Manufacturer
Licenses Its Name

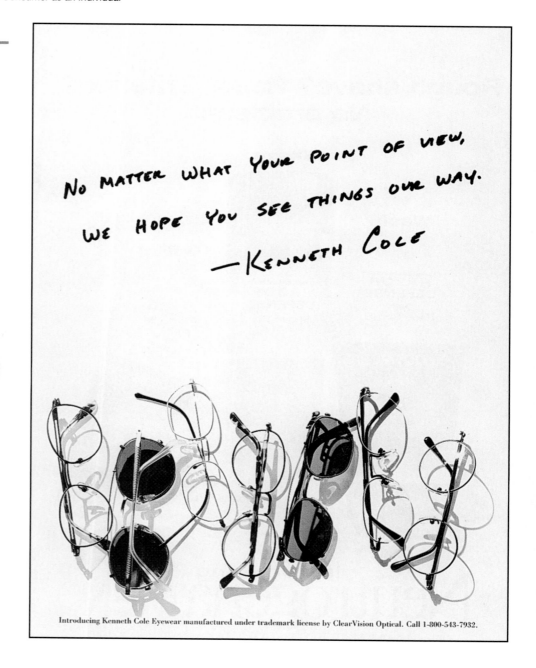

Introducing Kenneth Cole Eyewear manufactured under trademark license by ClearVision Optical. Call 1-800-543-7932.

corporations, and even cartoon characters are attached for a fee (i.e., "rented") to a variety of products, enabling the licensees to achieve instant recognition and implied quality for the licensed products. Some successful licensors include Liz Claiborne, Tommy Hilfiger, Calvin Klein, and Christian Dior, whose names appear on an exceptionally wide variety of products, from sheets to shoes and luggage to perfume. Figure 7-8 shows an ad for eyeglasses bearing the name of the well-known shoe manufacturer Kenneth Cole.

Corporations also license their names and trademarks, usually for some form of brand extension, where the name of the corporation is licensed to the maker of a related product and thereby enters a new product category (e.g., Godiva chocolates licensed its name for Godiva liqueur). Corporations also license their names for purely promotional licensing, in which popular company logos (such as "Always Coca-Cola") are stamped on clothing, toys, coffee mugs, and the like. Some magazines have also licensed their names to manufacturers of products similar to the magazines' own publishing focus (e.g., *Better Homes and Gardens* gardening tools and *Popular Mechanics* work boots). Municipal and state governments have begun licensing their names to achieve new sources of revenue. The Vatican Library licenses its name for a variety of products from luggage to bed linens, the Mormon Church has expanded its licensing activities to apparel and home decorating items, and Britain's Queen Elizabeth II has agreed to extend the licensed name "House of Windsor" to furniture and Scottish throw rugs.

The increase in licensing has made counterfeiting a booming business, as counterfeiters add well-known licensor names to a variety of products without benefit of contract or quality control. Aside from the loss of sales revenue because of counterfeiting, the authentic brands also suffer the consequences associated with zero quality control over counterfeit products that bear their names. It is also increasingly difficult to identify fakes of such expensive and upscale goods as Christian Dior bags, Gucci shoes, and Chanel No. 5 perfume. Many firms are now legally pursuing retailers that sell counterfeit branded goods; many also are employing specialized technology to make their products more counterfeit-proof.[6]

Stimulus Discrimination **Stimulus discrimination** is the opposite of stimulus generalization and results in the selection of a specific stimulus from among similar stimuli. The consumer's ability to discriminate among similar stimuli is the basis of positioning strategy (discussed in Chapter 6), which seeks to establish a unique image for a brand in the consumer's mind.

Positioning In our overcommunicated society, the key to stimulus discrimination is effective **positioning,** a major competitive advantage. The image—or position—that a product or service holds in the mind of the consumer is critical to its success. When a marketer targets consumers with a strong communications program that stresses the unique ways in which its product will satisfy the consumer's needs, it wants the consumer to differentiate its product from among competitive products on the shelf. Unlike the imitator who hopes consumers will *generalize* their perceptions and attribute special characteristics of the market leader's products to its own products, market leaders want the consumer to *discriminate* among similar stimuli. Major marketers are constantly vigilant concerning store brand look-alikes, and they quickly file suit against retailers that they believe are cannibalizing their sales. They want their products to be recognized as uniquely fulfilling consumers' needs. Studies have shown that the favorable attitudes resulting from effective positioning and stimulus discrimination are usually retained long enough to influence future purchase behavior.[7]

Product Differentiation Most product differentiation strategies are designed to distinguish a product or brand from that of competitors on the basis of an attribute that is relevant, meaningful, and valuable to consumers. However, many marketers also successfully differentiate their brands on an attribute that may actually be irrelevant to creating the implied benefit, such as a noncontributing ingredient or a color.[8]

It often is quite difficult to unseat a brand leader once stimulus discrimination has occurred. One explanation is that the leader is usually first in the market and has had a longer period to "teach" consumers (through advertising and selling) to associate the brand name with the product. In general, the longer the period of learning—of associating a brand name with a specific product—the more likely the consumer

FIGURE 7-9

Stimulus Discrimination

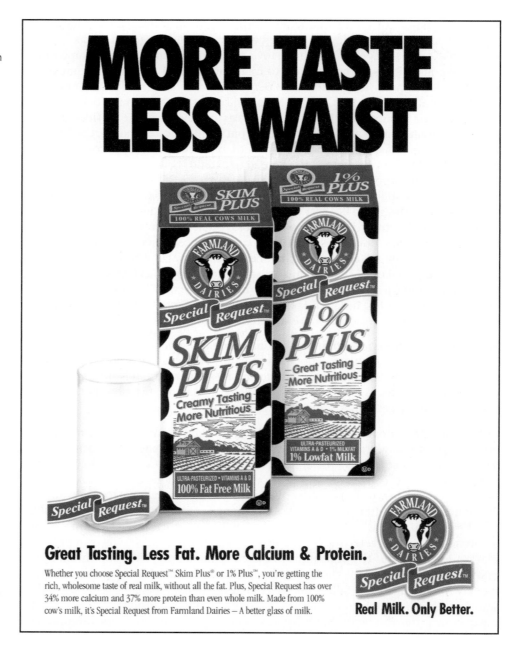

is to discriminate and the less likely to generalize the stimulus. Figure 7-9 is an example of stimulus discrimination.

The principles of classical conditioning provide the theoretical underpinnings for many marketing applications. Repetition, stimulus generalization, and stimulus discrimination are all major applied concepts that help to explain consumer behavior in the marketplace. However, they do not explain all behavioral consumer learning. Although a great deal of consumer behavior (e.g., the purchase of branded convenience goods) is shaped to some extent by repeated advertising messages stressing a unique competitive advantage, a significant amount of purchase behavior results from careful evaluation of product alternatives. Our assessments of products are often based on the degree of satisfaction—the rewards—we experience as a result of making specific purchases; in other words, from instrumental conditioning.

INSTRUMENTAL CONDITIONING

Like classical conditioning, **instrumental conditioning** requires a link between a stimulus and a response. However, in instrumental conditioning, the stimulus that results in the most satisfactory response is the one that is learned.

Instrumental learning theorists believe that learning occurs through a trial-and-error process, with habits formed as a result of rewards received for certain responses or behaviors. This model of learning applies to many situations in which consumers learn about products, services, and retail stores. For example, consumers learn which stores carry the type of clothing they prefer at prices they can afford to pay by shopping in a number of stores. Once they find a store that carries clothing that meets their needs, they are likely to patronize that store to the exclusion of others. Every time they purchase a shirt or a sweater there that they really like, their store loyalty is rewarded (*reinforced*), and their patronage of that store is more likely to be repeated. Whereas classical conditioning is useful in explaining how consumers learn very simple kinds of behaviors, instrumental conditioning is more helpful in explaining complex, goal-directed activities.

The name most closely associated with instrumental (*operant*) conditioning is that of the American psychologist B. F. Skinner. According to Skinner, most individual learning occurs in a controlled environment in which individuals are "rewarded" for choosing an appropriate behavior. In consumer behavior terms, instrumental conditioning suggests that consumers learn by means of a trial-and-error process in which some purchase behaviors result in more favorable outcomes (i.e., rewards) than other purchase behaviors. A favorable experience is "instrumental" in teaching the individual to repeat a specific behavior.

Like Pavlov, Skinner developed his model of learning by working with animals. Small animals, such as rats and pigeons, were placed in his "Skinner box"; if they made appropriate movements (e.g., if they depressed levers or pecked keys), they received food (a positive reinforcement). Skinner and his many adherents have done amazing things with this simple learning model, including teaching pigeons to play Ping-Pong and even to dance. In a marketing context, the consumer who tries several brands and styles of jeans before finding a style that fits her figure (positive reinforcement) has engaged in instrumental learning. Presumably, the brand that fits best is the one she will continue to buy. This model of instrumental conditioning is presented in Figure 7-10.

Reinforcement of Behavior

Skinner distinguished two types of reinforcement (or reward) that influence the likelihood that a response will be repeated. The first type, **positive reinforcement,** consists of events that strengthen the likelihood of a specific response. Using a shampoo that leaves your hair feeling silky and clean is likely to result in a repeat purchase of the shampoo. **Negative reinforcement** is an unpleasant or negative outcome that also serves to encourage a specific behavior. An advertisement that shows a model with wrinkled skin is designed to encourage consumers to buy and use the advertised skin cream.

Fear appeals in ad messages are examples of negative reinforcement. Many life insurance commercials rely on negative reinforcement to encourage the purchase of life insurance. The ads warn husbands of the dire consequences to their wives and children in the event of their sudden death. Marketers of headache remedies use

FIGURE 7-10

A Model of
Instrumental
Conditioning

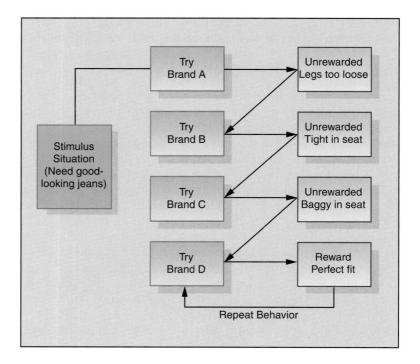

negative reinforcement when they illustrate the unpleasant symptoms of an unrelieved headache, as do marketers of mouthwash when they show the loneliness suffered by someone with bad breath. In each of these cases, the consumer is encouraged to avoid the negative consequences by buying the advertised product.

Either positive or negative reinforcement can be used to elicit a desired response. However, negative reinforcement should not be confused with punishment, which is designed to discourage behavior. For example, parking tickets are not negative reinforcement; they are a form of "punishment" designed to discourage drivers from parking illegally.

Forgetting and Extinction When a learned response is no longer reinforced, it diminishes to the point of *extinction,* that is, to the point at which the link between the stimulus and the expected reward is eliminated. If a consumer is no longer satisfied with the service a retail store provides, the link between the stimulus (the store) and the response (expected satisfaction) is no longer reinforced, and there is little likelihood that the consumer will return. When behavior is no longer reinforced, it is "unlearned." There is a difference, however, between extinction and *forgetting.* A person who has not visited a once favorite restaurant for a very long time may simply forget how much he used to enjoy eating there and not think to return. Thus, his behavior is unlearned because of lack of use rather than lack of reinforcement. Forgetting is often related to the passage of time; this is known as the process of *decay.* Marketers can overcome forgetting through repetition and can combat extinction through the deliberate enhancement of consumer satisfaction.

Strategic Applications of Instrumental Conditioning

Marketers effectively utilize the concepts of consumer instrumental learning when they provide positive reinforcement by assuring customer satisfaction with the product, the service, and the total buying experience.

Customer Satisfaction (Reinforcement) The objective of all marketing efforts should be to maximize customer satisfaction. Marketers must be certain to provide the best possible product for the money and to avoid raising consumer expectations for product (or service) performance beyond what the product can deliver. Aside from the experience of using the product itself, consumers can receive reinforcement from other elements in the purchase situation, such as the environment in which the transaction or service takes place, the attention and service provided by employees, and the amenities provided. For example, an upscale beauty salon, in addition to a beautiful environment, may offer coffee and soft drinks to waiting clients and provide free local telephone service at each hairdressing station. Even if the styling outcome is not so great, the client may feel so pampered with the atmosphere and service that she looks forward to her next visit. On the other hand, even with the other positive reinforcements in place, if the salon's employees are so busy talking with each other while the service is being rendered that the client feels ignored, she is not likely to return.

Some hotels provide reinforcement to guests in the form of small amenities, such as chocolates on the pillow or bottled water on the dresser; others send platters of fruit or even bottles of wine to returning guests to show their appreciation for continued patronage. Most frequent shopper programs are based on enhancing positive reinforcement and encouraging continued patronage. The more a consumer uses the service, the greater the rewards. Kellogg's provides a frequent user program by including coupons on the top of its cereal boxes that can be accumulated and exchanged for various premiums, such as a coffee mug or denim shirt emblazoned with the company's logo.

Relationship marketing—developing a close personalized relationship with customers—is another form of nonproduct reinforcement. Knowing that she will be advised of a forthcoming sale or that selected merchandise will be set aside for her next visit cements the loyalty that a consumer may have for a retail store. The ability to telephone his "personal" banker to transfer funds between accounts or to make other banking transactions without coming into the bank reinforces the satisfaction a consumer may have with his bank.

Reinforcement Schedules Marketers have found that product quality must be consistently high and provide customer satisfaction with each use for desired consumer behavior to continue. However, they have also discovered that some nonproduct rewards do not have to be offered each time the transaction takes place; even an occasional reward provides reinforcement and encourages consumer patronage. For example, airlines may occasionally upgrade a passenger at the gate, or a clothing discounter may from time to time announce a one-hour sale over the store sound system. The promise of possibly receiving a reward provides positive reinforcement and encourages consumer patronage.

Marketers have identified three types of reinforcement schedules: total (or continuous) reinforcement, systematic (fixed ratio) reinforcement, and random (variable ratio) reinforcement. An example of a total (or continuous) reinforcement schedule is the free after-dinner drink or fruit plate always served to patrons at certain restaurants. Needless to say, the basic product or service rendered is expected to provide total satisfaction (reinforcement) each time it is used.

A *fixed ratio* reinforcement schedule provides reinforcement every "*n*th" time the product or service is purchased (say, every third time). For example, a retailer may send a credit voucher to account holders every three months based on a percentage of the previous quarter's purchases. A *variable ratio* reinforcement schedule rewards consumers on a random basis or on an average frequency basis (such as every third or tenth transaction). Gambling casinos operate on the basis of variable ratios. People pour money into slot machines (which are programmed to pay off on a variable ratio), hoping for the big win. Variable ratios tend to engender high rates of desired behavior and are somewhat resistant to extinction—perhaps because, for many consumers, hope springs eternal. Other examples of variable ratio schedules include lotteries, sweepstakes, door prizes, and contests that require certain consumer behaviors for eligibility.

Shaping Reinforcement performed *before* the desired consumer behavior actually takes place is called **shaping.** Shaping increases the probabilities that certain desired consumer behavior will occur. For example, retailers recognize that they must first attract customers to their stores before they can expect them to do the bulk of their shopping there. Many retailers provide some form of preliminary reinforcement (shaping) to encourage consumers to visit only their store. For example, some retailers offer loss leaders—popular products at severely discounted prices—to the first hundred or so customers to arrive, since those customers are likely to stay to do much of their shopping. By reinforcing the behavior that's needed to enable the targeted consumer behavior to take place, marketers increase the probability that the desired behavior will occur. Car dealers recognize that in order to sell new model cars, they must first encourage people to visit their showrooms and to test-drive their cars. Hopefully, the test drive will result in a sale. Using shaping principles, many car dealers encourage showroom visits by providing small gifts (such as key chains and DVDs), larger gifts (e.g., a $10 check) to test-drive the car, and a rebate check upon placement of an order. They use a multistep shaping process to achieve desired consumer learning.

Massed Versus Distributed Learning As illustrated previously, *timing* has an important influence on consumer learning. Should a learning schedule be spread out over a period of time (*distributed learning*), or should it be "bunched up" all at once (*massed learning*)? The question is an important one for advertisers planning a media schedule, because massed advertising produces more initial learning, whereas a distributed schedule usually results in learning that persists longer. When advertisers want an immediate impact (e.g., to introduce a new product or to counter a competitor's blitz campaign), they generally use a massed schedule to hasten consumer learning. However, when the goal is long-term repeat buying on a regular basis, a distributed schedule is preferable. A distributed schedule, with ads repeated on a regular basis, usually results in more long-term learning and is relatively immune to extinction.

MODELING OR OBSERVATIONAL LEARNING

Learning theorists have noted that a considerable amount of learning takes place in the absence of direct reinforcement, either positive or negative, through a process psychologists call **modeling** or **observational learning** (also called *vicarious learning*). Consumers often observe how others behave in response to certain situations (stimuli) and the ensuing results (reinforcement) that occur, and they imitate (model) the positively reinforced behavior when faced with similar situations. Modeling is *the process through which individuals learn behavior by observing the behavior of others and the consequences of such behavior.* Their role models are usually people they admire because of such traits as appearance, accomplishment, skill, and even social class.

Advertisers recognize the importance of observational learning in their selection of models—whether celebrities or unknowns. If a teenager sees an ad that depicts social success as the outcome of using a certain brand of shampoo, she will want to buy it. If her brother sees a commercial that shows a muscular young athlete eating Wheaties—"the breakfast of champions"—he will want some, too. Indeed, vicarious (or observational) learning is the basis of much of today's advertising. Consumer models with whom the target audience can identify are shown achieving positive outcomes to common problem situations through the use of the advertised product. Children learn much of their social behavior and consumer behavior by observing their older siblings or their parents. They imitate the behavior of those they see rewarded, expecting to be rewarded similarly if they adopt the same behavior. Figure 7-11 depicts an ad portraying modeling to advertise an upscale product.

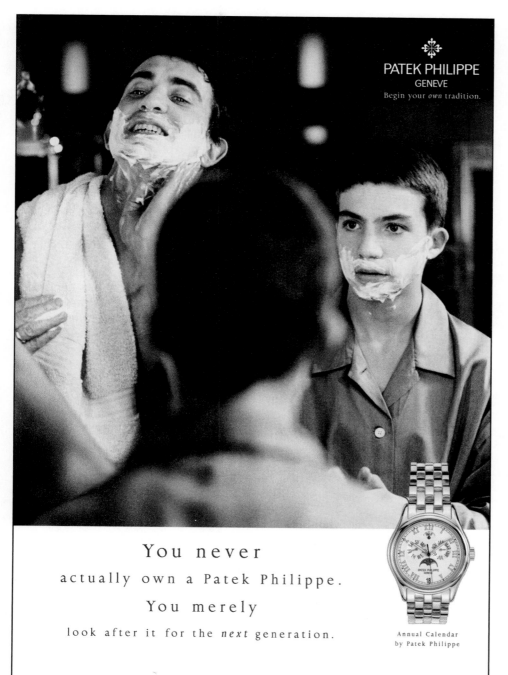

FIGURE 7-11

Consumers Learn
by Modeling
Courtesy of Patek Philippe.

Sometimes ads depict negative consequences for certain types of behavior. This is particularly true of public policy ads, which may show the negative consequences of smoking, of driving too fast, or taking drugs. By observing the actions of others and the resulting consequences, consumers learn vicariously to recognize appropriate and inappropriate behavior.

Cognitive Learning Theory

Not all learning takes place as the result of repeated trials. A considerable amount of learning takes place as the result of consumer thinking and problem solving. Sudden learning is also a reality. When confronted with a problem, we sometimes see the solution instantly. More often, however, we are likely to search for information on which to base a decision, and we carefully evaluate what we learn in order to make the best decision possible for our purposes.

Learning based on mental activity is called **cognitive learning.** Cognitive learning theory holds that the kind of learning most characteristic of human beings is *problem solving,* which enables individuals to gain some control over their environment. Unlike behavioral learning theory, cognitive theory holds that learning involves complex *mental processing of information.* Instead of stressing the importance of repetition or the association of a reward with a specific response, cognitive theorists emphasize the role of motivation and mental processes in producing a desired response. Figure 7-12 presents an ad designed to appeal to cognitive processing.

INFORMATION PROCESSING

Just as a computer processes information received as input, so too does the human mind process the information it receives as input. **Information processing** is related to both the consumer's cognitive ability and the complexity of the information to be processed. Consumers process product information by attributes, brands, comparisons between brands, or a combination of these factors. Although the attributes included in the brand's message and the number of available alternatives influence the intensity or degree of information processing, consumers with higher cognitive ability apparently acquire more product information and are more capable of integrating information on several product attributes than consumers with lesser ability.

Individuals also differ in terms of **imagery**—that is, in their ability to form mental images—and these differences influence their ability to recall information. Individual differences in imagery processing can be measured with tests of *imagery vividness* (the ability to evoke clear images), *processing style* (preference for and frequency of visual versus verbal processing), and *daydream (fantasy) content* and *frequency.*[9]

The more experience a consumer has with a product category, the greater his or her ability to make use of product information. Greater familiarity with the product category also increases cognitive ability and learning during a new purchase decision, particularly with regard to technical information. Some consumers learn by analogy; that is, they transfer knowledge about products they are familiar with to new or unfamiliar products in order to enhance their understanding.[10] One study found that when people exerted more cognitive effort in processing information about an alternative, they experienced a process-induced negative effect toward that alternative and were more likely to choose a product that required less effort to evaluate. However, the negative effect did not influence product choice for a clearly superior product.[11]

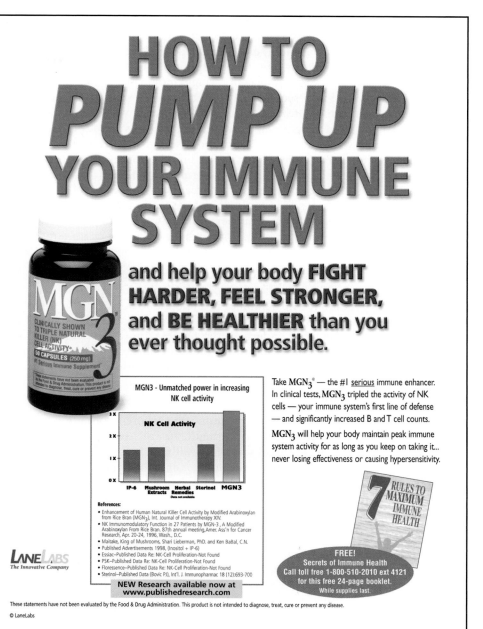

FIGURE 7-12

Appeal to Cognitive
Processing
Courtesy of LaneLabs.

How Consumers Store, Retain, and Retrieve Information

Of central importance to the processing of information is the human memory. A
basic research concern of most cognitive scientists is discovering how information
gets stored in memory, how it is retained, and how it is retrieved.

Structure of Memory Because information processing occurs in stages, it is generally believed that there are separate and sequential "storehouses" in memory where
information is kept temporarily before further processing: a sensory store, a short-
term store, and a long-term store.

Sensory Store All data come to us through our senses; however, the senses do not transmit whole images as a camera does. Instead, each sense receives a fragmented piece of information (such as the smell, color, shape, and feel of a flower) and transmits it to the brain in parallel, where the perceptions of a single instant are synchronized and perceived as a single image, in a single moment of time. The image of a sensory input lasts for just a second or two in the mind's **sensory store.** If it is not processed, it is lost immediately. As noted in Chapter 6, we are constantly bombarded with stimuli from the environment and subconsciously block out a great deal of information that we do not "need" or cannot use. For marketers, this means that although it is relatively easy to get information into the consumer's sensory store, it is difficult to make a lasting impression. Furthermore, studies suggest that the brain automatically and subconsciously "tags" all perceptions with a value, either positive or negative; this evaluation, added to the initial perception in the first microsecond of cognition, tends to remain unless further information is processed.[12] This would explain why first impressions tend to last and why it is hazardous for a marketer to introduce a product prematurely into the marketplace.

Short-Term Store The **short-term store** (known as "working memory") is the stage of real memory in which information is processed and held for just a brief period. Anyone who has ever looked up a number in a telephone book, only to forget it just before dialing, knows how briefly information lasts in short-term storage. If information in the short-term store undergoes the process known as *rehearsal* (i.e., the silent, mental repetition of information), it is then transferred to the long-term store. The transfer process takes from 2 to 10 seconds. If information is not rehearsed and transferred, it is lost in about 30 seconds or less. The amount of information that can be held in short-term storage is limited to about four or five items.

Long-Term Store In contrast to the short-term store, where information lasts only a few seconds, the **long-term store** retains information for relatively extended periods of time. Although it is possible to forget something within a few minutes after the information has reached long-term storage, it is more common for data in long-term storage to last for days, weeks, or even years. Almost all of us, for example, can remember the name of our first-grade teacher. Figure 7-13 depicts the transfer of information received by the sensory store, through the short-term store, to long-term storage.

Rehearsal and Encoding The amount of information available for delivery from short-term storage to long-term storage depends on the amount of **rehearsal** it is given. Failure to rehearse an input, either by repeating it or by relating it to other data, can result in fading and eventual loss of the information. Information can also be lost because of competition for attention. For example, if the short-term store receives a great number of inputs simultaneously from the sensory store, its capacity may be reduced to only two or three pieces of information.

FIGURE 7-13

Information Processing and Memory Stores

The purpose of rehearsal is to hold information in short-term storage long enough for encoding to take place. **Encoding** is the process by which we select a word or visual image to represent a perceived object. Marketers, for example, help consumers encode brands by using brand symbols. Kellogg's uses Tony the Tiger on its Frosted Flakes; the Green Giant Company has its Jolly Green Giant. Dell Computer turns the *e* in its logo on its side for quick name recognition; Microsoft uses a stylized window, presumably on the world.

"Learning" a picture takes less time than learning verbal information, but both types of information are important in forming an overall mental image. A print ad with both an illustration and body copy is more likely to be encoded and stored than an illustration without verbal information. A study that compared the effects of visual and verbal advertising found that, when advertising copy and illustrations focus on different product attributes, the illustrations disproportionately influence consumer inferences.[13] Another study found that high-imagery copy had greater recall than low-imagery copy, whether or not it was accompanied by an illustration; for low-imagery copy, however, illustrations were an important factor in audience recall.[14]

Researchers have found that the encoding of a commercial is related to the context of the TV program during (or adjacent to) which it is shown. Some parts of a program may require viewers to commit a larger portion of their cognitive resources to processing (e.g., when a dramatic event takes place versus a casual conversation). When viewers commit more cognitive resources to the program itself, they encode and store less of the information conveyed by a commercial. This suggests that commercials requiring relatively little cognitive processing may be more effective within or adjacent to a dramatic program setting than commercials requiring more elaborate processing.[15] Other research indicates that viewers who are very involved with a television show respond more positively to commercials adjacent to that show and have more positive purchase intentions.[16]

Men and women exhibit different encoding patterns. For example, although women are more likely than men to recall TV commercials depicting a social relationship theme, there is no difference in recall among men and women for commercials that focus on the product itself.[17]

When consumers are presented with too much information (called **information overload**), they may encounter difficulty in encoding and storing it all. Findings suggest that it is difficult for consumers to remember product information from ads for new brands in heavily advertised categories.[18] Consumers can become cognitively overloaded when they are given a lot of information in a limited time. The result of this overload is confusion, resulting in poor purchase decisions.

Retention Information does not just sit in long-term storage waiting to be retrieved. Instead, information is constantly organized and reorganized as new links between chunks of information are forged. In fact, many information-processing theorists view the long-term store as a network consisting of nodes (i.e., concepts), with links between and among them. As individuals gain more knowledge about a subject, they expand their network of relationships and sometimes their search for additional information. This process is known as *activation,* which involves relating new data to old to make the material more meaningful. Consumer memory for the name of a product may also be activated by relating it to the spokesperson used in its advertising. For many people, Michael Jordan means Nike sneakers. The total package of associations brought to mind when a cue is activated is called a *schema.*

Product information stored in memory tends to be brand based, and consumers interpret new information in a manner consistent with the way in which it is already organized. Consumers are confronted with thousands of new products each year, and their information search is often dependent upon how similar or dissimilar (discrepant) these products are to product categories already stored in memory. Therefore, consumers are more likely to recall the information they receive on new products bearing a familiar brand name, and their memory is less affected by exposure to competitive ads.

Consumers recode what they have already encoded to include larger amounts of information (chunking). For example, those individuals new to a chessboard must carefully contemplate their every move, whereas experienced chess players can readily anticipate their opponents' moves and make their own moves accordingly. Marketers should research the kinds and numbers of groupings (chunks) of information that consumers can handle. When the chunks offered in an advertisement do not match those in the consumer's frame of reference, information recall may be hampered. The degree of prior knowledge is also an important consideration. Knowledgeable consumers can take in more complex chunks of information than those who are less knowledgeable in the product category. Thus, the amount and type of technological information contained in a computer ad can be much more detailed in a magazine such as *PC Magazine* or *Wired* than in a general-interest magazine such as *Time*.

Information is stored in long-term memory in two ways: *episodically* (by the order in which it is acquired) and *semantically* (according to significant concepts). We may remember having gone to a movie last Saturday because of our ability to store data episodically, and we may remember the plot, the stars, and the director because of our ability to store data semantically. Learning theorists believe that memories stored semantically are organized into frameworks by which we integrate new data with previous experience. For information about a new brand or model of printer to enter our memory, for example, we would have to relate it to our previous experience with printers in terms of such qualities as speed, print quality, resolution, and memory.

Retrieval **Retrieval** is the *process by which we recover information from long-term storage.* For example, when we are unable to remember something with which we are very familiar, we are experiencing a failure of the retrieval system. Marketers maintain that consumers tend to remember the product's benefits rather than its attributes, suggesting that advertising messages are most effective when they link the product's attributes with the benefits that consumers seek from the product; this view is consistent with the previous discussion of product positioning strategies (Chapter 6). Consumers are likely to spend time interpreting and elaborating on information they find relevant to their needs and to activate such relevant knowledge from long-term memory.[19]

Studies indicate that incongruent (or unexpected) message elements pierce consumers' perceptual screens and improve the memorability of an ad when these elements are relevant to the advertising message.[20] For example, an ad for a brand of stain-resistant, easy-to-clean carpet shows an elegantly dressed couple in a beautiful dining room setting where the man inadvertently knocks the food, the flowers, and the china crashing to the floor. The elegance of the actors and the upscale setting make the accident totally incongruous and unexpected, whereas the message remains highly relevant: The mess can be cleaned up easily without leaving a stain on the carpet.

Incongruent elements that are not relevant to an ad also pierce the consumer's perceptual screen but provide no memorability for the product. An ad showing a nude woman sitting on a piece of office furniture would very likely attract readers' attention, but would provide no memorability for the product or the advertiser because of the irrelevance of the nudity to the advertising message.

Interference The greater the number of competitive ads in a product category, the lower the recall of brand claims in a specific ad. These **interference effects** are caused by confusion with competing ads and make information retrieval difficult. Ads can also act as retrieval cues for a competitive brand. An example of such consumer confusion occurred when consumers attributed the long-running and attention-getting television campaign featuring the Eveready Energizer Bunny to the leader in the field, Duracell.

Advertisements for competing brands or for other products made by the same manufacturer can lower the consumer's ability to remember advertised brand information. Such effects occur in response to even a small amount of advertising for similar products. The level of interference experienced can depend on the consumer's previous experiences, prior knowledge of brand attribute information, and the amount of brand information available at the time of choice. There are actually two kinds of interference. New learning can interfere with the retrieval of previously stored material, and old learning can interfere with the recall of recently learned material. With both kinds of interference, the problem is the similarity of old and new information. Advertising that creates a distinctive brand image can assist in the retention and retrieval of message contents.

Limited and Extensive Information Processing

For a long time, consumer researchers believed that all consumers passed through a complex series of mental and behavioral stages in arriving at a purchase decision. These stages ranged from awareness (exposure to information) to evaluation (preference, attitude formation), to behavior (purchase), to final evaluation (adoption or rejection). This same series of stages is often presented as the *consumer adoption process* (discussed in Chapter 15).

A number of models have been developed over the years to express the same notion of sequential processing of information by consumers (see Table 7-1). Initially, marketing scholars believed that extensive and complex processing of information by consumers was applicable to all purchase decisions. However, on the basis of their own subjective experiences as consumers, some theorists began to realize that there were some purchase situations that simply did not call for extensive information processing and evaluation; that sometimes consumers simply went from awareness of a need to a routine purchase, without a great deal of information

TABLE 7-1 Models of Cognitive Learning

	PROMOTIONAL MODEL	TRICOMPONENT MODEL	DECISION-MAKING MODEL	INNOVATION ADOPTION MODEL	INNOVATION DECISION PROCESS
SEQUENTIAL STAGES OF PROCESSING	Attention	Cognitive	Awareness	Awareness	
			Knowledge		Knowledge
	Interest	Affective		Interest	
	Desire		Evaluation	Evaluation	Persuasion
	Action	Conative	Purchase	Trial	Decision
			Postpurchase Evaluation	Adoption	Confirmation

search and mental evaluation. Such purchases were considered of minimal personal relevance, as opposed to highly relevant, search-oriented purchases. Purchases of minimal personal importance were called *low-involvement purchases,* and complex, search-oriented purchases were considered *high-involvement purchases.* The following section describes the development of **involvement theory** and discusses its applications to marketing strategy.

INVOLVEMENT THEORY

Involvement theory developed from a stream of research called **hemispheral lateralization,** or split-brain theory. The basic premise of *split-brain theory* is that the right and left hemispheres of the brain "specialize" in the kinds of information they process. The left hemisphere is primarily responsible for cognitive activities such as reading, speaking, and attributional information processing. Individuals who are exposed to verbal information cognitively analyze the information through left-brain processing and form mental images. Unlike the left hemisphere, the right hemisphere of the brain is concerned with nonverbal, timeless, pictorial, and holistic information. Put another way, the left side of the brain is rational, active, and realistic; the right side is emotional, metaphoric, impulsive, and intuitive.[21] Figure 7-14 shows an ad literally depicting split-brain theory.

Involvement Theory and Media Strategy

Building on the notion of hemispheral lateralization, a pioneer consumer researcher theorized that individuals *passively* process and store right-brain (nonverbal, pictorial) information—that is, without active involvement.[22] Because TV is primarily a pictorial medium, TV viewing was considered a right-brain activity (passive and holistic processing of images viewed on the screen), and TV itself was therefore considered a low-involvement medium. This research concluded that **passive learning** occurs through repeated exposures to a TV commercial (i.e., low-involvement information processing) and produces changes in consumer behavior (e.g., product purchases) *prior* to changes in the consumer's attitude toward the product. This view contradicts the models presented in Table 7-1, all of which maintain that cognitive evaluation and favorable attitude toward a product take place before the actual purchase behavior.

To extend this line of reasoning, cognitive (verbal) information is processed by the left side of the brain; thus, print media (e.g., newspapers and magazines) and interactive media (the Internet) are considered high-involvement media. According to this theory, print advertising is processed in the complex sequence of cognitive stages depicted in classic models of information processing (i.e., high-involvement information processing).

The right-brain theory of passive processing of information is consistent with classical conditioning. Through repetition, the product is paired with a visual image (e.g., a distinctive package) to produce the desired response: purchase of the advertised brand. According to this theory, in situations of passive learning (generated by low-involvement media), repetition is the key factor in producing purchase behavior. In marketing terms, the theory suggests that television commercials are most effective when they are of short duration and repeated frequently, thus ensuring brand familiarity without provoking detailed evaluation of the message content. A study of Web banner advertising found important attitudinal effects among viewers even when they didn't click through to the hyperlinked ad.[23]

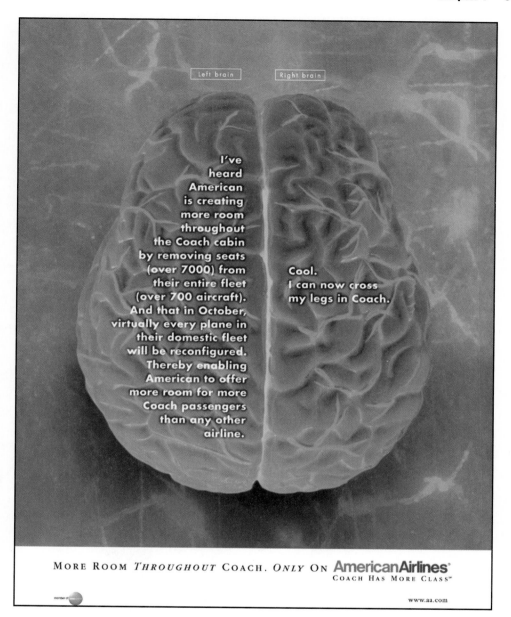

FIGURE 7-14

Ad Based on Split-Brain
Theory
Courtesy of American Airlines.
Image © Abrams
Lacagnina/Getty Images/
The Image Bank.

The right-brain processing theory stresses the importance of the *visual compo-nent* of advertising, including the creative use of symbols. Under this theory, highly visual TV commercials, packaging, and in-store displays generate familiarity with the brand and induce purchase behavior. Pictorial cues are more effective at gener-ating recall and familiarity with the product, whereas verbal cues (which trigger left-brain processing) generate cognitive activity that encourages consumers to evaluate the advantages and disadvantages of the product.

There are limitations to the application of split-brain theory to media strategy. Although the right and left hemispheres of the brain process different types of cues, they do not operate independently of each other but work together to process information. Some individuals are *integrated processors* (they readily engage both hemispheres during information processing). Integrated processors show greater overall recall of both the verbal and the visual portions of print ads than individuals who exhibit more "specialized" processing (i.e., right or left hemispheral processing).[24] Figure 7-15 presents an ad that builds on the notion of integrated processing; it shows an attention–getting fantasy illustration at the bottom of the page and a product illustration and block of copy at the top of the page explaining the product's benefits.

Involvement Theory and Consumer Relevance

From the conceptualization of high- and low-involvement media, involvement theory next focused on the consumer's involvement with products and purchases. It was briefly hypothesized that there are high- and low-involvement consumers; then, that there are high- and low-involvement purchases. These two approaches led to the notion that a consumer's level of involvement depends on the degree of personal relevance that the product holds for that consumer. Under this definition, high-involvement purchases are those that are very important to the consumer (e.g., in terms of perceived risk) and thus provoke extensive problem solving (information processing). An automobile and a dandruff shampoo both may represent high-involvement purchases under this scenario—the automobile because of high perceived financial risk, the shampoo because of high perceived social risk. Low-involvement purchases are purchases that are not very important to the consumer, hold little relevance, and have little perceived risk, and, thus, provoke very limited information processing. Highly involved consumers find fewer brands acceptable (they are called **narrow categorizers**); uninvolved consumers are likely to be receptive to a greater number of advertising messages regarding the purchase and will consider more brands (they are **broad categorizers**).

Central and Peripheral Routes to Persuasion

The theory of **central** and **peripheral routes to persuasion** illustrates the concepts of extensive and limited problem solving for high- and low-involvement purchase situations. The major premise of this theory is that consumers are more likely to carefully evaluate the merits and weaknesses of a product when the purchase is of high relevance to them. Conversely, the likelihood is great that consumers will engage in very limited information search and evaluation when the purchase holds little relevance or importance for them.[25] Thus, for high-involvement purchases, the *central route to persuasion,* which requires considered thought and cognitive processing, is likely to be the most effective marketing strategy. For low-involvement purchases, the *peripheral route to persuasion* is likely to be more effective. In this instance, because the consumer is less motivated to exert cognitive effort, learning is more likely to occur through repetition, the passive processing of visual cues, and holistic perception.

Various researchers have addressed the relationship between the theory of central and peripheral routes to persuasion and consumer information processing. A number of studies have found that high involvement with an issue produces more extensive processing of information. In these situations, the quality of the argument presented in the persuasive message is very influential to the decision outcome.[26] That would explain why highly involved consumers tend to use more attributes to evaluate brands, whereas less involved consumers apply very simple decision rules.

The Elaboration Likelihood Model The **elaboration likelihood model (ELM)** suggests that a person's level of involvement during message processing is a critical factor in determining which route to persuasion is likely to be effective. For example, as the message becomes more personally relevant (i.e., as involvement increases), people are more willing to expend the cognitive effort required to process the message arguments. Thus, when involvement is high, consumers follow the central route and base their attitudes or choices on the message arguments. When involvement is low, they follow the peripheral route and rely more heavily on other message elements (such as spokespersons or background music) to form attitudes or make product choices. The ad shown previously in Figure 7-12 to illustrate cognitive learning also illustrates using the central route to persuasion; Figure 7-16 shows an ad that takes

FIGURE 7-16

Peripheral Route to Persuasion
Courtesy of The Procter & Gamble Company. Used by permission.

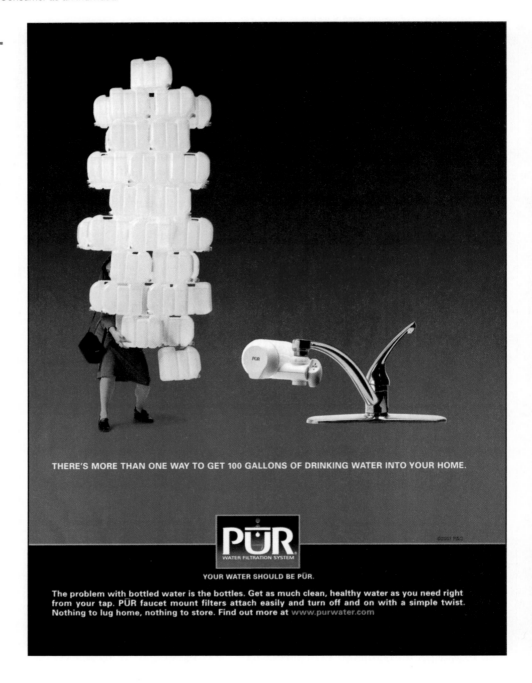

THERE'S MORE THAN ONE WAY TO GET 100 GALLONS OF DRINKING WATER INTO YOUR HOME.

PÜR
WATER FILTRATION SYSTEM

YOUR WATER SHOULD BE PÜR.

The problem with bottled water is the bottles. Get as much clean, healthy water as you need right from your tap. PÜR faucet mount filters attach easily and turn off and on with a simple twist. Nothing to lug home, nothing to store. Find out more at www.purwater.com

the peripheral route. One study found that comparative ads (see Chapter 9) are more likely to be processed centrally (purposeful processing of message arguments), whereas noncomparative ads are commonly processed peripherally (with little message elaboration and a response derived from other executional elements in the ad).[27] Another study found that the use of metaphors and figures of speech that deviate from the expected in print ads places added processing demands on the readers and increases the ad's persuasiveness and memorability. The metaphors examined in this study were such slogans as "It forced other car makers into the copier business" (Mercury Sable) and "In the Caribbean, there's no such thing as a

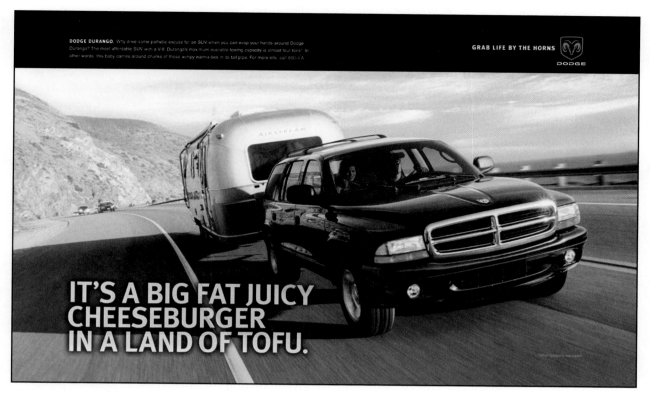

FIGURE 7-17

Unexpected Headline Metaphor Increases an Ad's Impact
Courtesy of DaimlerChrysler.

party of one" (Malibu Caribbean Rum).[28] Figure 7-17 uses a catchy metaphor head-line to advertise a Dodge Durango.

The marketing implications of the elaboration likelihood model are clear: For high-involvement purchases, marketers should use arguments stressing the strong, solid, high-quality attributes of their products, thus using the central (or highly cog-nitive) route. For low-involvement purchases, marketers should use the peripheral route to persuasion, focusing on the method of presentation rather than on the con-tent of the message (e.g., through the use of celebrity spokespersons or highly visual and symbolic advertisements).

Measures of Involvement

Given that involvement theory evolved from the notion of high- and low-involvement media, to high- and low-involvement consumers, to high- and low-involvement prod-ucts and purchases, to appropriate methods of persuasion in situations of high and low product relevance, it is not surprising to find there is great variation in the con-ceptualization and measurement of involvement itself. Researchers have defined and conceptualized involvement in a variety of ways, including ego involvement, commit-ment, communication involvement, purchase importance, extent of information search, persons, products, situations, and purchase decisions.[29] Some studies have tried to differentiate between brand involvement and product involvement.[30] Others differentiate between situational, enduring, and response involvement.[31]

TABLE 7-2	Measuring Involvement on a Semantic Differential Scale

TO ME, [INSERT PRODUCT OR PRODUCT CATEGORY **] IS:**

	1	2	3	4	5	6	7	
1. Important	—	—	—	—	—	—	—	Unimportant
2. Interesting	—	—	—	—	—	—	—	Boring
3. Relevant	—	—	—	—	—	—	—	Irrelevant
4. Exciting	—	—	—	—	—	—	—	Unexciting
5. Meaningful	—	—	—	—	—	—	—	Meaningless
6. Appealing	—	—	—	—	—	—	—	Unappealing
7. Fascinating	—	—	—	—	—	—	—	Ordinary
8. Priceless	—	—	—	—	—	—	—	Worthless
9. Involving	—	—	—	—	—	—	—	Uninvolving
10. Necessary	—	—	—	—	—	—	—	Unnecessary

Source: Adapted from Judith Lynne Zaichowsky, "The Personal Involvement Inventory: Reduction, Revision, and Application to Advertising," *Journal of Advertising,* 23, 4, (December 1994); 59–70. Reprinted by permission.

The lack of a clear definition about the essential components of involvement poses some measurement problems. Researchers who regard involvement as a cognitive state are concerned with the measurement of ego involvement, risk perception, and purchase importance. Researchers who focus on the behavioral aspects of involvement measure such factors as the search for and evaluation of product information. Others argue that involvement should be measured by the degree of importance the product has to the buyer.

Because of the many different dimensions and conceptualizations of involvement, many researchers agree that it makes more sense to develop an *involvement profile* rather than to measure a single involvement level. The suggested profile would include interest in the product category, the rewarding nature (perceived pleasure) of the product, its perceived ability to reflect the purchaser's personality, and the perceived risk associated with the purchase.[32] This view is consistent with the notion that involvement should be measured on a continuum rather than as a dichotomy consisting of two mutually exclusive categories of "high" and "low" involvement.[33] Table 7-2 presents a semantic differential scale designed to measure involvement. Table 7-3 shows a personal involvement inventory developed to measure a consumer's "enduring involvement" with a product.

Marketing Applications of Involvement

Involvement theory has a number of strategic applications for the marketer. For example, the left-brain (cognitive processing)/right-brain (passive processing) paradigm seems to have strong implications for the content, length, and presentation of both print and television advertisements. There is evidence that people process information extensively when the purchase is of high personal relevance and engage in limited information processing when the purchase is of low personal relevance. Uninvolved consumers appear to be susceptible to different kinds of persuasion than highly involved consumers.

By understanding the nature of low-involvement information processing, marketers can take steps to increase customer involvement with their ads. For example, advertisers can use sensory appeals, unusual stimuli, and celebrity endorsers to generate

TABLE 7-3	Product Involvement Inventory Measuring Consumers' Enduring Involvement with Products

1. I would be interested in reading about this product.
2. I would read a *Consumer Reports* article about this product.
3. I have compared product characteristics among brands.
4. I usually pay attention to ads for this product.
5. I usually talk about this product with other people.
6. I usually seek advice from other people prior to purchasing this product.
7. I usually take many factors into account before purchasing this product.
8. I usually spend a lot of time choosing what kind to buy.

Source: Edward F. McQuarrie and J. Michael Munson, "A Revised Product Involvement Inventory: Improved Usability and Validity," *Diversity in Consumer Behavior: Advances in Consumer Research*, vol. 19 (Provo, UT: Association for Consumer Research, 1992), pp. 108–15. Reprinted by permission.

more attention for their messages. Marketers should also focus on increasing customer involvement levels by creating bonds with their customers.[34] Of course, the best strategy for increasing the personal relevance of products to consumers is the same as the core of modern marketing itself: Provide benefits that are important and relevant to customers, improve the product and add benefits as competition intensifies, and focus on forging *bonds* and *relationships* with customers rather than just engaging in *transactions.*

Measures of Consumer Learning

For many marketers, the dual goals of consumer learning are increased market share and brand-loyal consumers. These goals are interdependent: Brand-loyal customers provide the basis for a stable and growing market share, and brands with larger market shares have proportionately larger groups of loyal buyers.[35] Marketers focus their promotional budgets on trying to teach consumers that their brands are best and that their products will best solve the consumers' problems and satisfy their needs. Thus, it is important for the marketer to measure how effectively consumers have "learned" its message. The following sections will examine various measures of consumer learning: *recognition* and *recall measures, cognitive measures,* and the *attitudinal and behavioral measures of brand loyalty.*

RECOGNITION AND RECALL MEASURES

Recognition and **recall tests** are conducted to determine whether consumers remember seeing an ad, the extent to which they have read it or seen it and can recall its content, their resulting attitudes toward the product and the brand, and their purchase intentions. Recognition tests are based on *aided recall,* whereas recall tests use *unaided recall.* In recognition tests, the consumer is shown an ad and asked whether he or she remembers seeing it and can remember any of its salient points. In recall tests, the consumer is asked whether he or she has read a specific magazine or watched a specific television show, and if so, can recall any ads or commercials seen, the product advertised, the brand, and any salient points about the product. Generally, brand names that convey specific and relevant advantages are more easily recognizable. For example, a recent study found that a brand name explicitly conveying a product benefit (such as Manhattan Mini-storage) leads to higher recall of an advertised benefit claim than a nonsuggestive brand name (Acme Storage).[36]

A number of syndicated research services conduct recognition and recall tests, such as the Starch Readership Service, which evaluates the effectiveness of magazine advertisements. After qualifying as having read a given issue of a magazine, respondents are presented with the magazine and asked to point out which ads they *noted,* which they *associated with the advertiser,* and which they *read most.* They are also asked which parts of the ads they *noted* and *read most.* An advertiser can gauge the effectiveness of a given ad by comparing its readership recognition scores to similar-sized ads, to competitive ads, and to the company's own prior ads. Figure 7-18 shows an example of a "Starched" ad.

FIGURE 7-18

Starch Readership
Scores Measure
Learning Through Ad
Recognition Tests
Courtesy of Buick.

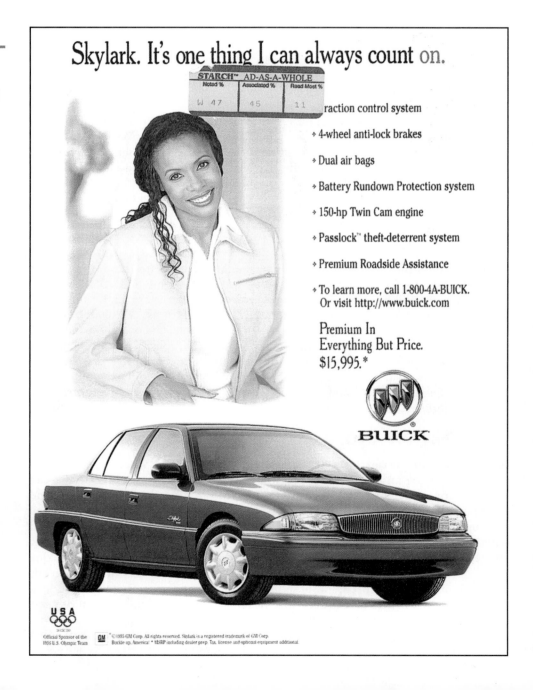

Skylark. It's one thing I can always count on.

STARCH™ AD-AS-A-WHOLE		
Noted %	Associated %	Read Most %
W 47	45	11

...raction control system

- 4-wheel anti-lock brakes
- Dual air bags
- Battery Rundown Protection system
- 150-hp Twin Cam engine
- Passlock™ theft-deterrent system
- Premium Roadside Assistance
- To learn more, call 1-800-4A-BUICK. Or visit http://www.buick.com

Premium In
Everything But Price.
$15,995.*

BUICK

Cognitive Responses to Advertising

Another measure of consumer learning is the degree to which consumers accurately comprehend the intended advertising message. **Comprehension** is a function of the message characteristics, the consumer's opportunity and ability to process the information, and the consumer's motivation (or level of involvement).[37] To ensure a high level of comprehension, many marketers conduct **copy testing** either *before* the advertising is actually run in media (called **pretesting**) or *after* it appears (**posttesting**). Pretests are used to determine which, if any, elements of an advertising message should be revised before major media expenses are incurred. Posttests are used to evaluate the effectiveness of an ad that has already run and to identify which elements, if any, should be changed to improve the impact and memorability of future ads.

Attitudinal and Behavioral Measures of Brand Loyalty

Brand loyalty is the ultimate desired outcome of consumer learning. However, there is no single definition of this concept. The varied definitions of brand loyalty reflect the models presented earlier in Table 7-1. They are summarized in Table 7-4, together with their shortcomings and weaknesses in the context of potential competitive responses.

Marketers agree that brand loyalty consists of both attitudes and actual behaviors toward a brand and that both must be measured. **Attitudinal measures** are concerned with consumers' overall feelings (i.e., evaluation) about the product and the brand and their purchase intentions. **Behavioral measures** are based on observable responses to promotional stimuli—repeat purchase behavior rather than attitude toward the product or brand. A recent study pointed out that marketers must distinguish between two attitudinal measures of brand loyalty (see Table 7-5); the study demonstrated that the degree of commitment toward buying the brand and the propensity to be brand loyal are two *separate* dimensions but did not conclusively determine which construct is more useful for explaining buying behavior.[38]

TABLE 7-4	Definitions of Brand Loyalty and Their Shortcomings

STAGE	IDENTIFYING MARKER	VULNERABILITIES
Cognitive	Loyalty to information such as price, features, and so forth.	Actual or imagined better competitive features or price through communication (e.g., advertising) and vicarious or personal experience. Deterioration in brand features or price. Variety seeking and voluntary trial.
Affective	Loyalty to a liking: "I buy it because I like it."	Cognitively–induced dissatisfaction. Enhanced liking for competitive brands, perhaps conveyed through imagery and association. Variety seeking and voluntary trial. Deteriorating performance.
Conative	Loyalty to an intention: "I'm committed to buying it."	Persuasive counterargumentative competitive messages. Induced trial (e.g., coupons, sampling, point-of-purchase promotions). Deteriorating performance.
Action	Loyalty to action, coupled with the overcoming of obstacles.	Induced unavailability (e.g., stocklifts—purchasing the entire inventory of a competitor's product from a merchant). Increased obstacles generally. Deteriorating performance.

Source: Richard L. Oliver, "Whence Brand Loyalty?" Journal of Marketing, 63 (1999), 33–44.

TABLE 7-5	Two Distinct Attitudinal Measures of Brand Loyalty

MEASURE DESCRIPTION

Attitude toward the act of purchasing the brand

Using a scale from 1 to 5, please tell me how committed you are to purchasing your preferred brand of directory advertising.

x_1 Uncommitted	1	2	3	4	5	Committed

Purchasing advertising with my preferred brand of directory in the next issue would be:

x_2 Bad	1	2	3	4	5	Good
x_3 Unpleasant	1	2	3	4	5	Pleasant
x_4 Unfavorable	1	2	3	4	5	Favorable
x_5 Negative	1	2	3	4	5	Positive
x_6 Undesirable	1	2	3	4	5	Desirable
x_7 Unwise	1	2	3	4	5	Wise
x_8 Unlikely	1	2	3	4	5	Likely

x_9 I would recommend my main brand to other people.

Unlikely	1	2	3	4	5	Likely

Propensity to be loyal

x_1 I would rather stick with a brand I usually buy than try something I am not very sure of.

x_2 If I like a brand, I rarely switch from it just to try something different.

x_3 I rarely introduce new brands and products to my colleagues.

x_4 I rarely take chances by buying unfamiliar brands even if it means sacrificing variety.

x_5 I buy the same brands even if they are only average.

x_6 I would rather wait for others to try a new brand than try it myself.

x_7 I would rather stick to well-known brands when purchasing directory advertising.

Behavioral loyalty includes the dimensions of preference and allegiance. It was operationalized as the amount of money spent on the preferred brand (preference) over time (allegiance).

Source: Rebekah Bennett and Sharyn Rundle-Thiele, "A Comparison of Attitudinal Loyalty Measurement Approaches," *Journal of Brand Management,* January 2002, 193–209.

Behavioral scientists who favor the theory of instrumental conditioning believe that brand loyalty results from an initial product trial that is reinforced through satisfaction, leading to repeat purchase. *Cognitive* researchers, on the other hand, emphasize the role of mental processes in building brand loyalty. They believe that consumers engage in extensive problem-solving behavior involving brand and attribute comparisons, leading to a strong brand preference and repeat purchase behavior. A recent study maintains that linking consumer satisfaction only to brand loyalty, as many marketers do, is shortsighted; it argues that brand loyalty is the synergy among such attitudinal components as perceived product superiority, personal fortitude, and bonding with the product or company.[39] However, one must not discount the value of satisfaction alone. A syndicated research company reported that 74 percent of its respondents resist promotional efforts by rival brands once they find a brand with which they are satisfied.[40]

Behavioral definitions (such as frequency of purchase or proportion of total purchases) lack precision, because they do not distinguish between the "real" brand-loyal buyer who is intentionally faithful and the spurious brand-loyal buyer who

FIGURE 7-19

Brand Loyalty as a Function of *Relative Attitude* and *Patronage Behavior*
Source: Alan S. Dick and Kunal Basu, "Customer Loyalty: Toward an Integrated Conceptual Framework," *Journal of the Academy of Marketing Science*, 22, 2 (1994), 101. Copyright © 1994 by *Journal of the Academy of Marketing Science*. Reprinted by permission of Sage Publications.

repeats a brand purchase because it is the only one available at the store. Often consumers buy from a mix of brands within their acceptable range (i.e., their **evoked set,** see Chapter 16). The greater the number of acceptable brands in a specific product category, the less likely the consumer is to be brand loyal to one specific brand. Conversely, products having few competitors, as well as those purchased with great frequency, are likely to have greater brand loyalty. Thus, a more favorable attitude toward a brand, service, or store, compared to potential alternatives, together with repeat patronage, are seen as the requisite components of customer loyalty. A recent study related the attitudinal and purchase aspects of brand loyalty to market share and the relative prices of brands. The study showed that brand trust and brand affect, combined, determine purchase loyalty and attitudinal loyalty. Purchase loyalty leads to a higher market share and attitudinal loyalty often enables the marketer to charge a higher price for the brand relative to competition.[41]

An integrated conceptual framework views consumer loyalty as the relationship between an individual's relative attitude toward an entity (brand, service, store, or vendor) and patronage behavior.[42] The consumer's relative attitude consists of two dimensions: the strength of the attitude and the degree of attitudinal differentiation among competing brands. As Figure 7-19 indicates, a consumer with a high relative attitude and high degree of repeat purchase behavior would be defined as *brand loyal;* a consumer with a low relative attitude and high repeat patronage would be considered *spuriously loyal.* This framework also reflects a correlation between brand loyalty and consumer involvement. High involvement leads to extensive information search and, ultimately, to brand loyalty, whereas low involvement leads to exposure and brand awareness and then possibly to brand habit (or spurious loyalty). Spuriously loyal consumers perceive little differentiation among brands and buy the brand repeatedly due to situational cues, such as package familiarity, shelf positioning, or special prices. On the other hand, truly brand-loyal consumers have a strong commitment to the brand and are less likely to switch to other brands in spite of the persuasive, promotional efforts of competitors.

Unlike tangible products where switching to another brand is relatively easy, it is often difficult to switch to another "brand" of service. For example, it is costly and time consuming to transfer one's business to a new attorney or accountant or even to get used to a new hair stylist. One study showed that the reasons that cause customers to switch service providers play a role in their loyalty behaviors toward subsequent providers. Thus, service marketers should research past customer behavior

FIGURE 7-20

Four Types of Loyalty Programs
Source: Grahame R. Dowling and Mark Uncles, "Do Customer Loyalty Programs Really Work?" *Sloan Management Review,* Summer 1997, 71–82.

	Timing of Reward	
	Immediate	Delayed
Directly Supports the Product's Value Position	**1** Retailer/Brand Manufacturer Promotions (Price Promotions)	**2** Airline Frequent Flyer Clubs, Coupons, and Tokens (GM card)
Type of Reward Other Indirect Types of Reward	**3** Competitions and Lotteries (Instant Scratches)	**4** Multiproduct Frequent Buyer Clubs (Fly Buys)

and use these data to increase the loyalty of new customers.[43] Loyalty programs are generally designed with the intention of forming and maintaining brand loyalty. One researcher argues that the objective of a sound loyalty program should be to build loyalty for the brand and product and not just the program itself. The study classifies loyalty programs into the four groups shown in Figure 7-20. The researcher argues that customers prefer immediate gratification programs (see sections 1 and 3 of the figure) over programs with delayed gratification (sections 2 and 4). On the other hand, marketers prefer programs that explicitly link the product and the program (sections 1 and 2) because they have a greater impact on purchase behavior.[44] It is essential to consider both perspectives in designing a loyalty program. Another study points out that loyalty programs for packaged goods are more effective when they offer more knowledge about the brand and increase the association between the loyalty program and the brand.[45]

Brand Equity

The term **brand equity** refers to the value inherent in a well-known brand name. This value stems from the consumer's perception of the brand's superiority and the social esteem that using it provides and the customer's trust and identification with the brand. For many companies, their most valuable assets are their brand names. Well-known brand names are referred to as **megabrands.** Among the best-known brands are Coca-Cola, Campbell's Soup, Hallmark Cards, and United Parcel Service. Their names have become "cultural icons" and enjoy powerful advantages over the competition.

Because of the escalation of new-product costs and the high rate of new-product failures, many companies prefer to leverage their brand equity through brand extensions rather than risk launching a new brand. Brand equity facilitates the acceptance of new products and the allocation of preferred shelf space and enhances perceived value, perceived quality, and premium pricing options. Researchers argue that brand equity is most important for low-involvement purchases, such as inexpensive consumer goods that are bought routinely and with little processing of cognitive information.[46] A recent study found that brand cues may actually "block" the learning of quality-related cues for specific product attributes.[47]

Because a brand that has been promoted heavily in the past retains a cumulative level of name recognition, companies buy, sell, and rent (i.e., license) their brand names, knowing that it is easier to buy than to create a brand name that has enduring strength. Brand equity enables companies to charge a price premium—an additional amount over and above the price of an identical store brand. A relatively new strategy among some marketers is **co-branding** (also called double branding). The basis of co-branding, in which two brand names are featured on a single product, is to use another product's brand equity to enhance the primary brand's equity. For example, Cranberry Newtons is a product of Nabisco and Ocean Spray, bearing both brand names. Some experts believe that using a second brand's equity may imply that the host brand can no longer stand on its own. Others question whether a co-branded product causes consumer confusion as to who actually makes the product and whether the host brand can survive if the second brand endorsement is taken away.

Brand equity reflects brand loyalty, which, as presented here, is a *learned* construct and one of the most important applications of learning theory to consumption behavior. Brand loyalty and brand equity lead to increased market share and greater profits. To marketers, the major function of learning theory is to teach consumers that their product is best, to encourage repeat purchase, and, ultimately, to develop loyalty to the brand name and brand equity for the company.

Summary

Consumer learning is the process by which individuals acquire the purchase and consumption knowledge and experience they apply to future related behavior. Although some learning is intentional, much learning is incidental. Basic elements that contribute to an understanding of learning are motivation, cues, response, and reinforcement.

There are two schools of thought as to how individuals learn—behavioral theories and cognitive theories. Both contribute to an understanding of consumer behavior. Behavioral theorists view learning as observable responses to stimuli, whereas cognitive theorists believe that learning is a function of mental processing.

Three major behavioral learning theories are classical conditioning, instrumental conditioning, and observational (vicarious) learning. The principles of classical conditioning that provide theoretical underpinnings for many marketing applications include repetition, stimulus generalization, and stimulus discrimination. Neo-Pavlovian theories view traditional classical conditioning as cognitive associative learning rather than as reflexive action.

Instrumental learning theorists believe that learning occurs through a trial-and-error process in which positive outcomes (i.e., rewards) result in repeat behavior. Both positive and negative reinforcement can be used to encourage the desired behavior. Reinforcement schedules can be total (consistent) or partial (fixed ratio or random). The timing of repetitions influences how long the learned material is retained. Massed repetitions produce more initial learning than distributed repetitions; however, learning usually persists longer with distributed (i.e., spread out) reinforcement schedules.

Cognitive learning theory holds that the kind of learning most characteristic of humans is problem solving. Cognitive theorists are concerned with how information is processed by the human mind: how it is stored, retained, and retrieved. A simple model of the structure and operation of memory suggests the existence of three separate storage units: the sensory store, short-term store (or working memory), and long-term store. The processes of memory include rehearsal, encoding, storage, and retrieval.

Involvement theory proposes that people engage in limited information processing in situations of low importance or relevance to them and in extensive information processing in situations of high relevance. Hemispheral lateralization theory gave rise to the theory that television is a low-involvement medium that results in passive learning and that print and interactive media encourage more cognitive information processing.

Measures of consumer learning include recall and recognition tests, cognitive responses to advertising, and attitudinal and behavioral measures of brand loyalty. A basic issue among researchers is whether to define brand loyalty in terms of the consumer's behavior or the consumer's attitude toward the brand. Brand equity refers to the inherent value a brand name has in the marketplace.

For marketers, the major reasons for understanding how consumers learn are to teach them that their brand is best and to develop brand loyalty.

Discussion Questions

1. How can the principles of (a) classical conditioning theory and (b) instrumental conditioning theory be applied to the development of marketing strategies?

2. Describe in learning terms the conditions under which family branding is a good policy and those under which it is not.

3. Neutrogena, the cosmetics company, has introduced a new line of shaving products for men. How can the company use stimulus generalization to market these products? Is instrumental conditioning applicable to this marketing situation? If so, how?

4. Which theory of learning (classical conditioning, instrumental conditioning, observational learning, or cognitive learning) best explains the following consumption behaviors: (a) buying a six-pack of Evian water, (b) preferring to purchase clothes at Gap, (c) buying a digital camera for the first time, (d) buying a new car, and (e) switching from one cellular phone service to another? Explain your choices.

5. a. Define the following memory structures: sensory store, short-term store (working memory), and long-term store. Discuss how each of these concepts can be used in the development of an advertising strategy.

   b. How does information overload affect the consumer's ability to comprehend an ad and store it in his or her memory?

6. Discuss the differences between low- and high-involvement media. How would you apply the knowledge of hemispheral lateralization to the design of TV commercials and print advertisements?

7. Why are both attitudinal and behavioral measures important in measuring brand loyalty?

8. What is the relationship between brand loyalty and brand equity? What role do both concepts play in the development of marketing strategies?

9. How can marketers use measures of recognition and recall to study the extent of consumer learning?

Exercises

1. Imagine you are the instructor in this course and that you are trying to increase student participation in class discussions. How would you use reinforcement to achieve your objective?

2. Visit a supermarket. Can you identify any packages where you think the marketer's knowledge of stimulus generalization or stimulus discrimination was incorporated into the package design? Note these examples and present them in class.

Key Terms

- Advertising wearout
- Attitudinal measures
- Behavioral learning theory
- Behavioral measures
- Brand equity
- Brand loyalty
- Broad categorizers versus narrow categorizers
- Central and peripheral routes to persuasion

- Classical versus instrumental conditioning
- Co-branding
- Cognitive associative learning
- Cognitive learning
- Cognitive learning theory
- Comprehension
- Conditioned learning
- Conditioned versus unconditioned stimuli

- Copy testing
- Cues
- Elaboration likelihood model (ELM)
- Encoding
- Evoked set
- Family branding
- Hemispheral lateralization
- Imagery
- Information overload

- **Information processing**
- **Instrumental conditioning**
- **Interference effects**
- **Involvement theory**
- **Learning**
- **Licensing**
- **Massed versus distributed learning**
- **Megabrands**
- **Modeling, observational, and vicarious learning**

- **Motivation**
- **Negative reinforcement versus positive reinforcement**
- **Neo-Pavlovian conditioning**
- **Passive learning**
- **Positioning**
- **Product category, product form and product line extensions**
- **Recognition and Recall tests**
- **Rehearsal**

- **Reinforcement**
- **Repetition**
- **Response**
- **Retrieval**
- **Sensory, short-term, and long-term stores**
- **Shaping**
- **Stimulus discrimination**
- **Stimulus generalization**
- **Stimulus-response theories**

Notes

1. The three product examples featured here are discussed in Robert M. McMath and Thom Forbes, *What Were They Thinking?* (New York: Time Business Random House, 1998).
2. N. J. Mackintosh, *Conditioning and Associative Learning* (New York: Oxford University Press, 1983), 10.
3. Terence A. Shimp, "Neo-Pavlovian Conditioning and Its Implications for Consumer Theory and Research," in *Handbook of Consumer Behavior*, ed. Thomas S. Robertson and Harold H. Kassarjian (Upper Saddle River, NJ: Prentice Hall, 1991), 162–187.
4. Chris Janiszewski and Luk Warlop, "The Influence of Classical Conditioning Procedures on Subsequent Attention to the Conditioned Brand," *Journal of Consumer Research*, 20, September 1993, 171–189.
5. Curtis P. Haugtvedt, David W. Schumann, Wendy L. Schneier, and Wendy L. Warren, "Advertising Repetition and Variation Strategies: Implications for Understanding Attitude Strength," *Journal of Consumer Research*, 21, June 1994, 176–189.
6. Ken Bensinger, "Can You Spot the Fake?" *Wall Street Journal*, February 16, 2001, W1, W14.
7. For example, Randi Priluck Grossman and Brian D. Till, "The Persistence of Classically Conditioned Brand Attitudes," *Journal of Advertising*, 27, 1, Spring 1998, 23–31.
8. Gregory S. Carpenter, Rashi Glazer, and Kent Nakamoto, "Meaningful Brands from Meaningless Differentiation: The Dependence on Irrelevant Attributes," *Journal of Marketing Research*, 31, August 1994, 339–350.
9. Michael D. Johnson and Claes Fornell, "The Nature and Methodological Implications of the Cognitive Representation of Products," *Journal of Consumer Research*, 14, September 1987, 214–227.
10. Jennifer Gregan Paxton and Deborah Roedder John, "Consumer Learning by Analogy: A Model of Internal Knowledge Transfer," *Journal of Consumer Research*, 24, December 1997, 266–284.
11. Ellen C. Garbarino and Julie A. Edell, "Cognitive Effort, Affect, and Choice," *Journal of Consumer Research*, 24, September 1997, 147–158.
12. Daniel Goleman, "Brain May Tag All Perceptions with a Value," *New York Times*, August 8, 1995, C1.
13. Ruth Ann Smith, "The Effects of Visual and Verbal Advertising Information on Consumers' Inferences," *Journal of Advertising*, 20, 4, December 1991, 13–23.
14. H. Rao Unnava and Robert E. Burnkrant, "An Imagery-Processing View of the Role of Pictures in Print Advertisements," *Journal of Marketing Research*, 28, May 1991, 226–231.
15. Kenneth R. Lord and Robert E. Burnkrant, "Television Program Elaboration Effects on Commercial Processing," in *Advances in Consumer Research*, vol. 15, ed. Michael Houston (Provo, UT: Association for Consumer Research, 1988), 213–218.
16. Kevin J. Clancy, "CPMs Must Bow to 'Involvement' Measurement," *Advertising Age*, January 20, 1992, 26.
17. Joan Meyers-Levy and Durairaj Maheswaran, "Exploring Differences in Males' and Females' Processing Strategies," *Journal of Consumer Research*, 18, June 1991, 63–70.
18. Robert J. Kent and Chris T. Allen, "Competitive Interference Effects in Consumer Memory for Advertising: The Role of Brand Familiarity," *Journal of Marketing*, 58, July 1994, 97–105.
19. Kevin Lane Keller, "Memory and Evaluation Effects in Competitive Advertising Environments," *Journal of Consumer Research*, 17, March 1991, 463–476.
20. For example, Susan E. Heckler and Terry L. Childers, "The Role of Expectancy and Relevancy in Memory for Verbal and Visual Information: What Is Incongruency?" *Journal of Consumer Research*, 18, March 1992, 475–492.

21. Flemming Hansen, "Hemispheral Lateralization: Implications for Understanding Consumer Behavior," *Journal of Consumer Research,* 8, June 1981, 23–36; Peter H. Lindzay and Donald Norman, *Human Information Processing* (New York: Academic Press, 1977); and Merlin C. Wittrock, *The Human Brain* (Upper Saddle River, NJ: Prentice Hall, 1977).

22. Herbert E. Krugman, "The Impact of Television Advertising: Learning Without Involvement," *Public Opinion Quarterly,* 29, Fall 1965, 349–356; "Brain Wave Measures of Media Involvement," *Journal of Advertising Research,* 11, February 1971, 3–10; and "Memory Without Recall, Exposure Without Perception," *Journal of Advertising Research,* Classics 1, September 1982, 80–85.

23. Rex Briggs and Nigel Hollis, "Advertising on the Web: Is There Response Before Click Through?" *Journal of Advertising Research,* 37, 2, March–April 1997, 33–45.

24. Susan E. Heckler and Terry L. Childers, "Hemispheric Lateralization: The Relationship of Processing Orientation with Judgment and Recall Measures for Print Advertisements," in *Advances in Consumer Research,* vol. 14, ed. M. Wallendorf and P. F. Anderson (Provo, UT: Association for Consumer Research, 1987), 46–50.

25. John T. Cacioppo, Richard E. Petty, Chuan Feng Kao, and Regina Rodriguez, "Central and Peripheral Routes to Persuasion: An Individual Difference Perspective," *Journal of Personality and Social Psychology,* 51, 5, 1986, 1032–1043.

26. See, for example, Richard E. Petty and John T. Cacioppo, "Issues Involvement Can Increase or Decrease Persuasion by Enhancing Message-Relevant Cognitive Responses," *Journal of Personality and Social Psychology,* 37, 1979, 1915–1926; Cacioppo and Petty, "The Need for Cognition," *Journal of Personality and Social Psychology,* 42, 1982, 116–131; and Cacioppo, Petty, and Katherine J. Morris, "Effects of Need for Cognition on Message Evaluation, Recall and Persuasion," *Journal of Personality and Social Psychology,* 45, 1983, 805–818.

27. Sanjay Putrevu and Kenneth R. Lord, "Comparative and Noncomparative Advertising: Attitudinal Effects Under Cognitive and Affective Involvement Conditions," *Journal of Advertising,* 23, 2, June 1994, 77–91.

28. Mark Toncar and James Munch, "Consumer Responses to Tropes in Print Advertising," *Journal of Advertising,* Spring 2001, 55–65.

29. Theo B. C. Poiesz and J. P. M. de Bont, "Do We Need Involvement to Understand Consumer Behavior?" *Advances in Consumer Research,* 22, 1995, 448–452. See also the following articles in *Advances in Consumer Research,* 11 ed. Thomas C. Kinnear (Provo, UT: Association for Consumer Research, 1984); James A. Muncy and Shelby D. Hunt, "Consumer Involvement: Definitional Issues and Research Directions," 193–196; John H. Antil, "Conceptualization and Operationalization of Involvement," 203–209; and Michael L. Rothschild, "Perspectives on Involvement: Current Problems and Future Directions," 216–217; Judith L. Zaichkowsky, "Conceptualizing Involvement," *Journal of Advertising,* 15, 2, 1986, 4–34.

30. Banwari Mittal and Myung Soo Lee, "Separating Brand Choice Involvement from Product Involvement via Consumer Involvement Profiles," in *Advances in Consumer Research,* vol. 15, ed. Michael Houston (Provo, UT: Association for Consumer Research, 1988), 43–49.

31. See Marsha L. Richins, Peter H. Bloch, and Edward F. McQuarrie, "How Enduring and Situational Involvement Combine to Create Involvement Responses," *Journal of Consumer Psychology,* 1, 2, 1992, 143–153.

32. Gilles Laurent and Jean Noel Kapferer, "Measuring Consumer Involvement Profiles," *Journal of Marketing Research,* 22, February 1985, 41–53; Jean Noel Kapferer and Gilles Laurent, "Consumer Involvement Profiles: A New Practical Approach to Consumer Involvement," *Journal of Advertising Research,* 25, 6, December 1985–January 1986, 48–56.

33. Kenneth Schneider and William Rodgers, "An 'Importance' Subscale for the Consumer Involvement Profile," *Advances in Consumer Research,* vol. 23, ed. Kim Corfman and John Lynch (Provo, UT: Association for Consumer Research, 1996), 249–254.

34. Simon Walls and David W. Schumann, "Measuring the Customer's Perception of the Bond Between the Customer and the Company," *American Marketing Association Educators' Conference Proceedings,* 12, 2001, 388–400.

35. For example, Alan Dick and Kunai Basu, "Customer Loyalty: Toward an Integrated Conceptual Framework," *Journal of the Academy of Marketing Science,* 22, Spring 1994, 99–113; Grahame R. Dowling and Mark Uncles, "Do Customer Loyalty Programs Really Work?" *Sloan Management Review,* Summer 1997, 71–82.

36. Kevin Lane Keller, Susan E. Heckler, and Michael J. Houston, "The Effects of Brand Name Suggestiveness on Advertising Recall," *Journal of Marketing,* 62, January 1998, 48–57.

37. David Glen Mick, "Levels of Subjective Comprehension in Advertising Processing and Their Relations to Ad Perceptions, Attitudes, and Memory," *Journal of Consumer Research,* 18, March 1992, 411–424.

38. Rebekah Bennett and Sharyn Rundle-Thiele, "A Comparison of Attitudinal Loyalty Measurement Approaches," *Journal of Brand Management,* January 2002, 193–209.

39. Richard L. Oliver, "Whence Brand Loyalty?" *Journal of Marketing,* 63, 1999, 33–44.

40. Diane Crispell and Kathleen Brandenburg, "What's in a Brand," *American Demographics,* May 1993, 28.

41. Arjun Chaudhuri and Morris B. Holbrook, "The Chain of Effects from Brand Trust and Brand Affect to Brand Performance: The Role of Brand Loyalty," *Journal of Marketing,* April 2001, 81–93.

42. Alan S. Dick and Kunal Basu, "Customer Loyalty: Toward an Integrated Conceptual Framework," *Journal of the Academy of Marketing Science,* 22, 2, 1994, 99–113.

43. Jaishankar Ganesh, Mark J. Arnold, and Kristy E. Reynolds, "Understanding the Customer Base of Service Providers: An Examination of the Differences Between Switchers and Stayers," *Journal of Marketing,* July 2000, 65–87.

44. Grahame R. Dowling and Mark Uncles, "Do Customer Loyalty Programs Really Work?" *Sloane Management Review,* Summer 1997, 71–82.

45. Michelle L. Roehm, Ellen Bolman Pullins, and Harper A. Roehm, Jr., "Designing Loyalty-Building Programs for Packaged Goods Brands," *Journal of Marketing Research,* May 2002, 202–213.

46. Katherine N. Lemon, Roland T. Rust, and Valerie A. Zeithaml, "What Drives Customer Equity," *Marketing Management,* 10, 1, September 2001, 20–25.

47. Stijn M. J. Van Osselaer and Joseph W. Alba, "Consumer Learning and Brand Equity," *Journal of Consumer Research,* 27, June 2000, 1–16.

At least one thing today will exceed your expectations.

Mandarin
Chicken™
Salad

Wendy's® New Garden Sensations™   We've Raised The Bar On Salads.

8

Consumer Attitude Formation and Change

As consumers, each of us has a vast number of attitudes toward products, services, advertisements, direct mail, the Internet, and retail stores. Whenever we are asked whether we like or dislike a product (e.g., a Sony DVD player), a service (e.g., DSL broadband Internet service from the telephone company), a particular retailer (e.g., Sears), a specific direct marketer (e.g., Amazon.com), or an advertising theme (e.g., "tommy girl—a declaration of independence"), we are being asked to express our **attitudes.**

Within the context of consumer behavior, an appreciation of prevailing attitudes has considerable strategic merit. For instance, there has been very rapid growth in the sales of natural ingredient bath, body, and cosmetic products throughout the world. This trend seems linked to the currently popular attitude that things "natural" are good and things "synthetic" are bad. Yet, in reality, the positive attitude favoring things natural is not based on any systematic evidence that natural cosmetic products are any safer or better for consumers.

To get at the heart of what is driving consumers' behavior, *attitude research* has been used to study a wide range of strategic marketing questions. For example, attitude research is frequently undertaken to determine whether consumers will accept a proposed new-product idea, to gauge why a firm's target audience has not reacted more favorably to its new promotional theme, or to learn how target customers are likely to react to a proposed change in the firm's packaging design. To illustrate, major athletic shoe marketers such as Nike (**www.nike.com**), or Reebok (**www.reebok.com**) frequently conduct research among target consumers of the different types of athletic footwear products that they market. They seek attitudes of target consumers with respect to size, fit, comfort, and fashion elements of their footwear, as well as test reactions to potential new designs or functional features. They also regularly gauge reactions to their latest advertising and other marketing messages designed to form and change consumer attitudes. All these marketing activities are related to the important task of impacting consumers' attitudes.

In this chapter we will discuss the reasons why attitude research has had such a pervasive impact on consumer behavior. We also will discuss the properties that have made attitudes so attractive to consumer researchers, as well as some of the common frustrations encountered in attitude research. Particular attention will be paid to the central topics of attitude formation, attitude change, and related strategic marketing issues.

What Are Attitudes?

Consumer researchers assess attitudes by asking questions or making inferences from behavior. For example, if a researcher determines from questioning a consumer that she consistently buys Almay hypoallergenic skin care products (www.almay.com) and even recommends them to friends, the researcher is likely to infer that the consumer possesses a positive attitude toward Almay products. This example illustrates that attitudes are not directly observable but must be inferred from what people say or what they do.

Moreover, the illustration suggests that a whole universe of consumer behaviors—consistency of purchases, recommendations to others, top rankings, beliefs, evaluations, and intentions are related to attitudes. What, then, are attitudes? In a consumer behavior context, an *attitude is a learned predisposition to behave in a consistently favorable or unfavorable way with respect to a given object.* Each part of this definition describes an important property of an attitude and is critical to understanding the role of attitudes in consumer behavior.

THE ATTITUDE "OBJECT"

The word *object* in our consumer-oriented definition of attitude should be interpreted broadly to include specific consumption- or marketing-related concepts, such as product, product category, brand, service, possessions, product use, causes or issues, people, advertisement, Internet site, price, medium, or retailer.

In conducting attitude research, we tend to be *object specific.* For example, if we were interested in learning consumers' attitudes toward three major brands of DVD players, our "object" might include Sony, Toshiba, and Panasonic; if we were examining consumer attitudes toward major brands of cellular telephones, our "object" might include Nokia, Ericsson, Samsung, Kyocera, LG, Panasonic, and Motorola.

ATTITUDES ARE A LEARNED PREDISPOSITION

There is general agreement that attitudes are *learned.* This means that attitudes relevant to purchase behavior are formed as a result of direct experience with the product, word-of-mouth information acquired from others, or exposure to mass-media advertising, the Internet and various forms of direct marketing (e.g., a retailer's catalog). It is important to remember that although attitudes may result from behavior, they are not synonymous with behavior. Instead, they reflect either a favorable or an unfavorable evaluation of the attitude object. As *learned predispositions,* attitudes have a motivational quality; that is, they might propel a consumer *toward* a particular behavior or repel the consumer *away* from a particular behavior.

ATTITUDES HAVE CONSISTENCY

Another characteristic of attitudes is that they are relatively consistent with the behavior they reflect. However, despite their *consistency,* attitudes are not necessarily permanent; they do change. (Attitude change is explored later in this chapter.)

It is important to illustrate what we mean by consistency. Normally, we expect consumers' behavior to correspond with their attitudes. For example, if a French consumer reported preferring Japanese over Korean electronics, we would expect that the individual would be more likely to buy a Japanese brand when his current VCR needed to be replaced. In other words, when consumers are free to act as they wish, we anticipate that their actions will be consistent with their attitudes. However, circumstances often preclude consistency between attitudes and behavior. For example, in the case of our French consumer, the matter of affordability may intervene, and the consumer would find a particular Korean VCR to be a more cost-effective choice than a Japanese VCR. Therefore, we must consider possible *situational* influences on consumer attitudes and behavior.

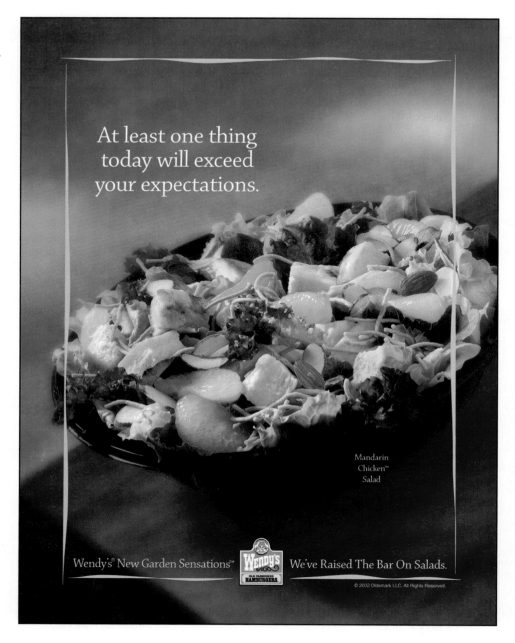

ATTITUDES OCCUR WITHIN A SITUATION

It is not immediately evident from our definition that attitudes occur within and are affected by the *situation*. By situation, we mean events or circumstances that, at a particular point in time, influence the relationship between an attitude and behavior. A specific situation can cause consumers to behave in ways seemingly inconsistent with their attitudes. For instance, let us assume that Reid purchases a different brand of deodorant each time the brand he is using runs low. Although his brand-switching behavior may seem to reflect a negative attitude or dissatisfaction with the brands he tries, it actually may be influenced by a specific situation, for example, his wish to economize. Thus, he will buy whatever is the least expensive brand. Consider the recent slowdown in the U.S. economy. For the first time in more than 65 years, the market share of popularly priced Suave brand hair care products topped 10 percent, while other manufacturers cut prices on their premium-priced offerings.[1]

The opposite can also be true. If Noah stays at a Hampton Inn each time he goes out of town on business, we may erroneously infer that he has a particularly favorable attitude toward Hampton Inn. On the contrary, Noah may find Hampton Inn to be "just okay." However, because he owns his own business and travels at his own expense, he may feel that Hampton Inn is "good enough," given that he may be paying less than he would be paying if he stayed at a Marriott, Sheraton, or Hilton hotel.

Indeed, individuals can have a variety of attitudes toward a particular behavior, each corresponding to a particular situation. Dana may feel it is alright to eat lunch at Taco Bell but does not consider it appropriate for dinner. In this case, Taco Bell has its "time and place," which functions as a boundary delineating the situations when Dana considers Taco Bell acceptable. However, if Dana is coming home late from school one night, feels exhausted and hungry, and spots a Taco Bell, she may just decide to have "dinner" there. Why? Because it is late, she is tired and hungry, and Taco Bell is convenient. Has she changed her attitude? Probably not.

It is important to understand how consumer attitudes vary from situation to situation. For instance, it is useful to know whether consumer preferences for different burger chains (e.g., Burger King, McDonald's, Wendy's) vary in terms of eating situations (i.e., lunch or snack, evening meal when rushed for time, or evening meal with family when not rushed for time). Consumer preferences for the various burger restaurants might depend on the anticipated eating situation. Wendy's, for example, might be favored by a segment of consumers as a good place to have dinner with their families. This suggests that its management might position Wendy's restaurants as a nice place to take the family for a leisurely (and inexpensive) dinner. Figure 8-1 is an example of Wendy's systematic effort to provide more main-course salads as a way of distancing itself from its more traditional competition. It also seems to be a logical way to win more dinner-time customers.

Clearly, when measuring attitudes, it is important to consider the situation in which the behavior takes place, or we can misinterpret the relationship between attitudes and behavior. Table 8-1 presents additional examples of how specific

TABLE 8-1	Examples of How Situations Might Influence Attitudes	
PRODUCT/SERVICE	**SITUATION**	**ATTITUDE**
Advil Migraine	Migraine headache	"I've got to get rid of this headache fast because I've got a midterm in three hours."
Mutual of Omaha Insurance	Financial planning	"If anything happens to my spouse, I've got to have enough money to get the kids through college."
BMW Automobile	Shopping for a new car	"I want to drive the car Pierce Brosnan drove in that James Bond movie."
Dove Soap	Rough skin	"My skin gets dry in winter, so I want to use a soap with moisturizer in it."
Invisalign Braces	Crooked teeth	"I need braces but don't want the world to know I'm wearing them."
Diet Pepsi Twist	Thirst	"Why bother to put lemon in the drink when you can get it that way straight from the bottle?"
Wizard Air Freshener	Bathroom odors	"Since the bathroom has no exhaust fan, I'd better keep a can of air freshener on the sink counter."

situations might influence consumer attitudes toward specific brands of products or services.

Structural Models of Attitudes

Motivated by a desire to understand the relationship between attitudes and behavior, psychologists have sought to construct models that capture the underlying dimensions of an attitude.[2] To this end, the focus has been on specifying the composition of an attitude to better explain or predict behavior. The following section examines several important attitude models: the *tricomponent attitude model,* the *multiattribute attitude models,* the *trying-to-consume model,* and the *attitude-toward-the-ad models.* Each of these models provides a somewhat different perspective on the number of component parts of an attitude and how those parts are arranged or interrelated.

TRICOMPONENT ATTITUDE MODEL

According to the **tricomponent attitude model,** attitudes consist of three major components: a *cognitive* component, an *affective* component, and a *conative* component (see Figure 8-2).

The Cognitive Component

The first part of the tricomponent attitude model consists of a person's *cognitions,* that is, the knowledge and perceptions that are acquired by a combination of direct experience with the *attitude object* and related information from various sources. This knowledge and resulting perceptions commonly take the form of *beliefs;* that is, the consumer believes that the attitude object possesses various attributes and that specific behavior will lead to specific outcomes.

Although it captures only a part of Ralph's belief system about two types of broadband Internet connections (e.g., cable and DSL), Figure 8-3 illustrates the composition of a consumer's belief system about these two alternatives. Ralph's

FIGURE 8-2

A Simple Representation of the Tricomponent Attitude Model

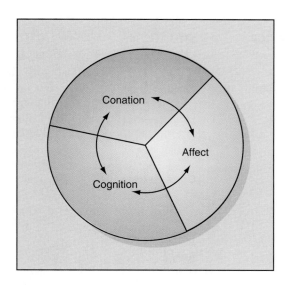

Product	BROADBAND INTERNET ACCESS							
Brand	Cable Internet Access				DSL Internet Access			
Attributes	Speed	Availability	Reliability	Other Features	Speed	Availability	Reliability	Other Features
Beliefs	Faster than DSL	Offered now by my cable company	As reliable as my cable TV	No choice of provider and slows down when lots of subscribers are online	Slower than a cable modem but faster than dial-up service	Offered now by my local telephone company	Can be spotty	Bandwidth varies less than with a cable connection but can be more difficult to install and troubleshoot
Evaluations	(++++)	(+++)	(+++)	(−)	(++)	(+++)	(−)	(+)

FIGURE 8-3

A Consumer's Belief System for Two Methods of Broadband Internet Access
Source: Adapted from Todd Spangler, "Crossing the Broadband Divide," *PC Magazine*, February 12, 2001, 92–103.

belief system for both types of connections consists of the same basic four attributes: speed, availability, reliability, and "other" features. However, Ralph has somewhat different beliefs about the two broadband alternatives with respect to these attributes. For instance, he knows from friends that the local cable company's broadband connection is much faster than DSL, but he does not like the fact that he will also have to begin subscribing to cable TV if he does not want to pay an extra $20 a month for the broadband Internet connection. Ralph is thinking of asking a few of his friends about the differences between cable and DSL broadband Internet service and will also go online to a number of Web sites that discuss this topic (e.g., www.cnet.com).

The Affective Component

A consumer's *emotions* or *feelings* about a particular product or brand constitute the *affective component* of an attitude. These emotions and feelings are frequently treated by consumer researchers as primarily *evaluative* in nature; that is, they capture an individual's direct or global assessment of the attitude object (i.e., the extent to which the individual rates the attitude object as "favorable" or "unfavorable," "good" or "bad"). To illustrate, Table 8-2 shows a series of evaluative (affective) scale items that might be used to assess consumers' attitudes toward Lubriderm Skin Therapy Moisturizing Lotion.

Affect-laden experiences also manifest themselves as *emotionally charged states* (e.g., happiness, sadness, shame, disgust, anger, distress, guilt, or surprise). Research indicates that such emotional states may enhance or amplify positive or negative experiences and that later recollections of such experiences may impact what comes to mind and how the individual acts.[3] For instance, a person visiting an outlet mall is likely to be influenced by his or her emotional state at the time. If the outlet mall shopper is feeling particularly joyous at the moment, a positive response to the outlet mall may be amplified. The emotionally enhanced response to the outlet mall

TABLE 8-2	Selected Evaluative Scale Used to Gauge Consumers' Attitudes Toward Lubriderm Skin Therapy Moisturizing Lotion

Compared to other skin moisturizing lotions, Lubriderm Skin Therapy Moisturizing Lotion is:

Good	[1]	[2]	[3]	[4]	[5]	[6]	[7]	Bad
Positive	[1]	[2]	[3]	[4]	[5]	[6]	[7]	Negative
Pleasant	[1]	[2]	[3]	[4]	[5]	[6]	[7]	Unpleasant
Appealing	[1]	[2]	[3]	[4]	[5]	[6]	[7]	Unappealing

may lead the shopper to recall with great pleasure the time spent at the outlet mall. It also may influence the individual shopper to persuade friends and acquaintances to visit the same outlet mall and to make the personal decision to revisit the mall.

In addition to using direct or global evaluative measures of an attitude object, consumer researchers can also use a battery of affective response scales (e.g., that measure feelings and emotions) to construct a picture of consumers' overall feelings about a product, service, or ad. Table 8-3 gives an example of a five-point scale that measures affective responses.

The Conative Component

Conation, the final component of the tricomponent attitude model, is concerned with the *likelihood* or *tendency* that an individual will undertake a specific action or behave in a particular way with regard to the attitude object. According to

TABLE 8-3	Measuring Consumers' Feelings and Emotions with Regard to Using Lubriderm Skin Therapy Moisturizing Lotion

For the past 30 days you have had a chance to try Lubriderm. We would appreciate it if you would identify how your skin felt after using the product during this 30-day trial period.

For each of the words below, we would appreciate it if you would mark an "X" in the box corresponding to how your skin felt after using Lubriderm during the past 30 days.

	VERY				NOT AT ALL
Relaxed	[ ]	[ ]	[ ]	[ ]	[ ]
Beautiful	[ ]	[ ]	[ ]	[ ]	[ ]
Tight	[ ]	[ ]	[ ]	[ ]	[ ]
Smooth	[ ]	[ ]	[ ]	[ ]	[ ]
Supple	[ ]	[ ]	[ ]	[ ]	[ ]
Clean	[ ]	[ ]	[ ]	[ ]	[ ]
Refreshed	[ ]	[ ]	[ ]	[ ]	[ ]
Younger	[ ]	[ ]	[ ]	[ ]	[ ]
Revived	[ ]	[ ]	[ ]	[ ]	[ ]
Renewed	[ ]	[ ]	[ ]	[ ]	[ ]

TABLE 8-4	Two Examples of Intention-to-Buy Scales

Which of the following statements best describes the chance that you will buy
Lubriderm Lotion the next time you purchase a skin care product?

_____ I definitely will buy it.

_____ I probably will buy it.

_____ I am uncertain whether I will buy it.

_____ I probably will not buy it.

_____ I definitely will not buy it.

How likely are you to buy Lubriderm Lotion during the next three months?

_____ Very likely

_____ Likely

_____ Unlikely

_____ Very unlikely

some interpretations, the conative component may include the actual behavior itself.

In marketing and consumer research, the conative component is frequently treated as an expression of the consumer's *intention to buy.* Buyer intention scales are used to assess the likelihood of a consumer purchasing a product or behaving in a certain way. Table 8-4 provides several examples of common **intention-to-buy scales.** Interestingly, consumers who are asked to respond to an intention-to-buy question appear to be more likely to actually make a brand purchase for positively evaluated brands (e.g., "I will buy it"), as contrasted to consumers who are not asked to respond to an intention question.[4] This suggests that a positive brand commitment in the form of a positive answer to an attitude intention question impacts in a positive way on the actual brand purchase.

MULTIATTRIBUTE ATTITUDE MODELS

Multiattribute attitude models portray consumers' attitudes with regard to an attitude object (e.g., a product, a service, a direct-mail catalog, or a cause or an issue) as a function of consumers' perception and assessment of the key attributes or beliefs held with regard to the particular attitude object. Although there are many variations of this type of attitude model, we have selected the following three models to briefly consider here: the *attitude-toward-object model,* the *attitude-toward-behavior model,* and the *theory-of-reasoned-action model.*

The Attitude-Toward-Object Model

The **attitude-toward-object model** is especially suitable for measuring attitudes toward a *product* (or *service*) category or specific *brands.*[5] According to this model, the consumer's attitude toward a product or specific brands of a product is a function of the presence (or absence) and evaluation of certain product-specific beliefs and/or attributes. In other words, consumers generally have favorable attitudes toward those brands that they believe have an adequate level of attributes that they evaluate as positive, and they have unfavorable attitudes toward those brands they feel do not have an adequate level of desired attributes or have too many negative or undesired attributes. As an illustration, we return to the broadband Internet connection example (see Figure 8-3). Each alternative has a different "mix" of features (a "feature set"). The defining features might include speed, reliability, cost, availability of 24/7 technical assistance, maximum file size that can be e-mailed, and so on. For instance, one of the two types of connections might be found to excel on core features, whereas the other may be really good on a few of the core features but offer more additional features. It is also possible that neither the cable nor the DSL carriers may be more than "second rate." However, what consumers will purchase is likely to be a function "how much they know," "what they feel are important features for them," and in the current example, their "awareness as to which type of broadband service possesses (or lacks) the valued attributes."

Conducting consumer attitude research with children, especially gauging their attitudes toward products and brands, is an ongoing challenge. What is needed are new and effective measurement approaches that allow children to express their attitudes toward brands. To this end, researchers have labored to develop an especially simple and short attitude measurement instrument for questioning children between 8 and 12 years of age. In the case of the example presented in Table 8-5, the questionnaire is set up to assess children's attitudes toward the Kellogg's brand.[6]

The Attitude-Toward-Behavior Model

The **attitude-toward-behavior** model is the individual's *attitude toward behaving* or *acting* with respect to an object rather than the attitude toward the object itself.[7] The appeal of the attitude-toward-behavior model is that it seems to correspond somewhat more closely to actual behavior than does the attitude-toward-object model. For instance, knowing Howard's attitude about the act of purchasing a top-of-the-line BMW (i.e., his attitude toward the *behavior*) reveals more about the potential act of purchasing than does simply knowing his attitude toward expensive German cars or specifically BMWs (i.e., the attitude toward the *object*). This seems logical, for a consumer might have a positive attitude toward an expensive BMW but a negative attitude as to his prospects for purchasing such an expensive vehicle.

TABLE 8-5 **A Scale Used to Measure Attitude Toward Brands for 8- to 12-Year-Olds**

	DEFINITELY DISAGREE	DISAGREE	AGREE	DEFINITELY AGREE
Kellogg's—I like it.	☐	☐	☐	☐
Kellogg's—It is fun.	☐	☐	☐	☐
Kellogg's—It is great.	☐	☐	☐	☐
Kellogg's—It is useful.	☐	☐	☐	☐
Kellogg's—I like it very much.	☐	☐	☐	☐
Kellogg's—It is practical/handy.	☐	☐	☐	☐
Kellogg's—It is useless.	☐	☐	☐	☐

Source: Claude Pecheux and Christian Derbaix, "Children and Attitude Toward the Brand. A New Measurement Scale," *Journal of Advertising Research*, July/August 1999, 19–27.

Theory-of-Reasoned-Action Model

The **theory of reasoned action** represents a comprehensive integration of attitude components into a structure that is designed to lead to both better explanation and better predictions of behavior. Like the basic tricomponent attitude model, the theory-of-reasoned-action model incorporates a *cognitive* component, an *affective* component, and a *conative* component; however, these are arranged in a pattern different from that of the tricomponent model (see Figure 8-4).

In accordance with this expanded model, to understand *intention* we also need to measure the *subjective norms* that influence an individual's intention to act. A subjective norm can be measured directly by assessing a consumer's feelings as to what relevant others (family, friends, roommates, co-workers) would think of the action being contemplated; that is, would they look favorably or unfavorably on the anticipated action? For example, if a graduate student was considering purchasing a new VW Beetle and stopped to ask himself what his parents or girlfriend would think of such behavior (i.e., approve or disapprove), such a reflection would constitute his subjective norm.

Consumer researchers can get behind the *subjective norm* to the underlying factors that are likely to produce it. They accomplish this by assessing the *normative beliefs* that the individual attributes to relevant others, as well as the individual's *motivation to comply* with each of the relevant others. For instance, consider the graduate student contemplating the purchase of a new VW Beetle. To understand his subjective norm about the desired purchase, we would have to identify his relevant others (parents and girlfriend); his beliefs about how each would respond to his

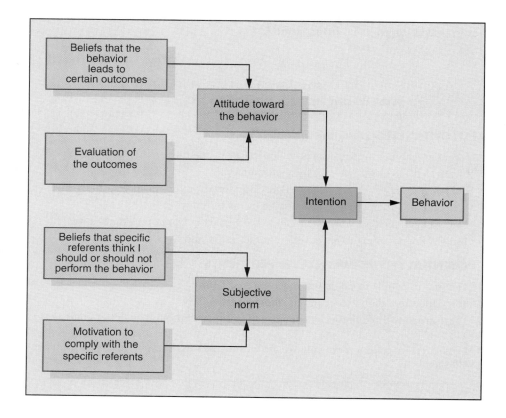

FIGURE 8-4

A Simplified Version of the Theory of Reasoned Action
Source: Adapted from Icek Ajzen and Martin Fishbein, *Understanding Attitudes and Predicting Social Behavior* (Upper Saddle River, NJ: Prentice Hall, 1980), 84, © 1980. Adapted by permission of Prentice Hall, Inc.

purchase of the Beetle (e.g., "Dad would consider the car an unnecessary luxury, but my girlfriend would love it"); and, finally, his motivation to comply with his parents and/or his girlfriend.[8]

THEORY OF TRYING-TO-CONSUME MODEL

There has been an effort underway to extend attitude models so that they might better accommodate consumers' goals as expressed by their "trying" to consume.[9] The **theory of trying to consume** is designed to account for the many cases in which the action or outcome is not certain but instead reflects the consumer's attempts to consume (i.e., purchase). A classic example of trying ("not") to consume is attempting to diet and lose weight. Xenadrine EFX seems particularly responsive to the dual challenge of easily and quickly losing weight (see Figure 8-5). In trying to consume, there are often *personal impediments* (a consumer is trying to find just the right necktie to go with a newly purchased suit for under $50 or trying to lose weight but loves potato chips) and/or *environmental impediments* (only the first 200 in line will be able to purchase this $300 DVD player for the special Saturday 8:00 A.M. to 9:00 A.M. price of $179) that might prevent the desired action or outcome from occurring. Again, the key point is that in these cases of trying, the outcome (e.g., purchase, possession, use, or action) is not and cannot be assumed to be certain. Table 8-6 lists a few examples of possible personal and environmental impediments that might negatively impact the outcome for a consumer trying to consume. Researchers have recently extended this inquiry by examining those situations in which consumers do <u>not</u> try to consume—that is, *fail to try to consume*. In this case, consumers appear to (1) fail to see or are ignorant of their options and (2) make a conscious effort not to consume; that is, they might seek to self-sacrifice or defer gratification to some future time.[10]

TABLE 8-6	Selected Examples of Potential Impediments That Might Impact on Trying

POTENTIAL PERSONAL IMPEDIMENTS

"I wonder whether my fingernails will be longer by the time of my wedding."

"I want to try to lose 15 pounds by next summer."

"I'm going to try to get tickets for a Broadway show for your birthday."

"I'm going to attempt to give up smoking by my birthday."

"I am going to increase how often I go to the gym from two to four times a week."

"Tonight I'm not going to have dessert at the restaurant."

POTENTIAL ENVIRONMENTAL IMPEDIMENTS

"The first 10 people to call in will receive a free T-shirt."

"Sorry, the shoes didn't come in this shipment from Italy."

"There are only three bottles of champagne in our stockroom. You better come in sometime today."

"I am sorry. We cannot serve you. We are closing the restaurant because of a problem with the oven."

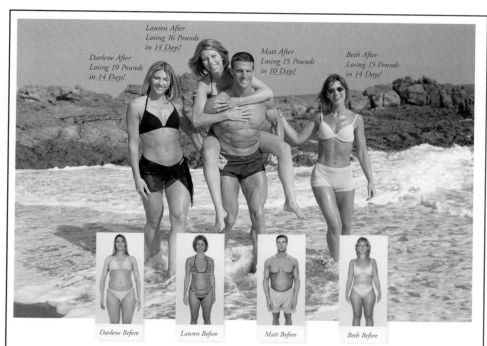

FIGURE 8-5

Ad Illustrating the
Theory of Trying to
"Consume"
Courtesy of Cytodyne
Technologies.

ATTITUDE-TOWARD-THE-AD MODELS

In an effort to understand the impact of advertising or some other promotional
vehicle (e.g., a catalog) on consumer attitudes toward particular products or brands,
considerable attention has been paid to developing what has been referred to as
attitude-toward-the-ad models.

Figure 8-6 presents a schematic of some of the basic relationships described by
an attitude-toward-the-ad model. As the model depicts, the consumer forms various
feelings (affects) and judgments (cognitions) as the result of exposure to an ad.

FIGURE 8-6

A Conception of the
Relationship Among
Elements in an
Attitude-Toward-the-
Ad Model
Source: Inspired by and based
on Julie A. Edell and Marian
Chapman Burke, "The Power
of Feelings in Understanding
Advertising Effects," *Journal
of Consumer Research,* 14,
December 1987, 431.
Reprinted by permission of
University of Chicago Press as
publisher.

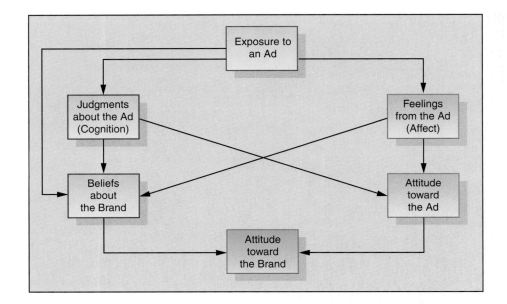

These feelings and judgments in turn affect the consumer's *attitude toward the ad* and *beliefs about the brand* acquired from exposure to the ad. Finally, the consumer's attitude toward the ad and beliefs about the brand influence his or her *attitude toward the brand.*[11]

Research among Asian Indian U.S. immigrants have explored attitudes toward 12 advertisements and purchase intention of six different products that the ads feature. The study found a positive relationship between attitude toward the advertisement and purchase intention for each of the advertised products; that is, if consumers "like" the ad, they are more likely to purchase the product.[12]

Additional research reveals that for a novel product (e.g., contact lens for pets) consumers' attitude toward the ad has a *stronger* impact on brand attitude and purchase intention than for a familiar product (e.g., pet food).[13] This same research found that beliefs about a brand (brand cognition) that result from ad exposure play a much stronger role in determining attitudes toward the brand for a familiar product. Thus, it is important to consider the nature of the attitude object in assessing the potential impact of advertising exposure.

Finally, consumer socialization has also shown itself to be an important determinant of a consumer's attitudes toward advertising. One study, for example, found that parental communication, peer communication, social utility of advertising, amount of television watched, gender, and race were all associated with attitude toward advertising. African Americans and women were found to have more positive attitudes toward advertising.[14]

Attitude Formation

How do people, especially young people, form their initial *general* attitudes toward "things"? Consider their attitudes toward clothing they wear, for example, underwear, casual wear, and business attire. On a more specific level, how do they form attitudes toward Fruit of the Loom or Calvin Klein underwear, or Levi's or Gap casual wear, or Anne Klein or Emporium Armani business clothing? Also, what about where such clothing is purchased? Would they buy their underwear, casual wear, and business clothing at Wal-Mart, Sears, JC Penney, or Macy's? How do family members and friends, admired celebrities, mass-media advertisements, even cultural memberships, influence the formation of their attitudes concerning consuming or not consuming each of these types of apparel items? Why do some attitudes seem to persist indefinitely while others change fairly often? The answers to such questions are of vital importance to marketers, for without knowing how attitudes are formed, they are unable to understand or to influence consumer attitudes or behavior.

Our examination of attitude formation is divided into three areas: *how attitudes are learned,* the *sources of influence* on attitude formation, and the impact of *personality* on attitude formation.

HOW ATTITUDES ARE LEARNED

When we speak of the formation of an attitude, we refer to the shift from having no attitude toward a given object (e.g., a digital camera) to having *some* attitude toward it (e.g., having a digital camera is great when you want to e-mail photos to friends). The shift from no attitude to an attitude (i.e., the *attitude formation*) is a result of learning (see Chapter 7 for detailed exploration of learning theories).

Consumers often purchase new products that are associated with a favorably viewed brand name. Their favorable attitude toward the brand name is frequently the result of repeated satisfaction with other products produced by the same company. In terms of *classical conditioning,* an established brand name is an *unconditioned* stimulus that through past positive reinforcement resulted in a favorable brand attitude. A new product, yet to be linked to the established brand, would be the *conditioned* stimulus. To illustrate, by giving a new moisturizing body wash the benefit of its well-known and respected family name, Oil of Olay is counting on an extension of the favorite attitude already associated with the brand name to the new product (see Figure 8-7). They are counting on stimulus generalization from the brand name to the new product. Research suggests that the "fit" between a parent brand (e.g., in this case Oil of Olay) and a brand extension (e.g., in this case Daily Renewal Moisturizing Body Wash) is a function of two factors: (1) the similarity between the preexisting product categories already associated with the parent brand (i.e., mostly products related to hair care) and the new extension and (2) the fit or match between the images of the parent brand and the new extension.[15]

Sometimes attitudes *follow* the purchase and consumption of a product. For example, a consumer may purchase a brand name product *without* having a prior attitude toward it because it is the only product of its kind available (e.g., the last bottle of aspirin in a gas station mini-mart). Consumers also make trial purchases of new brands from product categories in which they have little personal involvement (see Chapter 7). If they find the purchased brand to be satisfactory, then they are likely to develop a favorable attitude toward it.

In situations in which consumers seek to solve a problem or satisfy a need, they are likely to form attitudes (either positive or negative) about products on the basis of information exposure and their own cognition (knowledge and beliefs). In general, the more information consumers have about a product or service, the more likely they are to form attitudes about it, either positive or negative. However, regardless of available information, consumers are not always ready or

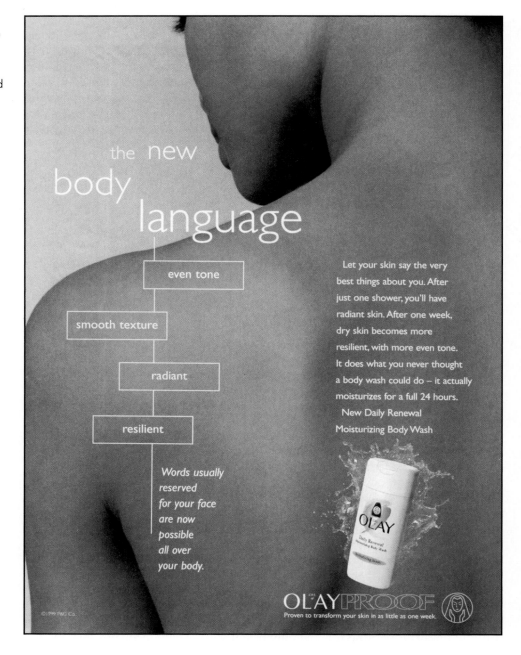

willing to process product-related information. Furthermore, consumers often use only a limited amount of the information available to them. Research suggests that only two or three important beliefs about a product dominate in the formation of attitudes and that less important beliefs provide little additional input.[16] This important finding suggests that marketers should fight off the impulse to include *all* the features of their products and services in their ads; rather, they should focus on the few key points that are at the heart of what distinguishes their product from the competition.

SOURCES OF INFLUENCE ON ATTITUDE FORMATION

The formation of consumer attitudes is strongly influenced by *personal experience,* the *influence* of family and friends, *direct marketing,* and *mass media.*

The primary means by which attitudes toward goods and services are formed is through the consumer's direct experience in trying and evaluating them.[17] Recognizing the importance of direct experience, marketers frequently attempt to stimulate trial of new products by offering cents-off coupons or even free samples. Figure 8-8 illustrates this strategy; the ad for Acuvue contact lenses includes a coupon for $50 off with the consumer's first purchase of Acuvue Toric lenses. In such cases, the marketer's objective is to get consumers to try the product and then to evaluate it. If a product proves to be to their liking, then it is probable that consumers will form a positive attitude and be likely to repurchase the product. In addition, from the information on the coupon (e.g., name and address) the marketer is able to create a database of interested consumers.

As we come in contact with others, especially family, close friends, and admired individuals (e.g., a respected teacher), we form attitudes that influence our lives.[18] The family is an extremely important source of influence on the formation of attitudes, for it is the family that provides us with many of our basic values and a wide range of less central beliefs. For instance, young children who are rewarded for good behavior with sweet foods and candy often retain a taste for (and positive attitude toward) sweets as adults.

Marketers are increasingly using highly focused direct-marketing programs to target small consumer niches with products and services that fit their interests and lifestyles. (Niche marketing is sometimes called *micromarketing.*) Marketers very carefully target customers on the basis of their demographic, psychographic, or geo-demographic profiles with highly personalized product offerings (e.g., hunting rifles for left-handed people) and messages that show they understand their special needs and desires. Direct-marketing efforts have an excellent chance of favorably influencing target consumers' attitudes, because the products and services offered and the promotional messages conveyed are very carefully designed to address the individual segment's needs and concerns and, thus, are able to achieve a higher "hit rate" than mass marketing.

In countries where people have easy access to newspapers and a variety of general and special-interest magazines and television channels, consumers are constantly exposed to new ideas, products, opinions, and advertisements. These mass-media communications provide an important source of information that influences the formation of consumer attitudes. Other research indicates that for consumers who lack direct experience with a product, exposure to an emotionally appealing advertising message is more likely to create an attitude toward the product than for consumers who have beforehand secured direct experience with the product category.[19] The net implications of these findings appear to be that emotional appeals are most effective with consumers who lack product experience.

Still another issue with regard to evaluating the impact of advertising messages on attitude formation is the level of realism that is provided. Research has shown that attitudes that develop through *direct experience* (e.g., product usage) tend to be more confidently held, more enduring, and more resistant to attack than those developed via *indirect experience* (e.g., reading a print ad). And just as television provided the advertiser with more realism than is possible in a radio or print ad, the

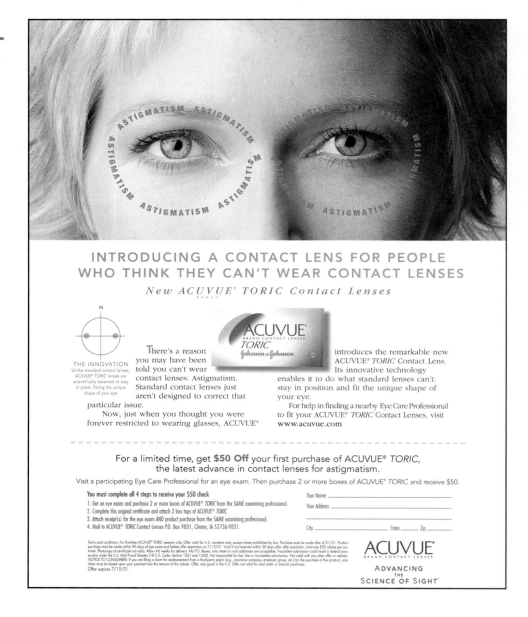

Internet has an even greater ability to provide telepresence, which is the simulated perception of direct experience. The World Wide Web also has the ability to provide the "flow experience," which is a cognitive state occurring when the individual is so involved in an activity that nothing else matters. Research on telepresence suggests that "perceptions of telepresence grew stronger as levels of interactivity and levels of vividness (i.e., the way an environment presents information to the senses) of web sites increased."[20]

PERSONALITY FACTORS

Personality also plays a critical role in attitude formation. For example, individuals with a high *need for cognition* (i.e., those who crave information and enjoy thinking) are likely to form positive attitudes in response to ads or direct mail that are rich in product-related information. On the other hand, consumers who are relatively *low in need for cognition* are more likely to form positive attitudes in response to ads that feature an attractive model or well-known celebrity. In a similar fashion, attitudes toward new products and new consumption situations are strongly influenced by specific personality characteristics of consumers.

Strategies of Attitude Change

It is important to recognize that much of what has been said about *attitude formation* is also basically true of attitude change. That is, attitude changes are *learned;* they are influenced by *personal experience* and other *sources of information,* and *personality* affects both the receptivity and the speed with which attitudes are likely to be altered.

Altering consumer attitudes is a key strategy consideration for most marketers. For marketers who are fortunate enough to be market leaders and to enjoy a significant amount of customer goodwill and loyalty, the overriding goal is to fortify the existing positive attitudes of customers so that they will not succumb to competitors' special offers and other inducements designed to win them over. For instance, in many product categories (e.g., canned soups, in which Campbell's has been the leader, or wet shaving systems, in which Gillette has dominated), most competitors take aim at the market leaders when developing their marketing strategies. Their objective is to change the attitudes of the market leaders' customers and win them over. Among the *attitude-change strategies* that are available to them are (1) changing the consumer's basic motivational function, (2) associating the product with an admired group or event, (3) resolving two conflicting attitudes, (4) altering components of the multiattribute model, and (5) changing consumer beliefs about competitors' brands.

CHANGING THE BASIC MOTIVATIONAL FUNCTION

An effective strategy for changing consumer attitudes toward a product or brand is to make particular needs prominent. One method for changing motivation is known as the **functional approach.**[21] According to this approach, attitudes can be classified in terms of four functions: the **utilitarian function,** the **ego-defensive function,** the **value-expressive function,** and the **knowledge function.**

The Utilitarian Function

We hold certain brand attitudes partly because of a brand's utility. When a product has been useful or helped us in the past, our attitude toward it tends to be favorable. One way of changing attitudes in favor of a product is by showing people that it can serve a utilitarian purpose that they may not have considered. For example, the ad for Clorox Disinfecting Spray (Figure 8-9) points out that this product will work for 24 hours, whereas its competitor, Lysol, does not.

The Ego-Defensive Function

Most people want to protect their self-images from inner feelings of doubt—they want to replace their uncertainty with a sense of security and personal confidence.[22] Ads for cosmetics and personal care products, by acknowledging this need, increase both their relevance to the consumer and the likelihood of a favorable attitude change by offering reassurance to the consumer's self-concept. For example, the ad in Figure 8-10 for Suave Performance Series Anti-Perspirant stresses in its headline "In a 24-7 World, Your Anti-Perspirant Does Not Get To Knock Off Early." Another example would be the ongoing advertising campaign for the Zippo lighter, designed to counter the trend toward disposable lighters. In an effort to equate the long-lasting

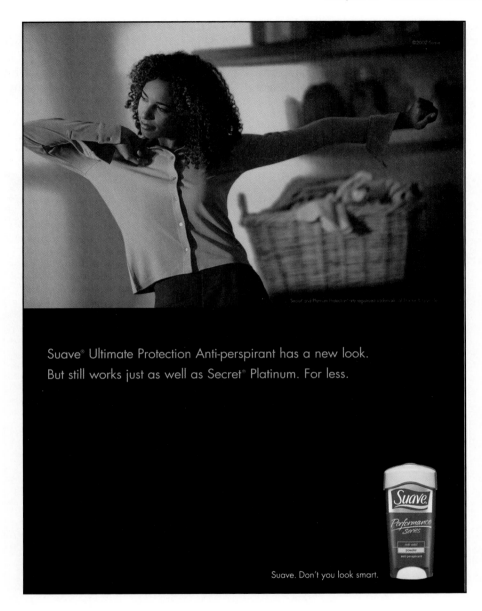

FIGURE 8-10

Suave Uses Ego-
Defensive Appeal

relationship a consumer can have with his Zippo lighter with other things in life, the campaign uses headlines such as "True love is not disposable" (the ad shows a Zippo with an engraved love poem).[23]

The Value-Expressive Function

Attitudes are an expression or reflection of the consumer's general values, lifestyle, and outlook. If a consumer segment generally holds a positive attitude toward owning the latest personal communications devices (e.g., owning the smallest cellular telephone), then their attitudes toward new electronic devices are likely to reflect that orientation. Similarly, if a segment of consumers has a positive attitude toward being "in fashion," then their attitudes toward high-fashion clothing are likely to reflect this viewpoint. Thus, by knowing target consumers' attitudes, marketers can better anticipate their values, lifestyle, or outlook and can reflect these characteristics in their advertising and direct marketing efforts. The advertisement for ACDelco in Figure 8-11 addresses target consumers' attitudes and outlooks by stating "You haven't missed a day of work in 12 years." It then appeals to the attitude by stating: "So it comes as no surprise that your auto parts are ACDelco."

FIGURE 8-11

ACDelco Uses a Value-Expressive Appeal
Courtesy of General Motors.

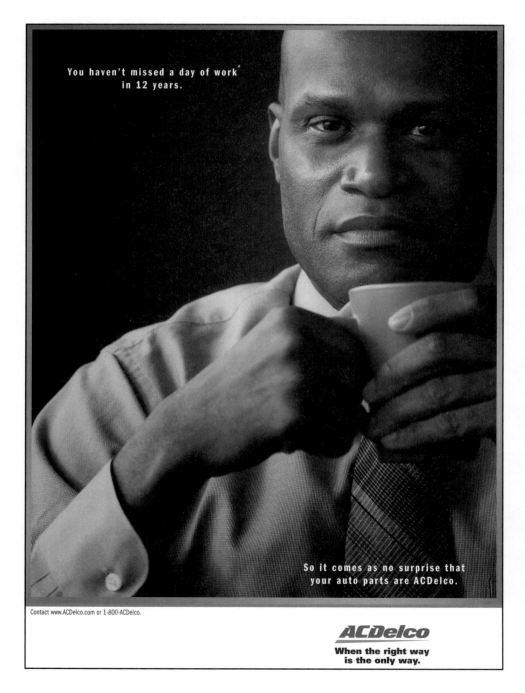

The Knowledge Function

Individuals generally have a strong need to know and understand the people and things they encounter. The consumer's "need to know," a cognitive need, is important to marketers concerned with product positioning. Indeed, many product and brand positionings are attempts to satisfy the *need to know* and to improve the consumer's attitudes toward the brand by emphasizing its advantages over competitive brands. For instance, a message for an advanced-design toothbrush might point out how it is superior to other toothbrushes in controlling gum disease by removing more plaque and that this is so important to overall good health. The message might even use a bar graph to contrast its plaque removal abilities to other leading toothbrushes. Figure 8-12 is an ad for Celestial Seasonings that points out that Green Tea is loaded with antioxidants, which are good for you. It supports its claims with some evidence (the bar graph) and an incentive (a cents-off coupon). An important characteristic of the advertising is its appeal to consumers' *need to know.*

Combining Several Functions

Because different consumers may like or dislike the same product or service for different reasons, a functional framework for examining attitudes can be very useful. For instance, three consumers may all have positive attitudes toward Suave hair care products. However, one may be responding solely to the fact that the products work well (the utilitarian function); the second may have the inner confidence to agree with the point "When you know beautiful hair doesn't have to cost a fortune" (an ego-defensive function). The third consumer's favorable attitudes might reflect the realization that Suave has for many years stressed value (equal or better products for less)—the *knowledge function.*

ASSOCIATING THE PRODUCT WITH A SPECIAL GROUP, EVENT, OR CAUSE

Attitudes are related, at least in part, to certain groups, social events, or causes. It is possible to alter attitudes toward products, services, and brands by pointing out their relationships to particular social groups, events, or causes. Ben & Jerry's ice cream factory, for example, may be the number-one tourist attraction in the State of Vermont, but, more importantly, the company is well recognized for giving approximately 7.5 percent of its pretax profits to a variety of causes (see **www.benjerry.com**), for establishing employee-led community action teams that work on local public service projects, and for distributing small grants to community groups within the State of Vermont.

Companies regularly include mention in their advertising of the civic and public acts that they sponsor to let the public know about the good that they are trying to do. For instance, Folgers® coffee sponsors a program "Wakin' up the Music," which supports a music appreciation program for youngsters in grades K–3, created by the GRAMMY® Foundation. Similarly, Crest sponsors a program that promotes good oral care to children through the Boys and Girls Clubs of America.

RESOLVING TWO CONFLICTING ATTITUDES

Attitude-change strategies can sometimes resolve actual or potential conflict between two attitudes. Specifically, if consumers can be made to see that their negative attitude toward a product, a specific brand, or its attributes is really not in conflict with another attitude, they may be induced to change their evaluation of the brand (i.e., moving from negative to positive).

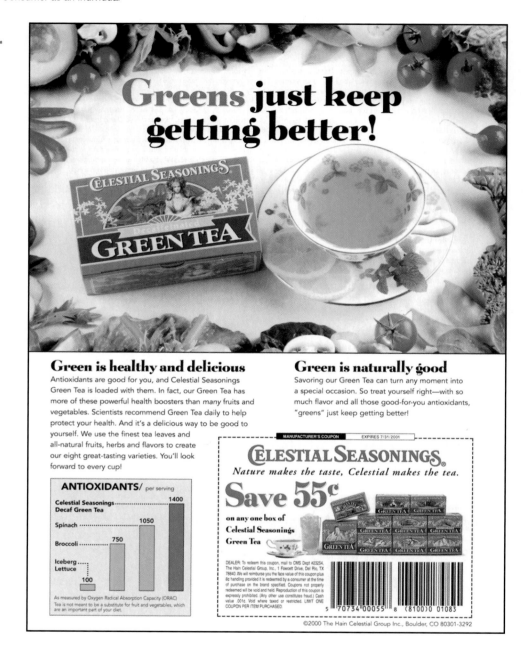

For example, Stanley is a serious amateur photographer who has been thinking of moving from 35mm photography into the realm of medium format photography in order to take advantage of the larger negative size. However, with the growth of digital photography, Stanley is unsure of whether his move to the medium format will be worthwhile. Stanley loves the idea of having a bigger negative to work with in his darkroom (attitude 1), but he may feel that purchasing a medium format camera is an unwise investment because these cameras may be supplanted in the near future by digital photography (attitude 2). However, if Stanley learns that Mamiya makes a medium format camera that offers both a film capability and a digital capability, he might change his mind and thereby resolve his conflicting attitudes (see Figure 8-13).

FIGURE 8-13

Resolving Two
Conflicting Attitudes
Courtesy of Mamiya America
Corporation.

Film or digital. The New Mamiya 645**AFD**.

The new Mamiya 645AFD is the world's first true cross-platform camera. Whether you're shooting film or digital, it is the most technologically advanced medium format camera. Responding to the most demanding photographers, the 645AFD is loaded with over 30 enhancements as compared to the original 645AF. Handling like a 35mm SLR, it incorporates features found only on sophisticated 35mm cameras, yet it offers the advantage of a format that's 2.7X larger than 35mm. Ready to conquer the digital world, the 645AFD offers exclusive data transfer from the camera to the digital back utilizing its digital intelligence via MSC (Mamiya Serial Communication). All exposure and digital capture information is displayed in both the viewfinder and main LCD panel on the camera. With exclusive Infrared Autofocus Assist and 10 World-Class AF lenses including 2 zooms, you get the best for both worlds. Choose interchangeable film magazines for 120, 220 or Polaroid film… or, switch to digital capture just by changing the back without changing your entire camera system. Sound extraordinary? It is. **The New Mamiya** 645**AFD… Part of your Future.**

MAMIYA AMERICA CORPORATION
8 Westchester Plaza, Elmsford, NY 10523
Phone: 914-347-3300 • Toll free FAX: 800-321-2205
E-mail: info@mamiya.com

Mamiya
master of the medium

ALTERING COMPONENTS OF THE MULTIATTRIBUTE MODEL

Earlier in this chapter we discussed a number of multiattribute attitude models. These models have implications for attitude-change strategies; specifically, they provide us with additional insights as to how to bring about attitude change: (1) changing the relative evaluation of attributes, (2) changing brand beliefs, (3) adding an attribute, and (4) changing the overall brand rating.

Changing the Relative Evaluation of Attributes

The overall market for many product categories is often set out so that different consumer segments are offered different brands with different features or benefits. For instance, within a product category such as deodorants, there are brands such as Mitchum that stress potency and brands such as Secret that stress gentleness. These two brands of deodorants have historically appealed to different segments of the overall deodorant market. Similarly, when it comes to cola, the market can be divided into regular colas and diet colas, or when it comes to teas, there is the division between regular teas and herbal teas.

In general, when a product category is naturally divided according to distinct product features or benefits that appeal to a particular segment of consumers, marketers usually have an opportunity to persuade consumers to "cross over," that is, to persuade consumers who prefer one version of the product (e.g., a standard "soft" contact lens) to shift their favorable attitudes toward another version of the product (e.g., a disposable contact lens), and possibly vice versa.

Changing Brand Beliefs

A second cognitive-oriented strategy for changing attitudes concentrates on changing beliefs or perceptions about the brand itself. This is by far the most common form of advertising appeal. Advertisers constantly are reminding us that their product has "more" or is "better" or "best" in terms of some important product attribute. As a variation on this theme of "more," ads for Palmolive dishwashing liquid are designed to *extend* consumers' brand attitudes with regard to the product's gentleness by suggesting that it be used for hand washing of fine clothing items. The Hewlett Packard computer ad (see Figure 8-14) challenges the notion that computers have to be difficult to use and difficult for a firm's IT department to manage by stating that the product is "Simple to the point of 'duh.'" It terms the computer as being "fast and lean," and claims that this machine will prove that "if there is less to go wrong, less will." In a similar fashion, Pantene hair care products challenge the notion that you have to be stuck with "flat hair." Pantene suggests that when consumers use its volume care products, they can increase volume by as much as 80 percent.

Within the context of brand beliefs, there are forces working to stop or slow down attitude change. For instance, consumers frequently resist evidence that challenges a strongly held attitude or belief and tend to interpret any ambiguous information in ways that reinforce their preexisting attitudes.[24] Therefore, information suggesting a change in attitude needs to be compelling and repeated enough to overcome the natural resistance to letting go of established attitudes.

Adding an Attribute

Another cognitive strategy consists of *adding an attribute*. This can be accomplished either by adding an attribute that previously has been ignored or one that represents an improvement or technological innovation.

The first route, adding a previously ignored attribute, is illustrated by the point that yogurt has more potassium than a banana (a fruit associated with a high quantity of potassium). For consumers interested in increasing their intake of potassium, the comparison of yogurt and bananas has the power of enhancing their attitudes toward yogurt.

The second route of adding an attribute that reflects an actual product change or technological innovation is easier to accomplish than stressing a previously

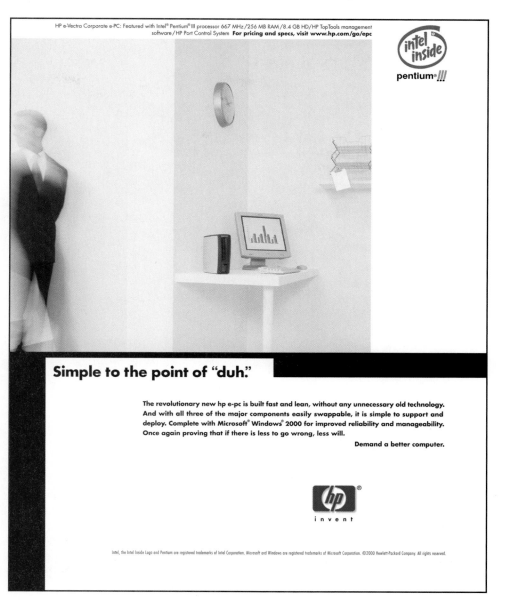

FIGURE 8-14

Changing Attitudes by Altering Beliefs About a Brand
Copyright 2000 Hewlett-Packard Company. Photo by: John Offenbach/Stockland Martel. Reproduced with permission.

ignored attribute. An example is Dove Nutrium. Not only does it clean and moisturize like regular Dove, but it also replenishes the skin's nutrients because it contains vitamin E lotion (see Figure 8-15). Sometimes eliminating a characteristic or feature has the same enhancing outcome as adding a characteristic or attribute. For instance, a number of skin care or deodorant manufacturers offer versions of their products that are unscented (i.e., *deleting an ingredient*). Indeed, Dove also markets an unscented version of its original Dove product.

Changing the Overall Brand Rating

Still another cognitive-oriented strategy consists of attempting to alter consumers' *overall assessment of the brand* directly, without attempting to improve or change their

FIGURE 8-15

Changing Attitudes by
Adding an Attribute

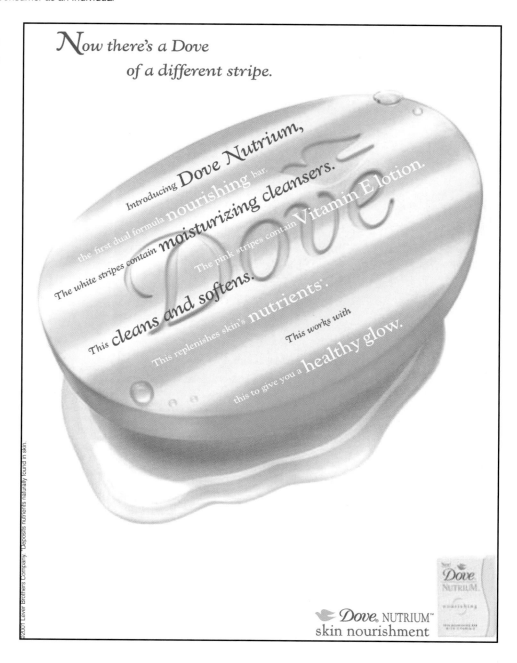

evaluation of any single brand attribute. Such a strategy frequently relies on some form of global statement that "this is the largest-selling brand" or "the one all others try to imitate," or a similar claim that sets the brand apart from all its competitors. This strategy has regularly been part of Honda's advertising approach of affirming that its cars are used by other auto manufacturers as the "standard" to live up to. It is also currently being used by Excedrin® Migraine, when it states that it is the number-one doctor-recommended brand for the relief of migraine pain.

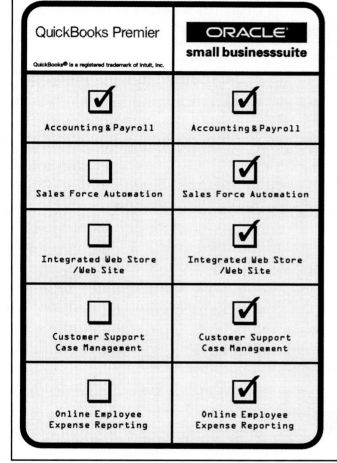

What Are You Waiting For?

QuickBooks Premier	ORACLE small businesssuite
QuickBooks® is a registered trademark of Intuit, Inc.	
☑ Accounting & Payroll	☑ Accounting & Payroll
☐ Sales Force Automation	☑ Sales Force Automation
☐ Integrated Web Store /Web Site	☑ Integrated Web Store /Web Site
☐ Customer Support Case Management	☑ Customer Support Case Management
☐ Online Employee Expense Reporting	☑ Online Employee Expense Reporting

Oracle Small Business Suite is the one, easy-to-use, totally complete system to run your entire company more efficiently. And you can import all your QuickBooks data with just a few clicks. Take Control of Your Business.

"★★★★★"
5 Stars
PC Magazine
March 2002

Call 1-800-SmallBiz or visit oraclesmallbusiness.com for a Free Trial.

FIGURE 8-16

Changing Attitudes by Changing Beliefs About a Competitor's Brand
Courtesy of Netledger.

CHANGING BELIEFS ABOUT COMPETITORS' BRANDS

Another approach to attitude-change strategy involves changing consumer beliefs about the *attributes of competitive* brands or product categories. For instance, an ad for Advil makes a dramatic assertion of product superiority over aspirin and Tylenol: The ad claims that Advil lasts longer and is gentler than aspirin and that two Advil work better than Extra Strength Tylenol. Similarly, consider the Oracle Small Business Suite advertisement presented in Figure 8-16. Clearly, the purpose of this ad is to create the attitude that the Oracle Small Business Suite is a superior product to QuickBooks, a principal competitor. In general, this strategy must be used with caution. Comparative advertising can boomerang by giving visibility to competing brands and claims. (Chapter 9 discusses comparative advertising in greater depth.)

THE ELABORATION LIKELIHOOD MODEL (ELM)

Compared to the various specific strategies of attitude change that we have reviewed, the **elaboration likelihood model (ELM)** proposes the more global view that consumer attitudes are changed by two distinctly different "routes to persuasion": a central route or a peripheral route (see also Chapter 7).[25] The *central route* is particularly relevant to attitude change when a consumer's motivation or ability to assess the attitude object is *high;* that is, attitude change occurs because the consumer actively seeks out information relevant to the attitude object itself. When consumers are willing to exert the effort to comprehend, learn, or evaluate the available information about the attitude object, learning and attitude change occur via the central route.

In contrast, when a consumer's motivation or assessment skills are low (e.g., low involvement), learning and attitude change tend to occur via the *peripheral route* without the consumer focusing on information relevant to the attitude object itself. In such cases, attitude change often is an outcome of secondary inducements (e.g., cents-off coupons, free samples, beautiful background scenery, great packaging, or the encouragement of a celebrity endorsement). Research indicates that even in low-involvement conditions (e.g., such as exposure to most advertising), in which both central and secondary inducements are initially equal in their ability to evoke similar attitudes, it is the central inducement that has the greatest "staying power"—that is, over time it is more persistent.[26]

Behavior Can Precede or Follow Attitude Formation

Our discussion of attitude formation and attitude change has stressed the traditional "rational" view that consumers develop their attitudes before taking action (e.g., "Know what you are doing before you do it"). There are alternatives to this "attitude precedes behavior" perspective, alternatives that, on careful analysis, are likely to be just as logical and rational. For example, *cognitive dissonance theory* and *attribution theory* each provide a different explanation as to why behavior might precede attitude formation.

COGNITIVE DISSONANCE THEORY

According to **cognitive dissonance theory,** discomfort or dissonance occurs when a consumer holds conflicting thoughts about a belief or an attitude object. For instance, when consumers have made a commitment—made a down payment or placed an order for a product, particularly an expensive one such as an automobile or a personal computer—they often begin to feel cognitive dissonance when they think of the unique, positive qualities of the brands not selected ("left behind"). When cognitive dissonance occurs after a purchase, it is called *postpurchase dissonance.* Because purchase decisions often require some amount of compromise, postpurchase dissonance is quite normal. Nevertheless, it is likely to leave consumers with an uneasy feeling about their prior beliefs or actions—a feeling that they would seek to resolve by changing their attitudes to conform with their behavior.

Thus, in the case of postpurchase dissonance, attitude change is frequently an *outcome* of an action or behavior. The conflicting thoughts and dissonant information following a purchase are prime factors that induce consumers to change their attitudes so that they will be consonant with their actual purchase behavior.

What makes postpurchase dissonance relevant to marketing strategists is the premise that *dissonance* propels consumers to reduce the unpleasant feelings created by the rival thoughts. A variety of tactics are open to consumers to reduce postpurchase dissonance. The consumer can rationalize the decision as being wise, seek out advertisements that support the choice (while avoiding dissonance-creating competitive ads), try to "sell" friends on the positive features of the brand, or look to known satisfied owners for reassurance. For example, consider the response of a young man who just purchased an engagement ring for his girlfriend to the following headline: "How can you make two months' salary last forever?" (see Figure 8-17). This thought and the rest of the message are likely to catch his attention. It says to him that although an engagement ring costs a great deal of money, it lasts forever because the future bride will cherish it for the rest of her life. Such a message is bound to help him reduce any lingering dissonance that he might have about how much he just spent on the ring.

In addition to such consumer-initiated tactics to reduce postpurchase uncertainty, a marketer can relieve consumer dissonance by including messages in its advertising specifically aimed at reinforcing consumers' decisions by complimenting their wisdom, offering stronger guarantees or warranties, increasing the number and effectiveness of its services, or providing detailed brochures on how to use its products correctly.

ATTRIBUTION THEORY

As a group of loosely interrelated social psychological principles, **attribution theory** attempts to explain how people assign causality (e.g., blame or credit) to events on the basis of either their own behavior or the behavior of others.[27] In other words, a person might say, "I contributed to Care, Inc. because it really helps people in need," or "She tried to persuade me to buy that unknown autofocus camera because she'd make a bigger commission." In attribution theory, the underlying question is why: "Why did I do this?" "Why did she try to get me to switch brands?" This process of making inferences about one's own or another's behavior is a major component of attitude formation and change.

Self-Perception Theory

Of the various perspectives on attribution theory that have been proposed, **self-perception theory**—individuals' inferences or judgments as to the causes of their own behavior—is a good beginning point for a discussion of attribution.

In terms of consumer behavior, self-perception theory suggests that attitudes develop as consumers *look at and make judgments about their own behavior.* Simply stated, if a young physician observes that she routinely purchases *The Chicago Tribune* on her way to the clinic, she is apt to conclude that she likes *The Chicago Tribune* (i.e., she has a positive attitude toward this newspaper).[28] Drawing inferences from one's own behavior is not always as simple or as clear-cut as the newspaper

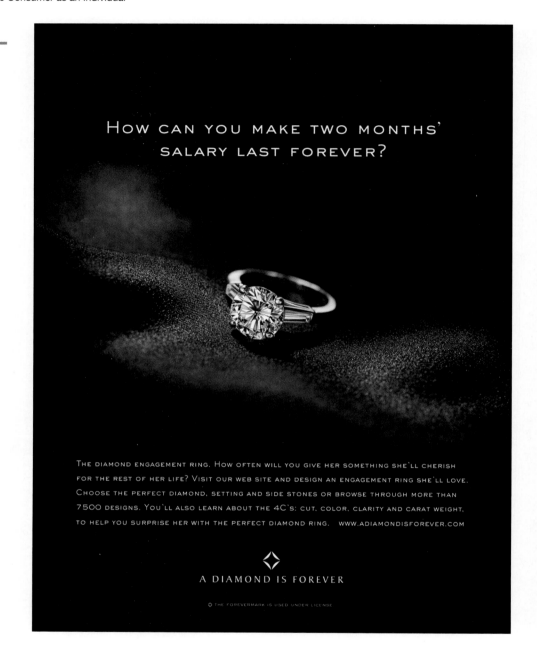

example might suggest. To appreciate the complexity of self-perception theory, it is useful to distinguish between **internal and external attributions.** Let us assume that Ralph has just finished using a popular computer presentation program (e.g., Microsoft's PowerPoint) for the first time and that his slide show is well received by his audience. If, after the presentation, he says to himself, "I'm really a natural at making great presentations," this statement would be an example of an *internal attribution*. It is an internal attribution because he is giving himself credit for the outcome (e.g., his ability, his skill, or his effort). That is, he is saying, "This slide presentation is good because of me." On the other hand, if Ralph concluded that the successful presentation was due to factors beyond his control (e.g., a user-friendly program, the assistance of a friend, or just "luck"), this would be an example of an *external attribution.* In this case, he might be saying, "My great presentation is beginner's luck."

This distinction between internal and external attributions can be of strategic marketing importance. For instance, it would generally be in the best interests of the firm that produces the presentation program if the users, especially inexperienced users, *internalized* their successful use of the graphics package. If they internalized such a positive experience, it is more likely that they will repeat the behavior and become a satisfied regular user. Alternatively, however, if they were to *externalize* their success, it would be preferable that they attribute it to the particular program rather than to an incidental environmental factor such as "beginner's luck" or a friend's "foolproof" instructions.

According to the principle of **defensive attribution,** consumers are likely to accept credit personally for success (internal attribution) and to credit failure to others or to outside events (external attribution). For this reason, it is crucial that marketers offer uniformly high-quality products that allow consumers to perceive themselves as the reason for the success; that is, "I'm competent." Moreover, a company's advertising should serve to reassure consumers, particularly inexperienced ones, that its products will not let them down but will make them heroes instead.

Foot-in-the-Door Technique Self-perception theorists have explored situations in which consumer compliance with a minor request affects subsequent compliance with a more substantial request. This strategy, which is commonly referred to as the **foot-in-the-door technique,** is based on the premise that individuals look at their prior behavior (e.g., compliance with a minor request) and conclude that they are the kind of person who says "yes" to such requests (i.e., an internal attribution). Such self-attribution serves to increase the likelihood that they will agree to a similar more substantial request. Someone who donates five dollars to cancer research might be persuaded to donate a much larger amount when properly approached. The initial donation is, in effect, the *foot in the door.*

Research into the foot-in-the-door technique has concentrated on understanding how specific incentives (e.g., cents-off coupons of varying amounts) ultimately influence consumer attitudes and subsequent purchase behavior. It appears that different-size incentives create different degrees of internal attribution which, in turn, lead to different amounts of attitude change. For instance, individuals who try a brand without any inducements or individuals who buy a brand repeatedly are more likely to infer increasingly positive attitudes toward the brand from their respective behaviors (e.g., "I buy this brand because I like it"). In contrast, individuals who try a free sample are less committed to changing their attitudes toward the brand ("I tried this brand because it was free").

Thus, contrary to what might be expected, it is not the biggest incentive that is most likely to lead to positive attitude change. If an incentive is too big, marketers run the risk that consumers might externalize the cause of their behavior to the incentive and be *less* likely to change their attitudes and *less* likely to make future purchases of the brand. Instead, what seems most effective is a *moderate* incentive, one that is just big enough to stimulate initial purchase of the brand but still small enough to encourage consumers to internalize their positive usage experience and allow a positive attitude change to occur.[29]

Attributions Toward Others

In addition to understanding self-perception theory, it is important to understand **attributions toward others** because of the variety of potential applications to consumer behavior and marketing. As already suggested, every time a person asks "why?" about a statement or action of another or "others"—a family member, a friend, a salesperson, a direct marketer, a shipping company—attribution theory is relevant. To illustrate, in evaluating the words or deeds of others, say, a salesperson, a consumer tries to determine if the salesperson's motives are in the consumer's best interests. If the salesperson's motives are viewed as favorable to the consumer, the consumer is likely to respond favorably. Otherwise, the consumer is likely to reject the salesperson's words and go elsewhere to make a purchase. In another case, a consumer orders a new DVD player from a major direct marketer such as **Amazon.com** or **Buy.com**. Because the consumer wants it immediately, she agrees to pay an extra $5 to $10 for next-day delivery by FedEx or UPS. If the next day the package with the DVD player fails to show up as expected, the consumer has two possible "others" to which she might attribute the failure—that is, the direct marketer (failing to get the product out on time) or the delivery service (failing to get the package to the consumer on time). In addition, she might blame them both (a dual failure); or if the weather was really bad, she might conclude that it was the bad weather (an attribution that neither of them was at fault).[30]

Attributions Toward Things

Consumer researchers also are interested in consumers' **attributions toward things** because products (or services) can readily be thought of as "things." It is in the area of judging product performance that consumers are most likely to form product attributions. Specifically, they want to find out why a product meets or does not meet their expectations. In this regard, they could attribute the product's successful performance (or failure) to the product itself, to themselves, to other people or situations, or to some combination of these factors.[31] To recap an earlier example, when Ralph developed an excellent computer slide presentation, he could attribute his success to the PowerPoint software program (product attribution), to his own skill (self or internal attribution), or to his friend who helped him (external attribution).

How We Test Our Attributions

After making initial attributions about a product's performance or a person's words or actions, we often attempt to determine whether the inference we made is correct. According to a leading attribution theorist, individuals acquire conviction about particular observations by acting like "naive scientists," that is, by collecting additional information in an attempt to confirm (or disconfirm) prior inferences. In collecting such information, consumers often use the following criteria:[32]

1. *Distinctiveness—The consumer attributes an action to a particular product or person if the action occurs when the product (or person) is present and does not occur in its absence.*
2. *Consistency over time—Whenever the person or product is present, the consumer's inference or reaction must be the same, or nearly so.*
3. *Consistency over modality—The inference or reaction must be the same, even when the situation in which it occurs varies.*
4. *Consensus—The action is perceived in the same way by other consumers.*

The following example illustrates how each of these criteria might be used to make inferences about product performance and people's actions.

If Nancy, a retired elementary school teacher who loved to cook and bake, observes that her apple pies seem to bake more evenly in her new Whirlpool gas range/oven (**www.whirlpool.com**), she is likely to credit the new Whirlpool appliance with the improved appearance of her pies (i.e., distinctiveness). Furthermore, if Nancy finds that her new Whirlpool gas range/oven produces the same high-quality results each time she uses it, she will tend to be more confident about her initial observation (i.e., the inference has consistency over time). Similarly, she will also be more confident if she finds that her satisfaction with the Whirlpool appliance extends across a wide range of other related tasks, from cooking turkeys in the oven to cooking pasta on the gas range (i.e., consistency over modality). Finally, Nancy will have still more confidence in her inferences to the extent that her friends who own Whirlpool gas ranges/ovens also have similar experiences (i.e., consensus).

Much like Nancy, we go about gathering additional information from our experiences with people and things, and we use this information to test our initial inferences.

Summary

An attitude is a learned predisposition to behave in a consistently favorable or unfavorable way with respect to a given object (e.g., a product category, a brand, a service, an advertisement, a Web site, or a retail establishment). Each property of this definition is critical to understanding why and how attitudes are relevant in consumer behavior and marketing.

Of considerable importance in understanding the role of attitudes in consumer behavior is an appreciation of the structure and composition of an attitude. Four broad categories of attitude models have received attention: tricomponent attitude model, multiattribute attitude model, trying-to-consume attitude model, and attitude-toward-the-ad model.

The tricomponent model of attitudes consists of three parts: a cognitive component, an affective component, and a conative component. The cognitive component captures a consumer's knowledge and perceptions (i.e., beliefs) about products and services. The affective component focuses on a consumer's emotions or feelings with respect to a particular product or service. Evaluative in nature, the affective component determines an individual's overall assessment of the attitude object in terms of some kind of favorableness rating. The conative component is concerned with the likelihood that a consumer will act in a specific fashion with respect to the attitude object. In marketing and consumer behavior, the conative component is frequently treated as an expression of the consumer's intention to buy.

Multiattribute attitude models (i.e., attitude-toward-object, attitude-toward-behavior, and the theory-of-reasoned-action models) have received much attention from consumer researchers. As a group, these models examine consumer beliefs about specific product attributes (e.g., product or brand features or benefits). Recently, there has been an effort to better accommodate consumers' goals as expressed by their "trying to consume" (i.e., a goal the consumer is trying or planning to accomplish). The theory of trying is designed to account for the many cases in which the action or outcome is not certain. The attitude-toward-the-ad models examine the influence of advertisements on the consumer's attitudes toward the brand.

How consumer attitudes are formed and how they are changed are two closely related issues of considerable concern to marketing practitioners. When it comes to attitude formation, it is useful to remember that attitudes are learned and that different learning theories provide unique insights as to how attitudes initially may be formed. Attitude formation is facilitated by direct personal experience and influenced by the ideas and experiences of friends and family members and exposure to mass media. In addition, it is likely that an individual's personality plays a major role in attitude formation.

These same factors also have an impact on attitude change; that is, attitude changes are learned, and they are influenced by personal experiences and the information gained from various personal and impersonal sources. The consumer's own personality affects both the acceptance and the speed with which attitudes are likely to be altered.

Strategies of attitude change can be classified into six distinct categories: (1) changing the basic motivational function, (2) associating the attitude object with a specific group or event, (3) relating the attitude object to conflicting attitudes, (4) altering components of the multiattribute model, (5) changing beliefs about competitors' brands, and (6) the elaboration likelihood model. Each of these strategies provides the marketer with alternative ways of changing consumers' existing attitudes.

Most discussions of attitude formation and attitude change stress the traditional view that consumers develop attitudes before they act. However, this may not always, or even usually, be true. Both cognitive dissonance theory and attribution theory provide alternative explanations of attitude formation and change that suggest that behavior might precede attitudes. Cognitive dissonance theory suggests that the conflicting thoughts, or dissonant information, following a purchase decision might propel consumers to change their attitudes to make them consonant with their actions. Attribution theory focuses on how people assign causality to events and how they form or alter attitudes as an outcome of assessing their own behavior or the behavior of other people or things.

Discussion Questions

1. Explain how situational factors are likely to influence the degree of consistency between attitudes and behavior.

2. Because attitudes are learned predispositions to respond, why don't marketers and consumer researchers just measure purchase behavior and forget attitudes?

3. Explain a person's attitude toward visiting Disney World in terms of the tricomponent attitude model.

4. How can the marketer of a "nicotine patch" (a device that assists individuals to quit smoking) use the *theory of trying* to segment its market? Using this theory, identify two segments that the marketer should target and propose product positioning approaches to be directed at each of the two segments.

5. Explain how the product manager of a breakfast cereal might change consumer attitudes toward the company's brand by (a) changing beliefs about the brand, (b) changing beliefs about competing brands, (c) changing the relative evaluation of attributes, and (d) adding an attribute.

6. The Department of Transportation of a large city is planning an advertising campaign that encour-ages people to switch from private cars to mass transit. Give examples of how the department can use the following strategies to change commuters' attitudes: (a) changing the basic motivational function, (b) changing beliefs about public transportation, (c) using self-perception theory, and (d) using cognitive dissonance.

7. The Saturn Corporation is faced with the problem that many consumers perceive compact and mid-size American cars to be of poorer quality than comparable Japanese cars. Assuming that Saturn produces cars that are of equal or better quality than Japanese cars, how can the company per-suade consumers of this fact?

8. Should the marketer of a popular computer graph-ics program prefer consumers to make internal or external attributions? Explain your answer.

9. A college student has just purchased a new per-sonal computer. What factors might cause the student to experience postpurchase dissonance? How might the student try to overcome it? How can the retailer who sold the computer help reduce the student's dissonance? How can the computer's manufacturer help?

Exercises

1. Find two print ads, one illustrating the use of the affective component and the other illustrating the cognitive component. Discuss each ad in the con-text of the tricomponent model. In your view, why has each marketer taken the approach it did in each of these ads?

2. What sources influenced your attitude about this course before classes started? Has your initial attitude changed since the course started? If so, how?

3. Describe a situation in which you acquired an atti-tude toward a new product through exposure to

an advertisement for that product. Describe a situation in which you formed an attitude toward a product or brand on the basis of personal influence.

4. Find advertisements that illustrate each of the four motivational functions of attitudes. Distinguish between ads that are designed to rein-

force an existing attitude and those aimed at changing an attitude.

5. Think back to the time when you were selecting a college. Did you experience dissonance immediately after you made a decision? Why or why not? If you did experience dissonance, how did you resolve it?

Key Terms

- **Attitudes**
- **Attitude-toward-behavior model**
- **Attitude-toward-object model**
- **Attitude-toward-the-ad model**
- **Attributions toward others**
- **Attributions toward things**
- **Attribution theory**
- **Cognitive dissonance theory**

- **Defensive attribution**
- **Ego-defensive function**
- **Elaboration likelihood model (ELM)**
- **Foot-in-the-door technique**
- **Functional approach**
- **Intention-to-buy scales**
- **Internal and external attributions**

- **Knowledge function**
- **Multiattribute attitude models**
- **Self-perception theory**
- **Theory of reasoned action**
- **Theory of trying to consume**
- **Tricomponent attitude model**
- **Utilitarian function**
- **Value-expressive function**

Notes

1. Jack Neff, "Suave Strokes," *Advertising Age,* August 20, 2001, 12.
2. Richard J. Lutz, "The Role of Attitude Theory in Marketing," in Harold H. Kassarjian and Thomas S. Robertson, eds., *Perspectives in Consumer Behavior,* 4th ed. (Upper Saddle River, NJ: Prentice-Hall, 1991), 317–339.
3. Joel B. Cohen and Charles S. Areni, "Affect and Consumer Behavior," in Harold H. Kassarjian and Thomas S. Robertson, eds., *Perspectives in Consumer Behavior,* 188–240; and Madeline Johnson and George M. Zinkhan, "Emotional Responses to a Professional Service Encounter," *Journal of Service Marketing,* 5, Spring 1991, 5–16. Also see John Kim, Jeen-Su Iim, and Mukesh Bhargava, "The Role of Affect in Attitude Formation: A Classical Condition Approach," *Journal of the Academy of Marketing Science,* 26 (1998), 143–152.
4. Jaideep Sengupta, "Perspectives on Attitude Strength" (a special session summary), in Joseph W. Alba and J. Wesley Hutchinson, eds., *Advances in Consumer Research,* 25 (Provo, UT: Association for Consumer Research, 1998), 63–64.
5. Martin Fishbein, "An Investigation of the Relationships Between Beliefs About an Object and the Attitude Toward the Object," *Human Relations,*

16, (1963), 233–240; and Martin Fishbein, "A Behavioral Theory Approach to the Relations Between Beliefs About an Object and the Attitude Toward the Object," in Martin Fishbein, ed., *Readings in Attitude Theory and Measurement* (New York: Wiley, 1967), 389–400.
6. Claude Pecheux and Christian Derbaix, "Children and Attitude Toward the Brand: A New Measurement Scale," *Journal of Advertising Research,* July/August 1999, 19–27.
7. Icek Ajzen and Martin Fishbein, *Understanding Attitudes and Predicting Social Behavior* (Upper Saddle River, NJ: Prentice-Hall, 1980); and Martin Fishbein and Icek Ajzen, *Belief, Attitude, Intentions, and Behavior* (Reading, MA: Addison-Wesley, 1975), 62–63. Also see Robert E. Burnkrant, H. Rao Unnava, and Thomas J. Page, Jr., "Effects of Experience on Attitude Structure," in Rebecca H. Holman and Michael R. Solomon, eds., *Advances in Consumer Research,* 18 (Provo, UT: Association for Consumer Research, 1991), 28–29.
8. Terence A. Shimp and Alican Kavas, "The Theory of Reasoned Action Applied to Coupon Usage," *Journal of Consumer Research,* 11, December 1984, 795–809; Blair H. Sheppard, Jon Hartwick, and Paul R. Warshaw, "The Theory of Reasoned Action: A Meta-Analysis of Past Research with

Recommendations for Modifications and Future Research," *Journal of Consumer Research,* 15, September 1986, 325–343; Sharon E. Beatly and Lynn R. Kahle, "Alternative Hierarchies of the Attitude-Behavior Relationship: The Impact of Brand Commitment and Habit," *Journal of the Academy of Marketing Science,* 16, Summer 1988, 1–10; Richard P. Bagozzi, Hans Baumgartner, and Youjae Yi, "Coupon Usage and the Theory of Reasoned Action," in Rebecca H. Holman and Michael R. Solomon, eds., *Advances in Consumer Research,* 18 (Provo, UT: Association for Consumer Research, 1991), 24–27; and Hee Sun Park, "Relationships Among Attitudes and Subjective Norms: Testing the Theory of Reasoned Action Across Cultures," *Communication Studies,* 51, 2, Summer 2000, 162–175.

9. Richard P. Bagozzi and Paul R. Warshaw, "Trying to Consume," *Journal of Consumer Research,* 17, September 1990, 127–140; Richard P. Bagozzi, Fred D. Davis, and Paul R. Warshaw, "Development and Test of a Theory of Technological Learning and Usage," *Human Relations,* 45(7), July 1992, 659–686; and Anil Mathur, "From Intentions to Behavior: The Role of Trying and Control," in Barbara B. Stern and George M. Zinkan, eds., *1995 AMA Educators' Proceedings* (Chicago: American Marketing Association, 1995), 374–375.

10. Stephen J. Gould, Franklin S. Houston, and Jonel Mundt, "Failing to Try to Consume: A Reversal of the Usual Consumer Research Perspective," in Merrie Brucks and Deborah J. MacInnis, eds., *Advances in Consumer Research* (Provo, UT: Association for Consumer Research, 1997), 211–216.

11. Rajeev Batra and Michael L. Ray, "Affective Responses Mediating Acceptance of Advertising," *Journal of Consumer Research,* 13, September 1986, 236–239; Julie A. Edell and Marian Chapman Burke, "The Power of Feelings in Understanding Advertising Effects," *Journal of Consumer Research,* 14, December 1987, 421–433; and Marian Chapman Burke and Julie A. Edell, "The Impact of Feelings on Ad-Based Affect and Cognition," *Journal of Marketing Research,* 26, February 1989, 69–83.

12. Durriya Z. Khairullah and Zahid Y. Khairullah, "Relationships Between Acculturation, Attitude Toward the Advertisement, and Purchase Intention of Asian-Indian Immigrants," *International Journal of Commerce and Management,* 9, 3/4, 1999, 46–65.

13. Dena Saliagas Cox and William B. Locander, "Product Novelty: Does It Moderate the Relationship Between Ad Attitudes and Brand Attitudes?" *Journal of Advertising,* 16, 1987, 39–44. Also see Cynthia B. Hanson and Gabriel J. Biehal, "Accessibility Effects on the Relationship Between Attitude Toward the Ad and Brand Choice," in Frank R. Kardes and Mita Sujan, eds., *Advances in Consumer Research,* 22 (Provo, UT: Association for Consumer Research, 1995), 152–158.

14. Alan J. Bush, Rachel Smith, and Craig Martin, "The Influence of Consumer Socialization Variables on Attitude Toward Advertising: A Comparison of African-Americans and Caucasians," *Journal of Advertising,* 28, 3, Fall 1999, 13–24.

15. Subodh Bhat and Srinivas K. Reddy, "Investigating the Dimensions of the Fit Between a Brand and Its Extensions," *1997 AMA Winter Educators' Conference Proceedings,* 8 (Chicago: American Marketing Association, 1997), 186–194.

16. Morris B. Holbrook, David A. Velez, and Gerard J. Tabouret, "Attitude Structure and Search: An Integrative Model of Importance-Directed Information Processing," in Kent B. Monroe, ed., *Advances in Consumer Research,* 8 (Ann Arbor, MI: Association for Consumer Research, 1981), 35–41.

17. Richard P. Bagozzi, Hans Baumgartner, and Youjae Yi, "Coupon Usage and the Theory of Reasoned Action," in Rebecca H. Holman and Michael R. Solomon, eds., *Advances in Consumer Research,* 18 (Provo, UT: Association for Consumer Research, 1991), 24–27.

18. For an interesting article on the impact of social interaction on attitude development, see Daniel J. Howard and Charles Gengler, "Emotional Contagion Effects on Product Attitudes," *Journal of Consumer Research,* 28, September 2001, 189–201.

19. Haksik Lee, Gilbert D. Harrell, and Cornelia L. Droge, "Product Experiences and Hierarchy of Advertising Effects," in *2000 AMA Winter Educators' Conference,* 11, eds., John P. Workman and William D. Perreault (Chicago: American Marketing Association, 2000), 41–42.

20. James R. Coyle and Esther Thorson, "The Effects of Progressive Levels of Interactivity and Vividness in Web Marketing Sites," *Journal of Advertising,* 30, 3, Fall 2001, 65–77; and Lynn C. Dailey and C. Edward Heath, "Creating the Flow Experience Online: The Role of Web Atmospherics," in *2000 AMA Winter Educators' Conference,* 11, eds., John P. Workman and William D. Perreault (Chicago: American Marketing Association, 2000), 58.

21. Daniel Katz, "The Functional Approach to the Study of Attitudes," *Public Opinion Quarterly,* 24, Summer 1960, 163–191; Sharon Shavitt, "Products, Personality and Situations in Attitude Functions: Implications for Consumer Behavior," in Thomas K. Srull, ed., *Advances in Consumer Research,* 16 (Provo, UT: Association for Consumer Research, 1989), 300–305; and Richard Ennis and Mark P. Zanna, "Attitudes, Advertising, and Automobiles: A Functional Approach," in Leigh McAlister and Michael L. Rothschild, eds., *Advances in Consumer Research,* 20

(Provo, UT: Association for Consumer Research, 1992), 662–666.

22. Maria Knight Lapinski and Franklin J. Boster, "Modeling the Ego-Defensive Function of Attitudes," *Communication Monographs*, 68, 3, September 2001, 314–324.

23. Cara Beardi, "Zippo's Eternal Flame," *Advertising Age*, August 13, 2001, 4.

24. Geoffrey L. Cohen, Joshua Aronson, and Claude M. Steele, "When Beliefs Yield to Evidence: Reducing Biased Evaluation by Affirming the Self," *Personality and Social Psychology Bulletin*, 26, 9, September 2000, 1151–1164.

25. Richard E. Petty, et al., "Theories of Attitude Change," in Harold Kassarjian and Thomas Robertson, eds., *Handbook of Consumer Theory and Research* (Upper Saddle River, NJ: Prentice Hall, 1991); and Richard E. Petty, John T. Cacioppo, and David Schumann, "Central and Peripheral Routes to Advertising Effectiveness: The Moderating Role of Involvement," *Journal of Consumer Research*, 10, September 1983, 135–146. Also see Curtis P. Haugtvedt and Alan J. Strathman, "Situational Product Relevance and Attitude Persistence," in Marvin E. Goldberg, Gerald Gorn, and Richard W. Pollay, eds., *Advances in Consumer Research*, 17 (Provo, UT: Association for Consumer Research, 1990), 766–769; and Scott B. Mackenzie and Richard A. Spreng, "How Does Motivation Moderate the Impact of Central and Peripheral Processing on Brand Attitudes and Intentions?" *Journal of Consumer Research*, 18, March 1992, 519–529.

26. Jaideep Sgupta, Ronald C. Goldstein, and David S. Boninger, "All Cues Are Not Created Equal: Obtaining Attitude Peristence Under Low-Involvement Conditions," *Journal of Consumer Reserach*, 23, March 1997, 351–361.

27. Edward E. Jones, et al., *Attribution: Perceiving the Causes of Behavior* (Morristown, NJ: General Learning Press, 1972); and Bernard Weiner, "Attributional Thoughts About Consumer Behavior," *Journal of Consumer Research*, 27, 3, December 2000, 382–387.

28. Chris T. Allen and William R. Dillon, "Self-Perception Development and Consumer Choice Criteria: Is There a Linkage?" in Richard P. Bagozzi and Alice M. Tybout, eds., *Advances in Consumer Research*, 10 (Ann Arbor, MI: Association for Consumer Research, 1983), 45–50.

29. See, for example, Leslie Lazar Kanuk, *Mail Questionnaire Response Behavior as a Function of Motivational Treatment* (New York: CUNY, 1974).

30. John R. O'Malley, Jr., "Consumer Attributions of Product Failures to Channel Members," in Kim P. Corfman and John F. Lynch, Jr., eds., *Advances in Consumer Research*, 23 (Provo, UT: Association for Consumer Research, 1996), 342–345. Also see Charmine Hartel, Janet R. Mccoll-Kennedy, and Lyn McDonald, "Incorporating Attributional Theory and the Theory of Reasoned Action Within an Affective Events Theory Framework to Produce a Contingency Predictive Model of Consumer Reactions to Organizational Mishaps," in Joseph W. Alba and J. Wesley Hutchinson, eds., *Advances in Consumer Research*, 25 (Provo, UT: Association for Consumer Research, 1998), 428–432.

31. Valerie S. Folkes, "Consumer Reactions to Product Failure: Attributional Approach," *Journal of Consumer Research*, 10, March 1984, 398–409; and "Recent Attribution Research in Consumer Behavior: A Review and New Dimensions," *Journal of Consumer Research*, 14, March 1988, 548–565.

32. Harold H. Kelley, "Attribution Theory in Social Psychology," in David Levine, ed., *Nebraska Symposium on Motivation*, 15 (Lincoln: University of Nebraska Press, 1967), 197.

EGYPT

Be patient.

ITALY

What exactly do you mean?

GREECE

That's just perfect.

Never underestimate the importance of local knowledge.

To truly understand a country and its culture, you have to be part of it. That's why, at HSBC, all our offices around the world are staffed by local people. In fact, you'll find we've got local people in more countries than any other bank. It's their insight that allows us to recognize financial opportunities invisible to outsiders.

But those opportunities don't benefit just our local customers. Innovations and ideas are shared throughout the HSBC network, so that everyone who banks with us can benefit.

Think of it as local knowledge that just happens to span the globe.

HSBC

The world's local bank

9

Communication and Consumer Behavior

O n September 11, 2001, and for several days afterward, mass communications ruled the daily lives of most Americans. Billions of people watched, for the most part in real time, as commercial passenger jets, turned into lethal weapons, hit prominent buildings in New York City and Washington, DC, and killed thousands of people. In fact, the president of the United States learned of the attacks during a TV appearance. Most likely, the terrorists who initiated and planned the attacks also watched the results of their diabolical acts on TV. Other forms of communications provided us with even more horrific images and sounds than the TV cameras. Cell phone calls from people trapped in the burning buildings, instantly reported in the media, made the images we saw even more frightening and grave. Audiovisual segments recorded by bystanders and shown on TV provided views of the disasters from almost every possible viewing angle. On September 11, 2001, communication technologies made historic events a reality for the population of the world. In a sense, communication tools on that day did not merely report history— they *were* the history.

Over many decades now, thanks to rapidly improving communications tools, American movies, TV shows, and music have dominated the world's pop culture. The emergence of global cable TV channels such as CNN and MTV, and the demise of control over communications in many totalitarian regimes in the 1980s, have enabled most of the world's inhabitants to learn about, and in many cases adopt, American culture, values, and consumption patterns. Advanced technologies, such as the Internet and personal satellite dishes, have eliminated many of the final barriers to global communications once set by distance, location, or dictators seeking to control their people through isolation and ignorance. Within hours of the September 11 terrorist attacks on New York and Washington, Americans watched the forces and faces behind this incredible disaster. We watched people in the Middle East cheering as the World Trade Center towers collapsed. We even watched the evil mastermind behind the destruction and mass murder calmly discuss his feelings on the day he watched the horrific aftermath of his deeds on TV. To Americans, self-assured about their country's position as a political, economic, and cultural superpower, the disaster broadcast on September 11, 2001, and on commercial-free TV for many days thereafter, was both inexplicable and tragic. These events shattered the notion that the earth had become a "global village"—a planet whose people increasingly adopted similar values and behaviors due to the dominance and impact of mass communications. Although the events of 9/11 have shown that the world is still divided by centuries-old hate and distrust, they have also shown that this planet is united by instant and relentless communications.

In addition to being a global force, communication is the unique tool that marketers use to persuade consumers to act in a desired way (e.g., to vote, to make a purchase, to make a donation, to patronize a retail store). Communication takes many forms: It can be *verbal* (either written or spoken), *visual* (an illustration, a picture, a product demonstration, a frown), or a combination of the two. It can also be symbolic—represented, say, by a high price, premium packaging, or memorable logo—and convey special meaning that the marketer wants to impart. Communication can evoke emotions that put consumers in more receptive frames of mind, and it can encourage purchases that help consumers solve problems or avoid negative outcomes. In short, communication is the bridge between marketers and consumers and between consumers and their sociocultural environments.

Components of Communication

Although there are many ways to define communication, most marketers agree that **communication** is *the transmission of a message from a sender to a receiver via a medium (or channel) of transmission.* In addition to these four basic components— sender, receiver, medium, and message—the fifth essential component of communication is *feedback,* which alerts the sender as to whether the intended message was, in fact, received. Figure 9-1 depicts this basic communications model.

THE SENDER

The sender, as the initiator of the communication, can be a formal or an informal source. A **formal communications source** is likely to represent either a for-profit (commercial) or a not-for-profit organization; an **informal source** can be a parent or friend who gives product information or advice. Consumers often rely on informal communications sources in making purchase decisions because, unlike formal sources, the sender is perceived as having nothing to gain from the receiver's subsequent actions. For that reason, **word-of-mouth communications** tend to be highly persuasive. Many studies recommend that marketers should encourage detailed, positive word-of-mouth about their products and services among consumers.[1]

THE RECEIVER

The **receiver** of formal marketing communications is likely to be a targeted prospect or a customer (e.g., a member of the marketer's target audience). *Intermediary* and *unintended* audiences are also likely to receive marketers' communications. Examples of intermediary audiences are wholesalers, distributors, and retailers, who

FIGURE 9-1

Basic Communication Model

receive trade advertising from marketers designed to persuade them to order and stock merchandise, and relevant professionals (such as architects or physicians), who are sent *professional advertising* in the hopes that they will specify or prescribe the marketer's products. Unintended audiences include everyone who is exposed to the message who is not specifically targeted by the sender. Unintended receivers of marketing communications often include publics that are important to the marketer, such as shareholders, creditors, suppliers, employees, bankers, and the local community. It is important to remember that the audience—no matter how large or how diverse—is composed of individual receivers, each of whom interprets the message according to his or her own personal perceptions and experiences.

THE MEDIUM

The **medium,** or communications channel, can be **impersonal** (e.g., a mass medium) or **interpersonal** (a formal conversation between a salesperson and a customer or an informal conversation between two or more people that takes place face-to-face, by telephone, by mail, or online).

Mass media are generally classified as *print* (newspapers, magazines, billboards), *broadcast* (radio, television), or *electronic* (primarily the Internet). New modes of *interactive communication* that permit the audiences of communication messages to provide direct feedback are beginning to blur the distinction between interpersonal and impersonal communications. For example, most companies encourage consumers to visit their Web sites to find out more about the product or service being advertised or to order online, but not all visitors receive the same message. The information visitors see or the ordering links they are routed to depend on their selections, in the form of clicking patterns, during that visit or even past visits to the site. **Direct marketers**—often called *database marketers*—also seek individual responses from advertisements they have placed in all the mass media: broadcast, print, and online, as well as from **direct mail.** Home shopping networks are expanding dramatically as consumers demonstrate their enthusiasm for TV shopping. Direct marketers use data regarding recent buying behavior of some consumers to generate purchases from subsequent consumers.

THE MESSAGE

The **message** can be **verbal** (spoken or written), **nonverbal** (a photograph, an illustration, or a symbol), or a combination of the two. A verbal message, whether it is spoken or written, can usually contain more specific product (or service) information than a nonverbal message. However, a verbal message combined with a nonverbal message often provides more information to the receiver than either would alone.

Nonverbal information takes place in both interpersonal channels and in impersonal channels and often takes the form of symbolic communication. Marketers often try to develop logos or symbols that are associated exclusively with their products and that achieve high recognition. The Coca-Cola Company, for example, has trademarked both the word *Coke* in a specific typographic style and the shape of the traditional Coke bottle, and both are instantly recognizable to consumers as symbols of the company's best-selling soft drink.[2] In 1994, the Supreme Court ruled that even a color that distinguishes a product (and serves no other function) can be registered as a trademark.[3] Figure 9-2 depicts an ad portraying nonverbal, symbolic communications (in the form of hand gestures) in three different cultures.

FIGURE 9-2

Ad Depicting
Nonverbal
Communication
Courtesy of HSBC Bank.

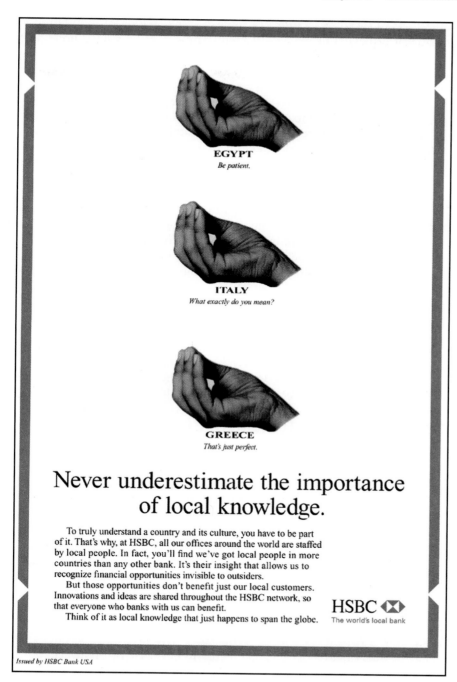

FEEDBACK

Feedback is an essential component of both interpersonal and impersonal communications. Prompt feedback permits the sender to reinforce, to change, or to modify the message to ensure that it is understood in the intended way. Generally, it is easier to obtain feedback (both verbal and nonverbal) from interpersonal communications than impersonal communications. For example, a good salesperson usually is alert to nonverbal feedback provided by consumer prospects. Such feedback may take the form of facial expressions (a smile, a frown, a look of total boredom, an expression of disbelief) or body movements (finger tapping, head nodding, head shaking, or clenched hands). Because of the high cost of space and time in impersonal media, it is very important for sponsors of impersonal communications to devise methods to obtain feedback as promptly as possible, so that they may revise a message if its meaning is not being received as intended.

An excellent example of marketing based on shoppers' feedback, in the form of "body language," is the selling method employed at the rapidly growing Diesel jeans stores. Unlike other clothing stores, Diesel stores are not user friendly because the company believes that a disoriented customer is the best prospect. Diesel stores feature loud techno music and large TV screens playing videos unrelated to the merchandise sold. There are no signs directing customers to different departments, no obvious salespeople, and jeans items have strange names accompanied by confusing charts intended to explain the clothing options. In the midst of this chaos, young and hip-looking salespeople who are trained to spot "wayward-looking," overwhelmed, and confused shoppers, "rescue" them by becoming their "shopping friends" and, of course, sell them as many pairs of jeans as possible.[4]

The Communications Process

In general, a company's marketing communications are designed to make the consumer aware of the product, induce purchase or commitment, create a positive attitude toward the product, give the product a symbolic meaning, or show how it can solve the consumer's problem better than a competitive product (or service).

THE MESSAGE INITIATOR (SOURCE)

The sponsor (initiator) of the message first must decide to whom the message should be sent and what meaning it should convey. Then the sponsor must *encode* the message in such a way that its meaning is interpreted by the targeted audience in precisely the intended way. The sources of *impersonal communications* usually are organizations (either for-profit or not-for-profit) that develop and transmit appropriate messages through special departments (e.g., marketing or public relations) or spokespersons. The targets, or receivers, of such messages usually are a specific audience or several audiences that the organization is trying to inform, influence, or persuade. For example, AOL wants to attract both online users and advertisers; a museum may wish to target both donors and visitors; and a mail-order company may want to persuade consumers to call a toll-free number for a copy of its catalog.

Marketers have a large arsenal from which to draw in encoding their messages: They can use words, pictures, symbols, spokespersons, and special channels. They can buy space or time in carefully selected media to advertise or broadcast their message, or they can try to have their message appear in space or time usually reserved for editorial messages. (The latter, called **publicity,** usually is the result of public relations efforts and tends to be more believable because its commercial origins and intent are not readily apparent.)

Credibility

The *credibility of the source* affects the *decoding* of the message. The sponsor of the communication—and his or her perceived honesty and objectivity—have an enormous influence on how the communication is accepted by the receiver(s). When the source is well respected and highly thought of by the intended audience, the message is much more likely to be believed. Conversely, a message from a source considered unreliable or untrustworthy is likely to be received with skepticism and may be rejected.

Credibility is built on a number of factors, of which the most important are the perceived intentions of the source. Receivers ask themselves, "Just what does he (or she) stand to gain if I do what is suggested?" If the receiver perceives any type of personal gain for the message sponsor as a result of the proposed action or advice, the message itself becomes suspect: "He wants me to buy that product just to earn a commission."

Credibility of Informal Sources One of the major reasons that informal sources such as friends, neighbors, and relatives have a strong influence on a receiver's behavior is simply that they are perceived as having nothing to gain from a product transaction that they recommend. That is why word-of-mouth communication is so effective. Interestingly enough, informal communications sources, called **opinion leaders,** often do profit psychologically, if not tangibly, by providing product information to others. A person may obtain a great deal of ego satisfaction by providing solicited as well as unsolicited information and advice to friends. This ego gratification may actually improve the quality of the information provided, because the opinion leader often deliberately seeks out the latest detailed information in order to enhance his or her position as "expert" in a particular product category. The fact that the opinion leader does not receive material gain from the recommended action increases the likelihood that the advice will be seriously considered.

Even with informal sources, however, intentions are not always what they appear to be. Individuals who experience postpurchase dissonance often try to alleviate their uncertainty by convincing others to make a similar purchase. Each time they persuade a friend or an acquaintance to make the same brand selection as they did, they are somewhat reassured that their own product choice was a wise one. The receiver, on the other hand, regards product advice from "the person who owns one" as totally objective, because the source is able to speak from actual experience. Thus, the increased credibility accorded the informal source may not really be warranted, despite the aura of perceived objectivity.

Credibility of Formal Sources Not-for-profit sources generally have more credibility than for-profit (commercial) sources. Formal sources that are perceived to be "neutral"—such as *Consumer Reports* or newspaper articles—have greater credibility than commercial sources because of the perception that they are more objective in their product assessments. That is why publicity is so valuable to a manufacturer: Citations of a product in an editorial context, rather than in a paid advertisement, give the reader much more confidence in the message. One study discovered that the perceived trustworthiness of publicity was higher when the message involved stressed the company's altruistic motives (e.g., launching a recycling program because of "good corporate citizenship") than when the message stressed a commercial corporate motive (e.g., launching a recycling venture in the form of a subsidiary).[5]

Because consumers recognize that the intentions of commercial sources (e.g., manufacturers, service companies, financial institutions, retailers) are clearly profit oriented, they judge commercial **source credibility** on such factors as past performance, reputation, the kind and quality of service they are known to render, the quality and image of other products they manufacture, the image and attractiveness of the spokesperson used, the type of retail outlets through which they sell, and their position in the community (e.g., evidence of their commitment to such issues as social responsibility or equal employment).

Firms with well-established reputations generally have an easier time selling their products than do firms with lesser reputations. The ability of a quality image to invoke credibility is one of the reasons for the growth of family brands.

Manufacturers with favorable brand images prefer to give their new products the existing brand name in order to obtain ready acceptance from consumers. Furthermore, a quality image permits a company to experiment more freely in many more areas of marketing than would otherwise be considered prudent, such as free-standing retail outlets, new price levels, and innovative promotional techniques. Recognizing that a manufacturer with a good reputation generally has high credibility among consumers, many companies spend a sizable part of their advertising budget on **institutional advertising,** which is designed to promote a favorable company image rather than to promote specific products.

Many companies sponsor special entertainment and sports events to enhance their image and credibility with their target audiences. The nature and quality of these sponsorships constitute a subtle message to the consumer: "We're a great (kind, good-natured, socially responsible) company; we deserve your business." For example, such firms as American Express, Avon Products, and Estée Lauder sponsor concerts in the park, athletic events, and walks to support cancer research. Other kinds of corporate-sponsored special events include marching bands, fireworks displays, parades, laser shows, and traveling art exhibits.

Credibility of Spokespersons and Endorsers Consumers sometimes regard the spokesperson who gives the product message as the source (or initiator) of the message. Thus, the "pitchman" (whether male or female) who appears in person or in a commercial or advertisement has a major influence on message credibility. This accounts for the increasing use of celebrities to promote products. Many studies have investigated the relationship between the effectiveness of the message and the spokesperson or endorser employed. Here are some of the key findings of this body of research:

- The effectiveness of the spokesperson is related to the message itself. For example, when message comprehension is low, receivers rely on the spokesperson's credibility in forming attitudes toward the product, but when comprehension (and, thus, systematic information processing) is high, the expertise of the spokesperson has far less impact on a receiver's attitudes.[6]
- The synergy between the endorser and the type of product or service advertised is an important factor. One study found that, for attractiveness-related products (such as cosmetics), a physically attractive celebrity spokesperson significantly enhanced message credibility and attitude toward the ad; for attractiveness-unrelated products (e.g., a camera) an attractive endorser had little or no effect. This suggests a "match-up" hypothesis for celebrity advertising.[7] Another study found that a celebrity endorser was more effective in terms of source credibility and consumer attitudes toward the ad for a hedonistic and "experiential" service (e.g., a restaurant) than for a utilitarian service (e.g., a bank).[8]
- Endorsers who have demographic characteristics (e.g., age, social class, and ethnicity) that are similar to those of the target audience are viewed as more credible and persuasive than those that do not. Also, consumers with strong ethnic identification are more likely to be persuaded by endorsers with similar ethnicity than individuals with weaker ethnic identification.[9]
- The endorser's credibility is not a substitute for corporate credibility. One study discovered that although the endorser's credibility strongly impacted the audience's *attitudes toward the ad,* the perceived corporate credibility had a strong impact on *attitudes toward the advertised brand.*[10] This study supports the development of multiple measures to evaluate the credibility and persuasiveness of advertising messages, such as attitudes toward the ad, toward the brand, and consumer purchase intentions.
- Marketers who use celebrities to give testimonials or endorse products must be sure that the specific wording of the endorsement lies within the recognized com-

petence of the spokesperson. A tennis star can believably endorse a brand of analgesic with comments about how it relieves sore muscle pain; however, a recitation of medical evidence supporting the brand's superiority over other brands is beyond his expected knowledge and expertise and, thus, may reduce (rather than enhance) message credibility. Somewhat surprisingly, one study of advertising agencies found that none of the agencies surveyed had a written strategy regarding the selection of celebrity endorsers. The study's authors recommended a long list of factors to be considered in selecting celebrity endorsers, such as a careful match with the target audience, product and brand, the celebrity's overall image, prior endorsements, trustworthiness, familiarity, expertise, profession, physical attractiveness, and whether the celebrity is a brand user.[11]

In interpersonal communications, consumers are more likely to be persuaded by salespersons who engender confidence and who give the impression of honesty and integrity. Consumer confidence in a salesperson is created in diverse ways, whether warranted or not. A salesperson who "looks you in the eye" often is perceived as more honest than one who evades direct eye contact. For many products, a sales representative who dresses well and drives an expensive, late-model car may have more credibility than one without such outward signs of success (and inferred representation of a best-selling product). For some products, however, a salesperson may achieve more credibility by dressing in the role of an expert. For example, a man selling home improvements may achieve more credibility by looking like someone who just climbed off a roof or out of a basement than by looking like a banker.

Message Credibility The reputation of the retailer who sells the product has a major influence on message credibility. Products sold by well-known quality stores seem to carry the added endorsement (and implicit guarantee) of the store itself (e.g., "If Macy's carries it, it must be good."). The aura of credibility generated by reputable retail advertising reinforces the manufacturer's message as well. That is why so many national ads (i.e., manufacturer-initiated ads) carry the line, "Sold at better stores everywhere."

The reputation of the medium that carries the advertisement also enhances the credibility of the advertiser. For example, the image of a prestige magazine like *Fortune* confers added status on the products advertised within. The reputation of the medium for honesty and objectivity also affects the believability of the advertising. Consumers often think that a medium they respect would not accept advertising for products it did not "know" were good. Because specialization in an area implies knowledge and expertise, consumers tend to regard advertising they see in special-interest magazines with more credibility than those they note in general-interest magazines.

However, there is no single answer as to which medium has the most credibility, especially at a time when new forms of media (such as the Web) and traditional media in new forms (such as online editions of well-established newspapers) are emerging and evolving. One study discovered that persons interested in politics are shifting from television to the Web for political information.[12] Another study reported that the public generally considers opinion polls reported in traditional news media as more credible than online polls,[13] and still another study reported that cable television newscasts are viewed as the most credible and that differences in the perceived credibility of various media were related to age.[14] As the number and types of media continue to evolve and grow, print, broadcast, and digital media executives should survey their audiences periodically on such factors as perceived fairness, balance, and accuracy in order to maximize their credibility with audiences and their attractiveness to advertisers.

The consumer's previous experience with the product or the retailer has a major impact on the credibility of the message. Fulfilled product expectations tend to increase the credibility accorded future messages by the same advertiser; unfulfilled product claims or disappointing product experiences tend to reduce the credibility of future messages. Thus, the key basis for message credibility is the ability of the product, service, or brand to deliver consistent quality, value, and satisfaction to consumers.

Effects of Time on Source Credibility: The Sleeper Effect The persuasive effects of high-credibility sources do not endure over time. Although a high-credibility source is initially more influential than a low-credibility source, research suggests that both positive and negative credibility effects tend to disappear after six weeks or so. This phenomenon has been termed the **sleeper effect.**[15] Consumers simply forget the source of the message faster than they forget the message itself. Studies attribute the sleeper effect to disassociation (i.e., the consumer disassociates the message from its source) over time, leaving just the message content. The theory of *differential decay* suggests that the memory of a negative cue (e.g., a low-credibility source) simply decays faster than the message itself, leaving behind the primary message content.[16] However, reintroduction of the same or similar message by the source serves to jog the audience's memory, and the original effect remanifests itself; that is, the high-credibility source remains more persuasive than the low-credibility source.[17] The implication for marketers who use high-credibility spokespersons is that they must repeat the same series of ads or commercials regularly in order to maintain a high level of persuasiveness. Somewhat surprisingly, the sleeper effect supports the use of negative attack advertising in political campaigns. The results of a study applying the sleeper effect to political advertising showed that the effectiveness of the attack ad increases considerably over a period of weeks, while the audience's initial negative perception of the political assailant as having low credibility fades and has only a temporary negative impact on the ad.[18]

THE TARGET AUDIENCE (RECEIVERS)

Receivers decode the messages they receive on the basis of their personal experiences and personal characteristics. If Mrs. Brown receives shoddy merchandise from an online retailer, she may be reluctant to buy online again. At the same time, her neighbor, Mrs. Greene, may be so pleased with the merchandise she receives from a reliable online retailer (such as L.L. Bean) in terms of quality, service, and fit that she vows to do even more of her shopping online in the future. The level of trust each neighbor displays toward online communications is based on her own prior experience.

A number of factors affect the decoding and comprehension of persuasive messages, including the receiver's personal characteristics, involvement with the product or product category, the congruency of the message with the medium, and the receiver's mood.

Personal Characteristics and Comprehension

The amount of meaning accurately derived from the message is a function of the message characteristics, the receiver's opportunity and ability to process the message, and the receiver's motivation. In fact, all of an individual's personal characteristics (described in earlier chapters) influence the accuracy with which the individual decodes a message. A person's demographics (such as age, gender, marital status), sociocultural memberships (social class, race, religion), and lifestyle are key determinants in how a message is interpreted. A bachelor may interpret a friendly comment from his unmarried neighbor as a "come-on"; a student may interpret a professor's comments as an indication of grading rigor. Personality, attitudes, and prior learning all affect how a message is decoded. Perception, based as it is on expectations, motivation, and past experience, certainly influences message interpretation. Not everyone reads and understands the marketing communications they receive in the same way that the sender intended.

One study examined the impact of illiteracy on comprehension and discovered that one-third of the recipients of a direct-mail advertising piece written at an eighth-grade reading level were unable to comprehend the intended message.[19] Another study, focused on gender-based differences in responding to charity ads, reported that women found altruistic appeals that stressed helping others more persuasive, whereas men tended to choose self-oriented themes that stressed helping oneself.[20]

Involvement and Congruency

A person's level of involvement (see Chapter 7) plays a key role in how much attention is paid to the message and how carefully it is decoded. People who have little interest (i.e., a low level of involvement) in golf, for example, may not pay much attention to an ad for a specially designed putter; people who are very interested (highly involved) in golf may read every word of a highly technical advertisement describing the new golf club. Thus, a target audience's level of involvement is an important consideration in the design and content of persuasive communications. One study discovered a relationship between level of involvement and the style and context of an ad. Subjects with low involvement with the product preferred messages placed within a congruent context (e.g., a humorous ad within a humorous TV series) while persons highly involved with the product preferred messages that contrasted the style of ad and the context within which it was placed (e.g., a humorous ad within a rational context such as a TV documentary).[21] Another study showed that the congruency between the nature of the television program and the advertisement affected the level of viewer recall. Cognitively involving commercials shown in a cognitively involving program context had higher recall than low-involvement commercials placed within an affective program context.[22]

Mood

Mood, or affect, plays a significant role in how a message is decoded. A consumer's mood (e.g., cheerfulness or unhappiness) affects the way in which an advertisement is perceived, recalled, and acted upon. Marketers of many image-centered products such as perfume, fashion, and liquor have found that appeals focused on emotions and feelings associated with these products are more effective than rational appeals depicting the product's benefits. Advertisers have found that emotional appeals work well even for technologically complex products. For example, Apple Computer encourages consumers to "Think Different"; Intel uses the "Intel Inside" theme to differentiate its product.[23] After the September 11, 2001, terrorist attacks, many marketers adapted the mood of their advertising to reflect the newly somber, patriotic spirit of the country.[24]

Many studies have investigated the impact of mood on message comprehension and effectiveness. In one study, the subjects' moods were manipulated by showing humorous ads (generating a positive mood) to some subjects and informational ads (generating a neutral mood) to other subjects. The study found that a positive mood enhanced the learning of brand names and the product categories to which they belong.[25] Also, research indicates that the consumer's mood often is influenced by the *content* of the ad and by the *context* in which the advertising message appears (such as the accompanying TV program or adjacent newspaper story); these in turn affect the consumer's evaluation and recall of the message.[26] One study showed that consumers with low familiarity with a service category prefer ads based on story appeals rather than lists of attributes and that such appeals work better when the receivers are in a happy mood while decoding the message.[27]

Barriers to Communication

Various "barriers" to communication may affect the accuracy with which consumers interpret messages. These include selective perception and psychological noise.

Selective Exposure to Messages Consumers selectively perceive advertising messages and tend to ignore advertisements that have no special interest or relevance to them. Furthermore, technology provides consumers with increasingly sophisticated means to control their exposure to media. TV remote controls offer viewers the ability to "wander" among program offerings with ease (often referred to as *grazing*), to *zap* commercials by muting the audio, and to *channel surf*—switch channels to check out other program offerings during commercial breaks. Some marketers try to overcome channel surfing during commercials by *roadblocking* (i.e., playing the same commercial simultaneously on competing channels).

The VCR enables viewers to fast-forward (*zip*) through commercials of prerecorded programs. The majority of consumers zip indiscriminately through videotapes to avoid all commercials, without first evaluating the commercials they zap. More recently, digital video recorders and services such as *TiVo* and *ReplayTV* allow consumers to watch programs whenever they want. These devices are much easier to use than VCRs and worried broadcasters are actively pursuing legislation that will limit their capabilities to affect advertising exposure.[28] Caller ID, phone answering machines, and other devices allow consumers to screen out telemarketing and other unsolicited contacts from marketers.

Psychological Noise Just as telephone static can impair reception of a message, so too can **psychological noise** (e.g., competing advertising messages or distracting thoughts). A viewer faced with the clutter of nine successive commercial messages during a program break may actually receive and retain almost nothing of what he has seen. Similarly, an executive planning a department meeting while driving to work may be too engrossed in her thoughts to "hear" a radio commercial. On a more familiar level, a student daydreaming about a Saturday night date may simply not "hear" a direct question by the professor. The student is just as much a victim of noise—albeit psychological noise—as another student who literally cannot hear a question because of construction noise from the building next door. There are various strategies that marketers's use to overcome psychological noise:

- Repeated exposure to an advertising message (through *repetition* or *redundancy* of the advertising appeal) helps surmount psychological noise and facilitates message reception. Thus, repeating an ad several times is a must. (The effects of repetition on learning were discussed in Chapter 7.) The principle of redundancy also is seen in advertisements that use both illustrations and copy to emphasize the same points.
- Copywriters often use *contrast* to break through the psychological noise and advertising clutter. Contrast (discussed in Chapter 6) entails using features within the message itself to attract additional attention. Such strategies include featuring an unexpected outcome, increasing the amount of sensory input (such as color, scent, or sound), and using tested message appeals that tend to attract more attention (discussed later in this chapter).
- Broadcasters and marketers also use *teasers* to overcome noise. For example, trivia quizzes shown at the beginning of a commercial break are designed to engage viewers in sticking with the channel in order to find out at the end of the break whether their own answers were right.

- Where possible, marketers place ads in *specialized media* where there is less psychological noise. For example, studies show that ads placed within the context of computer and video games and in movie theaters are recalled better than similar ads placed in more general media.[29]

Of course, the most effective way to ensure that a promotional message stands out and is received and decoded appropriately by the target audience is through effective *positioning* and a *unique selling proposition*. Advertisements for products that are perceived to provide better value than competitive products are more likely to be received in their intended ways than other promotional messages within the advertising clutter.

FEEDBACK—THE RECEIVER'S RESPONSE

Since marketing communications are usually designed to persuade a target audience to act in a desired way (e.g., to purchase a specific brand or product, to vote for a presidential candidate, to pay income taxes early), the ultimate test of marketing communications is the receiver's response. For this reason, it is essential for the sender to obtain **feedback** as promptly and as accurately as possible. Only through feedback can the sender determine whether and how well the message has been received.

As noted earlier, an important advantage of interpersonal communications is the ability to obtain immediate feedback through verbal as well as nonverbal cues. Experienced speakers are very attentive to feedback and constantly modify their messages based on what they see and hear from the audience. Immediate feedback is the factor that makes personal selling so effective. It enables the salesperson to tailor the sales pitch to the expressed needs and observed reactions of each prospect. Similarly, it enables a political candidate to stress specific aspects of his or her platform selectively in response to questions posed by prospective voters in face-to-face meetings. Immediate feedback in the form of inattention serves to alert the college professor to jolt a dozing class awake; thus, the professor may make a deliberately provocative statement such as: "This material will probably appear on your final exam."

Obtaining feedback is as important in *impersonal* (mass) communications as it is in *interpersonal* communications. Indeed, because of the high costs of advertising space and time in mass media, many marketers consider impersonal communications feedback to be even more essential. The organization that initiates the message must develop some method for determining *a priori* whether its mass communications are received by the intended audience, understood in the intended way, and effective in achieving the intended objectives.

Unlike interpersonal communications feedback, mass communications feedback is rarely direct; instead, it is usually inferred. Senders infer how persuasive their messages are from the resulting action (or inaction) of the targeted audience. Receivers buy (or do not buy) the advertised product; they renew (or do not renew) their magazine subscriptions; they vote (or do not vote) for the political candidate. Another type of feedback that companies seek from mass audiences is the degree of customer satisfaction (or dissatisfaction) with a product purchase. They try to discover and correct as swiftly as possible any problems with the product in order to retain their brand's image of reliability. Many companies have established 24-hour hot lines to encourage comments and questions from their consumers and also solicit consumer feedback through online contact. Figure 9-3 shows a comprehensive model of the options and relationships among the basic communications elements discussed above.

Advertising Effectiveness Research

In evaluating the impact of advertising, marketers must measure the *persuasion effects* (i.e., was the message received, understood, and interpreted correctly?) and the *sales*

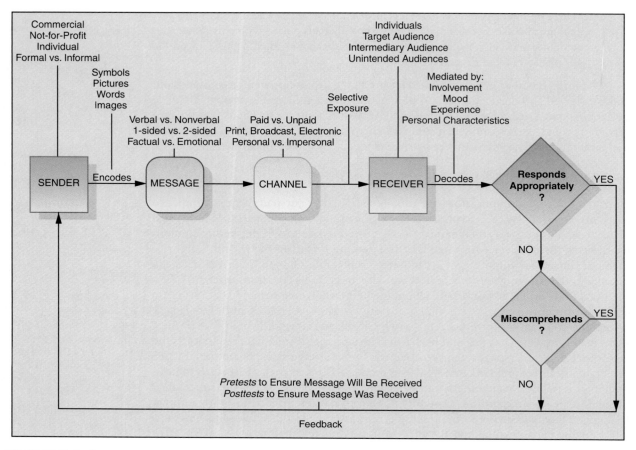

FIGURE 9-3

Comprehensive Communication Model

effects (i.e., did the ad increase sales?) of their advertising messages. Advertisers gauge the *persuasion effects* of their messages by conducting audience research to find out which media are read, which television programs are viewed, and which advertisements are remembered by their target audience(s). Should feedback indicate that the audience does not note or miscomprehends an ad, an alert sponsor modifies or revises the message so that the intended communication does, in fact, take place.

Unlike interpersonal communications between, say, a retail salesperson and a customer, in which the feedback (e.g., the customer's purchase or nonpurchase) is immediate, impersonal communications feedback is much less timely. Therefore, the *sales effects* of mass communications are difficult to assess (although retailers usually can assess the effectiveness of their morning newspaper ads by midday on the basis of sales activity for the advertised product). A widely used method of measuring the sales effects of food and other packaged goods advertising is based on the Universal Product Code (UPC), which is tied to computerized cash registers. Supermarket scanner data can be combined with data from other sources (e.g., media and promotional information) to measure the correlation between advertisements, special promotions, and sales.

Generally, persuasion effects are measured through *exposure, attention, interpretation,* and *recall.* Selected measures of these factors are described in Table 9-1.

TABLE 9-1 Measures of Advertising Effectiveness

MEDIA AND MESSAGE EXPOSURE MEASURES

Some of these measures assess *how many* consumers received the message and others focus on *who* received it. Data collected via both types of measures are offered for sale by syndicated services. For example, Mediamark Research Inc. (MRI) provides, for a given magazine, data on its *circulation* as well as a descriptive *audience profile* (a breakdown of its readers by gender, median age, and household income). MRI's Web Site Profiles provide advertisers and media buyers with data that compare the composition of a specific Web site audience with the characteristics and behaviors of the total online adult population.

The weekly Nielsen Ratings rank TV programs by the size of their audiences. A "top ranking" means that the program was watched by more people than any other program at that time during the week. In order to measure who watched a given program, some of the households in the Nielsen sample are also equipped with *People Meters*—small boxes that are placed on or near each TV set in the household. The boxes have buttons and lights that are assigned to each household member. When a viewer begins watching TV, he or she pushes the assigned button which changes the indicator light from red to green. When viewers finish watching, they push their button again (and the indicator changes back to red). To measure the audiences of local TV, Nielsen uses *diaries* in which viewers record the programs watched each day and who in the household watched each program. Nielsen//NetRatings uses a sample of consumers with Internet access to determine which Web sites are visited most often and the average duration of visit to each site.[a]

ATTENTION MEASURES

Physiological measures track bodily responses to stimuli. *Eye tracking* uses a camera to track the movement of the eye across a TV commercial or a print ad. It records the sequence in which various parts of the ad are viewed, the parts that were studied or ignored, and how much time was spent on each part. *Brain wave analysis* tracks the degree of attention paid to the components of messages through headsets that consumers wear while viewing commercials. These data are used to construct an "engagement index" showing the flow of attention across an ad. A method called MindView tracks the *skin's subtle reactions* to messages via tiny sensors placed on the upper palm of one hand. These data are used to generate a "viewer involvement profile" regarding the message tested.[b] In *theater tests,* TV programs or commercials are shown in a theater setting and viewers use dials (located in their armrests) to indicate their levels of interest or disinterest during the showing of the program or advertisement. *Web site usability tests* allow researchers to "peek over the shoulders" of visitors to record how quickly they find specific information, which components of the site draw more attention, and which parts lead to more clicks.[c] The *Starch Readership Survey* (discussed in Chapter 7) is a measure of attention as well as recall.

MESSAGE INTERPRETATION MEASURES

Attention measures, including sophisticated physiological techniques, measure the degrees of consumer arousal and involvement but do not assess the reasons behind their levels of engagement with the messages tested. Generally, researchers use *attitudinal measures* (see Figure 2-4 in Chapter 2), placed within *copy pretests* or *posttests* to assess whether respondents like the message, understand it correctly, and regard it as effective and persuasive. Researchers are also interested in measuring the emotions and feelings provoked by ads. One study tested the use of *Facial Electromyography* (Facial EMG)—a method that tracks the electrical activity and subtle movements of facial muscles—to gauge the emotions generated by different types of TV commercials. This research concluded that facial EMG is more effective in measuring emotional responses than self-reported cognitive responses because it goes beyond the biases and limitations of the commonly used (but much cheaper and easier to administer) self-report technique.[c]

MESSAGE RECALL MEASURES

In addition to the *recall and recognition* measures discussed in Chapter 7, researchers use *day-after recall tests* in which viewers of TV shows or listeners to radio broadcasts are interviewed a day after watching or listening to a given program. Participants are asked to describe which commercials they recall. The recall of a commercial and its central theme is evidence of its attention-getting and persuasive power.

Sources: [a] www.mriplus.com, www.nielsenmedia.com; [b] Patricia Winters Lauro, "Research Methods Are Being Developed to Help Advertisers Find Out What You Really Think," *New York Times* (April 13, 2000): C1; [c] Richard H. Hazlett and Sasha Yassky, "Emotional Response to Television Commercials: Facial EMG vs. Self Reports," *Journal of Advertising Research* (March/April 1999): 7–23.

Designing Persuasive Communications

In order to create persuasive communications, the sponsor (who may be an individual, a for-profit company, or a not-for-profit organization) must first establish the objectives of the communication, then select the appropriate audiences for the message and the appropriate media through which to reach them, and then design (encode) the message in a manner that is appropriate to each medium and to each audience. As noted earlier, the communications strategy should also include an *a priori* feedback mechanism that alerts the sponsor to any need for modifications or adjustments to the media or the message.

COMMUNICATIONS STRATEGY

In developing its communications strategy, the sponsor must establish the primary communications objectives. These might consist of creating awareness of a service, promoting sales of a product, encouraging (or discouraging) certain practices, attracting retail patronage, reducing postpurchase dissonance, creating goodwill or a favorable image, or any combination of these and other communications objectives.

There are numerous models claiming to depict how persuasive communications work. The *cognitive models* (presented previously in Table 7-1) depict a process in which exposure to a message leads to interest and desire for the product and, ultimately, to buying behavior. For many decades, this general model had been widely adopted by advertisers. A more recent and sophisticated model of advertising is shown in Figure 9-4. The authors of this paradigm maintain that it reflects the interrelationship among the key factors of persuasion—*perception, experience,* and *memory*—in a manner more consistent with how the human mind really works than the older cognitive models, and that advertising messages based on this model are more likely to generate consumption behavior.[30] The existence of these and many other models that claim to explain how persuasion works reflects the complexity of

FIGURE 9-4

The Three Phases and Flow of the Perception/Experience/Memory Model of Advertising

Source: Bruce F. Hall, "A New Model for Measuring Advertising Effectiveness," *Journal of Advertising Research* (March/April 2002): 23–31.

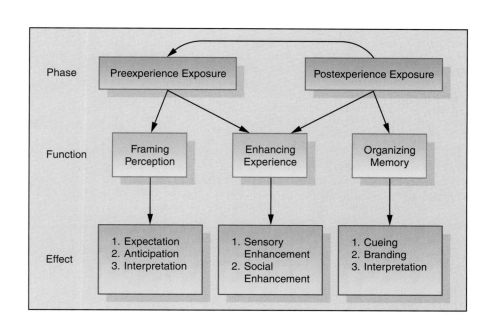

human information processing and the resulting challenges faced by advertisers trying to influence consumption behavior.

TARGET AUDIENCE

An essential component of a communications strategy is selecting the appropriate audience. It is important to remember that an audience is made up of individuals—in many cases, great numbers of individuals. Because each individual has his or her own traits, characteristics, interests, needs, experience, and knowledge, it is essential for the sender to segment the audience into groups that are homogeneous in terms of some relevant characteristic. Segmentation enables the sender to create specific messages for each target group and to run them in specific media that are seen, heard, or read by the target group. It is unlikely that a marketer could develop a single message that would appeal simultaneously to its total audience. Efforts to use "universal" appeals phrased in simple language that everyone can understand invariably result in unsuccessful advertisements to which few people relate.

Companies that have many diverse audiences sometimes find it useful to develop a communications strategy that consists of an overall (or umbrella) communications message to all their audiences, from which they spin off a series of related messages targeted directly to the specific interests of individual segments. In addition, to maintain positive communications with all of their publics, most large organizations have public relations departments or employ public relations counselors to provide favorable information about the company and to suppress unfavorable information.

MEDIA STRATEGY

Media strategy is an essential component of a communications plan. It calls for the placement of ads in the specific media read, viewed, or heard by each targeted audience. To accomplish this, advertisers develop, through research, a **consumer profile** of their target customers that includes the specific media they read or watch. Media organizations regularly research their own audiences in order to develop descriptive **audience profiles.** A cost-effective media choice is one that closely matches the advertiser's consumer profile to a medium's audience profile.

Before selecting specific media vehicles, advertisers must select general media categories that will enhance the message they want to convey. Which media categories the marketer selects depends on the product or service to be advertised, the market segments to be reached, and the marketer's advertising objectives. Rather than select one media category to the exclusion of others, many advertisers use a multimedia campaign strategy, with one primary media category carrying the major burden of the campaign and other categories providing supplemental support. Table 9-2 compares the potential persuasive impact of major advertising media along the dimensions of *targeting precision* (i.e., the ability to reach exclusively the intended audience), constructing a *persuasive message,* degree of *psychological noise, feedback,* and relative *cost.*

MESSAGE STRATEGIES

The message is the thought, idea, attitude, image, or other information that the sender wishes to convey to the intended audience. In trying to encode the message in a form that will enable the audience to understand its precise meaning, the sender must know exactly what he or she is trying to say and why (what the objectives are

TABLE 9-2	Persuasive Capabilities and Limitations of Major Advertising Media

	TARGETING PRECISION	MESSAGE DEVELOPMENT AND EXECUTION	DEGREE OF PSYCHOLOGICAL NOISE	OBTAINING FEEDBACK	RELATIVE COST
Newspapers	Access to large audiences. Not very selective in reaching consumers with specific demographics. Effective for reaching local consumers.	Flexible. Messages can be designed and published quickly. Limited production quality and short message life.	High clutter. Many messages competing for attention.	Sales volume. Redemptions of special promotions and level of store traffic provide immediate feedback.	Determined by size of ad and the medium's circulation. Affordable for local businesses. Permits joint (cooperative) advertising by national manufacturers and local sellers.
Magazines	High geographic and demographic selectivity. *Selective binding*[a] allows more precise targeting of subscribers with the desired demographics.	High quality of production. High credibility of ads in special-interest magazines. Long message life and pass-along readership. Long lead time required.	High clutter. Some magazines may not guarantee ad placement in a particular position within the magazine.	Delayed and indirect feedback, such as the Starch scores that measure recall and attention.	Determined by cost of page and circulation. Top magazines charge very high rates.
Television	Reaches very large audiences. Many programs lack audience selectivity.	Appeals to several senses. Enables messages that draw attention and generate emotion. Short-duration messages must be repeated. Long lead time.	High clutter. Viewers can avoid message exposures by channel surfing or using advanced technologies such as TiVo.	Day-after recall tests measure how many consumers were exposed to the message and, to a lesser degree, their characteristics.	Very high costs based on how many consumers watch a given program.
Radio	High geographic and demographic audience selectivity.	Audio messages only. Short exposure. Relatively short lead time.	High clutter. Listeners can easily switch among stations during commercials.	Delayed feedback, such as day-after recall tests.	Based on size of the audience reached. Local radio may be relatively inexpensive.
Internet	Potential for great audience selectivity. Audience may be demographically skewed. Enables tracking customers and building databases. Privacy issues make targeting more difficult.	Increasingly more advanced messages can be designed and shown relatively quickly. Marketers recognize that their home pages are advertisements and must be designed as persuasive tools.	Very high degree of clutter. Visitors can easily escape promotional messages. Banner ads and home pages can reinforce and expand promotional messages featured in other media.	Interactive medium with potential for gathering immediate feedback. Click rates on ads do not measure their impact accurately (since exposure to the brands featured occurs even without a click).	Great variation in establishing advertising rates since there is no standard measure of the impact of online advertising.

TABLE 9-2	(Continued)

	TARGETING PRECISION	MESSAGE DEVELOPMENT AND EXECUTION	DEGREE OF PSYCHOLOGICAL NOISE	OBTAINING FEEDBACK	RELATIVE COST
Direct Mail[b]	High audience selectivity. Enables personalization. Perceived by many as "junk mail."	Enables novel, visually appealing, and dramatic messages (including the addition of sensory inputs).	No competing messages within the mailing.	Easy to measure feedback through limited pretests and cost-per-inquiry and cost-per-order. Delayed feedback.	Relatively high cost per person per mailing due to "junk mail" image.
Direct Marketing[c]	Marketers can build and constantly refine an electronic database of qualified buyers based on inquiries and direct orders. Permits the development of highly selective customer segments. Privacy concerns makes this practice difficult.	A function of the medium used to solicit the direct response from the customer.	Can be relatively free of clutter, even in media where there is generally a lot of noise. For example, infomercials provide advertisers with a "clutter-free" environment.	Generates measurable responses and enables marketers to measure the profitability of their efforts directly.	Determined through such variables as cost-per-inquiry, cost-per-sale, and revenue-per-advertisement.

Notes: [a] Selective binding is a technique that enables publishers to narrowly segment their subscription bases. When readers subscribe, they are asked to provide demographic information, which the publisher enters into a database. Through a sophisticated computerized system, the publisher is able to select specific subscribers, based on reader demographic profiles, to receive special sections that are bound into a limited number of magazines.
[b] Direct mail includes catalogs, letters, brochures, promotional offers, and any materials mailed directly to customers at their homes or offices.
[c] Direct marketing is not a medium but an interactive marketing technique that uses various media (such as mail, print, broadcast, telephone, and cyberspace) for the purpose of soliciting a direct response from a consumer. Electronic shopping (through home-shopping TV channels or interactive cable) is also considered direct marketing.

and what the message is intended to accomplish). The sender must also know the target audience's personal characteristics in terms of education, interests, needs, and experience. The sender must then design a message strategy through words and/or pictures that will be perceived and accurately interpreted (decoded) by the targeted audience. Table 9-3 presents a list of message elements designed to appeal to three personality types, defined as the *righteous buyer* (who looks to recommendations from independent sources such as *Consumer Reports*), the *social buyer* (who relies on the recommendations of friends, on celebrity endorsements, and testimonials), and the *pragmatic buyer* (who looks for the best value for the money, though not necessarily the least expensive).[31]

Nonverbal stimuli (such as photographs or illustrations) tend to reinforce verbal message arguments. A number of studies have tried to manipulate the proportions of visual and verbal information used in print ads to determine the relative impact on recall and persuasion, but the findings have been inconclusive. In some instances, body copy alone induces more favorable consumer evaluations than body copy and visuals used together; in other instances the reverse is true. One study

TABLE 9-3	The Righteous, Social, and Pragmatic Buyer: A Comparative Analysis		
	RIGHTEOUS	**SOCIAL**	**PRAGMATIC**
Copy Appeals	Describe quality. Note achievements, awards, community and environmental positions.	Offer quality-of-life enhancements, exclusivity.	Benefit-driven. Focus on bottom line.
Copy Length	Wants information. Detailed copy facilitates decisions.	Provide short, lively copy.	Repeat benefits and price. Keep it to the point. Bottom-line oriented.
Endorsements	Highly important when from an independent source.	Impressed with credible celebrity endorsements.	Not important.
Visuals	Show the product fully. Use detail in comparison charts.	Show people having fun. Whimsical!	Include charts for comparison. Show practical use of product.
Pricing	Emphasize fair price, value.	Full retail price easily accepted.	Offer a discount or a special deal.
Guarantees	Provide strongly worded guarantees.	Important, and a decision tie-breaker.	Provide strongly worded guarantees.
Free Trial	"I can test it myself!"	"I can show it off!"	"I can use it and return it if I don't like it!"
Shipping and Handling	Show fairness. Wants costs itemized.	Include in price.	Ship it free.
Premiums	Relate to purchase.	Appeal to the ego. Fun.	Emphasize giving something free.
Time Limits of Offer	Don't ever break your word.	Helps incite action now.	There's always another deal.
Sweepstakes/ Contests	No great appeal.	Dreams of winning and impressing others.	Wants something for nothing.
Charter Membership	Provides some appeal.	"I'm the first to have it!"	Appeals if there's a special deal.

Source: Adapted from Gary Hennerberg, "The Righteous, Social, and Pragmatic Buyer," *Direct Marketing*, May 1993, 31–32. Reprinted with permission from *Direct Marketing* magazine, 224 Seventh Street, Garden City, NY 11330, 516-746-6700.

found that when verbal information was low in imagery, the inclusion of visual examples in the ad increased consumer recall of the verbal information.[32]

Involvement Theory

Involvement theory (see Chapter 7) suggests that individuals are more likely to devote active cognitive effort to evaluating the pros and cons of a product in a high-involvement purchase situation and more likely to focus on peripheral message cues in low-involvement situations. The *Elaboration Likelihood Model* (ELM) proposes that, for high-involvement products, marketers should follow the **central route to persuasion;** that is, they should present advertisements with strong, well-documented, issue-relevant arguments that encourage cognitive processing. When involvement is low, marketers should follow the **peripheral route to persuasion** by emphasizing noncontent visual or symbolic material (e.g., background scenery, music, or celebrity spokespersons) that provide the consumer with pleasant, indirect associations with the product and provoke favorable inferences about its merits (see Figure 9-5).

FIGURE 9-5

Central Route to
Persuasion
Courtesy of Bose Corporation.

Message Structure and Presentation

Some of the decisions that marketers must make in designing the message include the use of *resonance, positive or negative message framing, one-sided or two-sided messages, comparative advertising,* and the *order* of presentation.

Resonance **Advertising resonance** is defined as wordplay, often used to create a double meaning, used in combination with a relevant picture (see Figure 9-6). Other examples of advertising resonance are the phrase "absolut masterpiece" appearing next to a bottle of Absolut Vodka, and Pepsi's slogan "hit the beach topless" next to a Pepsi bottle cap lying in the sand. Using insights provided by semiotics, researchers have found that by manipulating the resonance in an ad, they can

FIGURE 9-6

Resonance in
Advertising

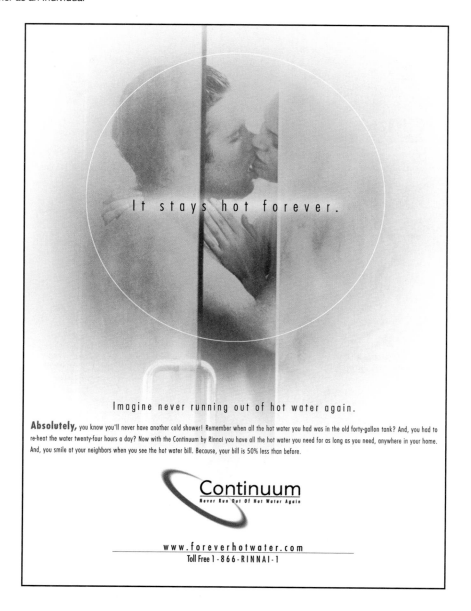

It stays hot forever.

Imagine never running out of hot water again.

Absolutely, you know you'll never have another cold shower! Remember when all the hot water you had was in the old forty-gallon tank? And, you had to re-heat the water twenty-four hours a day? Now with the Continuum by Rinnai you have all the hot water you need for as long as you need, anywhere in your home. And, you smile at your neighbors when you see the hot water bill. Because, your bill is 50% less than before.

Continuum
Never Run Out Of Hot Water Again

www.foreverhotwater.com
Toll Free 1-866-RINNAI-1

improve consumer attitudes toward the ad and the brand, and unaided recall of advertising headlines.[33] They also found that small changes in the ad format (resonance) can have a positive and measurable impact on consumer response.

Message Framing Should a marketer stress the benefits to be gained by using a specific product (**positive message framing**) or the benefits to be lost by not using the product (**negative message framing**)? Research suggests that the appropriate message framing decision depends on the consumer's attitudes and characteristics as well as the product itself. For example, one study found that positively framed messages are more persuasive in low-involvement situations in which there is little emphasis on detailed cognitive processing, and negatively framed messages were more persuasive in high-involvement situations that encourage detailed information processing.[34] Another study found that an individual's self-image impacts the type of framing that he or she finds more persuasive. Individuals with an independent self-image (i.e., who view themselves as defined by unique characteristics) were more persuaded by messages stressing an approach goal (positive framing), and those with an interdependent self-view (i.e., who view themselves as defined by others) found messages that stress avoidance goals more convincing (negative framing).[35]

A study of a credit card company's customers who had not used their cards in the preceding three months found that negative message framing (i.e., what the consumer might lose by not using the credit card) had a much stronger effect on subsequent usage behavior than positive message framing.[36] A study of advertised products that enabled the early detection of disease indicated that positively framed anecdotal messages were less persuasive than negatively framed anecdotal messages.[37] Another study discovered that argument-based, negatively framed messages are particularly effective in new markets, whereas emotion-based, positively framed messages are more persuasive in older markets.[38]

One-Sided Versus Two-Sided Messages   Should marketers tell their audiences only the good points about their products, or should they also tell them the bad (or the commonplace)? Should they pretend that their products are the only ones of their kind, or should it acknowledge competing products? These are very real strategy questions that marketers face every day, and the answers depend on the nature of the audience and the nature of the competition.

If the audience is friendly (e.g., if it uses the advertiser's products), if it initially favors the communicator's position, or if it is not likely to hear an opposing argument, then a *one-sided (supportive) message* that stresses only favorable information is most effective. However, if the audience is critical or unfriendly (e.g., if it uses competitive products), if it is well educated, or if it is likely to hear opposing claims, then a *two-sided (refutational) message* is likely to be more effective. Two-sided advertising messages tend to be more credible than one-sided advertising messages because they acknowledge that the advertised brand has shortcomings. Two-sided messages can also be very effective when consumers are likely to see competitors' negative counterclaims or when consumer attitudes toward the brand are already negative.[39]

Some marketers stress only positive factors about their products and pretend that competition does not exist. However, when competition does exist and when it is likely to be vocal, such advertisers tend to lose credibility with the consumer. The credibility of an advertised claim can often be enhanced by actually disclaiming superiority of some product features in relation to a competing brand or by not claiming that the product is a universal cure. For example, an ad for Rogaine noted that, at the conclusion of a 12-month clinical test, almost half the men using the product experienced modest to dense hair regrowth, about a third experienced minimal hair regrowth, and about one-sixth had no regrowth whatever (see Figure 9-7). The admission that the product did not always work enhanced the credibility of the ad. In political marketing, a candidate will sometimes argue in generalities that a particular course of action is the correct one but give no details with which the audience can analyze, discuss, or rebut the argument (a one-sided argument). Using a two-sided argument, the candidate may say something favorable about the reasonableness of an opponent's position

FIGURE 9-7

Two-Sided Appeal

John's losing his hair.
His mission: get it back.

ASAP!
But how?
Weaving? No.
Transplant?
Not for him.
A hairpiece?
Never, never.
What John really
wants is his
own hair back.
And now he's learned,
**for male pattern
baldness, only
Rogaine has been
proven to regrow hair.**

Normal hair grows and rests in cycles. The exact mechanism by which *Rogaine* Topical Solution (minoxidil topical solution 2%) stimulates hair growth is unknown. But many scientists believe that *Rogaine* works, in part, by taking advantage of the existing hair's growth cycle. Prolong the growth cycle so that more hairs grow longer and thicker at the same time, and you may see improved scalp coverage.

Will *Rogaine* work for you?

Dermatologists conducted 12-month clinical tests. After 4 months, 26% of patients using *Rogaine* reported moderate to dense hair regrowth, compared with 11% of those using a placebo (a similar solution without minoxidil — the active ingredient in *Rogaine*). After 1 year of use, almost half of the men who continued using *Rogaine* in the study rated their regrowth as moderate (40%) to dense (8%). Thirty-six percent reported minimal regrowth. The rest (16%) had no regrowth.

Side effects were minimal: 7% of those who used *Rogaine* had itching of the scalp. (Roughly 5% of those using a placebo

reported the same minor irritations.) *Rogaine* should only be applied to a normal, healthy scalp (not sunburned or irritated).

Make a commitment to see results.

Studies indicate that *at least 4 months of twice-daily treatment with Rogaine are usually necessary before there is evidence of regrowth.* So why not make it part of your normal routine when you wake up and go to bed, like brushing your teeth.

As you'd expect, if you're younger, have been losing your hair for a shorter period of time, and have less initial hair loss, you're more likely to have a better response.

Rogaine is a treatment, not a cure. So further progress is only possible by using it continuously. If you stop using it, you will probably shed the newly regrown hair within a few months.

Get your free Information Kit, plus a $10 incentive to see a doctor.

Why wait? Find out whether *Rogaine* is for you. Call **1-800-965-1199** for a free Information Kit about the product and how to use it. **And because *Rogaine* requires a prescription,** we'll include a list of nearby dermatologists or other doctors experienced in treating hair loss, plus a $10 incentive to visit a doctor soon.

Call
1-800-965-1199

for your free Information Kit
on *Rogaine* and a $10
incentive to see a doctor.

Rogaine®
TOPICAL
SOLUTION minoxidil 2%

See next page for important additional information.

©1994 The Upjohn Company USJ 2659.00 January 1995

before attacking it, thus gaining credibility by appearing objective, open-minded, and fair in examining the issues.

Comparative Advertising **Comparative advertising** is a widely used marketing strategy in which a marketer claims product superiority for its brand over one or more explicitly named or implicitly identified competitors, either on an overall basis or on selected product attributes (see Figure 9-8). Comparative advertising is useful for product positioning, for target market selection, and for brand positioning strate-

FIGURE 9-8

Comparative Advertising

gies. Figure 9-9 presents an ad in which Saab compares its automobile to the Saab military aircraft, thus positioning the car as the land equivalent of its precision manufactured military aircraft.

Some critics of the technique maintain that comparative ads often assist recall of the competitor's brand at the expense of the advertised brand. However, the wide use of comparative advertising and the research into its strategic effects do not support this view. Studies have found that comparative ads are capable of exerting more positive effects on brand attitudes, purchase intentions, and purchase than noncomparative advertisements.[40] Studies of comparative advertising using an information-processing perspective found that comparative ads elicited higher levels of cognitive processing, had better recall, and were perceived as more relevant than noncomparative ads.[41] Another study of the mental images formed by noncomparative versus comparative ads supported the use of comparative advertising as an effective positioning strategy.[42]

A study that tested the degree of negativity in comparative messages (by using positive, negative, and mildly negative comparative messages) for several products reported that negative elements in an ad contributed to its effectiveness as long as they were believable or were offset by some elements that made the ad appear

FIGURE 9-9

Comparative
Advertising

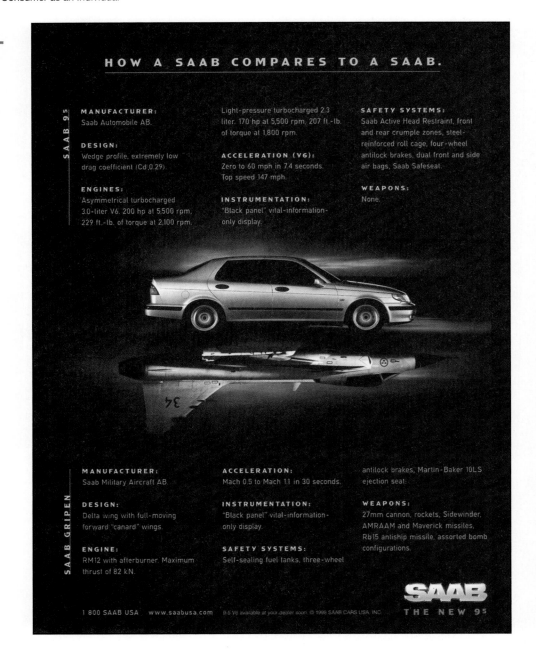

neutral.[43] There has been considerable concern expressed regarding the ability of comparative advertising to mislead consumers, including several legal actions against companies by the Federal Trade Commission. A recent study advocates the development of concrete measures designed to gauge a comparative ad's ability to mislead consumers.[44]

Order Effects Is it best to present your commercial first or last? Should you give the bad news first or last? Communications researchers have found that the **order** in which a message is presented affects audience receptivity. For this reason, politicians and other professional communicators often jockey for position when they address an audience sequentially; they are aware that the first and last speeches are more likely to be retained in the audience's memory than those in between. On TV, the position of a commercial in a commercial pod can be critical. The commercials shown first are recalled the best, whereas those in the middle are recalled the least.

When just two competing messages are presented, one after the other, the evidence as to which position is more effective is somewhat conflicting. Some researchers have found that the material presented first produces a greater effect (*primacy effect*), whereas others have found that the material presented last is more effective (*recency effect*). One study found that in situations that foster high levels of cognitive processing, the initial message tends to be more influential (primacy effect), whereas in situations of low message elaboration, the second message had a greater impact (recency effect).[45] Magazine publishers recognize the impact of order effects by charging more for ads on the front, back, and inside covers of magazines than for the inside magazine pages because of their greater visibility and recall.

Order is also important in listing product benefits within an ad. If audience interest is low, the most important point should be made first to attract attention. However, if interest is high, it is not necessary to pique curiosity, so product benefits can be arranged in ascending order, with the most important point mentioned last. When both favorable information and unfavorable information are to be presented (as in an annual stockholders' report), placing the favorable material first often produces greater tolerance for the unfavorable news. It also produces greater acceptance and better understanding of the total message.

Repetition   **Repetition** is an important factor in learning. Thus, it is not surprising that repetition, or frequency of the ad, affects persuasion, ad recall, brand name recall, and brand preferences. It also increases the likelihood that the brand will be included in the consumer's *consideration set*. One study found that multiple message exposures gave consumers more opportunity to internalize product attributes, to develop more or stronger cue associations, more positive attitudes, and increased willingness to resist competitive counterpersuasion efforts.[46] Another study found that in low-involvement situations, individuals are more likely to regard message claims that are repeated frequently as more truthful than those repeated with less frequency.[47] A study that examined the effects of repetition of the same ad versus repetition of varied ad executions (holding the number of repetitions for each variable constant) found that varied ad executions enhanced memory for the brand name over repeated same-ad executions. The study supported the *encoding variability hypothesis,* which attributes the superior memorability of varied executions to the multiple paths laid down in memory between the brand name and other concepts, providing alternative retrieval routes that increase access to the brand name.[48]

Advertising Appeals

Sometimes objective, *factual appeals* are more effective in persuading a target audience; at other times *emotional appeals* are more effective. It depends on the kind of audience to be reached and their degree of involvement in the product category. In general, however, logical, reason-why appeals are more effective in persuading educated audiences, and emotional appeals are more effective in persuading less-educated consumers. The following section examines the effectiveness of several frequently used emotional appeals.

Fear Fear is an effective appeal often used in marketing communications. Some researchers have found a negative relationship between the intensity of fear appeals and their ability to persuade, so that strong fear appeals tend to be less effective than mild fear appeals. (See also the discussion of *assimilation-contrast theory* in Chapter 8.) A number of explanations have been offered for this phenomenon. Strong fear appeals concerning a highly relevant topic (such as cigarette smoking) cause the individual to experience cognitive dissonance, which is resolved either by rejecting the practice or by rejecting the unwelcome information. Because giving up a comfortable habit is difficult, consumers more readily reject the threat. This they do by a variety of techniques, including denial of its validity ("There still is no real proof that smoking causes cancer"), the belief that they are immune to personal disaster ("It can't happen to me"), and a diffusing process that robs the claim of its true significance ("I play it safe by smoking only filter cigarettes"). Therefore, marketers should use reasonable but not extreme fear appeals and also recognize that fear appeals are not always appropriate. For example, a study of warning information labels affixed to full-fat, reduced-fat, and nonfat products concluded that, for products with credible and familiar risks, information labels were more effective than warning labels because they do not arouse *psychological reactance.*[49] Another study of adolescent responses to fear communications found that adolescents are more persuaded to avoid drug use by messages that depict negative social consequences of drug use rather than physical threats to their bodies.[50]

There is no single explanation of the relationship between fear appeals and persuasiveness. One theory proposes that individuals cognitively appraise the available information regarding the severity of the threat, then they appraise the likelihood that the threat will occur; they evaluate whether coping behavior can eliminate the threat's danger, and if so, whether they have the ability to perform the coping behavior. This theory is called the *Ordered Protection Motivation* (OPM) model. The study also found that the personality variable "sensation seeking" affected the processing of fear appeals. A high sensation seeker is more likely to use drugs and also to react negatively to fear-focused antidrug messages, feeling that he or she is immortal.[51]

Marketers must also consider that the mention of possible detrimental effects of using a product while proclaiming its benefits may result in negative attitudes toward the product itself. For example, if a luxury automobile company features a new 24-hour emergency hot line in a series of advertisements (as an "added value" product feature), some consumers may be "turned off" by even the suggestion that a brand-new, expensive car would experience roadside mechanical problems—particularly late at night on a dark and lonely road.

Humor Many marketers use humorous appeals in the belief that humor will increase the acceptance and persuasiveness of their advertising communications. By some estimates, up to 24 percent of TV ads in the United States use humor, but there are some risks associated with using this appeal.[52] For example, the effects of humorous ads vary by the audience's demographics, level of involvement (humor is more effective for promoting low-involvement products), and attitudes (humor is more effective when the audience already has positive attitudes toward the brand).[53] Table 9-4 summarizes some research findings on the impact of humor on advertising.

TABLE 9-4	Impact of Humor on Advertising

- *Humor attracts attention.*
- *Humor does not harm comprehension.* (In some cases it may even aid comprehension.)
- *Humor is not more effective at increasing persuasion.*
- *Humor does not enhance source credibility.*
- *Humor enhances liking.*
- *Humor that is relevant to the product is superior to humor that is unrelated to the product.*
- *Audience demographic factors (e.g., gender, ethnicity, age) affect the response to humorous advertising appeals.*
- *The nature of the product affects the appropriateness of a humorous treatment.*
- *Humor is more effective with existing products than with new products.*
- *Humor is more appropriate for low-involvement products and feeling-oriented products than for high-involvement products.*

Source: Marc G. Weinberger and Charles S. Gulas, "The Impact of Humor in Advertising: A Review," *Journal of Advertising* 21, 4 (December 1992): 35–59. Reprinted by permission.

Marketers believe that younger, better-educated, upscale, and professional people tend to be receptive audiences for humorous messages (see Figure 9-10). A study of how humor actually works within ads discovered that surprise is almost always needed to generate humor and that the effectiveness of humorous ads is also influenced by such message elements as warmth and playfulness.[54]

Abrasive Advertising How effective can unpleasant or annoying ads be? Studies of the sleeper effect, discussed earlier, suggest that the memory of an unpleasant commercial that antagonizes listeners or viewers may dissipate over time, leaving only the brand name in the minds of consumers.

All of us have at one time or another been repelled by so-called agony commercials, which depict in diagrammatic detail the internal and intestinal effects of heartburn, indigestion, clogged sinus cavities, hammer-induced headaches, and the like. Nevertheless, pharmaceutical companies often run such commercials with great success because they appeal to a certain segment of the population that suffers from ailments that are not visible and thus elicit little sympathy from family and friends. Their complaints are legitimized by commercials with which they immediately identify. With the sponsor's credibility established ("They really understand the misery I'm going through"), the message itself tends to be highly persuasive in getting consumers to buy the advertised product.

Sex in Advertising In our highly permissive society, sensual advertising seems to permeate the print media and the airwaves. Advertisers are increasingly trying to provoke attention with suggestive illustrations, crude language, and nudity in their efforts to appear "hip" and contemporary. In today's advertising, there is a lot of explicit and daring sexual imagery, extending far beyond the traditional product categories of fashion and fragrance into such categories as shampoo, beer, cars, and home construction.

There is little doubt that sexual themes have attention-getting value, but studies show that they rarely encourage actual consumption behavior. A widely quoted study that examined the effects of sexual advertising appeals on cognitive processing and communications effectiveness found that sexual appeals interfere with message comprehension, particularly when there is substantial information to be processed. It also found that more product-related thinking occurs in response to nonsexual appeals and that visual sexual elements in an ad are more likely to be processed than its verbal content, drawing cognitive processing away from product or message evaluation.[55] Some researchers have concluded that nudity may negatively impact the product

FIGURE 9-10

Humor to Baby
Boomers

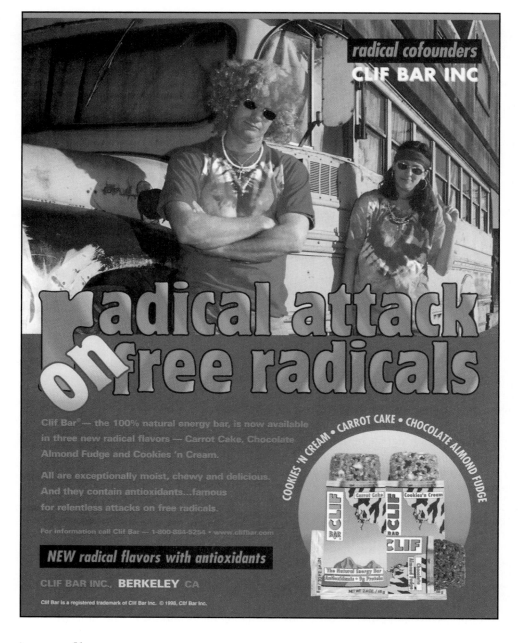

message.[56] These and other findings support the theory that sexual advertising appeals often detract from the processing of message content.

The type of interest that sexual-advertising evokes often stops exactly where it starts—with sex. If a sexually suggestive or explicit illustration is not relevant to the product advertised, it has little effect on consumers' buying intentions. This highlights the potential risk of sexually oriented advertising: The advertiser may be giving up persuasiveness to achieve "stopping power." When using sex to promote a product, the advertiser must be sure that the product, the ad, the target audience, and the use of sexual themes and elements all work together. When sex is relevant to the product, it can be an extremely potent copy theme. For example the advertisers of Perrier Jouët champagne show a beautiful nude tattooed with the company's

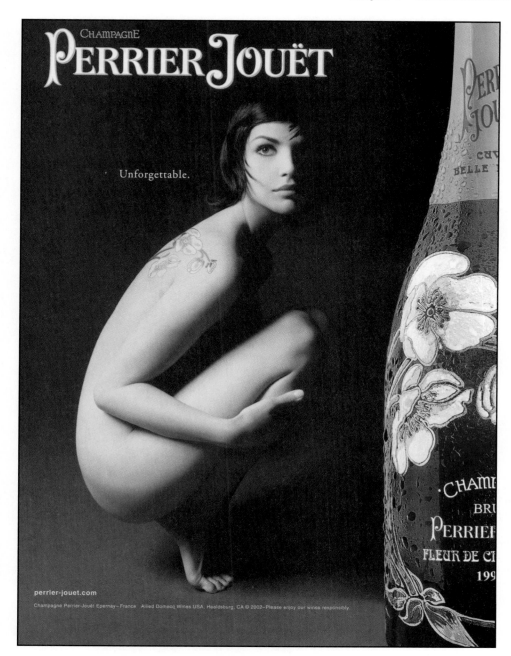

FIGURE 9-11

Sexual Appeal

logo and the single word "Unforgettable" to suggest a romantic, exciting, and unforgettable evening drinking their champagne (see Figure 9-11).

Audience Participation Earlier we spoke about the importance of feedback in the communications process. The provision of feedback changes the communications process from one-way to two-way communication. This is important to senders because it enables them to determine whether and how well communication has taken place. But feedback also is important to receivers because it enables them to participate, to be involved, to experience in some way the message itself. Participation by the receiver reinforces the message. An experienced communicator asks questions and opinions of an audience to draw them into the discussion. Many professors use the participative approach in classrooms rather than the more sterile lecture format because they recognize that student participation tends to facilitate internalization of the information covered.

Although participation is easily accomplished in interpersonal and online communications, it takes a great deal of ingenuity to achieve in impersonal communications. Thus, it is a challenge for imaginative marketers to get consumers actively engaged in their advertising as soon as they see it. An example of a clever ad appealing to audience participation is featured in Figure 9-12.

FIGURE 9-12

Audience Participation Appeal
Reprinted by permission of Kate Spade.

· W O R D   S E A R C H ·
have courage

PLEASE FIND THE WORDS BELOW HIDDEN WITHIN OUR PUZZLE.

```
A B H N I A R A K I N O P
Y H C O M M U N I T Y I E
O N O T P O H O I Y P L A
R L U H T E P T E R M T C
E P R H T G N E R T S I E
I T A R A F R I M L T P S
T R G A D S Y T E G O R L
E P E R S E V E R A N C E
Y U T E L A N Y L I M A F
H F R I E N D S E H I M O
```

hope   peace   friends   community
strength   family   courage   perseverance

kate spade
NEW YORK

new york chicago san francisco greenwich manhasset boston www.katespade.com ©2002 kate spade®

THE "HAVE COURAGE" MEDIUM SHOPPER IN WOOL,
AVAILABLE IN RED/NAVY, NAVY/RED, AND CHARCOAL/NAVY, $195

Summary

This chapter has described how the consumer receives and is influenced by marketing communications. There are five basic components of communication: the sender, the receiver, the medium, the message, and feedback (the receiver's response). In the communications process, the sender encodes the message using words, pictures, symbols, or spokespersons and sends it through a selected channel (or medium). The receiver decodes (interprets) the message based on his or her personal characteristics and experience, and responds (or does not respond) based on such factors as selective exposure, selective perception, comprehension, and psychological noise.

There are two types of communications: interpersonal and impersonal (or mass) communications. Interpersonal communications occur on a personal level between two or more people and may be verbal or nonverbal, formal or informal. In mass communications, there is no direct contact between source and receiver. Interpersonal communications take place in person, by telephone, by mail, or by e-mail; mass communications occur through such impersonal media as television, radio, newspapers, and magazines. Feedback is an essential component of all types of communications because it provides the sender with some notion as to whether and how well the message has been received.

The credibility of the source, a vital element in message persuasiveness, often is based on the source's perceived intentions. Informal sources and neutral or editorial sources are considered to be highly objective and, thus, highly credible. The credibility of a commercial source is more problematic and usually is based on a composite evaluation of its reputation, expertise, and knowledge and that of the medium, the retail channel, and company spokespersons.

Media selection depends on the product, the audience, and the advertising objectives of the campaign. Each medium has advantages and shortcomings that must be weighed in the selection of media for an advertising campaign.

The manner in which a message is presented influences its impact. For example, one-sided messages are more effective in some situations and with some audiences; two-sided messages are more effective with others. High-involvement products (those with great relevance to a consumer segment) are best advertised through the central route to persuasion, which encourages active cognitive effort. Low-involvement products are best promoted through peripheral cues, such as background scenery, music, or celebrity spokespersons.

Emotional appeals frequently used in advertising include fear, humor, and sexual appeals. When sexual themes are relevant to the product, they can be very effective; when used solely as attention-getters, they rarely achieve brand recall. Audience participation is a very effective communications strategy because it encourages internalization of the advertising message. Future research is needed to identify the many product, audience, and situational variables that mediate the effects of message order and presentation in persuading consumers to buy.

Discussion Questions

1. Explain the differences between feedback from interpersonal communications and feedback from impersonal communications. How can the marketer obtain and use each kind of feedback?

2. List and discuss the effects of psychological noise on the communications process. What strategies can a marketer use to overcome psychological noise?

3. List and discuss factors that affect the credibility of formal communications sources of product information. What factors influence the perceived credibility of an informal communications source?

4. What are the implications of the sleeper effect for the selection of spokespersons and the scheduling of advertising messages?

5. Should marketers use more body copy than artwork in print ads? Explain your answer.

6. For what kinds of audiences would you consider using comparative advertising? Why?

Exercises

1. Bring two print advertisements to class: one illustrating a one-sided message and the other a two-sided message. Which of the measures discussed in the chapter would you use to evaluate the effectiveness of each ad? Explain your answers.

2. Find one example of each of the following two advertising appeals: fear and sex. One example must be a print ad and the other a TV commercial. Analyze the placement of each ad in the medium where it appeared according to the media selection criteria presented in Table 9-2.

3. Watch one hour of TV on a single channel during prime time and also tape the broadcast. Immediately after watching the broadcast, list all the commercials you can recall seeing. For each commercial, identify (a) the message framing approach used, and (b) whether the message was one-sided or two-sided. Compare your list with the actual taped broadcast. Explain any discrepancies between your recollections and the actual broadcast on the basis of concepts discussed in this chapter.

4. For three of the commercials you watched in the preceding exercise, identify whether the marketer used the central or peripheral route to persuasion. Explain your answer and speculate on why each marketer chose the approach it used to advertise the product or service.

Key Terms

- **Advertising resonance**
- **Audience versus consumer profiles**
- **Communication**
- **Comparative advertising**
- **Central and peripheral routes to persuasion**
- **Direct marketing versus direct mail**
- **Feedback**
- **Formal versus informal communications sources**
- **Institutional advertising**
- **Interpersonal versus impersonal communications**
- **One-sided versus two-sided messages**
- **Opinion leaders**
- **Order**
- **Positive versus negative framing strategies**
- **Psychological noise**
- **Publicity**
- **Receiver**
- **Repetition**
- **Sleeper effect**
- **Source credibility**
- **Verbal versus nonverbal messages**
- **Word-of-mouth communications**

Notes

1. For example, L. Jean Harrison-Walker, "The Measurement of Word-of-Mouth Communication and an Investigation of Service Quality and Customer Commitment as Potential Antecedents," *Journal of Service Research* (August 2001): 60–75.

2. For an empirical analysis of some 200 logos designed to achieve corporate image and communication goals, see Pamela W. Henderson and Joseph A. Cote, "Guidelines for Selecting or Modifying Logos," *Journal of Marketing* (April 1998): 14–30.

3. See Paul N. Bloom and Torger Reve, "Transmitting Signals to Consumers for Competitive Advantage," *Business Horizons* (July–August 1990): 58–66; and Linda Greenhouse, "High Court Ruling Upholds Trademarking of a Color," *New York Times* (March 29, 1994): D1.

4. Warren St. John, "A Store Lures Guys Who Are Graduating from Chinos," *New York Times on the Web* (July 14, 2002).

5. Lynne M. Sallot, "What the Public Thinks About Public Relations: An Impression Management

Experiment," *Journalism and Mass Communication Quarterly* (Spring 2002): 150–171.

6. S. Ratneshwar and Shelly Chaiken, "Comprehension's Role in Persuasion: The Case of Its Moderating Effect on the Persuasive Impact of Source Cues," *Journal of Consumer Research* 18 (June 1991): 52–62.

7. Michael A. Kamins, "An Investigation into the 'Match Up' Hypothesis in Celebrity Advertising: When Beauty May Be Only Skin Deep," *Journal of Advertising* 19, 1 (1990): 4–13. See also Marsha L. Richins, "Social Comparison and the Idealized Images of Advertising," *Journal of Consumer Research* 18 (June 1991): 71–83.

8. Marla Royne Stafford, Thomas F. Stafford, and Ellen Day, "A Contingency Approach: The Effects of Spokesperson Type and Service Type on Service Advertising," *Journal of Advertising* (Summer 2000): 17–32.

9. Laura M. Arpan, "When in Rome? The Effects of Spokesperson Ethnicity on Audience Evaluation of Crisis," *The Journal of Business Communication* (July 2002): 314–339; Osei Appiah, "Ethnic Identification and Adolescents' Evaluations of Advertisements," *Journal of Advertising Research* (September/October 2001): 7–22; Oscar W. DeShields Jr. and Ali Kara, "The Persuasive Effect of Spokesperson Similarity Moderated by Source Credibility," *2000 American Marketing Association Education Proceedings,* Vol 11, 132–143.

10. Ronald E. Goldsmith, Barbara A. Lafferty, and Stephen J. Newell, "The Impact of Corporate Credibility and Celebrity Credibility on Consumer Reaction to Advertisements and Brands," *Journal of Advertising* (Fall 2000): 43–54.

11. B. Zafer Erdogan, Michael J. Baker, and Stephen Tagg, "Selecting Celebrity Endorsers: The Practitioner's Perspective," *Journal of Advertising Research* (May/June 2001): 39–48.

12. Thomas J. Robinson and Barbara K. Kaye, "Using Is Believing: The Influence of Reliance on the Credibility of Online Political Information Among Politically Interested Internet Users," *Journalism and Mass Communication Quarterly* (Winter 2000): 865–879.

13. Sung Tae Kim, David Weaver, and Lars Willnat, "Media Reporting and Perceived Credibility of Online Polls," *Journalism and Mass Communication Quarterly* (Winter 2000): 846–864.

14. Mineabere Ibelema and Lary Powell, "Cable Television News Viewed as Most Credible," *Newspaper Research Journal* (Winter 2001): 41–51.

15. Carl I. Hovland, Arthur A. Lumsdaine, and Fred D. Sheffield, *Experiments on Mass Communication* (New York: Wiley, 1949): 182–200.

16. See Joseph W. Alba, Howard Marmorstein, and Amitava Chattopadhyay, "Transitions in Preference

over Time: The Effects of Memory on Message Persuasiveness," *Journal of Marketing Research* 29 (November 1992): 414.

17. Darlene B. Hannah and Brian Sternthal, "Detecting and Explaining the Sleeper Effect," *Journal of Consumer Research* 11 (September 1984): 632–642.

18. Ruth Ann Weaver Lariscy and Spencer F. Tinkham, "The Sleeper Effect and Negative Political Advertising," *Journal of Advertising* (Winter 1999): 13–30.

19. Jean Harrison-Walker, "The Import of Illiteracy to Marketing Communication," *Journal of Consumer Marketing* 12, 1 (1995): 50–64.

20. Frédéric F. Brunel and Michelle R. Nelson, "Explaining Gender Responses to 'Help-Self' and 'Help-Others' Charity Ads Appeals: The Mediating Role of World-Views," *Journal of Advertising* (Fall 2000): 15–27.

21. Patrick De Pelsmacker, Maggie Geuens, and Pascal Anckaert, "Media Context and Advertising Effectiveness: The Role of Context Appreciation and Context/Ad Similarity," *Journal of Advertising* (Summer 2002): 49–61.

22. Andrew Sharma, "Recall of Television Commercials as a Function of Viewing Context: The Impact of Program-Commercial Congruity on Commercial Messages," *Journal of General Psychology* (October 2000): 383–396.

23. Vijay Mahajan and Yoram Wind, "Got Emotional Product Positioning?" *Marketing Management* (May/June 2002): 36–41.

24. Anna Wilde Mathews, "Patriotism Edges Out Promotion in Messages Designed to Unite U.S.," *Wall Street Journal* (September 18, 2001): B6.

25. Angela Y. Lee and Brian Sternthal, "The Effects of Positive Mood on Memory," *Journal of Consumer Research* (September 1999): 115–129.

26. See Mahima Mathur and Amitava Chattopadhyay, "The Impact of Moods Generated by Television Programs on Responses to Advertising," *Psychology and Marketing* 8, 1 (Spring 1991): 59–77.

27. Anna S. Mattila, "The Role of Narratives in the Advertising of Experiential Services," *Journal of Service Research* (August 2000): 35–45.

28. Brad Stone, "The War Over Your TV," *Newsweek* (July 29, 2002): 46–47.

29. For example, Michael T. Ewing, Erik Du Plessis, and Charles Foster, "Cinema Advertising Reconsidered," *Journal of Advertising Research* (January/February 2001): 78–85; Michelle R. Nelson, "Recall of Brand Placements in Computer/Video Games," *Journal of Advertising Research* (March/April 2002): 80–92.

30. Bruce F. Hall, "A New Model for Measuring Advertising Effectiveness," *Journal of Advertising Research* (March/April 2002): 23–31.

31. Gary Hennerberg, "The Righteous, Social, and Pragmatic Buyer," *Direct Marketing* (May 1993): 31–34.

32. H. Rao Unnava and Robert E. Burnkrant, "An Imagery Processing View of the Role of Pictures in Print Advertisements," *Journal of Marketing Research* 28 (May 1991): 226–231.

33. Edward F. McQuarrie and David Glen Mick, "On Resonance: A Critical Pluralistic Inquiry into Advertising Rhetoric," *Journal of Consumer Research* 19 (September 1992): 180–197.

34. Durairaj Maheswaran and Joan Meyers Levy, "The Influence of Message Framing and Issue Involvement," *Journal of Marketing Research* 27 (August 1990): 361–367.

35. Jennifer L. Aaker and Angela Y. Lee, " 'I' Seek Pleasure and 'We' Avoid Pains: The Role of Self-Regulatory Goals in Information Processing and Persuasion," *Journal of Consumer Research* (June 2001): 33–49.

36. Yoav Ganzach and Nili Karsahi, "Message Framing and Buying Behavior: A Field Experiment," *Journal of Business Research* 32 (1995): 11–17.

37. Dena Cox and Anthony D. Cox, "Communicating the Consequences of Early Detection: The Role of Evidence and Framing," *Journal of Marketing* (July 2001): 91–103.

38. Rajesh K. Chandy, Gerard J. Tellis, Deborah J. MaCinnis, and Pattana Thaivanich, "What to Say When: Advertising Appeals in Evolving Markets," *JMR, Journal of Marketing Research* (November 2001): 399–414.

39. Ayn E. Crowley and Wayne D. Hoyer, "An Integrative Framework for Understanding Two–Sided Persuasion," *Journal of Consumer Research* 20 (March 1994): 561–574.

40. Randall L. Rose, Paul W. Miniard, Michael J. Barone, Kenneth C. Manning, and Brian D. Till, "When Persuasion Goes Undetected: The Case of Comparative Advertising," *Journal of Marketing Research* 30 (August 1993): 315–330; see also Cornelia Pechmann and S. Ratneshwar, "The Use of Comparative Advertising for Brand Positioning: Association versus Differentiation," *Journal of Consumer Research* 18 (September 1991): 145–160, and Cornelia Pechmann and David W. Stewart, "The Effects of Comparative Advertising on Attention, Memory, and Purchase Intentions," *Journal of Consumer Research* 17 (September 1990): 180–191.

41. Darrel D. Muehling, Jeffrey J. Stoltman, and Sanford Grossbart, "The Impact of Comparative Advertising on Levels of Message Involvement," *Journal of Advertising* 19, 4 (1990): 41–50; see also Jerry B. Gotlieb and Dan Sarel, "Comparative Advertising Effectiveness: The Role of Involvement and Source Credibility," *Journal of Advertising* 20, 1 (1991): 38–45.

42. Kenneth C. Manning, Paul W. Miniard, Michael J. Barone, and Randall L. Rose, "Understanding the Mental Representations Created by Comparative Advertising," *Journal of Advertising* (Summer 2001): 27–39.

43. Alina B. Sorescu and Betsy D. Gelb, "Negative Comparative Advertising: Evidence Favoring Fine-Tuning," *Journal of Advertising* (Winter 2000): 25–40.

44. Michael J. Barone, Randall L. Rose, Paul W. Miniard, and Kenneth C. Manning, "Enhancing the Detection of Misleading Comparative Advertising," *Journal of Advertising Research* (September/October 1999): 43–50.

45. Curtis P. Haugtvedt and Duane T. Wegener, "Message Order Effect in Persuasion: An Attitude Strength Perspective," *Journal of Consumer Research* 21 (June 1994): 205–218.

46. Curtis P. Haugtvedt et al., "Advertising Repetition and Variation Strategies: Implications for Understanding Attitude Strength," *Journal of Consumer Research* 21 (June 1994): 176–189.

47. Scott A. Hawkins and Stephen J. Hoch, "Low Involvement Learning: Memory Without Evaluation," *Journal of Consumer Research* 19 (September 1992): 212–225.

48. H. Rao Unnava and Robert E. Burnkrant, "Effects of Repeating Varied Ad Executions on Brand Name Memory," *Journal of Marketing Research* 28 (November 1991): 406–416.

49. Brad J. Bushman, "Effects of Warning and Information Labels on Consumption of Full Fat, Reduced Fat, and No Fat Products," *Journal of Applied Psychology* 83, 1 (1998): 97–101.

50. Denise D. Schoenbachler and Tommy E. Whittler, "Adolescent Processing of Social and Physical Threat Communications," *Journal of Advertising* 35, 4 (Winter 1996): 37–54.

51. James B. Hunt, John F. Tanner Jr., and David R. Eppright, "Forty Years of Fear Appeal Research: Support for the Ordered Protection Motivation Model," *American Marketing Association* 6 (Winter 1995): 147–153.

52. Dana L. Alden, Ashesh Mukherjee, and Wayne D. Hoyer, "The Effects of Incongruity, Surprise and Positive Moderators on Perceived Humor in Advertising," *Journal of Advertising* (Summer 2000): 1–15.

53. Ibid.

54. Ibid.

55. Jessica Severn, George E. Belch, and Michael A. Belch, "The Effects of Sexual and Non-Sexual Advertising Appeals and Information Level on Cognitive Processing and Communication Effectiveness," *Journal of Advertising* 19, 1 (1990): 14–22.

56. Michael S. LaTour, Robert E. Pitts, and David C. Snook Luther, "Female Nudity, Arousal, and Ad Response: An Experimental Investigation," *Journal of Advertising* 19, 4 (1990): 51–62.

III

Consumers in Their Social and Cultural Settings

PART 3 DISCUSSES THE CONSUMER IN THEIR SETTINGS.

The five chapters in Part 3 are designed to provide the reader with a detailed picture of the social and cultural dimensions of consumer behavior. Chapters 10 through 14 explain how social and cultural concepts affect the attitudes and behavior of individuals in the United States and the world beyond, and show how these concepts are employed by marketing practitioners to achieve their marketing objectives.

The training wheels
of good nutrition.

Get them started on the road to healthy snacking.
Great fruity taste. And no artificial flavors.

www.dannon.com

Reference Groups and Family Influences

With the exception of those very few people who are classified as hermits, most individuals interact with other people on a daily basis, especially with members of their own families.

In the first part of this chapter, we will consider how group involvements and memberships influence our actions as consumers—that is, impact consumers' decision making, shopping activities, and actual consumption. The second part of this chapter deals with how the family influences its members' consumer behavior. For instance, a child learning the uses and value of money is often a "family matter"; so are decisions about a new car, a vacation trip, or whether to go to a local or an out-of-town college. The family commonly provides the opportunity for product exposure and trial and imparts consumption values to its members. As a major consumption group, the family is also a prime target for many products and services.

This chapter begins with a discussion of the basic concepts of group dynamics and how reference groups both directly and indirectly influence consumer behavior. We then examine some basic family concepts. Next we discuss family consumer decision making and consumption behavior; last we explore the marketing implications of the family life cycle. (The four chapters that follow discuss other social and societal *groupings* that influence consumer buying processes: social class, culture, subculture, and cross-cultural exposure.)

What Is a Group?

A **group** may be defined as two or more people who interact to accomplish either individual or mutual goals. The broad scope of this definition includes an intimate group of two co-workers who each week attend a Weight Watchers class together (**www.weightwatchers.com**) and a larger, more formal group, such as a local scuba diving club, whose members are mutually interested in scuba equipment, scuba training, and scuba diving trips and vacations. Included in this definition, too, is a kind of "one-sided grouping" in which an individual consumer observes the appearance or actions of others, who unknowingly serve as consumption-related role models.

Sometimes groups are classified by membership status. A group to which a person either belongs or would qualify for membership in is called a *membership group*. For example, the group of women with whom a young executive plays tennis weekly would be considered, for her, a membership group. There are also groups in which an individual is not likely to receive membership, despite acting like a member by adopting the group's values, attitudes, and behavior. This is considered a **symbolic group.** For instance, professional golfers may constitute a symbolic group for an amateur golfer who identifies with certain players by imitating their behavior whenever possible (e.g., by purchasing a specific brand of golf balls or golf clubs). However, the amateur golfer does not (and probably never will) qualify for membership as a professional golfer because he has neither the skills nor the opportunity to compete professionally.

Understanding the Power of Reference Groups

Within the context of consumer behavior, the concept of reference groups is an extremely important and powerful idea. A **reference group** is any person or group that serves as a point of comparison (or reference) for an individual in forming either general or specific values, attitudes, or a specific guide for behavior. This basic concept provides a valuable perspective for understanding the impact of other people on an individual's consumption beliefs, attitudes, and behavior. It also provides insight into the methods marketers sometimes use to effect desired changes in consumer behavior.

From a marketing perspective, *reference groups* are groups that serve as *frames of reference* for individuals in their purchase or consumption decisions. The usefulness of this concept is enhanced by the fact that it places no restrictions on group size or membership, nor does it require that consumers identify with a tangible group (i.e., the group can be symbolic such as owners of successful small businesses, leading corporate chief executive officers, rock stars, or golf celebrities).

Reference groups that influence general or broadly defined values or behavior are called **normative reference groups.** An example of a child's normative reference group is the immediate family, which is likely to play an important role in molding the child's general consumer values and behavior (such as which foods to select for good nutrition, appropriate ways to dress for specific occasions, how and where to shop, or what constitutes "good" value).

Reference groups that serve as benchmarks for specific or narrowly defined attitudes or behavior are called **comparative reference groups.** A comparative reference group might be a neighboring family whose lifestyle appears to be admirable and worthy of imitation (the way they maintain their home, their choice of home furnishings and cars, their taste in clothing, or the number and types of vacations they take).

Both normative and comparative reference groups are important. Normative reference groups influence the development of a basic code of behavior; comparative reference groups influence the expression of specific consumer attitudes and behavior. It is likely that the specific influences of comparative reference groups to some measure depend on the basic values and behavior patterns established early in a person's development by normative reference groups.

A BROADENED PERSPECTIVE ON REFERENCE GROUPS

The meaning of "reference group" has changed over the years. As originally used, reference groups were narrowly defined to include only those groups with which a person interacted on a direct basis (such as family and close friends). However, the concept gradually has broadened to include both direct and indirect individual or group influences. **Indirect reference groups** consist of those individuals or groups with whom a person does not have direct face-to-face contact, such as movie stars, sports heroes, political leaders, TV personalities, or even well-dressed and interesting-looking people on the street. It is the power of the indirect reference group that helps sell the Nike clothing, golf balls, and golf equipment used by Tiger Woods (**www.nike.com**).

Referents a person might use in evaluating his or her own general or specific attitudes or behavior vary from one individual to several family members, to a broader kinship or from a voluntary association to a social class, a profession, an ethnic group, a community, an age category, or even a nation or culture. As Figure 10-1 indicates, the major societal groupings that influence an individual's consumer behavior are family, friends, social class, various subcultures, one's own culture, and even other cultures. For instance, within the scope of selected subcultures, we would include various age categories (teenagers or baby boomers) that might serve as a reference group for their own or others' behavior.

FACTORS THAT AFFECT REFERENCE GROUP INFLUENCE

The degree of influence that a reference group exerts on an individual's behavior usually depends on the nature of the individual and the product and on specific social factors. This section discusses how and why some of these factors influence consumer behavior. Table 10-1 presents a broad view of the factors that influence conformity.

Information and Experience

An individual who has firsthand experience with a product or service, or can easily obtain full information about it, is less likely to be influenced by the advice or example of others. On the other hand, a person who has little or no experience with a product or service and does not expect to have access to objective information about it (e.g., a person who believes that advertising may be misleading or deceptive) is more likely to seek out the advice or example of others. For instance, when a young corporate sales rep wants to impress his client, he may take her to a restaurant that

FIGURE 10-1

Major Consumer
Reference Groups

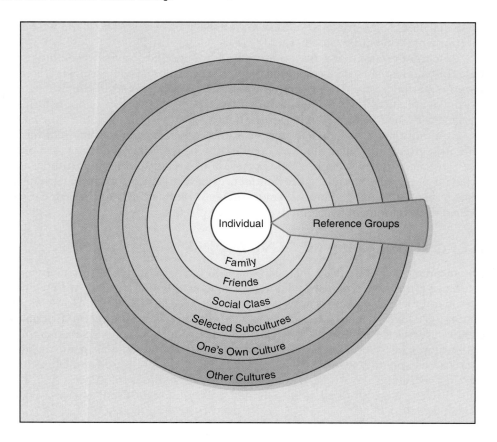

TABLE 10-1   Selective Factors That Positively Influence Conformity

CHARACTERISTICS	POSITIVE (+) EFFECT
Task/situational characteristics	Difficulty/complexity Ambiguity/subjectivity
Brand characteristics	No information Limited choice Prior conformity Crisis/emergency
Group characteristics	Attractiveness Expertise Credibility Clarity of group goals Likely future interaction with group Past success
Personal characteristics	Tendency to conform Need for affiliation Need to be liked Desire for control Fear of negative evaluation

Source: Based on Dana-Nicoleta Lascu and George Zinkhan, "Consumer Conformity: Review and Applications for Marketing Theory and Practice," *Journal of Marketing Theory and Practice,* Summer 1999, 1–12.

he knows from experience to be good or to one that has been highly recommended by the local newspaper's Dining Out Guide. If he has neither personal experience nor information he regards as valid, he may seek the advice of a friend or a parent or imitate the behavior of others by taking her to a restaurant he knows is frequented by young business executives whom he admires.

Credibility, Attractiveness, and Power of the Reference Group

A reference group that is perceived as credible, attractive, or powerful can induce consumer attitude and behavior change. For example, when consumers are concerned with obtaining accurate information about the performance or quality of a product or service, they are likely to be persuaded by those whom they consider trustworthy and knowledgeable. That is, they are more likely to be persuaded by sources with *high credibility*.

When consumers are primarily concerned with the acceptance or approval of others they like, with whom they identify, or who offer them status or other benefits, they are likely to adopt their product, brand, or other behavioral characteristics. When consumers are primarily concerned with the power that a person or group can exert over them, they might choose products or services that conform to the norms of that person or group in order to avoid ridicule or punishment. However, unlike other reference groups that consumers follow because they are credible or because they are attractive, *power groups* are not as likely to cause attitude change. Individuals may conform to the behavior of a powerful person or group but are not as likely to experience a change in their own attitudes.

Different reference groups may influence the beliefs, attitudes, and behavior of an individual at different points in time or under different circumstances. For example, the dress habits of a young male executive may vary, depending on his place and role. He may conform to the dress code of his office by wearing dress shirts and conservative business suits by day and drastically alter his mode of dress after work by wearing more trendy, flamboyant styles.

Conspicuousness of the Product

The potential influence of a reference group on a purchase decision varies according to how visually or verbally conspicuous the product is to others. A visually *conspicuous product* is one that will stand out and be noticed (such as a luxury item or novelty product); a verbally conspicuous product may be highly interesting, or it may be easily described to others. Products that are especially conspicuous and status revealing (a new automobile, fashion clothing, sleek laptop computer, or home furniture) are most likely to be purchased with an eye to the reactions of relevant others. Privately consumed products that are less conspicuous (fruit yogurt or laundry soaps) are less likely to be purchased with a reference group in mind.

Walk down any street in America (and almost anywhere else) and you are likely to see someone wearing a hat, T-shirt, or jacket emblazoned with the logo of a favorite sports team. Similarly, while in a car, just look at the license plates of other cars on the road. It will not be long before you start seeing license plates containing the name and logo of universities, favorite sports teams, environmental groups, and many other institutions and causes. Research has found that among those attending a sporting event (e.g., baseball or basketball game), the more an individual identifies with a particular team, the greater the likelihood that he or she will purchase the products of the companies that sponsor that team (e.g., a particular brand of beer, hot dogs, or newspapers).[1]

Reference Groups and Consumer Conformity

Marketers may have divergent goals with regard to **consumer conformity.** Some marketers, especially market leaders, are interested in the ability of reference groups to change consumer attitudes and behavior by encouraging *conformity*. To be capable of such influence, a reference group must accomplish the following:

1. *Inform or make the individual aware of a specific product or brand*
2. *Provide the individual with the opportunity to compare his or her own thinking with the attitudes and behavior of the group*
3. *Influence the individual to adopt attitudes and behavior that are consistent with the norms of the group*
4. *Legitimize the decision to use the same products as the group*

In contrast, marketers, especially those responsible for a new brand or a brand that is not the market leader, may wish to elect a strategy that asks consumers to strike out and be different and not just *follow the crowd* when making a purchase decision.

In reality the nonconformity appeal can be thought of as a request to shift one's reference (attitudes or behavior) from one grouping (brand A users) to another reference (non–brand A users or brand B users).

Selected Consumer-Related Reference Groups

As already mentioned, consumers are potentially influenced by a diverse range of people that they come in contact with or observe. We will consider the following five specific reference groups because they give us a kind of cross section of the types of groups that influence consumers' attitudes and behavior: (1) friendship groups, (2) shopping groups, (3) work groups, (4) virtual groups or communities, and (5) consumer-action groups. The family, possibly the most compelling reference group for consumer behavior, will be fully covered in the second part of this chapter.

FRIENDSHIP GROUPS

Friendship groups are typically classified as **informal groups** because they are usually unstructured and lack specific authority levels. In terms of relative influence, after an individual's family, his or her friends are most likely to influence the individual's purchase decisions.

Seeking and maintaining friendships is a basic drive of most people. Friends fulfill a wide range of needs: They provide companionship, security, and opportunities to discuss problems that an individual may be reluctant to discuss with family members. Friendships are also a sign of maturity and independence, for they represent a breaking away from the family and the forming of social ties with the outside world.

The opinions and preferences of friends are an important influence in determining the products or brands a consumer ultimately selects. Marketers of products such as brand-name clothing, fine jewelry, snack foods, and alcoholic beverages recognize the power of peer group influence and frequently depict friendship situations in their ads.

SHOPPING GROUPS

Two or more people who shop together, whether for food, for clothing, or simply to pass the time, can be called a **shopping group.** Such groups are often offshoots of family or friendship groups and, therefore, they function as what has been referred to as *purchase pals*.[2] The motivations for shopping with a purchase pal range from a primarily social motive (to share time together and enjoy lunch after shopping) to helping reduce the risk when making an important decision (having someone along whose expertise will reduce the chance of making an incorrect purchase). In instances where none of the members of the shopping group knows much about the product under consideration (such as an expensive home entertainment center), a shopping group may form for defensive reasons; members may feel more confident with a collective decision.

A special type of shopping group is the in-home shopping party, which typically consists of a group that gathers together in the home of a friend to attend a "party" devoted to demonstrating and evaluating a specific line of products. The in-home party approach provides marketers with an opportunity to demonstrate the features of their products simultaneously to a group of potential customers. Early purchasers tend to create a bandwagon effect: Undecided guests often overcome a reluctance to buy when they see their friends make positive purchase decisions. Furthermore, some of the guests may feel obliged to buy because they are in the home of the sponsoring host or hostess. Given the spirit and excitement of "consumer gatherings" or "parties," Tupperware, for example, generates 90 percent of its $1 billion in annual sales from such consumer parties.[3]

WORK GROUPS

The sheer amount of time that people spend at their jobs, frequently more than 35 hours per week, provides ample opportunity for work groups to serve as a major influence on the consumption behavior of members.

Both the formal work group and the informal friendship-work group can influence consumer behavior. The *formal work group* consists of individuals who work together as part of a team and, thus, have a sustained opportunity to influence each other's consumption-related attitudes and actions. Informal friendship-work groups consist of people who have become friends as a result of working for the same firm, whether or not they work together as a team. Members of informal work groups may influence the consumption behavior of other members during coffee or lunch breaks or at after-work meetings.

Recognizing that work groups influence consumers' brand choices and that many women now work outside of their homes, firms that in the past sold their products exclusively through direct calls on women in their homes now are redirecting their sales efforts to offices and plants during lunch-hour visits. For instance, Avon (**www.avon.com**) and Tupperware (**www.tupperware.com**), two leading direct-to-home marketers, encourage their sales representatives to reach working women at their places of employment.

VIRTUAL GROUPS OR COMMUNITIES

Thanks to computers and the Internet, we are witnessing the emergence of a new type of group—virtual groups or communities. Both adults and children are turning on their computers, logging onto the Web, and visiting special-interest Web sites, often with chat rooms. If you're a skier, you can chat online with other skiers; if you're an amateur photographer, you can chat online with others who share your interest. Local newspapers everywhere run stories from time to time about singles who met online, typically accompanied by a picture of their wedding. An Internet provider such as America Online even lets its members create *Buddy Lists*,™ so when they sign onto AOL they immediately know which of their friends are currently online and can send and receive instant messages. An elderly person in Chicago, for example, might not make it to the local senior citizen center when it's freezing outside and snowing, but he or she can always log on.[4]

Whereas 50 years ago the definition of a community stressed the notion of geographic proximity and face-to-face relationships, today's communities are much more broadly defined as "sets of social relations among people."[5] In this spirit, there is also today rather wide-scale access to what is known as "Internet communities" or "virtual communities." These terms refer to Web-based consumer groups (e.g., www.well.com, www.geocities.com, www.ivillage.com, www.bigplanet.com, www. planetall.com, and www.icq.com). These communities provide their members with access to extensive amounts of information, fellowship, and social interaction covering an extremely wide range of topics and issues (e.g., vegetarianism, cooking, collecting, trading, finance, filmmaking, romance, politics, technology, art, hobbies, spiritualism, age grouping, online game playing, voice-video chats, free e-mail, tech assistance, travel and vacations, educational opportunities, living with illnesses, and a host of lifestyle options). Virtual communities provide an opportunity for a marketer to address consumers with a particular common interest, can be one of the primary pleasures a consumer has online, and also have the ability to enhance the consumption experience (via discussion with others).[6]

The exchange of knowledge that can take place within a virtual community can help a good product sell faster and a poor product fail faster. Indeed, there are a number of "knowledge exchanges" that permit registered members and others to ask questions of experts on subjects germane to that exchange. For example, EXP.com offers expertise in 300 subjects and does so without a subscription fee—the customer or expert can determine the prices for answers.[7] And some virtual communities, hosted by a commercial source, are aimed at particular ethnic groups and contain online content targeted to a distinct ethnic community. Startec Global Communications Corporation (www.startec.com) already operates virtual communities for Arab, Iranian, Turkish, Indian, and Chinese consumers. Its DragonSurf.com site, for instance, concentrates on the needs and interests of young, educated Chinese Web surfers in China and elsewhere around the world.[8]

When visiting such communities, it does not matter if you are tall or short, thin or fat, handsome or plain-looking. On the Internet, people are free to express their thoughts, to be emotional and intimate with those they do not know and have never met, and even to escape from those they normally interact with by spending time on the Internet. The anonymity of the Web gives its users the freedom to express whatever views they wish and to also benefit from savoring the views of others. Because of this anonymity, Internet users can say things to others that they would not say in face-to-face interactions.[9] Communicating over the Internet permits people to explore the boundaries of their personalities (see the related discussion in Chapter 5) and to shift from one persona to another. For example, investigators have found that there are a surprisingly large number of men who adopt female personae online ("gender swapping").[10] Some community Web sites have attempted to control the limits of what is deemed appropriate and inappropriate by instituting codes of behavior. For example, fans of the canceled TV program *Dr. Quinn, Medicine Woman* are not only part of an e-mail discussion list, but also new members are sent a "conduct code" when they subscribe.[11]

Brand Communities

Although relationship marketing has been discussed earlier in the text (see Chapter 7), the next step in its evolution is the establishment of brand communities. As one recent newspaper article noted, "There is a definite feeling among marketers that if you want to build up loyalty to your brand, your product has to have an active social life."[12] Examples of such brand communities include the group of runners who get together at the Niketown store in Boston on Wednesday evenings for a run (www.nike.com), Saturn automobile reunions and barbeques (www.saturn.com), and Harley-Davidson owner groups (www.harleydavidson.com). A *brand community* has been defined as "a specialized, non-geographically bound community, based on a structured set of social relationships among admirers of a brand . . . it is marked by a shared consciousness, rituals and traditions, and a sense of moral responsibility."[13] It is this sense of community, for example, that causes Saab owners (www.saabusa.com) to beep or flash their lights at another Saab on the road (i.e., a greeting ritual).

Consider how Jeep has developed its brand community. The company offers multiple opportunities for Jeep owners to get to know each other, get to know their vehicles, and get to know the company. Jeep (www.jeep.com) conducts Jeep Jamborees (regional rallies that concentrate on off-road driving), Camp Jeep (national rallies offering off-road driving and product-related activities), and Jeep 101 (an off-road driving course with product-related activities and displays). At both Camp Jeep and Jeep 101 there are "camp counselors" who provide participants with free beverages, free product information, and free off-road trail recommendations.[14] The result is that Jeep has fostered involvement in its brand community, so that a bond exists between the Jeep owner and (1) the product, (2) the brand, (3) the company, and (4) other Jeep owners. The brand community is, therefore, "customer centric"; it is the customer experience that provides meaning to the brand community rather than the brand itself. Consider the following comment from a Jeep owner attending Jeep 101:[15]

> *I've been very happy. I get a lot of communications from Jeep, which I've been so impressed with. Usually you buy a car and then you're a forgotten soul. Its kinda like they want you to be part of the family. As soon as I got the invitation for Jeep 101, I registered. I was very excited. But I was nervous. I didn't think I would end up driving. I was very relieved to see someone in the car with you, 'cause it gave you the confidence to do what you're supposed to. Otherwise, I had visions of abandoning the truck on the hill and saying "I can't do it!" I thought I might wimp out, but I didn't.*

CONSUMER-ACTION GROUPS

A particular kind of consumer group—a **consumer-action group**—has emerged in response to the consumerist movement. Today there are a very large number of such groups that are dedicated to providing consumers with assistance in their effort to make the right purchase decisions, consume products and services in a healthy and responsible manner, and to generally add to the overall quality of their lives. The following are just a few examples of the diverse range of consumer concerns being addressed by private and public consumer-action groups: neighborhood crime watch, youth development, forests and wildlife concerns, children and advertising, race and ethnicity, community volunteerism, legal assistance, public health, disaster relief, energy conservation, education, smoking, the environment, access to telecommunications, science in the public interest, credit counseling, privacy issues, and children and the Internet.

Consumer-action groups can be divided into two broad categories: (1) those that organize to correct a specific consumer abuse and then disband and (2) those that organize to address broader, more pervasive problem areas and operate over an extended or indefinite period of time. A group of irate parents who band together to protest the opening of an X-rated movie theater in their neighborhood or a group of neighbors who attend a meeting of the local highway department to protest how poorly the streets in their area have been cleared of snow are examples of temporary, cause-specific consumer-action groups. An example of an enduring consumer-action group is Mothers Against Drunk Driving (MADD), a group founded in 1980 and operating today throughout the United States within local community groups. MADD representatives serve on numerous public advisory boards and help establish local task forces to combat drunk driving. Additionally, the organization supports actions to restrict alcoholic beverage advertising and is opposed in general to any advertising and products that may have a negative impact on youth.

The overriding objective of many consumer-action groups is to bring sufficient pressure to bear on selected members of the business community to make them correct perceived consumer abuses.

Celebrity and Other Reference Group Appeals

Appeals by celebrities and other similar reference groups are used very effectively by advertisers to communicate with their markets. Celebrities can be a powerful force in creating interest or actions with regard to purchasing or using selected goods and services. This identification may be based on admiration (of an athlete), on aspiration (of a celebrity or a way of life), on empathy (with a person or a situation), or on recognition (of a person—real or stereotypical—or of a situation). In some cases, the prospective consumer may think, "If she uses it, it must be good. If I use it, I'll be like her." In other cases, the prospective consumer says to himself, "He has the same problems that I have. What worked for him will work for me."

Five major types of reference group appeals in common marketing usage are *celebrity appeals, expert appeals, common-man appeals, executive and employee appeals,* and *trade or spokes-character appeals.* These appeals, as well as less frequently employed appeals, are often operationalized in the form of testimonials or endorsements. In the case of the common man, they may be presented as *slice-of-life* commercials.

CELEBRITIES

Celebrities, particularly movie stars, TV personalities, popular entertainers, and sports icons, provide a very common type of reference group appeal. Indeed, it has been estimated that 25 percent of U.S. commercials include celebrity endorsers.[16] To their loyal followers and to much of the general public, celebrities represent an idealization of life that most people imagine that they would love to live. Advertisers spend enormous sums of money to have celebrities promote their products, with the expectation that the reading or viewing audience will react positively to the celebrity's association with their products. One discussion about celebrity endorsers noted that "famous people hold the viewer's attention," and this is why the World Chiropractic Alliance recently began a search to find doctors with famous patients and to use such associations in their marketing efforts.[17] Do you remember when Michael Jordan first retired from basketball for about two years? His return to the NBA resulted in the firms whose products he endorses to increase their stock market value by $1 billion, and he is under contract with Nike until the year 2023.[18] But many experts believe that today it is Tiger Woods, and not Michael Jordan, who is the number-one celebrity endorser. His five-year deal with Buick is estimated at $30 million, and his $40 million deal with Nike is expected to double because he has now switched to Nike brand golf balls.[19]

Do you or one of your friends own a Microsoft Xbox? When the Xbox was introduced into the Japanese market in February 2002, 50,000 limited edition versions were available. In addition to a black translucent case, the limited edition versions included a silver-plated key chain with the engraved signature of Bill Gates, CEO of Microsoft. It was hoped that this key chain would separate the Xbox from its Sony and Nintendo rivals.[20] And are you aware that the number of Americans who practiced yoga in 1998 represented a 300 percent increase over 1990? This was due in part to celebrities such as actress Gwyneth Paltrow and model Christy Turlington and to Madonna playing a yoga instructor in her film *The Next Best Thing.*[21]

   A firm that decides to employ a celebrity to promote its product or service has the choice of using the celebrity to give a **testimonial** or an **endorsement** as an **actor** in a commercial or as a company **spokesperson.** Table 10-2 distinguishes among these different types of celebrity appeals, and Table 10-3 lists some currently popular celebrity endorsers and the client products or services they have represented. Figure 10-2 presents the findings of a recent study that explored what marketing practitioners in the United Kingdom look for in selecting a celebrity endorser. What is apparent is that the importance of certain celebrity characteristics varies depending on whether the product being promoted is technical (e.g., PCs) or nontechnical

TABLE 10-2   Types of Celebrity Appeals

TYPES	DEFINITION
Testimonial	Based on personal usage, a celebrity attests to the quality of the product or service.
Endorsement	Celebrity lends his or her name and appears on behalf of a product or service with which he or she may or may not be an expert.
Actor	Celebrity presents a product or service as part of character endorsement.
Spokesperson	Celebrity represents the brand or company over an extended period of time.

TABLE 10-3   Popular Celebrities and Their Products/Services

CELEBRITY	PRODUCT/SERVICE
Charles Barkley	Coors Beer
Christie Brinkley	Results for Women
Cindy Crawford	Diet Pepsi
Dorothy Hamil	ChapStick
Jennifer Love Hewitt	Neutrogena
Faith Hill	CoverGirl
Paul Hogan	Subaru Automobiles
Michael Jordan	Hanes Men's Underwear
Anna Kournikova	Lycos.com
Michelle Kwan	Exprèsse from Yoplait
Mark Martin	Viagra
Vincent Pastore	Don Diego Cigars
Mr. T	1-800-COLLECT
Steven Tyler	Got Milk?

FIGURE 10-2

Importance of Celebrity Characteristics According to Product Types

Source: B. Zafer Erdogan, Michael J. Baker, and Stephen Tagg, "Selecting Celebrity Endorsers: The Practitioner's Perspective," *Journal of Advertising Research,* May/June 2001, 46.

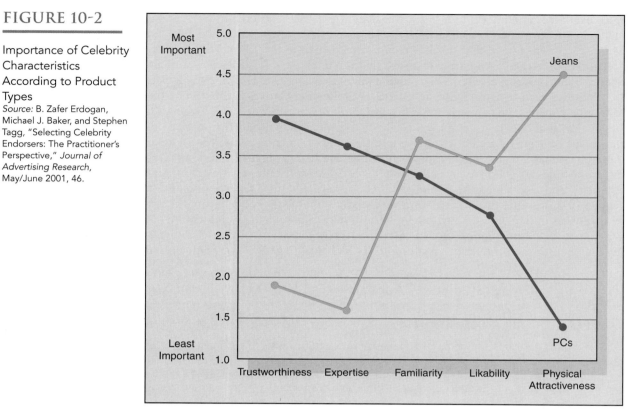

(e.g., jeans) in nature. Specifically, for a product like a PC the "trustworthiness" of a celebrity is considered to be most important, whereas for a clothing item like jeans the "physical attractiveness" of the celebrity is viewed as most important.

Of all the benefits that a celebrity might contribute to a firm's advertising program—fame, talent, credibility, or charisma—celebrity credibility with the consumer audience is the most important. By **celebrity credibility** we mean the audience's perception of both the celebrity's *expertise* (how much the celebrity knows about the product area) and *trustworthiness* (how honest the celebrity is about what he or she says about the product).[22] To illustrate, when a celebrity endorses only one product, consumers are likely to perceive the product in a highly favorable light and indicate a greater intention to purchase it. In contrast, when a celebrity endorses a variety of products, his or her perceived credibility is reduced because of the apparent economic motivation underlying the celebrity's efforts.[23] A recent study also found that endorser credibility had its strongest impact with respect to influencing a consumer's attitude toward the ad, but that corporate credibility (the credibility of the company paying for the advertisement) had a stronger impact on attitude toward the brand.[24]

Not all companies feel that using celebrity endorsers is the best way to advertise. Some companies avoid celebrities because they fear that if the celebrity gets involved in some undesirable act or event (e.g., an ugly matrimonial problem, a scandal, or a criminal case), the news or press coverage will negatively impact the sale of the endorsed brand. For example, researchers recently compiled a list of 48 undesirable events occurring between 1980 and 1994 that involved celebrity endorsers hired by publicly traded companies. The list included such notables as Mike Tyson, Michael Jackson, and Jennifer Capriati.[25]

FIGURE 10-3

An Expert Appeal

THE EXPERT

A second type of reference group appeal used by marketers is the *expert,* a person who, because of his or her occupation, special training, or experience, is in a unique position to help the prospective consumer evaluate the product or service that the advertisement promotes. For example, an advertisement for a quality frying pan may feature the endorsement of a chef, an ad for fishing tackle may contain the endorsement of a professional fishing guide, or an ad for an allergy medication may contain the endorsement of a professional golfer (see Figure 10-3).

THE "COMMON MAN"

A reference group appeal that uses the testimonials of satisfied customers is known as the *common-man* approach. The advantage of the common-man appeal is that it demonstrates to prospective customers that someone just like them uses and is satisfied with the product or service being advertised. The common-man appeal is especially effective in public health announcements (such as antismoking or high blood pressure messages), for most people seem to identify with people like themselves when it comes to such messages.[26]

Many television commercials show a typical person or family solving a problem by using the advertised product or service. These commercials are known as *slice-of-life commercials* because they focus on real-life situations with which the viewer can identify. For example, one commercial focuses on how a laundry detergent can deodorize clothes; another talks about how a certain breakfast cereal provides enough energy to get an individual through a hectic morning. When viewers identify with the situation, they are likely to adopt the solution that worked in the TV commercial. Figure 10-4 presents an ad for Xenadrine EFX

FIGURE 10-4

Customers Providing Testimonials
Courtesy of Cytodyne Technologies.

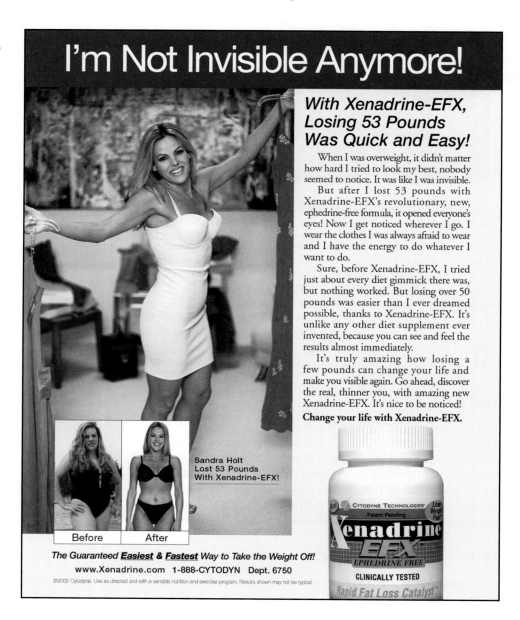

(www.xenadrine.com) that effectively uses the endorsement of a satisfied customer who personally lost 53 pounds.

THE EXECUTIVE AND EMPLOYEE SPOKESPERSON

During the past two decades, an increasing number of firms have used their top executives as spokespersons in consumer ads. The popularity of this type of advertising probably is due to the success and publicity received by a number of executive spokespersons. For instance, early in the history of this type of advertising, Lee Iacocca, former CEO of Chrysler, was a highly effective corporate spokesperson in persuading consumers that Chrysler automobiles were worthy of their purchase consideration. Similarly, the now retired Frank Perdue (Perdue chickens), who has been replaced by his son, and the deceased David Thomas (Wendy's) were both very popular and effective spokespersons for their company's products.

Like celebrity spokespersons, executive spokespersons seem to be admired by the general population because of their achievements and the status implicitly conferred on business leaders in the United States. The appearance of a company's chief executive in its advertising seems to imply that someone at the top is watching over the consumers' best interests, and it encourages consumers to have more confidence in the firm's products or services.

TRADE OR SPOKES-CHARACTERS

Trade or spokes-characters (e.g., M&M People, Tony the Tiger, or Capt'n Crunch), as well as familiar cartoon characters (Ninja Turtles, Mr. Magoo, Bart Simpson), serve as quasi-celebrity endorsers. These trade spokes-characters present an idealized image and dispense information that can be very important for the product or service that they "work for."[27] Figure 10-5 shows the Green Giant as a trade or spokes-character for The Green Giant Company.

With few exceptions, trade characters serve as exclusive spokespersons for a particular product or service. They sometimes provide a kind of personality for the product or service and make the product appear friendlier (Ronald McDonald). Betty Crocker now even has her own Web site to offer recipes, personalized weekly menus, and household hints (www.bettycrocker.com). This Web site is the modern-day extension of the fact that Betty Crocker started answering letters from consumers in the 1920s and got her own toll-free telephone number in 1980. According to the company, the purpose of the Web site "is not to push Betty Crocker, not to sell products, but to provide content that offers ideas and solves problems, so people consider the site a valuable resource."[28]

OTHER REFERENCE GROUP APPEALS

A variety of other promotional strategies can function creatively as frames of reference for consumers. Respected retailers and the editorial content of selected special-interest magazines can also function as frames of reference that influence consumer attitudes and behavior. For instance, a customer might feel that if a leading fashion-oriented store such as Nordstrom depicts Tommy Bahama casual shirts on its Web site (store.nordstrom.com), then such clothing must be acceptable and in good taste. Similarly, a regular reader of *GQ* might see unstructured and relaxed sport coats as appropriate to wear to work if the magazine were to feature them in office surroundings. In these two instances, the retailer and the magazine are functioning as frames of reference that influence consumer behavior. And some marketers try to get

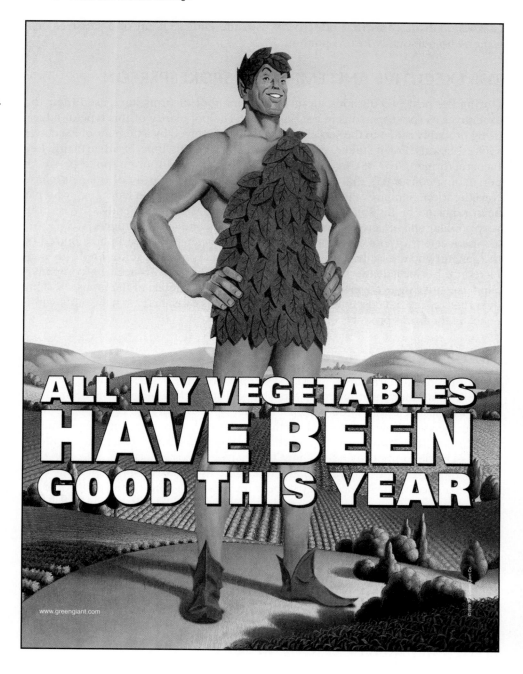

a placement for their product or service in a movie. Verizon Wireless, for example, was reported to have "scored big" when in the movie *Hannibal* the film's main character breaks into the apartment of an FBI agent and finds the agent's Verizon Wireless telephone bill.[29]

Finally, *seals of approval* and even objective product ratings can serve as positive endorsements that encourage consumers to act favorably toward certain products. For instance, many parents of young children look for the American Dental Association's seal of approval before selecting a brand of toothpaste. A high rating by an objective rating magazine, such as *Consumer Reports,* can also serve as an endorsement for a brand.

The remainder of this chapter concentrates on the family—arguably the most important group influencing human behavior in general and consumer behavior in particular.

The Family Is a Concept in Flux

Although the term **family** is a basic concept, it is not easy to define because family composition and structure, as well as the roles played by family members, are almost always in transition. Traditionally, however, *family* is defined as *two or more persons related by blood, marriage, or adoption who reside together.* In a more dynamic sense, the individuals who constitute a family might be described as members of the most basic social group who live together and interact to satisfy their personal and mutual needs. Today in the United States, 68 percent of the 105.5 million households are families.[30] According to many sources, the *family* remains the central or dominant institution in providing for the welfare of its members.

Although **families** sometimes are referred to as **households,** not all households are families. For example, a household might include individuals who are not related by blood, marriage, or adoption, such as unmarried couples, family friends, roommates, or boarders. However, within the context of consumer behavior, households and families usually are treated as synonymous, and we will continue this convention.

In most Western societies, three types of families dominate: the married couple, the nuclear family, and the extended family. The simplest type of family, in number of members, is the *married couple*—a husband and a wife. As a household unit, the married couple generally is representative of either new marrieds who have not yet started a family and older couples who have already raised their children.

A husband and wife and one or more children constitute a **nuclear family.** This type of family is still commonplace but has been on the decline. The nuclear family, together with at least one grandparent living within the household, is called an **extended family.** Within the past 30 years the incidence of the extended family has also declined because of the geographic mobility that splits up families. Moreover, because of divorce, separation, and out-of-wedlock births, there has been a rapid increase in the number of **single-parent family** households consisting of one parent and at least one child.

Not surprisingly, the type of family which is most typical can vary considerably from culture to culture. For instance, in an individualistic society such as that in Canada, the nuclear family is most common. In a kinship culture (with extended families) such as that in Thailand, a family would commonly include a head of household, married adult children, and grandchildren.[31]

THE CHANGING U.S. FAMILY

Important demographic changes reflect the dynamic nature of the family. For example, recent newspaper articles point out that 55 percent of career women who are 35 years old are childless, between a third and half of 40-year-old career women have no children, and the number of childless women between the ages of 40 and 44 has doubled during the past 20 years.[32] Moreover, 49 percent of female corporate executives earning $100,000 or more annually are childless (but only 10 percent of high-income male executives have no children).

FIGURE 10-6

Evidence of the
Dynamic Nature of U.S.
Households
Source: Marketing to Women,
January 2000, 3.

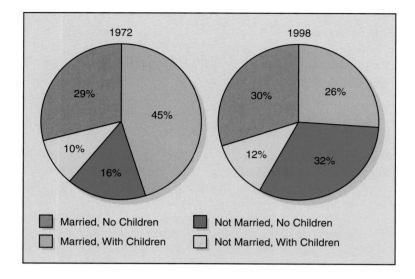

There is no doubt that the "typical" or "traditional" family or household has changed. Although 45 percent of households in 1972 were "married, with children," by 1998 this percentage was reduced to 26 percent, and "not married, no children" households rose from 16 percent in 1972 to 32 percent in 1998, making it the most common type of household in the United States (see Figure 10-6).[33] Still further, in 1972, 73 percent of children lived in a household with two parents, but this number had decreased to 51 percent in 1998; and whereas in 1972 nearly 75 percent of adults were married, only 56 percent of adults were married in 1998.[34] The fact that the divorce rate has risen 30 percent since 1970 undoubtedly has had an impact on the American family. Indeed, in 1996 almost 23 million children under the age of 21 were living with only one parent, and about one-third of all children in the United States live in remarried or cohabiting stepfamily households.[35] Because of these changes in family dynamics, companies such as American Greetings sell Mother's Day cards for single moms, divorced moms, stepmothers, foster mothers, caregivers, guardians, and others who play a maternal role.[36]

Attitudes with respect to children and child-rearing have also been changing. Consider the information presented in Table 10-4, which compares the attitudes toward children of Gen-Xers (25- to 37-year-olds), Baby Boomers, and Pre-Boomers. The results, for example, show that while 37 percent of Gen-Xers "believe preschool kids suffer if mother works," 46 percent of Baby Boomers and 57 percent of Pre-Boomers share this view.[37]

Socialization of Family Members

The **socialization of family members,** ranging from young children to adults, is a central family function. In the case of young children, this process includes imparting to children the basic values and modes of behavior consistent with the culture. These generally include moral and religious principles, interpersonal skills, dress and grooming standards, appropriate manners and speech, and the selection of suitable educational and occupational or career goals. Table 10-5 presents the results of a study by SmartGirl Internette that looks at the household chores performed by girls

TABLE 10-4	How Different Generations Feel About Children		
	GEN-XERS	**BABY BOOMERS**	**PRE-BOOMERS**
Ideal number of children is two	52%	55%	50%
Ideal number of children is three	27%	21%	30%
Favor spanking to discipline a child	74%	76%	76%
Favor sex ed in public schools	91%	87%	80%
Believe preschool kids suffer if mother works	37%	46%	57%
Believe it's better for the man to work and the woman to tend home	29%	37%	64%
Believe a working mother doesn't hurt children	67%	63%	52%
Believe a wife should help husband put career first	12%	15%	32%
I spend too little time with my kids	45%	46%	25%
Divorce laws should be tougher	50%	52%	59%

Source: Pamela Paul, "Meet the Parents," *American Demographics*, January 2002, 46. Reprinted by permission of Primedia.

TABLE 10-5	Household Chores Performed by Girls Age 11 to 17
CHORE	**% WHO SAY THEY PERFORM IT**
Picking things up in my room	95%
Picking things up around the house	84%
Vacuuming	72%
Washing/drying the dishes	66%
Loading or unloading the dishwasher	65%
Doing laundry	61%
Sweeping	55%
Dusting	55%
Cleaning the bathtub, shower, or sink	54%
Washing the windows or mirrors	48%
Cleaning the kitchen	46%
Cleaning the toilet	41%
Mopping the bathroom or kitchen floor	39%
Ironing	37%

Source: Marketing to Women, January 2000, 3. Courtesy of SmartGirl.org. Copyright 2002 SmartGirl Internette Inc.

11 to 17 years of age. The findings indicate that over one-half of the girls in this age category claim that they "dust and sweep."

A recent Dutch study found that younger juveniles spend most of their leisure time with their family, whereas older juveniles spend most of their leisure time with peers.[38] The transition period between these two age groups was 13, with 13-year-olds dividing their leisure time between parents, peers, and being alone. The results further indicate that 14- and 15-year-old boys, especially from the higher social classes, were strongly focused on peer groups, whereas girls the same age preferred dyadic friendships.

GIVE YOUR KIDS THE RIGHT TOOLS AND THERE'S NO TELLING HOW FAR THEY'LL GO.

Help your kids really succeed with new Microsoft® Encarta® Reference Library 2003 and Microsoft Office XP Standard for Students and Teachers. Together they give your kids all the tools they need to create reports that will wow their teachers. Too bad there wasn't stuff like this when you were a kid. Get your copies of Encarta and Office XP today and help support the PTA. Find out how at microsoft.com/pta

Encarta Reference Library offers comprehensive, up-to-date content, new research and learning tools, and the latest multimedia features. Your kids will do so well in school that they may even be able to teach you a thing or two.

Office XP helps kids take all that information and quickly turn regular projects into shining masterpieces complete with pictures and charts. Plus it's almost 70% off for students,* so your kids won't be the only ones looking smart.

FIGURE 10-7

Computer-Related Products Are Sought After by Parents of Young Children
Microsoft Encarta Reference Library 2003 and Microsoft Office XP Standard for Students and Teachers ® are registered trademarks of Microsoft Corporation. Reprinted with permission from Microsoft Corporation.

Parental socialization responsibility seems to be constantly expanding. For instance, parents are often anxious to see their young children possess adequate computer skills, almost before they are able to talk or walk—as early as 12 months after their birth. Because of parents' intensive interest in their young children learning about using a computer, hardware and software developers are regularly developing products targeted at parents seeking to buy such items for their children (see Figure 10-7).

Another sign of parents' constant pressure to help their young children secure an "advantage" or "keep ahead" are the demanding daily schedules that rule the lives of many children (e.g., daily preschool classes, after-school classes, play dates, weekend enrichment, and/or sports programs). Such hectic schedules foster a concentration on competition and results and not on having fun or on being creative. In contrast, as kids their parents might have built forts out of blankets or pillows. However, with the structured activities of today and with the child constantly surrounded by media, there is little opportunity for the child to explore his or her world in such an imaginative fashion.[39]

Marketers frequently target parents looking for assistance in the task of socializing their children. To this end, marketers are sensitive to the fact that the socialization of young children provides an opportunity to establish a foundation on which later experiences continue to build throughout life. These experiences are reinforced and modified as the child grows into adolescence, the teenage years, and eventually into adulthood.

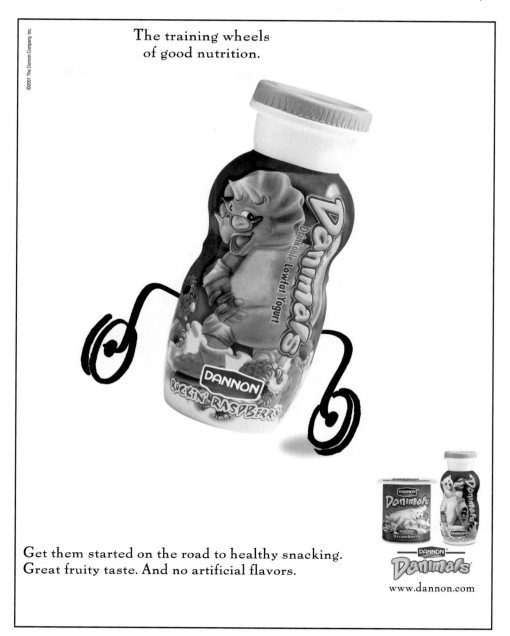

The training wheels
of good nutrition.

Get them started on the road to healthy snacking.
Great fruity taste. And no artificial flavors.

www.dannon.com

FIGURE 10-8

Consumer and
Consumption-Related
Socialization
Courtesy of Dannon.

CONSUMER SOCIALIZATION OF CHILDREN

The aspect of childhood socialization that is particularly relevant to the study of
consumer behavior is **consumer socialization,** which is defined as the *process by
which children acquire the skills, knowledge, attitudes and experiences necessary to
function as consumers* (see Figure 10-8). A variety of studies have focused on how
children develop consumption skills. Many preadolescent children acquire their
consumer behavior norms through observation of their parents and older siblings,
who function as role models and sources of cues for basic consumption learning.
In contrast, adolescents and teenagers are likely to look to their friends for models of acceptable consumption behavior.[40] Other research has shown that younger

children generally also react positively to advertisements employing a spokesperson who seems to fulfill a parental role, whereas teens often like products for the simple reason that their parents disapprove of them.[41]

Shared shopping experiences (i.e., coshopping when mother and child shop together) also give children the opportunity to acquire in-store shopping skills. Possibly because of their more harried lifestyles, working mothers are more likely to undertake coshopping with their children than are nonworking mothers. Coshopping is a way of spending time with one's children while at the same time accomplishing a necessary task. Research has also shown that children influence family purchases for many different types of products that the family purchases and that this influence can be significant.[42]

Consumer socialization also serves as a tool by which parents influence other aspects of the socialization process. For instance, parents frequently use the promise or reward of material goods as a device to modify or control a child's behavior. A mother may reward her child with a gift when the child does something to please her, or she may withhold or remove it when the child disobeys. Research conducted by one of the authors supports this behavior-controlling function. Specifically, adolescents reported that their parents frequently used the promise of chocolate candy as a means of controlling their behavior (such as getting them to complete homework or to clean their rooms).

It is important to mention that consumer socialization of children does not function identically in all cultures. For example, a recent study found that American mothers emphasize autonomy more than Japanese mothers and want their children to develop independent consumption skills at an early age. In contrast, Japanese mothers maintain greater control over their children's consumption and, therefore, their offspring's understanding of how advertising works and other consumer-related skills develop at a somewhat later age.[43]

ADULT CONSUMER SOCIALIZATION

The socialization process is not confined to childhood; rather, it is an ongoing process. It is now accepted that socialization begins in early childhood and extends throughout a person's entire life. For example, when a newly married couple establishes their own household, their adjustment to living and consuming together is part of this continuing process. Similarly, the adjustment of a retired couple who decide to move to Florida or Arizona is also part of the ongoing socialization process. Even a family that is welcoming a pet into their home as a new family member must face the challenge of socializing the pet so that it fits into the family environment. Recent survey research reveals that pet owners commonly treat their pets as full-fledged family members. For instance, 58 percent of those surveyed indicated that they have sent or received a holiday card from their dog or cat; and 78 percent regularly talk in a different voice ("I wov you") to their pets.[44]

INTERGENERATIONAL SOCIALIZATION

It appears that it is quite common for certain product loyalties or brand preferences to be transferred from one generation to another—*intergenerational brand transfer*—maybe for even three or four generations within the same family. For instance, specific brand preferences for products such as peanut butter, mayonnaise, ketchup, coffee, and canned soup are all product categories that are frequently passed on from one generation to another generation. The following are selected

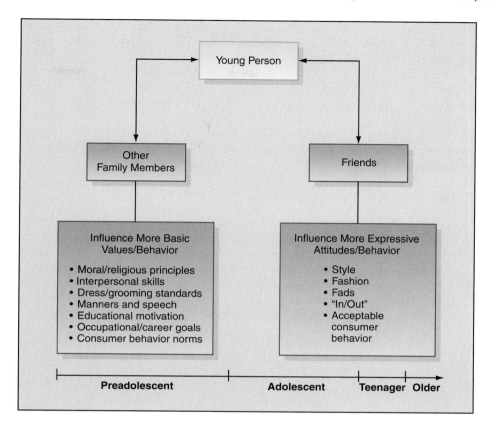

FIGURE 10-9

A Simple Model of the
Socialization Process

verbatims from research with college-aged consumers as to how they feel about
product usage extending over several generations:[45]

> *My mother stills buys almost every brand that her mother did. She is scared to try
> anything else, for it will not meet the standards, and (she) would feel bad not buy-
> ing something that has been with her so long. (Respondent is an Italian-American
> male in his early twenties.)*
>
> *I find it hard to break away from the things I've been using since I was little,
> like Vaseline products, Ivory soap, Lipton tea, and corn flakes. I live on campus so
> I have to do my own shopping, and when I do I see a lot of my mother in myself. I
> buy things I'm accustomed to using . . . products my mother buys for the house.
> (Respondent is West Indian American female.)*

Figure 10-9 presents a simple model of the socialization process that focuses on
the socialization of young children but that can be extended to family members of
all ages. Note that the arrows run both ways between the young person and other
family members and between the young person and his or her friends. This two-
directional arrow signifies that socialization is really a two-way street, in which the
young person is both socialized and influences those who are doing the socializing.
Supporting this view is the reality that children of all ages often influence the opinions and behavior of their parents. As an example, recent research with elementary
school-aged children has found that parental warmth relates positively to (1) the
extent to which a child's interest in the Internet serves as a catalyst for increased
parental Internet interest, (2) how much the child teaches a parent about the
Internet, and (3) whether the child acts as the parent's Internet broker (e.g., the

child shops for the parent on the Internet).[46] Because children are often more comfortable than their parents with digital and electronic media, they are often the ones in the family who do the teaching.

Other Functions of the Family

Three other basic functions provided by the family are particularly relevant to a discussion of consumer behavior. These include economic well-being, emotional support, and suitable family lifestyles.

ECONOMIC WELL-BEING

Although families in affluent nations of North America, Europe, and Asia are no longer formed primarily for economic security, providing financial means to its dependents is unquestionably a basic family function (see Figure 10-10). How the family divides its responsibilities for providing economic well-being has changed considerably during the past 25 years. No longer are the traditional roles of husband as economic provider and wife as homemaker and child rearer still valid. For instance, it is very common for married women with children in the United States

FIGURE 10-10

Appealing to the Responsibility of Providing for Future Family Financial Need
Courtesy of Lincoln National Corporation. Image © Craig Perman.

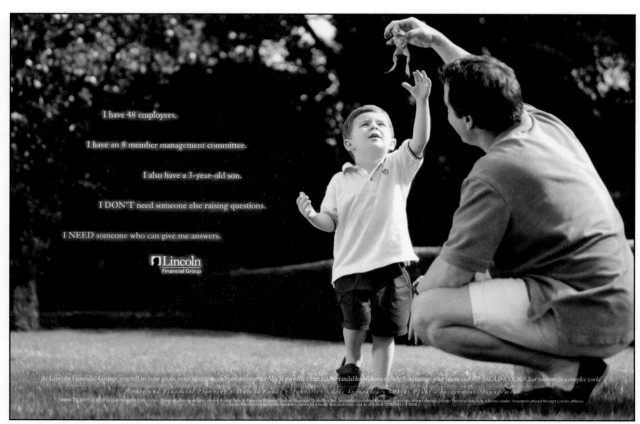

I have 48 employees.

I have an 8 member management committee.

I also have a 3-year-old son.

I DON'T need someone else raising questions.

I NEED someone who can give me answers.

Lincoln
Financial Group

and other industrial countries to be employed outside the home and for their husbands to share household responsibilities. In part, this may be why more than 70 percent of women in the United States who are over the age of 18 claim that it is more difficult to be a mother now than it was 20 or 30 years ago.[47]

The 1990s witnessed a growth in women's contributions to family income, as more and more women, now college educated, had careers rather than just jobs. According to some sociologists, the net effects of this income growth were largely positive on family outcomes and did not result in a decrease in the importance of men's earnings. The positive effects included greater marital stability and greater marital equality.[48]

The economic role of children also has changed. Today, despite the fact that many teenage children work, they rarely assist the family financially. Instead, many teenagers are expected to pay for their own amusements; others contribute to the costs of their formal education and prepare themselves to be financially independent. It is of interest to note that a recent study found that when parents are involved in a college student's acquisition of a credit card, credit card balances tend to be lower.[49]

EMOTIONAL SUPPORT

The provision of emotional nourishment (including love, affection, and intimacy) to its members is an important core function of the contemporary family. In fulfilling this function, the family provides support and encouragement and assists its members in coping with decision making and with personal or social problems.[50] To make it easier for working parents to show their love, affection, and support to their children, greeting card companies have been increasingly creating cards for parents to give to their children (or vice versa).

The *San Francisco Chronicle* asked its younger readers: "What is the key to happiness?" Many responses dealt specifically with the child's family:[51]

> *My key to happiness is to be with my family, because they're the only ones that understand my feelings, and also they're the only ones that care for me.*
> *The key to happiness is when my dad is making me laugh.*
> *The key to my happiness is my family, because they love and trust me.*
> *My family is a very good family. My mom and dad are very nice and listen to me. My sisters both have babies, so I'm even happier than I was before. Also, my grandpa lives with us. That's my key to happiness.*

If the family cannot provide adequate assistance when it is needed, it may turn to a counselor, psychologist, or other helping professional as an alternative. For instance, in most communities, educational and psychological centers are available that are designed to assist parents who want to help their children improve their learning and communication skills or to generally better adjust to their environments.

SUITABLE FAMILY LIFESTYLES

Another important family function in terms of consumer behavior is the establishment of a suitable *lifestyle* for the family. Upbringing, experience, and the personal and jointly held goals of the spouses determine the importance placed on education or career, on reading, on television viewing, on the learning of computer skills, on the frequency and quality of dining out, and on the selection of other entertainment and recreational activities. Researchers have identified a shift in the nature of family "togetherness." Whereas a family being together once meant doing things together, today it means being in the same household and each person doing his or her own thing.[52]

Family lifestyle commitments, including the allocation of time, are greatly influencing consumption patterns. For example, a series of diverse pressures on moms has

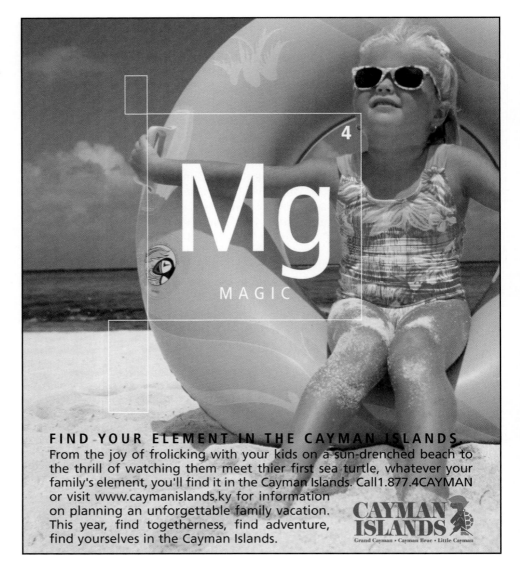

reduced the time that they have available for household chores and has created a market for convenience products and fast-food restaurants. Also, with both parents working, an increased emphasis is being placed on the notion of "quality time" rather than on the "quantity of time" spent with children and other family members. Realizing the importance of quality family time, the Cayman Islands is telling its audience that you can "come back from your family vacation without needing one" (see Figure 10-11).

Family Decision Making and Consumption-Related Roles

Although many marketers recognize the family as the basic consumer decision-making unit, they most frequently examine the attitudes and behavior of the one family member whom they believe to be the major *decision maker*. In some cases, they also examine the attitudes and behavior of the person most likely to be the primary *user* of the product or service. For instance, in the case of men's underwear, which is frequently purchased by women for their husbands and unmarried sons, it is commonplace to seek the views of both the men who wear the underwear and the women who buy it. By considering both the likely user and the likely purchaser, the marketer obtains a richer picture of the consumption process.

KEY FAMILY CONSUMPTION ROLES

For a family to function as a cohesive unit, tasks such as doing the laundry, preparing meals, setting the dinner table, taking out the garbage, and walking the dog must be carried out by one or more family members. In a dynamic society, family-related duties are constantly changing (such as the greater performance of household tasks by men). However, we can identify eight distinct roles in the *family decision-making process,* as presented in Table 10-6. A look at these roles provides further insight into how family members interact in their various consumption-related roles.

The number and identity of the family members who fill these roles vary from family to family and from product to product. In some cases, a single family member will independently assume a number of roles; in other cases, a single role will be performed jointly by two or more family members. In still other cases, one or more of these basic roles may not be required. For example, a family member may be walking down the snack food aisle at a local supermarket when he picks out an interesting new chocolate candy. His selection does not directly involve the influence of other family members. He is the *decider,* the *buyer* and, in a sense, the *gatekeeper;* however, he may or may not be the sole consumer (or user). Products may be consumed by a single family member (deodorant, razor), consumed or used directly by two or more family members (orange juice, shampoo), or consumed indirectly by the entire family (central air conditioning, DVD player, or art glass collection).

A study of children's influence on family decision making with respect to eating out found that about 17 percent of the 9- to 12-year-old children studied considered themselves to be the main decision maker with respect to the decision to go to a restaurant,

| TABLE 10-6 | The Eight Roles in the Family Decision-Making Process |

ROLE	DESCRIPTION
Influencers	Family member(s) who provide information to other members about a product or service
Gatekeepers	Family member(s) who control the flow of information about a product or service into the family
Deciders	Family member(s) with the power to determine unilaterally or jointly whether to shop for, purchase, use, consume, or dispose of a specific product or service
Buyers	Family member(s) who make the actual purchase of a particular product or service
Preparers	Family member(s) who transform the product into a form suitable for consumption by other family members
Users	Family member(s) who use or consume a particular product or service
Maintainers	Family member(s) who service or repair the product so that it will provide continued satisfaction
Disposers	Family member(s) who initiate or carry out the disposal or discontinuation of a particular product or service

TABLE 10-7	Who Makes the Decision to go to a Restaurant? Children's Perceptions by Family Type			
	CHILD	**FATHER**	**MOTHER**	**TOTAL**
Traditional	12.0	52.0	36.0	100% 75.8
Nontraditional	25.0	12.5	62.5	100% 24.2
Total	15.2	42.4	42.4	100% 100%

Source: JoAnne Labrecque and Line Ricard, "Children's Influence on Family Decision Making: A Restaurant Study," *Journal of Business Research*, 54, November 2001, 175. With permission of Elsevier Science.

whereas 40 percent thought of themselves as the main decision maker with respect to the choice of restaurants.[53] In contrast, 30 percent of the parents of these children felt that their offspring were the main decision makers in deciding to eat out, and almost an equal number, 29 percent, felt that the child (or children) also was the main decision maker with regard to which restaurant was patronized. Additionally, in traditional families, children most often felt that it was the father who makes the decision to go to a restaurant, whereas in nontraditional families it was most often the mother (see Table 10-7). The results also reveal that in nontraditional households a child was twice as likely to make the decision to go to a restaurant than in a traditional household.

DYNAMICS OF HUSBAND–WIFE DECISION MAKING

Marketers are interested in the relative amount of influence that a husband and a wife have when it comes to family consumption choices. Most husband–wife influence studies classify family consumption decisions as **husband dominated, wife dominated, joint** (either equal or syncratic), and **autonomic** (either solitary or unilateral).[54]

The relative influence of a husband and wife on a particular consumer decision depends in part on the product and service category. For instance, during the 1950s, the purchase of a new automobile was strongly husband dominated, whereas food and financial banking decisions more often were wife dominated. Forty years later, the purchase of the family's principal automobile is still often husband dominated in many households. However, in other contexts or situations (such as a second car or a car for a single or working woman), female car buyers are a rapidly expanding segment of the automobile market, a segment to which many car manufacturers are currently paying separate marketing attention. Also, in the case of financial decision making, there has been a general trend over the past decade to have the female head of household make financial decisions (see Figure 10-12).[55]

Husband–wife decision making also appears to be related to cultural influence. Research comparing husband–wife decision-making patterns in the People's Republic of China and in the United States reveals that among Chinese there were substantially fewer "joint" decisions and more "husband-dominated" decisions for many household purchases.[56] However, when limiting the comparison to urban and rural Chinese households (i.e., a "within-China" comparison), the research showed that in a larger city such as Beijing, married couples were more likely than rural couples to share equally in purchase decisions. Still further, because of China's "one child" policy and the ensuing custom of treating a single child as a "little emperor," many of the parents' purchase decisions are influenced by the input of their child.[57]

In another recent cross-cultural study, husband–wife decision making was studied among three groups: Asian Indians living in India, Asian Indians living in the United

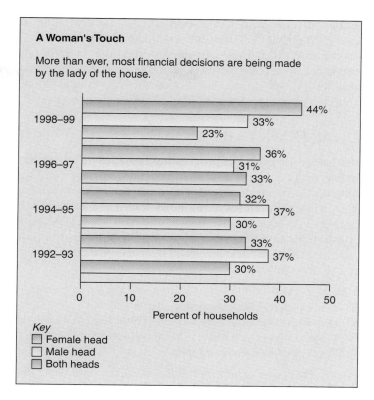

FIGURE 10-12

Household Financial
Decision Making
Source: Joan Raymond, "For
Richer and for Poorer,"
American Demographics, July
2000, 61. Reprinted by per-
mission of Primedia.

States, and American nationals. Results show a decrease in husband-dominated decisions and an increase in wife-dominated decisions, going from Asian Indians in India,
to Asian Indians in the United States, to American nationals. This pattern seems to
indicate the impact of assimilation on decision making.[58]

The Family Life Cycle

Sociologists and consumer researchers have long been attracted to the concept of the
family life cycle (FLC) as a means of depicting what was once a rather steady and
predictable series of stages through which most families progressed. However, with
the advent of many diverse family and lifestyle arrangements, what was the rule has
been on the decline. This decline in the percentage of families that progress through
a traditional FLC (to be explored shortly) seems to be caused by a host of societal
factors, including an increasing divorce rate, the explosive number of out-of-wedlock
births, and the 35-year decline in the number of extended families that transpired as
many young families moved to advance their job and career opportunities.

The notion of the FLC remains a useful marketing tool when one keeps in mind
that there are family and lifestyle arrangements that are not fully accounted for by
the traditional representation. FLC analysis enables marketers to segment families
in terms of a series of stages spanning the life course of a family unit. The FLC is a
composite variable created by systematically combining such commonly used
demographic variables as *marital status, size of family, age of family members* (focusing on the age of the oldest or youngest child), and *employment status* of the head of
household. The ages of the parents and the relative amount of disposable income
usually are inferred from the stage in the family life cycle.

To reflect the current realities of a wide range of family and lifestyle arrangements, our treatment of the FLC concept is divided into two sections. The first section considers the traditional FLC schema. This model is increasingly being challenged because it fails to account for various important family living arrangements. To rectify these limitations, the second section focuses on alternative FLC stages, including increasingly important nontraditional family structures.

TRADITIONAL FAMILY LIFE CYCLE

The **traditional family life cycle** is a progression of stages through which many families pass, starting with bachelorhood, moving on to marriage (and the creation of the basic family unit), then to family growth (with the birth of children), to family contraction (as grown children leave the household), and ending with the dissolution of the basic unit (due to the death of one spouse). Although different researchers have expressed various preferences in terms of the number of FLC stages, the traditional FLC models proposed over the years can be synthesized into just five basic stages, as follows:

> *Stage I: Bachelorhood—young single adult living apart from parents*
> *Stage II: Honeymooners—young married couple*
> *Stage III: Parenthood—married couple with at least one child living at home*
> *Stage IV: Postparenthood—an older married couple with no children living at home*
> *Stage V: Dissolution—one surviving spouse*

The following discussion examines the five stages in detail and shows how they lend themselves to market segmentation strategies.

Stage I: Bachelorhood

The first FLC stage consists of young single men and women who have established households apart from their parents. Although most members of this FLC stage are fully employed, many are college or graduate students who have left their parents' homes. Young single adults are apt to spend their incomes on rent, basic home furnishings, the purchase and maintenance of automobiles, travel and entertainment, and clothing and accessories. Members of the bachelorhood stage frequently have sufficient disposable income to indulge themselves. Marketers target singles for a wide variety of products and services.

In most large cities, there are travel agents, housing developments, health clubs, sports clubs, and other service and product marketers that find this FLC stage a lucrative target niche. *Meeting, dating,* and *mating* are prominent concerns of many young adults who typically are beginning their working lives after recently completing college or some other form of career or job training. It is relatively easy to reach this segment because many special-interest publications target singles. For example, *GQ, Details,* and *Playboy* are directed to a young, sophisticated, single male audience, whereas *Cosmopolitan, Allure,* and *Glamour* are directed to young single females.

It is interesting to note how the perceptions of 18- to 29-year-olds have been changing with respect to marriage. Whereas in 1991, 72 percent of this group felt that a happy marriage is part of the good life, by 1996 the number had risen to 86 percent. This growth in percentage is higher than for any other age group of U.S. adults.[59]

Marriage marks the transition from the bachelorhood stage to the honeymooner stage. Engaged and soon-to-be-married couples have a combined income of more than $48,000 (30 percent greater than the average U.S. household); therefore, they are the target for many products and services (the bridal industry is a $32-billion-a-year market—see Figure 10-13).[60] And they want their wedding to be special,

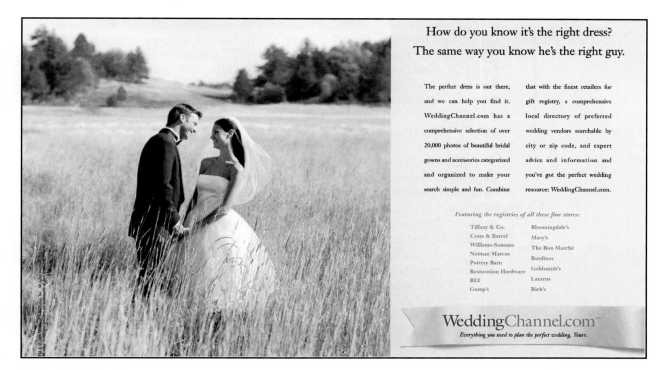

How do you know it's the right dress?
The same way you know he's the right guy.

The perfect dress is out there, and we can help you find it. WeddingChannel.com has a comprehensive selection of over 20,000 photos of beautiful bridal gowns and accessories categorized and organized to make your search simple and fun. Combine that with the finest retailers for gift registry, a comprehensive local directory of preferred wedding vendors searchable by city or zip code, and expert advice and information and you've got the perfect wedding resource: WeddingChannel.com.

Featuring the registries of all these fine stores:

Tiffany & Co.
Crate & Barrel
Williams-Sonoma
Neiman Marcus
Pottery Barn
Restoration Hardware
REI
Gump's

Bloomingdale's
Macy's
The Bon Marché
Burdines
Goldsmith's
Lazarus
Rich's

WeddingChannel.com
Everything you need to plan the perfect wedding. Yours.

FIGURE 10-13

Targeting the "To Be Married" Market
Courtesy of WeddingChannel.com, Inc.

which explains the recent trend in wedding sites that are far from home—an exotic Carribean island or a major European capital city. For example, a Wyoming company, Bonham Western Weddings, arranges ceremonies at local ranches and also sells wedding outfits with a Western design. The owner of the company claims, "A lot of people from back East come out here."[61]

Stage II: Honeymooners

The *honeymoon* stage starts immediately after the marriage vows are taken and generally continues until the arrival of the couple's first child. This FLC stage serves as a period of adjustment to married life. Because many young husbands and wives both work, these couples have available a combined income that often permits a lifestyle that provides them with the opportunities of more indulgent purchasing of possessions or allows them to save or invest their extra income.

Honeymooners have considerable start-up expenses when establishing a new home (major and minor appliances, bedroom and living room furniture, carpeting, drapes, dishes, and a host of utensils and accessory items). During this stage, the advice and experience of other married couples are likely to be important to newlyweds. Also important as sources of new product information are the so-called shelter magazines, such as *Better Homes and Gardens* and *Metropolitan Home*.

Stage III: Parenthood

When a couple has its first child, the honeymoon is considered over. The *parenthood* stage (sometimes called the full-nest stage) usually extends over more than a 20-year period. Because of its long duration, this stage can be divided into shorter phases: the preschool phase, the elementary school phase, the high school phase, and the college phase. Throughout these parenthood phases, the interrelationships of family members and the structure of the family gradually change. Furthermore, the financial resources of the family change significantly, as one (or both) parents progress in a career and as child-rearing and educational responsibilities gradually increase and finally decrease as children become self-supporting.

An increase in the number of births among baby boomers (born between 1946 and 1964) has resulted in a "baby boomlet." These parents are older, better educated, more affluent, and more socially aware than previous generations. Many feel that they are better parents to their children than their parents were to them. Their children often become the focus of their lives, and they spend money accordingly. "Boomer" parents have become an important target for companies that serve the baby market. They also are an important market for many investment and insurance services. There is even a company called Cover Concepts Marketing Services that distributes product samples, coupons, and other promotions to boomer parents and their preschool children at more than 22,000 day care centers.[62] The purpose here is to secure product and service exposure among this important group of consumers.

Many magazines cater to the information and entertainment needs of parents and children. For example, there are many other special-interest publications, such as *Humpty Dumpty,* designed for the young child just learning to read; *Scholastic Magazine,* for the elementary school pupil; *Boy's Life,* for young boys; and *American Girl, Seventeen, Glamour,* and *Mademoiselle,* for teen and young adult girls interested in fashion.

Stage IV: Postparenthood

Because parenthood extends over many years, it is only natural to find that *post-parenthood,* when all the children have left home, is traumatic for some parents and liberating for others. This so-called *empty-nest stage* signifies for many parents almost a "rebirth," a time for doing all the things they could not do while the children were at home and they had to worry about soaring educational expenses. For the mother, it may be a time to further her education, to enter or reenter the job market, or to seek new interests. For the father, it is a time to indulge in new hobbies. For both, it is the time to travel, to entertain, perhaps to refurnish their home or to sell it in favor of a new home or condominium.

It is during this stage that married couples tend to be most comfortable financially. Today's empty nesters have more leisure time. They travel more frequently, take extended vacations, and are likely to purchase a second home in a warmer climate. They have higher disposable incomes because of savings and investments, and they have fewer expenses (no mortgage or college tuition bills). They look forward to being involved grandparents. For this reason, families in the postparenthood stage are an important market for luxury goods, new automobiles, expensive furniture, and vacations to faraway places.

Many empty nesters retire while they are still in good health. Retirement provides the opportunity to pursue new interests, to travel, and to fulfill unsatisfied needs. Hotels, airlines, and car-leasing companies have responded to this market with discounts to consumers over 60; some airlines have established special travel clubs with unlimited mileage for a flat fee. Adult communities have sprung up in many parts of the nation (see Figure 10-14). Of course, for older retired couples who do not have adequate savings or income, retirement is far different and very restrictive.

Older consumers tend to use television as an important source of information and entertainment. They favor programs that provide the opportunity to "keep up with what's happening," especially news and public affairs programs. In addition, a

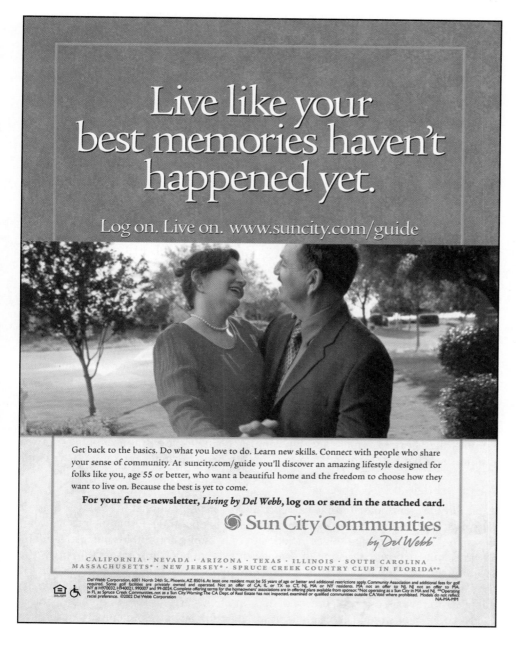

FIGURE 10-14

Targeting the
Postparenthood Stage
of FLC Sun City
Communities
Courtesy of Sun City
Communities by Del Webb.

number of special-interest magazines cater exclusively to this market, such as *Modern Maturity*. (Chapter 13 contains a more detailed discussion of the older consumer as a subcultural market segment.)

Stage V: Dissolution

Dissolution of the basic family unit occurs with the death of one spouse. When the surviving spouse is in good health, is working or has adequate savings, and has supportive family and friends, the adjustment is easier. The surviving spouse (usually, the wife) often tends to follow a more economical lifestyle. Many surviving spouses seek each other out for companionship; others enter into second (or third and even fourth) marriages.

Marketing and the Traditional FLC

Whereas the foregoing discussion of the traditional family life cycle concept indicated the types of products and services that a household or family might be most interested in at each stage, it is also possible to trace how the FLC concept impacts a single product or service over time. A recent study employed an eight-stage FLC scheme to investigate how consumers choose a bank.[63] As part of the research, the 3,100 respondents were asked to rate the relative importance of 18 product/service characteristics that might impact on their choice of a bank. Table 10-8 presents the findings of the study. The research reveals that location is very important to all respondents (i.e., it was always ranked either first or second), but other bank attributes tended to be much more important to some FLC segments than others. For instance, "fast service," was ranked fifth by bachelor stage individuals and twelfth or thirteenth by full-nest II, empty-nest I, and empty-nest II respondents.

MODIFICATIONS—THE NONTRADITIONAL FLC

As we already noted, the traditional FLC model has lost its ability to fully represent the progression of stages through which current family and lifestyle arrangements move. To compensate for these limitations, consumer researchers have been attempting to search out expanded FLC models that better reflect diversity of family and lifestyle arrangements.[64] Figure 10-15 presents an FLC model that depicts along the main horizontal row the stages of the traditional FLC and above and below the main horizontal row are selected alternative FLC stages that account for some important nontraditional family households that marketers are increasingly targeting. The underlying sociodemographic forces that drive this expanded FLC model include divorce and later marriages, with and without the presence of children. Although somewhat greater reality is provided by this modified FLC model, it only recognizes families that started in marriage, ignoring such single-parent households as unwed mothers and families formed because a single person or single persons adopt a child.

Nontraditional FLC Stages

Table 10-9 presents an extensive categorization of nontraditional FLC stages that are derived from the dynamic sociodemographic forces operating during the past 25 years or so. These nontraditional stages include not only family households but also nonfamily households: those consisting of a single individual and those consisting of two or more unrelated individuals. At one time, nonfamily households were so uncommon that it was not really important whether they were considered or not. However, as Table 10-10 reveals, over 30 percent of all households are currently nonfamily households (i.e., men or women living alone or with another person as an unmarried couple). The table points out how FLC stages have shifted so that today nonfamily households actually outnumber married couples with children, the once stereotypical family.

Consumption in Nontraditional Families

When households undergo status changes (divorce, temporary retirement, a new person moving into the household, or the death of a spouse), they often undergo spontaneous changes in consumption-related preferences and, thus, become attractive targets for many marketers. For example, divorce often requires that one (or both) former spouses find a new residence, get new telephones (with new telephone numbers), buy new furniture, and perhaps find a job. These requirements mean that a divorced person might need to contact real estate agents, call the local and long-distance telephone companies, visit furniture stores, and possibly contact a personnel

TABLE 10-8 Choosing a Bank—Average Service Attribute Importance for Different FLC Stages

Attitude	Bachelor Stage: Young, single	Newly married couples: Young, no children	Full-nest I: youngest child under 6	Full-nest II: youngest child 6 or over	Full-nest III: Older married couples with children	Empty-nest I: Older married couples, no children with them, head in labor force	Empty-nest II: Older married couples, no children living at home, head retired	Single head of households
	S1 Rank	S2 Rank	S3 Rank	S4 Rank	S5 Rank	S6 Rank	S7 Rank	S8 Rank
Located near home	1	2	1	1	1	1	2	1
Overall quality of service	2	9	7	7	6	7	10	4
Good reputation	3	1	2	2	8	6	9	2
Ease of qualifying for free checking account by maintaining a minimum balance	4	10	9	13	11	11	5	3
Fast service	5	8	10	12	10	12	13	10
Being able to obtain all financial services at one location	6	11	11	10	13	9	8	12
Paying highest rates on savings	7	5	8	8	5	5	4	5
Availability of auto/personal loans	8	7	6	4	12	10	14	7

Source: Rajshekhar G. Javalgi and Paul Dion, "A Life Cycle Segmentation Approach to Marketing Financial Products and Services," *The Services Industries Journal*, 19, no. 3, July 1999, 78–79. Reprinted by permission.

FIGURE 10-15

An Extended Family
Life Cycle Schema
Accounts for
Alternative Consumer
Lifestyle Realities
Source: Patrick E. Murphy and
William A. Staples, "A
Modern-Sized Family Life
Cycle," *Journal of Consumer
Research,* 6 June 1979, 17.
Reprinted by permission of
The University of Chicago
Press as publisher.

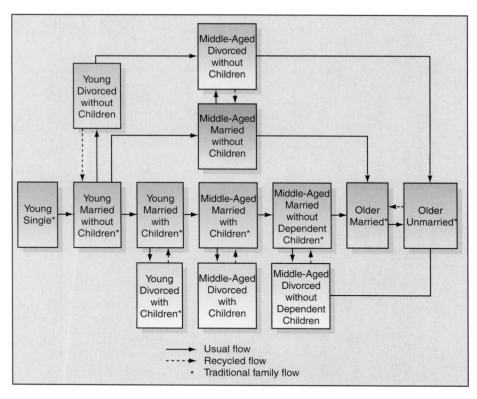

TABLE 10-9	Noteworthy Nontraditional FLC Stages

ALTERNATIVE FLC STAGES	**DEFINITION/COMMENTARY**
FAMILY HOUSEHOLDS	
Childless couples	It is increasingly acceptable for married couples to elect not to have children. Contributing forces are more career-oriented married women and delayed marriages.
Couples who marry later in life (in their late 30s or later)	More career-oriented men and women and greater occurrence of couples living together. Likely to have fewer or even no children.
Couples who have first child later in life (in their late 30s or later)	Likely to have fewer children. Stress quality lifestyle: "Only the best is good enough."
Single parents I	High divorce rates (about 50 percent) contribute to a portion of single-parent households.
Single parents II	Young man or woman who has one or more children out of wedlock.
Single parents III	A single person who adopts one or more children.
Extended family	Young single-adult children who return home to avoid the expenses of living alone while establishing their careers. Divorced daughter or son and grandchild(ren) return home to parents. Frail elderly parents who move in with children. Newlyweds living with in-laws.
NONFAMILY HOUSEHOLDS	
Unmarried couples	Increased acceptance of heterosexual and homosexual couples.
Divorced persons (no children)	High divorce rate contributes to dissolution of households before children are born.
Single persons (most are young)	Primarily a result of delaying first marriage; also, men and women who never marry.
Widowed persons (most are elderly)	Longer life expectancy, especially for women, means more over-75 single-person households.

TABLE 10-10	Family and Nonfamily Households		
	NUMBER OF HOUSEHOLDS BY TYPE IN 2000 (IN 000S)	**DISTRIBUTION OF HOUSEHOLDS BY TYPE**
ALL HOUSEHOLDS	**105,480**	**100.0%**
Family Households	**71,787**	**68.1%**
Married couples	54,493	51.7%
with own children under 18	24,836	23.5%
Female householder		
(no husband present)	12,900	12.2%
Nonfamily Households	**33,693**	**31.9%**
Householder living alone	27,230	25.8%
Average household size = 2.59		
Average family size = 3.14		

Source: U.S. Census Bureau (factfinder.census.gov/bf/_lang= en_vt_name= DEC_2000_SF1_U_DP1_geo_id= 01000US.html).

agency or career consultant. There are also the special needs of the children who are experiencing the divorce.

In another sphere, the substantial increase in dual-income households (in which both the husband and wife work) has also tended to muddy the lifestyle assumptions implicit in the traditional FLC. Most dual-income families have children (the majority of those children are between 11 and 20 years of age). The most affluent dual-income segment is, not surprisingly, the "crowded nesters." This dual-income couple, with an adult child living at home, has the advantage of an additional potential source of income to contribute to the general well-being of the household.

The side-by-side existence of traditional and nontraditional FLC stages is another example of our recurring observation that the contemporary marketplace is complex in its diversity, and it is a challenge to segment and serve.

Summary

Almost all individuals regularly interact with other people who directly or indirectly influence their purchase decisions. Thus, the study of groups and their impact on the individual is of great importance to marketers concerned with influencing consumer behavior.

Consumer reference groups are groups that serve as frames of reference for individuals in their purchase decisions. Examples of reference groups include (1) friendship groups, (2) shopping groups, (3) work groups, (4) virtual groups or communities, and (5) consumer-action groups. Reference groups that influence general values or behavior are called normative reference groups; those that influence specific attitudes are called comparative reference groups. The concept of consumer reference groups has been broadened to include groups with which

consumers have no direct face-to-face contact, such as celebrities, political figures, and social classes.

The credibility, attractiveness, and power of the reference group affect the degree of influence it has. Reference group appeals are used very effectively by some advertisers in promoting their goods and services because they subtly induce the prospective consumer to identify with the pictured user of the product.

The five types of reference group appeals most commonly used in marketing are celebrities, experts, the common man, the executive and employee spokesperson, and the trade spokes-character. Celebrities are used to give testimonials or endorsements as actors or as company spokespersons. Experts may be recognized experts in the product category or actors playing the part of experts (such as an automobile mechanic). The common-man approach is designed to show that individuals who are just like the prospect are satisfied with the advertised product. Increasingly, firms are using their top executives as spokespersons because their appearance in company advertisements seems to imply that someone at the top is watching over the consumer's interest.

For many consumers their family is their primary reference group for many attitudes and behaviors. The family is the prime target market for most products and product categories. As the most basic membership group, families are defined as two or more persons related by blood, marriage, or adoption who reside together. There are three types of families: married couples, nuclear families, and extended families. Socialization is a core function of the family. Other functions of the family are the provision of economic and emotional support and the pursuit of a suitable lifestyle for its members.

The members of a family assume specific roles in their everyday functioning; such roles or tasks extend to the realm of consumer purchase decisions. Key consumer-related roles of family members include influencers, gatekeepers, deciders, buyers, preparers, users, maintainers, and disposers. A family's decision-making style often is influenced by its lifestyle, roles, and cultural factors.

The majority of consumer studies classify family consumption decisions as husband-dominated, wife-dominated, joint, or autonomic decisions. The extent and nature of husband–wife influence in family decisions depend, in part, on the specific product or service and selected cultural influences.

Classification of families by stage in the family life cycle (FLC) provides valuable insights into family consumption-related behavior. The traditional FLC begins with bachelorhood, moves on to marriage, then to an expanding family, to a contracting family, and to an end with the death of a spouse. Dynamic sociodemographic changes in society have resulted in many non-traditional stages that a family or nonfamily household might pass through (such as childless couples, couples marrying later in life, single parents, unmarried couples, or single-person households). These nontraditional stages are becoming increasingly important to marketers in terms of specific market niches.

Discussion Questions

1. As a marketing consultant, you have been asked to evaluate a new promotional campaign for a large retail chain. The campaign strategy is aimed at increasing group shopping. What recommendations would you make?

2. Many celebrities who are considered to be persuasive role models often appear in TV beer commercials. Does the use of such celebrities in beer advertising constitute an unethical marketing practice? Discuss.

3. You are the marketing vice president of a large soft-drink company. Your company's advertising agency is in the process of negotiating a contract to employ a superstar female singer to promote your product. Discuss the reference group factors that you would raise before the celebrity is hired.

4. How does the family influence the consumer socialization of children? What role does television advertising play in consumer socialization?

5. As a marketing consultant, you were retained by the Walt Disney Company to design a study investigating how families make vacation decisions. Whom, within the family, would you interview? What kind of questions would you ask? How would you assess the relative power of each family member in making vacation-related decisions?

6. Which of the five stages of the traditional family life cycle constitute the most lucrative segment(s) for the following products and services: (a) telephone party lines, (b) a Club Med vacation, (c) Domino's pizza, (d) compact disc players, (e) mutual funds, and (f) motor homes? Explain your answers.

7. As the marketing manager of a high-quality, fairly expensive line of frozen dinners, how would you use the nonfamily household information listed in Table 10-9 to segment the market and position your product?

8. A domestic airline's frequent-flyer program states that award tickets are transferable only to family members. As the airline executive charged with reevaluating this policy, how would you use the census data listed in Table 10-10 to decide whether or not to change the present policy?

Exercises

1. Prepare a list of formal and informal groups to which you belong and give examples of purchases for which each served as a reference group. In which of the groups you listed is the pressure to conform the greatest? Why?

2. With a paper and pencil, spend one hour watching a network television channel during prime time. Record the total number of commercials that aired. For each commercial using a celebrity endorser, record the celebrity's name, the product or service advertised, and whether the celebrity was used in a testimonial, as an endorser, as an actor, or as a spokesperson.

3. Think of a recent major purchase your family has made. Analyze the roles performed by the various family members in terms of the following consumption roles: influencers, gatekeepers, deciders, buyers, preparers, users, maintainers, and disposers.

4. Select three product categories and compare the brands you prefer to those your parents prefer. To what extent are the preferences similar? Discuss the similarities in the context of consumer socialization.

5. Identify one traditional family and one nontraditional family (or household) featured in a TV sitcom or series. (The two families households can be featured in the same or in different TV shows.) Classify the traditional group into one stage of the traditional FLC. Classify the nontraditional group into one of the categories described in Table 10-9. Select two characters of the same gender and approximate age, one from each group, and compare their consumption behavior (such as clothes, furniture, or stated or implied attitudes toward spending money).

Key Terms

- Actor
- Autonomic (unilateral) decisions
- Celebrity credibility
- Comparative reference groups
- Consumer-action group
- Consumer conformity
- Consumer socialization
- Endorsement
- Extended family

- Family
- Family life cycle
- Group
- Husband-dominated decisions
- Indirect reference groups
- Informal groups
- Joint (syncratic) decisions
- Normative reference groups
- Nuclear family

- Reference group
- Shopping group
- Single-parent family
- Socialization of family members
- Spokesperson
- Symbolic group
- Testimonial
- Traditional family life cycle
- Wife-dominated decisions

Notes

1. Robert Madrigal, "The Influence of Social Alliances with Sports Teams on Intentions to Purchase Corporate Sponsors' Products," *Journal of Advertising,* 29, Winter 2000, 13–24.

2. Pamela Kicker and Cathy L. Hartman, "Purchase Pal Use: Why Buyers Choose to Shop with Others," in *1993 AMA Winter Educators' Proceedings,* 4, eds.

Rajan Varadarajan and Bernard Jaworski (Chicago: American Marketing Association, 1993), 378–384.

3. Eve M. Kahn and Julie Lasky, "Out of the Pantry and Partying On," *New York Times,* November 8, 2001, F9.

4. Amitai Etzioni, "E-Communities Build New Ties, But Ties That Bind," *New York Times,* February 10, 2000, G7.

5. Cara Okleshen and Sanford Grossbart, "Usenet Groups, Virtual Community and Consumer Behavior," in *Advances in Consumer Research*, 25, eds. Joseph W. Alba and J. Wesley Hutchinson (Provo, UT: Association for Consumer Research, 1998), 276–282.

6. Birud Sindhav, "A Sociological Perspective on Web-Related Consumer Marketing," in *1999 AMA Educators Proceedings*, 10, eds., Stephen P. Brown and D. Sudharshan (Chicago: American Marketing Association, 1999), 226–227.

7. John Harney, "Cyber Bazaars," *IntelligentKM*, March 8, 2001, 58–62.

8. "Startec Acquires Chinese Web Community," *PR Newswire*, March 7, 2000, 1.

9. Eileen Fischer, Julia Bristor, and Brenda Gainer, "Creating or Escaping Community? An Exploratory Study of Internet Consumers' Behaviors," *Advances in Consumer Research*, 23 (Provo, UT: Association for Consumer Research, 1996), 178–182; Siok Kuan Tambyah, "Life on the Net: The Reconstruction of Self and Community," *Advances in Consumer Research*, 23 (Provo, UT: Association for Consumer Research, 1996), 172–177.

10. "Is the Net Redefining Our Identity?" *Business Week*, May 12, 1997, 100–101.

11. S. Elizabeth Bird, "Chatting on Cynthia's Porch: Creating Community in an E-Mail Fan Group," *Southern Communication Journal*, 65, no. 1, Fall 1999, 49–65.

12. Kendra Nordin, *Christian Science Monitor*, February 26, 2001, 16.

13. Albert M. Muniz, Jr. and Thomas C. O'Guinn, "Brand Community," *Journal of Consumer Research*, 27, March 2001, 412–432.

14. James H. McAlexander, John W. Schouten, and Harold F. Koenig, "Building Brand Community," *Journal of Marketing*, 66, January 2002, 38–54.

15. Ibid., 46.

16. B. Zafer Erdogan, Michael J. Baker, and Stephen Tagg, "Selecting Celebrity Endorsers: The Practitioner's Perspective," *Journal of Advertising Research*, May/June 2001, 39–48.

17. "D.C.s with Celebrity Patients Sought for PR Campaign," *The Chiropractic Journal*, March 2002, 26.

18. Lynette Knowles Mathur, Ike Mathur, and Nanda Rangan, "The Wealth Effects Associated with a Celebrity Endorser: The Michael Jordan Phenomenon," *Journal of Advertising Research*, 37, 3, May–June 1997, 25; and Jeff Manning, "Jordan, Nike Linked Until 2023," *The Oregonian*, January 14, 1999, D1.

19. David Nielsen, "Tiger on Verge of Becoming No. 1 Pitchman in Sports," *Cincinnati Post*, June 21, 2000, 8B.

20. Jay Greene, "Next, Bill Gates Air Fresheners?" *Business Week*, February 11, 2002, 16.

21. Bonnie Tsui, "Yoga Magazine Gets Boost from Spirituality Surge," *Advertising Age*, September 4, 2000, 20.

22. Roobina Ohanian, "The Impact of Celebrity Spokespersons: Perceived Image on Consumers' Intention to Purchase," *Journal of Advertising Research*, February–March, 1991, 46–54.

23. Carolyn Tripp, Thomas D. Jensen, and Les Carlson, "The Effects of Multiple Product Endorsements by Celebrities on Consumers' Attitudes and Intentions," *Journal of Consumer Research*, 20, March 1994, 535–547; and David C. Bojanic, Patricia K. Voli, and James B. Hunt, "Can Consumers Match Celebrity Endorsers with Products?" in *Developments in Marketing Science*, ed. Robert L. King (Richmond, VA: Academy of Marketing Science, 1991), 303–307.

24. Ronald E. Goldsmith, Barbara A. Lafferty, and Stephen J. Newell, "The Impact of Corporate Credibility and Celebrity Credibility on Consumer Reaction to Advertisements and Brands," *Journal of Advertising*, 29, no. 3, Fall 2000, 43–54.

25. Richard Morin, "When Celebrity Endorsers Go Bad," *The Washington Post*, February 3, 2002, B5.

26. "Study Identifies Qualities of Effective Public Health Service Announcements," *Marketing News*, April 1981, 7.

27. Margaret F. Callcott and Wei-Na Lee, "Establishing the Spokes-Character in Academic Inquiry: Historical Overview and Framework for Definition," in *Advances in Consumer Research*, 22, eds. Frank R. Kardes and Mita Sujan (Provo, UT: Association for Consumer Research, 1995), 144–151.

28. Stuart Elliott, "Betty Crocker Sets Up House in Cyberspace," *New York Times*, August 11, 1997, B1, B8.

29. Andrea Petersen, "If Products's Invisible, Can It Be Placed?" *Wall Street Journal*, April 9, 2001, B1.

30. U.S. Census Bureau (factfinder.census.gov/bf/_lang=en_vt_name=DEC_2000_SF1_U_DP1_geo_id=01000US.html).

31. Terry L. Childers and Akshay R. Rao, "The Influence of Familial and Peer-Based Reference Groups on Consumer Decisions," *Journal of Consumer Research*, 19, September 1992, 198–211.

32. Maureen Dowd, "The Baby Bust," *New York Times*, April 10, 2001, A27; and Nancy Gibbs, "Making Time for a Baby," *Time Magazine*, 159, no. 15, April 15, 2002, 48–54.

33. Rebecca Gardyn, "Unmarried Bliss," *American Demographics*, December 2000, 56–61.

34. "Data Reveal Another Change in U.S. Families," *The Houston Chronicle*, November 24, 1999, 3; and Sara Eckel, "Single Mothers," *American Demographics*, May 1999, 63–66.

35. Barbara LeBey, "American Families Are Drifting Apart," *USA Today*, September 2001, 20–22; and Marilyn Coleman and Lawrence H. Ganong, "Changing Families, Changing Responsibilities?" *National Forum*, 80, i3, Summer 2000, 34–37.

36. "The Business of Mother's Day," *PR Newswire*, April 18, 2001, 1.

37. Pamela Paul, "Meet the Parents," *American Demographics*, January 2002, 43–47.

38. Elke Zeijl, Yolanda te Poel, Manuela du Bois-Reymond, Janita Ravesloot, and Jacqueline J. Meulman, "The Role of Parents and Peers in the Leisure Activities of Young Adolescents," *Journal of Leisure Research,* 32, no. 3, 2000, 281–302.

39. Pamela Kruger, "Why Johnny Can't Play," *Fast Company,* August 2000, 271–272.

40. Deborah Roedder John, "Consumer Socialization of Children: A Retrospective Look at Twenty-Five Years of Research," *Journal of Consumer Research,* 26, December 1999, 183–213.

41. Amy Rummel, John Howard, Jennifer M. Swinton, and D. Bradley Seymour, "You Can't Have That! A Study of Reactance Effects and Children's Consumer Behavior," *Journal of Marketing Theory and Practice,* Winter 2000, 38–45.

42. Kay M. Palan and Russell N. Laczniak, "The Relationship Between Advertising Exposure and Children's Influence Strategies," in *2001 AMA Winter Educators' Conference,* 12, eds. Ram Krishnan and Madhu Viswanathan (Chicago: American Marketing Association, 2001), 28–36.

43. Gregory M. Rose, "Consumer Socialization, Parental Style, and Developmental Timetables in the United States and Japan," *Journal of Marketing,* 63, July 1999, 105–119.

44. John Fetto, "Woof Woof" Means, "I Love You," *American Demographics,* February 2002, 11.

45. Barbara Olsen, "Brand Loyalty and Lineage: Exploring New Dimensions for Research," in *Advances in Consumer Research,* 20, eds. Leigh McAlister and Michael L. Rothschild (Provo, UT: Association for Consumer Research, 1993), 575–579; Marilyn Lavin, "Husband-Dominant, Wife-Dominant, Joint," *Journal of Consumer Marketing,* 10 (1993), 33–42; and Vern L. Bengtson, "Beyond the Nuclear Family: The Increasing Importance of Multigenerational Bond," *Journal of Marriage and Family* (February 2001), 1–16.

46. Sanford Grossbart, Stephanie McConnell Hughes, Cara Okleshen, Stephanie Nelson, Les Carlson, Russell N. Laczniak, and Darrel Muehling, "Parents, Children, and the Internet: Socialization Perspectives," in *2001 AMA Winter Educators' Conference,* 12, eds. Ram Krishnan and Madhu Viswanathan (Chicago: American Marketing Association, 2001), 379–385.

47. Kevin Heubusch, "A Tough Job Gets Tougher," *American Demographics,* September 1997, 39.

48. Lynn White and Stacy J. Rogers, "Economic Circumstances and Family Outcomes: A Review of the 1990s," *Journal of Marriage and the Family,* 62, November 2000, 1035–1051.

49. Todd Starr Palmer, Mary Beth Pinto, and Diane H. Parente, "College Students' Credit Card Debt and the Role of Parental Involvement: Implications for Public Policy," *Journal of Public Policy and Marketing,* 20 (1), Spring 2001, 105–113.

50. Jonghee Park, Patriya Tanshuhaj, Eric R. Spangenberg, and Jim McCullough, "An Emotion-Based Perspective of Family Purchase Decisions," in *Advances in Consumer Research,* 22, eds. Frank R. Kardes and Mita Sujan (Provo, UT: Association for Consumer Research 1995), 723–728.

51. Janice Greene, "Dogs, Dads and Laughter Bring Happiness to Kids," *San Francisco Chronicle,* November 2, 2001, 2.

52. Leah Haran, "Families Together Differently Today," *Advertising Age,* October 23, 1995, 1, 12.

53. J. Labrecque and L. Ricard, "Children's Influence on Family Decision-Making: A Restaurant Study," *Journal of Business Research,* 54, November 2001, 173–176.

54. Kim P. Corfman, "Perceptions of Relative Influence: Formation and Measurement," *Journal of Marketing Research,* 28, May 1991, 125–136. Also, for additional articles on family decision-making roles and structures, see Christina Kwai-Choi and Roger Marshall, "Who Do We Ask and When: A Pilot Study About Research in Family Decision Making," in *Developments in Marketing Science,* 16, eds. Michael Levy and Dhruv Grewal (Coral Gables, FL: Academy of Marketing Science, 1993), 30–35.

55. Joan Raymond, "For Richer and for Poorer," *American Demographics,* July 2000, 58–64.

56. John B. Ford, Michael S. LaTour, and Tony L. Henthorne, "Perception of Marital Roles in Purchase Decision Processes: A Cross-Cultural Study," *Journal of the Academy of Marketing Science,* 23, 2 (1995), 120–131; and Tony L. Henthorne, Michael S. LaTour, and Robert Matthews, "Perception of Marital Roles in Purchase Decision Making: A Study of Japanese Couples," *Proceedings* (Chicago: American Marketing Association, 1995), 321–322.

57. James U. McNeal and Chyon-Hwa Yeh, "Development of Consumer Behavior Patterns among Chinese Children," *Journal of Consumer Marketing,* 14 (1997), 45–59.

58. Gopala Ganesh, "Spousal Influence in Consumer Decisions: A Study of Cultural Assimilation," *Journal of Consumer Marketing,* 14 (1997), 132–145.

59. "Romantic Resurgence," *American Demographics,* August 1997, 35.

60. Dee Miller, "'Til Death Do They Part," *Marketing News,* March 27, 1995, 1–2; and Nellie S. Huang, "No More Toasters, Please," *Smart Money,* April 1993, 133–135.

61. Jeff Zeleny, "Trips Down the Aisle Turn into Vacations as More Couples Marry Far from Home," *Wall Street Journal,* June 20, 1996, B1, B10.

62. Paulette Thomas, "Show and Tell: Advertisers Take Pitches to Preschools," *Wall Street Journal,* October 28, 1996, B1, B5.

63. Rajshekhar G. Javalgi and Paul Dion, "A Life Cycle Segmentation Approach to Marketing Financial Products and Services," *The Services Industries Journal,* 19, no. 3, July 1999, 74–96.

64. Charles M. Schaninger and William D. Danko, "A Conceptual and Empirical Comparison of Alternative Household Life Cycle Models," *Journal of Consumer Research,* 19, March 1993, 580–594.

A good vibe.

A new Vibe.™

Pontiac's got a new Vibe. Check it out at pontiac.com/vibe.

Social Class and Consumer Behavior

S ome form of class structure or social stratification has existed in all societies throughout the history of human existence. In contemporary societies, an indication that social classes exist is the common reality that people who are better educated or have more prestigious occupations such as physicians and lawyers often are more highly valued than those who are truck drivers and farmhands. This is so, even though all four occupations are necessary for a society's well-being. Moreover, as will be discussed later, a wide range of differences in values, attitudes, and behavior exists among members of different social classes.

The major topics that will be explored in this chapter are a definition of social class and how it is measured, lifestyle profiles of the social classes, social-class mobility, geodemographic clustering, the affluent and nonaffluent consumer, the arrival of the "techno-class," and how social-class-linked attitudes and behavior influence consumer behavior.

What Is Social Class?

Although **social class** can be thought of as a continuum—a range of social positions on which each member of society can be placed—researchers have preferred to divide the continuum into a small number of specific social classes, or *strata*. Within this framework, the concept of social class is used to assign individuals or families to a social-class category. Consistent with this practice, social class is defined as *the division of members of a society into a hierarchy of distinct status classes, so that members of each class have relatively the same status and members of all other classes have either more or less status.*

To appreciate more fully the complexity of social class, we will briefly consider several underlying concepts pertinent to this definition.

SOCIAL CLASS AND SOCIAL STATUS

Researchers often measure social class in terms of **social status;** that is, they define each social class by the amount of status the members of that class have in comparison with members of other social classes. In social-class research (sometimes called *social stratification*), *status is frequently thought of as the relative rankings of members of each social class in terms of specific status factors.* For example, relative *wealth* (amount of economic assets), *power* (the degree of personal choice or influence over others), and *prestige* (the degree of recognition received from others) are three status factors frequently used when estimating social class.

To secure an understanding of how status operates within the minds of consumers, researchers have explored the idea of *social comparison theory.* According to this social-psychological concept, individuals quite normally compare their own material possessions with those owned by others in order to determine their relative social standing. This is especially important in a marketing society where status is often associated with consumers' purchasing power (or how much can be purchased). Simply stated, individuals with more purchasing power or a greater ability to make purchases have more status. Those who have more restrictions on what they can or cannot buy have less status. Because visible or conspicuous possessions are easy to spot, they especially serve as markers or indicators of one's own status and the status of others. Not surprisingly, recent research confirmed that a key ingredient of status is a consumer's possessions compared with others' similar possessions (possibly one's home versus another person's home).[1] In making such a comparison, an individual consumer might decide to compare himself with someone who is worse off (i.e., a downward comparison) in order to bolster his self-esteem; or alternatively a consumer might elect to *compare upward* with another consumer "with more" or some idealized media image (e.g., a beautiful home in a magazine advertisement), which is likely to make the consumer feel somewhat inferior.

A related concept is *status consumption*—the process by which consumers endeavor to increase their social standing through conspicuous consumption or possessions.[2] A number of research studies have validated the status consumption scale presented in Table 11-1. As the market for luxury or status products continues to grow, there is an even greater need for marketers to identify and understand which consumers especially seek out such status-enhancing possessions, as well as the relationship between status consumption and social class.[3]

Although *social comparison theory* and its related activity of *status consumption* have the potential of being very enlightening about status and how it oper-

TABLE 11-1	A Five-Question Status Consumption Scale[a]

1. I would buy a product just because it has status.
2. I am interested in new products with status.
3. I would pay more for a product if it had status.
4. The status of a product is irrelevant to me (negatively worded).
5. A product is more valuable to me if it has some snob appeal.

[a] Each of the five items is measured on 7-point Likert (agree–disagree) scale.
Source: Jacqueline K. Eastman, Ronald E. Goldsmith, and Leisa Reinecke Flynn, "Status Consumption in Consumer Behavior: Scale Development and Validation," *Journal of Marketing Theory and Practice,* Summer 1999, 44.

ates, consumer and marketing researchers most often approach the actual study of status in terms of one or more of the following convenient demographic (more precisely socioeconomic) variables: *family income, occupational status,* and *educational attainment.* These socioeconomic variables, as expressions of status, are used by marketing practitioners on a daily basis to measure social class.

SOCIAL CLASS IS HIERARCHICAL AND A NATURAL FORM OF SEGMENTATION

Social-class categories usually are ranked in a hierarchy, ranging from low to high status. Thus, members of a specific social class perceive members of other social classes as having either more or less status than they do. To many people, therefore, social-class categories suggest that others are either equal to them (about the same social class), superior to them (higher social class), or inferior to them (lower social class).

Within this context, social-class membership serves consumers as a frame of reference (or a reference group) for the development of their attitudes and behavior. In the context of reference groups, members of a specific social class may be expected to turn most often to other members of the same class for cues (or clues) regarding appropriate behavior. In other cases, members of a particular social class (e.g., upper-lower class) may aspire to advance their social-class standing by emulating the behavior of members of the middle class. To accomplish this goal, they might read middle-class magazines, do "middle-class things" (such as visit museums and advance their education), and hang out at middle-class restaurants so that they can observe middle-class behavior.[4]

The hierarchical aspect of social class is important to marketers. Consumers may purchase certain products because these products are favored by members of either their own or a higher social class (e.g., a luxury imported automobile), and consumers may avoid other products because they perceive the products to be "lower-class" products (e.g., a digital readout wristwatch as a dress watch). Thus, the various social-class strata provide a natural basis for market segmentation for many products and services. In many instances, consumer researchers have been able to relate aspects of product usage to social-class membership.

The classification of society's members into a small number of social classes has also enabled researchers to note the existence of shared values, attitudes, and behavioral patterns among members within each social class and differing values, attitudes, and behavior *between* social classes. Consumer researchers have been able to relate social-class standing to consumer attitudes concerning specific products and to examine social-class influences on the actual consumption of products.

SOCIAL-CLASS CATEGORIES

Little agreement exists among sociologists on how many distinct class divisions are necessary to adequately describe the class structure of the United States. Most early studies divided the members of specific communities into five or six social-class groups. However, other researchers have found nine-, four-, three-, and even two-class schemas suitable for their purposes. The choice of how many separate classes to use depends on the amount of detail that the researcher believes is necessary to explain adequately the attitudes or behavior under study. Marketers are interested in the social-class structures of communities that are potential markets for their products and in the specific social-class level of their potential customers. Table 11-2 illustrates the number and diversity of social-class schemas, whereas Table 11-3 shows the distribution of the U.S. population according to a recently generated five-category subdivision.

Table 11-3 also reveals the small size of the upper class, which is the reason why most mass marketers simply ignore it (or combine it with the upper-middle class). On the other hand, its small size and highly cultivated tastes make the upper class a particularly desirable target market for specialty firms with a specific expertise and the ability to cater to the small number of particularly affluent consumers (see Figure 11-1).

TABLE 11-2 **Variations in the Number and Types of Social-Class Categories**

TWO-CATEGORY SOCIAL-CLASS SCHEMAS

- *Blue collar, white collar*
- *Lower, upper*
- *Lower, middle*

THREE-CATEGORY SOCIAL-CLASS SCHEMAS

- *Blue collar, gray collar, white collar*
- *Lower, middle, upper*

FOUR-CATEGORY SOCIAL-CLASS SCHEMA

- *Lower, lower-middle, upper-middle, upper*

FIVE-CATEGORY SOCIAL-CLASS SCHEMAS

- *Lower, working class, lower-middle, upper-middle, upper*
- *Lower, lower-middle, middle, upper-middle, upper*

SIX-CATEGORY SOCIAL-CLASS SCHEMA

- *Lower-lower, upper-lower, lower-middle, upper-middle, lower-upper, upper-upper*

SEVEN-CATEGORY SOCIAL-CLASS SCHEMA

- *Real lower-lower, a lower group of people but not the lowest, working class, middle class, upper-middle, lower-upper, upper-upper*

NINE-CATEGORY SOCIAL-CLASS SCHEMA

- *Lower-lower, middle-lower, upper-lower, lower-middle, middle-middle, upper-middle, lower-upper, middle-upper, upper-upper*

TABLE 11-3 Percent Distribution of Five-Category Social-Class Measure

SOCIAL CLASSES	PERCENTAGE
Upper	4.3
Upper-middle	13.8
Middle	32.8
Working	32.3
Lower	16.8
Total percentage	100.0

Source: Eugene Sivadas, George Mathew, and David J. Curry, "A Preliminary Examination of the Continued Significance of Social Class to Marketing: A Geodemographic Replication," *Journal of Consumer Marketing,* 14, 6 (1997), 469. Reprinted by permission.

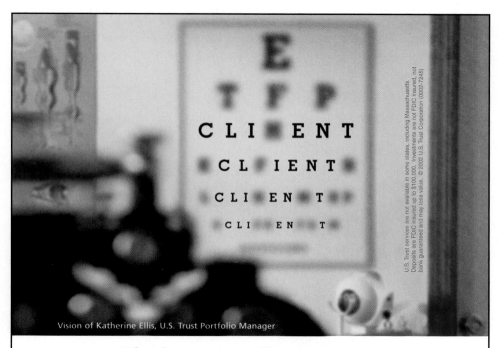

FIGURE 11-1

Financial Services Company Targeting Upscale Customers
Courtesy of U.S. Trust Company.

The Measurement of Social Class

There is no general agreement on how to measure social class. To a great extent, researchers are uncertain about the underlying dimensions of social-class structure. To attempt to resolve this dilemma, researchers have used a wide range of measurement techniques that they believe give a fair approximation of social class.

Systematic approaches for measuring social class fall into the following broad categories: **subjective measures, reputational measures,** and **objective measures** of social class.

SUBJECTIVE MEASURES

In the *subjective* approach to measuring social class, individuals are asked to estimate their own social-class positions. Typical of this approach is the following question:

Which one of the following four categories best describes your social class: the lower class, the lower-middle class, the upper-middle class, or the upper class?

Lower class	[ ]
Lower-middle class	[ ]
Upper-middle class	[ ]
Upper class	[ ]
Do not know/refuse to answer	[ ]

The resulting classification of social-class membership is based on the participants' self-perceptions or self-images. Social class is treated as a personal phenomenon, one that reflects an individual's sense of belonging or identification with others. This feeling of social-group membership is often referred to as **class consciousness.**

Subjective measures of social-class membership tend to produce an overabundance of people who classify themselves as middle class (thus understating the number of people—the "fringe people"—who would, perhaps, be more correctly classified as either lower or upper class).[5] Moreover, it is likely that the subjective perception of one's social-class membership, as a reflection of one's self-image, is related to product usage and consumption preferences (see Chapter 5). This is not only an American phenomenon. Every year in Japan, a "Life of the Nation" survey asks citizens to place themselves into one of five social-class categories: upper, upper-middle, middle-middle, lower-middle, and lower class. Whereas in the late 1950s over 70 percent of respondents placed themselves into one of the three middle-class categories, by the late 1960s, and continuing on through today, close to 90 percent categorize themselves as "middle class."[6] Again, this demonstrates the tendency for consumers to report seeing themselves as "middle class."

REPUTATIONAL MEASURES

The *reputational* approach for measuring social class requires selected community informants to make initial judgments concerning the social-class membership of others within the community. The final task of assigning community members to social-class positions, however, belongs to the trained researcher.

Sociologists have used the reputational approach to obtain a better understanding of the specific class structures of communities under study. Consumer researchers, however, are concerned with the measurement of social class to understand markets and consumption behavior better, not social structure. In keeping with this more focused goal, the reputational approach has proved to be impractical.

OBJECTIVE MEASURES

In contrast to the subjective and reputational methods, which require people to envision their own class standing or that of other community members, *objective* measures consist of selected demographic or socioeconomic variables concerning the individual(s) under study. These variables are measured through questionnaires that ask respondents several factual questions about themselves, their families, or their places of residence. When selecting objective measures of social class, most researchers favor one or more of the following variables: occupation, amount of income, and education. To these socioeconomic factors they sometimes add geodemographic clustering data in the form of zip code and residence-neighborhood information. These socioeconomic indicators are especially important as a means of locating concentrations of consumers with specific social-class membership.

Socioeconomic measures of social class are of considerable value to marketers concerned with segmenting markets. Marketing managers who have developed socioeconomic profiles of their target markets can locate these markets (i.e., identify and measure them) by studying the socioeconomic data periodically issued by the United States Bureau of the Census and numerous commercial geodemographic data services. To reach a desired target market, marketers match the *socioeconomic profiles* of their target audiences to the *audience profiles* of selected advertising media. Socioeconomic audience profiles are regularly developed and routinely made available to potential advertisers by most of the mass media (see Table 11-4). Readers' median income data for a selection of print media are presented in Table 11-5.

TABLE 11-4   Socioeconomic Profile of *Esquire* Readers

	TOTAL	PERCENT	(U.S. AVERAGE = 100)
Total Adults	2,866,000	100.0%	100
Gender			
Men		58.2	121
Women		41.8	80
Age			
18–34		37.3	116
25–44		35.0	108
25–54		66.2	112
Median Age		**39.7**	
Income			
HHI $100,000+		19.6	143
HHI $75,000+		31.2	123
HHI $50,000+		53.6	116
Median HHI (Household income)		**$52,873**	
Occupational Position			
Top management		7.0	171
Professional/managerial		26.9	133
Education			
Postgraduate Studies/degree		12.1	159
College degree		29.4	129
Base = Adults			

Source: MRI Doublebase 2001: Index 100 = Total U.S. Adults and *Esquire* Magazine at www.esquiremediakit.com.

| TABLE 11-5 | Readers' Median Household Income for Selected Publications |

NEWSPAPER/MAGAZINE	MEDIAN HOUSEHOLD INCOME
Barron's	$98,137.7
Inc.	92,817.8
New York Times Sunday	91,112.3
Forbes	88,889.8
Architectural Digest	86,923.2
Money	78,044.7
New Yorker	73,597.8
PC Magazine	70,997.0
Smithsonian	67,861.3
Newsweek	66,935.9
Time	64,172.3
Car & Driver	62,610.4
People	59,654.1
Town & Country	57,905.5
Cosmopolitan	55,024.8
Esquire	50,828.6
Playboy	50,383.4
Field & Stream	49,761.1
Hunting	45,582.7
Family Circle	48,956.1
Soap Opera Digest	42,623.2
Star	39,016.9
Country Music	36,367.7
True Story	25,984.0

Source: From *2002 Magazine Audience Estimates* (New York: Mediamark Research, Inc.). Reprinted by permission.

Objective measures of social class fall into two basic categories: **single-variable indexes** and **composite-variable indexes.**

Single-Variable Indexes

A single-variable index uses just one socioeconomic variable to evaluate social-class membership. Some of the variables that are used for this purpose are discussed next.

Occupation Occupation is a widely accepted and probably the best-documented measure of social class because it reflects occupational status.[7] The importance of occupation as a social-class indicator is dramatized by the frequency with which people ask others they meet for the first time, "What do you do for a living?" The response to this question serves as a guide in sizing up (or evaluating and forming opinions of) others.

More important, marketers frequently think in terms of specific occupations when defining a target market for their products (such as "Teachers are our best customers for summer cruises") or broader occupational categories ("We target our vacation resort club to executives and professionals"). Still further, the likelihood that particular occupations would be receptive to certain products or services often

TABLE 11-6	Occupational Rankings in Terms of Honesty and Ethical Standards	

OCCUPATION	2001 RANK	COMBINED PERCENT[a]
Firefighters	1	90
Nurses	2	84
Members of U.S. military	3	81
Police officers	4	68[b]
Druggists/pharmacists	5	68[b]
Medical doctors	6	66
Clergy	7	64
Engineers	8	60
College teachers	9	58
Dentists	10	56
Accountants	11	41
Bankers	12	34
Journalists	13	29
Congressmen/Congresswomen	14	25[b]
Business executives	15	25[b]
Senators	16	25[b]
Auto mechanics	17	22
Stockbrokers	18	19
Lawyers	19	18
Labor union leaders	20	17
Insurance salespeople	21	13
Advertising practitioners	22	11
Car salespeople	23	8

[a]Rank is based on the combination of "very high" and "high" ratings.
[b]Tie breakers: (1) Largest percent "very high" (2) smallest percent combination of "low/very low."
Source: The Gallup Poll Monthly, December 2001. Reprinted by permission.

provides the basis for an occupational screener requirement for participation in focus groups or survey research and for marketers to select occupational databases to target with direct-marketing campaigns (e.g., a list of female attorneys practicing in Denver, Colorado).

Table 11-6 presents findings from a continuing survey undertaken by the Gallup organization that estimates the relative honesty and perceived ethical standards that people assign to a sample of basic occupational titles. Because this ranking is based more on respect or societal prestige (a form of status) than on wealth, it is not surprising that the rankings only somewhat suggest that occupations toward the top half of the table earn greater incomes or require more formal education than those toward the bottom half. Moreover, in its 2001 assessment of a range of occupations, researchers at Gallup added three occupations that were especially relevant to the heroic rescue and recovery efforts in the September 11, 2001, terrorist attack in New York and Washington, DC (i.e., firefighters, nurses, and members of the U.S. military). Not too surprisingly, these three occupations immediately received top rating by a fairly big margin.

TABLE 11-7 The Relationship Between Formal Education and Household Income

	TOTAL	LESS THAN 9TH GRADE	SOME HIGH SCHOOL	HIGH SCHOOL GRADUATE	SOME COLLEGE (NO DEGREE)	ASSOCIATES DEGREE	BACHELOR'S DEGREE OR MORE
All Households	100%	100%	100%	100%	100%	100%	100%
Under $10,000	8.7	26.3	20.6	9.2	5.8	4.5	2.8
$10,000 to $14,999	7.1	17.4	14.0	8.4	5.6	5.3	2.4
$15,000 to $24,999	13.6	22.3	21.8	16.9	13.8	10.8	5.6
$25,000 to $34,999	12.4	13.5	14.9	14.5	13.2	13.0	8.0
$35,000 to $49,999	15.8	9.7	13.7	17.6	18.4	17.2	13.7
$50,000 to $74,999	18.8	7.4	10.5	19.0	21.2	23.5	21.5
$75,000 and over	23.5	3.4	4.5	14.4	22.1	25.7	46.1
Number of households (000's)	98,845	6,800	8,974	30,846	17,986	7,755	26,484
Median income	$42,038	$17,261	$21,737	$35,744	$44,149	$49,279	$69,804

Source: U.S. Bureau of the Census, *Statistical Abstract of the United States: 2001*, Washington, DC, 434.

Within the domain of occupational status, there has also been an increasing trend toward self-employment among business and professional people. Specifically, it appears that business executives and professionals who are self-employed or entrepreneurs are substantially more likely to be *very wealthy* than their counterparts who work for someone else.[8] This link between self-employment and higher incomes is consistent with the trend of increasing numbers of business school graduates seeking to work for themselves rather than going to work for a "big business."

Still further, it is also noteworthy to keep in mind that although the status of a particular occupation may change significantly over time, evidence suggests that when it comes to the status of some 40 occupations (studied between 1976 and 2000) a high degree of *status consistency* was found.[9] Specifically, certain occupations (e.g., U.S. Supreme Court justices and physicians) were consistently ranked high over the many years of the research, whereas other occupations (e.g., farmhands and taxi drivers) were consistently ranked low during the same period of time.

Education The level of a person's formal education is another commonly accepted approximation of social-class standing. Generally speaking, the more education a person has, the more likely it is that the person is well paid (or has a higher income) and has an admired or respected position (high occupational status).[10] Using U.S. census data, Table 11-7 supports the close relationship between educational attainment and amount of household income.

Income Individual or family income is another socioeconomic variable frequently used to approximate social-class standing. Researchers who favor income as a measure of social class use either *amount* or *source* of income. Table 11-8 illustrates the types of categories used for each of these income variables. Available research suggests that income works best in accounting for leisure consumption when measured in terms of ("engaging in" or "doing or not doing") a particular leisure activity (such as snow skiing, bowling, or playing basketball or golf).[11]

TABLE 11-8	Typical Categories Used for Assessing Amount or Source of Income	

AMOUNT OF INCOME	SOURCE OF INCOME
Under $25,000 per year	Public welfare
$25,000 to $49,999	Private financial assistance
$50,000 to $74,999	Wages (hourly)
$75,000 to $99,999	Salary (yearly)
$100,000 to $124,999	Profits or fees
$125,000 to $149,999	Earned wealth
$150,000 to $174,999	Inherited wealth, interest, dividends, royalties
$175,000 to $199,999	
$200,000 and over	

Although income is a popular estimate of social-class standing, not all consumer researchers agree that it is an appropriate index of social class. Some argue that a blue-collar automobile mechanic and a white-collar assistant bank manager may both earn $53,000 a year, yet because of (or as a reflection of) social-class differences, each will spend that income in a different way. How they decide to spend their incomes reflects different values. Within this context, it is the difference in values that is an important discriminant of social class between people, not the amount of income they earn.

Substantiating the importance of consumers' personal values, rather than amount of income, is the observation that affluence may be more a function of attitude or behavior than of income level.[12] These "adaptational affluent" consumers represent a broad segment who do not have the income needed to be considered affluent in today's society, yet they desire to have the best. They buy less but buy better quality, assigning priorities and gradually working their way toward having everything they want.

Other Variables Quality of neighborhood and dollar value of residence are rarely used as sole measures of social class. However, they are used informally to support or verify social-class membership assigned on the basis of occupational status or income.

Finally, possessions have been used by sociologists as an index of social class.[13] The best-known and most elaborate rating scheme for evaluating possessions is **Chapin's Social Status Scale,** which focuses on the presence of certain items of furniture and accessories in the living room (types of floor or floor covering, drapes, fireplace, library table, telephone, or bookcases) and the condition of the room (cleanliness, organization, or general atmosphere).[14] Conclusions are drawn about a family's social class on the basis of such observations. To illustrate how home decorations reflect social-class standing, lower-class families are likely to place their television sets in the living room and bedrooms, whereas middle- and upper-class families usually place their television sets in one or more of the following rooms: bedrooms, family room, or a media room (*but* **not** *in the living room*). The marketing implications of such insights suggest that advertisements for television sets targeted at lower-class consumers should show the set in a living room, whereas advertisements directed to middle- or upper-class consumers should show the set in a bedroom, a family room,

FIGURE 11-2

Targeting the Upper-Class Consumer
Courtesy of eBay™. eBay and the eBay logo are trademarks of eBay Inc.

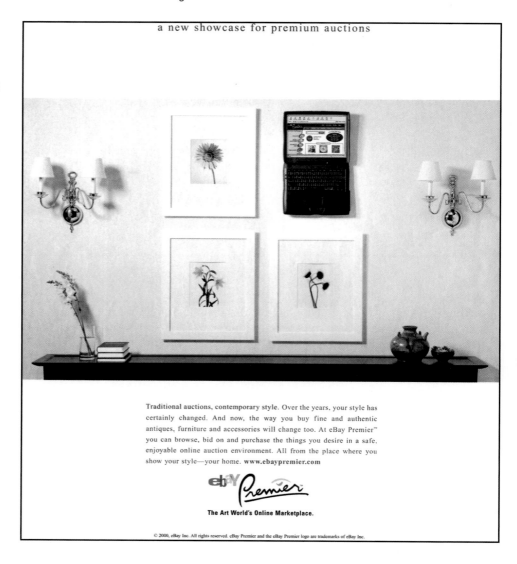

or a media room. Figure 11-2 presents an ad for eBay Premier (www.ebaypremier.com) that is targeting upper-class consumers seeking access to auctions featuring authentic antiques, furniture, and accessories.

Composite-Variable Indexes

Composite indexes systematically combine a number of socioeconomic factors to form one overall measure of social-class standing. Such indexes are of interest to consumer researchers because they may better reflect the complexity of social class than single-variable indexes. For instance, research exploring consumers' perceptions of mail and phone order shopping reveals that the *higher* the socioeconomic status (in terms of a composite of income, occupational status, and education), the more positive are the consumers' ratings of mail and phone order buying, relative to in-store shopping.[15] The same research also found that downscale consumers (a composite of lower scores on the three variables) were less positive toward magazine and catalog shopping and more positive toward in-store shopping than more upscale socioeconomic groupings. Armed with such information, retailers such as

Kmart, Wal-Mart, and Target that especially target *working-class* consumers would have a real challenge using direct-marketing catalogs and telephone-selling approaches. In contrast, retailers concentrating on upscale consumers, such as Neiman Marcus and Saks, have been especially effective in developing catalog programs targeted to specific segments of affluent or upscale consumers.

Two of the more important composite indexes are the **Index of Status Characteristics** and the **Socioeconomic Status Score:**

1. Index of Status Characteristics. *A classic composite measure of social class is Warner's Index of Status Characteristics (ISC).*[16] *The ISC is a weighted measure of the following socioeconomic variables: occupation, source of income (not amount of income), house type, and dwelling area (quality of neighborhood).*
2. Socioeconomic Status Scores. *The United States Bureau of the Census developed the Socioeconomic Status Score (SES), which combines three basic socioeconomic variables: occupation, family income, and educational attainment.*[17]

Lifestyle Profiles of the Social Classes

Consumer research has found evidence that within each of the social classes, there is a constellation of specific lifestyle factors (shared beliefs, attitudes, activities, and behaviors) that tends to distinguish the members of each class from the members of all other social classes.

To capture the lifestyle composition of the various social-class groupings, Table 11-9 presents a consolidated portrait, pieced together from numerous sources, of the members of the following six social classes: upper-upper class, lower-upper class, upper-middle class, lower-middle class, upper-lower class, and lower-lower class. Each of these profiles is only a generalized picture of the class. People in any class may possess values, attitudes, and behavioral patterns that are a hybrid of two or more classes.

CHINA: PURSUING A MIDDLE-CLASS LIFESTYLE

In recent years, established marketers from all over the world have singled out China as a highly desirable growth market for their brands. These marketers have been anxious to satisfy China's rapidly expanding urban middle class's appetite for consumer goods. Specifically, the wealthiest 20 percent of urban Chinese households (about 80 million people) constitutes a highly attractive market. These relatively affluent urban Chinese consumers are primarily composed of the two following segments: (1) "little rich"—those 15 percent with annual household income of about $3,200, and (2) "yuppies"—those 5 percent with annual household income of about $9,500.[18] Although household incomes between $3,200 and $9,500, on first glance, do not seem like much, this conclusion can be a real error. With small families and housing and other costs subsidized by the government, an urban Chinese family is able to have a relatively good lifestyle on a relatively small income. The "secret" is that a fairly large amount of a family's income is discretionary income (i.e., income that can be spent on a wide range of nonnecessities). Table 11-10 reveals more about the lifestyles of these two urban Chinese middle-class consumer groups, and Table 11-11 presents a comparison of their consumption patterns for selected products. Interestingly, the two middle-class segments tend to differ more in terms of their consumption patterns than in terms of their attitudes, lifestyles and media behavior.

TABLE 11-9	Social-Class Profiles

THE UPPER-UPPER CLASS—COUNTRY CLUB ESTABLISHMENT

- *Small number of well-established families*
- *Belong to best country clubs and sponsor major charity events*
- *Serve as trustees for local colleges and hospitals*
- *Prominent physicians and lawyers*
- *May be heads of major financial institutions, owners of major long-established firms*
- *Accustomed to wealth, so do not spend money conspicuously*

THE LOWER-UPPER CLASS—NEW WEALTH

- *Not quite accepted by the upper crust of society*
- *Represent "new money"*
- *Successful business executives*
- *Conspicuous users of their new wealth*

THE UPPER-MIDDLE CLASS—ACHIEVING PROFESSIONALS

- *Have neither family status nor unusual wealth*
- *Career oriented*
- *Young successful professionals, corporate managers, and business owners*
- *Most are college graduates, many with advanced degrees*
- *Active in professional, community, and social activities*
- *Have a keen interest in obtaining the "better things in life"*
- *Their homes serve as symbols of their achievements*
- *Consumption is often conspicuous*
- *Very child oriented*

THE LOWER-MIDDLE CLASS—FAITHFUL FOLLOWERS

- *Primarily nonmanagerial white-collar workers and highly paid blue-collar workers*
- *Want to achieve respectability and be accepted as good citizens*
- *Want their children to be well-behaved*
- *Tend to be churchgoers and are often involved in church-sponsored activities*
- *Prefer a neat and clean appearance and tend to avoid faddish or highly styled clothing*
- *Constitute a major market for do-it-yourself products*

THE UPPER-LOWER CLASS—SECURITY-MINDED MAJORITY

- *The largest social-class segment*
- *Solidly blue collar*
- *Strive for security (sometimes gained from union membership)*
- *View work as a means to "buy" enjoyment*
- *Want children to behave properly*
- *High wage earners in this group may spend impulsively*
- *Interested in items that enhance their leisure time (e.g., TV sets, hunting equipment)*
- *Husbands typically have a strong "macho" self-image*
- *Males are sports fans, heavy smokers, beer drinkers*

THE LOWER-LOWER CLASS—ROCK BOTTOM

- *Poorly educated, unskilled laborers*
- *Often out of work*
- *Children are often poorly treated*
- *Tend to live a day-to-day existence*

TABLE 11-10 Two Urban Socioeconomic Segments in China: Psychographic, Lifestyle Activities and Media Behavior

SEGMENTS/DIMENSIONS	LITTLE RICH	YUPPIES
CONSUMER ATTITUDES		
Work hard and get rich	43%	32%
Satisfaction with life	73%	80%
Live one's own life	37%	48%
Live a pure and honest life	10%	5%
Willing to pay for brands	43%	68%
Prefer foreign goods	28%	48%
LIFESTYLE ACTIVITIES		
Reading	88%	80%
Going to movies	48%	51%
Going to parks	45%	60%
Domestic travel	53%	68%
Karaoke bar	48%	50%
MEDIA USE (MINUTES)		
Television time	143	146
Radio time	41	42
Newspaper time	52	60
Magazine time	67	61

Note: Based on media used the previous day and the amount of time each medium was used.
Source: Geng Cui and Qiming Liu, "Executive Insights: Emerging Market Segments in a Transitional Economy: A Study of Urban Consumers in China," Journal of International Marketing, 9, no. 1, 2001, 91. Reprinted with permission.

TABLE 11-11 Two Urban Socioeconomic Segments in China: Selective Consumption Patterns

SEGMENTS/PRODUCTS	LITTLE RICH	YUPPIES
Color TV	94%	100%
Microwave oven	12%	22%
Air conditioner	19%	47%
Compact disc player	32%	55%
Mobile telephone	12%	33%
Computer	5%	14%
Private car	5%	12%
Tea	92%	92%
Ice cream	34%	37%
Soft drinks	47%	60%
Beer	50%	72%
Credit card	11%	40%
Life insurance	42%	41%

Note: Based on media used the previous day and the amount of time each medium was used.
Source: Geng Cui and Qiming Liu, "Executive Insights: Emerging Market Segments in a Transitional Economy: A Study of Urban Consumers in China," Journal of International Marketing, 9, no. 1, 2001, 94. Reprinted with permission.

Social-Class Mobility

Social-class membership in the United States is not as hard and fixed as it is in some other countries and cultures. Although individuals can move either up or down in social-class standing from the class position held by their parents, Americans have primarily thought in terms of **upward mobility** because of the availability of free education and opportunities for self-development and self-advancement. Indeed, the classic Horatio Alger tale of a penniless young orphan who managed to achieve great success in business and in life is depicted over and over again in American novels, movies, and television shows. Today many young men and women with ambition to get ahead dream of going to college and eventually starting their own successful businesses.

Because upward mobility has commonly been attainable in American society, the higher social classes often become reference groups for ambitious men and women of lower social status. Familiar examples of upward mobility are the new management trainee who strives to dress like the boss; the middle manager who aspires to belong to the status country club; or the graduate of a municipal college who wants to send his daughter to Princeton. The ad for The Peninsula Group of hotels in Figure 11-3 is targeted to successful upwardly mobile individuals striving to express their personal vision. As part of the advertisement, supporting copy makes the point that this is a small group of luxury hotels that are uniquely able to fuse different cultures and provide its clients with "peace of mind."

Recognizing that individuals often aspire to the lifestyle and possessions enjoyed by members of a higher social class, marketers frequently incorporate the symbols of higher-class membership, both as products and props in advertisements targeted to lower social-class audiences. For example, ads often present or display marketers' products within an upper-class setting: The products are displayed on a table in front of a fireplace with a beautiful mantle (a board game), shown on the desk of an elegantly appointed executive office (a new desktop computer), shown being consumed by fashionably (European) dressed models (a domestic wine), shown appearing on an exquisitely set dining room table (a bottle of jam), and shown parked outside of a famous exclusive restaurant (a new model automobile). Sometimes a more direct appeal to consumers' sense of having products that are normally restricted to members of other social classes is an affective message. For instance, if a direct marketer of consumer electronics were to promote a top-of-the-line flat-panel monitor (such as a high-end Sony 18-inch LCD display), usually purchased by business executives, as "now it's your turn to have what business executives have enjoyed" (it's been marked down about 50 percent of original price), this would be a marketing message that encourages household consumers to have a "dream monitor" on their desks.

Another characteristic of social-class mobility is that products and services traditionally within the realm of one social class may filter down to lower social classes. For instance, plastic surgery was once affordable only for movie stars and other wealthy consumers. Today, however, consumers of all economic strata undergo cosmetic procedures.

SOME SIGNS OF DOWNWARD MOBILITY

Although the United States is frequently associated with *upward mobility,* because it was the "rule" for much of its history that each generation within a family tended

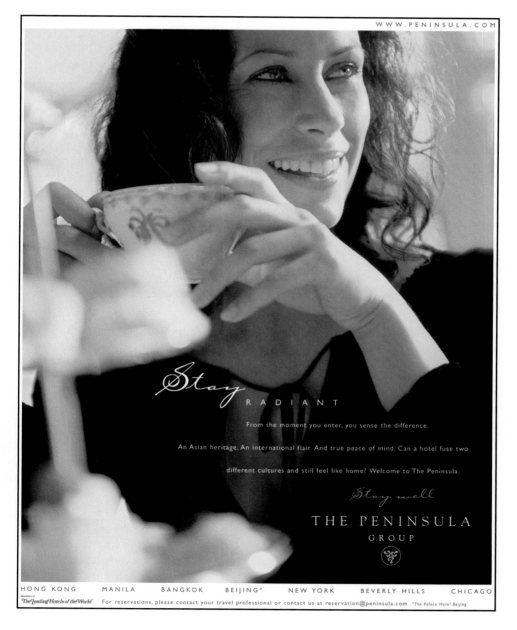

FIGURE 11-3

Appealing to Upward
Mobility
Courtesy of The Peninsula
Group.

to "do better" than the last generation, there now are signs of some **downward mobility.** Social commentators have suggested that some young adults (such as members of the X-Generation described in Chapter 13) are not only likely to find it difficult to "do better" than their successful parents (e.g., to get better jobs, own homes, have more disposable income, and have more savings) but also may *not* even do as well as their parents.

There is some evidence of such a slide in social-class mobility. Specifically, researchers have found that the odds that young men's income will reach middle-class levels by the time they reach their thirtieth birthday have been slowly declining.[19] This regressive pattern holds true, regardless of race, parents' income, and young persons' educational level.

Geodemographic Clustering

In recent years, traditional social-class measures have been enhanced by linking consumer-related geographic and socioeconomic data to create more powerful **geodemographic clusters.** The underlying rationale for geodemographic clustering is that "birds of a feather flock together."

One of the most popular clustering services is **PRIZM** (www.claritas.com), which identifies a variety of socioeconomic and demographic factors (education, income, occupation, family life cycle, ethnicity, housing, and urbanization) drawn from U.S. census data. This material is combined with survey and panel data on actual consumer behavior (e.g., product purchase and usage, mail-order buying, and media-exposure habits) to locate concentrations of consumers with similar characteristics. Experts point to the benefits of marketing to consumer clusters:[20]

> *America has become a nation of such diversity that the clusters are essential to finding people most interested in your products and services. For consumers, the value of clusters is that they don't have to wade through a lot of junk mail that misses the target. What's the point of an apartment dweller getting a pitch for buying a lawn mower?*

PRIZM assigns every one of the microneighborhoods in the United States (zip code + 4 areas) to one of 62 PRIZM clusters, which can be further collapsed into 15 groups (S1 through R3). Table 11-12 shows seven examples of PRIZM cluster segments drawn from specific socioeconomic categories. Marketers can superimpose these geodemographic clusters onto a host of product and service usage data, media-exposure data, and lifestyle data (such as VALS, discussed in Chapter 5) to create a sharp, refined picture of their target markets. To illustrate the usefulness of such information, Table 11-13 presents an overview profile of the "Urban Gold Coast" PRIZM cluster.

The Affluent Consumer

Affluent households constitute an especially attractive target segment because its members have incomes that provide them with a disproportionately larger share of all discretionary income—the "extras" that allow the purchase of luxury cruises, foreign sports cars, time-sharing ski-resort condos, fine jewelry, and ready access to home PCs, laptops, and surfing on the Internet. It has also been pointed out there is a strong positive relationship between health and economic status—that is, "the healthiest people are those who are economically advantaged" and "poverty is bad for you."[21]

The wealth of Americans grew dramatically during the 1990s partially due to the longest bull market in U.S. history. By the year 2000, the total personal wealth in America was more than $25 trillion, with more than 7 million households having a net worth of over $1 million, and 600,000 households having a net worth of over $5 million.[22] The affluent market is increasingly attracting marketers. Whirlpool Corporation, for example, the leading home appliance manufacturer in the United States, realizes that as more and more consumers own household appliances, it can no longer rely on volume to increase profits. So the firm now focuses on upscale products that are so profitable they can sell fewer appliances and still make money.

TABLE 11-12 Sample PRIZM Cluster Segments Drawn from All 62 Clusters to Reflect a Range of Socioeconomic Groups

GROUP CODES	CLUSTER NUMBER	CLUSTER NICKNAME/ DESCRIPTION	PERCENT OF U.S. HOUSEHOLDS	SOCIOECONOMIC CATEGORY/INCOME RANGE OF HEAD OF HOUSEHOLD	KEY EDUCATION LEVEL	KEY OCCUPATIONAL LEVEL	PREDOMINANT AGE RANGE(S)
S1 Elite Suburbs (Suburban)	01	Blue Blood Estates/Privileged superrich families	1.20%	Elite (1)[a]	College grad	White collar	45–64
	04	Pools & Patios/ Established empty nesters	1.80%	Affluent (9)	College grad	White collar	45+
U1 Urban Uptown (Urban)	10	Bohemian Mix/ Bohemian singles and couples	1.50%	Middle (17)	College grad	White collar	25–44
S2 The Affluentials (Suburban)	22	Blue-Chip Blues/ Upscale blue-collar families	2.00%	Upper middle (30)	High school/ Some college	White collar/ Blue collar	35–64
C2 2nd City Centers (Urban)	34	Starter Families/ Young middle-class families	1.50%	Middle (36)	High school/ Some college	Blue collar	Under 18, 25–34
T3 Working Towns (Urban)	54	Mines & Mills/ Older families, mine and mill towns	2.10%	Poor (56)	Less than high school/ High school	Blue collar	65+
R3 Rustic Living (Rural)	62	Hard Scrabble/ Families in poor isolated areas	2.0%	Poor (58)	Less than high school/High school	Blue collar/ Farming	Under 18, 55+

[a]Socioeconomic rank, for example, "(1)" = ranked first out of 62 clusters, and "(58)" = ranked 58 out of 62 clusters.
Source: © 2000, Claritas Inc. PRIZM and Claritas are registered trademarks of Claritas, Inc. The 62 PRIZM cluster nicknames ("Blue Blood Estates," "Big Sky Families," "Country Squires," etc.) are trademarks of Claritas, Inc.

TABLE 11-13	A Profile of PRIZM Cluster: "Urban Gold Coast" (Cluster 06)

SOCIOECONOMIC FACTORS

Percent of U.S. households	0.60%
Predominant age range	Mixed
Socioeconomic group	Affluent
Demographic caption	Professional urban singles and couples
Housing type	Renters, multiunit housing
Education	College graduates
Occupation	White collar
Race/Ethnicity	White, Asian

LIFESTYLE

Purchased 10+ audio books last year
Use Web TV online
Listed to golden oldies
Watch *Politically Incorrect*
Read *New York Magazine*

Source: © 2000, Claritas Inc. PRIZM and Claritas are registered trademarks of Claritas, Inc. The 62 PRIZM cluster nicknames are trademarks of Claritas, Inc.

Its Duet line, a $2,200 washer-dryer set, sold so well in the first six months after its introduction that Whirlpool had to double its sales projections.[23]

For over 25 years, Mendelsohn Media Research has conducted an annual study of the **affluent market** (currently defined in terms of three affluent segments: those with household incomes of $75,000 to $99,999 per year—the "least affluent," those with incomes of $100,000 to $199,999 per year—the "medium affluent," and those with incomes of $200,000 or more per year—the "most affluent"). Although it consists of only 25 percent of all households, this upscale market segment consumed more wine (2.4 drinks per week per adult), took more domestic airline flights (7.4 flights annually per adult), owned more vehicles (2.5 per household), and held more securities ($224,000 per household) than nonaffluent households. The average household income for these consumers is $139,000, and 62 percent of this group who are employed in either a professional or managerial capacity.[24] Figure 11-4 presents additional information as to average household expenditures for selected purchases for the three affluent segments. The results reveal that although the first two segments of affluent consumers certainly spend ample amounts purchasing a wide variety of products, in most cases the "most affluent" purchasers spend significantly more. For instance, when it comes to desktop, laptop, and handheld computers, the "least affluent" spent $1,512 and the "medium affluent" spent $1,816, whereas the "most affluent" spent $2,911. Substantiating this expenditure pattern, Forrester Research, which specializes in technology-related market research, reports that affluent customers have an affinity for technology, especially when it comes to the task of managing their finances.[25] Figure 11-5 presents some further insights about affluent consumers in terms of a comparison of the sports participation of the three

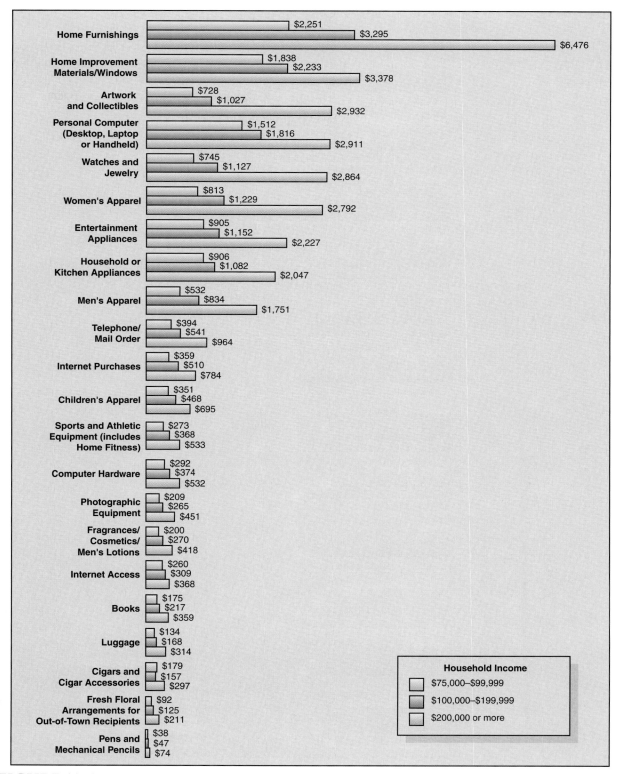

FIGURE 11-4

Three Segments of Affluent Consumers' Average Household Expenditures (among purchasing households)
Source: 2002 Mendelsohn Affluent Survey (New York: Mendelsohn Media Research, Inc., 2002), 11.

FIGURE 11-5

Affluent Consumers'
Participation in
Selected Sports (num-
ber of days in past year,
indexed to each of the
three income segments)
Source: 2002 Mendelsohn
Affluent Survey (New York:
Mendelsohn Media Research,
Inc., 2002).

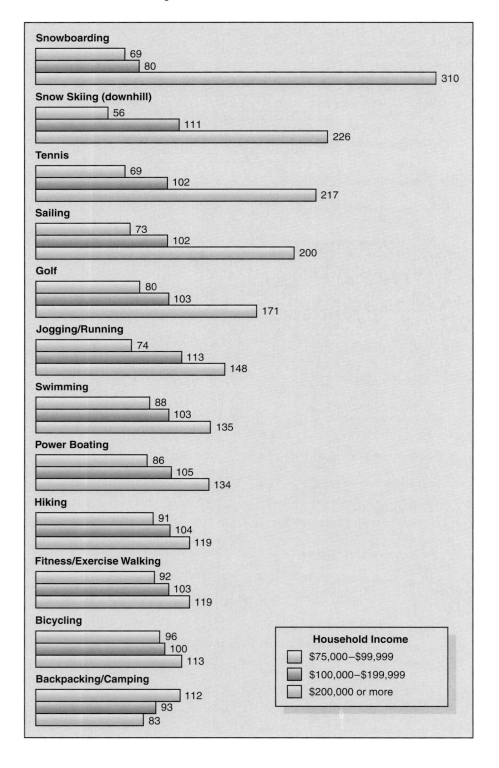

segments of affluent consumers. The results reveal that the "most affluent" are more likely than members of the two other affluent consumer segments to participate in a sampling of sports.[26] An examination of these two figures explains why marketers are eager to target affluent consumers.

Still further, a growing subcategory of the affluent are *millionaires.* Currently, more than 3 million U.S. households have a net worth of more than $1 million.[27] Contrary to common stereotypes, these millionaires are quite similar to nonmillionaires. They are typically first generation wealthy, often working for themselves in "ordinary" nonglamour businesses. They work hard and frequently live in nonpretentious homes, often next door to nonmillionaires.

In the United Kingdom, the affluent are often empty nesters with high disposable incomes and small or paid-off mortgages. They have an abundance of money, but are time poor and are interested in improving the quality of their lives with overseas vacations and sports cars.[28] Moreover, researchers who have examined affluent consumers, in both the United Kingdom and United States, have found that they are likely to focus on saving or reducing time and effort and, not unsurprisingly, are willing to pay for many things that provide such convenience.[29]

THE MEDIA EXPOSURE OF THE AFFLUENT CONSUMER

As might be expected, the media habits of the affluent differ from those of the general population.[30] For example, those households earning more than $75,000 a year view less TV per day than less affluent households. A profile of the media habits of $75,000-plus affluent adult householders shows they read 6.1 different publications; they listen to 12.5 hours of weekday radio and watch 24.7 hours of TV per week; and 92 percent of them subscribe to cable TV. Magazines that cater to the tastes and interests of the affluent include *Architectural Digest, Condé Nast Traveler, Gourmet, Southern Accents,* and *Town & Country.* Table 11-14 presents a selection of magazines and reveals the median household incomes of their readers who have incomes of $75,000 or more. (See Table 11-5 for a more general selection of print media and corresponding median incomes.)

SEGMENTING THE AFFLUENT MARKET

The affluent market is not one single market. Contrary to popular stereotypes, the wealth in America is not found only behind "the tall, cloistered walls of suburban country clubs."[31] Wealth is spread among niches, including Asian immigrants, single women, and young Cuban Americans, to name a few.

Because not all affluent consumers share the same lifestyles (i.e., activities, interests, and opinions), various marketers have tried to isolate meaningful segments of the affluent market. One scheme, for example, has divided the affluent into two groups—the *upbeat enjoyers* who live for today and the *financial positives* who are conservative and look for value. Still further, it has been commented that "most people who have money are fairly conservative, and have accumulated wealth because they are very good savers."[32]

To assist the many marketers interested in reaching subsegments of the affluent market, Mediamark Research, Inc. (MRI) has developed the following affluent market-segmentation schema for the *Upper Deck* consumers (defined as the top 10 percent of households in terms of income):[33]

1. Well-feathered nests: *Households that have at least one high-income earner and children present (38% of the Upper Deck).*

| TABLE 11-14 | Affluent Readers' ($75,000+ Median Household Income) for Selected Publications |

NEWSPAPER/MAGAZINE	MEDIAN HOUSEHOLD INCOME ($)
Allure	$112,100
Architectural Digest	$124,300
Better Homes and Gardens	$108,200
Boating	$118,400
Bon Appétit	$125,300
Business Week	$126,400
Cigar Aficionado	$126,000
Condé Nast Traveler	$135,200
Elle	$115,300
Esquire	$120,800
Fortune	$135,600
Golf Magazine	$116,900
Gourmet	$127,000
GQ Gentlemen's Quarterly	$121,000
House & Garden	$108,500
Martha Stewart Living	$112,600
National Geographic	$111,900
Newsweek	$114,100
Self	$109,800
Southern Accents	$124,400
Town & Country	$120,200
Travel & Leisure	$123,400
U.S. News & World Report	$112,000
Vanity Fair	$123,500
Vogue	$117,500
W	$138,900

Source: From 2002 Mendelsohn Affluent Survey (New York: Mendelsohn Media Research, Inc.). Reprinted by permission.

2. No strings attached: *Households that have at least one high-income earner and no children (35% of the Upper Deck).*
3. Nanny's in charge: *Households that have two or more earners, none earning high incomes, and children present (9% of the Upper Deck).*
4. Two careers: *Households that have two or more earners, neither earning high incomes, and no children present (11% of the Upper Deck).*
5. The good life: *Households that have a high degree of affluence with no person employed or with the head of household not employed (7% of the Upper Deck).*

Armed with such affluent lifestyle segments, MRI provides subscribing firms with profiles of users of a variety of goods and services frequently targeted to the affluent consumer (e.g., domestic and foreign travel, leisure clothing, lawn care services, rental cars, and various types of recreational activities). For instance, in terms of recreation, the well-feathered nester can be found on the tennis court, the good lifer may be playing golf, while the two-career couple may be off sailing.[34]

With few local marketers vying for their business, the *rural affluent* represent an untapped (and somewhat difficult to pinpoint) subsegment of the affluent market. The rural affluent fall into four categories:[35]

1. Suburban transplants: *Those who move to the country but still commute to a high-paying urban job.*
2. Equity-rich suburban expatriates: *Urbanites who sell their homes for a huge profit, buy a far less expensive home in a small town, and live off the difference.*
3. City folks with country homes: *Wealthy snowbirds and vacationers who spend winters or summers in scenic rural areas, especially mountainous and coastal areas.*
4. Wealthy landowners: *Wealthy farmers and other natives who make a comfortable living off the land.*

Middle-Class Consumers

It is not easy to define the boundaries of what is meant by "middle class." Although the U.S. Bureau of the Census does *not* have a definition of middle class, there have nevertheless been many attempts to define it. For instance, "middle market" has been defined as the "middle" 50 percent of household incomes—that is, about 49 million households earning between $25,000 and $75,000.[36] Realistically, the upper boundary of the middle-class household is likely to be rapidly approaching $85,000 (which is about 52 percent of all U.S. households). Still another definition of "middle class" envisions households composed of college-educated adults, who in some way use computers to make a living, are involved in their children's education, and are confident that they can maintain the quality of their family's life.[37]

For many marketers "middle class" can be thought of as including households that range from lower-middle to middle-middle class in terms of some acceptable variable or combination of variables (e.g., income, education, and/or occupation). This view of middle class does *not* include the upper-middle class, which over the years has increasingly been treated as a segment of affluent consumers.

Adding to the challenge of defining "middle class" is the reality that luxury and technological products have been becoming more affordable for more consumers (often because of the introduction of near-luxury models by major luxury-brand firms and/or the downward price trend for many technology products) and, therefore, more middle-class consumers have access to products and brands that where once considered beyond their reach.[38] Table 11-15 shows the historical trend with respect to the average number of hours of labor needed to purchase specific consumer products. For instance, when it was first introduced, a microwave oven required over 200 hours of labor to be able to purchase. Today, its cost is equal to about 15 hours of work.

Still further, the dynamic nature of social class in the United States has been working against the middle class. In particular, there is mounting evidence that the middle-class American is slowly disappearing. It appears that middle-class consumers are increasingly moving upstream to the ranks of the upper-middle class, and another smaller segment is losing ground and slipping backward to the ranks of the working class—creating a distribution that looks like an "hourglass."[39]

Although the middle class has been shrinking in the United States, there has been a fairly rapid increase in the number of middle-class consumers in selective

TABLE 11-15	Products Show an Inclination to Move from New Luxury to Wide-Mass Ownership

Average number of hours' labor needed to purchase various products

YEAR	PRODUCT	EARLY LABOR COST	1970 LABOR COST	1997 LABOR COST
1908	Automobile	4,696	1,397	1,365
1915	Refrigerator	3,162	112	68
1915	Long-distance call	90	0.40	0.03
1917	Movie ticket	0.48	0.47	0.32
1919	Air travel (1,000 miles)	221	18	11
1919	Chicken, 3-lb fryer	2.6	0.40	0.20
1947	Microwave oven	2,467	176	15
1954	Color television	562	174	23
1971	Soft contact lenses	95	n/a	4
1972	VCR	365	n/a	15
1984	Cellular phone	456	n/a	9
1984	Computer (millions of instructions per minute)	57	n/a	0.40

Source: Federal Reserve Bank of Dallas, from W. Michael Cox, "The Low Cost of Living, *The Voluntarist,* October 1999, 3.

Asian and Eastern European countries. For example, within the past few years, Tropicana and other fruit juice companies have been successfully positioning their products to the expanding middle-class Indian consumers who are seeking more health-oriented products.[40] Similarly, General Motors is now manufacturing automobiles in China, hoping that China's growing middle class will be attracted to purchasing its vehicles.

The Working Class and Other Nonaffluent Consumers

Although many advertisers would prefer to show their products as part of an affluent lifestyle, working-class or blue-collar people represent a vast group of consumers that marketers cannot ignore. In fact, households earning $34,000 or less control more than 30 percent of the total income in the United States. Lower-income, or **downscale consumers** (frequently defined as having household incomes of $30,000 or less) may actually be more brand loyal than wealthier consumers, because they can not afford to make mistakes by switching to unfamiliar brands.

Understanding the importance of speaking to (not *at*) the downscale consumers, companies such as RC Cola, MasterCard, and McDonald's target "average Joes" (and Janes) with ads reflecting the modest lifestyles of some of their customers.[41] For instance, marketers need to be sensitive to the reality that downscale consumers often spend a higher percentage of their available incomes on food than do their middle-class counterparts. Moreover, food is a particularly important purchase area for low-income consumers because it represents an area of "indulgence." For this reason, they periodically trade-up the foods they purchase — especially favorite ethnic and natural foods — "where taste and authenticity matter."[42]

The Arrival of the "Techno-Class"

The degree of literacy, familiarity, and competency with technology, especially computers and the Internet, appears to be a new basis for a kind of "class standing," or status or prestige. Those who are unfamiliar with or lack computer skills are being referred to as "technologically underclassed."[43] Educators, business leaders, and government officials have warned that the inability to adequately use technology is negatively impacting lifestyles and the quality of life of those who are not computer literate.

Not wanting to see their children left out of the "sweep of computer technology," parents in all social-class groupings are seeking out early computer exposure for their children. Either based on their positive experiences using computers (or possibly on fears produced as result of a lack of personal computer experience), parents sense that an understanding of computers is a necessary tool of competitive achievement and success. At the other end of the life and age spectrum, even 55-year-old professionals, who were initially reluctant to "learn computers," are now seeking personal computer training—they no longer want to be left out, nor do they want to be further embarrassed by having to admit that they "don't know computers."

Consumers throughout the world have come to believe that it is critical to acquire a functional understanding of computers in order to ensure that they do not become obsolete or hinder themselves socially or professionally. In this sense, there is a technological class structure that centers around the amount of computer skills that one possesses. It appears that those without necessary computer skills will increasingly find themselves to be "underclassed" and "disadvantaged." As *Wired* magazine wrote when it began publishing in 1993, "The Digital Revolution is whipping through our lives like a Bengali typhoon."[44]

THE GEEK GETS STATUS

The importance of the computer and the prominent role it now plays in our lives has resulted in somewhat of a reversal of fortune, in that the "geek" is now often viewed by his or her peers as "friendly and fun." The increasingly positive image of geeks has made them and their lifestyles the target of marketers' messages designed to appeal to their great appetite for novel technological products (see Figure 11-6).

Indeed, according to a recent British National Opinion Poll (NOP) of 7- to 16-year-olds, "Computer geeks are now the coolest kids in class."[45] The poll found that the archetypical geek is most typically a 14- to 16-year-old boy who is the family computer expert, and he is willing to teach his parents, siblings, and teachers about computers. Interestingly, in an environment where children naturally take to computers, it is often the parents who find themselves technologically disenfranchised. To remedy this situation, some schools are offering classes to bring parents up to speed in the use of computers.[46]

Selected Consumer Behavior Applications of Social Class

Social-class profiles provide a broad picture of the values, attitudes, and behavior that distinguish the members of various social classes. This section focuses on specific consumer research that relates social class to the development of marketing strategy.

FIGURE 11-6

Appealing to the Geek-Oriented Consumer
Courtesy of General Motors.

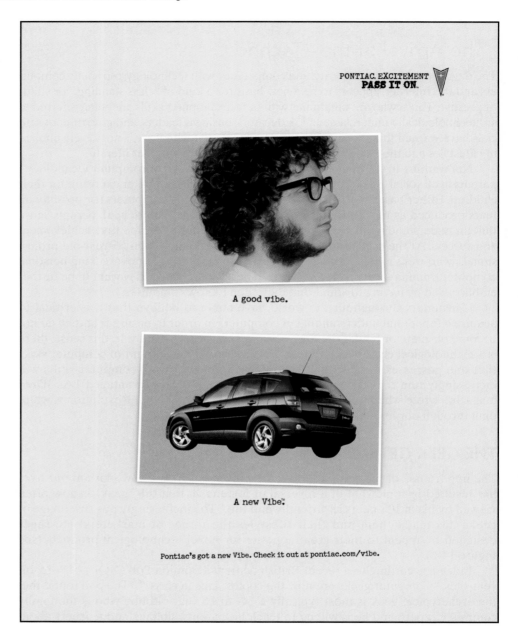

PONTIAC. EXCITEMENT
PASS IT ON.

A good vibe.

A new Vibe.

Pontiac's got a new Vibe. Check it out at pontiac.com/vibe.

CLOTHING, FASHION, AND SHOPPING

A Greek philosopher once said, "Know, first, who you are; and then adorn yourself accordingly."[47] This bit of wisdom is relevant to clothing marketers today, because most people dress to fit their self-image, which includes their perceptions of their own social-class membership. However, for many consumers, the notion of "keeping up with the Joneses" (i.e., trying to be like one's neighbors) has been replaced by looking to more upscale reference groups that they would like to emulate (most often, people earning substantially more than they do).

Members of specific social classes differ in terms of what they consider fashionable or in good taste. For instance, lower-middle-class consumers have a strong preference for T-shirts, caps, and other clothing that offer an *external point of identification,* such as the name of an admired person or group (the Seattle Mariners), a respected company or brand name (Budweiser), or a valued trademark (Tommy Hilfiger). These consumers are prime targets for licensed goods (with well-known logos). In contrast, upper-class consumers are likely to buy clothing that is free from such supporting associations. Upper-class consumers also seek clothing with a more subtle look, such as the kind of sportswear found in an L.L. Bean, Land's End, or Talbots catalog, rather than designer jeans.

Social class is also an important variable in determining where a consumer shops. People tend to avoid stores that have the image of appealing to a social class very different from their own. In the past, some mass merchandisers who tried to appeal to a higher class of consumers found themselves alienating their traditional customers. This implies that retailers should pay attention to the social class of their customer base and the social class of their store appeal to ensure that they send the appropriate message through advertising. For instance, Gap has been rapidly rolling out the Old Navy clothing stores in an effort to attract working-class families who usually purchased their casual and active wear clothing from general merchandise retailers such as Kmart, Wal-Mart, or Target. For Gap, trading down to the lower-income consumer with Old Navy has resulted in bigger sales, more leverage with suppliers, and increased traffic volume. It let Gap create a "knock-off" of itself before anybody else got the chance.[48] However, in creating a lower-price alternative to itself, Gap has also tended to cannibalize itself—shifting loyal Gap customers to the Old Navy outlets. Different department stores also target different social-class consumers. For example, Neiman Marcus and Nordstrom target upscale consumers, whereas JCPenney and Dillards are appealing to middle-class shoppers, and Kmart and Wal-Mart tend to target more of a working-class customer.

In exploring the social-class image or perception of retailers, researchers have discovered that consumers rate shirts purchased at Nordstrom, for example, to have higher status than shirts sold at Kmart.[49] In another study examining the social-class perceptions of five retail stores among whites, Korean Americans, and African Americans, researchers found that both whites and Koreans perceived JCPenney to be more lower-middle class in its appeal than did African American consumers.[50] Moreover, Korean respondents imagined Dillards, Nordstrom, and Macy's to each be in a lower social-class position than the social-class perceptions of whites and African American consumers. All three subcultural groups, however, had a similar social-class image of Wal-Mart—that is, as a "lower-middle" or "upper-lower" class store. Given that consumers' social-class perceptions of clothing brands and retail stores' prestige may impact their choices, researchers have developed a 19-item instrument (the PRE-CON scale) to gauge the following underlying factors of consumer preference: brand, quality, status, fashion involvement, and store atmosphere (see Table 11-16).[51]

THE PURSUIT OF LEISURE

Social-class membership is also closely related to the choice of recreational and leisure-time activities. For instance, upper-class consumers are likely to attend the theater and concerts, to play bridge, and to attend college football games. Lower-class consumers tend to be avid television watchers and fishing enthusiasts, and they enjoy drive-in movies and baseball games. Furthermore, the lower-class consumer spends more time on commercial types of activities (bowling, playing pool or billiards, or visiting taverns) and craft activities (model building, painting, and woodworking projects) rather than cerebral activities (reading, visiting museums). In any case, whether we are describing middle-class or working-class consumers, there

TABLE 11-16	The PRECON Scale for Measuring Clothing Preferences and Store Prestige
Brand	I consider the brand name when purchasing clothing for myself.
	I will pay a higher price for clothing that is made by a popular designer or manufacturer.
	I look my best when wearing brand-name clothing.
	Clothing made by a well-known designer or manufacturer is worth more money.
Quality	I prefer to shop at stores that carry high-quality merchandise.
	I usually buy high-quality clothing.
	When I buy clothes for others or as a gift, I buy clothes of superior quality.
Status	It is important to shop in the same clothing stores as my friends.
	Sometimes I would like to know where important people buy their clothes.
	I like to shop in the same clothing stores as people I admire.
	I often ask friends where they buy their clothes.
Fashion Involvement	Planning and selecting my wardrobe can be included among my favorite activities.
	I enjoy clothes as much as some people enjoy books, records, and movies.
	If I were to suddenly receive more money than I have now, I would spend it on clothes.
	I like to shop for clothes.
Store Atmosphere	It is important to me that a clothing store have a warm, inviting atmosphere.
	It is important to me that the clothing store I shop in has great service.
	Personal service is important to me when buying clothes.
	I shop at stores that have artistic-looking displays.

Source: Dawn R. Deeter-Schmelz, Jesse N. Moore, and Daniel J. Goebel, "Prestige Clothing Shopping by Consumers: A Confirmatory Assessment and Refinement of the PRECON Scale with Managerial Implications," *Journal of Marketing Theory and Practice,* Fall 2000, 51.

appears to be a trend toward more spending on "experiences" that bring the family together (family vacations or activities) and less spending on "things."[52]

Over the past decade or so, however, a number of changes are increasingly being observed that point to a further blurring of social-class lines with regard to leisure interests, especially with regard to arts and media preference. More specifically, only with the increased numbers of the suburban middle-class viewers could wrestling have become one of cable TV's most popular programming areas. Similarly, the presumedly sophisticated consumers who read magazines such as *The New Yorker* also like to attend theme parks and shoot billiards.[53] Figure 11-7 presents these and other preferences in terms of a perceptual map of 100 arts, media, and leisure pursuits.

SAVING, SPENDING, AND CREDIT

Saving, spending, and credit card usage all seem to be related to social-class standing. Upper-class consumers are more future oriented and confident of their financial acumen; they are more willing to invest in insurance, stocks, and real estate. In comparison, lower-class consumers are generally more concerned with immediate gratification; when they do save, they are primarily interested in safety and security. Therefore, it is not surprising that when it comes to bank credit card usage, members of the lower social classes tend to use their bank credit cards for installment purchases, whereas members of the upper social classes pay their credit card bills in full each month. In other words, lower-class purchasers tend to use their credit cards to "buy now and pay later" for things they might not otherwise be able to afford, whereas upper-class purchasers use their credit cards as a convenient substitute for cash.

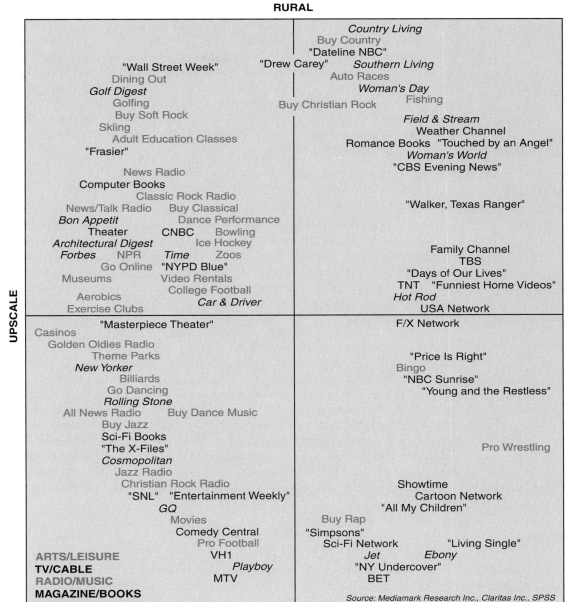

RURAL

Country Living
Buy Country
"Dateline NBC"
"Drew Carey"   *Southern Living*
Auto Races
Woman's Day
Buy Christian Rock   Fishing

"Wall Street Week"
Dining Out
Golf Digest
Golfing
Buy Soft Rock
Skiing
Adult Education Classes
"Frasier"

Field & Stream
Weather Channel
Romance Books "Touched by an Angel"
Woman's World
"CBS Evening News"

News Radio
Computer Books
Classic Rock Radio
News/Talk Radio   Buy Classical
Bon Appetit   Dance Performance
Theater   CNBC   Bowling
Architectural Digest   Ice Hockey
Forbes   NPR   *Time*   Zoos
Go Online   "NYPD Blue"
Museums   Video Rentals
Aerobics   College Football
Exercise Clubs   *Car & Driver*

"Walker, Texas Ranger"

Family Channel
TBS
"Days of Our Lives"
TNT   "Funniest Home Videos"
Hot Rod
USA Network

"Masterpiece Theater"   F/X Network
Casinos
Golden Oldies Radio
Theme Parks   "Price Is Right"
New Yorker   Bingo
Billiards   "NBC Sunrise"
Go Dancing   "Young and the Restless"
Rolling Stone
All News Radio   Buy Dance Music
Buy Jazz
Sci-Fi Books
"The X-Files"   Pro Wrestling
Cosmopolitan
Jazz Radio
Christian Rock Radio   Showtime
"SNL"   "Entertainment Weekly"   Cartoon Network
GQ   "All My Children"
Movies   Buy Rap
Comedy Central   "Simpsons"
Pro Football   Sci-Fi Network   "Living Single"
ARTS/LEISURE   VH1   *Jet*   *Ebony*
TV/CABLE   *Playboy*   "NY Undercover"
RADIO/MUSIC   MTV   BET
MAGAZINE/BOOKS

Source: Mediamark Research Inc., Claritas Inc., SPSS

URBAN

The computer-generated preference space above, based on the preferences of Americans for 100 arts, media, and leisure pursuits, reveals omnivorous culture buffs among consumers who are upscale, downscale, urban, or rural.

UPSCALE   **DOWNSCALE**

FIGURE 11-7

Preferences of Americans for 100 Arts, Media, and Leisure Pursuits
Source: Michael J. Weiss, Morris B. Holbrook, and John Habich, "Death of the Arts Snob?" *American Demographics,* June 2001, 44. All rights reserved. Reprinted by permission.

SOCIAL CLASS AND COMMUNICATION

Social-class groupings differ in terms of their media habits and in how they transmit and receive communications. Knowledge of these differences is invaluable to marketers who segment their markets on the basis of social class.

When it comes to describing their world, lower-class consumers tend to portray it in rather personal and concrete terms, whereas middle-class consumers are able to describe their experiences from a number of different perspectives. A simple example illustrates that members of different social classes tend to see the world differently. The following responses to a question asking where the respondent usually purchases gasoline were received:

> *Upper-middle-class answer: At Mobil or Shell.*
> *Lower-middle-class answer: At the station on Main and Fifth Street.*
> *Lower-class answer: At Ed's.*

Such variations in response indicate that middle-class consumers have a broader or more general view of the world, while lower-class consumers tend to have a narrow or personal view—seeing the world through their own immediate experiences.

Regional differences in terminology, choice of words and phrases, and patterns of usage also tend to increase as we move down the social-class ladder. Therefore, in creating messages targeted to the lower classes, marketers try to word advertisements to reflect particular regional preferences that exist (e.g., "soda" is "pop" in the Midwest).

Selective exposure to various types of mass media differs by social class. In the selection of specific television programs and program types, higher-social-class members tend to prefer current events and drama, whereas lower-class individuals tend to prefer soap operas, quiz shows, and situation comedies. Higher-class consumers tend to have greater exposure to magazines and newspapers than do their lower-class counterparts. Lower-class consumers are likely to have greater exposure to publications that dramatize romance and the lifestyles of movie and television celebrities. For example, magazines such as *True Story* appeal heavily to blue-collar or working-class women, who enjoy reading about the problems, fame, and fortunes of others. Middle-class consumers are more likely to read a newspaper and to prefer movies and late-night programs than their lower-class counterparts.[54]

Summary

Social stratification, the division of members of a society into a hierarchy of distinct social classes, exists in all societies and cultures. Social class usually is defined by the amount of status that members of a specific class possess in relation to members of other classes. Social-class membership often serves as a frame of reference (a reference group) for the development of consumer attitudes and behavior.

The measurement of social class is concerned with classifying individuals into social-class groupings. These groupings are of particular value to marketers, who use social classification as an effective means of identifying and segmenting target markets. There are three basic methods for measuring social class: subjective measurement, reputational measurement, and objective measurement. Subjective measures rely on an individual's self-perception; reputational measures rely on an individual's perceptions of others; and objective measures use specific socioeconomic measures, either alone (as a single-variable index) or in combination with others (as a composite-variable index). Composite-variable indexes, such as the Index of Status Characteristics and the Socioeconomic Status Score, combine a number of socioeconomic factors to form one overall measure of social-class standing.

Class structures range from two-class to nine-class systems. A frequently used classification system consists of six classes: upper-upper, lower-upper, upper-middle, lower-middle, upper-lower, and lower-

lower classes. Profiles of these classes indicate that the socioeconomic differences among classes are reflected in differences in attitudes, in leisure activities, and in consumption habits. This is why segmentation by social class is of special interest to marketers.

In recent years, some marketers have turned to geodemographic clustering as an alternative to a strict social-class typology. Geodemographic clustering is a technique that combines geographic and socioeconomic factors to locate concentrations of consumers with particular characteristics. Particular

attention currently is being directed to affluent consumers, who represent the fastest-growing segment in our population; however, some marketers are finding it extremely profitable to cater to the needs of nonaffluent consumers.

Research has revealed social-class differences in clothing habits, home decoration, and leisure activities, as well as saving, spending, and credit habits. Thus, astute marketers tailor specific product and promotional strategies to each social-class target segment.

Discussion Questions

1. Marketing researchers generally use the objective method to measure social class rather than the subjective or reputational methods. Why is the objective method preferred by researchers?

2. Under what circumstances would you expect income to be a better predictor of consumer behavior than a composite measure of social class (e.g., based on income, education, and occupation)? When would you expect the composite social-class measure to be superior?

3. Describe the correlation between social status (or prestige) and income. Which is a more useful segmentation variable? Discuss.

4. Which status-related variable—occupation, education, or income—is the most appropriate segmentation base for: (a) expensive vacations, (b) opera subscriptions, (c) *People* magazine subscriptions, (d) fat-free foods, (e) personal computers, (f) pocket-size cellular telephones, and (g) health clubs?

5. Consider the Rolex watch, which has a retail price range starting at about $2,000 for a stainless-steel model to thousands of dollars for a solid-gold model. How might the Rolex company use geodemographic clustering in its marketing efforts?

6. How would you use the research evidence on affluent households presented in this chapter to segment the market for (a) home exercise equipment, (b) vacations, and (c) banking services?

7. How can a marketer use knowledge of consumer behavior to develop financial services for affluent consumers? For downscale consumers?

8. You are the owner of two furniture stores, one catering to upper-middle-class consumers and the other to lower-class consumers. How do social-class differences influence each store's (a) product lines and styles, (b) advertising media selection, (c) the copy and communications style used in the ads, and (d) payment policies?

Exercises

1. Copy the list of occupations in Table 11-6 and ask students majoring in areas other than marketing (both business and nonbusiness) to rank the relative prestige of these occupations. Are any differences in the rankings related to the students' majors? Explain.

2. Find three print ads in one of the publications listed in Table 11-5. Using the social-class char-

acteristics listed in Table 11-9, identify the social class targeted by each ad and evaluate the effectiveness of the advertising appeals used.

3. Select two households featured in two different TV series or sitcoms. Classify each household into one of the social classes discussed in the text and analyze its lifestyle and consumption behavior.

Key Terms

- **Affluent market**
- **Chapin's Social Status Scale**
- **Class consciousness**
- **Composite-variable indexes**
- **Downscale consumers**
- **Downward mobility**

- **Geodemographic clusters**
- **Index of Status Characteristics**
- **Objective measures**
- **PRIZM**
- **Reputational measures**

- **Single-variable index**
- **Social class**
- **Social status**
- **Socioeconomic Status Score**
- **Subjective measures**
- **Upward mobility**

Notes

1. Shaun Saunders, "Fromm's Marketing Character and Rokeach Values," *Social Behavior and Personality,* 29 (2), 2001, 191–196.
2. Jacqueline K. Eastman, Ronald E. Goldsmith, and Leisa Reinecke Flynn, "Status Consumption in Consumer Behavior: Scale Development and Validation," *Journal of Marketing Theory and Practice,* Summer 1999, 41–52.
3. Ibid., 43.
4. Douglas B. Holt, "Does Cultural Capital Structure American Consumption?" *Journal of Consumer Research,* 25, June 1998, 19.
5. Malcolm M. Knapp, "Believing 'Myth of the Middle Class' Can Be Costly Misreading of Consumer Spending," *Nation's Restaurant News,* January 1, 2001, 36.
6. Takashina Shuji, "The New Inequality," *Japan Echo,* August 2000, 38–39.
7. Rebecca Piirto Heath, "The New Working Class," *American Demographics,* January 1998, 52.
8. John P. Dickson and R. Bruce Lind, "The Stability of Occupational Prestige as a Key Variable in Determining Social Class Structure: A Longitudinal Study 1976–2000," in *2001 AMA Winter Educators' Conference,* 12, eds. Ram Krishnan and Madhu Viswanathan (Chicago: American Marketing Association, 2001), 38–44.
9. Rebecca Piirto Heath, "Life on Easy Street," *American Demographics,* April 1997, 33–38.
10. Diane Crispell, "The Real Middle Americans," *American Demographics,* October 1994, 28–35.
11. Eugene Sivadas, George Mathew, and David J. Curry, "A Preliminary Examination of the Continued Significance of Social Class to Marketing: A Geodemographic Replication," *Journal of Consumer Marketing,* 14, 6, 1997, 469.
12. Dennis Rodkin, "Wealthy Attitude Wins over Healthy Wallet: Consumers Prove Affluence Is a State of Mind," *Advertising Age,* July 9, 1990, S4, S6.
13. Janeen Arnold Costa and Russell W. Belk, "Nouveaux Riches as Quintessential Americans: Case Studies of Consumption in an Extended Family," *Advances in Nonprofit Marketing,* 3 (Greenwich, CT: JAI Press, 1990), 83–140.
14. F. Stuart Chapin, *Contemporary American Institutions* (New York: Harper, 1935), 373–397.
15. Robert B. Settle, Pamela L. Alreck, and Denny E. McCorkle, "Consumer Perceptions of Mail/Phone Order Shopping Media," *Journal of Direct Marketing,* 8, Summer 1994, 30–45.
16. W. Lloyd Warner, Marchia Meeker, and Kenneth Eells, *Social Class in America: Manual of Procedure for the Measurement of Social Status* (New York: Harper & Brothers, 1960).
17. *Methodology and Scores of Socioeconomic Status,* Working Paper No. 15 (Washington, DC: U.S. Bureau of the Census, 1963).
18. Geng Cui and Quiming Liu, "Executive Insights: Emerging Market Segments in a Transitional Economy: A Study of Urban Consumers in China," *Journal of International Marketing,* 9, no. 1, 2001, 84–106.
19. Randy Kennedy, "For Middle Class, New York Shrinks as Home Prices Soar," *New York Times,* April 1, 1998, A1, B6; "Two Tier Marketing," *Business Week,* March 17, 1997, 82–90; and Keith Bradsher, "America's Opportunity Gap," *New York Times,* June 4, 1995, 4.
20. Lynn Kahle, "Zip Decoder Giving a Salescerk Your Postal Code Is Only the First Step for Marketers to Sort the Citizenry into 'Clusters,' the Better for Firms to Know and Target Their Customers," *The Oregonian,* December 21, 1999, C01.

21. Paul Bruder, "Economic Health: The Key Ingredient in the Personal Health of Global Communities," *Hospital Topics,* 79, no. 1, Winter 2001, 32–35.

22. Bill Merrick, "Coming Soon: A Wealth of Riches," *Credit Union Magazine,* June 2001, 64–69.

23. Lisa Singhania, "Whirlpool Looks to Innovation to Boost Appliance Sales," *The Grand Rapids Press,* February 6, 2000, F1; and Gregory L. White and Shirley Leung, "Stepping Up: Middle Market Shrinks as Americans Migrate Toward the High End— Shifting Consumer Values Create 'Hourglass' Effect'; Quality Gets Easier to Sell—Six Air Bags, 22 Bath Towels," *Wall Street Journal,* March 29, 2002, A1.

24. *The Mendelsohn Affluent Survey 2002* (New York: Mendelsohn Media Research, Inc., 2002).

25. "New Forrester Report Advises How to Win Affluent Consumers in the Economic Slump," *Business Wire,* August 1, 2001, 1.

26. Op. Cit, The Mendelsohn Affluent Survey 2002.

27. Anita Sharpe, "The Rich Aren't So Different After All," *Wall Street Journal,* November 12, 1996, B1, B10; and Rebecca Piirto Heath, "Life on Easy Street," *Wall Street Journal,* November 12, 1996, 33.

28. Geoffrey Holliman, "Once a Teenager, Now Affluent and Best Not Ignored," *Marketing,* December 2, 1999, 22.

29. Martha R. McEnally and Charles Bodkin, "A Comparison of Convenience Orientation Between U.S. and U.K. Households," in *2001 AMA Winter Educators' Conference,* 12, eds. Ram Krishnan and Madhu Viswanathan (Chicago: American Marketing Association, 2001), 332–338.

30. Op. Cit, The Mendelsohn Affluent Survey 2002.

31. "Marketing to Affluents: Hidden Pockets of Wealth," *Advertising Age,* July 9, 1990, S1.

32. Jeanie Casison, "Wealthy and Wise," *Incentive,* January 1999, 78–81.

33. *The Upper Deck* (Mediamark Research, Inc., 2001).

34. For some further insights about the affluence of dual-income households, see Diane Crispell, "The Very Rich Are Sort of Different," *American Demographics,* March 1994, 11–13.

35. Sharon O'Malley, "Country Gold," *American Demographics,* July 1992, 26–34.

36. Gayle Gerhardt and Pete Jacques, "Is the Middle Market Still in the Middle?" *Life Insurance Marketing & Research Association's Market Facts Quarterly,* Fall 2001, 18–21.

37. Debra Goldman, "Paradox of Pleasure," *American Demographics,* May 1999, 50–53.

38. W. Michael Cox, "The Low Cost of Living," *The Voluntaryist,* October 1999, 3.

39. White and Leung, "Stepping Up," A1.

40. Rasul Bailay, "Juice Processors See Fruitful Future in India—Companies Hope to Lure Country's Middle Class—'The Taste of Good Health'," *Wall Street Journal,* November 17, 2000, 28; and Clay Chandler, "GM to Make Small Cars in China; Buick Sail, Similar to Opel, Will Be Aimed at Middle Class," *The Washington Post,* October 24, 2000, E1.

41. Karen Benezra, "Hardworking RC Cola," *Brandweek,* May 25, 1998, 18–19.

42. "Small Budgets Yield Big Clout for Food Companies—10.1 Million Low Income Consumers Can't (or Shouldn't) Be Ignored," *PR Newswire,* August 22, 2002, 1.

43. Steve Rosenbush, "Techno Leaders Warn of a 'Great Divide'," *USA Today,* June 17, 1998, B1.

44. Steve Lohr, "A Time Out for Technophilia," *New York Times,* November 18, 2001, 4.

45. "Computer Geeks Now the Cool Kids in Class," *The Press* (Christchurch, New Zealand), July 20, 2000, 31.

46. Sophia Lezin Jones, "Parent Technology Nights: Classes to Help Boost Computer Savvy Riverside Elementary Moms, Dads Invited," *The Atlanta Journal—Constitution,* October 19, 1999, JJ1.

47. Epictetus, "Discourses" (second century) in *The Enchiridon,* 2nd ed., trans. Thomas Higginson (Indianapolis: Bobbs-Merrill, 1955).

48. Mike Duff, "Old Navy: The Master of Downmarket Apparel Dollars," *DSN Retailing Today,* May 8, 2000, 89–90.

49. D. F. Baugh, and L. L. Davis. "The Effect of Store Image on Consumers' Perceptions of Designer and Private Label Clothing," *Clothing and Textiles Research Journal,* 7, no. 3, 1989, 15–21.

50. Youn-Kyung Kim and Seunghae Han, "Perceived Images of Retail Stores and Brands: Comparison Among Three Ethnic Consumer Groups," *Journal of Family and Consumer Sciences,* 92, no. 3, 2000, 58–61.

51. Dawn R. Deeter-Schmelz, Jesse N. Moore, and Daniel J. Goebel, "Prestige Clothing Shopping by Consumers: A Confirmatory Assessment and Refinement of the PRECON Scale with Managerial Implications," *Journal of Marketing Theory and Practice,* Fall 2000, 43–58.

52. Christina Duff, "Indulging in Inconspicuous Consumption," *Wall Street Journal,* April 14, 1997, B1, B2; and Christina Duff, "Two Family Budgets: Different Means, Similar Ends," *Wall Street Journal,* April 14, 1997, B1, B2.

53. Michael J. Weiss, Morris B. Holbrook, and John Habich, "Death of the Arts Snob?" *American Demographics,* June 2001, 40–42.

54. Kim and Han, "Perceived Images of Retail Store Brands," 59.

WORK HARD. BE SUCCESSFUL.

GO SOMEPLACE WHERE NONE OF THAT MATTERS.

There are places in this world where you are not a CEO, a mogul, a player, or even a hotshot. Places where all you are is a human being. The question you must now ask yourself is, "How can I get there?" With Range Rover's permanent four-wheel drive, electronic air suspension and unique off-road navigation system, the answer may be, "Quite easily." Visit a Land Rover Centre and see what a Range Rover is made of.

LAND-ROVER

RANGE ROVER

12

The Influence of Culture on Consumer Behavior

T he study of culture is a challenging undertaking because its primary focus is on the broadest component of social behavior—*an entire society.* In contrast to the psychologist, who is principally concerned with the study of individual behavior, or the sociologist, who is concerned with the study of groups, the anthropologist is primarily interested in identifying the very fabric of society itself.

This chapter explores the basic concepts of culture, with particular emphasis on the role that culture plays in influencing consumer behavior. We will first consider the specific dimensions of culture that make it a powerful force in regulating human behavior. After reviewing several measurement approaches that researchers use to understand the impact of culture on consumption behavior, we will show how a variety of core American cultural values influence consumer behavior.

This chapter is concerned with the general aspects of culture; the following two chapters focus on subculture and on cross-culture and show how marketers can use such knowledge to shape and modify their marketing strategies.

What Is Culture?

Given the broad and pervasive nature of **culture,** its study generally requires a detailed examination of the character of the total society, including such factors as language, knowledge, laws, religions, food customs, music, art, technology, work patterns, products, and other artifacts that give a society its distinctive flavor. In a sense, culture is a society's personality. For this reason, it is not easy to define its boundaries.

Because our objective is to understand the influence of culture on consumer behavior, we define culture as the *sum total of learned beliefs, values, and customs that serve to direct the consumer behavior of members of a particular society.*

The *belief* and *value* components of our definition refer to the accumulated feelings and priorities that individuals have about "things" and possessions. More precisely, *beliefs* consist of the very large number of mental or verbal statements (i.e., "I believe . . . ") that reflect a person's particular knowledge and assessment of something (another person, a store, a product, a brand). *Values* also are beliefs. Values differ from other beliefs, however, because they meet the following criteria: (1) They are relatively few in number; (2) they serve as a guide for culturally appropriate behavior; (3) they are enduring or difficult to change; (4) they are not tied to specific objects or situations; and (5) they are widely accepted by the members of a society.

Therefore, in a broad sense, both values and beliefs are mental images that affect a wide range of specific attitudes that, in turn, influence the way a person is likely to respond in a specific situation.[1] For example, the criteria a person uses to evaluate alternative brands in a product category (such as Volvo versus Jaguar automobiles), or his or her eventual preference for one of these brands over the other, are influenced by both a person's general values (perceptions as to what constitutes quality and the meaning of country of origin) and specific beliefs (particular perceptions about the quality of Swedish-made versus English-made cars).

In contrast to beliefs and values, customs are *overt modes of behavior that constitute culturally approved or acceptable ways of behaving in specific situations.* Customs consist of everyday or routine behavior. For example, a consumer's routine behavior, such as adding sugar and milk to coffee, putting ketchup on hamburgers, putting mustard on frankfurters, and having a salad *after* rather than *before* the main course of a meal, are customs. Thus, whereas beliefs and values are guides for behavior, customs are *usual and acceptable ways of behaving.*

By our definition, it is easy to see how an understanding of various cultures of a society helps marketers predict consumer acceptance of their products.

The Invisible Hand of Culture

The impact of culture is so natural and automatic that its influence on behavior is usually taken for granted. For instance, when consumer researchers ask people why they do certain things, they frequently answer, "Because it's the right thing to do." This seemingly superficial response partially reflects the ingrained influence of culture on our behavior. Often it is only when we are exposed to people with different cultural values or customs (as when visiting a different region or a different country) that we become aware of how culture has molded our own behavior. Thus, a true appreciation of the influence that culture has on our daily life requires some knowledge of at least one other society with different cultural characteristics. For example, to understand that brushing our teeth twice a day with flavored toothpaste is a cultural phenomenon requires some awareness that members of another society either do not brush their teeth at all or do so in a distinctly different manner than our own society.

Perhaps the following statement expresses it best:[2]

Consumers both view themselves in the context of their culture and react to their environment based upon the cultural framework that they bring to that experience. Each individual perceives the world through his own cultural lens.

Culture Satisfies Needs

Culture exists to satisfy the needs of the people within a society. It offers order, direction, and guidance in all phases of human problem solving by providing "tried-and-true" methods of satisfying physiological, personal, and social needs. For example, culture provides standards and "rules" about when to eat ("not between meals"), where to eat ("in a busy restaurant, because the food is likely to be good"), what is appropriate to eat for breakfast (juice and cereal), lunch (a sandwich), dinner ("something hot and good and healthy"), and snacks ("something with quick energy"); and what to serve to guests at a dinner party ("a formal sit-down meal"), at a picnic (barbecued "franks and hamburgers"), or at a wedding (champagne). Culture is also associated with what a society's members consider to be a necessity and what they view as a luxury. For instance, 55 percent of American adults consider a microwave to be a necessity, and 36 percent consider a remote control for a TV or VCR to be a necessity.[3]

Similarly, culture also provides insights as to suitable dress for specific occasions (such as what to wear around the house, what to wear to school, to work, to church, at a fast-food restaurant, or to a movie theater). Dress codes have shifted dramatically; people are dressing more casually most of the time. Today, only a few big-city restaurants and clubs have business dress requirements. With the relaxed dress code in the corporate work environment, fewer men are wearing dress shirts, ties, and business suits, and fewer women are wearing dresses, suits, and panty hose. In their place casual slacks, sports shirts and blouses, jeans, and the emerging category of "dress casual" have been increasing in sales.

Soft-drink companies would prefer that consumers received their morning "jolt" of caffeine from one of their products rather than from coffee. Because most Americans do not consider soda a suitable breakfast beverage, the real challenge for soft-drink companies is to overcome culture, not competition. Indeed, coffee has been challenged on all fronts by juices, milk, teas (hot and iced), a host of different types of soft drinks, and now even caffeinated waters. Not resting on their "cultural advantage" as a breakfast drink and the namesake of the "coffee break," coffee marketers have been fighting back by targeting gourmet and specialty coffees (e.g., espresso, cappuccino, and café mocha) to young adults (those 18 to 24 years of age). These efforts have been paying off as young adults (an important segment of the soft-drink market) have been responding positively to gourmet coffees.[4]

Cultural beliefs, values, and customs continue to be followed as long as they yield satisfaction. When a specific standard no longer satisfies the members of a society, however, it is modified or replaced, so that the resulting standard is more in line with current needs and desires. For instance, it was once considered a sign of a fine hotel that it provided down or goose feather pillows in rooms. Today, with so many guests allergic to such materials, synthetic polyfill pillows are becoming more the rule. Thus, culture gradually but continually evolves to meet the needs of society.

Culture Is Learned

Unlike innate biological characteristics (e.g., sex, skin, hair color, or intelligence), culture is learned. At an early age, we begin to acquire from our social environment a set of beliefs, values, and customs that make up our culture. For children, the learning of these acceptable cultural values and customs is reinforced by the process of playing with their toys. As children play, they act out and rehearse important cultural lessons and situations. This cultural learning prepares them for later real-life circumstances.

HOW CULTURE IS LEARNED

Anthropologists have identified three distinct forms of cultural learning: *formal learning,* in which adults and older siblings teach a young family member "how to behave"; *informal learning,* in which a child learns primarily by imitating the behavior of selected others, such as family, friends, or TV heroes and *technical learning,* in which teachers instruct the child in an educational environment about what should be done, how it should be done, and why it should be done. Although a firm's advertising can influence all three types of cultural learning, it is likely that many product advertisements enhance informal cultural learning by providing the audience with a model of behavior to imitate. This is especially true for visible or conspicuous products and products that are evaluated in public settings (such as designer clothing, cell phones, or status golf clubs), where peer influence is likely to play an important role.[5]

The repetition of advertising messages creates and reinforces cultural beliefs and values. For example, many advertisers continually stress the same selected benefits of their products or services. Ads for wireless phone service often stress the clarity of their connection, or the nationwide coverage of their service, as well as the flexibility of their pricing plans. It is difficult to say whether wireless phone subscribers *inherently* desire these benefits from their wireless service providers or whether, after several years of cumulative exposure to advertising appeals stressing these benefits, they have been taught by marketers to desire them. In a sense, although specific product advertising may reinforce the benefits that consumers want from the product (as determined by consumer behavior research), such advertising also "teaches" future generations of consumers to expect the same benefits from the product category.

Figure 12-1 shows that cultural meaning moves from the culturally constituted world to consumer goods and from there to the individual consumer by means of various *consumption-related vehicles* (e.g., advertising or observing or imitating others' behavior). Imagine the ever-popular T-shirt and how it can furnish cultural meaning and identity for wearers. T-shirts can function as *trophies* (as proof of participation in sports or travel) or as self-proclaimed labels of *belonging to a cultural category* ("Super Bowl XXXVI Attendee," "Retired"). T-shirts can also be used as a means of *self-expression,* which may provide wearers with the additional benefit of serving as a "topic" initiating social dialogue with others. Still further, although we might expect that a Las Vegas T-shirt would be worn by a person who has been to Las Vegas (or has received it as a gift from someone else who has visited Las Vegas), this is not necessarily so. In such a world of "virtual identities," consumers can now just buy a Las Vegas T-shirt at a local retailer and create the impression that they have been there.[6]

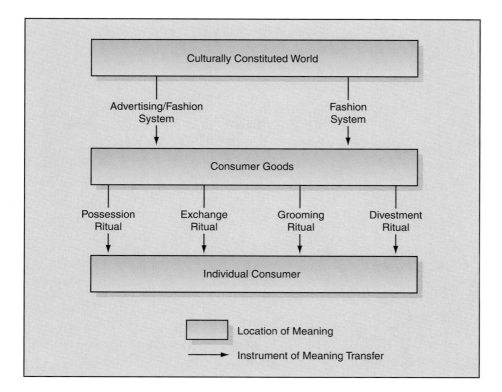

FIGURE 12-1

The Movement of
Cultural Meaning
Source: Grant McCracken,
"Culture and Consumption: A
Theoretical Account of the
Structure and Movement of
the Cultural Meaning of
Consumer Goods," *Journal of
Consumer Research,* 13, June
1986, 72. Reprinted by per-
mission of The University of
Chicago Press as publishers.

ENCULTURATION AND ACCULTURATION

When discussing the acquisition of culture, anthropologists often distinguish between the learning of one's own, or native, culture and the learning of some "new" (other) culture. The learning of one's own culture is known as **enculturation.** The learning of a new or foreign culture is known as **acculturation.** In Chapter 14, we will see that acculturation is an important concept for marketers who plan to sell their products in foreign or multinational markets. In such cases, marketers must study the specific culture(s) of their potential target markets to determine whether their products will be acceptable to its members and, if so, how they can best communicate the characteristics of their products to persuade the target market to buy.

LANGUAGE AND SYMBOLS

To acquire a common culture, the members of a society must be able to communicate with each other through a common language. Without a common language, shared meaning could not exist, and true communication would not take place (see Chapter 9).

To communicate effectively with their audiences, marketers must use appropriate **symbols** to convey desired product images or characteristics (see Figure 12-2). These symbols can be verbal or nonverbal. Verbal symbols may include a television announcement or an advertisement in a magazine. Nonverbal communication includes the use of such symbols as figures, colors, shapes, and even textures to lend

FIGURE 12-2

Ad Using Visual Imagery as a Symbol
Courtesy of The Procter & Gamble Company. Used by permission.

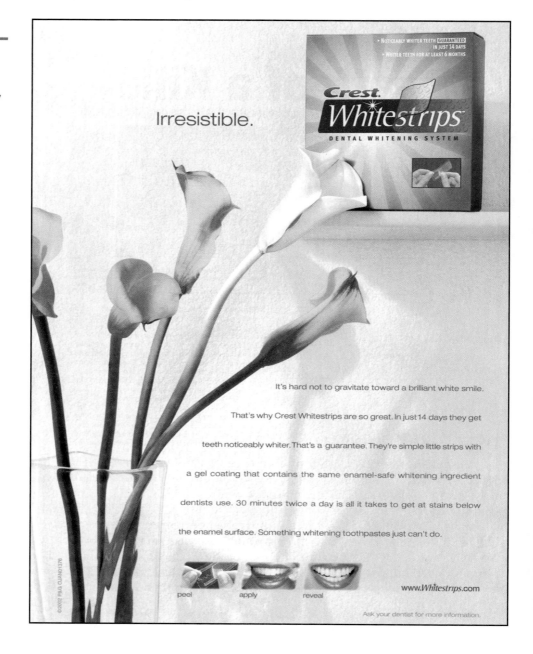

additional meaning to print or broadcast advertisements, to trademarks, and to packaging or product designs.

Basically, the symbolic nature of human language sets it apart from all other animal communication. A symbol is anything that stands for something else. Any word is a symbol. The word *razor* calls forth a specific image related to an individual's own knowledge and experience. The word *hurricane* calls forth the notion of wind and rain and also has the power to stir us emotionally, arousing feelings of danger and the need for protection and safety. Similarly, the word *jaguar* has symbolic meaning: To some it suggests a fine luxury automobile, to others it implies wealth and status; to still others it suggests a sleek, wild animal to be seen at the zoo.

Because the human mind can process symbols, it is possible, for example, for a person to "experience" cognitively a visualization for a product, like the advertisement for Edge skin moisturizing gel, which contrasts two scenes—one of a parched desert without the gel and one of a rich green landscape with the gel. Such a comparison presents the idea that a skin-moisturizing gel will transform a person's dry skin to a comfortable moist state. The capacity to learn symbolically is primarily a human phenomenon; most other animals learn by direct experience. Clearly, the ability of humans to understand symbolically how a product, service, or idea can satisfy their needs makes it easier for marketers to sell the features and benefits of their offerings. Through a shared language and culture, individuals already know what the image means; thus, an association can be made without actively thinking about it.

A symbol may have several, even contradictory, meanings, so the advertiser must ascertain exactly what the symbol is communicating to its intended audience. For example, the advertiser who uses a trademark depicting an old craftsman to symbolize careful workmanship may instead be communicating an image of outmoded methods and lack of style. The marketer who uses slang in an advertisement to attract a teenage audience must do so with great care; slang that is misused or outdated will symbolically date the marketer's firm and product.

Price and channels of distribution also are significant symbols of the marketer and the marketer's product. For example, price often implies quality to potential buyers. For certain products (such as clothing), the type of store in which the product is sold also is an important symbol of quality. In fact, all the elements of the marketing mix—the product, its promotion, price, and the stores at which it is available—are symbols that communicate ranges of quality to potential buyers.

RITUAL

In addition to language and symbols, culture includes various ritualized experiences and behaviors that until recently have been neglected by consumer researchers. A **ritual** is a type of symbolic activity consisting of a series of steps (multiple behaviors) occurring in a fixed sequence and repeated over time.[7]

In practice, rituals extend over the human life cycle from birth to death, including a host of intermediate events (such as confirmation, graduations, and marriage). These rituals can be very public, elaborate, religious, or civil ceremonies, or they can be as mundane as an individual's grooming behavior or flossing.[8] Ritualized behavior is typically rather formal and often is scripted behavior (as a religious service requiring a prayer book or the code of proper conduct in a court of law). It is also likely to occur repeatedly over time (such as singing the national anthem before a basketball game).

Most important from the standpoint of marketers is the fact that rituals tend to be replete with ritual artifacts (products) that are associated with or somehow enhance the performance of the ritual. For instance, tree ornaments, stockings, and various food items are linked to the ritual of Christmas celebration; other rituals (such as a graduation, a wedding or wedding anniversary, a Thursday night card game (see Figure 12-3), or a Saturday afternoon visit to the hair salon) have their own specific artifacts associated with them. For special occasions, such as wedding anniversaries, some types of artifacts are perceived as more

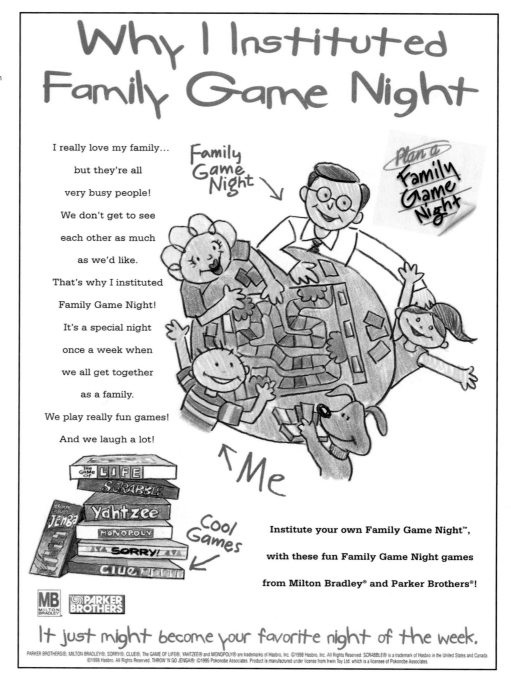

appropriate as gifts than others, for example, jewelry rather than everyday household items (Table 12-1).

In addition to a ritual, which is the way that something is traditionally done, there is also *ritualistic behavior*, which can be defined as any behavior that is made into a ritual. For example, a baseball player may swing his bat a certain number of times and kick the dirt near home plate before a pitch to ensure a good swing. Table 12-2 describes a young woman's ritualistic behavior with respect to facial beauty care.

TABLE 12-1	Selected Rituals and Associated Artifacts

SELECTED RITUALS	TYPICAL ARTIFACTS
Wedding	White gown (something old, something new, something borrowed, something blue)
Birth of child	U.S. savings bond, silver baby spoon
Birthday	Card, present, cake with candles
50th wedding anniversary	Catered party, card and gift, display of photos of the couple's life together
Graduation	Pen, U.S. savings bond, card, wristwatch
Valentine's Day	Candy, card, flowers
New Year's Eve	Champagne, party, fancy dress
Thanksgiving	Prepare a turkey meal for family and friends
Going to the gym	Towel, exercise clothes, water, portable tape player
Sunday football	Beer, potato chips, pretzels
Super Bowl party	Same as Sunday football (just more)
Starting a new job	Get a haircut, buy some new clothing
Get a job promotion	Taken out to lunch by coworkers, receive token gift
Retirement	Company party, watch, plaque
Death	Send a card, give to charity in the name of the deceased

TABLE 12-2	Facial Beauty Ritual of a Young TV Advertising Sales Representative

1. I pull my hair back with a headband.
2. I take all my makeup off with L'Oréal eye makeup remover.
3. Next, I use a Q-tip with some moisturizer around my eyes to make sure all eye makeup is removed.
4. I wash my face with Noxzema facial wash.
5. I apply Clinique Dramatically Different Lotion to my face, neck, and throat.
6. If I have a blemish, I apply Clearasil Treatment to the area to dry it out.
7. Twice weekly (or as necessary) I use Aapri Facial Scrub to remove dry and dead skin.
8. Once a week I apply Clinique Clarifying Lotion 2 with a cotton ball to my face and throat to remove deep-down dirt and oils.
9. Once every three months I get a professional salon facial to deep-clean my pores.

Source: From "Culture and Consumption: A Theoretical Account of the Structure and Movement of the Cultural Meaning of Consumer Goods," by Grant McCracken in *Journal of Consumer Research,* Vol. 13, June 1986. Reprinted by permission of the publisher.

CULTURE IS SHARED

To be considered a cultural characteristic, a particular belief, value, or practice must be shared by a significant portion of the society. Thus, culture frequently is viewed as group *customs* that link together the members of a society. Of course, common language is the critical cultural component that makes it possible for people to share values, experiences, and customs.

Various social institutions within a society transmit the elements of culture and make the sharing of culture a reality. Chief among such institutions is the *family,* which serves as the primary agent for enculturation—the passing along of basic cultural beliefs, values, and customs to society's newest members. A vital part of the enculturation role of the family is the consumer socialization of the young (see Chapter 10). This includes teaching such basic consumer-related values and skills as the meaning of money; the relationship between price and quality; the establishment of product tastes, preferences, and habits; and appropriate methods of response to various promotional messages.

In addition to the family, two other institutions traditionally share much of the responsibility for the transfer of selected aspects of culture: *educational institutions* and *houses of worship.* Educational institutions specifically are charged with imparting basic learning skills, history, patriotism, citizenship, and the technical training needed to prepare people for significant roles within society. Religious institutions provide and perpetuate religious consciousness, spiritual guidance, and moral training. Although the young receive much of their consumer training within the family setting, the educational and religious systems reinforce this training by teaching economic and ethical concepts.

A fourth, frequently overlooked, social institution that plays a major role in the transfer of culture throughout society is the mass media. Given the extensive exposure of the American population to both print and broadcast media, as well as the easily ingested, entertaining format in which the contents of such media usually are presented, it is not surprising that the mass media are powerful vehicles for imparting a wide range of cultural values.

We are exposed daily to advertising, an important component of the media. Advertising not only underwrites, or makes economically feasible, the editorial or programming contents of the media, but it also transmits much about our culture. Without advertising, it would be almost impossible to disseminate information about products, ideas, and causes.

Consumers receive important cultural information from advertising. For example, it has been hypothesized that one of the roles of advertising in sophisticated magazines such as *Vanity Fair* (**www.vanityfair.com**), *Wine Spectator* (**www.winespectator.com**), and *Martha Stewart Living* (**www.marthastewart.com**) is to instruct readers how to dress, how to decorate their homes, and what foods and wines to serve guests, or in other words, what types of behavior are most appropriate to their particular social class.

Thus, although the scope of advertising is often considered to be limited to influencing the demand for specific products or services, in a cultural context advertising has the expanded mission of reinforcing established cultural values and aiding in the dissemination of new tastes, habits, and customs. In planning their advertising, marketers should recognize that advertising is an important agent for social change in our society.

Culture Is Dynamic

To fulfill its need-gratifying role, culture continually must evolve if it is to function in the best interests of a society. For this reason, the marketer must carefully monitor the sociocultural environment in order to market an existing product more effectively or to develop promising new products.

TABLE 12-3	Food: What's In and What's Out

WHAT'S IN WITH FOODS	WHAT'S OUT WITH FOODS
Multiethnic cuisine	Nouvelle cuisine
Artisanal cheeses	Flourless chocolate cake
Lemon butter sauces, salsa, au jus	Hollandaise, Bearnaise, heavy gravy
Comfort food, bistro cuisine	Fat-free foods
Soy beverages	Chai tea
Tapas	Sushi
Flavored mashed potatoes	Rice pilaf
Prepared/partially prepared foods	Cooking from scratch
Authentic regional cuisine	Generic international cuisine
Hot and spicy dishes	Blackened fish and chicken

Source: American Demographics, November 2001, 24. Copyright © 2001 Media Central Inc., a Primedia Company. All rights reserved. Reprinted by permission.

This is not an easy task because many factors are likely to produce cultural changes within a given society (new technology, population shifts, resource shortages, wars, changing values, and customs borrowed from other cultures). For example, major ongoing cultural changes in American society reflect the expanded role options open to women. Today, most women work outside the home, frequently in careers that once were considered exclusively male oriented. These career women are increasingly not waiting for marriage and a man to buy them luxury items—such as fur coats, expensive wristwatches, and diamond rings. More and more such women are saying, "I earn a good living, why wait? I will buy it for myself."[9]

The changing nature of culture means that marketers have to consistently reconsider *why* consumers are now doing what they do, *who* the purchasers and the users of their products are (males only, females only, or both), *when* they do their shopping, *how* and *where* they can be reached by the media, and *what* new product and service needs are emerging. Marketers who monitor cultural changes also often find new opportunities to increase corporate profitability. For example, marketers of such products and services as life insurance, financial and investment advice, casual clothing, toy electric trains, and cigars are among those who have attempted to take advantage of shifts in what is feminine and how to communicate with female consumers.

From time to time, a number of magazines publish lists of "what's hot" and "what's not." Table 12-3 presents a recent example of such a comparative list of what is "in" and what is "out" when it comes to food items. Such lists reflect the dynamic nature of a particular society or culture.

The Measurement of Culture

A wide range of measurement techniques are used in the study of culture. Some of these techniques were described in Chapter 2. For example, the projective tests used by psychologists to study motivation and personality and the attitude measurement techniques used by social psychologists and sociologists are relatively popular tools in the study of culture.

In addition, *content analysis, consumer fieldwork,* and *value measurement instruments* are three research approaches that are frequently used to examine culture and to spot cultural trends. There are also several commercial services that track emerging values and social trends for businesses and governmental agencies.

CONTENT ANALYSIS

Conclusions about a society, or specific aspects of a society, or a comparison of two or more societies sometimes can be drawn from examining the content of particular messages. **Content analysis,** as the name implies, focuses on the content of verbal, written, and pictorial communications (such as the copy and art composition of an ad).

Content analysis can be used as a relatively objective means of determining what social and cultural changes have occurred in a specific society or as a way of contrasting aspects of two different societies. A content analysis of 263 ads appearing in eight issues of *Seventeen* magazine, four Japanese issues and four American issues, found that teenage girls are portrayed differently. The research concluded that these "differences correspond to each country's central concepts of self and society." Whereas American teen girls are often associated with images of "independence and determination," Japanese teen girls are most often portrayed with a "happy, playful, childlike girlish image."[10] In another content analysis study—this one comparing American and Chinese television commercials targeted to children—the research revealed that 82 percent of the Chinese ads aimed at children were for food products, whereas 56 percent of the ads directed at American children were for toys.[11]

Content analysis is useful to both marketers and public policy makers interested in comparing the advertising claims of competitors within a specific industry, as well as for evaluating the nature of advertising claims targeted to specific audiences (e.g., women, the elderly, or children).

CONSUMER FIELDWORK

When examining a specific society, anthropologists frequently immerse themselves in the environment under study through **consumer fieldwork.** As trained researchers, they are likely to select a small sample of people from a particular society and carefully observe their behavior. Based on their observations, researchers draw conclusions about the values, beliefs, and customs of the society under investigation. For example, if researchers were interested in how men select neckties, they might position trained observers in department and clothing stores and note how neckties are selected (solid versus patterned, striped versus paisley, and so on). The researchers also may be interested in the degree of search that accompanies the choice, that is, how often consumers tend to take a necktie off the display, examine it, compare it to other neckties in the store, and place it back again before selecting the necktie that they finally purchase.

The distinct characteristics of **field observation** are that (1) it takes place within a natural environment; (2) it is performed sometimes without the subject's awareness; and (3) it focuses on observation of behavior. Because the emphasis is on a natural environment and observable behavior, field observation concerned with consumer behavior often focuses on in-store shopping behavior and, less frequently, on in-home preparation and consumption.

In some cases, instead of just observing behavior, researchers become **participant-observers** (i.e., they become active members of the environment that they are studying). For example, if researchers were interested in examining how consumers select computer software, they might take a sales position in a computer superstore to observe directly and even to interact with customers in the transaction process.

Today there are consumer research firms that specialize in studying consumer rituals and values. For example, E-Lab LLC specializes in videotaping subjects at work, at home, in their cars, and in public places. Its research suggests: "Ask a teenager why he's buying a certain backpack, and you might not get a useful answer. Watch a teenager as he shops for that backpack, and you might learn a few things." This type of research, used by Nissan in the 1990s when it was designing its line of Infinity automobiles, discovered that the Japanese notion of luxury was very different than the American version—whereas the Japanese crave simplicity, Americans crave visible opulence.[12]

Both field observation and participant-observer research require highly skilled researchers who can separate their own emotions from what they actually observe in their professional roles. Both techniques provide valuable insight that might not easily be obtained through survey research that simply asks consumers questions about their behavior.

In addition to fieldwork methods, depth interviews and focus-group sessions (see Chapter 2) are also often used by marketers to get a "first look" at an emerging social or cultural change. In the relatively informal atmosphere of focus group discussions, consumers are apt to reveal attitudes or behavior that may signal a shift in values that, in turn, may affect the long-run market acceptance of a product or service. For instance, focus group studies can be used to identify marketing programs that reinforce established customer loyalty and goodwill (or relationship marketing). A common thread running throughout these studies showed that established customers, especially for services (such as investment and banking services), want to have their loyalty acknowledged in the form of *personalized services*. These observations have led various service and product companies to refine or establish loyalty programs that are more personalized in the way that they treat their established customers (e.g., by recognizing the individuality of such core customers). This is just one of numerous examples showing how focus groups and depth interviews are used to spot social trends.

VALUE MEASUREMENT SURVEY INSTRUMENTS

Anthropologists have traditionally observed the behavior of members of a specific society and inferred from such behavior the dominant or underlying values of the society. In recent years, however, there has been a gradual shift to measuring values directly by means of survey (questionnaire) research. Researchers use data collection instruments called *value instruments* to ask people how they feel about such basic personal and social concepts as freedom, comfort, national security, and peace.

A variety of popular value instruments have been used in consumer behavior studies, including the **Rokeach Value Survey,** the *List of Values (LOV,)* and the *Values and Lifestyles—VALS* (discussed in Chapter 3). The widely used Rokeach Value Survey is a self-administered value inventory that is divided into two parts, each part measuring different but complementary types of personal values (see Table 12-4). The first part consists of 18 *terminal value* items, which are designed to measure the relative importance of end states of existence (or personal goals). The second part consists of 18 *instrumental value* items, which measure basic approaches an individual might take to reach end-state values. Thus, the first half of the measurement instrument deals with ends, and the second half considers means.

Using the Rokeach Value Survey, adult Brazilians were categorized into six distinctive value segments.[13] For example, Segment A (representing 13 percent of the sample) was most concerned with "world peace," followed by "inner harmony" and

TABLE 12-4	The Rokeach Value Survey Instrument

TERMINAL VALUES	INSTRUMENTAL VALUES
A Comfortable Life (a prosperous life)	Ambitious (hardworking, aspiring)
An Exciting Life (a stimulating, active life)	Broad-Minded (open-minded)
A World at Peace (free of war and conflict)	Capable (competent, effective)
Equality (brotherhood, equal opportunity for all)	Cheerful (lighthearted, joyful)
Freedom (independence and free choice)	Clean (neat, tidy)
Happiness (contentedness)	Courageous (standing up for your beliefs)
National Security (protection from attack)	Forgiving (willing to pardon others)
Pleasure (an enjoyable life)	Helpful (working for the welfare of others)
Salvation (saved, eternal life)	Honest (sincere, truthful)
Social Recognition (respect and admiration)	Imaginative (daring, creative)
True Friendship (close companionship)	Independent (self-reliant, self-sufficient)
Wisdom (a mature understanding of life)	Intellectual (intelligent, reflective)
A World of Beauty (beauty of nature and the arts)	Logical (consistent, rational)
Family Security (taking care of loved ones)	Loving (affectionate, tender)
Mature Love (sexual and spiritual intimacy)	Obedient (dutiful, respectful)
Self-Respect (self-esteem)	Polite (courteous, well-mannered)
A Sense of Accomplishment (lasting contribution)	Responsible (dependable, reliable)
Inner Harmony (freedom from inner conflict)	Self-Controlled (restrained, self-disciplined)

Source: Modified and reproduced by special permission of the publisher, Consulting Psychologists Press, Inc., Palo Alto, CA 94303 from *Rokeach Value Survey* by Milton Research. Copyright 1983 by Milton Rokeach. All rights reserved. Further reproduction is prohibited without the publisher's written consent.

"true friendship." Members of this segment were found to be especially involved in domestic-oriented activities (such as gardening, reading, and going out with the family to visit relatives). Because of their less materialistic and nonhedonistic orientation, this segment also may be the least prone to experiment with new products. In contrast, Segment B (representing 9 percent of the sample) was most concerned with self-centered values such as self-respect, a comfortable life, pleasure, an exciting life, a sense of accomplishment, and social recognition. They were least concerned with values related to the family, such as friendship, love, and equality. These self-centered, achievement-oriented, pleasure seekers were expected to prefer provocative clothes in the latest fashion, to enjoy an active lifestyle, and to be more likely to try new products.

The LOV is a related measurement instrument that is also designed to be used in surveying consumers' personal values. The LOV scale asks consumers to identify their two most important values from a nine-value list (such as "warm relationships with others," "a sense of belonging," or "a sense of accomplishment") that is based on the terminal values of the Rokeach Value Survey.[14]

American Core Values

What is the American culture? In this section, we identify a number of **core values** that both affect and reflect the character of American society. This is a difficult undertaking for several reasons. First, the United States is a diverse country, consisting of a variety of **subcultures** (religious, ethnic, regional, racial, and economic groups), each of which interprets and responds to society's basic beliefs and values in its own specific way. Second, America is a dynamic society that has undergone almost constant change in response to the development of new technology. This element of rapid change makes it especially difficult to monitor changes in cultural values. Finally, the existence of contradictory values in American society is somewhat confusing. For instance, Americans traditionally embrace freedom of choice and individualism, yet simultaneously they show great tendencies to conform (in dress, in furnishings, and in fads) to the rest of society. In the context of consumer behavior, Americans like to have a wide choice of products and prefer those that uniquely express their personal lifestyles. Yet, there is often a considerable amount of implicit pressure to conform to the values of family members, friends, and other socially important groups. It is difficult to reconcile these seemingly inconsistent values; their existence, however, demonstrates that America is a complex society with numerous paradoxes.

When selecting the specific core values to be examined, we were guided by three criteria:

1. The value must be pervasive. *A significant portion of the American people must accept the value and use it as a guide for their attitudes and actions.*
2. The value must be enduring. *The specific value must have influenced the actions of the American people over an extended period of time (as distinguished from a short-run trend).*
3. The value must be consumer related. *The specific value must provide insights that help us to understand the consumption actions of the American people.*

Meeting these criteria are a number of basic values that expert observers of the American scene consider the "building blocks" of that rather elusive concept called the "American character."

ACHIEVEMENT AND SUCCESS

In a broad cultural context, achievement is a major American value, with historical roots that can be traced to the traditional religious belief in the Protestant work ethic, which considers hard work to be wholesome, spiritually rewarding, and an appropriate end in itself. Indeed, substantial research evidence shows that the achievement orientation is closely associated with the technical development and general economic growth of American society.[15]

Individuals who consider a "sense of accomplishment" an important personal value tend to be achievers who strive hard for success. Although historically associated with men, especially male business executives, today *achievement* is very important for women, who are increasingly enrolled in undergraduate and graduate business programs and are more commonly seeking top-level business careers.

Success is a closely related American cultural theme. However, achievement and success do differ. Specifically, achievement is its own direct reward (it is implicitly satisfying to the individual achiever), whereas success implies an extrinsic reward (such as luxury possessions, financial compensation, or status improvement). Moreover, it is a widespread embracing of achievement and success that has led to the great success and progress of the United States.[16]

Both achievement and success influence consumption. They often serve as social and moral justification for the acquisition of goods and services. For example, "You owe it to yourself," "You worked for it," and "You deserve it" are popular achievement themes used by advertisers to coax consumers into purchasing their products

FIGURE 12-4

An Achievement-
Success Appeal
Courtesy of Land Rover.

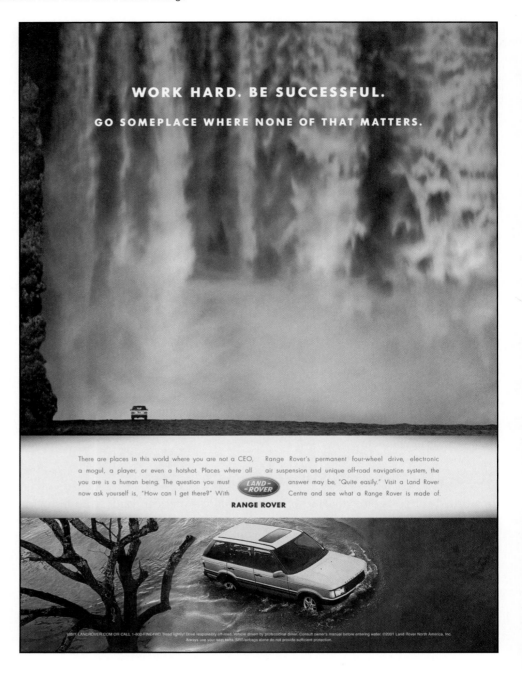

(see Figure 12-4). Regardless of gender, achievement-oriented people often enjoy conspicuous consumption because it allows them to display symbols of their personal achievement. When it comes to personal development and preparation for future careers, the themes of achievement and success are also especially appropriate.

It is of interest to mention that the theories of colonialism and dependency were once used to explain the differences between the poor countries and the rich countries of the globe. However, these theories are given little credence today, and the current paradigm used to explain the differences between "have" and "have-not" nations is culture.

ACTIVITY

Americans attach an extraordinary amount of importance to being *active* or *involved*. Keeping busy is widely accepted as a healthy and even necessary part of the American lifestyle. The hectic nature of American life is attested to by foreign visitors, who frequently comment that they cannot understand why Americans are always "on the run" and seemingly unable to relax.

The premium placed on activity has had both positive and negative effects on the popularity of various products. For example, a principal reason for the enormous growth of fast-food chains, such as McDonald's and Kentucky Fried Chicken, is that so many people want quick, prepared meals when they are away from the house. Americans rarely eat a full breakfast because they usually are too rushed in the morning to prepare and consume a traditional morning meal. In fact, bagels, which can be prepared quickly and easily, have been stealing sales away from sit-down cereal breakfasts because they can be eaten on the run.[17]

Recent research suggests that "being busy," in and of itself, just is not enough and is not necessarily healthy. For example, some researchers have reported that although it is important for elderly people to "keep busy," it is important that the activities that they engage in be fulfilling. Similarly, it is being questioned whether keeping young children busy all the time is healthy for them—it's been suggested that kids need time to relax![18]

EFFICIENCY AND PRACTICALITY

With a basic philosophy of down-to-earth pragmatism, Americans pride themselves on being efficient and practical. When it comes to *efficiency,* they admire anything that saves time and effort. In terms of *practicality,* they generally are receptive to any new product that makes tasks easier and can help solve problems. For example, today it is possible for manufacturers of many product categories to offer the public a wide range of interchangeable components. Thus, a consumer can design his or her own customized wall unit from such standard components as compatible metals and woods, legs, door facings, and style panels at a cost not much higher than a completely standardized unit. The capacity of manufacturers to create mass-produced components offers consumers the practical option of a customized product at a reasonable price. If you are unfamiliar with such furniture, just browse through an IKEA catalog or the "virtual catalog" on the IKEA Web site (**www.ikea.com**).

Another illustration of Americans' attentiveness to efficiency and practicality is the extreme importance attached to *time* (see Figure 12-5). Americans seem to be convinced that "time waits for no one," which is reflected in their habitual attention to being prompt. Another sign of America's preoccupation with time is the belief that time is in increasingly short supply.[19] Americans place a great deal of importance on getting there first, on the value of time itself, on the notion that time is money, on the importance of not wasting time, and on identifying "more" time. In our attempt to get more and more out of each day, one author has concluded that we may become trapped in a vicious circle in which we feel as if we are getting less and less out of each day.[20]

The frequency with which Americans look at their watches and the importance attached to having an accurate timepiece tend to support the American value of *punctuality.* Similarly, the broad consumer acceptance of the microwave oven and microwaveable foods are also examples of Americans' love affair with products that save time and effort by providing efficiency and practicality.

Ad Stressing Saving Time and Money

PROGRESS

Progress is another watchword of American society. Americans respond favorably to the promise of progress. Receptivity to progress appears to be closely linked to the other core values already examined (*achievement, success, efficiency,* and *practicality*) and to the central belief that people can always improve themselves, that tomorrow should be better than today. In a consumption-oriented society, such as that of the United States, progress often means the acceptance of change, new products, or services designed to fulfill previously undersatisfied or unsatisfied needs. A new type of counselor, the "life coach" or "personal coach," works with individuals in order to help them improve themselves and seek "fulfillment and balance in careers, family, health, and hobbies."[21] The coach tracks the client's progress and tries to

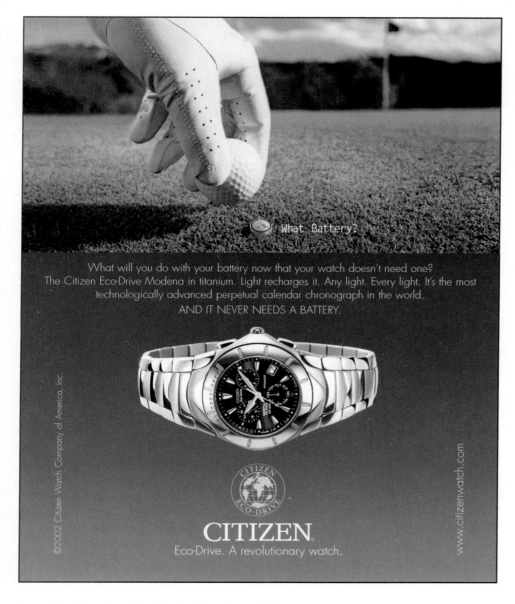

FIGURE 12-6

Progress Is a Winning Appeal
Courtesy of Citizen Watch Company of America.

keep the client heading in the direction of his or her fulfillment. Ideally, the coach makes the client excited about prospects for the future.

In the name of progress, Americans appear to be receptive to product claims that stress "new," "improved," "longer-lasting," "speedier," "quicker," "smoother and closer," and "increased strength" (see Figure 12-6).

MATERIAL COMFORT

For most Americans (even young children), *material comfort* signifies the attainment of "the good life," a life that may include a new car, a dishwasher, an air conditioner, a hot tub, and an almost infinite variety of other convenience-oriented and pleasure-providing goods and services.[22] It appears that consumers' idea of material comfort is largely a *relative* view; that is, consumers tend to define their own satisfaction with the amount of material goods they have in terms of a comparison of what they have to what others have. If a comparison suggests that they have more than others do, then they are more likely to be satisfied.[23] On the other hand, as many popular songs point out, the ownership of material goods does not always lead to happiness. For instance, many people, especially affluent people, might be willing to trade money for more free time to spend with family and friends.

A relatively new company, Indulge.com (www.indulge.com), claims to be the first online specialty store "that redefines indulgence for the 21st century." Consider the company mission and the lifestyle it attempts to foster:[24]

> The Indulge.com mission is to be the premier on-line "specialty store" and destination of choice for savvy consumers by providing the most unique and satisfying shopping experience; and the products and services that fulfill their desire for style, beauty, and everyday indulgences. . . . It values detail, nuance and the unexpected touch—those qualities that elevate a product from a basic to that of a basic luxury.

Material comfort has often been associated with "bigger quantities of things" or "more of something." Recently, however, there has been a noticeable shift away from such a "more is better" viewpoint to a "better is better" vision—one that stresses better quality and better design. Americans today increasingly want better, and better looking, products. Such a state of affairs has been referred to as "the design economy"—that is, an economy that is based on the interaction of four elements: sustained prosperity, ongoing technology, a culture open to change, and marketing expertise.[25] Consider, for example, how the famous designer, Michael Graves, has helped Target (mass-merchandise retailer) accomplish its goal of being a standout provider of finely designed products at mass-market prices.

INDIVIDUALISM

Americans place a strong value on "being themselves." Self-reliance, self-interest, self-confidence, self-esteem, and self-fulfillment are all exceedingly popular expressions of individualism. Striving for individualism seems to be linked to the rejection of dependency; that is, it is better to rely on oneself than on others.

In terms of consumer behavior, an appeal to individualism frequently takes the form of reinforcing the consumer's sense of identity with products or services that both reflect and emphasize that identity. For example, advertisements for high-style clothing and cosmetics usually promise that their products will enhance the consumer's exclusive or distinctive character and set him or her apart from others.

FREEDOM

Freedom is another very strong American value, with historical roots in such democratic ideals as freedom of speech, freedom of the press, and freedom of worship. As an outgrowth of these democratic beliefs in freedom, Americans have a strong preference for freedom of choice, the opportunity to choose from a wide range of alternatives. This preference is reflected in the large number of competitive brands and product variations that can be found on the shelves of the modern supermarket or department store. For many products, consumers can select from a wide variety of sizes, colors, flavors, features, styles, and even special ingredients (such as all-natural-ingredient toothpaste without sugar). It also explains why many companies offer consumers many choices (see Figure 12-7).

However, there are decision-making situations when consumers are faced with too many choices. In such cases they may feel overwhelmed by the shear number of choices and respond by running away from the stressful situation (see Chapter 16).

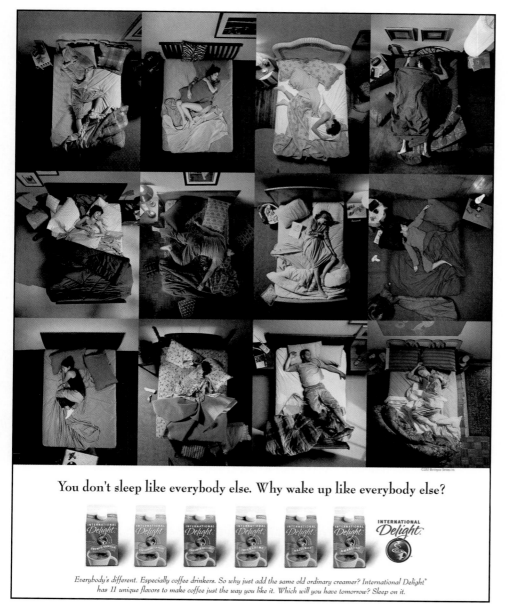

FIGURE 12-7

Ad Featuring the
"Freedom of Choice"
Courtesy of Dean Foods.

You don't sleep like everybody else. Why wake up like everybody else?

INTERNATIONAL
Delight.

Everybody's different. Especially coffee drinkers. So why just add the same old ordinary creamer? International Delight
has 11 unique flavors to make coffee just the way you like it. Which will you have tomorrow? Sleep on it.

Recent research with 1,000 English consumers found that many of the respondents reported feeling bewildered and irritated by the fact that they were being offered "too much choice."[26]

EXTERNAL CONFORMITY

Although Americans deeply embrace freedom of choice and individualism, they nevertheless accept the reality of conformity. *External conformity* is a necessary process by which the individual adapts to society.

In the realm of consumer behavior, conformity (or uniformity) takes the form of standardized goods and services. Standardized products have been made possible by mass production. The availability of a wide choice of standardized products places the consumer in the unique position of being *individualistic* (by selecting specific products that close friends do not have) or of *conforming* (by purchasing a similar or identical product). In this context, individualism and conformity exist side by side as choices for the consumer.

An interesting example of the "Ping-Pong" relationship between seeking individualism and accepting conformity is the widespread acceptance of more casual dressing in the workplace (already discussed in this chapter). For instance, male and female executives are conforming less to workplace dress codes (i.e., there are more "total" dress options open to business executives). For instance, some male executives are wearing casual slacks and sport shirts to work; others are wearing blazers and slacks rather than business suits. Greater personal confidence and an emphasis on comfort appear to be the reasons that many executives are wearing less traditional business attire. Nevertheless, in some companies the appearance of male executives in blue blazers and gray slacks does seem like a "business uniform" (which is a kind of conformity). Consumer research examining the types of clothing that men and women wear to the office suggests that the majority of American workers are wearing some type of casual clothing to work.[27] For men, it is commonly "everyday casual" (jeans, shorts, T-shirts, etc.); for women it is "casual" (casual pants with or without a jacket, sweaters, separates, and pantsuits). Moreover, more than 50 percent of workers surveyed feel that it increases their productivity to wear casual clothing to work.

HUMANITARIANISM

Americans are often generous when it comes to giving to those in need. They support with a passion many humane and charitable causes, and they sympathize with the underdog who must overcome adversity to get ahead. They also tend to be charitable and willing to come to the aid of people who are less fortunate than they are. To make the study of charitable giving more fruitful, consumer researchers have recently validated two scales that deal with *attitudes toward helping others* (AHO) and *attitudes toward charitable organizations* (ACO).[28] Table 12-5 presents the nine-item scale used to measure AHO and ACO.

Within the context of making charitable decisions, the Web site of the Planned Giving Design Center (**www.pgdc.net**) assists charities in their efforts to establish and cultivate relationships with professionals who advise clients in a position to make charitable contributions (e.g., lawyers, financial planners, trust officers).[29] Other Web sites are designed to provide individual givers with assistance in donating to specific charities (e.g., **www.charityguide.org**, **www.guidestar.org**, and **www.charitynavigator.org**).

Beyond charitable giving, other social issues have an impact on both what consumers buy and where they invest. For example, some investors prefer mutual funds that screen companies for such social concerns as military contracts, pollution problems, and equal opportunity employment. Investments in socially conscious mutual funds are now quite commonplace. Many companies try to appeal to consumers by emphasizing their concern for environmental or social issues.

YOUTHFULNESS

Americans tend to place an almost sacred value on *youthfulness*. This emphasis is a reflection of America's rapid technological development. In an atmosphere where "new" is constantly stressed, "old" is often equated with being outdated. This is in contrast to traditional European, African, and Asian societies, in which the elderly are revered for having the wisdom of experience that comes with age.

Youthfulness should not be confused with youth, which describes an age grouping. Americans are preoccupied with *looking* and *acting* young, regardless of their

TABLE 12-5	A Scale to Measure Attitude Toward Helping Others (AHO) and Attitude Toward Charitable Organizations (ACO)

SCALE ITEM

ATTITUDE TOWARD HELPING OTHERS (AHO)

People should be willing to help others who are less fortunate.

Helping troubled people with their problems is very important to me.

People should be more charitable toward others in society.

People in need should receive support from others.

ATTITUDE TOWARD CHARITABLE ORGANIZATIONS (ACO)

The money given to charities goes for good causes.

Much of the money donated to charity is wasted. (R)

My image of charitable organizations is positive.

Charitable organizations have been quite successful in helping the needy.

Charity organizations perform a useful function for society.

Note: (R) = reverse scored.
Source: Deborah J. Webb, Corliss L. Green, and Thomas G. Brashear, "Development and Validation of Scales to Measure Attitudes Influencing Monetary Donations to Charitable Organizations," *Journal of the Academy of Marketing Science,* 28, no. 12, Spring 2000, 299–309. Reprinted by permission of the publisher.

chronological age. For Americans, youthfulness is a state of mind and a state of being, sometimes expressed as being "young at heart," "young in spirit," or "young in appearance." Figure 12-8 presents an ad for Olay® Total Effects that depicts a woman who is "declaring war" on aging.

A great deal of advertising is directed to creating a sense of urgency about retaining one's youth and fearing aging.[30] Hand-cream ads talk about "young hands"; skin-treatment ads state "I dreaded turning 30 . . . "; fragrance and makeup ads stress looking "sexy and young" or "denying your age"; detergent ads ask the reader, "Can you match their hands with their ages?" These advertising themes, which promise the consumer the benefits of youthfulness, reflect the high premium Americans place on appearing and acting young.

Consider what one writer concludes after examining examples of "midlife consciousness" in American literature of the late nineteenth and early twentieth centuries:[31]

Since the early nineteenth century, Americans have tended to sentimentalize youth; aging represents a loss beyond sentimentalizing . . . middle age is represented as the stuff of jokes, taken seriously only when linked to catastrophe. Even today, middle age represents a crisis to be resolved. This crisis mentality is the aftereffect of the culture's sentimentalizing of youth.

FITNESS AND HEALTH

Americans' preoccupation with *fitness* and *health* has emerged as a core value. This value has manifested itself in a number of ways, including tennis, racquetball, and jogging, and the continued increases in sales of vitamins. Added to these trends is an enhanced consciousness on the part of Americans that "You are what you eat" (see Figure 12-9).

FIGURE 12-8

Fighting the Signs of
Aging
Courtesy of The Procter &
Gamble Company. Used by
permission.

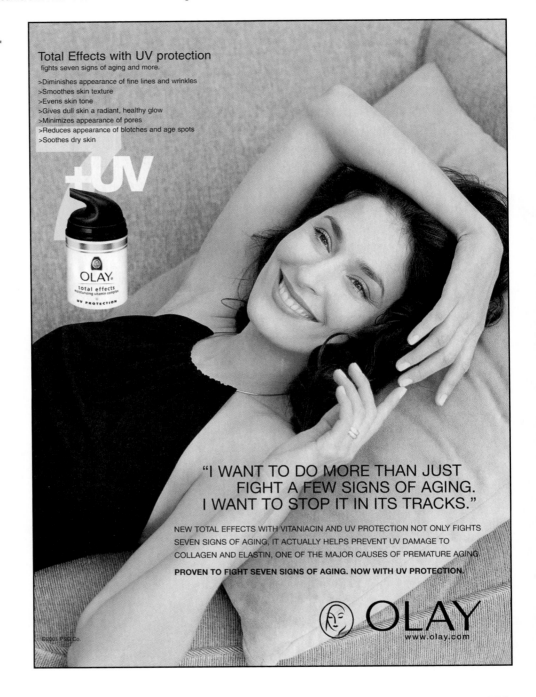

Fitness and health are becoming lifestyle choices for many consumers. This trend has stimulated Reebok to open a series of exercise-retail complexes that seek to build a cultural connection with consumers that goes beyond the normal marketing approach. Traditional food manufacturers have begun modifying their ingredients to cater to the health-conscious consumer. Frozen dinners have become more nutritious in recent years, and manufacturers of traditional "junk food" are trying to make it more healthful. "Light" or "fat-free" versions of snack chips or pretzels, along with "low-sodium," "no-cholesterol," "no-preservative" snack products, are an

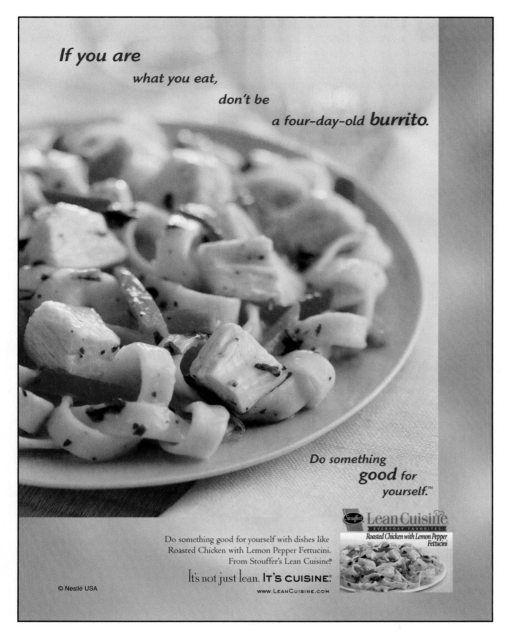

attempt to provide consumers with tasty and healthy options. There are even Web
sites for the fitness-minded consumer (see **www.fitnessonline.com**) offering work-
out tips, nutritional information, and fitness-related products and services. And the
Wall Street Journal has reported that 100 million Americans sought health information over the Internet in the year 2000—up 30 million from the prior year.[32]

Although there is no denying the "fitness and healthy living" trend in American
society, there is evidence that consumers find it difficult "to be good" in terms of their
personal health. For instance, people miss their desserts. Research suggests that more
than 75 percent of American consumers think about dessert between one and eight
times a day. The main activities that seem to put people in the mood for desserts are
exercise, working, entertainment, eating, and studying.[33] Also, many Americans are

unwilling to compromise on flavor for health benefits, with the result being a kind of reverse trend toward full-flavored, rich foods. This countertrend reveals the diversity of preferences that exist side by side within the marketplace.[34] It points up that low-fat and low-cholesterol food products are not for everyone and that there is an important market segment whose members seek to indulge their taste buds and their waistlines. Indeed, AC Nielsen data for food, drug, and mass-merchandising outlet sales indicated that recently fat-free potato chip sales were down 33 percent, fat-free cookies and margarine sales were down 12 percent, and fat-free ice cream sales were down 22 percent.[35] And the World Health Organization has released a report stating that obesity is an increasing problem in both developed and developing countries.

CORE VALUES ARE NOT AN AMERICAN PHENOMENON

The cultural values just examined are not all uniquely or originally American. Some were borrowed, particularly from European society, as people emigrated to the United States. Some values that originated in America are now part of the fabric of other societies. For example, there is evidence that the good life may be a universal notion and that global brands are used as an external sign of attaining the good life.[36]

In addition, not all Americans necessarily accept each of these values. However, as a whole, these values do account for much of the American character. Table 12-6 summarizes a number of American core values and indicates their relevance to consumer behavior.

TABLE 12-6   Summary of American Core Values

VALUE	GENERAL FEATURES	RELEVANCE TO CONSUMER BEHAVIOR
Achievement and Success, Activity	Hard work is good; success flows from hard work	Acts as a justification for acquisition of goods ("You deserve it")
	Keeping busy is healthy and natural	Stimulates interest in products that are time-savers and enhance leisure time
Efficiency and Practicality	Admiration of things that solve problems (e.g., save time and effort)	Stimulates purchase of products that function well and save time
	People can improve themselves; tomorrow should be better than today	Stimulates desire for new products that fulfill unsatisfied needs; ready acceptance of products that claim to be "new and improved"
Material Comfort	"The good life"	Fosters acceptance of convenience and luxury products that make life more comfortable and enjoyable
Individualism	Being oneself (e.g., self-reliance, self-interest, self-esteem)	Stimulates acceptance of customized or unique products that enable a person to "express his or her own personality"
Freedom	Freedom of choice	Fosters interest in wide product lines and differentiated products
External Conformity	Uniformity of observable behavior; desire for acceptance	Stimulates interest in products that are used or owned by others in the same social group
Humanitarianism	Caring for others, particularly the underdog	Stimulates patronage of firms that compete with market leaders
Youthfulness	A state of mind that stresses being "young at heart" and having a youthful appearance	Stimulates acceptance of products that provide the illusion of maintaining or fostering youthfulness
Fitness and Health	Caring about one's body, including the desire to be physically fit and healthy	Stimulates acceptance of food products, activities, and equipment perceived to maintain or increase physical fitness.

Summary

The study of culture is the study of all aspects of a society. It is the language, knowledge, laws, and customs that give that society its distinctive character and personality. In the context of consumer behavior, culture is defined as the sum total of learned beliefs, values, and customs that serve to regulate the consumer behavior of members of a particular society. Beliefs and values are guides for consumer behavior; customs are usual and accepted ways of behaving.

The impact of culture on society is so natural and so ingrained that its influence on behavior is rarely noted. Yet, culture offers order, direction, and guidance to members of society in all phases of human problem solving. Culture is dynamic and gradually and continually evolves to meet the needs of society.

Culture is learned as part of social experience. Children acquire from their environment a set of beliefs, values, and customs that constitutes culture (i.e., they are encultured). These are acquired through formal learning, informal learning, and technical learning. Advertising enhances formal learning by reinforcing desired modes of behavior and expectations; it enhances informal learning by providing models for behavior.

Culture is communicated to members of society through a common language and through commonly shared symbols. Because the human mind has the ability to absorb and to process symbolic communication, marketers can successfully promote both tangible and intangible products and product concepts to consumers through mass media.

All the elements in the marketing mix serve to communicate symbolically with the audience. Products project an image of their own; so does promotion. Price and retail outlets symbolically convey images concerning the quality of the product.

The elements of culture are transmitted by three pervasive social institutions: the family, the church, and the school. A fourth social institution that plays a major role in the transmission of culture is the mass media, both through editorial content and through advertising.

A wide range of measurement techniques is used to study culture. The range includes projective techniques, attitude measurement methods, field observation, participant observation, content analysis, and value measurement survey techniques.

A number of core values of the American people are relevant to the study of consumer behavior. These include achievement and success, activity, efficiency and practicality, progress, material comfort, individualism, freedom, conformity, humanitarianism, youthfulness, and fitness and health.

Because each of these values varies in importance to the members of our society, each provides an effective basis for segmenting consumer markets.

Discussion Questions

1. Distinguish among beliefs, values, and customs. Illustrate how the clothing a person wears at different times or for different occasions is influenced by customs.

2. A manufacturer of fat-free granola bars is considering targeting school-age children by positioning its product as a healthy, nutritious snack food. How can an understanding of the three forms of cultural learning be used in developing an effective strategy to target the intended market?

3. The Citrus Growers of America is planning a promotional campaign to encourage the drinking of orange and grapefruit juice in situations in which many consumers normally consume soft drinks. Using the Rokeach Value Survey (Table 12-4), identify relevant cultural, consumption-specific, and product-specific values for citrus juices as an alternative to soft drinks. What are the implications of these values for an advertising campaign designed to increase the consumption of citrus juices?

4. For each of the following products and activities:
   a. Identify the core values most relevant to their purchase and use.
   b. Determine whether these values encourage or discourage use or ownership.

c. Determine whether these core values are shifting and, if so, in what direction. The products and activities are:

1. Donating money to charities
2. Donating blood
3. Compact disk players
4. Telephone answering machines
5. Toothpaste
6. Diet soft drinks
7. Foreign travel
8. Suntan lotion
9. Cellular phones
10. Interactive TV home-shopping services
11. Fat-free foods
12. Products in recyclable packaging

Exercises

1. Identify a singer or singing group whose music you like and discuss the symbolic function of the clothes that person (or group) wears.

2. Think of various routines in your everyday life (such as grooming or food preparation). Identify one ritual and describe it. In your view, is this ritual shared by others? If so, to what extent? What are the implications of your ritualistic behavior to the marketer(s) of the product(s) you use during your routine?

3. a. Summarize an episode of a weekly television series that you watched recently. Describe how the program transmitted cultural beliefs, values, and customs.

b. Select and describe three commercials that were broadcast during the program mentioned in 3a. Do these commercials create or reflect cultural values? Explain your answer.

4. a. Find two different advertisements for deodorants in two magazines that are targeted to different audiences. Content-analyze the written and pictorial aspects of each ad, using any core values discussed in this chapter. How are these values portrayed to the target audiences?

b. Identify symbols used in these ads and discuss their effectiveness in conveying the desired product image or characteristics.

Key Terms

- **Acculturation**
- **Consumer fieldwork**
- **Content analysis**
- **Core values**

- **Culture**
- **Enculturation**
- **Field observation**
- **Participant-observers**

- **Ritual**
- **Rokeach Value Survey**
- **Subculture**
- **Symbols**

Notes

1. Thomas C. O'Guinn and L. J. Shrum, "The Role of Television in the Construction of Consumer Reality," *Journal of Consumer Research*, 23, March 1997, 278–295.
2. Linda C. Ueltschy and Robert F. Krampf, "Cultural Sensitivity to Satisfaction and Service Quality Measures," *Journal of Marketing Theory and Practice*, Summer 2001, 14–31.
3. "Demo Memo," *American Demographics*, February 1998, 41.
4. "U.S. Coffee Consumption Highest in Decade-Survey," *Forbes.Com*, June 14, 2002, at www.forbes.com/business/newswire/2002/06/14rtr632507.html.
5. Gwen Rae Bachmann, Deborah Roedder John, and Akshay Rao, "Children's Susceptibility to Peer Group Purchase Influence: An Exploratory Investigation," in *Advances in Consumer Research*, vol. 20, eds. Leigh McAlister and Michael L. Rothschild (Provo, UT: Association for Consumer Research 1993), 463–468.
6. Shaila K. Dewan, "Can't Afford Hawaii? Get the Shirt," *New York Times*, July 21, 2001, B1, B6.
7. Dennis W. Rook, "The Ritual Dimension of Consumer Behavior," *Journal of Consumer Research*, 12, December 1985, 251–264.

8. Dennis W. Rook, "Ritual Behavior and Consumer Symbolism," in *Advances in Consumer Research,* vol. 11, ed. Thomas C. Kinnear (Ann Arbor, MI: Association for Consumer Research, 1984), 279–284.

9. Tara Parker-Pope, "All That Glitters Isn't Purchased by Men," *Wall Street Journal,* January 7, 1997, B1; and Dana Canedy, "As the Purchasing Power of Women Rises, Marketers Start to Pay Attention to Them," *New York Times,* July 2, 1998, D6.

10. Michael L. Maynard and Charles R. Taylor, "Girlish Images Across Cultures: Analyzing Japanese Versus U.S. *Seventeen* Magazine Ads," *Journal of Advertising,* 28, no. 1, Spring 1999, 39–45.

11. Mindy F. Ji and James U. McNeal, "How Chinese Children's Commercials Differ from Those of the United States: A Content Analysis," *Journal of Advertising,* 30, no. 3, Fall 2001, 79–92.

12. Lawrence Osborne, "Consuming Rituals of the Suburban Tribe," *New York Times Magazine,* January 13, 2002, 28–31; Margaret Littman, "Science Shopping," *Crain's Chicago Business,* January 11, 1999, 3; and Marvin Matises, "Top of Mind: Send Ethnographers into New-SKU Jungle," *Brandweek,* September 25, 2000, 32–33.

13. Wagner A. Kamakura and Jose Afonso Mazzon, "Value Segmentation: A Model for the Measurement of Values and Value Systems," *Journal of Consumer Research,* 18, September 1991, 208–218.

14. Lynn R. Kahle, ed., *Social Values and Social Change: Adaption of Life in America* (New York: Praeger, 1983); Sharon E. Beatty et al., "Alternative Measurement Approaches to Consumer Values: The List of Values and the Rokeach Value Survey," *Psychology & Marketing,* 2, 1985, 181–200; and Lynn R. Kahle, Roger P. McIntyre, Reid P. Claxton, and David B. Jones, "Empirical Relationships Between Cognitive Style and LOV: Implications for Values and Value Systems," in *Advances in Consumer Research,* vol. 22, eds. Frank R. Kardes and Mita Sujan (Provo, UT: Association for Consumer Research 1995), 141–146.

15. David C. McClelland, *The Achieving Society* (New York: Free Press, 1961), 150–151.

16. Lawrence E. Harrison, "Culture Matters," *The National Interest,* 60, Summer 2000, 55–65.

17. James P. Miller, "Cereal Makers Fight Bagels with Price Cuts," *Wall Street Journal,* June 20, 1996, B1.

18. "Just Keeping Busy in Old Age Isn't the Key to Actively Enjoying Life; Seniors: The Quality and Purpose of Their Activities Determine Whether the Elderly Are Just Going Through the Motions or Truly Fulfilled, a Researcher Has Found," *The Los Angeles Times,* November 26, 1999, 5C; and Evelyn Petersen, "Being Busy All The Time Isn't Healthy Series: Booked Solid," *Syracuse Herald American,* October 17, 1999, A13.

19. Corina Cristea, "Now Everybody's a Busy Body," *Brandweek,* July 6, 1998, 18–19.

20. Peter Rojas, "Time-Out Guide," *Red Herring,* December 1999, 114.

21. Kate Gurnett, "Life Coaches Help People Move into Winner's Circle," *Times Union,* March 3, 2002, S21.

22. William J. Havlena and Susan L. Holak, "Children's Images and Symbols of Wealth: An Exploration Using Consumer Collages," *1997 AMA Winter Educators' Conference,* eds. Debbie Thorne LeClair and Michael Hartline (Chicago: American Marketing Association, 1997), 1–2.

23. Ramesh Venkat and Harold J. Ogden, "Material Satisfaction: The Effects of Social Comparison and Attribution," in *1995 AMA Educators' Proceedings,* eds. Barbara B. Stern and George M. Zinkan (Chicago: American Marketing Association, 1995), 314–349.

24. "Indulge.com to Launch with a Multi-Million Dollar Ad Campaign; Arnell Group Creates Their First Internet Campaign," *PR Newswire,* November 16, 1999, 1.

25. Frank Gibney, Jr. and Belinda Luscombe, "The Redesigning of America," *Time,* June 26, 2000, unnumbered insert section.

26. Virginia Matthews, "Simplicity Is the Consumer's Choice: Marketing Product Innovation: Shoppers Complain of Confusion as Companies Blitz Them with a Host of New Products, Writes Virginia Matthews," *Financial Times* (London), December 10, 1999, 16.

27. "Casual Clothes Are Workplace Trend," *Brandweek,* July 18, 1994, 17. Also, see Ellen Neuborne, "Fashion on Menu at T.G.I. Friday's," *USA Today,* February 27, 1996, B1.

28. Deborah J. Webb, Corliss L. Green, and Thomas G. Brashear, "Development and Validation of Scales to Measure Attitudes Influencing Monetary Donations to Charitable Organizations," *Journal of the Academy of Marketing Science,* 28, 2, Spring 2000, 299–309.

29. George R. Reis, "Building Bridges," *Fund Raising Management,* 30, 6, August 1999, 19–23.

30. Richard A. Lee "The Youth Bias in Advertising," *American Demographics,* January 1997, 47–50.

31. Dale M. Bauer, "Refusing Middle Age," *ANQ,* 15, 1, Winter 2002, 46–60.

32. Laura Landro, "More People Are Using Internet Health Sites, But Fewer Are Satisfied," *Wall Street Journal,* December 29, 2000, A9.

33. "The Big Scoop on Just Desserts," *Advertising Age,* October 2, 1995, 3.

34. Sean Mehegan, "As Indulgence Roars Back with a Vengeance, Low-Fat Candies Beat a Strategic Retreat," *Brandweek,* March 2, 1998, 12.

35. Jeffrey A. Tannenbaum, "Fat-Free Store Pushes to Gain Weight in U.S.—Small New York Firm Targets Shrinking Market," *Asian Wall Street Journal,* February 14, 2001, N5; and Normita Thongtham, "You Are What You Eat," *The Bangkok Post,* March 2, 2002, 1.

36. George M. Zinkhan and Penelope J. Prenshaw, "Good Life Images and Brand Name Associations: Evidence from Asia, America, and Europe," in *Advances in Consumer Research,* vol. 21, eds. Chris T. Allen and Deborah Roedder John (Provo, UT: Association for Consumer Research, 1994), 496–500.

Cellular Case No. 1074

Aug. 15, 3:52pm: Buffalo, New York.

"It was either static or my girlfriend pretending ther was static—either way there's a problem."

It's about time somebody cleared things up around here.

The last thing you need in your life is more static. That's why Sprint PCS built the only all-digital, all-PCS nationwide network from the ground up, serving more than 280 major metropolitan areas. So no matter who you're talking to, your calls will be clear. The conversation, on the other hand, is up to you. **1-800-480-4PCS** or visit **www.sprintpcs.com**

 Sprint®

The clear alternative to cellular.℠

Sprint PCS®

13

Subcultures and Consumer Behavior

C ulture has a potent influence on all consumer behavior. Individuals are brought up to follow the beliefs, values, and customs of their society and to avoid behavior that is judged unacceptable or considered taboo. In addition to segmenting in terms of cultural factors, marketers also segment overall societies into smaller subgroups (subcultures) that consist of people who are similar in terms of their ethnic origin, their customs, and the ways they behave. These subcultures provide important marketing opportunities for astute marketing strategists.

Our discussion of subcultures, therefore, has a narrower focus than the discussion of culture. Instead of examining the dominant beliefs, values, and customs that exist within an entire society, this chapter explores the marketing opportunities created by the existence of certain beliefs, values, and customs shared by members of specific subcultural groups within a society.

These subcultural divisions are based on a variety of sociocultural and demographic variables, such as nationality, religion, geographic locality, race, age, and sex.

What Is Subculture?

The members of a specific **subculture** possess beliefs, values, and customs that set them apart from other members of the same society. In addition, they adhere to most of the dominant cultural beliefs, values, and behavioral patterns of the larger society. We define subculture, then, as *a distinct cultural group that exists as an identifiable segment within a larger, more complex society.*

Thus, the cultural profile of a society or nation is a composite of two distinct elements: (1) the unique beliefs, values, and customs subscribed to by members of specific subcultures; and (2) the central or core cultural themes that are shared by most of the population, regardless of specific subcultural memberships. Figure 13-1 presents a simple model of the relationship between two subcultural groups (geographic or regional subcultures—i.e., Easterners and Westerners) and the larger culture. As the figure depicts, each subculture has its own unique traits, yet both groups share the dominant traits of the overall American culture.

Let us look at it in another way: Each American is, in large part, a product of the "American way of life." Each American, however, is at the same time a member of various subcultures. For example, an 11-year-old boy may simultaneously be Hispanic American, Catholic, a preteen, and a South Carolinian. We would expect that membership in each different subculture would provide its own set of specific beliefs, values, attitudes, and customs. Table 13-1 lists typical subcultural categories and corresponding examples of specific subcultural groups. This list is by no means exhaustive: Elementary school teachers, Republicans, Girl Scouts, and millionaires—in fact, any group that shares common beliefs and customs—may be classified as a subculture.

Subcultural analysis enables the marketing manager to focus on sizable and natural market segments. When carrying out such analyses, the marketer must determine whether the beliefs, values, and customs shared by members of a specific subgroup make them desirable candidates for special marketing attention. Subcultures, therefore, are relevant units of analysis for market research. And these subcultures are dynamic—for example, as presented in Figure 13-2, the different ethnic groups that comprise the U.S. population have been changing and will continue to change in size and economic power in the coming years. For instance, the

FIGURE 13-1

Relationship Between
Culture and Subculture

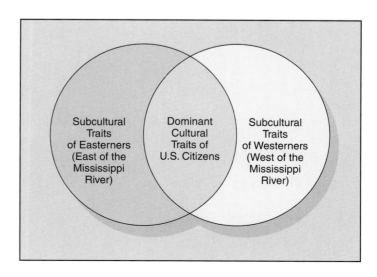

Subcultural
Traits
of Easterners
(East of the
Mississippi
River)

Dominant
Cultural
Traits of
U.S. Citizens

Subcultural
Traits
of Westerners
(West of the
Mississippi
River)

TABLE 13-1	Examples of Major Subcultural Categories

CATEGORIES	EXAMPLES
Nationality (i.e., birthplace of ancestors)	Jamaican, Vietnamese, French
Religion	Mormon, Baptist, Catholic
Geographic region	Northeast, Southwest, Midwest
Race	Pacific Islander, Native American, Caucasian
Age	Senior citizen, teenager, Xers
Gender	Female, male
Occupation	Bus driver, mechanic, engineer
Social class	Lower, middle, upper

white (non-Hispanic) population of the Unites States, which made up 71 percent of Americans in the year 2000, is projected to represent about 53 percent of the U.S. population by the year 2050.[1] Frequently a "window on the future," the State of California in 1999 reported that the state's multicultural or combined minority population became the state's majority population.[2]

A recent study of ethnic media usage in California also found that 84 percent of Asian American, African American, and Hispanic American respondents claimed to get information from ethnic television, radio, and publications. Furthermore, 68 percent preferred ethnic-language TV stations over English channels for news, and 40 percent reported paying greater attention to ethnic language ads than English-language ads.[3]

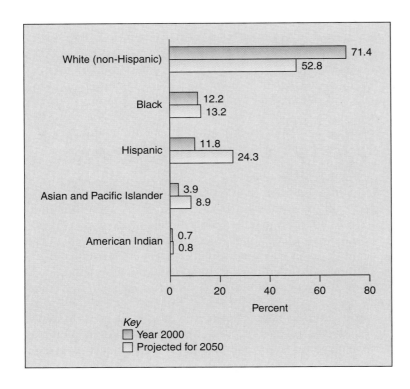

Key
Year 2000
Projected for 2050

FIGURE 13-2

Ethnic Groups as a Percentage of the U.S. Population
Source: Victor Wishna, "Getting with the Program," *Restaurant Business,* March 1, 2000, 39; as based on U.S. Census Bureau data.

The following sections examine a number of important subcultural categories: nationality, religion, geographic location, race, age, and sex. (Occupational and social-class subgroups were discussed in detail in Chapter 11.)

Nationality Subcultures

For many people, **nationality** is an important subcultural reference that guides what they value and what they buy. This is especially true for the population of a country like the United States that has a history of attracting people from all over the globe. Supporting this pattern are the results of the 2000 U.S. Census, which found that about one in ten Americans is foreign born.[4] For these Americans, as well as Americans born in the United States, there is frequently a strong sense of identification and pride in the language and customs of their ancestors.

When it comes to consumer behavior, this ancestral pride is manifested most strongly in the consumption of ethnic foods, in travel to the "homeland," and in the purchase of numerous cultural artifacts (ethnic clothing, art, music, foreign-language newspapers). Interest in these goods and services has expanded rapidly as younger Americans attempt to better understand and more closely associate with their ethnic roots. To illustrate the importance of ethnic origin as a subcultural market segment, the following section examines the **Hispanic American subculture.**

HISPANIC SUBCULTURES

The 2000 U.S. Census found that the number of Hispanic Americans (of all races) had grown by more than 60 percent during the 1990s (compared to an overall U.S. population growth of 13.2 percent). These 35.3 million Americans represent about 12 percent of the U.S. population and an estimate of Hispanic purchasing power in 2001 was $452 billion.[5] In contrast to other American population segments, Hispanic Americans are younger—35 percent of Hispanics are 18 years old or younger, whereas only 26 percent of the U.S. population is 18 or younger. The median age for Hispanics is almost 26 years of age, whereas the median age for the rest of America is 35 years of age. Hispanic Americans also tend to be members of larger families (average Hispanic household size is 3.7 people compared to an average U.S. household size of 2.5 people). They are also more likely to live in an extended family household consisting of several generations of family members. Not only are Hispanic households more likely than black or non-Hispanic American white families to contain children, but also Hispanics spend more time caring for their children.[6]

By the year 2005, the Hispanic American subculture is expected to grow to over 38 million individuals and will then be the largest minority in the United States (supplanting African Americans as the largest American minority group).[7] Indeed, the 10 metro areas with the largest Hispanic populations are also the cities with the greatest gains in their Hispanic populations; they attracted more than half of all new Hispanic residents and together are the home to 58 percent of the Hispanic population of the United States.[8] Interestingly, though, new immigrants from Central America and Mexico have been moving into places such as North Carolina, Iowa, and Georgia.[9]

This subcultural group can be considered as a single market, based on a common language and culture, or as separate subcultural markets that correspond to different Hispanic countries of origin. There are 12 Hispanic subgroups identified in the United States. The three largest Hispanic subcultural groups consist of Mexican Americans (about 64 percent of total Hispanic Americans), Puerto Ricans (approximately 10 percent of the total), and Cubans (about 4 percent of the total). These subcultures are heavily concentrated geographically, with more than 70 percent of their members residing in California, Texas, New York, and Florida; Los Angeles alone is home to one-fifth of the Hispanic population of the United States. Also, whereas more than 60 percent of all Mexican Americans (the largest Hispanic group) were born in the United States, 72 percent of Cuban Americans were born in Cuba.[10]

Understanding Hispanic Consumer Behavior

Available evidence indicates that Hispanic and Anglo consumers differ in terms of a variety of important buyer behavior variables. For instance, Hispanic consumers have a strong preference for well-established brands and traditionally prefer to shop at smaller stores. In the New York metropolitan area, for example, Hispanic consumers spend 55 percent of their food budgets in over 8,000 *bodegas* (relatively small food specialty stores), despite the fact that supermarket prices generally are lower. Table 13-2 presents these and other distinctive characteristics of the overall Hispanic market.

Although mindful of their tradition, Hispanic Americans, like other major subcultural groups, are a dynamic and evolving portion of the overall society. For this reason, a growing number of Hispanic consumers are shifting their food shopping to nonethnic, large, American-style supermarkets. They appear to be engaged in a process of acculturation; that is, they are gradually adopting the consumption patterns of the majority of U.S. consumers. Similarly, when it comes to clothes shopping, Hispanic youths are more fashion conscious and are more likely to seek out and be loyal to well-known brands and to generally like the act of shopping more than their non-Hispanic counterparts.[11] And although only 39 percent of Hispanics currently own a computer (as compared to 63 percent of the U.S. population), fully one-third of these non-PC owners plan to purchase one within the next 12 months.[12] Perhaps one of the reasons why Mattel has introduced a Spanish-language "Barbie" site targeted to young girls (**www.barbielatina.com**) is because of the increasing number of Hispanic households with personal computers.[13]

TABLE 13-2	Traditional Characteristics of the Hispanic American Market

Prefer well-known or familiar brands

Buy brands perceived to be more prestigious

Are fashion conscious

Historically prefer to shop at smaller personal stores

Buy brands advertised by their ethnic-group stores

Tend not to be impulse buyers (i.e., are deliberate)

Increasingly clipping and using cents-off coupons

Likely to buy what their parents bought

Prefer fresh to frozen or prepared items

Tend to be negative about marketing practices and government intervention in business

| TABLE 13-3 | Ways in Which "Hispanic" Has Been Defined |

NAME OF INDICATOR	NATURE/SCOPE AND COMMENTARY
Spanish surname	Not a definitive; since a non-Hispanic person might have a Spanish surname, or a Hispanic person might have a non-Spanish surname.
Country of origin	The birthplace of persons born in the United States of Hispanic parents (e.g., of Puerto Rican parentage) would not reveal their Hispanic background.
Country of family ancestry	Includes those individuals who may not be Hispanic despite coming from a particular Spanish-Latin country (e.g., people of German parentage who may be brought up in a Latin country).
Spanish spoken at home	A significant minority of Hispanic households may speak English at home, yet consider themselves to be culturally Hispanic.
Self-identification	It is reasonable that if an adequate number of self-report choices are offered, a person might identify himself or herself as "Hispanic."
Degree of identification	This measure captures the "degree" of personal identification as "Hispanic" and augments the self-identification measure.

Defining and Segmenting the Hispanic Market

Marketers who are targeting the diversity within the Hispanic subcultures are concerned with finding the best ways to define and segment this overall subculture. In terms of definition, Table 13-3 presents six variables marketers have used to determine who is Hispanic. Of these measures, the combination of *self-identification* and *degree of identification* are particularly appealing, because they permit consumers to define or label themselves. Research shows that those who strongly identify with being Hispanic (*Strong Hispanic Identifiers*) are more frequent users of Spanish-language media, are more brand loyal, are more likely to buy prestige brands, are more likely to seek the advice of another and to more often be influenced by friends or family, and are more likely to buy brands advertised to Hispanics than Weak Hispanic Identifiers.[14] This pattern suggests that the degree of Hispanic identification is a useful segmentation variable when targeting the Hispanic market. Even among Hispanics who are bilingual at home, 55 percent feel that it is important for their salesperson to speak Spanish—and a full 34 percent of Hispanics who mainly speak English at home feel similarly.[15]

In addition, the Hispanic market can be segmented by using a combination of *country of origin* and *geographic concentration in the United States* (e.g., about 65 percent of Hispanic Americans of Mexican origin are concentrated in California and Texas; about 30 percent of those of Puerto Rican origin live in New York; and 67 percent of Cuban Americans live in Florida).[16] Some marketers feel that it is worthwhile to target each Hispanic American market separately. Other marketers, including Anheuser-Busch, Coca-Cola, American Honda, Sears, Coors, Colgate-Palmolive, McDonald's, Toyota, and Philip Morris, have targeted the Hispanic market as a single market, using Spanish-language mass media. Procter & Gamble, in an attempt to close up the 7-point market share gap between its brands in the overall U.S. market and its market share among Hispanic Americans and African Americans, moved its U.S. Hispanic marketing unit to Puerto Rico and employs several multicultural advertising agencies.[17]

FIGURE 13-3

Targeting Hispanic
American Consumers
Courtesy of The Procter &
Gamble Company. Used by
permission.

The Spanish language is often regarded as the bridge that links the various
Hispanic subcultures. Even with this common language, however, there is considerable variation among Hispanics regarding their language preferences (such as
Spanish only, Spanish preferred, English only, or English preferred). This language
categorization provides still another basis for segmenting the Hispanic American
market. Available research indicates that Hispanic Americans spend the most time
with mass media in the first language that they learn to speak. So those whose first
language is Spanish tend to prefer TV, radio, magazines, and newspapers in Spanish
(see Figure 13-3), whereas those Hispanic Americans who first learn English prefer

FIGURE 13-4

Hispanic Linguistic Challenge: Preferences Vary in Getting the Message
Source: Laurel Wentz, "Reverse English," *Advertising Age*, November 19, 2001, S1&S2 (based on research supplied by Strategy Research Corp).

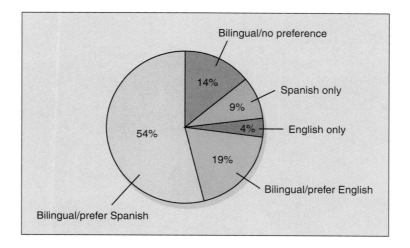

their media exposure to be in English.[18] However, there is also some evidence that Hispanic assimilation is a myth, especially with regard to Spanish-language television. Even second- and third-generation Hispanics in the United States, people who are completely bilingual and who speak English without a trace of an accent, are big viewers of Spanish-language television. This fact seems to hold true regardless of the Hispanic household's income. As the program director of Telemundo (one of the two Spanish-language TV networks operating in the United States) has observed, "After nearly 40 years, Spanish remains a more powerful force than assimilation."[19] Accordingly, Univision and Telemundo, two Spanish-language TV networks, together air about $1.7 billion worth of Hispanic television advertising, and Hispanic radio stations in New York, Miami, and Los Angeles successfully compete against mass market stations for top ratings.[20] Figure 13-4 presents the language preferences of Hispanic Americans with respect to receiving advertising messages. It clearly indicates that the largest segment of bilingual consumers prefer Spanish.

Each of the major Hispanic subcultural groups appears to have some distinct beliefs, values, and customs; thus, a marketing strategy that may be successful with Puerto Ricans in New York might fail with Cubans in Miami. For this reason some marketers segment the Hispanic market by appealing to the distinct cultural values of a specific nationality. Others segment the Hispanic market in terms of the degree of *acculturation* to the dominant American cultural values, customs, artifacts, and rituals.

Religious Subcultures

The United States reportedly has more than 200 different organized **religious subcultures.** Of this number, Protestant denominations, Roman Catholicism, and Judaism are the principal organized religious faiths. The members of all these religious groups at times are likely to make purchase decisions that are influenced by their religious identity. Commonly, consumer behavior is directly affected by religion in terms of products that are *symbolically* and *ritualistically* associated with the celebration of various religious holidays. For example, Christmas has become the major gift-purchasing season of the year.

Religious requirements or practices sometimes take on an expanded meaning beyond their original purpose. For instance, dietary laws for an observant

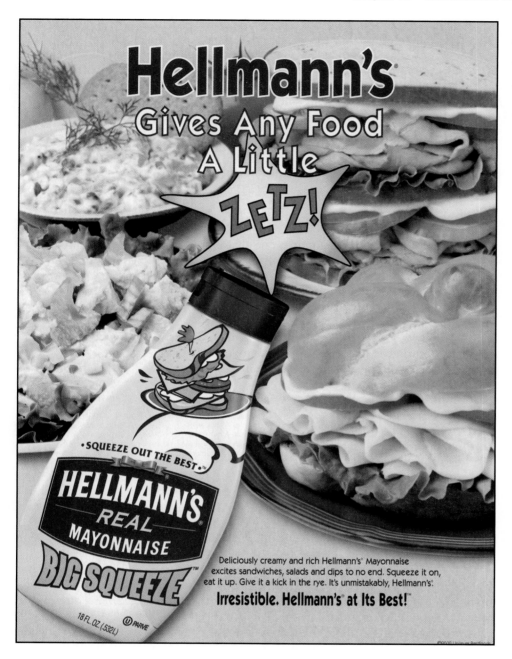

Jewish family represent an obligation, so there are toothpastes and artificial sweeteners that are kosher for Passover. The *U* and *K* marks on food packaging are symbols that the food meets Jewish dietary laws. For nonobservant Jews and an increasing number of non-Jews, however, these marks often signify that the food is pure and wholesome—a kind of "Jewish *Good Housekeeping* Seal of Approval." In response to the broader meaning given to kosher-certified products, a number of national brands, such as Coors beer and Pepperidge Farm cookies, have secured kosher certification for their products. Indeed, most Kosher food is consumed by non-Jews.[21] Figure 13-5 shows an ad for Hellmann's Real

Mayonnaise. Note that the label displays a *U* inside a circle and the word *parve*. This tells the shopper that the product is kosher and that it can be eaten with either meat or dairy products (but not both). Targeting specific religious groups with specially designed marketing programs can be really profitable. For instance, the Shaklee Corporation, a multilevel marketer of the Shaklee Performance drink mix, recruits salespeople from a variety of different religious groups (e.g., Hasidic Jews, Amish, and Mennonites) to sell its products to members of their communities.[22] It is likely that such shared religious identity and membership aid a salesperson in his or her effort to communicate with and persuade potential customers.

Geographic and Regional Subcultures

The United States is a large country, one that enjoys a wide range of climatic and geographic conditions. Given the country's size and physical diversity, it is only natural that many Americans have a sense of **regional** identification and use this identification as a way of describing others (such as "he is a true Southerner"). These labels often assist us in developing a mental picture and supporting *stereotype* of the person in question.

Anyone who has traveled across the United States has probably noted many regional differences in consumption behavior, especially when it comes to food and drink. For example, a *mug* of black coffee typifies the West, while a *cup* of coffee with milk and sugar is preferred in the East. There also are geographic differences in the consumption of a staple food such as bread. Specifically, in the South and Midwest, soft white bread is preferred, whereas on the East and West coasts, firmer breads (rye, whole wheat, and French and Italian breads) are favored. And regional differences also include brand preferences. Why do you suppose Skippy is the best-selling brand of peanut butter on both the East and West coasts, while Peter Pan sells best in the South and Jif sells best in the Midwest?[23] And for some food categories, there is even a difference between states in the same general region of the country. For example, what could explain the fact that 27 percent of Alabama residents consider pecan pie to be their favorite Thanksgiving dessert, whereas only 9 percent of Georgia residents and 10 percent of Tennessee residents feel similarly?[24]

Consumer research studies document regional differences in consumption patterns. For instance, Table 13-4 illustrates that differences in product purchase, ownership, or usage levels occur between major metropolitan areas. This distribution helps redefine local markets in terms of specific urban lifestyles. A more detailed illustration of regional preferences is presented in Table 13-5, which reports where Americans tend to go to get a cup of coffee. Specifically, 41 percent of Northeasterners head for a bagel or donut shop, as compared to 14 percent of Westerners, who are much more likely to buy their cup of coffee in a coffee specialty shop like Starbucks or Gloria Jean's.[25] Still further, Table 13-6 reveals that San Francisco leads the nation's 25 largest markets when it comes to shopping on the Internet. These examples provide strong evidence supporting marketers who argue that it is important to take geographic consumption patterns into account when planning marketing and promotional efforts.

In general, large metropolitan areas, with a substantial number of affluent middle-age households, dominate many, but not all, consumer-spending categories. Two examples are the San Jose, California, metro area, which leads in apparel purchasing,

| TABLE 13-4 | Product Purchase/Usage by Leading Metropolitan Market |

PRODUCT PURCHASE/USAGE	HIGHEST PURCHASE/USAGE	LOWEST PURCHASE/USAGE
Dental floss	San Francisco	Dallas–Fort Worth
Own a domestic vehicle	Detroit	New York
Own an imported vehicle	Los Angeles	Detroit
Dessert toppings	Chicago	San Francisco
Ready-to-drink iced tea	New York	Dallas–Fort Worth
Snack mix	Detroit	New York
Own a camcorder	Chicago	Boston
Cat treat	Cleveland	Dallas–Fort Worth
Car rental—business use	San Francisco	New York
Ready-to-drink iced cappuccino	Los Angeles	Detroit
Shoe polish	New York	Boston
Own 4-plus TV sets	Detroit	San Francisco
Low/no alcohol beer	Los Angeles	Dallas–Fort Worth
Grated cheese	Philadelphia	Los Angeles
Pre-electric shave lotion	Washington, DC	San Francisco

Source: Doublebase Mediamark Research, Inc. 2001 Doublebase Report. All rights reserved. Reprinted by permission.

and Nassau-Suffolk counties in New York, which lead in purchasing of insurance and pension programs.[26] Also, demonstrating local and regional differences, consumer research reveals that Irwindale, California, is the "king of the Big Mac." This California community is home of the greatest per capita sales of Big Macs—double or triple the sales of the four next largest markets.[27] Does anyone know why?

Regional differences also exist with respect to entertainment and entertainment/electronic products. Consider the following:[28]

- *The gritty TV drama Law & Order: Special Victims Unit is strong with viewers in the Northeast but does just so-so in the more conservative South.*
- *The eerie Stir of Echoes and other horror films are top choices in North Dakota video stores, but foreign films are the favorites in Hawaii.*
- *Rock 'n' roll, whose dominance has declined in recent years, remains king on the radio in one area: the Rocky Mountain states.*

| TABLE 13-5 | Where Americans Go for a Cup of Coffee |

	MIDWEST	NORTHEAST	SOUTH	WEST
A diner or sit-down restaurant	55%	42%	46%	47%
A coffee shop like Starbucks or Gloria Jean's	34%	28%	27%	42%
A convenience store	26%	28%	28%	24%
A bagel or donut shop	18%	41%	21%	14%
A fast-food chain	23%	12%	22%	17%
At work	14%	8%	11%	14%

Source: Katarzyna Dawidowska, "Caffeine Overload," *American Demographics,* 24, i4, April 2002, 16. © Media Central Inc., a Primedia Company. All rights reserved. Reprinted by permission.

TABLE 13-6	Percentage of consumer from Selected Major Market Areas That Purchased Online During Past 30 Days

Of the 25 largest U.S. markets, the San Francisco Bay Area leads the nation in shopping online.

DMA (DESIGNATED MARKET AREA)	PURCHASED ONLINE LAST 30 DAYS
San Francisco	22.3%
Washington, DC	18.9%
Boston	18.5%
Seattle–Tacoma	18.4%
Dallas–Fort Worth	18.2%
Chicago	16.2%
Houston	15.9%
New York	15.2%
Phoenix	15.0%
Atlanta	14.9%

Source: John Fetto, "Online Shopping Spree," *American Demographics*, 24, 2, February 2002, 14. © Media Central Inc., a Primedia Company. All rights reserved. Reprinted by permission.

Additionally, consumers in some geographic areas of the United States appear to have more trouble operating entertainment products (e.g., VCRs and TVs) and electronic products (e.g., mobile phone, computer) than others. For instance, Midwesterners, more than the residents of any other region, report that they are able to operate most household electronics, while Northeasterners appear to be somewhat "technologically challenged" (see Table 13-7).

TABLE 13-7	Regional Differences in Who Needs the Most Help Around the Home[a]

	TOTAL	SOUTH	NORTHEAST	WEST	MIDWEST
Television	82%	86%	79%	78%	83%
VCR	59%	58%	53%	56%	70%
Mobile phone	44%	41%	40%	43%	53%
Stereo	77%	78%	73%	74%	76%
Home security system	45%	53%	47%	53%	27%
Remote control	68%	69%	64%	60%	76%
Microwave	78%	76%	70%	81%	83%
Computer	44%	40%	38%	46%	53%
Answering machine	73%	76%	67%	74%	73%

[a]Based on the question: "I fully understand how to operate my _____ and all its features."
Source: John Fetto, "Can You Set Your VCR?" *American Demographics*, 24, 3, March 2002, 9. © Media Central Inc., a Primedia Company. All rights reserved. Reprinted by permission.

Racial Subcultures

The major **racial subcultures** in the United States are Caucasian, African American, Asian American, and American Indian. Although differences in lifestyles and consumer-spending patterns exist among these groups, the vast majority of racially oriented consumer research has focused on consumer differences between African Americans and Caucasians. More recently, particular research attention has been given to Asian American consumers.

THE AFRICAN AMERICAN CONSUMER

The U.S. Census Bureau estimates the African American population of the United States to be more than 36 million people, or nearly 13 percent of the U.S. population. As such, **African American consumers** currently constitute the largest racial minority in the United States.[29] With a purchasing power estimated to be $572 billion, African American consumers are sought after by marketers who target over $1.3 billion in advertising, promotions, and events to communicate specifically with them.[30] However, this important subcultural grouping is frequently portrayed as a single, undifferentiated African American market, consisting of consumers who have a uniform set of consumer needs. In reality they are a diverse group, consisting of numerous subgroups, each with distinctive backgrounds, needs, interests, and opinions. For example, in addition to the African Americans who have been in the United States for many generations, there are Caribbean Americans, from such islands as Jamaica and Haiti, who have recently immigrated to the United States.[31] Therefore, just as the white majority has been divided into a variety of market segments, each with its own distinctive needs and tastes, so, too, can the African American market be segmented.

Consumer Behavior Characteristics of African American Consumers

Although there are many similarities between African Americans and the rest of America in terms of consumer behavior, there are also some meaningful differences in terms of product preferences and brand purchase patterns. African American consumers tend to prefer popular or leading brands, are brand loyal, and are unlikely to purchase private-label and generic products. One study, for example, found that almost two-thirds of African Americans are willing to pay more to get "the best," even if the brand or product is not widely recognized (only 51 percent of whites were reported to feel this way), and African Americans have been reported to buy high fashions and name brands "as signals of their success."[32] Still further, African American consumers tend to make more trips during the course of a week to the grocery store (2.2 trips versus 1.8 trips for the average shopper), and they also spend more per week ($94 versus $85 for the average shopper) than other consumers.[33]

Some meaningful differences exist among Anglo-White, African American, and Hispanic American consumers in the purchase, ownership, and use of a diverse group of products (see Table 13-8). For marketers, these findings confirm the wisdom of targeting racial market segments.

Reaching the African American Audience

A question of central importance to marketers is how to best reach *African American consumers*. Traditionally, marketers have subscribed to one of two distinct marketing strategies. Some have followed the policy of running all their advertising

| TABLE 13-8 | Comparison of Purchase Patterns of Anglo-White, African American, and Hispanic American Households |

PRODUCT/ACTIVITY	ANGLO-WHITE	AFRICAN AMERICAN	HISPANIC AMERICAN
Dental floss	102	86	98
Mouthwash	97	124	105
Hand and body cream	98	117	100
Vitamin/mineral supplements	103	77	86
Energy drinks	96	124	132
Car rental—business use	94	131	78
Camera film	104	66	89
Greeting card	103	83	85
Instant breakfast	97	112	105
Barbeque and seasoning sauces	100	103	89
Ready-to-drink iced cappuccino	95	113	121
Cat treat	110	42	84
Charcoal	93	148	109
Attend movies/last 6 months	101	90	106
Went camping/past 12 months	110	31	89
Own a full-size van	112	19	130
Own a camera	106	60	83

Source: Mediamark Research, Inc. Doublebase 2001 Report. All rights reserved. Reprinted by permission.

in general mass media in the belief that African Americans have the same media habits as whites; others have followed the policy of running additional advertising in selected media directed exclusively to African Americans.

Both strategies may be appropriate in specific situations and for specific product categories. For products of very broad appeal (as aspirin or toothpaste), it is possible that the mass media (primarily television) may effectively reach all relevant consumers, including African American and white. For other products (such as personal grooming products or food products), marketers may find that mass media do not communicate effectively with the African American market. Because the media habits of African American consumers differ from those of the general population, media specifically targeted to African Americans are likely to be more effective. The notion that African Americans have cultural values subtly different from the U.S. population as a whole is supported by a Yankelovich survey in which a majority of African Americans believe that most advertising is designed for white people.[34] Furthermore, a recent study of ethnic identification found that African American adolescents with a stronger sense of black ethnic identity tend to identify more closely with black models or characters appearing in ads than do African American adolescents with weaker ethnic identification.[35] Research studies have also concluded that the socializing effects of the media may be greater for African Americans than for Caucasians. For example, some African American children watch more than 40 hours of TV weekly, and both children and adolescents often use television as a source of guidance (e.g., African American adolescents use TV to learn about occupations and to learn dating behavior).[36] Other research reveals that African American adults tend to place a great deal of trust in African American centric media (i.e., black magazines, black TV news, black-owned local newspapers, and black radio news) as source of information about companies and their products.[37]

Many marketers supplement their general advertising with advertisements in magazines, newspapers, and other media directed specifically to African Americans. For example, L'eggs especially targets African American women by running ads in such publications as *Ebony, Essence,* and *Heart & Soul.* This is the first time since the mid-1980s that L'eggs has conducted such a targeted campaign, which makes sense because African American women wear panty hose at twice the rate of other women.[38] And Volvo automobiles recently inaugurated its first campaign targeted to the African American car buyer—a $6 million effort consisting of print, radio, and an in-school educational component to promote the use of seat belts.[39] To create these campaigns, major advertisers targeting the African American market have increasingly used specialized services of African American advertising agencies. These specialized agencies generally provide marketers wanting to target African Americans with the distinctive advantage of access to a staff of African American marketing professionals who thoroughly know the values and customs of this market and its specific subsegments.

With respect to reaching the African American consumer, Table 13-9 presents a number of Internet usage differences among whites, Hispanic Americans, and African Americans. Note, for example, how African Americans are more likely to be on the Internet "just for fun" and to look for a job or to play a game. Additionally, whereas 76 percent of the general market would "feel comfortable" making an online purchase with a credit card, only 39 percent of African Americans and 47 percent of Hispanic Americans feel similarly.[40]

ASIAN AMERICAN CONSUMERS

The **Asian American** population is currently about 12 million in size and is the fastest-growing American minority (on a percentage basis). It is expected that immigration should push the Asian American population to over 13 million in 2005—a population that grew by more than 54 percent between 1990 and 2001.[41] According to the 2000 census, six different ethnicities make up about 88 percent of the Asian American population: Chinese (2.4 million), Filipinos (1.9 million), Indian (1.7 million), Vietnamese (1.12 million), Korean (1.1 million), and Japanese (797,000).[42]

Asian Americans currently represent about 4 percent of the U.S. population and they are expected to grow to nearly 5 percent by the year 2005. Because Asian Americans are largely family oriented, highly industrious, and strongly driven to achieve a middle-class lifestyle, they are an attractive market for increasing numbers of marketers. Indeed, about 60 percent of Asian Americans have incomes of at least $60,000, and about 50 percent hold professional positions.[43]

Where Are the Asian Americans?

Asian Americans are largely urban people concentrated in neighborhoods situated in and around a small number of large American cities (93 percent live in metropolitan areas). Nearly half of all Asian Americans live in Los Angeles, San Francisco, and New York, and at present, more than 10 percent of California's population is Asian American. The stereotype that most Chinese live in "Chinatown" is incorrect. Most Chinese, as well as most other Asian Americans, do not live in downtown urban areas; they live in the suburbs.[44]

TABLE 13-9	Online Behavior of White, African American, and Hispanic American Consumers		
ACTIVITY	**WHITES**	**BLACKS**	**HISPANICS**
E-mail	93%	88%	87%
Hobby	76%	68%	70%
Product information	73%	71%	73%
Travel information	65%	64%	63%
Arts information	63%	66%	70%
Weather	63%	53%	55%
Just for fun	61%	73%	69%
Get news	59%	62%	58%
Health information	55%	52%	48%
School research	54%	65%	59%
Work research	49%	48%	51%
Buy product	48%	35%	42%
Use video/audio clip	47%	60%	50%
Financial information	45%	40%	36%
Instant messaging	44%	51%	51%
Visit government Web site	41%	38%	36%
Look for a job	37%	51%	41%
Sports	35%	44%	37%
Political information	33%	34%	33%
Play a game	33%	48%	36%
Listen to music	32%	54%	44%
Buy travel product	29%	28%	29%
Place to live information	27%	35%	29%
Chat	23%	38%	30%
Download music	21%	29%	37%
Religious information	20%	33%	21%
Banking	17%	19%	20%
Auction	14%	6%	8%
Buy/sell stocks	9%	8%	7%
Gamble/play game	5%	5%	4%

Source: Michael J. Weiss, "Online America," *American Demographics*, March 2001. Reprinted with permission of Primedia.

Understanding the Asian American Consumer

Local newspapers and weekly news magazines frequently portray the accomplishments of Asian Americans, who have shown themselves to be hardworking, very family oriented, and strivers for excellence in educational pursuits (for themselves and their children). Indeed, throughout the United States, Asian American children have consistently won a substantial share of academic awards and scholarships.

Supporting this profile, U.S. Census Bureau data reveal that more Asian Americans, on a per capita basis, own their own businesses than non–Asian American minorities (e.g., over half of all minority-owned businesses grossing over $1 million are owned by Asian Americans).[45] Those who do not own their own businesses are largely in professional, technical, or managerial occupations. Additionally, many Asian Americans are young and live a good part of their lives in multi-income households. Asian Americans also tend to be better educated (i.e., 37 percent have at least a bachelor's degree) and are more computer literate than the general population. English-speaking Asian Americans are more likely than other Americans to get their news and information online. Asian Americans who go online also tend to be young—whereas 41 percent of the entire Internet population is between 18 and 34 years of age, fully 63 percent of all Asians online fall into this age category. Still further, whereas only about 24 percent of Hispanic and African American households have Internet access, fully 57 percent of Asian American households are wired.[46] Two general-interest Internet sites, **www.Click2Asia.com** and **www.AsianAvenue.com**, have helped create cyberspace communities for Asian Americans.[47]

Asian Americans as Consumers

From 1990 to 2000, the buying power of the Asian American community experienced a 125 percent rise to $254 billion. Asian Americans value quality (frequently associated with well-known brands) and are willing to pay for it. This population segment tends to be loyal customers, frequently more male oriented when it comes to consumption decisions, and attracted to retailers that make it known that they welcome Asian American patronage.

It is important to remember that Asian Americans are really drawn from diverse cultural backgrounds. Therefore, although Asian Americans have many similarities, marketers should avoid treating Asian Americans as a single market because they are far from being so homogeneous. For example, Vietnamese Americans are more likely to follow the traditional model, wherein the man makes the decision for large purchases; however, Chinese American husbands and wives are more likely to share in the decision-making process.[48] Vietnamese Americans also frown on credit, because in their culture owing money is viewed negatively. In contrast, Korean Americans and Chinese Americans, many of whom have been in the United States for years, accept credit as the American way.[49]

The use of Asian American models in advertising is effective in reaching this market segment. Research reveals that responses to an ad for stereo speakers featuring an Asian model were significantly more positive than responses to the same ad using a Caucasian model.[50] Additionally, the percentage of Asian Americans who prefer advertisements that are not in the English language varies among different Asian American groups. For instance, according to Table 13-10, 93 percent of

TABLE 13-10 Language Preference of Specific Asian American Groups

ASIAN AMERICAN GROUP	% WHO PREFER NATIVE LANGUAGE	% SPEAKING NATIVE LANGUAGE AT HOME
Vietnamese	93	71
Chinese	83	66
Korean	81	66
Filipino	66	56
Asian Indian	55	59
Japanese	42	29

Source: www.ewowfacts.com/pdfs/chapters/61.pdf (page 609); and *Orienting the U.S. Food and Beverage Market: Strategies Targeting Asian Americans to 2010* (Alexandria, VA: Promar International), June 2000, 87.

Vietnamese consumers prefer ad messages in the Vietnamese language, whereas only 42 percent of Japanese Americans prefer such messages in Japanese.

ge Subcultures

It's not difficult to understand why each major age subgrouping of the population might be thought of as a separate subculture. After all, don't you listen to different music than your parents and grandparents, dress differently, read different magazines, and enjoy different TV shows? Clearly, important shifts occur in an individual's demand for specific types of products and services as he or she goes from being a dependent child to a retired senior citizen. In this chapter, we will limit our examination of **age subcultures** to four age groups, moving from youngest to oldest: **Generation Y, Generation X, baby boomers,** and **seniors.** These four age segments have been singled out because their distinctive lifestyles qualify them for consideration as subcultural groups.

THE GENERATION Y MARKET

This age cohort (a cohort is a group of individuals born over a relatively short and continuous period of time) includes the approximately 71 million Americans born between the years 1977 and 1994 (i.e., the children of baby boomers). Members of Generation Y (also known as "echo boomers" and the "millennium generation") can be divided into three subsegments: Gen Y adults (age 19–24), Gen Y teens (age 13–18), and Gen Y kids, or "tweens" (age 8–12).[51]

Members of Generation Y are often described as pragmatic, savvy, socially and environmentally aware, and open to new experiences.

Appealing to Generation Y

The teen segment of Generation Y spends over $150 billion annually and influences purchases by their parents of several times this amount. They have grown up in a media-saturated environment and tend to be aware of "marketing hype." For example, they would tend to immediately understand that when a shopping center locates popular teen stores at opposite ends of the mall they are being encouraged "to walk the mall."[52]

This age cohort has shifted some of its TV viewing time to the Internet and, when compared with their parents, they are less likely to read newspapers and often do not trust the stores that their parents shop in.[53] Smart retailers have found it profitable to develop Web sites specifically targeted to the interests of the Gen Y consumer (see Figure 13-6). For example, Limited Too (www.limitedtoo.com), Rave Girl (www.goravegirl.com), and Abercrombie & Fitch (www.abercrombiekids.com) have all developed sites targeted to the tween market, despite the fact that a person is supposed to be at least 18 years old to place an order.[54]

THE GENERATION X MARKET

This age grouping—often referred to as *Xers, busters,* or *slackers*—consists of the approximately 46 million individuals born between about 1965 and 1979 (different experts quote different starting and ending years). As consumers, these 23- to 37-year-olds spend about $125 billion yearly.[55] They do not like labels, are cynical and

FIGURE 13-6

Ad Appealing
to the Young Adult
Subsegment of Gen Y
Courtesy of Sprint.

do not want to be singled out and marketed to. They matured during an era of soaring divorce rates and "latchkey children."[56]

Also, unlike their parents, who are frequently baby boomers, they are in no rush to marry, start a family, or work excessive hours to earn high salaries. For Generation X consumers, job satisfaction is typically more important than salary. It has been said, for example, that "Baby Boomers live to work, Gen Xers work to live!" Xers reject the values of older coworkers who may neglect their families while striving to secure higher salaries and career advancement, and many have observed their parents getting laid off after many years of loyalty to an employer. They, therefore, are not particularly interested in long-term employment with a single company but instead prefer to work for a company that can offer some worklife flexibility and can bring some fun aspects into the environment. Gen Xers understand the necessity of money but do not view salary as a sufficient reason for staying with a company—the quality of the work itself and the relationships built on the job are much more important.[57] For Generation X, it is more important to enjoy life and to have a lifestyle that provides freedom and flexibility.

Appealing to Generation X

Members of Generation X often pride themselves on their sophistication. Although they are not necessarily materialistic, they do purchase good brand names (such as Sony) but not necessarily designer labels. They want to be recognized by marketers as a group in their own right and not as mini–baby boomers. Therefore, advertisements targeted to this audience must focus on their style in music, fashions, and language. One key for marketers appears to be sincerity. Xers are not against advertising but only opposed to insincerity.

Baby boomer media does not work with Generation X members. For example, while 65 percent of 50- to 64-year-olds, and 55 percent of 30- to 49-year-olds read a newspaper regularly, only 39 percent of adults under 30 (the younger Xers) regularly read a newspaper.[58] Xers are the MTV generation, and whereas the three major U.S. TV networks attract an average of only 18 percent of the 18- to 29-year-old group, the Fox network claims that 38 percent of its viewers are in this age group.

THE BABY BOOMER MARKET

Marketers have found baby boomers a particularly desirable target audience because (1) they are the single largest distinctive age category alive today; (2) they frequently make important consumer purchase decisions; and (3) they contain small subsegments of trendsetting consumers (sometimes known as yuppies, or young upwardly mobile professionals) who have influence on the consumer tastes of other age segments of society.[59]

Who Are the Baby Boomers?

The term *baby boomers* refers to the age segment of the population that was born between 1946 and 1964. Thus, baby boomers are in the broad age category that extends from about mid-30s to mid-50s. These 78 million or so baby boomers represent more than 40 percent of the adult population. The magnitude of this statistic alone would make them a much sought-after market segment. However, they also are valued because they comprise about 50 percent of all those in professional and managerial occupations and more than one-half of those with at least a college degree.

In addition, although each year more baby boomers turn 50 years of age (see Figure 13-7), they do not necessarily like the idea. Increases in health club memberships and a boom in the sales of vitamin and health supplements are evidence that these consumers are trying hard to look and feel "young"—they do not want to age gracefully but will fight and kick and pay whatever is necessary to look young. For example, 35- to 50-year-olds are the largest market for plastic surgery, and the majority of cosmetic dentistry patients are 40 to 49 years of age.[60]

Consumer Characteristics of Baby Boomers

Baby boomers tend to be motivated consumers. They enjoy buying for themselves, for their homes or apartments, and for others—they are consumption oriented. As

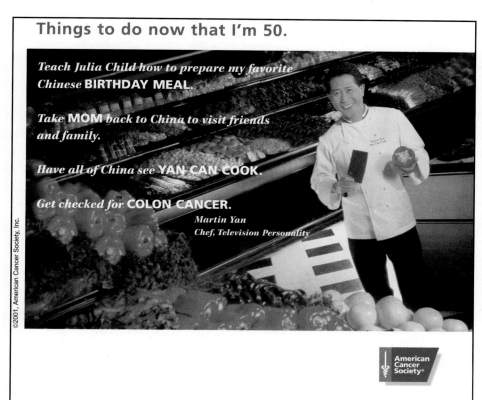

FIGURE 13-7

Appealing to Baby
Boomers' Sense of Self

baby boomers age, the nature of the products and services they most need or desire changes. For example, because of the aging of this market segment, sales of "relaxed fit" jeans, and "lineless" bifocal glasses are up substantially, as is the sales of walking shoes. Men's and women's pants with elastic waistbands are also enjoying strong sales. Recently, bank marketers and other financial institutions are also paying more attention to assisting boomers who are starting to think about retirement, St. Joseph's Aspirin has switched its target from babies to boomers, and Disney has ads to entice baby boomers to vacation at their theme parks without their kids.[61]

Yuppies are by far the most sought-after subgroup of baby boomers. Although constituting only 5 percent of the population, they generally are well off financially,

FIGURE 13-8

Appealing to Yuppies'
Sense of Seeking
Enriching Experiences
Courtesy of Williams Labadie.

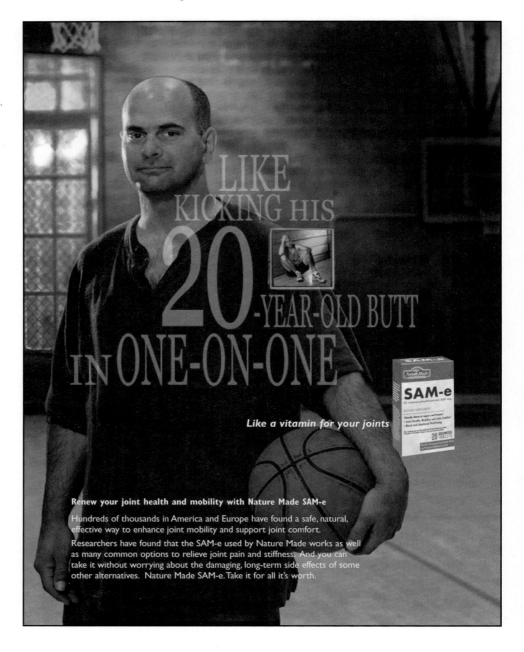

well educated, and in enviable professional or managerial careers. They often are associated with status brand names, such as BMWs or Volvo station wagons, Rolex watches, cable TV, and Cuisinart food processors. Today, as many yuppies are maturing, they are shifting their attention away from expensive status-type possessions to travel, physical fitness, planning for second careers, or some other form of new directions for their lives (see Figure 13-8).

Gen Yers, Gen Xers, and baby boomers differ in their purchasing behavior, attitudes toward brands, and behavior toward ads. Table 13-11 captures some of the differences among these three age cohorts.

TABLE 13-11   Comparison of Selected Age Cohorts Across Marketing-Related Issues

THEMES	GENERATION Y	GENERATION X	BOOMERS
Purchasing behavior	Savvy, pragmatic	Materialistic	Narcissistic
Coming of age technology	Computer in every home	Microwave in every home	TV in every home
Price–quality attitude	Value oriented: weighing price–quality relationships	Price oriented: concerned about the cost of individual items	Conspicuous consumption: buying for indulgence
Attitude toward brands	Brand embracing	Against branding	Brand loyal
Behavior toward ads	Rebel against hype	Rebel against hype	Respond to image-building type

Source: Stephanie M. Noble and Charles H. Noble, "Getting to Know Y: The Consumption Behaviors of a New Cohort," *AMA Winter Educators' Conference 11* (Chicago: American Marketing Association, 2000), *Marketing Theory,* Conference Proceedings, 294.

OLDER CONSUMER

America is aging. Some baby boomers are well into their 50s (or "mature adults"), and there are plenty of preboomers—those 57 to 65 years old. According to the 2000 U.S. Census, there are almost 35 million people in this country who are 65 years of age or older (12.4 percent of the population). More important, by the year 2030 one out of every five Americans (about 70 million people) will be in this age bracket. From the start to the end of the twentieth century, life expectancy in the United States rose from 47.3 years to 76.9 years, and whereas a 65-year-old in 1900 could expect, on average, to live 11.9 more years, a 65-year-old in 2000 can expect 17.9 more years of life. And whereas the 65-plus age segment of the U.S. population increased 12 percent between 1990 and 2000, this segment is projected to increase by 35.3 percent between 2010 and 2020 (as a large number of baby boomers turn 65 years old).[62]

It should also be kept in mind that "later adulthood" (i.e., those who are 50 years of age or older) is the longest adult life stage for most consumers (i.e., often 29 or more years in duration).[63] This is in contrast to "early adulthood" (i.e., those who are 18 to 34 years of age), a stage lasting 16 years, and "middle adulthood" (i.e., those who are 35 to 49 years of age), a stage lasting 14 years. Remember that people over age 50 comprise about one-third of the adult U.S. market.

Although some people think of older consumers as consisting of people without substantial financial resources, in generally poor health, and with plenty of free time on their hands, the fact is that 31 percent of men and 20 percent of women aged 65 to 69 were employed in 2001, as were 19 percent of men and 12 percent of women aged 70 to 74. Additionally, millions of seniors are involved in the daily care of a grandchild, and many do volunteer work.[64] The annual discretionary income of this group amounts to 50 percent of the discretionary income of the United States, and these older consumers are major purchasers of luxury products such as cars, alcohol, vacations, and financial products. Americans over 65 now control 70 percent of the nation's wealth, which amounts to about $70 trillion.[65]

Defining "Older" in Older Consumer

Driving the growth of the elderly population are three factors: the declining birthrate, the aging of the huge baby boomer segment, and improved medical diagnoses and treatment. In the United States, "old age" is officially assumed to begin with a person's 65th birthday (or when the individual qualifies for full Social Security and Medicare). However, people over age 60 tend to view themselves as being 15 years younger than their chronological age.

Research consistently suggests that people's perceptions of their ages are more important in determining behavior than their chronological ages (or the number of years lived).[66] In fact, people may at the same time have a number of different perceived or **cognitive ages.** Specifically, elderly consumers perceive themselves to be younger than their chronological ages on four perceived age dimensions: *feel age* (how old they feel); *look age* (how old they look); *do age* (how involved they are in activities favored by members of a specific age group); and *interest age* (how similar their interests are to those of members of a specific age group).[67] The results support other research that indicates that elderly consumers are more likely to consider themselves younger (to have a younger cognitive age) than their chronological age.

For marketers, these findings underscore the importance of looking beyond chronological age to perceived or cognitive age when appealing to mature consumers and to the possibility that cognitive age might be used to segment the mature market. The "New-Age Elderly," when compared to the "Traditional Elderly," are more adventurous, more likely to perceive themselves to be better off financially, and more receptive to marketing information.[68]

Segmenting the Elderly Market

The elderly are by no means a homogeneous subcultural group. There are those who, as a matter of choice, do not have color TVs or Touch-Tone telephone service, whereas others have the latest desktop computers and spend their time surfing the Internet (cyberseniors will be discussed later in this section).

One consumer gerontologist has suggested that the elderly are more diverse in interests, opinions, and actions than other segments of the adult population.[69] Although this view runs counter to the popular myth that the elderly are uniform in terms of attitudes and lifestyles, both gerontologists and market researchers have repeatedly demonstrated that age is not necessarily a major factor in determining how older consumers respond to marketing activities.

With an increased appreciation that the elderly constitute a diverse age segment, more attention is now being given to identifying ways to segment the elderly into meaningful groupings.[70] One relatively simple segmentation scheme partitions the elderly into three chronological age categories: the *young-old* (65 to 74 years of age), the *old* (those 75 to 84); and the *old-old* (those 85 years of age and older). This market segmentation approach provides useful consumer-relevant insights.

The elderly can also be segmented in terms of motivations and *quality-of-life orientation*. Table 13-12 presents a side-by-side comparison of new-age elderly consumers and the more traditional older consumers. The increased presence of the new-age elderly suggests that marketers need to respond to the value orientations of older consumers whose lifestyles remain relatively ageless. Clearly, the new-age elderly are individuals who feel, think, and do according to a cognitive age that is younger than their chronological age. An examination of several recent studies on aging suggests an "erosion of chronological age as a central indicator of the experience of aging."[71]

Cyberseniors

Although some people might think of older Americans as individuals who still use rotary phones and are generally resistant to change, this stereotype is far from the

TABLE 13-12	Comparison of New-Age and Traditional Elderly

NEW-AGE ELDERLY	TRADITIONAL/STEREOTYPICAL ELDERLY
• *Perceive themselves to be different in outlook from other people their age*	• *Perceive all older people to be about the same in outlook*
• *Age is seen as a state of mind*	• *See age as more of a physical state*
• *See themselves as younger than their chronological age*	• *See themselves at or near their chronological age*
• *Feel younger, think younger, and "do" younger*	• *Tend to feel, think, and do things that they feel match their chronological age*
• *Have a genuinely youthful outlook*	• *Feel that one should act one's age*
• *Feel there is a considerable adventure to living*	
• *Feel more in control of their own lives*	• *Normal sense of being in control of their own lives*
• *Have greater self-confidence when it comes to making consumer decisions*	• *Normal range of self-confidence when it comes to making consumer decisions*
• *Less concerned that they will make a mistake when buying something*	• *Some concern that they will make a mistake when buying something*
• *Especially knowledgeable and alert consumers*	• *Low-to-average consumer capabilities*
• *Selectively innovative*	• *Not innovative*
• *Seek new experiences and personal challenges*	• *Seek stability and a secure routine*
• *Less interested in accumulating possessions*	• *Normal range of interest in accumulating possessions*
• *Higher measured life satisfaction*	• *Lower measured life satisfaction*
• *Less likely to want to live their lives over differently*	• *Have some regrets as to how they lived their lives*
• *Perceive themselves to be healthier*	• *Perceive themselves to be of normal health for their age*
• *Feel financially more secure*	• *Somewhat concerned about financial security*

Source: Reprinted by permission from "The Value Orientation of New-Age Elderly: The Coming of an Ageless Market" by Leon G. Schiffman and Elaine Sherman in *Journal of Business Research* 22, April 1991, 187–194. Copyright 1991 by Elsevier Science Publishing Co., Inc.

truth. Few older consumers are fearful of new technology, and there are more Internet users over the age of 50 than under the age of 20. Research studies have found that those over 55 are more likely than the average adult to use the Internet to purchase books, stocks, and computer equipment—92 percent of surfing seniors have shopped online and 78 percent have purchased online.[72]

What's the attraction for seniors to go online? Certainly, the Internet is a great way to communicate with friends and family members living in other states, including grandchildren in college. But the Web is also a place to find information (e.g., stock prices, health and medication-related information), entertainment, and a sense of community. There also appears to be a relationship between the amount of time an older adult spends on the Internet and his or her level of out-of-home mobility (using the Internet may serve as a substitute for going out of the house). Having a computer and modem "empowers" older consumers—it allows them to regain some of the control that was lost due to the physical and/or social deterioration in their lives. For example, a consumer can pay bills, shop, and e-mail friends. This may be part of the reason why the American Association of Retired Persons (AARP) claims that 2 million of its members are computer users.[73]

Marketing to the Older Consumer

Older consumers do want to be marketed to, but only for the "right" kinds of products and services and using the "right" advertising presentation. For example, older models tend to be underrepresented in advertisements or are often shown as being infirm or feeble. Part of the problem, according to some writers on the subject, is that the advertising professionals who create the ads are often in their 20s and 30s and have little understanding or empathy for older consumers. Seniors often want to be identified not for what they did in the past but by what they would like to accomplish in the future. Retirement or moving to a sunbelt community is viewed as the opening of a new chapter in life and not a quiet withdrawal from life. In the same vein, the increase in the number of older adults taking vacation cruises and joining health clubs signifies a strong commitment to remaining "functionally young."[74]

Sex as a Subculture

Because **sex roles** have an important cultural component, it is quite fitting to examine **gender** as a subcultural category.

SEX ROLES AND CONSUMER BEHAVIOR

All societies tend to assign certain traits and roles to males and others to females. In American society, for instance, aggressiveness and competitiveness often were considered traditional *masculine traits;* neatness, tactfulness, gentleness, and talkativeness were considered traditional *feminine traits.* In terms of role differences, women have historically been cast as homemakers with responsibility for child care and men as the providers or breadwinners. Because such traits and roles are no longer relevant for many individuals, marketers are increasingly appealing to consumers' broader vision of gender-related role options.

CONSUMER PRODUCTS AND SEX ROLES

Within every society, it is quite common to find products that are either exclusively or strongly associated with the members of one sex. In the United States, for example, shaving equipment, cigars, pants, ties, and work clothing were historically male products; bracelets, hair spray, hair dryers, and sweet-smelling colognes generally were considered feminine products. For most of these products, the **sex role** link has either diminished or disappeared; for others, the prohibition still lingers. An interesting product category with regard to the blurring of a gender appeal is men's fragrances. Although men are increasingly wearing fragrances, it is estimated that 30 percent of men's fragrances are worn by women.[75] Also, although women have historically been the major market for vitamins, men are increasingly being targeted for vitamins exclusively formulated for men.

In terms of its appeal, men and women seem to differ in their attraction to the Internet. For instance, women go online to seek out reference materials, online books, medical information, cooking ideas, government information, and chatting. In contrast, men tend to focus on exploring, discovery, identifying free software, and investments. This provides further support for the notion that men are "hunters," whereas women are "nurturers."[76] Still further, although men and women are equally likely to browse commercial sites, women are less likely to purchase online (32% for men versus 19% for women). Evidence suggests that the lower incidence of women purchasing online is due to their heightened concerns with online security

TABLE 13-13	Male and Female Internet User Segments	
	KEY USAGE SITUATION	**FAVORITE INTERNET MATERIALS**
FEMALE SEGMENTS		
Social Sally	Making friends	Chat and personal Web page
New Age Crusader	Fight for causes	Books and government information
Cautious Mom	Nurture children	Cooking and medical facts
Playful Pretender	Role play	Chat and games
Master Producer	Job productivity	White Pages and government information
MALE SEGMENTS		
Bits and Bytes	Computers and hobbies	Investments, discovery, software
Practical Pete	Personal productivity	Investments, company listings
Viking Gamer	Competing and winning	Games, chat, software
Sensitive Sam	Help family and friends	Investments, government information
World Citizen	Connecting with world	Discovery, software, investments

Source: Scott M. Smith and David B. Whitlark, "Men and Women Online: What Makes them Click?" *Marketing Research*, 13, 2, Summer 2001, 23.

and privacy.[77] Table 13-13 presents a gender-oriented segmentation scheme that accounts for the type of online materials favored by specific subsegments of males and specific subsegments of females.

THE WORKING WOMAN

Marketers are keenly interested in the **working woman,** especially the married working woman. They recognize that married women who work outside of the home are a large and growing market segment, one whose needs differ from those of women who do not work outside the home (frequently self-labeled "stay-at-home moms"). It is the size of the working woman market that makes it so attractive. Approximately 60 percent of American women 16 years of age and older are in the labor force, which represents a market of over 65 million individuals. Whereas more than half of all women with children under the age of 1 are working (55 percent), almost 78 percent of women with children ages 6 to 17 are employed.[78]

Because 40 percent of all business travelers today are women, hotels have begun to realize that it pays to provide the services women want, such as healthy foods, gyms, and spas and wellness centers. Female business travelers are also concerned about hotel security and frequently use room service because they do not want to go to the hotel bar or restaurant. The Paris Hilton, for example, discreetly hands key cards to female patrons, offers valet parking, and allows women to receive guests in an executive lounge located on the hotel's business floor. And bathrooms feature roses, shampoos, and bath gels.[79]

Segmenting the Working Woman Market

To provide a richer framework for segmentation, marketers have developed categories that differentiate the motivations of working and nonworking women. For instance, a number of studies have divided the female population into four segments: *stay-at-home* housewives; *plan-to-work* housewives; *just-a-job* working women; and *career-oriented* working women.[80] The distinction between "just-a-job" and "career-oriented" working women is particularly meaningful. "Just-a-job" working women seem to be motivated to work primarily by a sense that the family requires the additional income, whereas "career-oriented" working women, who tend to be in a managerial or professional position, are driven more by a need to achieve and succeed in their chosen careers. Today, though, with more and more female college graduates in the workforce, the percentage of career-oriented working women is on the rise. As evidence of this fact, 25 percent of all working women bring home a paycheck that is larger than their husband's (10 years ago it was only 17 percent).[81]

Working women spend less time shopping than nonworking women. They accomplish this "time economy" by shopping less often and by being brand and store loyal. Not surprisingly, working women also are likely to shop during evening hours and on weekends, as well as to buy through direct-mail catalogs.

Businesses that advertise to women should also be aware that magazines are now delivering a larger women's audience than television shows. Whereas early 1980s' TV shows had higher ratings than popular magazines, today the top 25 women's magazines have larger audiences than the top 25 television shows targeted to females.[82]

Subcultural Interaction

All consumers are simultaneously members of more than one subcultural segment (e.g., a consumer may be a young, Hispanic, Catholic homemaker living in the Midwest). For this reason, marketers should strive to understand how multiple *subcultural* memberships *interact* to influence target consumers' relevant consumption behavior. Promotional strategy should not be limited to target a single subcultural membership.

Summary

Subcultural analysis enables marketers to segment their markets to meet the specific needs, motivations, perceptions, and attitudes shared by members of a specific subcultural group. A subculture is a distinct cultural group that exists as an identifiable segment within a larger, more complex society. Its members possess beliefs, values, and customs that set them apart from other members of the same society; at the same time, they hold to the dominant beliefs of the overall society. Major subcultural categories in this country include nationality, religion, geographic location, race, age, and sex. Each of these can be broken down into smaller segments that can be reached through special copy appeals and selective media choices. In some cases (such as the elderly consumer), product characteristics can be tailored to the specialized needs of the market segment. Because all consumers simultaneously are members of several subcultural groups, the marketer must determine for the product category how specific subcultural memberships interact to influence the consumer's purchase decisions.

Discussion Questions

1. Why is subcultural analysis especially significant in a country such as the United States?

2. Discuss the importance of subcultural segmentation to marketers of food products. Identify a food product for which the marketing mix should be regionalized. Explain why and how the marketing mix should be varied across geographic areas of the United States.

3. How can marketers of the following products use the material presented in this chapter to develop promotional campaigns designed to increase market share among African American, Hispanic, and Asian American consumers? The products are (a) compact disk players, (b) ready-to-eat cereals, and (c) designer jeans.

4. Asian Americans are a small proportion of the total U.S. population. Why are they an important market segment? How can a marketer of personal computers effectively target Asian Americans?

5. Sony is introducing a new 27-inch TV with a picture-in-picture feature. How should the company position and advertise the product to (a) Generation X consumers and (b) affluent baby boomers?

6. In view of the anticipated growth of the over-50 market, a leading cosmetics company is reevaluating the marketing strategy for its best-selling moisturizing face cream for women. Should the company market the product to younger (under-50) as well as older women? Would it be wiser to develop a new brand and formula for consumers over 50 rather than target both age groups with one product? Explain your answer.

7. Marketers realize that people of the same age often exhibit very different lifestyles. Using the evidence presented in this chapter, discuss how developers of retirement housing can use older Americans' lifestyles to more effectively segment their markets.

8. a. How should marketers promote products and services to working women? What appeals should they use? Explain.

   b. As the owner of a Saturn automobile dealership, what kind of marketing strategies would you use to target working women?

Exercises

1. Using one of the subculture categories listed in Table 13-1, identify a group that can be regarded as a subculture within your university or college.
   a. Describe the norms, values, and behaviors of the subculture's members.
   b. Interview five members of that subculture regarding attitudes toward the use of credit cards.
   c. What are the implications of your findings for marketing credit cards to the group you selected?

2. Interview one baby boomer and one Generation X consumer regarding the purchase of a car. Prepare a report on the differences in attitudes between the two individuals. Do your findings support the text's discussion of the differences between boomers and busters? Explain.

3. Many of your perceptions regarding price versus value are likely to be different from those of your parents or grandparents. Researchers attribute such differences to cohort effects,

which are based on the premise that consumption patterns are determined early in life. Therefore, individuals who experienced different economic, political, and cultural environments during their youth are likely to be different types of consumers as adults. Describe instances in which your parents or grandparents disagreed with or criticized purchases you had made. Describe the cohort effects that explain each party's position during these disagreements.

4. Find two good and two bad examples of advertising directed toward elderly consumers. To what degree are these ads stereotypical? Do they depict the concept of perceived age? How could these ads be improved by applying some of this chapter's guidelines for advertising to elderly consumers?

Key Terms

- **African American consumers**
- **Age subcultures**
- **Asian American consumers**
- **Baby boomers**
- **Cognitive ages**
- **Gender subcultures**

- **Generation X consumers**
- **Generation Y**
- **Hispanic American subculture**
- **Nationality subcultures**
- **Racial subcultures**

- **Regional subcultures**
- **Religious subcultures**
- **Seniors**
- **Sex roles**
- **Subcultural interaction**
- **Subculture**

Notes

1. Victor Wishna, "Getting with the Program," *Restaurant Business,* March 1, 2000, 36–44.
2. Saul Gitlin, "Ground Shifts in California," *Advertising Age,* September 25, 2000, 78.
3. Pui-Wing Tam, "Ethnic Media Muy Popular in California," *Wall Street Journal,* April 23, 2002, B1.
4. Eric Schmitt, "New Census Shows Hispanics Are Even with Blacks in U.S.," *New York Times,* March 8, 2001, A1, A21.
5. "Using Diversity Marketing in the U.S. to Create Product Awareness in Latin America," *Healthcare PR & Marketing News,* 9, 21, October 26, 2000, 1; "Two-Thirds of Major Advertisers Missing Opportunities," *PR Newswire,* April 19, 2002, 1; Burney Simpson, "The Future Cardholder," *Credit Card Management,* 14, 13, March 2002, 36–42; and Schmitt, "New Census Shows Hispanics Are Even with Blacks in U.S.," A21.
6. Jeanie Casison, "Snapshot of America," *Incentive,* October 2001, 33–36; Lynn Petrak, "Cultured Products," *Dairy Field,* April 2001, 34–38; and John Robinson, Bart Landry, and Ronica Rooks, "Time and the Melting Pot," *American Demographics,* June 1998, 18–24.
7. See U.S. Census Bureau, Projections Table NP-T5-B (www.census.gov/population/projections/nation/summary/np-t5-b.txt).
8. William H. Frey, "The Diversity Myth," *American Demographics,* June 1998, 39.
9. Schmitt, "New Census Shows Hispanics Are Even with Blacks in U.S.," A21.
10. Brad Edmondson, "Hispanic Americans in 2001," *American Demographics,* January 1997, 17.
11. Soyeon Shim and Kenneth C. Gehrt, "Native American and Hispanic Adolescent Consumers: Examination of Shopping Orientation, Socialization Factors and Social Structure Variables," in *1995 AMA Educators' Proceedings,* eds. Barbara B. Stern and George M. Zinkan (Chicago: American Marketing Association, 1995), 297–298.
12. Sandra Yin, "Hola, You've Got Mail!" *American Demographics,* 23, 12, December 2001, 13–16.
13. Catharine P. Taylor, "Barbie Latina Says 'Hola' to Net," *Advertising Age,* October 1, 2001, 54.
14. Rohit Deshpandè, Wayne D. Hoyer, and Naveen Donthu, "The Intensity of Ethnic Affiliation: A Study of the Sociology of Hispanic Consumption," *Journal of Consumer Research,* 13, September 1986,

214–220; and Cynthia Webster, "The Role of Hispanic Ethnic Identification on Reference Group Influence," in *Advances in Consumer Research,* 21, eds. Chris T. Allen and Deborah Roedder John (Provo, UT: Association for Consumer Research, 1994), 458–463.

15. Yin, "Hola, You've Got Mail!" 15.
16. www.hispanichandbook.com/file/02-hisppop 1990-2000.pdf, based on 2000 U.S. Census.
17. Jack Neff and Laurel Wentz, "Diversity Drive," *Advertising Age,* May 21, 2001, 3, 28.
18. Marcia Mogelonsky, "First Language Comes First," *American Demographics,* October 1995, 21.
19. "Assimilation No Threat to Hispanic Media," *Advertising Age,* March 31, 1997, A2, A4.
20. Laurel Wentz, "Marketing to Hispanics," *Advertising Age,* September 10, 2001, S1; and Jeffrey D. Zbar, "Marketing to Hispanics," *Advertising Age,* September 18, 2000, S1, S15.
21. Kevin Michael Grace, "Is This Kosher," *Report Newsmagazine,* 27, 1, May 8, 2000, 37; Laura Bird, "Major Brands Look for the Kosher Label," *Adweek's Marketing Week,* April 1, 1991, 18–19; and Judith Waldrop, "Everything's Kosher," *American Demographics,* March 1991, 4.
22. Heidi J. Shrager, "Closed-Circle Commerce," *Wall Street Journal,* November 19, 2001, B1, B11.
23. Florence Fabricant, "The Geography of Taste," *New York Times Magazine,* March 10, 1996, 40–41.
24. Anne Marie Chaker, "Thanksgiving: Thanksgiving Is More Than Turkey," *Wall Street Journal,* November 10, 1999, S4.
25. Katarzyna Dawidowska, "Caffeine Overload," *American Demographics,* 24, 4, April 2002, 16.
26. Marcia Mogelonsky, "America's Hottest Market," *American Demographics,* January 1996, 20–31, 55.
27. Anne R. Curey and Sam Ward, "Big Mac Capital of the USA," *USA Today,* September 9, 1998, 1B.
28. Anthony DeBarros, "Boundaries of Taste Shape Entertainment," *USA Today,* April 3, 2000, 1A.
29. U.S. Census Bureau, Projections Table NP-T5-B.
30. Burney Simpson, "The Future Cardholder," 36–42; and Alan J. Bush, Rachel Smith, and Craig Martin, "The Influence of Consumer Socialization Variables on Attitude Towards Advertising: A Comparison of African-Americans and Caucasians," *Journal of Advertising,* 28, 3, Fall 1999, 13–24.
31. "Understanding Nuances of Language and Culture Is Key in Marketing to Minority Women," *Marketing to Women,* 13, 2, February 2000, S1.
32. Youn-Kyung Kim and Seunghae Han, "Perceived Images of Retail Stores and Brands: Comparison Among Three Ethnic Consumer Groups," *Journal of Family and Consumer Sciences,* 92, 3, 2000, 58–61; and Christy Fisher, "Black, Hip, and Primed (to Shop)," *American Demographics,* September 1996, 52–58.
33. Gerda Gallop-Goodman, "Check This Out," *American Demographics,* 23, 5, May 2001, 14–17.
34. Kari Van Hoof, "Surveys Point to Group Differences," *Brandweek,* March 7, 1994, 32–33.
35. Osei Appiah, "Ethnic Identification on Adolescents' Evaluations of Advertisements," *Journal of Advertising Research,* 41, 5, September/October 2001, 7–22.
36. Bush, Smith, and Martin, "The Influence of Consumer Socialization Variables," 13–24.
37. "Understanding nuances of language and culture are key in marketing to minority women," S3.
38. Becky Ebenkamp, "L'eggs Goes Multicultural in Spring," *Brandweek,* February 16, 1998, 4.
39. Jean Halliday, "Volvo to Buckle Up African-Americans," *Advertising Age,* February 14, 2000, 28.
40. Becky Ebenkamp, "Divide and Culture," *Brandweek,* January 29, 2001, 16–18; and Michael J. Weiss, "Online America," *American Demographics,* March 2001, 53–60.
41. Burney Simpson, "The Future Cardholder," 38.
42. Ibid., 36; and U.S. Census Bureau, Projections Table NP-T5-B; and see www.ewowfacts.com/pdfs/chapters/61.pdf.
43. Brad Edmondson, "Asian Americans in 2001," *American Demographics,* February 1997, 16–17; and see www.census.gov/prod/2002pubs/01statab/income.pdf.
44. www.ewowfacts.com/pdfs/chapters/61.pdf.
45. Ibid.
46. John Fetto, "Cyber Tigers," *American Demographics,* 24, 3, March 2002, 9–10; and Sheila Thorne, "Reaching the Minority Majority," *Pharmaceutical Executive,* 21, 4, April 2001, 156–158.
47. "Orienting the U.S. Food and Beverage Market: Strategies Targeting Asian Americans to 2010," Promar International, Alexandria, VA, June 2000.
48. John Steere, "How Asian-Americans Make Purchase Decisions," *Marketing News,* March 13, 1995, 9.
49. Simpson, "The Future Cardholder," 36–42.
50. Judy Cohen, "White Consumer Response to Asian Models in Advertising," *Journal of Consumer Marketing,* Spring 1992, 17–27.
51. Stephanie M. Noble and Charles H. Noble, "Getting to Know Y: The Consumption Behaviors of a New Cohort," in *2000 AMA Winter Educators' Conference,* 11, eds., John P. Workman and William D. Perreault (Chicago: American Marketing Association, 2000), 293–303; and Pamela Paul, "Getting Inside Gen Y," *American Demographics,* 23, 9, September 2001, 42–49.
52. Lauren Keating, "The In Crowds," *Shopping Center World,* 29, 5, May 2000, 160–165.
53. Joyce M. Wolburg and James Pokrywczynski, "A Psychographic Analysis of Generation Y College Students," *Journal of Advertising Research,* 41, 5, September/October 2001, 33–52.

54. Chantal Todè, "Evolution of Tweens' Tastes Keeps Retailers on Their Toes," *Advertising Age,* February 12, 2001, S6.

55. See www.jour.unr.edu/outpost/specials/genx.overvw1.html.

56. Keating, "The In Crowds," 163.

57. Judi E. Loomis, "Generation X," *Rough Notes,* 143, 9, September 2000, 52–54.

58. Paula M. Poindexter and Dominic L. Lasorsa, "Generation X: Is Its Meaning Understood?" *Newspaper Research Journal,* 20, 4, Fall 1999, 28–36.

59. "Boomer Facts," *American Demographics,* January 1996, 14. Also see Diane Crispell, "U.S. Population Forecasts Decline for 2000, but Rise Slightly for 2050," *Wall Street Journal,* March 25, 1996, B3.

60. Cindy Hearn and Doug Hammond, "Cosmetic Dentistry: The 'Boom' Is upon Us!" *Dental Economics,* 91, 9, September 2001, 118–122.

61. Abbey Klaassen, "St. Joseph: From Babies to Boomers," *Advertising Age,* July 9, 2001, 1, 38; and Bob Garfield, "Disney's Quest for Boomers Shows a Bit of Imagineering," *Advertising Age,* August 13, 2001, 29.

62. Christine L. Himes, "Elderly Americans," *Population Bulletin,* 56, 4, December 2001, 3–40; and "Profiles of General Demographic Characteristics 2000," U.S. Department of Commerce, May 2001, accessed via www.census.gov/prod/cen2000/dp1/2kh00.pdf.

63. John Nielson and Kathy Curry, "Creative Strategies for Connecting with Mature Individuals," *Journal of Consumer Marketing,* 14, 4, 1997, 320.

64. Ibid., 3–40.

65. Marylyn Carrigan and Isabelle Szmigin, "The Representation of Older People in Advertisements," *Journal of the Market Research Society (London),* 41, 3, July 1999, 311–326; and Ilana Polyak, "The Center of Attention," *American Demographics,* 22, 11, November 2000, 30–32.

66. Kelly Tepper, "The Role of Labeling Processes in Elderly Consumers' Responses to Age Segmentation Cues," *Journal of Consumer Research,* March 1994, 503–519; and Candace Corlett, "Building a Successful 50+ Marketing Program," *Marketing Review,* January 1996, 10–11, 19.

67. Benny Barak and Leon G. Schiffman, "Cognitive Age: A Nonchronological Age Variable," in *Advances in Consumer Research,* 8, ed. Kent B. Monroe (Ann Arbor, MI: Association for Consumer Research, 1981), 602–606; Elaine Sherman, Leon G. Schiffman, and William R. Dillon, "Age/Gender Segments and Quality of Life Differences," in *1988 Winter Educators' Conference,* ed. Stanley Shapiro and A. H. Walle (Chicago: American Marketing Association, 1988), 319–320; Stuart Van Auken and Thomas E. Barry, "An

Assessment of the Trait Validity of Cognitive Age," *Journal of Consumer Psychology,* 1995, 107–132; Robert E. Wilkes, "A Structural Modeling Approach to the Measurement and Meaning of Cognitive Age," *Journal of Consumer Research,* September 1992, 292–301; and Chad Rubel, "Mature Market Often Misunderstood," *Marketing News,* August 28, 1995, 28–29.

68. Elaine Sherman, Leon G. Schiffman, and Anil Mathur, "The Influence of Gender on the New-Age Elderly's Consumption Orientation," *Psychology & Marketing,* 18, 10, October 2001, 1073–1089.

69. Elaine Sherman, quoted in David B. Wolfe, "The Ageless Market," *American Demographics,* July 1987, 26–28, 55–56.

70. Carol M. Morgan and Doran J. Levy, "Understanding Mature Consumers," *Marketing Review,* January 1996, 12–13, 25; and Elaine Sherman and Leon G. Schiffman, "Quality-of-Life (QOL) Assessment of Older Consumers: A Retrospective Review," *Journal of Business and Psychology,* Fall 1991, 107–119.

71. Don E. Bradley and Charles F. Longino, Jr., "How Older People Think About Images of Aging in Advertising and the Media," *Generations,* 25, 3, Fall 2001, 17–21.

72. Isabelle Szmigin and Marylyn Carrigan, "Leisure and Tourism Services and the Older Innovator," *The Service Industries Journal (London),* 21, 3, July 2001, 113–129; and Polyak, "The Center of Attention," 32.

73. Charles A. McMellon and Leon G. Schiffman, "Cybersenior Empowerment: How Some Older Individuals Are Taking Control of Their Lives," *The Journal of Applied Gerontology,* 21, 2, June 2002, 157–175; and Charles A. McMellon and Leon G. Schiffman, "Cybersenior Mobility: Why Some Older Consumers May Be Adopting the Internet," *Advances in Consumer Research,* 27, 2000, 138–144.

74. Isabelle Szmigin and Marylyn Carrigan, "Learning to Love the Older Consumer," *Journal of Consumer Behaviour (London),* 1, 1, June 2001, 22–34; Bill Radford, "Age-Old Trend/Health-Conscious Seniors Displacing Younger Fitness-Club Patrons," *The Gazette,* November 12, 2001, LIFE1; and Bradley and Longino, "How Older People Think . . . ," 17–21.

75. Maxine Wilkie, "Scent of a Market," *American Demographics,* August 1995, 40–49.

76. Scott M. Smith and David B. Whitlark, "Men and Women Online: What Makes Them Click?" *Marketing Research,* 13, 2, Summer 2001, 20–25.

77. Kara A. Arnold and Lyle R. Wetsch, "Sex differences and Information Processing; Implications for Marketing on the Internet," in *2001 AMA Winter*

Educators' Conference, 12, eds. Ram Krishnan and Madhu Viswanathan (Chicago: American Marketing Association 2001), 357–365.

78. Rifka Rosenwein, "The Baby Sabbatical," *American Demographics,* February 2002, 36–40.

79. Anjuman Ali, "Women Travelers: Marooned No More," *Wall Street Journal Europe,* July 6–7, 2001, 29.

80. Thomas Barry, Mary Gilly, and Lindley Doran, "Advertising to Women with Different Career Orientations," *Journal of Advertising Research,* 25, April–May 1985, 26–35.

81. Alice Z. Cuneo, "Advertisers Target Women, but Market Remains Elusive," *Advertising Age,* November 10, 1997, 1, 24–26.

82. Alison Stein Wellner, "The Female Persuasion," *American Demographics,* 24, 2, February 2002, 24–29.

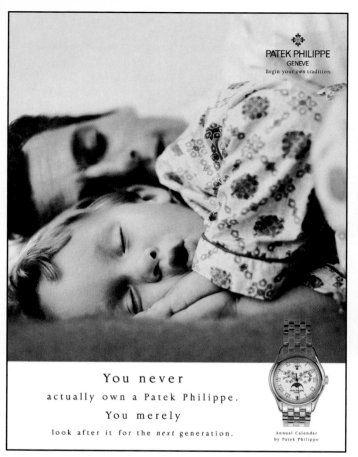

PATEK PHILIPPE
GENEVE
Begin your own tradition.

You never
actually own a Patek Philippe.
You merely
look after it for the *next* generation.

Annual Calendar
by Patek Philippe

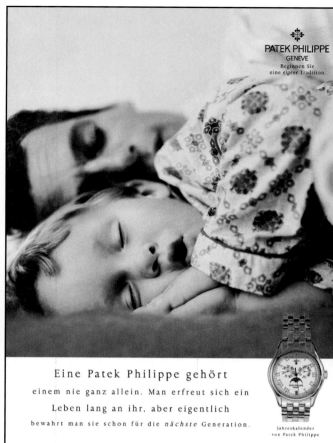

PATEK PHILIPPE
GENEVE
Beginnen Sie
eine *eigene* Tradition.

Eine Patek Philippe gehört
einem nie ganz allein. Man erfreut sich ein
Leben lang an ihr, aber eigentlich
bewahrt man sie schon für die *nächste* Generation.

Jahreskalender
von Patek Philippe

PATEK PHILIPPE
GENEVE
Begin your own tradition.

気持ちを刻み込んで、
その時計は受け継がれる。
父から子へ、世代から世代へ。

"年次カレンダー"
by Patek Philippe

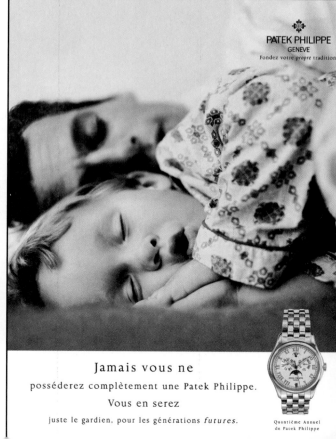

PATEK PHILIPPE
GENEVE
Fondez votre *propre* tradition.

Jamais vous ne
posséderez complètement une Patek Philippe.
Vous en serez
juste le gardien, pour les générations *futures*.

Quantième Annuel
de Patek Philippe

14

Cross-Cultural Consumer Behavior: An International Perspective

I n our examination of psychological, social, and cultural factors, we have consistently pointed out how various segments of the American consuming public differ. If so much diversity exists among segments of a single society, then even more diversity is likely to exist among the members of two or more societies. To succeed, international marketers must understand the nature and extent of differences between the consumers of different societies—"cross-cultural" differences—so that they can develop effective targeted marketing strategies to use in each foreign market of interest.

In this chapter, we broaden our scope of analysis and consider the marketing implications of cultural differences and similarities that exist between the people of two or more nations. We also compare the views that pit a global marketing perspective—one that stresses the *similarities* of consumers worldwide—against a localized marketing strategy that stresses the *diversity* of consumers in different nations and their specific cultural orientations. Our own view is that marketers must be aware of and sensitive to cross-cultural similarities and differences that can provide expanded sales and profit opportunities. Multinational marketers must be ready to tailor their marketing mixes to the specific customs of each nation that they want to target.

The Imperative to Be Multinational

Today, almost all major corporations are actively marketing their products beyond their original homeland borders. In fact, the issue is generally not *whether* to market a brand in other countries but rather *how* to do it (as the same product with the same "global" advertising campaign, or "tailored" products and localized ads for each country). Because of this emphasis on operating multinationally, the vocabulary of marketing now includes terms such as *glocal,* which refers to companies that are both "global" and "local"; that is, they include in their marketing efforts a blend of standardized and local elements in order to secure the benefits of each strategy.[1]

This challenge has been given special meaning by the efforts of the **European Union** (EU) to form a single market. Although the movement of goods and services among community members has been eased, it is unclear whether this diverse market will really be transformed into a single market of homogeneous "Euroconsumers" with the same or very similar wants and needs. Many people hope that the recent introduction of the euro as a common EU currency will help shape Europe into a huge, powerful, unified market. Furthermore, the rapid acceptance of capitalism by many Eastern European countries also presents a major opportunity and challenge to marketers. Firms such as Coca-Cola, General Motors, Nabisco, Gillette, and R.J. Reynolds have been investing extensive sums on product development and marketing to satisfy the needs of Eastern European consumer markets.[2]

The **North American Free Trade Agreement** (NAFTA), which currently consists of the United States, Canada, and Mexico, provides free-market access to more than 400 million consumers. The emerging Association of Southeast Asian Nations (ASEAN), consisting of Indonesia, Singapore, Thailand, the Philippines, Malaysia, Brunei, and Vietnam, is another important economic alliance that offers marketers new global markets. The members of this group have formed the ASEAN Free Trade Area (AFTA) to promote regional trade.

Many firms are developing strategies to take advantage of these and other emerging economic opportunities. A substantial number of firms are now jockeying for market share in foreign markets. Starbucks has opened a store within the Forbidden City in Beijing, China, and MTV Networks has formed a partnership with @JapanMedia to establish a new 24-hour Japanese language music TV channel.[3]

With the buildup of "multinational fever" and the general attractiveness of multinational markets, products or services originating in one country are increasingly being sought out by consumers in other parts of the world. For instance, a Kodak camera purchased by a tourist in France may contain a camera mechanism from a Kodak factory in China and film manufactured in the United States. But the camera was assembled and packaged in France. With Kodak's factories in France, Brazil, Mexico, Canada, India, China, Japan, and Britain, Kodak pays $200 million a year in tariffs for the film and cameras that cross national borders.[4]

Firms are selling their products worldwide for a variety of reasons. First, many firms have learned that overseas markets represent the single most important opportunity for their future growth when their home markets reach maturity. This realization is propelling them to expand their horizons and seek consumers scattered all over the world. Moreover, consumers all over the world are increasingly eager to try "foreign" products that are popular in different and far-off places. Consider the following story:[5]

> There was this Englishman who worked in the London office of a multinational corporation based in the United States. He drove home one evening in his Japanese car. His wife, who worked in a firm which imported German kitchen equipment, was already home. Her small Italian car was often quicker through the traffic. After a meal which included New Zealand lamb, California carrots, Mexican honey, French cheese and Spanish wine, they settled down to watch a program on their television set, which has been made in Finland. The program was a retrospective celebration of the war to recapture the Falkland Islands. As they watched it they felt warmly patriotic, and very proud to be British.

According to *Business Week,* Coca-Cola is the most valuable brand in the world, with a 2001 brand value of $68.9 billion. Table 14-1 presents *Business Week's* list of the world's 10 most valuable brands.

ACQUIRING EXPOSURE TO OTHER CULTURES

As more and more consumers come in contact with the material goods and lifestyles of people living in other parts of the world, they have the opportunity to adopt these different products and practices. How consumers in one culture secure exposure to the goods of other people living in other cultures is an important part of consumer behavior. It impacts the well-being of consumers worldwide and of marketers trying to gain acceptance for their products in countries that are often quite different from their home country.

A portion of consumers' exposure to different cultures tends to come about through consumers' own initiatives—their travel, their living and working in foreign countries, or even their immigration to a different country. Additionally, consumers obtain a "taste" of different cultures from contact with foreign movies, theater, art and artifacts and, most certainly, from exposure to unfamiliar and different products. This second major category of cultural exposure is often fostered by marketers seeking to expand their markets by bringing new products, services, practices, ideas,

| TABLE 14-1 | The World's Most Valuable Brands |

RANK	BRAND	2001 BRAND VALUE ($BILLIONS)
1	Coca-Cola	68.9
2	Microsoft	65.1
3	IBM	52.8
4	GE	42.4
5	Nokia	35.0
6	Intel	34.7
7	Disney	32.6
8	Ford	30.1
9	McDonald's	25.3
10	AT&T	22.8

Note: Only includes brands that sell at least 20% outside of their home country or region.
Source: Gerry Khermouch, Stanley Holmes, and Moon Ihlwan, "The Best Global Brands," *Business Week,* August 6, 2001, 50. Reprinted with special permission by The McGraw-Hill Companies, Inc.

and experiences to potential consumers residing in a different country and possessing a different cultural view. Within this context, international marketing provides a form of "culture transfer."

COUNTRY-OF-ORIGIN EFFECTS

When consumers are making purchase decisions, they may take into consideration the countries of origin of their choices. Researchers have shown that consumers use their knowledge of where products are made in the evaluation of their purchase options.[6] Such a country-of-origin effect seems to come about because consumers are often aware that a particular firm or brand name is associated with a particular country. For example, a recent article noted:[7]

> *It's hard to think of BMW or Mercedes except in the context of their being German; a Rover or a Jaguar is linked with Britishness (despite the fact that both brands are now under overseas ownership); and Ferrari is a brand that is Italian before it's anything else at all. . . . Brooklyn, Italy's leading brand of chewing gum, is manufactured near Milan by a company called Perfetti and, in its long history, has never been anywhere near the United States.*

In general, many consumers associate France with wine, fashion clothing, and perfume and other beauty products; Italy with pasta, designer clothing, furniture, shoes, and sports cars (see Figure 14-1); Japan with cameras and consumer electronics; and Germany with cars, tools, and machinery. Moreover, consumers tend to have an *attitude* or even a preference when it comes to a particular product being made in a particular country. This attitude might be positive, negative, or neutral, depending on perceptions or experience. For instance, a consumer in one country might positively value a particular product made in another country (e.g., affluent American consumers may feel that an Italian Prada handbag or a Swiss Rolex watch are worthwhile investments. In contrast, another consumer might be negatively influenced when he learns that a DVD player he is considering is made in a country he does not associate with fine electronics, such as a DVD player made in Italy). Such country-of-origin effects influence how consumers rate quality and which brands they will ultimately select.[8] Recent research suggests, though, that when consumer motivation is high and when a specific model of a product is being evaluated (as opposed to a range of products manufactured in a particular country), then consumers are *less* likely to base judgments on country-of-origin information.[9]

In addition to perceptions of a product's attributes based on its country of manufacture, research evidence exists that suggests that some consumers may refrain from purchasing products from particular countries due to animosity. A study of this issue found that *high-animosity consumers* in the People's Republic of China owned fewer Japanese products than *low-animosity consumers* (during World War II, Japan occupied parts of China). Although some Chinese consumers might consider Sony to be a high-end, high-quality brand (or perceptions of the product itself might be very positive), they might nevertheless refuse to bring a product manufactured in Japan into the home. Similarly, some Jewish consumers might avoid purchasing German-made products due to the Holocaust, and some New Zealand and Australian consumers might boycott French products due to France's nuclear tests in the South Pacific.[10]

The American Automobile Labeling Act of 1992 requires that all new cars sold in the United States must contain a label indicating component source country information if such foreign components exceed 15 percent of the total unit produc-

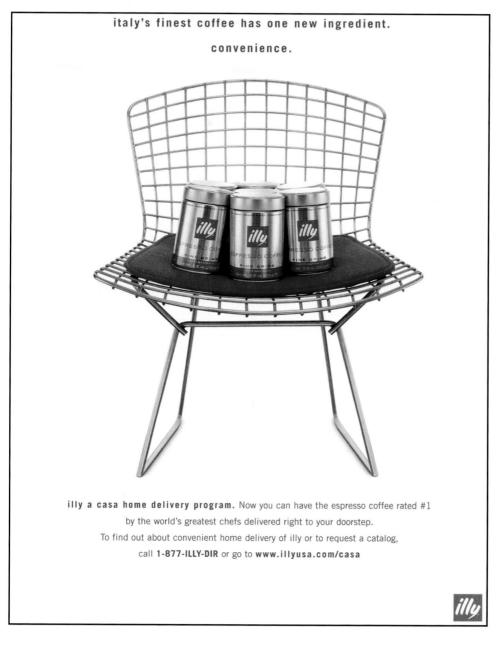

FIGURE 14-1

The Importance of
Country of Origin
Courtesy of illy caffe.

tion cost. But Americans are generally accepting of foreign-made products. Although in the late 1980s there were consumers who preferred a Japanese-made Honda to the same model made in the United States, today the general attitude is "As long as it's a Honda, it doesn't matter where it's made." A recent study asked both U.S. and Thai students, "Are you willing to buy a Sony product if it is 'made in China' at the same price as one 'made in Japan?'" Although 81 percent of the Thai students answered, "No," 81 percent of U.S. students answered "Yes."[11]

Cross-Cultural Consumer Analysis

To determine whether and how to enter a foreign market, marketers need to conduct some form of **cross-cultural consumer analysis.** Within the scope of this discussion, cross-cultural consumer analysis is defined as the effort to determine to what extent the consumers of two or more nations are similar or different. Such analyses can provide marketers with an understanding of the psychological, social, and cultural characteristics of the foreign consumers they wish to target, so that they can design effective marketing strategies for the specific national markets involved.

In a broader context, cross-cultural consumer analysis might also include a comparison of subcultural groups (see Chapter 13) within a single country (such as English and French Canadians, Cuban Americans and Mexican Americans in the United States, or Protestants and Catholics in Northern Ireland). For our purposes, however, we will limit our discussion of cross-cultural consumer analysis to comparisons of consumers of *different* countries.

SIMILARITIES AND DIFFERENCES AMONG PEOPLE

A major objective of cross-cultural consumer analysis is to determine how consumers in two or more societies are similar and how they are different. For instance, Table 14-2 presents at least a partial depiction of the differences between Chinese and American cultural traits. Such an understanding of the similarities and differences that exist between nations is critical to the multinational marketer who must devise appropriate strategies to reach consumers in specific foreign markets. The greater the similarity between nations, the more feasible it is to use relatively similar marketing strategies in each nation. On the other hand, if the cultural beliefs, values, and customs of specific target countries are found to differ widely, then a highly

TABLE 14-2 A Comparison of Chinese and American Cultures

CHINESE CULTURAL TRAITS	AMERICAN CULTURAL TRAITS
• Centered on a set of relationships defined by Confucian doctrine	• Centered on the individual
• Submissive to authority	• Greater emphasis on self-reliance
• Ancestor worship	• Resents class-based distinctions
• Passive acceptance of fate by seeking harmony with nature	• Active mastery in the person–nature relationship
• Emphasizes inner experiences of meaning and feeling	• Concerned with external experiences and the world of things
• A closed worldview, prizing stability and harmony	• An open view of the world, emphasizing change and movement
• Culture rests on kinship ties and tradition with a historical orientation	• Places primary faith in rationalism and is oriented toward the future
• Places weight on vertical interpersonal relationships	• Places weight on horizontal dimensions of interpersonal relationships
• Values a person's duties to family, clan, and state	• Values the individual personality

Source: Adapted from Carolyn A. Lin, "Cultural Values Reflected in Chinese and American Television Advertising," *Journal of Advertising,* 30, 4, Winter 2001, 83–94.

individualized marketing strategy is indicated for each country. To illustrate, in addition to IKEA furniture company's generic global Web site that uses English, the firm also offers 14 localized Web sites and 30 minisites that only provide contact information. And whereas the IKEA Italian Web site shows a group of people frolicking on their IKEA furniture (nudity is acceptable and commonplace in Italian advertising), the Saudi Arabian Web site uses extremely conservative photographs.[12] As another example, a recent study that examined brand choice and personal values among young British and Spanish girls (11- to 12-year-olds) found that the Spanish girls are seeking fun and individual satisfaction from snack food brands (individual pleasure seekers), whereas their British counterparts are seeking friendship, sociability, and a sense of well being (reassurance seekers).[13]

A firm's success in marketing a product or service in a number of foreign countries is likely to be influenced by how similar the beliefs, values, and customs are that govern the use of the product in the various countries. For example, the worldwide TV commercials of major international airlines (American Airlines, Continental Airlines, Air France, Lufthansa, Swissair, United Airlines, and British Airways) tend to depict the luxury and pampering offered their business-class and first-class international travelers. The reason for their general cross-cultural appeal is that these commercials speak to the same types of individuals worldwide—upscale international business travelers—who share much in common (Figure 14-2). In contrast, knowing that "typical" American advertising would not work in China, Nike hired Chinese-speaking art directors and copywriters to develop specific commercials that would appeal to the Chinese consumer within the boundaries of the Chinese culture. The resulting advertising campaign appealed to national pride in China.[14]

As another example of the importance of cultural differences or orientation, consider that Southeast Asia is frequently the largest market for prestige and luxury brands from the West, and that luxury brand companies such as Louis Vuitton, Rolex, Gucci, and Prada are looking to markets such as Hanoi and Guangzhou when they are thinking of expanding their market reach. Indeed, in fine tuning their marketing, these luxury brand marketers need to be especially responsive to cultural differences that compel luxury purchases in the Asian and Western markets. Specifically, research suggests that whereas Western consumers tend to "use" a prestige item to enhance their sense of individualism or serve as a source of personal pleasure, for Southeast Asian consumers that same prestige item might serve to further join the individual with others and to provide visible evidence of the person's value to others.[15]

Time Effects

When American businesspeople start dealing with their counterparts in other countries, one of the first things they must realize is that the pace of life differs from one nation to another. For example, whereas the average children's birthday party in the United States lasts approximately two hours, Brazilians are willing to wait a little more than two hours for a late arriver to show up at a birthday party. Consequently, Brazilians are still waiting for guests to arrive as parents of American children are coming to take their kids home. Interestingly, in contrast to the United States, fewer Brazilians wear watches.[16]

How time is spent on the job is also an issue that varies from country to country. In the United States, about 80 percent of work time is spent on the task and perhaps 20 percent is used for social activities. But in countries such as India and Nepal, the balance is closer to 50 percent on each; and in Japan, social time, such as having tea with peers in the middle of the day, is considered to be a part of work.[17] Research on the pace of life in 31 countries (basing overall pace on how long

FIGURE 14-2

The International Business Traveler Seeks to Be Pampered with Services

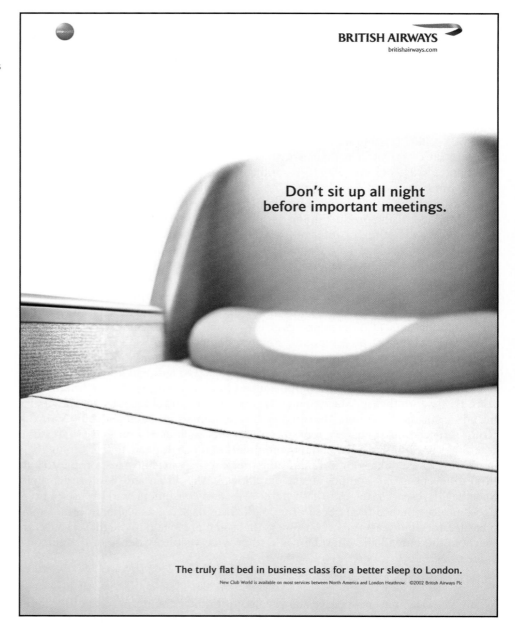

pedestrians take to walk 60 feet, the minutes it takes a postal clerk to complete a stamp-purchase transaction, and the accuracy of public clocks) reveals substantial cross-cultural differences—whereas Switzerland had the fastest pace of life, Mexico had the slowest. Table 14-3 presents a summary of these findings.

THE GROWING GLOBAL MIDDLE CLASS

The growing middle class in developing countries is a phenomenon that is very attractive to global marketers who are often eager to identify new customers for their products. The news media has given considerable coverage to the idea that the rapidly expanding middle class in countries of Asia, South America, and Eastern

| TABLE 14-3 | The Pace of Life in 31 Countries |

SPEED IS RELATIVE

(Rank of 31 countries for overall pace of life and for three measures: minutes downtown pedestrians take to walk 60 feet; minutes it takes a postal clerk to complete a stamp-purchase transaction; and accuracy in minutes of public clocks.)

	OVERALL PACE	WALKING 60 FEET	POSTAL SERVICE	PUBLIC CLOCK
Switzerland	1	3	2	1
Ireland	2	1	3	11
Germany	3	5	1	8
Japan	4	7	4	6
Italy	5	10	12	2
England	6	4	9	13
Sweden	7	13	5	7
Austria	8	23	8	3
Netherlands	9	2	14	25
Hong Kong	10	14	6	14
France	11	8	18	10
Poland	12	12	15	8
Costa Rica	13	16	10	15
Taiwan	14	18	7	21
Singapore	15	25	11	4
United States	16	6	23	20
Canada	17	11	21	22
South Korea	18	20	20	16
Hungary	19	19	19	18
Czech Republic	20	21	17	23
Greece	21	14	13	29
Kenya	22	9	30	24
China	23	24	25	12
Bulgaria	24	27	22	17
Romania	25	30	29	5
Jordan	26	28	27	19
Syria	27	29	28	27
El Salvador	28	22	16	31
Brazil	29	31	24	28
Indonesia	30	26	26	30
Mexico	31	17	31	26

Source: Robert Levine, "The Pace of Life in 31 Countries," *American Demographics*, November 1997, 20–29. Reprinted by permission of Primedia.

Europe is based on the reality that, although per capita income may be low, there is nevertheless considerable buying power in a country such as China, where $1,500 of income is largely discretionary income. This means that a Chinese family with $1,500 is middle class and is a target customer for TVs, VCRs, and computers. Indeed, this same general pattern of the growing middle class has also been observed in many parts of South America, Asia, and Eastern Europe.[18] In many parts of the world, an income equivalent to $5,000 is considered the point at which a person becomes "middle class," and it has been estimated that at the end of 2001, there were 1 billion people in the world's developing countries that met this income standard.[19]

Although a growing middle class may provide a market for products such as Big Macs and fries, it should always be remembered that the same product may have different meanings in different countries. For example, whereas a U.S. consumer wants his or her "fast food" to be fast, a Korean consumer is more likely to view a meal as a social or family-related experience. Consequently, convenient store hours may be valued more by a Korean consumer than shorter service time.[20]

Regulations in different countries may preclude the use of some of the marketing practices that a firm employs in the United States. For example, German advertising rules do not allow an ad to compare one brand to another, nor do they permit Lands' End to offer a "lifetime guarantee." And whereas consumers in the United States like to buy with plastic charge cards, the French prefer an invoice and the Germans prefer COD.[21]

ACCULTURATION IS A NEEDED MARKETING VIEWPOINT

Too many marketers contemplating international expansion make the strategic error of believing that if its product is liked by local or domestic consumers, then everyone will like it. This biased viewpoint increases the likelihood of marketing failures abroad. It reflects a lack of appreciation of the unique psychological, social, cultural, and environmental characteristics of distinctly different cultures. To overcome such a narrow and culturally myopic view, marketers must also go through an *acculturation process*. They must learn everything that is relevant about the usage or potential usage of their products and product categories in the foreign countries in which they plan to operate. Take the Chinese culture, for example. For Western marketers to succeed in China it is important for them to take into consideration *guo qing* (pronounced "gwor ching"), which means "to consider the special situation or character of China."[22] An example of *guo qing* for Western marketers is the Chinese policy of limiting families to one child. An appreciation of this policy means that foreign businesses will understand that Chinese families are open to particularly high-quality baby products for their single child (or "the little emperor").[23] One result of this one-child policy is that in the large cities in China, children are given more than $3 billion a year by their parents to spend as they wish and influence approximately 68 percent of their parents' spending. These Chinese children are also less culture bound than their parents and are, therefore, more open to Western ideas and products.[24]

In a sense, cross-cultural **acculturation** is a dual process for marketers. First, marketers must thoroughly orient themselves to the values, beliefs, and customs of the new society to appropriately position and market their products (being sensitive to and consistent with traditional or prevailing attitudes and values). Second, to gain acceptance for a culturally new product in a foreign society, they must develop a strategy that encourages members of that society to modify or even break with their own traditions (to change their attitudes and possibly alter their behavior). To illustrate the point, a social marketing effort designed to encourage consumers in developing nations to secure polio vaccinations for their children would require a two-step acculturation process. First, the marketer must obtain an in-depth picture of a society's present attitudes and customs with regard to preventive medicine and related concepts. Then the marketer must devise promotional strategies that will convince the members of a target market to have their children vaccinated, even if doing so requires a change in current attitudes.

Distinctive Characteristics of Cross-Cultural Analysis

It is often difficult for a company planning to do business in foreign countries to undertake **cross-cultural consumer research.** For instance, it is difficult in the Islamic countries of the Middle East to conduct Western-style market research. In Saudi Arabia, for instance, it is illegal to stop people on the streets, and focus groups are impractical because most gatherings of four or more people (with the exception of family and religious gatherings) are outlawed.[25] American firms desiring to do business in Russia have found a limited amount of information regarding consumer and market statistics. Similarly, marketing research information on China is generally inadequate, and surveys that ask personal questions arouse suspicion. So marketers have tried other ways to elicit the data they need. For example, Grey Advertising has given cameras to Chinese children so they can take pictures of what they like and do not like, rather than ask them to explain it to a stranger. Moreover, AC Nielsen conducts focus groups in pubs and children's playrooms rather than in conference rooms; and Leo Burnett has sent researchers to China to simply "hang out" with consumers.[26]

APPLYING RESEARCH TECHNIQUES

Although the same basic research techniques used to study domestic consumers are useful in studying consumers in foreign lands (see Chapter 2), in cross-cultural analysis an additional burden exists because language and word usage often differ from nation to nation. Another issue in international marketing research concerns scales of measurement. In the United States, a 5- or 7-point scale may be adequate, but in other countries a 10- or even 20-point scale may be needed. Still further, research facilities, such as telephone interviewing services, may or may not be available in particular countries or areas of the world.

To avoid such research measurement problems, consumer researchers must familiarize themselves with the availability of research services in the countries they are evaluating as potential markets and must learn how to design marketing research studies that will yield useful data. Researchers must also keep in mind that cultural differences may make "standard" research methodologies inappropriate. Table 14-4 identifies basic issues that multinational marketers must consider when planning cross-cultural consumer research.

Alternative Multinational Strategies: Global versus Local

Some marketers have argued that world markets are becoming more and more similar and that standardized marketing strategies are, therefore, becoming more feasible. For example, Exxon Mobil has launched a $150 million marketing campaign to promote its brands (Exxon, Esso, Mobil, and General), and the firm wants all the ads to carry the same look and feel, regardless of in which of 100 countries in the world the ad will appear.[27] In contrast, other marketers feel that differences between consumers of various nations are far too great to permit a standardized marketing strategy. In a practical sense, a basic challenge for many executives contemplating multinational marketing is to decide whether to use *shared needs and values* as a segmentation strategy (i.e., to appeal to consumers in different countries in terms of their "common" needs, values, and goals) or to use *national borders* as a segmentation strategy (i.e., to use relatively different, "local," or specific marketing strategies for members of distinctive cultures or countries).

TABLE 14-4	Basic Research Issues in Cross-Cultural Analysis

FACTORS	EXAMPLES
Differences in language and meaning	Words or concepts (e.g., "personal checking account") may not mean the same in two different countries.
Differences in market segmentation opportunities	The income, social class, age, and sex of target customers may differ dramatically between two different countries.
Differences in consumption patterns	Two countries may differ substantially in the level of consumption or use of products or services (e.g., mail catalogs).
Differences in the perceived benefits of products and services	Two nations may use or consume the same product (e.g., yogurt) in very different ways.
Differences in the criteria for evaluating products and services	The benefits sought from a service (e.g., bank cards) may differ from country to country.
Differences in economic and social conditions and family structure	The "style" of family decision making may vary significantly from country to country.
Differences in marketing research and conditions	The types and quality of retail outlets and direct-mail lists may vary greatly among countries.
Differences in marketing research possibilities	The availability of professional consumer researchers may vary considerably from country to country.

FAVORING A WORLD BRAND

An increasing number of firms have created **world brand** products that are manufactured, packaged, and positioned in exactly the same way regardless of the country in which they are sold. It is quite natural for a "world class" upscale brand of wristwatches such as Patek Philippe to create a global or uniform advertising campaign to reach its sophisticated worldwide target market (see Figure 14-3). Although the advertising copy is in specific target languages, one might speculate that many of Patek Philippe's affluent target customers do read and write English. Nevertheless, to maximize their "comfort zone," it is appropriate to speak to them in their native languages.

Marketers of products with a wide or almost mass-market appeal have also embraced a world branding strategy. For instance, Playtex has moved from a local strategy of nation-by-nation advertising to a global advertising strategy. Other multinational companies, such as General Motors, Gillette, Estée Lauder, Unilever, and Fiat, also use global advertising for various products and services.

Still other marketers selectively use a world branding strategy. For example, you might think that Procter & Gamble (P&G), which markets more than 300 brands worldwide, is a company with an abundance of world brands. Recently, though, it was revealed that of its 16 largest brands, only three are truly global brands—Always/Whisper, Pringles, and Pantene. Some of P&G's other brands, such as Pampers, Tide/Ariel, Safeguard, and Oil of Olay, are just starting to establish common positioning in the world market.[28]

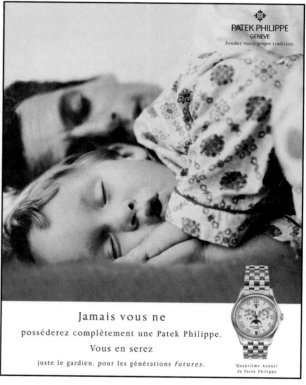

FIGURE 14-3

Leading Wristwatch Manufacturer Using a Global Advertising Strategy

ADAPTIVE GLOBAL MARKETING

In contrast to the marketing communication strategy that stresses a common message, some firms embrace a strategy that adapts their advertising messages to the specific values of particular cultures. McDonald's is an example of a firm that tries to localize its advertising to consumers in each of the cross-cultural markets in which it operates, making it a "glocal" company. For example, the Ronald McDonald that we all know has been renamed Donald McDonald in Japan, because the Japanese language does not contain the "R" sound. Additionally, the McDonald's menu in Japan has been localized to include corn soup and green tea milkshakes.[29] And in Sweden McDonald's developed a new package using woodcut illustrations and a softer design to appeal to the interest the consumers of that nation have in food value and the outdoors.[30]

Like McDonald's, Levi's and Reebok also tend to follow multilocal strategies that calculate cultural differences in creating brand images for their products. For instance, Levi's tends to position its jeans to American consumers, stressing a social-group image, whereas it uses a much more individualistic, sexual image when communicating with European consumers.[31] Still further, Yahoo!, one of the most important Web sites on the Internet, modifies both its content and communications for each of its 23 country-specific Web sites, and in a number of Coke's 146 world markets, what we know as Diet Coke is called Coca-Cola Light, because the word *diet* has an undesirable connotation or no relevance.[32] Also, Coca-Cola is currently testing flavored drinks containing vitamins and minerals that it hopes will find a large market among the 2 billion children of the world, primarily in underdeveloped nations, suffering from micronutrient deficiencies.[33] Responding to demanding market conditions, Coke's chairman-CEO has announced a new "Think local—Act local" edict.[34] Perhaps one result of this change in direction is the fact that Coke's best-selling beverage in Japan is not Coke Classic—it's Georgia Coffee—packaged in a can and available in more than 10 versions (e.g., black, black with sugar, with milk and sugar, and so on). Other marketers, too, feel that the world brand concept may be going too far. Specifically, the computer game Tomb Raider IV also had to be customized for different countries. Lara Croft, the heroine, was felt to be too tall and too British for the Japanese market, the Nazi icons had to be removed for the German market, and the naked priestess and zombies had to be clothed for the American market.[35]

Some firms follow a mixed or combination strategy. For instance, Unilever, Playtex, and Black & Decker have augmented their global strategies with local executions. In taking such an adaptive approach, global advertisers with a knowledge of cross-cultural differences can tailor their supplemental messages more effectively to suit individual local markets. For example, a study has indicated that while U.S. consumers focus more on the product-related claims made in advertisements, Taiwanese consumers focus more on the appropriateness of the ad, such as its aesthetic qualities.[36] There is also some evidence to suggest that Spanish ads may contain a larger proportion of affiliation appeals than U.S. ads do because of Spain's cultural inclination toward femininity in its societal norms (U.S. societal norms tend to reflect masculinity).[37] Because concepts and words often do not easily translate and many regions of the country have their own language, advertisements in China are likely to be more effective if they rely heavily on symbols rather than text.[38] It is also important to note that consumers in different countries of the world have vastly different amounts of exposure to advertisements. For instance, the daily amount of advertising aimed at Japanese consumers, at almost $6 a day, is 14 times the amount aimed at the average Laotian consumer in an entire year.[39]

A recent study of foreign advertisers in China found that 11 percent employed a standardized (or global) strategy, 12 percent used a localized strategy, and fully 77 percent favored a combination strategy. Of the seven advertising components that were studied, localizing language to blend with the local culture was considered to be the most important, followed by the need to localize product attributes, models, colors of ads, humor, scenic background, and music.[40]

FRAMEWORKS FOR ASSESSING MULTINATIONAL STRATEGIES

Multinational marketers face the challenge of creating marketing and advertising programs capable of communicating effectively with a diversity of target markets. To assist in this imposing task, various frameworks have been developed to determine the degree to which marketing and advertising efforts should be either globalized or localized.

To enable international marketers to assess the positions their products enjoy in specific foreign markets, Table 14-5 presents a five-stage continuum that ranges from mere awareness of a foreign brand in a local market area to complete global identification of the brand; that is, the brand is accepted "as is" in almost every market, and consumers do not think about its country of origin.

Table 14-6 presents a framework that focuses on four marketing strategies available to a firm contemplating doing business on a global basis. A firm might decide either to standardize or localize its product and either standardize or localize its communications program (thus forming a two-by-two matrix). The four possibilities that this decision framework considers range from a company incorporating a **global strategy** (or standardizing both product and communications program) to developing a completely **local strategy** (or customizing both the product and communications program) for each unique market. In the middle there are two *mixed strategies*. All four cells may represent growth opportunities for the firm. To

TABLE 14-5	A Product Recognition Continuum for Multinational Marketing
FACTORS	**EXAMPLES**
Stage One	Local consumers have heard or read of a brand marketed elsewhere but cannot get it at home; a brand is "alien" and unavailable but may be desirable [e.g., Rover (English autos), Havana cigars (made in Cuba), or medicine not approved by the FDA but sold in Europe].
Stage Two	Local consumers view a brand made elsewhere as "foreign," made in a particular country but locally available (e.g., Saab autos, French wine). The fact that the brand is foreign makes a difference in the consumer's mind, sometimes favorable, sometimes not.
Stage Three	Local consumers accord imported brand "national status"; that is, its national origin is known but does not affect their choice (e.g., Molson beer in the United States, Ford autos in southern Europe).
Stage Four	Brand owned by a foreign company is made (wholly or partly) domestically and has come to be perceived by locals as a local brand; its foreign origins may be remembered but the brand has been "adopted" ("naturalized"). Examples are Sony in the United States, Coca-Cola in Europe and Japan.
Stage Five	Brand has lost national identity and consumers everywhere see it as "borderless" or global; not only can people not identify where it comes from but they never ask this question. Examples include the Associated Press and CNN news services, Nescafé, Bayer aspirin.

Source: Adapted from George V. Priovolos, "How to Turn National European Brands into Pan-European Brands." Working paper. Hagan School of Business, Iona College, New Rochelle, NY.

TABLE 14-6	A Framework for Alternative Global Marketing Strategies

PRODUCT STRATEGY	COMMUNICATION STRATEGY	
	Standardized Communications	Localized Communications
Standardized Product	**Global Strategy:** Uniform Product/ Uniform Message	**Mixed Strategy:** Uniform Product/ Customized Message
Localized Product	**Mixed Strategy:** Customized Product/ Uniform Message	**Local Strategy:** Customized Product/ Customized Message

determine which cell represents the firm's best strategy, the marketer must conduct cross-cultural consumer analysis to obtain consumer reactions to alternative product and promotional executions. To illustrate the strategic importance of product uniformity, Frito-Lay, the U.S. snack-food giant, has been standardizing quality and reducing the many local brand names of potato chip companies that it owns throughout the world. This effort is moving the company along a common global visual appearance that features the Lay's logo as a global brand. Its efforts are driven by research that reveals that potato chips are a snack food that has widespread appeal throughout much of the world.[41]

Another orientation for assessing whether to use a global versus local marketing strategy concentrates on a high-tech to high-touch continuum. **Product standardization** appears to be most successful for high-involvement products that approach either end of the high-tech/high-touch continuum. In other words, products that are at either extreme are more suitable for positioning as global brands. In contrast, low-involvement products in the midrange of the high-tech/high-touch continuum are more suitably marketed as local brands, using market-by-market executions.[42] To illustrate, on a worldwide basis, consumers interested in high-involvement, high-tech products share a common language (such as "bytes" and "microprocessors"), whereas advertisements for high-involvement, high-touch products tend to use more emotional appeals and to emphasize visual images. In either case, according to this perspective (high-involvement products that are either high-tech or high-touch), such products are candidates for global promotional communications.

Some researchers have written that globalization (or standardization) and localization should be viewed as two ends of a continuum and that often the key to success is to "be global but to act local." It is also generally an error to assume that demographic segments in other nations would want to be or act like Americans. When looking for success in a foreign market, it has been suggested that a company should remember the following 3 P's—place, people, and product. Table 14-7 presents the specific elements of these 3 P's and cites the appropriate marketing strategy when using a standardization approach and when using a localization approach.[43]

When marketing high-tech products abroad, it is important to note that many industrialized nations lag behind the United States in computer usage. For example, although more than 90 percent of U.S. white-collar workers use a PC, only 55 per-

TABLE 14-7	Degree of Fit between Marketing Strategies and the 3 P's		
		Marketing Strategies	
THE 3 P'S	**SPECIFIC ELEMENTS**	**STANDARDIZATION**	**LOCALIZATION**
Place	Economy	Prosperous	Struggling
	Partners	Few	Plentiful
	Competition	Low	Intense
People	Tastes	Little preference	High preference
	Sophistication	High	Low
	Segments	Few	Many
	Classification	Industrial/consumer durables	Consumer nondurables
Products	Technology	High	Low
	Culture bound	Low	High
	Reputation	Sterling	Poor or unknown
	Product perception	High	Low

Source: Sangeeta Ramarapu, John E. Timmerman, and Narender Ramarapu, "Choosing Between Globalization and Localization as a Strategic Thrust for Your International Marketing Effort," *Journal of Marketing Theory and Practice*, 7, 2, Spring 1999, 101. Reprinted by permission.

cent of Western European white-collar workers do so. Often the goal in many European firms is to rise to a high enough position in the company so you do not have to use a PC (i.e., not using a PC is a status symbol).[44] Moreover, approximately 68 percent of all existing Web pages are in English, 6 percent are in Japanese, 6 percent are in German, and 4 percent are in Chinese (these are the top four languages on the Internet).[45]

Perhaps because of the dominance of English-language pages on the Internet, specific non–English-speaking European nations appear to be out to distinguish themselves and their cultures by designing Web sites that in some way or other reflect their countries and specific cultures. So German Web sites might employ bright colors and a geometrical layout to give it a "German feel"; a French Web site might have a black background; a Dutch Web site might offer video downloads; and a Scandinavian Web site might provide a variety of images of nature.[46]

Cross-Cultural Psychographic Segmentation

The paradox in cross-cultural consumer research is that although worldwide consumers may be similar in many ways (e.g., the increased number of women who work outside of the home), any differences in attitudes or behavior can be crucial in determining satisfaction and may provide an opportunity for segmenting consumers in terms of cultural differences. For example, although more than 50 percent of Japanese and American women work outside of the home (which enhances the need for many convenience and time-saving products), Japanese women have been slower to embrace the liberated attitudes of their counterpart working women in the United States.[47] Seen in this light, the determination of whether or not to market a time-saving cleaning device as a world brand is a critical strategic decision. Some firms might attempt to establish a global branding strategy, whereas others would design an individual or local marketing strategy—one that treats Japanese and American working women differently. One marketing authority aptly summed up the issues years ago by stating: "The only ultimate truth possible is that humans are both deeply the same and obviously different. . . ."[48]

This book endorses the same thesis. Earlier chapters have described the underlying similarities that exist between people and the external influences that serve to differentiate them into distinct market segments. If we believe in tailoring marketing strategies to specific segments of the American market, it follows then that we also believe in tailoring marketing strategies to the needs—psychological, social, cultural, and functional—of specific foreign segments.

Global psychographic research often reveals cultural differences of great importance to marketers. For example, Roper Starch Worldwide, a major multinational marketing research company, interviewed 35,000 consumers in 35 countries in order to identify shared values, irrespective of national borders. The research sought to uncover the bedrock values in peoples' lives in order to understand the motivations that drive both attitudes and behavior. After completing the interviews in North and South America, Asia, and Europe, six global value groups were uncovered: *Strivers, Devouts, Altruists, Intimates, Fun Seekers,* and *Creatives.*[49] Table 14-8 presents a brief description of each of these six global market segments.

Finally, a recent study of 18- to 56-year-olds in more than two dozen countries divided respondents into four generational cohorts: Core Boomers (born 1946 to 1954), Cuspers (born 1954 to 1964), Gen Xers (born 1965 to 1974), and Echo Boomers (born 1975 to 1994). Table 14-9 compares the responses of Core Boomers and Echo Boomers on a number of values. Note, for example, how 100 percent of the Mexican Core Boomers felt that today's emphasis on work is a bad thing, whereas in most other countries only 50 percent share this view. And on this same question 94 percent of the Echo Boomers in the Netherlands agreed, compared with only 28 percent of the participating Mexican Echo Boomers.[50]

TABLE 14-8	Six Global Consumer Market Segments	
SEGMENT NAME	**GLOBAL SIZE**	**DESCRIPTION**
Strivers	23%	Value wealth, status, ambition, and power, and products like cellular telephones and computers. They consider material things extremely important.
Devouts	22%	Have more traditional values, like faith, duty, obedience, and respect for elders. Least involved with the media and least likely to want Western brands. Concentrated in the Mideast, Africa, and Asia.
Altruists	18%	Very outer focused—interested in social issues and causes. Generally well educated, older (median age 44), and more female than the norm. Found in Russia and Latin America.
Intimates	15%	These are "people people," and focus on relationships close to home, such as spouses, significant others, family, and friends. Often found in England, Hungary, the Netherlands, and the United States. Very heavy users of media—gives them something to talk about to others.
Fun Seekers	12%	The youngest group. They value excitement, adventure, pleasure, and looking good, and spend time at bars, clubs, and restaurants. The group loves electronic media and is more global in its lifestyle, especially in music.
Creatives	10%	Dedicated to technology, knowledge, and learning, and are the highest consumers of media, especially books, magazines, and newspapers. Members of this group are global trendsetters in owning and using a PC and in surfing the Web.

Source: Stuart Elliott, "Research Finds Consumers Worldwide Belong to Six Basic Groups That Cross National Lines," *New York Times,* June 25, 1998, D8. Copyright © 1998 The New York Times. Reprinted by permission.

TABLE 14-9 Worldwide Cohorts

PERCENTAGE WHO AGREE THAT:	UK CORE	UK ECHO	Netherlands CORE	Netherlands ECHO	France CORE	France ECHO	Mexico CORE	Mexico ECHO	USA CORE	USA ECHO	Canada CORE	Canada ECHO	Australia CORE	Australia ECHO	Hong Kong CORE	Hong Kong ECHO
Today's emphasis on work is a bad thing. People need to slow down and enjoy life more.	56%	73%	50%	94%	82%	50%	100%	28%	54%	57%	43%	65%	50%	81%	50%	50%
I would rather lead a simple life than be rich and famous.	44%	32%	38%	22%	50%	64%	33%	38%	49%	40%	29%	35%	25%	19%	50%	50%
Life in 2001 is more stressful than life in 1951.	89%	44%	75%	61%	100%	55%	100%	79%	74%	52%	71%	48%	75%	65%	100%	65%
The morality of young people has gotten worse in my country over the course of my lifetime.	70%	78%	61%	67%	62%	36%	67%	72%	65%	80%	70%	65%	38%	74%	50%	80%
Most people I know in my age group grew up in a loving, stable family environment.	89%	37%	63%	39%	100%	27%	67%	45%	52%	32%	86%	44%	63%	52%	100%	60%

*Generational group samples in some countries were as small as 25 to 30 people.

Note: Core= Core Boomers: Echo= Echo Boomers

Source: Pamela Paul, "Global Generation Gap," American Demographics, 24, 3, March 2002, 19 (based on "Generations and Gaps" Euro RSCG Worldwide).

Marketing Mistakes: A Failure to Understand Differences

In most cases, the gamble for marketers in international marketing is not knowing whether the product, the promotional appeal, the pricing policy, or the retail channels that are effective in one country will work in other countries and in trying to determine what specific changes should be made to ensure acceptance in each foreign market. The following examples of some international marketing blunders illustrate that failure to adapt marketing strategy to the target market's distinctive cultural traits can lead to costly mistakes.

PRODUCT PROBLEMS

International marketers frequently neglect to modify their products to meet local customs and tastes. American marketers who sell food products in Japan frequently learn the hard way (through poor sales performance) that they must alter traditional product characteristics. For example, Snapple failed to sustain sales momentum in Japan because consumers preferred clearer, less sweet iced tea. It appears that Snapple was either unwilling or too slow to alter its ingredients to conform to local Japanese tastes.[51] Kellogg's, the giant cereal company, has attempted to avoid the numerous "cultural traps" that are associated with cross-cultural marketing of food-stuff in its international expansion. It has learned to draw careful distinctions between the Irish, who consume 17 pounds of cereal per person per year (the highest rate in the world), and the French, Italians, and Greeks, whose meager breakfasts tend not to include cereal.[52] Indeed, an article discussing Kellogg's attempt to market cereals in Europe was titled "Europe Is Deaf to Snap! Crackle! Pop!" The story did note that some European moms were purchasing cereal for their children, and that cultural changes on the Continent might make bigger breakfasts essential.[53]

Still another example showed that when Oreos were introduced in Japan, Nabisco reduced the amount of sugar in the cookie batter (the box promoted them as having a "bitter twist") to meet Japanese tastes. However, some Japanese consumers still considered them too sweet and told the company that they "just wanted to eat the base" without the cream. Nabisco belatedly introduced new Petit Oreo Non-Cream cookies that consisted of single wafers without the cream.[54] To avoid such problems, marketers must ascertain in advance whether the physical characteristics of their products will be acceptable to the new market. When IKEA opened its first store in the Philadelphia area, it sold European-sized curtains that did not fit American windows. The founder of IKEA once remarked, jokingly, that "Americans just won't lower their ceilings to fit our curtains."[55]

Color is also a critical variable in international marketing, because the same color often has different meanings in different cultures. For example, consider the color blue. In Holland, it stands for warmth; in Iran, it represents death; in Sweden, it connotes coldness; in India, it means purity. Furthermore, yellow, which represents warmth in the United States, connotes infidelity in France.[56] Pepsodent erred when it tried to sell its toothpaste in Southeast Asia by promising white teeth. In that part of the world, chewing betel nuts is considered an elite habit and, consequently, brownish-red teeth are viewed as a status symbol. Thus, Pepsodent's slogan, "You'll wonder where the yellow went," did not help to sell the product.[57] It is critical that the colors of products and packages convey the proper meaning in the countries in which they are marketed. For example, just before an American necktie manufacturer shipped its first order to Japan, its customer asked about the color of the gift boxes. When told they were white, the Japanese customer requested red. In Japan, the color white is associated with death.[58]

PROMOTIONAL PROBLEMS

When communicating with consumers in different parts of the world, the promotional message must be consistent with the language and customs of the particular target society. International marketers have faced various problems in communicating with widely different customer groups. For example, the 7-Up Company's highly successful "uncola" theme, developed for the U.S. market, was considered inappropriate for many foreign markets because it did not translate well into other languages. Similarly, learning from earlier mistakes, multinational firms like P&G and Ford now work harder to be responsive to particular tastes and values of local markets. For instance, they recently withdrew their sponsorship of television programming in some countries when the sex and violence of the shows were judged to be too strong.[59] And when Coke recently rolled out its "Life Tastes Good" advertising campaign, it was adopted by Coke operations all over the world but not in Japan. The Coke advertising slogan in Japan is "No Reason," which is based on the responses teenagers provided in Toyko focus groups when asked why they drink Coke.[60]

Product names and promotional phrases can also cause considerable problems for international marketers. The word *clock* in Chinese sounds like the word *death*. The Chevrolet Nova did not sell well in Latin America because in Spanish the word *nova* means "It doesn't run." GM also blundered with its "body by Fisher" tag line, which in Flemish translates into "corpse by Fisher." The U.S. government made a miscalculation when it moved to drop the word *North* from North American Free Trade Agreement (or to move from NAFTA to AFTA) so as to make it more inclusive. The trouble began when Brazil pointed out that in Portuguese AFTA sounded like the words that mean "an open mouth sore."[61]

PRICING AND DISTRIBUTION PROBLEMS

International marketers must adjust their pricing and distribution policies to meet local economic conditions and customs. For instance, in many developing nations, small-sized product packages often are a necessity because consumers cannot afford the cash outlay required for the larger sizes popular in the United States and other affluent countries. Even in developed nations, important differences do exist. For example, supermarkets are very popular in Switzerland, but in France, which is just across the border, consumers prefer smaller and more intimate stores for grocery shopping.

It should also be remembered that what Americans view as "low cost" may not be viewed similarly in other countries. For example, the U.S. fast-food franchises that operate in Mexico, such as McDonald's, Burger King, and Wendy's, are all considered upscale to the Mexican consumer. When Taco Bell tried to enter the Mexican market, it found that its taco prices were much higher than the standard Mexican taco (10 pesos versus 3 pesos). Moreover, what Taco Bell considered to be a taco was more in line with what Mexican consumers would call a burrito.[62]

Japan's traditional distribution system differs from the system in the United States in that a close, complex relationship exists among the larger Japanese manufacturers and their distributors and retailers. For example, it took 24 years from the time Japan allowed the introduction of U.S. apples until the apples actually reached the marketplace where Japanese consumers could buy them.[63] Thus, marketers must vary their distribution channels by nation.

Summary

With so much diversity present among the members of just one nation (as in the United States), it is easy to appreciate that numerous larger differences may exist between citizens of different nations having different cultures, values, beliefs, and languages. If international marketers are to satisfy the needs of consumers in potentially very distinct markets effectively, they must understand the relevant similarities and differences that exist between the peoples of the countries they decide to target.

When consumers make purchase decisions, they seem to take into consideration the countries of origin of the brands that they are assessing. Consumers frequently have specific attitudes or even preferences for products made in particular countries. These country-of-origin effects influence how consumers rate quality and, sometimes, which brands they will ultimately select.

As increasing numbers of consumers from all over the world come in contact with the material goods and lifestyle of people living in other countries and as the number of middle-class consumers grows in developing countries, marketers are eager to locate these new customers and to offer them their products. The rapidly expanding middle classes in countries of Asia, South America, and Eastern Europe possess relatively substantial buying power because their incomes are largely discretionary (for necessities like housing and medical care are often provided by the state at little or no cost).

For some international marketers, acculturation is a dual process: First, marketers must learn everything that is relevant to the product and product category in the society in which they plan to market, and then they must persuade the members of that society to break with their traditional ways of doing things to adopt the new product. The more similar a foreign target market is to a marketer's home market, the easier is the process of acculturation. Conversely, the more different a foreign target market, the more difficult the process of acculturation.

Some of the problems involved in cross-cultural analysis include differences in language, consumption patterns, needs, product usage, economic and social conditions, marketing conditions, and market research opportunities. There is an urgent need for more systematic and conceptual cross-cultural analyses of the psychological, social, and cultural characteristics concerning the consumption habits of foreign consumers. Such analyses would identify increased marketing opportunities that would benefit both international marketers and their targeted consumers.

Discussion Questions

1. Will the elimination of trade barriers among the countries of the European Union change consumer behavior in these countries? How can U.S. companies take advantage of the economic opportunities emerging in Europe?

2. With all the problems facing companies that go global, why are so many companies choosing to expand internationally? What are the advantages of expanding beyond the domestic market?

3. Are the cultures of the world becoming more similar or more different? Discuss.

4. What is cross-cultural consumer analysis? How can a multinational company use cross-cultural research to design each factor in its marketing mix? Illustrate your answer with examples.

5. What are the advantages and disadvantages of global promotional strategies?

6. Should Head & Shoulders shampoo be sold worldwide with the same formulation? In the same package? With the same advertising theme? Explain your answers.

7. a. If you wanted to name a new product that would be acceptable to consumers throughout the world, what cultural factors would you consider?

    b. What factors might inhibit an attempt by Apple to position a new laptop computer as a world brand?

8. An American company is introducing a line of canned soups in Poland. (a) How should the

company use cross-cultural research? (b) Should the company use the same marketing mix it uses in the United States to target Polish consumers? (c) Which, if any, marketing mix components should be designed specifically for marketing canned soups in Poland? Explain your answers.

9. Mercedes-Benz, a German car manufacturer, is using cross-cultural psychographic segmentation to develop marketing campaigns for a new two-seater sports car directed at consumers in different countries. How should the company market the car in the United States? How should it market the car in Japan?

10. What advice would you give to an American retailer who wants to sell women's clothing in Japan?

11. Select two of the marketing mistakes discussed in the text. Discuss how these mistakes could have been avoided if the companies involved had adequately researched some of the issues listed in Table 14-4.

Exercises

1. Have you ever traveled outside the United States? If so, please identify some of the differences in values, behavior, and consumption patterns you noted between people in a country you visited and Americans.

2. Interview a student from another culture about his or her use of (a) credit cards, (b) fast-food restaurants, (c) shampoo, and (d) sneakers. Compare your consumption behavior to that of the person you interviewed and discuss any similarities and differences you found.

3. Much has been written about the problems at Euro Disney, the Walt Disney Company's theme park and resort complex, which opened in France in April 1992. These difficulties were largely attributed to Disney's lack of understanding of European (particularly French) culture and the company's failure to modify its American theme-park concept to fit the preferences and customs of European visitors. Discuss how the Walt Disney Company could have used input from cross-cultural analysis in better designing and operating Euro Disney, using a computerized literature search about Euro Disney from your school's library.

4. Select one of the following countries: Mexico, Brazil, Germany, Italy, Israel, Kuwait, Japan, or Australia. Assume that a significant number of people in the country you chose would like to visit the United States and have the financial means to do so. Now, imagine you are a consultant for your state's tourism agency and that you have been charged with developing a promotional strategy to attract tourists from the country you chose. Conduct a computerized literature search of the databases in your school's library and select and read several articles about the lifestyles, customs, and consumption behavior of people in the country you chose. Prepare an analysis of the articles and, on the basis of what you read, develop a promotional strategy designed to persuade tourists from that country to visit your state.

Key Terms

- **Acculturation**
- **Cross-cultural consumer analysis**
- **Cross-cultural consumer research**
- **Cross-cultural psychographic segmentation**
- **European Union**
- **Global strategy versus local strategy**
- **Multinational strategies**
- **North American Free Trade Agreement**
- **Product standardization**
- **World brand**

Notes

1. Thomas L. Friedman, "Big Mac II," *New York Times,* December 11, 1996, A27.
2. Betsy McKay and Steven Gutterman, "For Ads, Russian Revolution Lives," *Advertising Age,* March 7, 1994, 40.
3. Larry Roellig, "Designing Global Brands: Critical Lessons," *Design Management Journal,* 12, 4, Fall 2001, 40–45; and "MTV: Music Television and H&Q Asia Pacific's @Japan Media Group to Launch New 24-Hour Channel in Japan," *PR Newswire,* August 29, 2000, 1.
4. Louis Uchitelle, "Globalization Marches On, as U.S. Eases Up on the Reins," *New York Times,* December 17, 2001, C12, C21.
5. Michael Silk and David L. Andrews, "Beyond a Boundary? Sport, Transnational Advertising, and the Reimagining of National Culture," *Journal of Sport and Social Issues,* 25, 2, May 2001, 180–201.
6. Sharyne Merritt and Vernon Staubb, "A Cross-Cultural Exploration of Country-of-Origin Preference," in *1995 AMA Winter Educators' Proceedings,* eds. David W. Stewart and Naufel J. Vilcassim (Chicago: American Marketing Association, 1995), 380; Jill Gabrielle Klein, Richard Ettenson, and Marlene D. Morris, "The Animosity Model of Foreign Product Purchase: An Empirical Test in the People's Republic of China," *Journal of Marketing,* 62, January 1998, 89–100; and Gillian Sullivan Mort, Hume Winzar, and C. Min Han, "Country Image Effects in International Services: A Conceptual Model and Cross-National Empirical Test," in *2001 AMA Educators' Proceedings,* 12, eds. Greg W. Marshall and Stephen J. Grove (Chicago: American Marketing Association, 2001), 43–44.
7. Simon Anholt, "The Nation as Brand," *Across the Board,* 37, 10, December 2000, 22–27.
8. Israel D. Nebenzahl, Eugene D. Jaffe, and Shlomo I. Lampert, "Towards a Theory of Country Image Effect on Product Evaluation," *Management International Review,* 37, 1997, 27–49.
9. Zeynep Gurhan-Canli and Durairaj Maheswaran, "Determinants of Country-of-Origin Evaluations," *Journal of Consumer Research,* 27, June 2000, 96–108.
10. Klein, Ettenson, and Morris, "The Animosity Model," 89–100.
11. Lyn S. Amine and Sang-Heun Shin, "A Comparison of Consumer Nationality as a Determinant of COO Preferences," *Multinational Business Review,* 10, 1, Spring 2002, 45–53; and Paul Chao, "The Moderating Effects of Country of Assembly, Country of Parts, and Country of Design on Hybrid Product Evaluations," *Journal of Advertising,* 30, 4, Winter 2001, 67–81.
12. Olin Lagon, "Culturally Correct Site Design," *Web Techniques,* 5, 9, September 2000, 49–51.
13. Anne Dibley and Susan Baker, "Uncovering the Links Between Brand Choice and Personal Values Among Young British and Spanish Girls," *Journal of Consumer Behavior (London),* 1, 1, June 2001, 77–93.
14. Robert G. Tian and Charles Emery, "Cross-Cultural Issues in Internet Marketing," *Journal of American Academy of Business,* 1, 2, March 2002, 217–224.
15. Nancy Y. Wong and Aaron C. Ahuvia, "Personal Taste and Family Face: Luxury Consumption in Confucian and Western Societies," *Psychology and Marketing,* 15, 5, August 1998, 423–441. Also see Sarah Ellison, "Sex-Themed Ads Often Don't Travel Well," *Wall Street Journal,* March 31, 2000, 87.
16. Robert Levine, "The Pace of Life in 31 Countries," *American Demographics,* November 1997, 20–29.
17. Robert Levine, "Re-Learning to Tell Time," *American Demographics,* January 1998, 20–25.
18. Chip Walker, "The Global Middle Class," *American Demographics,* September 1995, 40–46; Paula Kephart, "How Big Is the Mexican Market?" *American Demographics,* October 1995, 17–18; and Rahul Jacob, "The Big Rise," *Fortune,* May 30, 1994, 74–90.
19. Rainer Hengst, "Plotting Your Global Strategy," *Direct Marketing,* August 2000, 55.
20. Mookyu Lee and Francis M. Ulgado, "Consumer Evaluations of Fast-Food Services: A Cross-National Comparison," *The Journal of Services Marketing,* 11, 1, 1997, 39–52.
21. Hengst, "Plotting Your Global Strategy," 52–57.
22. Rick Yan, "To Reach China's Consumers, Adapt to Guo Qing," *Harvard Business Review,* September–October 1994, 66–67.
23. Kathy Chen, "Chinese Babies Are Coveted Consumers," *Wall Street Journal,* May 15, 1998, B1; and Fara Warner, "Western Markets Send Researchers to China to Plumb Consumers' Minds," *Wall Street Journal,* March 28, 1997, B5.
24. Mindy F. Ji and James U. McNeal, "How Chinese Childen's Commercials Differ from Those of the United States: A Content Analysis," *Journal of Advertising,* 30, 3, Fall 2001, 78–92.
25. Tara Parker-Pope, "Nonalcoholic Beer Hits the Spot in Mideast," *Wall Street Journal,* December 6, 1995, B1.
26. Warner, "Western Markets Send Researchers," B5.
27. Vanessa O'Connell, "Exxon 'Centralizes' New Global Campaign," *Wall Street Journal,* July 11, 2001, B6.
28. Robert L. Wehling, "Even at P&G, Only 3 Brands Make Truly Global Grade So Far," *Advertising Age International,* January 1998, 8.
29. Friedman, "Big Mac II," A27; and Drew Martin and Paul Herbig, "Marketing Implications of Japan's

Social-Cultural Underpinnings," *Journal of Brand Management,* 9, 3, January 2002, 171–179.

30. Pamela Buxton, "Helping Brands Take on the World," *Marketing (London),* May 13, 1999, 32.

31. Martin S. Roth, "The Effects of Culture and Socioeconomics on the Performance of Global Brand Image Strategies," *Journal of Marketing Research,* 32, 1995, 163–175.

32. Roellig, "Designing Global Brands," 43.

33. Betsy McKay, "Drinks for Developing Countries," *Wall Street Journal,* November 27, 2001, B1, B6.

34. Jack Neff, "Rethinking Globalism," *Advertising Age,* October 9, 2000, 1, 100; and Stevenson, 41.

35. Silk and Andrews, "Beyond a Boundary," 190.

36. Sharon Shavitt, Michelle R. Nelson, and Rose Mei Len Yuan, "Exploring Cross-Cultural Differences in Cognitive Responding to Ads," in *Advances in Consumer Research,* 24, eds. Merrie Brucks and Deborah J. MacInnis (Provo, UT: Association for Consumer Research, 1997), 245–250.

37. Michael A. Callow, Dawn B. Lerman, and Mayo de Juan Vigaray, "Motivational Appeals in Advertising: A Comparative Content Analysis of United States and Spanish Advertising," in *Proceedings of the Sixth Symposium on Cross-Cultural Consumer and Business Studies,* ed. Scott M. Smith (Honolulu, HI: Association of Consumer Research and the Society for Consumer Psychology, 1997), 392–396.

38. Dean Foster, "Playing with China Dollars," *Brandweek,* November 10, 1997, 20–23.

39. Kip D. Cassino, "A World of Advertising," *American Demographics,* November 1997, 60.

40. Jiafei Yin, "International Advertising Strategies in China: A Worldwide Survey of Foreign Advertisers," *Journal of Advertising Research,* 39, 6, November/ December 1999, 25–35.

41. Robert Frank, "Potato Chips to Go Global—or So Pepsi Bets," *Wall Street Journal,* November 30, 1995, B1.

42. Teresa Domzal and Lynette Unger, "Emerging Positioning Strategies in Global Marketing," *Journal of Consumer Marketing,* 4, Fall 1987, 27–29.

43. Sangeeta Ramarapu, John E. Timmerman, and Narender Ramarapu, "Choosing Between Globalization and Localization as a Strategic Thrust for Your International Marketing Effort," *Journal of Marketing Theory and Practice,* 7, 2, 97–105.

44. David Kirkpatrick, "Europe's Technology Gap Is Getting Scary," *Fortune,* March 17, 1997, 26–27.

45. Tian and Emory, "Cross-Cultural Issues in Internet Marketing," 217–224.

46. Ben Vickers, "In Internet Age, Europe Looks to Define Its Many Cultures Against U.S. Online," *Wall Street Journal,* April 2, 2001, B9F.

47. Jack Russel, "Working Women Give Japan Culture Shock," *Advertising Age,* January 16, 1995, 1–24.

48. Sidney J. Levy, "Myth and Meaning in Marketing," in *1974 Combined Proceedings,* ed. Ronald C. Curhan (Chicago: American Marketing Association, 1975), 555–556.

49. Stuart Elliott, "Research Finds Consumers World-wide Belong to Six Basic Groups That Cross National Lines," *New York Times,* June 25, 1998, D8.

50. Pamela Paul, "Global Generation Gap," *American Demographics,* 24, 3, March 2002, 18–19.

51. Norihiko Shirouzu, "Snapple in Japan: Splash Dried Up," *Wall Street Journal,* April 15, 1996, B1, B6.

52. John Tagliabue, "Spoon-to-Spoon Combat Overseas," *New York Times,* January 7, 1995, 17.

53. Ernest Beck and Rekha Balu, "Europe Is Deaf to Snap! Crackle! Pop!" *Wall Street Journal,* June 22, 1998, B1, B2.

54. Yumiko Ono, "Some Kids Won't Eat the Middle of an Oreo," *Wall Street Journal,* November 20, 1991, B1.

55. Julia Flynn and Lori Bongiorno, "IKEA's New Game Plan," *Business Week,* October 6, 1997, 99–102.

56. Linda J. Coleman, Ernest F. Cooke, and Chandra M. Kochunny, "What Is Meant by Global Marketing?" in *Developments in Marketing Science,* eds. J. M. Hawes and G. B. Gilsan (Akron, OH: Academy of Marketing Science, 1987), 10, 178.

57. Ibid., 179.

58. Toddi Gutner, "Never Give a Mandarin a Clock, and Other Rules," *Business Week,* December 9, 1996, 192.

59. Deborah Klosky, "Spanish Viewership Cries 'Foul' on Lurid TV," *Advertising Age,* April 17, 1995, 1–20.

60. Seth Stevenson, "I'd Like to Buy the World a Shelf-Stable Children's Lactic Drink," *New York Times Magazine,* March 10, 2002, 38–43.

61. David E. Sanger, "An Epidemic Adverted: Foot-in-Mouth Disease," *New York Times,* December 11, 1994, 22.

62. Gustavo Mendex-Kuhn, "MEXICO: What Bell?" *Brandweek,* May 5, 1997, 26.

63. Lisa A. Petrison, Masaru Ariga, and Paul Wang, "Strategies for Penetrating the Japanese Market," *Journal of Direct Marketing,* 8, Winter 1994, 44–58; and Sheryl WuDunn, "Japan Tastes Once-Forbidden Fruit," *New York Times,* January 11, 1995, A3.

PART FOUR

The Consumer's Decision-Making Process

Chapter 15 begins with a discussion of personal influence, opinion leadership, and the diffusion of innovations. The final chapter examines in detail a simple model of consumer decision making that ties together the psychological, social, and cultural concepts examined throughout the book. The book concludes with a discussion of various related aspects of consumption behavior (such as gift giving) and explores the outcomes of relationship marketing from the consumer's perspective.

Be first.

Exclusively @
CHAMPS
SPORTS

adidas

The new SL HOOPS from adidas. Where sport and style become one. August

Consumer Influence and the Diffusion of Innovations

This chapter deals with two interrelated issues of considerable importance to consumers and marketers alike—the informal influence that others have on consumers' behavior and the dynamic processes that impact consumers' acceptance of new products and services.

In the first part of this chapter we will examine the nature and dynamics of the influence that friends, neighbors, and acquaintances have on our consumer-related decisions. This influence is often called *word-of-mouth communications* or the *opinion leadership process* (the two terms will be used interchangeably here). We will also consider the personality and motivations of those who influence (opinion leaders) and those who are influenced (opinion receivers). In the second part of this chapter, we will explore factors that encourage and discourage acceptance (or rejection) of new products and services. For consumers, new products and services may represent increased opportunities to satisfy personal, social, and environmental needs and add to their quality of life. For the marketer, new products and services provide an important mechanism for keeping the firm competitive and profitable.

What Is Opinion Leadership?

The power and importance of personal influence are captured in the following comment by an ad agency executive: "Perhaps the most important thing for marketers to understand about word of mouth is its huge potential economic impact."[1]

Opinion leadership (or word-of-mouth communications) is the process by which one person (the opinion leader) informally influences the actions or attitudes of others, who may be opinion seekers or merely opinion recipients. The key characteristic of the influence is that it is interpersonal and informal and takes place between two or more people, *none of whom represents a commercial selling source that would gain directly from the sale of something.* Word of mouth implies personal, or face-to-face, communication, although it may also take place in a telephone conversation or within the context of e-mail or a chat group on the Internet. This communication process is likely, at times, to also be reinforced by nonverbal observations of the appearance and behavior of others.

One of the parties in a word-of-mouth encounter usually offers advice or information about a product or service, such as which of several brands is best or how a particular product may be used. This person, the **opinion leader,** may become an **opinion receiver** when another product or service is brought up as part of the overall discussion.

Individuals who actively seek information and advice about products sometimes are called **opinion seekers.** For purposes of simplicity, the terms *opinion receiver* and *opinion recipient* will be used interchangeably in the following discussion to identify both those who actively seek product information from others and those who receive unsolicited information. Simple examples of opinion leadership at work include the following:

1. *During a coffee break, a coworker talks about the movie he saw last night and recommends seeing it.*
2. *A person shows a friend photographs of his recent Australian Outback vacation, and the friend suggests that using a polarizing filter might produce better pictures of outdoor scenery.*
3. *A family decides that they would like a swimming pool for their backyard and they ask neighbors who have pools which pool construction company they should call.*

Most studies of opinion leadership are concerned with the measurement of the behavioral impact that opinion leaders have on the consumption habits of others. Available research, for example, suggests that "influentials" or opinion leaders are almost four times more likely than others to be asked about political and government issues, as well as how to handle teens; three times more likely to be asked about computers or investments; and twice as likely to be asked about health issues and restaurants.[2] There is also research to suggest that when an information seeker feels that he or she knows little about a particular product or service, a "strong-tie source" will be sought (such as a friend or family member), but when the consumer has some prior knowledge of the subject area, then a "weak-tie source" is acceptable (acquaintances or strangers).[3]

WORD OF MOUTH IN TODAY'S *ALWAYS IN CONTACT* WORLD

Over the past decade, with the proliferation of cell phone usage and e-mail (and the invention of combination devices like BlackBerry and Web-capable cell phones), many people find themselves, by choice, to be "always" available to friends, family, and business associates. Although Americans have been somewhat slower than con-

| TABLE 15-1 | Top 15 Countries in Terms of the Number of Internet Users by the End of Year 2000 | |

COUNTRY	NUMBER OF INTERNET USERS (IN MILLIONS)	PERCENTAGE OF TOTAL
United States	135.7	36.2
Japan	26.9	7.2
Germany	19.1	5.1
United Kingdom	17.9	4.8
China	15.8	4.2
Canada	15.2	4.1
South Korea	14.8	3.9
Italy	11.6	3.1
Brazil	10.1	2.8
France	9.0	2.4
Australia	8.1	2.2
Russia	6.6	1.8
Taiwan	6.5	1.7
Netherlands	5.4	1.5
Spain	5.2	1.4

Source: Eric Chi-Chung Shiu and John A. Dawson, "Cross-National Consumer Segmentation of Internet Shopping for Britain and Taiwan," *The Service Industries Journal (London)*, 22, January 2002, 155. Reprinted by permission.

sumers in other countries, most notably Japan, to embrace the notion of receiving e-mail via our cellular telephones, this may be due, in part, to the great number of PCs in use in the United States. For example, as Table 15-1 shows, whereas 36 percent of Americans are Internet users, the second-place nation, Japan, has only 7.2 percent of its citizens on the Web.[4] There are presently about 50 million Web-enabled cellular telephones in Japan, with some college students and teenagers getting 80 or more e-mail messages a day. In fact, sales of books and magazines in Japan have dropped, as more young adults read their cell phone e-mails on subways.[5]

Along with the explosion of Web-capable cellular telephones is the creation of the "thumb generation," which is known in Japan as *oya yubi sedai.* Young people in Japan learn to send e-mail messages from the cell phones by using their thumbs, and some Japanese TV stations have even held thumbing speed contests. This is just a natural extension of the thumb usage learned from using handheld computer games.[6]

Viral Marketing

Also known as "buzz marketing," "wildfire marketing," "avalanche marketing," or any one of a dozen other names, *viral marketing* "describes any strategy that encourages individuals to pass on a marketing message to others, creating the potential for exponential growth in the message's exposure and influence."[7] Viral marketing is the marriage of e-mail and word of mouth. It is also named "viral" because it allows a message to spread like a virus. Consider HotMail, the first free Web e-mail service. By giving away free e-mail addresses and services, and by attaching a tag to the bottom of every message that read "Get your private, free e-mail at http://www.hotmail.com," every time a HotMail user sent an e-mail, there was a good chance that the receiver of the e-mail would consider signing up for a free HotMail account. And with the expectation of 150 million Instant Messenger (IM) users by the year 2004, companies like ActiveBuddy create custom software

TABLE 15-2 A Profile of Adult Instant Messenger (IM) Users

	PERCENT
GENDER	
Men	50
Women	50
AGE	
18–29 years of age*	30
30–49 years of age	50
50–plus years of age	19
EDUCATION	
No college	36
Some college	34
College graduate	30
ANNUAL HOUSEHOLD INCOME*	
Less than $50,000	45
$50,000 to $75,000	19
More than $75,000	24

*Some respondents did not know or declined to answer.
Source: Marc Weingarten, "The Medium Is the Instant Message" (based on Pew Internet & American Life Project, March 2001), *Business 2.0,* February 2002, 99.

applications to connect IM users to information that they want, while "mimicking, in a crude way, the banter of a fellow IM user at the other end of the data link."[8] Table 15-2 presents the demographic characteristics of adult Instant Messenger users.

Consider some other recent examples of viral marketing in action. M80 Interactive Marketing (one of a number of viral marketing firms) has its employees surf the Web to locate enthusiastic music fans who can be used to generate "buzz" about Britney Spears, one of the firm's clients. These fans may be asked, for example, to swamp MTV's request line demanding the star's latest hit. Beanie Babies, the VW Beetle, the movie *The Blair Witch Project,* and ICQ (an Internet chat service) were also able to generate word-of-mouth hype that resulted in explosive consumer demand. Volkswagen even sold 2,000 Reflex Yellow and Vapor Blue Beetles online, and *only* online. Vespa, the Italian motor scooter manufacturer, has its in-house agency hire models to hang out on scooters outside trendy nightclubs and cafes in Los Angeles.[9] Procter & Gamble is using viral marketing in a big way. The company has developed kiosks for shopping malls that present and sell new P&G products— all in the hope that shoppers will tell their friends what they have seen. And if the shopper purchases a product at the kiosk, he or she is invited to join an "Innovator's Club" that offers discounts, a Web site, and puts the shopper into the P&G database for future new product introductions.[10]

Dynamics of the Opinion Leadership Process

The opinion leadership process is a very dynamic and powerful consumer force. As informal communication sources, opinion leaders are remarkably effective at influencing consumers in their product-related decisions. Some of the reasons for the effectiveness of opinion leaders are discussed next.

CREDIBILITY

Opinion leaders are highly credible sources of information because they usually are perceived as objective concerning the product or service information or advice they dispense. Their intentions are perceived as being in the best interests of the opinion recipients because they receive no compensation for the advice and apparently have no "ax to grind." Because opinion leaders often base their product comments on firsthand experience, their advice reduces for opinion receivers the perceived risk or anxiety inherent in buying new products. The average person is exposed to anywhere from 200 to 1,000 sales communications a day, but he or she is thousands of times more likely to act on the basis of a friend's or colleague's recommendation. Whereas the advertiser has a vested interest in the message being advertised, the opinion leader offers advice that does not have a commercial motive.[11]

POSITIVE AND NEGATIVE PRODUCT INFORMATION

Information provided by marketers is invariably favorable to the product and/or brand. Thus, the very fact that opinion leaders provide both favorable and unfavorable information adds to their credibility. An example of an unfavorable or negative product comment is, "The problem with those inexpensive digital cameras is that the images they produce are not nearly as sharp as those from a small point-and-shoot 35mm camera." Compared with positive or even neutral comments, negative comments are relatively uncommon. For this reason, consumers are especially likely to note such information and to avoid products or brands that receive negative evaluations. Over the years, a number of motion pictures have failed due to negative "buzz" about the film, and one study found that negative word of mouth about a food product retarded sales more than twice as much as positive word of mouth promoted sales.[12] Consumers, it turns out, are generally three to ten times more likely to share a negative experience than a positive one.[13] Figure 15-1 highlights the factors that lead to negative word-of-mouth behavior. (Note: If the word *negative* was changed to the word *positive* everywhere it appears in Figure 15-1, it seems to also work.)

INFORMATION AND ADVICE

Opinion leaders are the source of both information and advice. They may simply talk about their *experience* with a product, relate what they know about a product, or, more aggressively, *advise* others to buy or to avoid a specific product. The kinds of product or service information that opinion leaders are likely to transmit during a conversation include the following:

1. Which of several brands is best: *"In my opinion, when you consider cost, RCA offers the best value in TV."*
2. How to best use a specific product: *"I find that my photos look best when I use genuine Kodak processing."*
3. Where to shop: *"When Macy's has a sale, the values are terrific."*
4. Who provides the best service: *"Over the last 10 years, I've had my car serviced and repaired at Goodyear, and I think its service can't be beat."*

Many of the messages being sent and received these days deal with movies, restaurants, shopping, computer games, and other areas of interest to young adults—word-of-mouth communication in the form of telephone or e-mail.

FIGURE 15-1

The Factors Leading to
Negative Word-of-
Mouth Behavior
Source: Geok Theng Lau and
Sophia Ng, "Individual and
Situational Factors Influencing
negative word-of-mouth
Behavior," *Revue Canadienne
des Sciences de
l'Administration (Montreal),*
18, September 2001, 169.

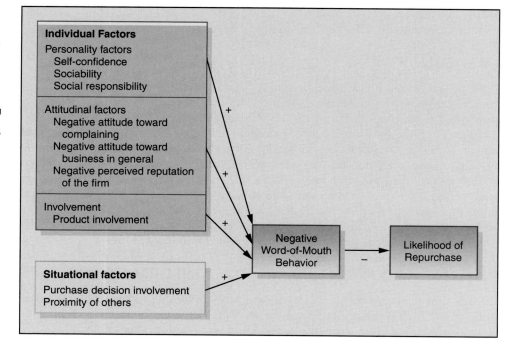

Figure 15-2 presents the results of a survey estimating the percentage of Americans that acted on a referral from an opinion leader for selected important product and service categories during the past year.

OPINION LEADERSHIP IS CATEGORY SPECIFIC

Opinion leadership tends to be *category specific;* that is, opinion leaders often "specialize" in certain product categories about which they offer information and advice.

FIGURE 15-2

Word of Mouth
in Action
Source: Business Week
(based on an online survey
of 1,000 adults, February
2002, Goodmind LLC), May 6,
2002, 10.

Restaurants
69%

Computer Hardware/Software
36%

Consumer Electronics
24%

Travel
22%

Automotive
18%

Financial Services
9%

When other product categories are discussed, however, they are just as likely to reverse their roles and become opinion receivers. A person who is considered particularly knowledgeable about boats may be an opinion leader in terms of this subject, yet when it comes to purchasing a VCR, the same person may seek advice from someone else—perhaps even from someone who has sought his advice on boats.

OPINION LEADERSHIP IS A TWO-WAY STREET

As the preceding example suggests, consumers who are opinion leaders in one product-related situation may become opinion receivers in another situation, even for the same product. Consider the following example. Bradley, a new homeowner contemplating the purchase of a lawnmower, may seek information and advice from other people to reduce his indecision about which brand to select. Once the lawnmower has been bought, however, he may experience postpurchase dissonance (see Chapter 8) and have a compelling need to talk favorably about the purchase to other people to confirm the correctness of his own choice. In the first instance, he is an opinion receiver (seeker); in the second, he assumes the role of opinion leader.

An opinion leader may also be influenced by an opinion receiver as the result of a product-related conversation. For example, a person may tell a friend about a favorite hotel getaway in Maui, Hawaii, and, in response to comments from the opinion receiver, come to realize that the hotel is too small, too isolated, and offers vacationers fewer amenities than other hotels.

The Motivation Behind Opinion Leadership

To understand the phenomenon of opinion leadership, it is useful to examine the motivation of those who provide and those who receive product-related information.

THE NEEDS OF OPINION LEADERS

What motivates a person to talk about a product or service? Motivation theory suggests that people may provide information or advice to others to satisfy some basic need of their own (see Chapter 4). However, opinion leaders may be unaware of their own underlying motives. As suggested earlier, opinion leaders may simply be trying to reduce their own postpurchase dissonance by confirming their own buying decisions. For instance, if Noah subscribes to DSL broadband service and then is uncertain that he made the right choice, he may try to reassure himself by "talking up" the service's advantages to others. In this way, he relieves his own psychological discomfort. Furthermore, when he can influence a friend or neighbor to also get DSL, he confirms his own good judgment in selecting the service first. Thus, the opinion leader's true motivation may really be self-confirmation or self-involvement. Furthermore, the information or advice that an opinion leader dispenses may provide all types of tangential personal benefits: It may confer attention, imply some type of status, grant superiority, demonstrate awareness and expertise, and give the feeling of possessing inside information and the satisfaction of "converting" less adventurous souls.

In addition to *self*-involvement, the opinion leader may also be motivated by *product* involvement, *social* involvement, and *message* involvement. Opinion leaders who are motivated by product involvement may find themselves so pleased or so disappointed with a product that they simply must tell others about it. Those who are motivated by social involvement need to share product-related experiences. In this type of situation, opinion leaders use their product-related conversations as expressions of friendship, neighborliness, and love.[14]

The pervasiveness of advertising in our society encourages message involvement. Individuals who are bombarded with advertising messages and slogans tend to discuss them and the products they are designed to sell. Such word-of-mouth conversation is typified by the popular use in everyday conversation of slogans such as Microsoft's "Where do you want to go today?", Nike's "Just do it!", or Chevrolet's "Like a rock."

THE NEEDS OF OPINION RECEIVERS

Opinion receivers satisfy a variety of needs by engaging in product-related conversations. First, they obtain new-product or new-usage information. Second, they reduce their perceived risk by receiving firsthand knowledge from a user about a specific product or brand. Third, they reduce the search time entailed in the identification of a needed product or service. Moreover, opinion receivers can be certain of receiving the approval of the opinion leader if they follow that person's product endorsement or advice and purchase the product. For all of these reasons, people often look to friends, neighbors, and other acquaintances for product information. Indeed, research examining the importance of four specific information sources on a hypothetical $100 purchase of consumer services revealed that *advice from others* was more important than the combined impact of sales representatives, advertising and promotion, and other sources.[15] Table 15-3 compares the motivations of opinion receivers with those of opinion leaders.

PURCHASE PALS

Researchers have also examined the influence of "purchase pals" as information sources who actually accompany consumers on shopping trips. Although purchase

---

TABLE 15-3   A Comparison of the Motivations of Opinion Leaders and Opinion Receivers

OPINION LEADERS	**OPINION RECEIVERS**
SELF-IMPROVEMENT MOTIVATIONS	
• *Reduce postpurchase uncertainty or dissonance*	• *Reduce the risk of making a purchase commitment*
• *Gain attention or status*	• *Reduce search time (e.g., avoid the necessity of*
• *Assert superiority and expertise*	*shopping around)*
• *Feel like an adventurer*	
• *Experience the power of "converting" others*	
PRODUCT-INVOLVEMENT MOTIVATIONS	
• *Express satisfaction or dissatisfaction with a product or service*	• *Learn how to use or consume a product*
	• *Learn what products are new in the marketplace*
SOCIAL-INVOLVEMENT MOTIVATIONS	
• *Express neighborliness and friendship by discussing products or services that may be useful to others*	• *Buy products that have the approval of others, thereby ensuring acceptance*
MESSAGE-INVOLVEMENT MOTIVATIONS	
• *Express one's reaction to a stimulating advertisement by telling others about it*	

pals were used only 9 percent of the time for grocery items, they were used 25 percent of the time for purchases of electronic equipment (e.g., computers, VCRs, TV sets).[16] Interestingly, male purchase pals are more likely to be used as sources of product category expertise, product information, and retail store and price information. Female purchase pals are more often used for moral support and to increase confidence in the buyer's decisions. Similarly, research evidence suggests that when a weak tie exists between the purchase pal and the shopper (e.g., neighbor, classmate, or work colleague), the purchase pal's main contribution tends to be functional—the source's specific product experiences and general marketplace knowledge are being relied on. In contrast, when strong ties exist (such as mother, son, husband, or wife), what is relied on is the purchase pal's familiarity and understanding of the buyer's individual characteristics and needs (or tastes and preferences).[17]

SURROGATE BUYERS VERSUS OPINION LEADERS

Although the traditional model of new product adoption shows opinion leaders influencing the purchase of many new products and services, there are instances in which surrogate buyers replace opinion leaders in this role. For example, working women are increasingly turning to wardrobe consultants for help in purchasing business attire, most new drugs start out requiring a doctor's prescription, and many service providers make decisions for their clients (e.g., your service station decides which brand of disk brake pads to install on your car). Consequently, in an increasing number of decision situations, it is a surrogate buyer who primarily influences the purchase.[18] Table 15-4 presents the key differences between opinion leaders and surrogate buyers.

TABLE 15-4 **Key Differences Between Opinion Leaders and Surrogate Buyers**

OPINION LEADER	SURROGATE BUYER
1. Informal relationship with end users	1. Formal relationship; occupation-related status
2. Information exchange occurs in the context of a casual interaction	2. Information exchange in the form of formal instructions/advice
3. Homophilous (to a certain extent) to end users	3. Heterophilus to end users (that in fact is the source of power)
4. Does not get paid for advice	4. Usually hired, therefore gets paid
5. Usually socially more active than end users	5. Not necessarily socially more active than end users
6. Accountability limited regarding the outcome of advice	6. High level of accountability
7. As accountability limited, rigor in search and screening of alternatives low	7. Search and screening of alternatives more rigorous
8. Likely to have (although not always) used the product personally	8. May not have used the product for personal consumption
9. More than one can be consulted before making a final decision	9. Second opinion taken on rare occasions
10. Same person can be an opinion leader for a variety of related product categories	10. Usually specializes for a specific product/service category

Source: Praveen Aggarwal and Taihoon Cha, "Surrogate Buyers and the New Product Adoption Process: A Conceptualization and Managerial Framework," *Journal of Consumer Marketing,* 14, 5, 1997; 394. Reprinted by permission.

Measurement of Opinion Leadership

Consumer researchers are interested in identifying and measuring the impact of the opinion leadership process on consumption behavior. In measuring opinion leadership, the researcher has a choice of four basic measurement techniques: (1) the *self-designating method,* (2) the *sociometric method,* (3) the *key informant method,* and (4) the *objective method.*

In the self-designating method, respondents are asked to evaluate the extent to which they have provided others with information about a product category or specific brand or have otherwise influenced the purchase decisions of others. Figure 15-3 shows two types of self-designating question formats that can be used to determine a consumer's opinion leadership activity. The first consists of a single question, whereas the second consists of a series of questions. The use of multiple questions enables the researcher to determine a respondent's opinion leadership more reliably because the statements are interrelated.[19] The self-designating technique is used more often than other methods for measuring opinion leadership because consumer researchers find it easy to include in market research questionnaires. Because this method relies on the respondent's self-evaluation, however, it may be open to bias should respondents perceive "opinion leadership" (even though the term is not used) to be a desirable characteristic and, thus, overestimate their own roles as opinion leaders.

The sociometric method measures the person-to-person informal communication of consumers concerning products or product categories. In this method, respondents are asked to identify (a) the specific individuals (if any) to whom they provided advice or information about the product or brand under study and (b) the specific individuals (if any) who provided them with advice or information about the product or brand under study. In the first instance, if respondents identify one or more individuals to whom they have provided some form of product information, they are tentatively classified as opinion leaders. In the second instance, respondents are asked to identify the individuals (if any) who provided them with information about a product under investigation. Individuals designated by the primary respondent are tentatively classified as opinion leaders. In both cases, the researcher attempts to validate the determination by asking the

---

FIGURE 15-3

Self-Designating Questions for Measuring Opinion Leadership

SINGLE-QUESTION APPROACH:
1. In the last six months have you been asked your advice or opinion about *golf equipment*?*
    Yes _____ No _____

MULTIPLE-QUESTION APPROACH:
(Measured on a 5-point bipolar "Agree/Disagree" scale)

1. Friends and neighbors frequently ask my advice about *golf equipment.*
2. I sometimes influence the types of *golf equipment* friends buy.
3. My friends come to me more often than I go to them about *golf equipment.*
4. I feel that I am generally regarded by my friends as a good source of advice about *golf equipment.*
5. I can think of at least three people whom I have spoken to about *golf equipment* in the past six months.

*Researchers can insert their own relevant product-service or product-service category.

individuals named whether they did, in fact, either provide or receive the relevant product information.

The sociometric approach to determining opinion leadership has useful applications to the study of consumer behavior. For example, consider the flow of opinion leadership among college students living in university housing. Each school year, dormitory students must select a long-distance telephone company. With this in mind, it would be useful for a long-distance company (e.g., AT&T, MCI, or Sprint) to undertake a sociometric study on a particular college campus to determine how word of mouth influences the selection of a long-distance telephone company. This information would provide the basis for subsequent promotional campaigns. On a more general level, any intact community (e.g., a college or an apartment house development) provides an opportunity to measure and evaluate the flow of word-of-mouth communications concerning a new product and its subsequent impact on product trial.

Opinion leadership can also be measured through the use of a key informant, a person who is keenly aware of or knowledgeable about the nature of social communications among members of a specific group. The key informant is asked to identify those individuals in the group who are most likely to be opinion leaders.

The key informant does not have to be a member of the group under study. For example, a professor may serve as the key informant for a college class, identifying those students who are most likely to be opinion leaders with regard to a particular issue. This research method is relatively inexpensive because it requires that only one individual or at most several individuals be intensively interviewed, whereas the self-designating and sociometric methods require that a consumer sample or entire community be interviewed. However, the key informant method is generally not used by marketers because of the difficulties inherent in identifying an individual who can objectively identify opinion leaders in a relevant consumer group.

The key informant method would seem to be of greatest potential use in the study of industrial or institutional opinion leadership. For example, a firm's salespeople might serve as key informants in the identification of specific customers who are most likely to influence the purchase decisions of other potential customers. Similarly, the purchasing agent of a specific firm might serve as a key informant by providing a supplier's salesperson with the names of those persons in the firm who are most likely to influence the purchase decision. In the study of consumers, possible key informants include knowledgeable community members, such as the president of the women's club, the head of the local school board, or a prominent local businessperson.

Finally, the objective method of determining opinion leadership is much like a "controlled experiment"—it involves placing new products or new-product information with selected individuals and then tracing the resulting "web" of interpersonal communication concerning the relevant product(s). In a practical sense, a new restaurant in a downtown business district might apply this approach to speed up the creation of a core customer base by sending out invitations to young, influential business executives to dine with their friends at a reduced introductory price any time during the first month of the restaurant's operations. If the restaurant's food and drink are judged to be superior, the restaurant is likely to enjoy the benefits of enhanced positive word of mouth generated by the systematic encouragement of the young clientele to "try it out" and who "talk it up" to their friends after experiencing the new restaurant.

Table 15-5 presents an overview of each of the four methods of measuring opinion leadership, together with advantages and limitations.

TABLE 15-5 **Methods of Measuring Opinion Leadership: Advantages and Limitations**

OPINION LEADERSHIP MEASUREMENT METHOD	DESCRIPTION OF METHOD	SAMPLE QUESTIONS ASKED	ADVANTAGES	LIMITATIONS
Self-Designating Method	Each respondent is asked a series of questions to determine the degree to which he or she perceives himself or herself to be an opinion leader.	"Do you influence other people in their selection of products?"	Measures the individual's own perceptions of his or her opinion leadership.	Depends on the objectivity with which respondents can identify and report their personal influence.
Sociometric Method	Members of a social system are asked to identify to whom they give advice and to whom they go for advice and information about a product category.	"Whom do you ask?" "Who asks you for information about that product category?"	Sociometric questions have the greatest degree of validity and are easy to administer.	It is very costly and analysis often is very complex. Requires a large number of respondents. Not suitable for sample design where only a portion of the social system is interviewed.
Key Informant Method	Carefully selected key informants in a social system are asked to designate opinion leaders.	"Who are the most influential people in the group?"	Relatively inexpensive and less time consuming than the sociometric method.	Informants who are not thoroughly familiar with the social system are likely to provide invalid information.
Objective Method	Artificially places individuals in a position to act as opinion leaders and measures results of their efforts.	"Have you tried the product?"	Measures individual's ability to influence others under controlled circumstances.	Requires the establishment of an experimental design and the tracking of the resulting impact on the participants.

Source: Adapted with the permission of The Free Press, a division of Simon & Schuster, from *Diffusion of Innovations.* Fourth Edition by Everett M. Rogers. Copyright © 1995 by Everett M. Rogers. Copyright © 1962, 1971, 1983 by the Free Press.

A Profile of the Opinion Leader

Just who are opinion leaders? Can they be recognized by any distinctive characteristics? Can they be reached through specific media? Marketers have long sought answers to these questions, for if they are able to identify the relevant opinion leaders for their products, they can design marketing messages that encourage them to communicate with and influence the consumption behavior of others. For this reason, consumer researchers have attempted to develop a realistic profile of the opinion leader. This has not been easy to do. As was pointed out earlier, opinion leadership tends to be category specific; that is, an individual who is an opinion *leader* in one product category may be an opinion *receiver* in another product category. Thus, the generalized profile of opinion leaders is likely to be influenced by the context of specific product categories.

TABLE 15-6	Profile of Opinion Leaders

GENERALIZED ATTRIBUTES ACROSS PRODUCT CATEGORIES	CATEGORY-SPECIFIC ATTRIBUTES
Innovativeness	Interest
Willingness to talk	Knowledge
Self-confidence	Special-interest media exposure
Gregariousness	Same age
Cognitive differentiation	Same social status
	Social exposure outside group

Although it is difficult to construct a generalized profile of the opinion leader without considering a particular category of interest (or a specific product or service category), Table 15-6 does present a summary of the generalized characteristics that appear to hold true regardless of product category. The evidence indicates that opinion leaders across all product categories generally exhibit a variety of defining characteristics. First, they reveal a keen sense of knowledge and interest in the particular product or service area, and they are likely to be consumer innovators. They also demonstrate a greater willingness to talk about the product, service, or topic; they are more self-confident; and they are more outgoing and gregarious ("more sociable"). Furthermore, within the context of a specific subject area, opinion leaders receive more information via nonpersonal sources and are considered by members of their groups to have expertise in their area of influence. Indeed, a recent study found expertise of the source (the opinion leader) to be strongly associated with likely influence on the information seeker's decision-making process.[20] They also usually belong to the same socioeconomic and age groups as their opinion receivers.

When it comes to their mass-media exposure or habits, opinion leaders are likely to read special-interest publications devoted to the specific topic or product category in which they "specialize." For example, photography opinion leaders read publications such as *Popular Photography, Balian's Outdoor & Nature PhotoWorld,* and *Petersen's Photographic.* These special-interest magazines serve not only to inform photography-oriented consumers about new cameras, films, and accessories that may be of personal interest but also provide them with the specialized knowledge that enables them to make recommendations to relatives, friends, and neighbors. Thus, the opinion leader tends to have greater exposure to media specifically relevant to his or her area of interest than the nonleader.

Frequency and Overlap of Opinion Leadership

Opinion leadership is not a rare phenomenon. Often more than one-third of the people studied in a consumer research project are classified as opinion leaders with respect to some self-selected product category. The frequency of consumer opinion leadership suggests that people are sufficiently interested in at least one product or product category to talk about it and give advice concerning it to others.

This leads to the interesting question: Do opinion leaders in one product category tend to be opinion leaders in other product categories? The answer to this question comes from an area of research aptly referred to as *opinion leadership overlap.* Accordingly, opinion leadership tends to overlap across certain combinations of interest areas. Overlap is likely to be highest among product categories that involve similar interests (such as televisions and VCRs, high-fashion clothing and cosmetics, household cleansers and detergents, expensive wristwatches and writing instruments, hunting gear and fishing tackle). Thus, opinion leaders in one product area often are opinion leaders in related areas in which they are also interested.

However, research does suggest the existence of a special category of opinion leader, the **market maven.**[21] These consumers possess a wide range of information about many different types of products, retail outlets, and other dimensions of markets. They both initiate discussions with other consumers and respond to requests for market information. Market mavens like to shop, and they also like to share their shopping expertise with others. However, although they appear to fit the profile of opinion leaders in that they have high levels of brand awareness and tend to try more brands, unlike opinion leaders their influence extends beyond the realm of high-involvement products. For example, market mavens may help diffuse information on such low-involvement products as razor blades and laundry detergent.[22] A recent study also found that market mavens are value conscious, which explains their greater coupon redemption behavior.[23]

Market mavens are also distinguishable from other opinion leaders because their influence stems not so much from product experience but from a more general knowledge or *market expertise* that leads them to an early awareness of a wide array of new products and services. Part of this early awareness may come from the fact that market mavens have a more favorable attitude than nonmavens toward direct mail as a source of information.

The Situational Environment of Opinion Leadership

Product-related discussions between two people do not take place in a vacuum. Two people are not likely to meet and spontaneously break into a discussion in which product-related information is sought or offered. Rather, product discussions generally occur within relevant situational contexts, such as when a specific product or a similar product is used or served or as an outgrowth of a more general discussion that touches on the product category. For example, while drinking tea, one person might tell the other person about a preferred brand of tea.

Moreover, it is not surprising that opinion leaders and opinion receivers often are friends, neighbors, or work associates, for existing friendships provide numerous opportunities for conversation concerning product-related topics. Close physical proximity is likely to increase the occurrences of product-related conversations. A local health club or community center, for example, or even the local supermarket, provides opportunities for neighbors to meet and engage in informal communications about products or services. In a similar fashion, the rapid growth in the use of the Internet is also creating a type of close "electronic proximity" or "communities"—one in which people of like minds, attitudes, concerns, backgrounds, and experiences are coming together in "chat sessions" to explore their common interests. For example, a recent study identified personal involvement and continuing relationship as two important factors when examining reactions to a Web site and noted that "information becomes a relationship on the WWW" (World Wide Web).[24] It has been our experience that a fair amount of information and advice, especially as to the strengths and limitations of products and services, is offered in these online chat sessions. Within this context, the Internet is proving to be a fertile environment for word-of-mouth communications of the kind that consumer marketers are interested in impacting. Because of this, a number of firms (e.g., Snap Portal, Xoom.com, Participate.com, TalkCity, Prospero) now offer chat room management services to businesses. For example, Participate.com was hired by the health site Accenthealth.com to manage its chat rooms, so that Accenthealth editors could focus on writing and health issues.[25]

The Interpersonal Flow of Communication

A classic study of voting behavior concluded that ideas often flow from radio and print media to opinion leaders and from them to the general public.[26] This so-called **two-step flow of communication theory** portrays opinion leaders as direct receivers of information from impersonal mass-media sources, who in turn transmit (and interpret) this information to the masses. This theory views the opinion leader as an intermediary between the impersonal mass media and the majority of society. Figure 15-4 presents a model of the two-step flow of communication theory. Information is depicted as flowing in a single direction (or one way) from the mass media to opinion leaders (Step 1) and then from the opinion leaders (who interpret, legitimize, and transmit the information) to friends, neighbors, and acquaintances, who constitute the "masses" (Step 2).

MULTISTEP FLOW OF COMMUNICATION THEORY

A more comprehensive model of the interpersonal flow of communication depicts the transmission of information from the media as a multistep flow. The revised model takes into account the fact that information and influence often are two-way processes in which opinion leaders both influence and are influenced by opinion receivers. Figure 15-5 presents a model of the **multistep flow of communication theory.** Steps 1a and 1b depict the flow of information from the mass media simultaneously to opinion

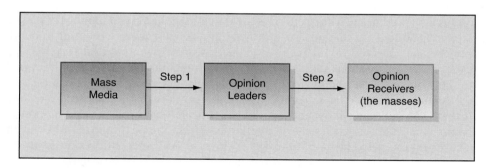

FIGURE 15-4

Two-Step Flow of Communication Theory

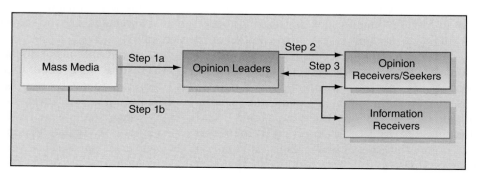

FIGURE 15-5

Multistep Flow of Communication Theory

leaders, opinion receivers/seekers, and information receivers (who neither influence nor are influenced by others). Step 2 shows the transmission of information and influence from opinion leaders to opinion receivers/seekers. Step 3 reflects the transfer of information and influence from opinion receivers to opinion leaders.

Opinion Leadership and the Firm's Marketing Strategy

Marketers have long been aware of the power that opinion leadership exerts on consumers' preferences and actual purchase behavior. For this reason many marketers look for an opportunity to encourage word-of-mouth communications and other favorable informal conversations concerning their products because they recognize that consumers place more credibility in informal communications sources than in paid advertising or a company's salespeople.

New-product designers take advantage of the effectiveness of word-of-mouth communication by deliberately designing products to have word-of-mouth potential. A new product should give customers something to talk about ("buzz potential"). Examples of products and services that have had such word-of-mouth appeal include the Polaroid camera, the Sony Walkman, the Motorola StarTAC cellular phone, Swatch watch, America Online, and Microsoft Windows programs. These revolutionary products have attained market share because consumers "sell" them to each other by means of word of mouth. Motion pictures also appear to be one form of entertainment in which word of mouth operates with some degree of regularity and a large degree of impact. It is very common to be involved directly or overhear people discussing which movies they liked and which movies they advise others to skip. Proof of the power of word of mouth are those cases in which critics hate a movie and the viewing public like it and tell their friends.

Consider Penny Nirider, who lives in Thorntown, Indiana. Several years ago she took a day job at Enduron handling the firm's accounts payables. Shortly thereafter, the company purchased Wilmarc, a small firm that manufactures a number of plastic products, including the Snow-Ease, a shovel that does not require the user to bend. When Penny received a call from an elderly woman who wanted to purchase another Snow-Ease (and couldn't find one locally), she put one in a box and shipped it to the woman for $10 below retail (these shovels had never before been distributed by mail order). After a particularly large snowstorm, the elderly purchaser called an AM radio talk show and praised her shovel. As a result of word of mouth, Wilmarc sold 2,100 snow shovels via mail order within the next four months—even after raising the price to its normal $29.95 level.[27] And then there's the story of Tickle Me Elmo, whose huge success was helped when Tyco Toys rushed the doll to Rosie O'Donnell to give to her 1-year-old son. Hundreds of other Elmos were then sent to Ms. O'Donnell's show for distribution to the in-studio audience (the show's TV audience is mainly stay-at-home mothers of preschoolers).[28]

Small marketers with limited resources are unable to spend millions of dollars promoting their products. So in today's world, they try to create a "buzz" about their product. As an example, although iced coffee has been slow to catch on in the United States (in contrast, Coca Cola's Georgia iced coffee is a very successful brand in Japan), the market is expanding because many young adults were raised drinking cold drinks in the morning. Planet Java (www.planet-java.com), a brand of iced coffee that should be available nationally by the time you read this, has been promoted via the Internet, product sampling, and event sponsorships. As another example, Starwood's W hotels relied heavily on word of mouth, the Internet, and alternative media for the opening of its Newark, California W Suites Hotel.[29]

For instances in which informal word of mouth does not spontaneously emerge from the uniqueness of the product or its marketing strategy, some marketers have deliberately attempted to stimulate or to simulate opinion leadership.

PROGRAMS DESIGNED TO STIMULATE OPINION LEADERSHIP

Advertising and promotional programs designed to persuade consumers to "tell your friends how much you like our product" are one way in which marketers encourage consumer discussions of their products or services. For instance, Daffy's, an off-price retailer operating in the New York metropolitan area, used an outdoor poster (at bus shelters and subway stations) to boldly state that "Friends don't let friends pay retail." Here the implication is that you should share your knowledge and experience with others.

In a promotional campaign for Hennessy Cognac, actors were paid to visit Manhattan bars and nightclubs and order Cognac martinis, made with Hennessy. Although they were instructed to act as if they were ordering a new fad drink, in reality they were attempting to create a new fad drink.[30] Finally, Big Fat Inc., a Manhattan-based firm, places undercover employees in stores and other public places to talk up new books, beverages, records, and so on.[31] The objective of a promotional strategy of stimulation is to run advertisements or a direct-marketing program that is sufficiently interesting and informative to provoke consumers into discussing the benefits of the product with others.

ADVERTISEMENTS SIMULATING OPINION LEADERSHIP

A firm's advertisements can also be designed to simulate product discussions by portraying people in the act of informal communication. This promotional tactic suggests that it is appropriate to discuss a particular subject or product. For example, simulated informal communications encounters between two or more women are often portrayed in TV advertising for personal care products to persuade women to discuss their use or contemplated use. Because these simulations often function as convenient substitutes, they reduce the need for consumers to actually seek product advice from others.

WORD OF MOUTH MAY BE UNCONTROLLABLE

Although most marketing managers believe that word-of-mouth communication is extremely effective, one problem that they sometimes overlook is the fact that informal communication is difficult to control. Negative comments, frequently in the form of rumors that are untrue, can sweep through the marketplace to the detriment of a product.

Indeed, a study by the White House Office of Consumer Affairs found that 90 percent or more of unhappy customers will not do business again with the company that is the source of their dissatisfaction. To make matters even worse, each dissatisfied customer will share his or her grievance with at least nine other people, and 13 percent of unhappy customers will tell more than 20 people about the negative experience.[32]

Some common rumor themes that have plagued marketers in recent years and unfavorably influenced sales include the following: (1) The product was produced under unsanitary conditions, (2) the product contained an unwholesome or culturally unacceptable ingredient, (3) the product functioned as an undesirable depressant or stimulant, (4) the product included a cancer-causing element or agent, and (5) the firm was owned or influenced by an unfriendly or misguided foreign country, governmental agency, or religious cult.

Some marketers have used toll-free telephone numbers in an attempt to head off negative word of mouth, displaying an 800 number prominently on their products' labels. Customer relations managers want dissatisfied customers to call their companies' 800 numbers and receive "satisfaction" instead of telling their complaints to friends and relatives. A particularly challenging form of "negative" word of mouth can be generated today over the Internet, when a dissatisfied consumer decides to post his or her story on a bulletin board for all to see. For example, a recent newspaper article cited a number of false Internet postings, including a former Sears employee who implied that the company ran sweatshops, a former Gateway 2000 employee who established a Web site to disparage the company's computer products, and a bulletin board posting that accused Tommy Hilfiger (the fashion designer) of making racist comments on the *Oprah Winfrey Show*.[33] As one consumer noted after she had complained about Blockbuster Video over the Internet, "Five minutes of my time to complain to thousands of people is a good turnaround . . . I vented and I felt better."[34] And just as every large firm today has its own Internet Web site, for many of these companies there is a corresponding "negative" Web site created by a disgruntled consumer. Such sites, which often take the form of chat rooms, provide customers who have had negative experiences with a product, service, or government agency a place to tell their "horror" stories to others (see, for example, **www.sucks500.com**).

CREATION OF OPINION LEADERS

Marketing strategists agree that promotional efforts would be significantly improved if they could segment their markets into opinion leaders and opinion receivers.[35] Then they could direct their promotional messages directly to the people most likely to "carry the word" to the masses. Because of the difficulties inherent in identifying appropriate opinion leaders, however, some researchers have suggested that it might be more fruitful to "create" product-specific opinion leaders.

In one classic study, a group of socially influential high school students (class presidents and sports captains) were asked to become members of a panel that would rate newly released musical recordings. As part of their responsibilities, panel participants were encouraged to discuss their record choices with friends. Preliminary examination suggested that these influentials would not qualify as opinion leaders for musical recordings because of their relatively meager ownership of the product category.[36] However, some of the records the group evaluated made the Top 10 charts in the cities in which the members of the group lived; these same recordings did not make the Top 10 charts in any other city. This study suggests that product-specific opinion leaders can be created by taking socially involved or influential people and deliberately increasing their enthusiasm for a product category.

A recent research effort explored the notion of increasing enthusiasm for a product category. Over a 12-week period of time, half the participants were assigned to look at corporate Web sites (i.e., marketer-generated information sources), and half were asked to look at online discussions (e.g., chat rooms, forums). Consumers who got their information from online discussions reported greater interest in the product category. It is felt that chat rooms and other forums provide consumers with personal experiences and may offer greater credibility, trustworthiness, relevance, and empathy than marketer-generated Internet Web sites.[37]

Diffusion of Innovations

The second part of this chapter examines a major issue in marketing and consumer behavior—the acceptance of new products and services. The framework for exploring consumer acceptance of new products is drawn from the area of research known as the **diffusion of innovations.** Consumer researchers who specialize in the diffusion of innovations are primarily interested in understanding two closely related processes: the **diffusion process** and the **adoption process.** In the broadest sense, diffusion is a macro process concerned with the spread of a new product (an innovation) from its source to the consuming public. In contrast, adoption is a micro process that focuses on the stages through which an individual consumer passes when deciding to accept or reject a new product. In addition to an examination of these two interrelated processes, we present a profile of **consumer innovators,** those who are the first to purchase a new product. The ability of marketers to identify and reach this important group of consumers plays a major role in the success or failure of new-product introductions.

And why are new-product introductions so important? Well, the policy of Gillette (www.gillette.com) is that 40 percent of sales must come from products introduced within the past five years. Similarly, fully half of Hewlett Packard's revenues (www.hp.com) are derived from products introduced to the market within the past 24 months.[38]

It is also of interest to note that diffusion models for particular types of goods and services may change over time. For example, until the 1960s, it was assumed that new fashions diffused in a top-down or trickle-down manner—new styles are first adopted by the upper-class elites and gradually diffuse to the middle and lower classes. However, since the 1960s, the bottom-up model has served as the better explanation of fashion diffusion—new styles develop in lower-status groups and are later adopted by higher-status groups. These innovative fashions typically emanate from urban communities that also serve as the seedbeds for other innovations, such as art and popular music.[39]

The Diffusion Process

The diffusion process is concerned with how innovations spread, that is, how they are assimilated within a market. More precisely, diffusion is the process by which the acceptance of an innovation (a new product, new service, new idea, or new practice) is spread by communication (mass media, salespeople, or informal conversations) to members of a social system (a target market) over a period of time. This definition includes the four basic elements of the diffusion process: (1) the innovation, (2) the channels of communication, (3) the social system, and (4) time.

THE INNOVATION

No universally accepted definition of the terms product **innovation** or *new product* exists. Instead, various approaches have been taken to define a new product or a new service; these can be classified as *firm-, product-, market-,* and *consumer-oriented definitions of innovations.*

Firm-Oriented Definitions

A *firm-oriented* approach treats the newness of a product from the perspective of the company producing or marketing it. When the product is "new" to the company, it is considered new. This definition ignores whether or not the product is actually new to the marketplace (i.e., to competitors or consumers). Consistent with this view, copies or modifications of a competitor's product would qualify as new. Although this definition has considerable merit when the objective is to examine the impact that a "new" product has on the firm, it is not very useful when the goal is to understand consumer acceptance of a new product.

Product-Oriented Definitions

In contrast to firm-oriented definitions, a *product-oriented* approach focuses on the features inherent in the product itself and on the effects these features are likely to have on consumers' established usage patterns. One product-oriented framework considers the extent to which a new product is likely to disrupt established behavior patterns. It defines the following three types of product innovations:[40]

1. A **continuous innovation** *has the least disruptive influence on established patterns. It involves the introduction of a modified product rather than a totally new product. Examples include the redesigned Toyota Camry, the latest version of Microsoft PowerPoint, reduced-fat Oreo cookies, the BOSE Wave radio, and Teflon (see Figure 15-6).*
2. A **dynamically continuous innovation** *is somewhat more disruptive than a continuous innovation but still does not alter established behavior patterns. It may involve the creation of a new product or the modification of an existing product. Examples include 8-mm camcorders, compact disk players, antilock automobile brakes, erasable-ink pens, and disposable diapers.*
3. A **discontinuous innovation** *requires consumers to adopt new behavior patterns. Examples include airplanes, radios, TVs, automobiles, fax machines, home computers, videocassette recorders, medical self-test kits, and the Internet.*

Figure 15-7 shows how the telephone, a discontinuous innovation of major magnitude, has produced a variety of both dynamically continuous and continuous innovations and has even stimulated the development of other discontinuous innovations.

Market-Oriented Definitions

A *market-oriented* approach judges the newness of a product in terms of how much exposure consumers have to the new product. Two market-oriented definitions of product innovation have been used extensively in consumer studies:

1. *A product is considered new if it has been purchased by a relatively small (fixed) percentage of the potential market.*
2. *A product is considered new if it has been on the market for a relatively short (specified) period of time.*

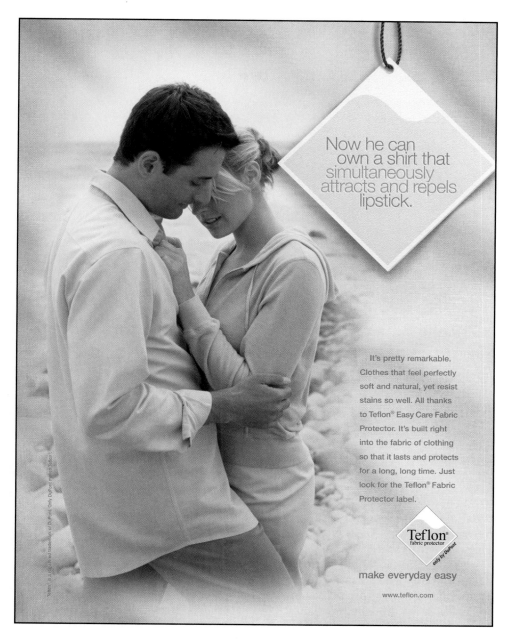

FIGURE 15-6

A Continuous
Innovation
Reprinted by permission of
DuPont and David Monaco.

Both of these market-oriented definitions are basically subjective because they leave the researcher with the task of establishing the degree of sales penetration within the market that qualifies the product as an "innovation" (such as the first 5 percent of the potential market to use the new product) or how long the product can be on the market and still be considered "new" (i.e., the first three months that the product is available).

Consumer-Oriented Definitions

Although each of the three approaches described have been useful to consumer researchers in their study of the diffusion of innovations, some researchers have

FIGURE 15-7

The Telephone Has Led
to Related Innovations

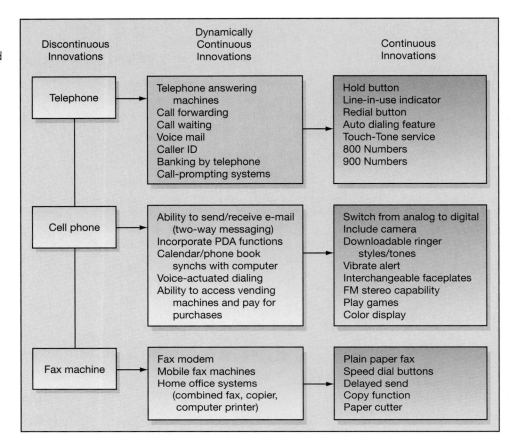

favored a *consumer-oriented* approach in defining an innovation.[41] In this context, a "new" product is any product that a potential consumer judges to be new. In other words, newness is based on the consumer's perception of the product rather than on physical features or market realities. Although the consumer-oriented approach has been endorsed by some advertising and marketing practitioners, it has received little systematic research attention.

Additionally, it should be pointed out that although this portion of the chapter deals primarily with what might be described as "purchase" innovativeness (or time of adoption), a second type of innovativeness, "use innovativeness," has been the subject of some thought and research. A consumer is being *use innovative* when he or she uses a previously adopted product in a novel or unusual way. In one study that dealt with the adoption of VCRs and PCs, early adopters showed significantly higher use innovativeness than those who adopted somewhat later along the cycle of acceptance of the innovation.[42]

Product Characteristics That Influence Diffusion

All products that are new do not have equal potential for consumer acceptance. Some products seem to catch on almost overnight (cordless telephones), whereas others take a very long time to gain acceptance or never seem to achieve widespread consumer acceptance (trash compactors).

The uncertainties of product marketing would be reduced if marketers could anticipate how consumers will react to their products. For example, if a marketer knew that a product contained inherent features that were likely to inhibit its acceptance, the marketer could develop a promotional strategy that would compensate for these features or decide not to market the product at all. Pickups trucks are now being designed for the female driver, and manufacturers are careful to design door handles that do not break nails. Ford even offers adjustable gas and brake pedals.[43]

Although there are no precise formulas by which marketers can evaluate a new product's likely acceptance, diffusion researchers have identified five product characteristics that seem to influence consumer acceptance of new products: (1) relative advantage, (2) compatibility, (3) complexity, (4) trialability, and (5) observability.[44] Based on available research, it has been estimated that these five product characteristics account for much of the dynamic nature of the rate or speed of adoption.[45]

Relative Advantage The degree to which potential customers perceive a new product as superior to existing substitutes is its *relative advantage*. For example, although many people carry beepers so that their business offices or families can contact them, a cellular telephone enables users to be in nearly instant communication with the world and allows users to both receive and place calls. The fax machine is another example of an innovation that offers users a significant relative advantage in terms of their ability to communicate. A document can be transmitted in as little as 15 to 18 seconds at perhaps one-tenth the cost of an overnight express service, which will not deliver the document until the following day.

Compatibility The degree to which potential consumers feel a new product is consistent with their present needs, values, and practices is a measure of its *compatibility*. For instance, an advantage of 3M's Scotch™ Pop-up Tape Strips is that they are easier to use than roll-tape for certain tasks (such as wrapping gifts), yet they represent no new learning for the user. Similarly, in the realm of shaving products, it is not too difficult to imagine that a few years ago when Gillette introduced the MACH3 razor, some men made the transition from inexpensive disposable razors and other men shifted from competitive nondisposable razors (including Gillette's own Sensor razors). This new product is fully compatible with the established wet-shaving rituals of many men. However, it is difficult to imagine male shavers shifting to a new depilatory cream designed to remove facial hair. Although potentially simpler to use, a cream would be basically *incompatible* with most men's current values regarding daily shaving practices.

A study of purchasers of CD players and other technology-based products (such as computers, VCRs, and telephone answering machines) found that the key factors inhibiting product adoption were incompatibility with existing values and poor product quality.[46] And although it is possible, in theory, to make a cellular telephone the size of a button (e.g., personal handy phones the size of a hairclip are popular in Japan), American consumers, according to phone manufacturer Ericsson, do not like the feeling of talking into empty space.[47]

Complexity Complexity, the degree to which a new product is difficult to understand or use, affects product acceptance. Clearly, the easier it is to understand and use a product, the more likely it is to be accepted. For example, the acceptance of such convenience foods as frozen french fries, instant puddings, and microwave dinners is generally due to their ease of preparation and use. Interestingly, although VCRs can be found in most American homes, millions of adults still need help from their children in programming the machine to record a particular television program. The recognition of this need has made the VCR Plus+ device a success.

The issue of complexity is especially important when attempting to gain market acceptance for high-tech consumer products. Four predominant types of "technological fear" act as barriers to new product acceptance: (1) fear of technical complexity, (2) fear of rapid obsolescence, (3) fear of social rejection, and (4) fear of

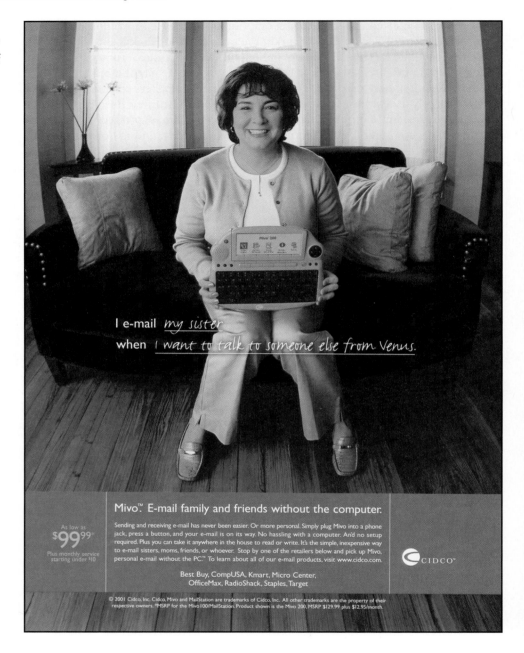

physical harm. Of the four, *technological complexity* was the most widespread concern of consumer innovators.[48] Figure 15-8 presents an advertisement for Cidco, a wireless e-mail solution that makes a point that it is easy to use and convenient.

Trialability *Trialability* refers to the degree to which a new product is capable of being tried on a limited basis. The greater the opportunity to try a new product, the easier it is for consumers to evaluate it and ultimately adopt it. In general, frequently purchased household products tend to have qualities that make trial relatively easy, such as the ability to purchase a small or "trial" size. Because a computer program cannot be packaged in a smaller size, many computer software companies offer free working models of their latest software to encourage computer users to try the program and subsequently buy the program.

Aware of the importance of trial, marketers of new supermarket products commonly use substantial cents-off coupons or free samples to provide consumers with direct product experience. On the other hand, durable items, such as refrigerators or ovens, are difficult to try without making a major commitment. This may explain why publications such as *Consumer Reports* are so widely consulted for their ratings of infrequently purchased durable goods.

Observability Observability (or communicability) is the ease with which a product's benefits or attributes can be observed, imagined, or described to potential consumers. Products that have a high degree of social visibility, such as fashion items, are more easily diffused than products that are used in private, such as a new type of deodorant. Similarly, a tangible product is promoted more easily than an intangible product (such as a service).

It is also important to recognize that a particular innovation may diffuse differently throughout different cultures. For example, although shelf-stable milk (milk that does not require refrigeration) has been successfully sold for years in Europe, Americans thus far have resisted the aseptic milk package.[49] Table 15-7 summarizes the product characteristics that influence diffusion.

Resistance to Innovation

What makes some new products almost instant successes, while others must struggle to achieve consumer acceptance? To help answer such a question, marketers look at the product characteristics of an innovation. Such characteristics offer clues to help determine the extent of consumer resistance, which increases when perceived relative advantage, perceived compatibility, trialability, and communicability are low, and perceived complexity is high. The term *innovation overload* is used to describe the situation in which the increase in information and options available to the consumer is so great that it seriously impairs decision making. As a result, the consumer finds it difficult to make comparisons among the available choices. In a world in

---

TABLE 15-7   Product Characteristics That Influence Diffusion

CHARACTERISTICS	DEFINITION	EXAMPLES
Relative Advantage	The degree to which potential customers perceive a new product as superior to existing substitutes	Air travel over train travel, cordless phones over corded telephones
Compatibility	The degree to which potential consumers feel a new product is consistent with their present needs, values, and practices	Gillette MACH3 over disposable razors, digital telephone answering machines over machines using tape to make recordings
Complexity	The degree to which a new product is difficult to understand or use	Products low in complexity include frozen TV dinners, electric shavers, instant puddings
Trialability	The degree to which a new product is capable of being tried on a limited basis	Trial size jars and bottles of new products, free trials of software, free samples, cents-off coupons
Observability	The degree to which a product's benefits or attributes can be observed, imagined, or described to potential customers	Clothing, such as a new Tommy Hilfiger jacket, a car, wristwatches, eyeglasses

which consumers often find themselves with too little time and too much stress, increased complexity of products wastes time and may delay the acceptance of the product.[50] Consider the fate of Sony's MiniDisc. Although a huge success in Japan, the product flopped in the United States a few years ago and is just now being reintroduced. The MiniDisk (MD) is small and thin and can hold 74 minutes of music. But most people in the United States are satisfied with their CDs and cassettes, and MDs cannot be easily played in a car (an adapter is needed). Added to the MD's problems is the existence of recordable CD units for personal computers (CD "burners").[51]

THE CHANNELS OF COMMUNICATION

How quickly an innovation spreads through a market depends to a great extent on communications between the marketer and consumers, as well as communication among consumers (word-of-mouth communication). Of central concern is the uncovering of the relative influence of impersonal sources (advertising and editorial matter) and interpersonal sources (salespeople and informal opinion leaders).

In recent years, a variety of new channels of communication have been developed to inform consumers of innovative products and services. Consider the growth of interactive marketing messages, in which the consumer becomes an important part of the communication rather than just a "passive" message recipient. For example, for the past several years, an increasing number of companies, such as the Ford Motor Company, General Motors, and other major automobile manufactures, have used floppy disks or CD-ROMs to promote their products. Another example of a new channel of communication is beauty parlors in New York City. Still further, many Web sites currently ask the Internet user if he or she would like to be informed about new products, discount offers, and so on, relevant to the focus of the site. If the answer is "yes," the consumer provides the Web site with an e-mail address and will then receive periodic information from this source.

Consider Nike's Presto line of sneakers. Although the company spends about $1 billion annually to promote its products, it was word of mouth that caused sales of the Presto to soar. Instead of ads in major publications and prime-time television, Nike used MTV and Comedy Central, offered a page of stickers in *YM* magazine, and rented a studio in Manhattan to display a wall containing 200 Presto sneakers. The firm also encouraged teens to log onto the Nike Web site to select Presto graphics, pair the graphics with music, and then e-mail the mini–music videos to their friends (i.e., an example of viral marketing).[52]

THE SOCIAL SYSTEM

The diffusion of a new product usually takes place in a social setting frequently referred to as a *social system*. In the context of consumer behavior, the terms *market segment* and target market may be more relevant than the term *social system* used in diffusion research. A social system is a physical, social, or cultural environment to which people belong and within which they function. For example, for a new hybrid seed corn, the social system might consist of all farmers in a number of local communities. For a new drug, the social system might consist of all physicians within a specific medical specialty (e.g., all neurologists). For a new special diet product, the social system might include all residents of a geriatric community. As these examples indicate, the social system serves as the *boundary* within which the diffusion of a new product is examined.

The orientation of a social system, with its own special values or norms, is likely to influence the acceptance or rejection of new products. When a social system is modern in orientation, the acceptance of innovations is likely to be high. In contrast, when a social system is traditional in orientation, innovations that are perceived as radical or as infringements on established customs are likely to be avoided. According to one authority, the following characteristics typify a *modern social system:*[53]

- *A positive attitude toward change*
- *An advanced technology and skilled labor force*
- *A general respect for education and science*
- *An emphasis on rational and ordered social relationships rather than on emotional ones*
- *An outreach perspective, in which members of the system frequently interact with outsiders, thus facilitating the entrance of new ideas into the social system*
- *A system in which members can readily see themselves in quite different roles*

The orientations of a social system (either modern or traditional) may be national in scope and may influence members of an entire society or may exist at the local level and influence only those who live in a specific community. The key point to remember is that a social system's orientation is the climate in which marketers must operate to gain acceptance for their new products. For example, in recent years, the United States has experienced a decline in the demand for beef. The growing interest in health and fitness throughout the nation has created a climate in which beef is considered too high in fat and in caloric content. At the same time, the consumption of chicken and fish has increased because these foods satisfy the prevailing nutritional values of a great number of consumers.

TIME

Time is the backbone of the diffusion process. It pervades the study of diffusion in three distinct but interrelated ways: (1) the *amount of purchase time,* (2) the identification of *adopter categories,* and (3) the *rate of adoption.*

Purchase Time

Purchase time refers to the amount of time that elapses between consumers' initial awareness of a new product or service and the point at which they purchase or reject it. Table 15-8 illustrates the scope of purchase time by tracking a hypothetical family's purchase of a new car.

Table 15-8 illustrates not only the length and complexity of consumer decision making but also how different information sources become important at successive steps in the process. Purchase time is an important concept because the average time a consumer takes to adopt a new product is a predictor of the overall length of time it will take for the new product to achieve widespread adoption. For example, when the individual purchase time is short, a marketer can expect that the overall rate of diffusion will be faster than when the individual purchase time is long. Some products, for example, are so attractive to consumers that supply cannot keep up with demand. For example, Miller Brewing Company had to introduce its plastic bottles to the national audience three months later than originally planned because demand for the bottles in sports arenas proved to be so strong. Still further, some car dealers were charging thousands of dollars above the sticker price for cars like the

TABLE 15-8	Time Line for Selecting a New Automobile

WEEK	**PRECIPITATING SITUATIONS/FACTORS**
0	The family (Mom and Dad are both school teachers and have two elementary school aged children) currently owns one car, a midsized sedan, which is 6 years old and has 75,000 miles on its odometer. A month ago, the wife's parents, who retired recently, sold their home and moved to Florida. They hope that their daughter and family will visit them Christmas week. But there is some concern that the family's current vehicle is too old to drive from Boston to Tampa.
	DECISION PROCESS BEGINS
1–4	For a few Saturday mornings, the family drives to a number of car dealerships to see, gather information about, test drive, and price a number of midprice, midsized family sedans.
5–9	The family's home oil burner breaks and has to be replaced. Because of the expense involved, the family puts the notion of buying a new car on the back burner for a while.
	INTEREST IS RETRIGGERED
10	As Christmas is now only two months away, the couple keeps being prodded by the wife's parents about driving down and spending the Christmas vacation with them in Florida. So they decide to once again think about buying a new car in time for such a vacation trip.
	CONSUMER ACQUIRES A MENTOR (OPINION LEADER)
	The husband asks one of his coworkers, a fellow teacher who knows a great deal about automobiles, to serve as his mentor (opinion leader) with respect to cars, and he agrees.
	FEATURES AND BRAND OPTIONS ARE REVIEWED
11	With the advice of the mentor, the couple narrows down their search to vehicles that have four-cylinder engines (for good gas mileage), offer cruise control (for the long trip to Florida), and are equipped with air bags and antilock braking systems. Consequently, the choice has narrowed to the Toyota Camry, Honda Accord, and VW Passat.
12–13	The couple spends time on the Internet at both manufacturers' Web sites and the Web sites of independent auto services, such as www.autoweb.com. They also return to their local Toyota, Honda, and VW dealers to again test drive these three vehicles.
14–15	After spending evenings pouring over brochures and information downloaded from the Internet, the couple decides that the VW Passat is the car they want to buy.
	ORDERING THE CAR
	The couple visits four VW dealers located in the greater Boston area, and three of them have the desired car (color, options, etc.) in stock. Volkswagen, through its dealers, is currently offering a low-interest, four-year financing plan, which the couple decides is the best way for them to pay for the car. After negotiating with the three dealerships that have the car they want, they decide to pay $100 more for the car (considering what the dealer wants for the new vehicle and what the dealer is willing to give them for their trade-in) than the lowest price they received, in order to purchase it from the dealership closest to their home. After signing the purchase agreement, the couple left the dealership singing "Florida, here we come!"

Lexus SC 430, Chrysler PT Cruiser, and the Ford Thunderbird when they were first introduced.[54]

Adopter Categories

The concept of **adopter categories** involves a classification scheme that indicates where a consumer stands in relation to other consumers in terms of time (or when the consumer adopts a new product). Five adopter categories are frequently cited in the diffusion literature: *innovators, early adopters, early majority, late majority,* and

TABLE 15-9   Adopter Categories

ADOPTER CATEGORY	DESCRIPTION	RELATIVE PERCENTAGE WITHIN THE POPULATION THAT EVENTUALLY ADOPTS
Innovators	*Venturesome*—very eager to try new ideas; acceptable if risk is daring; more cosmopolite social relationships; communicate with other innovators	2.5%
Early Adopters	*Respect*—more integrated into the local social system; the persons to check with before adopting a new idea; category contains greatest number of opinion leaders; are role models	13.5
Early Majority	*Deliberate*—adopt new ideas just prior to the average time; seldom hold leadership positions; deliberate for some time before adopting	34.0
Late Majority	*Skeptical*—adopt new ideas just after the average time; adopting may be both an economic necessity and a reaction to peer pressures; innovations approached cautiously	34.0
Laggards	*Traditional*—the last people to adopt an innovation; most "localite" in outlook; oriented to the past; suspicious of the new	16.0
		100.0%

Source: Adapted/Reprinted with the permission of The Free Press, a division of Simon & Schuster, from *Diffusion of Innovations,* 3rd edition, by Everett M. Rogers. Copyright © 1995 by Everett M. Rogers. Copyright © 1962, 1971, 1983 by The Free Press.

laggards. Table 15-9 describes each of these adopter categories and estimates their relative proportions within the total population that eventually adopts the new product. It should also be mentioned that the person first to buy an innovation is often an individual who serves as a bridge to other networks, an opinion broker between groups, rather than within groups.[55]

As Figure 15-9 indicates, the adopter categories are generally depicted as taking on the characteristics of a normal distribution (a bell-shaped curve) that describes the total population that ultimately adopts a product. Some argue that the bell curve is an erroneous depiction because it may lead to the inaccurate conclusion that 100 percent of the members of the social system under study (the target market) eventually will accept the product innovation. This assumption is not in keeping with marketers' experiences, because very few, if any, products fit the precise needs of all potential consumers. For example, all purchasers of prerecorded music could theoretically be expected to use (or try) compact disks (CDs). In fact, however, only a relatively small percentage of cassette users have adopted CDs, and it is unrealistic for the music industry to expect all prerecorded cassette purchasers to do so. For this reason, it is appropriate to add an additional category, that of *nonadopters.* The

FIGURE 15-9

The Sequence and
Proportion of Adopter
Categories Among the
Population That
Eventually Adopts
Source: Adapted/Reprinted
with the permission of The
Free Press, a division of Simon
& Schuster, from *Diffusion of
Innovations,* 3rd edition, by
Everett M. Rogers. Copyright
© 1995 by Everett M. Rogers.
Copyright © 1962, 1971, 1983
by The Free Press.

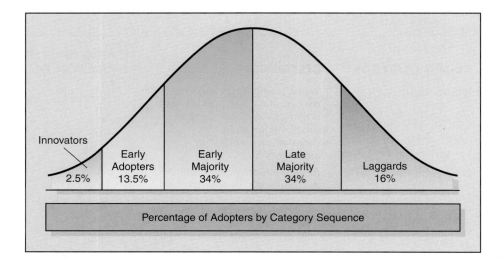

"nonadopter" category is in accord with marketplace reality—that *not* all potential consumers adopt a particular product or service innovation.

Instead of the classic five-category adopter scheme, many consumer researchers have used other classification schemes, most of which consist of two or three categories that compare *innovators* or *early triers* with *later triers* or nontriers. As we will see, this focus on the innovator or early trier has produced several important generalizations that have practical significance for marketers planning the introduction of new products.

Rate of Adoption

The rate of adoption is concerned with how long it takes a new product or service to be adopted by members of a social system, that is, how quickly it takes a new product to be accepted by those who will ultimately adopt it. The general view is that the rate of adoption for new products is getting faster or shorter. Fashion adoption is a form of diffusion, one in which the rate of adoption is important. Cyclical fashion trends or "fads" are extremely "fast," whereas "fashion classics" may have extremely slow or "long" cycles.

In general, the diffusion of products worldwide is becoming a more rapid phenomenon. For example, it took black-and-white TVs about 12 years longer to reach the same level of penetration in Europe and Japan as in the United States. For color TVs, the lag time dropped to about five years for Japan and several more years for Europe. In contrast, for VCRs there was only a three- or four-year spread, with the United States (with its emphasis on cable TV) lagging behind Europe and Japan. Finally, for compact disk players, penetration levels in all three countries were about even after only three years.[56] Table 15-10 presents the time required for a sample of electronic products to penetrate 10 percent of the mass market in the United Kingdom.

The objective in marketing new products is usually to gain wide acceptance of the product as quickly as possible. Marketers desire a rapid rate of product adoption to penetrate the market and quickly establish market leadership (obtain the largest share of the market) before competition takes hold. A *penetration policy* is usually accompanied by a relatively low introductory price designed to discourage competition from entering the market. Rapid product adoption also demonstrates to mar-

| **TABLE 15-10** | Time Required for Electronic Products to Penetrate 10 Percent of the Mass Market in the United Kingdom |

PRODUCT	**NUMBER OF YEARS**
Pager	41
Telephone	38
Cable television	25
Fax machine	22
VCR	9
Cellular phone	9
Personal computer	7
CD-ROM*	6
Wireless data service*	6
Screen-phone*	6
Interactive television*	3

*Predicted.
Source: Eric Chi-Chung Shiu and John A. Dawson, "Cross-National Consumer Segmentation of Internet Shopping for Britain and Taiwan," *The Service Industries Journal (London)*, 22, January 2002, 163. Reprinted by permission.

keting intermediaries (wholesalers and retailers) that the product is worthy of their full and continued support.

Under certain circumstances, marketers might prefer to avoid a rapid rate of adoption for a new product. For example, marketers who wish to use a pricing strategy that will enable them to recoup their development costs quickly might follow a *skimming policy:* They first make the product available at a very high price to consumers who are willing to pay top dollar and then gradually lower the price in a stepwise fashion to attract additional market segments at each price reduction plateau. For example, an examination of current newspaper advertisements in the New York area show that four-head, cable-ready, remote control VCRs can be purchased for $100 or less. But when VCRs were first marketed, two-head models, with no remote control functions, sold for $700 or more.

In addition to how long it takes from introduction to the point of adoption (or when the purchase actually occurs), it is useful to track the extent of adoption (the diffusion rate). For instance, a particular corporation might not upgrade its employees' computer systems to the Windows XP environment until after many other companies in the area have already begun to do so. However, once it decides to upgrade, it might install Windows XP software in a relatively short period of time on all of its employees' PCs. Thus, although the company was relatively "late" with respect to *time* of adoption, its *extent* of adoption was very high.

Although sales graphs depicting the adoption categories (again, see Figure 15-9) are typically thought of as having a normal distribution in which sales continue to increase prior to reaching a peak (at the top of the curve), some research evidence indicates that a third to a half of such sales curves, at least in the consumer electronics industry, involve an initial peak, a trough, and then another sales increase. Such a "saddle" in the sales curve has been attributed to the early market adopters and the main market adopters being two separate markets.[57] Figure 15-10 presents three examples of sales curves with saddles—PCs, VCR decks with stereo, and cordless telephones.

FIGURE 15-10

"Sales Saddle" Differentiates Early Market Adopters from the Main Market Adopters

Source: Jacob Goldenberg, Barak Libai, and Eitan Muller, "Riding the Saddle: How Cross-Market Communications Can Create a Major Slump in Sales," *Journal of Marketing*, 66, April 2002, 5.

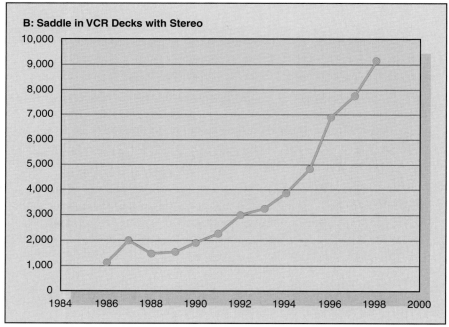

The Adoption Process

The second major process in the diffusion of innovations is *adoption*. The focus of this process is the stages through which an individual consumer passes while arriving at a decision to try or not to try or to continue using or to discontinue using a new product. (The *adoption process* should not be confused with *adopter categories*.)

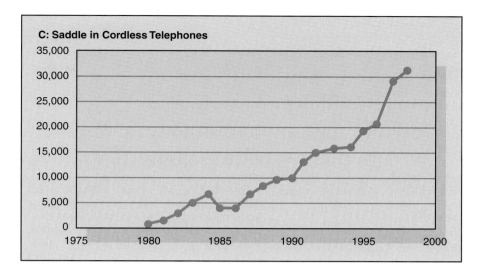

FIGURE 15-10

Continued

STAGES IN THE ADOPTION PROCESS

It is often assumed that the consumer moves through five stages in arriving at a decision to purchase or reject a new product: (1) awareness, (2) interest, (3) evaluation, (4) trial, and (5) adoption (or rejection). The assumption underlying the adoption process is that consumers engage in extensive information search (see Chapter 7), whereas consumer involvement theory suggests that for some products, a limited information search is more likely (for low-involvement products). The five **stages in the adoption process** are described in Table 15-11.

Although the traditional adoption process model is insightful in its simplicity, it does not adequately reflect the full complexity of the consumer adoption process. For one, it does not adequately acknowledge that there is quite often a need or problem-recognition stage that consumers face before acquiring an awareness of potential options or solutions (a need recognition preceding the awareness stage). Moreover, the adoption process does not adequately provide for the possibility of evaluation and rejection of a new product or service after each stage, especially after trial (i.e., a consumer may reject the product after trial or never use the product on a continuous basis). Finally, it does not explicitly include postadoption or postpurchase evaluation, which can lead to a strengthened commitment or to a decision to discontinue use. Figure 15-11 presents an enhanced representation of the adoption process model, one that includes the additional dimensions or actions described here.

The adoption of some products and services may have minimal consequences, whereas the adoption of other innovations may lead to major behavioral and lifestyle changes. Examples of innovations with such major impact on society include the automobile, the telephone, the electric refrigerator, the television, the airplane, and the personal computer.

THE ADOPTION PROCESS AND INFORMATION SOURCES

The adoption process provides a framework for determining which types of information sources consumers find most important at specific decision stages. For example, early subscribers to a computer-linked data service, such as CompuServe, might

TABLE 15-11   The Stages in the Adoption Process

NAME OF STAGE	WHAT HAPPENS DURING THIS STAGE	EXAMPLE
Awareness	Consumer is first exposed to the product innovation.	Janet sees an ad for a new MP3 player in a magazine she is reading.
Interest	Consumer is interested in the product and searches for additional information.	Janet reads about the MP3 player on the manufacturer's Web site and then goes to an electronics store near her apartment and has a salesperson show her the unit.
Evaluation	Consumer decides whether or not to believe that this product or service will satisfy the need—a kind of "mental trial."	After talking to a knowledgeable friend, Janet decides that this MP3 player will allow her to easily download the MP3 files that she has on her computer. She also feels that the unit's size is small enough to easily fit into her beltpack.
Trial	Consumer uses the product on a limited basis.	Since an MP3 player cannot be "tried" like a small tube of toothpaste, Janet buys the MP3 player online from Amazon.com, which offers a 30-day (from the date of shipment) full-refund policy.
Adoption (Rejection)	If trial is favorable, consumer decides to use the product on a full rather than a limited basis—if unfavorable, the consumer decides to reject it.	Janet finds that the MP3 player is easy to use and that the sound quality is excellent. She keeps the MP3 player.

first become aware of the service via mass-media sources (magazines and radio publicity). Then these early subscribers' final pretrial information might be an outcome of informal discussions with personal sources. The key point is that impersonal mass-media sources tend to be most valuable for creating initial product awareness; as the purchase decision progresses, however, the relative importance of these sources declines while the relative importance of interpersonal sources (friends, salespeople, and others) increases. Figure 15-12 depicts this relationship.

FIGURE 15-11

An Enhanced Adoption Process Model

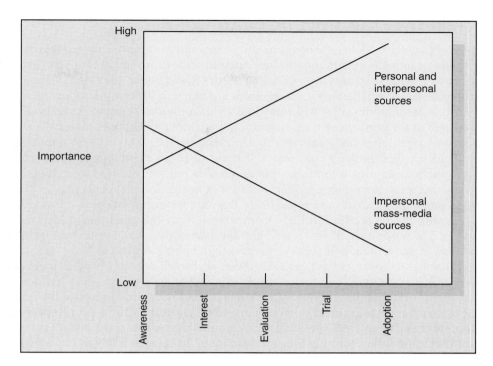

FIGURE 15-12

The Relative
Importance of Different
Types of Information
Sources in the
Adoption Process

A Profile of the Consumer Innovator

Who is the consumer innovator? What characteristics set the innovator apart from later adopters and from those who never purchase? How can the marketer reach and influence the innovator? These are key questions for the marketing practitioner about to introduce a new product or service.

DEFINING THE CONSUMER INNOVATOR

Consumer innovators can be defined as the relatively small group of consumers who are the earliest purchasers of a new product. The problem with this definition, however, concerns the concept of *earliest,* which is, after all, a relative term. Sociologists have treated this issue by sometimes defining innovators as the first 2.5 percent of the social system to adopt an innovation. In many marketing diffusion studies, however, the definition of the consumer innovator has been derived from the status of the new product under investigation. For example, if researchers define a new product as an innovation for the first three months of its availability, then they define the consumers who purchase it during this period as "innovators." Other researchers have defined innovators in terms of their *innovativeness,* that is, their purchase of some minimum number of new products from a selected group of new products. For instance, in the adoption of new fashion items, innovators can be defined as those consumers who purchase more than one fashion product from a group of 10 new fashion products. Noninnovators would be defined as those who purchase none or only one of the new fashion products. In other instances, researchers have defined innovators as those falling within an arbitrary proportion of the total market (e.g., the first 10 percent of the population in a specified geographic area to buy the new product).

INTEREST IN THE PRODUCT CATEGORY

Not surprisingly, consumer innovators are much more interested than either later adopters or nonadopters in the product categories that they are among the first to purchase. If what is known from diffusion theory holds true in the future, the earliest purchasers of small electric automobiles are likely to have substantially greater interest in automobiles (they will enjoy looking at automotive magazines and will be interested in the performance and functioning of automobiles) than those who purchased conventional small cars during the same period or those who purchased small electric cars during a later period. Recent research examining early adopters of products containing a nonfat synthetic cooking oil (i.e., olestra) were found to have a high interest in such a product because of health and diet concerns.[58]

Consumer innovators are more likely than noninnovators to seek information concerning their specific interests from a variety of informal and mass-media sources. They are more likely to give greater deliberation to the purchase of new products or services in their areas of interest than noninnovators.

Although innovators have generally been portrayed as heavy product category users, this may be true only for relatively continuous innovations. A recent study found that for discontinuous innovations, it is often novices that purchase the product, whereas experts in the subject area are often laggards with respect to product adoption. For example, serious amateur photographers with a great deal of camera knowledge and little computer literacy were found to be least likely to buy a digital camera, whereas individuals with high computer literacy and low photographic knowledge were most likely to purchase this product.[59] Therefore, it might be more important for the digital camera manufacturer to advertise in *PC Magazine* than in *Popular Photography*.

THE INNOVATOR IS AN OPINION LEADER

When discussing the characteristics of the opinion leader earlier in this chapter, we indicated a strong tendency for consumer opinion leaders to be innovators. In the present context, an impressive amount of research on the diffusion of innovations has found that consumer innovators provide other consumers with information and advice about new products and that those who receive such advice frequently follow it. Thus, in the role of opinion leader, the consumer innovator often influences the acceptance or rejection of new products.

When innovators are enthusiastic about a new product and encourage others to try it, the product is likely to receive broader and quicker acceptance. When consumer innovators are dissatisfied with a new product and discourage others from trying it, its acceptance will be severely limited, and it may die a quick death. For products that do not generate much excitement (either positive or negative), consumer innovators may not be sufficiently motivated to provide advice. In such cases, the marketer must rely almost entirely on mass media and personal selling to influence future purchasers; the absence of informal influence is also likely to result in a somewhat slower rate of acceptance (or rejection) of the new product. Because motivated consumer innovators can influence the rate of acceptance or rejection of a new product, they influence its eventual success or failure.

PERSONALITY TRAITS

In Chapter 5, we examined the personality traits that distinguish the consumer innovator from the noninnovator. In this section, we will briefly highlight what researchers have learned about the personality of the consumer innovator.

First, consumer innovators generally are *less dogmatic* than noninnovators. They tend to approach new or unfamiliar products with considerable openness and little anxiety. In contrast, noninnovators seem to find new products threatening to the point where they prefer to delay purchase until the product's success has been clearly established.

Consistent with their open-mindedness, it appears that innovative behavior is an expression of an individual's *need for uniqueness*.[60] Those new products, both branded and unbranded, that represent a greater change in a person's consumption habits were viewed as superior when it came to satisfying the need for uniqueness. Therefore, to gain more rapid acceptance of a new product, marketers might consider appealing to a consumer's need for uniqueness.

Still further, consumer innovators also differ from noninnovators in terms of *social character*. Consumer innovators are *inner-directed;* that is, they rely on their own values or standards when making a decision about a new product. In contrast, noninnovators are *other-directed,* relying on others for guidance on how to respond to a new product rather than trusting their own personal values or standards. Thus, the initial purchasers of a new line of automobiles might be inner-directed, whereas the later purchasers of the same automobile might be other-directed. This suggests that as acceptance of a product progresses from early to later adopters, a gradual shift occurs in the personality type of adopters from inner-directedness to other-directedness.

There also appears to be a link between *optimum stimulation level* and consumer innovativeness. Specifically, individuals who seek a lifestyle rich with novel, complex, and unusual experiences (high optimum stimulation levels) are more willing to risk trying new products, to be innovative, to seek purchase-related information, and to accept new retail facilities.

Researchers have isolated a link between *variety seeking* and purchase behavior that provides insights into consumer innovators. Variety-seeking consumers tend to be brand switchers and purchasers of innovative products and services. They also possess the following innovator-related personality traits: They are open-minded (or low in dogmatism), extroverts, liberal, low in authoritarianism, able to deal with complex or ambiguous stimuli, and creative.[61]

To sum up, consumer innovators seem to be more receptive to the unfamiliar and the unique; they are more willing to rely on their own values or standards than on the judgment of others. They also are willing to run the risk of a poor product choice to increase their exposure to new products that will be satisfying. For the marketer, the personality traits that distinguish innovators from noninnovators suggest the need for separate promotional campaigns for innovators and for later adopters.

Perceived Risk and Venturesomeness

Perceived risk, which is discussed in detail in Chapter 6, is another measure of a consumer's likelihood to try new brands or products. Perceived risk is the degree of uncertainty or fear about the consequences of a purchase that a consumer feels when considering the purchase of a new product. For example, consumers experience uncertainty when they are concerned that a new product will not work properly or as well as other alternatives. Research on perceived risk and the trial of new products overwhelmingly indicates that consumer innovators are low-risk perceivers; that is, they experience little fear of trying new products or services. Consumers who perceive little or no risk in the purchase of a new product are much more likely to make innovative purchases than consumers who perceive a great deal of risk. In other words, high-risk perception limits innovativeness.

Venturesomeness is a broad-based measure of a consumer's willingness to accept the risk of purchasing new products. Measures of venturesomeness have been used to evaluate a person's general values or attitudes toward trying new products. A typical measurement scale might include such items as:

- *I prefer to (try a toothpaste when it first comes out) (wait and learn how good it is before trying it).*
- *When I am shopping and see a brand of paper towels I know about but have never used, I am (very anxious or willing to try it), (hesitant about trying it), (very unwilling to try it).*
- *I like to be among the first people to buy and use new products that are on the market (measured on a five-point "agreement" scale).*

Research that has examined venturesomeness has generally found that consumers who indicate a willingness to try new products tend to be consumer innovators (as measured by their actual purchase of new products). On the other hand, consumers who express a reluctance to try new products are, in fact, less likely to purchase new products. Therefore, venturesomeness seems to be an effective barometer of actual innovative behavior.

Purchase and Consumption Characteristics

Consumer innovators possess purchase and usage traits that set them apart from noninnovators. For example, consumer innovators are *less* brand loyal; that is, they are more apt to switch brands. This is not surprising, for brand loyalty would seriously impede a consumer's willingness to try new products.

Consumer innovators are more likely to be *deal prone* (to take advantage of special promotional offers such as free samples and cents-off coupons). They are also likely to be *heavy users* of the product category in which they innovate. Specifically, they purchase larger quantities and consume more of the product than noninnovators. Finally, for products like VCRs, PCs, microwave ovens, 35-mm cameras, and food processors, usage variety is likely to be a relevant dimension of new-product diffusion. An understanding of how consumers might be "usage innovators"—that is, finding or "inventing" new uses for an innovation—might create entirely new market opportunities for marketers' products.

To sum up, a positive relationship exists between innovative behavior and heavy usage. Consumer innovators are not only an important market segment from the standpoint of being the first to use a new product, but they also represent a substantial market in terms of product volume. However, their propensity to switch brands or to use products in different or unique ways and their positive response to promotional deals also suggest that innovators will continue to use a specific brand only as long as they do not perceive that a new and potentially better alternative is available.

MEDIA HABITS

Comparisons of the media habits of innovators and noninnovators across such widely diverse areas of consumption as fashion clothing and new automotive services suggest that innovators have somewhat greater total exposure to magazines than noninnovators, particularly to special-interest magazines devoted to the product category in which they innovate. For example, fashion innovators are more likely to read magazines such as *Gentlemen's Quarterly* and *Vogue* than noninnovators; financial services innovators have greater exposure to such special-interest magazines as *Money* and *Financial World*.

FIGURE 15-13

Adidas Ad Calls Out to
Those Who Would Be
Fashion Innovators
Reprinted by permission of
Adidas America, Inc.

Consumer innovators are also less likely to watch television than noninnovators. This view is consistently supported by research that over the past decade or so has compared the magazine and TV exposure levels of consumer innovators. The evidence indicates that consumer innovators have higher-than-average magazine exposure (see Figure 15-13) and lower-than-average TV exposure. It will be interesting, though, to observe over the next few years what the impact of the convergence of computers and television will be. Studies concerning the relationship between innovative behavior and exposure to other mass media, such as radio and newspapers, have been too few, and the results have been too varied to draw any useful conclusions.

SOCIAL CHARACTERISTICS

Consumer innovators are more socially accepted and socially involved than noninnovators. For example, innovators are more socially integrated into the community, better accepted by others, and more socially involved; that is, they belong to more social groups and organizations than noninnovators. This greater social acceptance and involvement of consumer innovators may help explain why they function as effective opinion leaders.

DEMOGRAPHIC CHARACTERISTICS

It is reasonable to assume that the age of the consumer innovator is related to the specific product category in which he or she innovates; however, research suggests that consumer innovators tend to be younger than either late adopters or noninnovators. This is no doubt because many of the products selected for research attention (such as fashion, convenience grocery products, or new automobiles) are particularly attractive to younger consumers.

Consumer innovators have more formal education, have higher personal or family incomes, and are more likely to have higher occupational status (to be professionals or hold managerial positions) than late adopters or noninnovators. In other words, innovators tend to be more upscale than other consumer segments and can, therefore, better afford to make a mistake should the innovative new product or service being purchased prove to be unacceptable.

Table 15-12 summarizes the major differences between consumer innovators and late adopters or noninnovators. The table includes the major distinctions examined in our current presentation of the *consumer innovator profile*.

ARE THERE GENERALIZED CONSUMER INNOVATORS?

Do consumer innovators in one product category tend to be consumer innovators in other product categories? The answer to this strategically important question is a guarded "no." The overlap of innovativeness across product categories, like opinion leadership, seems to be limited to product categories that are closely related to the same basic interest area. Consumers who are innovators of one new food product or one new appliance are more likely to be innovators of other new products in the same general product category. In other words, although no single or generalized consumer-innovativeness trait seems to operate *across* broadly different product categories, evidence suggests that consumers who innovate *within* a specific product category will innovate again within the same product category. For example, up to the point of "innovator burnout" (i.e., "what I have is good enough"), a person who was an innovator in buying an original IBM PC for his or her home office in the early 1980s was most likely again an innovator in buying a PC with an Intel 80286 microprocessor, an Intel 80386 microprocessor, an Intel 80486 microprocessor, and an Intel Pentium microprocessor and is likely to again be an innovator when it comes to the next generation of microprocessors for personal computers. For the marketer, such a pattern suggests that it is generally a good marketing strategy to target a new product to consumers who were the first to try other products in the same basic product category.

In the realm of high-tech innovations, there is evidence suggesting that there is a generalized "high-tech" innovator—known as a "change leader."[62] Such individuals tend to embrace and popularize many of the innovations that are ultimately accepted by the mainstream population, such as computers, cellular telephones, and fax machines. They tend to have a wide range of personal and professional contacts

TABLE 15-12	Comparative Profiles of the Consumer Innovator and the Noninnovator or Late Adopter

CHARACTERISTIC	INNOVATOR	NONINNOVATOR (OR LATE ADOPTER)
PRODUCT INTEREST	More	Less
OPINION LEADERSHIP	More	Less
PERSONALITY		
Dogmatism	Open-minded	Closed-minded
Need for uniqueness	Higher	Lower
Social character	Inner-directed	Other-directed
Optimum stimulation level	Higher	Lower
Variety seeking	Higher	Lower
Perceived risk	Less	More
Venturesomeness	More	Less
PURCHASE AND CONSUMPTION TRAITS		
Brand loyalty	Less	More
Deal proneness	More	Less
Usage	More	Less
MEDIA HABITS		
Total magazine exposure	More	Less
Special-interest magazines	More	Less
Television	Less	More
SOCIAL CHARACTERISTICS		
Social integration	More	Less
Social striving (e.g., social, physical, and occupational mobility)	More	Less
Group memberships	More	Less
DEMOGRAPHIC CHARACTERISTICS		
Age	Younger	Older
Income	Higher	Lower
Education	More	Less
Occupational status	Higher	Lower

representing different occupational and social groups; most often these contacts tend to be "weak ties" or acquaintances. Change leaders also appear to fall into one of two distinct groups: a *younger group* that can be characterized as being stimulation seeking, sociable, and having high levels of fashion awareness or a *middle-aged group* that is highly self-confident and has very high information-seeking needs.

Similar to change leaders, "technophiles" are individuals who purchase technologically advanced products soon after their market debut. Such individuals tend to be technically curious people. Also, another group responding to technology are adults who are categorized as "techthusiasts"—people who are most likely to purchase or subscribe to emerging products and services that are technologically oriented. These consumers are typically younger, better educated, and more affluent.[63]

Summary

Opinion leadership is the process by which one person (the opinion leader) informally influences the actions or attitudes of others, who may be opinion seekers or merely opinion recipients. Opinion receivers perceive the opinion leader as a highly credible, objective source of product information who can help reduce their search time and perceived risk. Opinion leaders, in turn, are motivated to give information or advice to others, in part because doing so enhances their own status and self-image and because such advice tends to reduce any postpurchase dissonance that they may have. Other motives include product involvement, "other" involvement, and message involvement.

Market researchers identify opinion leaders by such methods as self-designation, key informants, the sociometric method, and the objective method. Studies of opinion leadership indicate that this phenomenon tends to be product specific; that is, individuals "specialize" in a product or product category in which they are highly interested. An opinion leader for one product category may be an opinion receiver for another.

Generally, opinion leaders are gregarious, self-confident, innovative people who like to talk. Additionally, they may feel differentiated from others and choose to act differently (or public individuation). They acquire information about their areas of interest through avid readership of special-interest magazines and by means of new-product trials. Their interests often overlap adjacent product areas; thus, their opinion leadership may extend into related areas. The market maven is an intense case of such a person. These consumers possess a wide range of information about many different types of products, retail outlets, and other dimensions of markets. They both initiate discussions with other consumers and respond to requests for market information over a wide range of products and services. Market mavens are also distinguishable from other opinion leaders, because their influence stems not so much from product experience but from a more general knowledge or market expertise that leads them to an early

awareness of a wide array of new products and services.

The opinion leadership process usually takes place among friends, neighbors, and work associates who have frequent physical proximity and, thus, have ample opportunity to hold informal product-related conversations. These conversations usually occur naturally in the context of the product-category usage.

The two-step flow of communication theory highlights the role of interpersonal influence in the transmission of information from the mass media to the population at large. This theory provides the foundation for a revised multistep flow of communication model, which takes into account the fact that information and influence often are two-way processes and that opinion leaders both influence and are influenced by opinion receivers.

Marketers recognize the strategic value of segmenting their audiences into opinion leaders and opinion receivers for their product categories. When marketers can direct their promotional efforts to the more influential segments of their markets, these individuals will transmit this information to those who seek product advice. Marketers try to both simulate and stimulate opinion leadership. They have also found that they can create opinion leaders for their products by taking socially involved or influential people and deliberately increasing their enthusiasm for a product category.

The diffusion process and the adoption process are two closely related concepts concerned with the acceptance of new products by consumers. The diffusion process is a macro process that focuses on the spread of an innovation (a new product, service, or idea) from its source to the consuming public. The adoption process is a micro process that examines the stages through which an individual consumer passes when making a decision to accept or reject a new product.

The definition of the term *innovation* can be firm oriented (new to the firm), product oriented (a continuous innovation, a dynamically continuous innovation, or a discontinuous innovation), market oriented (how long the product has been on the market or an arbitrary percentage of the potential target market that has purchased it), or consumer oriented (new to the consumer). Market-oriented definitions of innovation are most useful to consumer researchers in the study of the diffusion and adoption of new products.

Five product characteristics influence the consumer's acceptance of a new product: relative advantage, compatibility, complexity, trialability, and observability (or communicability).

Diffusion researchers are concerned with two aspects of communication—the channels through which word of a new product is spread to the consuming public and the types of messages that influence the adoption or rejection of new products. Diffusion is always examined in the context of a specific social system, such as a target market, a community, a region, or even a nation.

Time is an integral consideration in the diffusion process. Researchers are concerned with the amount of purchase time required for an individual consumer to adopt or reject a new product, with the rate of adoption, and with the identification of sequential adopters. The five adopter categories are innovators, early adopters, early majority, late majority, and laggards.

Marketing strategists try to control the rate of adoption through their new-product pricing policies. Marketers who wish to penetrate the market to achieve market leadership try to acquire wide adoption as quickly as possible by using low prices. Those who wish to recoup their developmental costs quickly use a skimming pricing policy but lengthen the adoption process.

The traditional adoption process model describes five stages through which an individual consumer passes to arrive at the decision to adopt or reject a new product: awareness, interest, evaluation, trial, and adoption. To make it more realistic, an enhanced model is suggested as one that considers the possibility of a preexisting need or problem, the likelihood that some form of evaluation might occur through the entire process, and that even after adoption there will be postadoption or purchase evaluation that might either strengthen the commitment or alternatively lead to discontinuation.

New-product marketers are vitally concerned with identifying the consumer innovator so that they may direct their promotional campaigns to the people who are most likely to try new products, adopt them, and influence others. Consumer research has identified a number of consumer-related characteristics, including product interest, opinion leadership, personality factors, purchase and consumption traits, media habits, social characteristics, and demographic variables that distinguish consumer innovators from later adopters. These serve as useful variables in the segmentation of markets for new-product introductions.

Discussion Questions

1. a. Why is an opinion leader a more credible source of product information than an advertisement for the same product?
   b. Are there any circumstances in which information from advertisements is likely to be more influential than word of mouth?

2. Why would a consumer who has just purchased an expensive fax machine for home use attempt to influence the purchase behavior of others?

3. A company that owns and operates health clubs across the country is opening a health club in your town. The company has retained you as its marketing research consultant and has asked you to identify opinion leaders for its service. Which of the following identification methods would you recommend: the self-designating method, the sociometric method, the key informant method, or the objective method? Explain your selection. In your answer, be sure to discuss the advantages and disadvantages of the four techniques as they relate to the marketing situation just described.

4. Do you have any "market mavens" among your friends? Describe their personality traits and behaviors. Describe a situation in which a market maven has given you advice regarding a

product or service and discuss what you believe was his or her motivation for doing so.

5. Describe how a manufacturer might use knowledge of the following product characteristics to speed up the acceptance of pocket-sized cellular telephones:
   a. Relative advantage
   b. Compatibility
   c. Complexity
   d. Trialability
   e. Observability

6. Toshiba has introduced an ultraslim laptop computer that weighs about two pounds, has a color screen, and has a powerful processor into which a full-size desktop screen and keyboard can be easily plugged. How can the company use the diffusion-of-innovations framework to develop promotional, pricing, and distribution strategies targeted to the following adopter categories?
   a. Innovators
   b. Early adopters
   c. Early majority
   d. Late majority
   e. Laggards

7. Is the curve that describes the sequence and proportion of adopter categories among the population (Figure 15-9) similar in shape to the product life cycle curve? Explain your answer. How would you use both curves to develop a marketing strategy?

8. Sony is introducing a 27-inch TV with a built-in VCR, a picture-in-picture feature, and a feature that allows the viewer to simultaneously view frozen frames of the last signals received from 12 channels.
   a. What recommendations would you make to Sony regarding the initial target market for the new TV model?
   b. How would you identify the innovators for this product?
   c. Select three characteristics of consumer innovators (as summarized in Table 15-12). Explain how Sony might use each of these characteristics to influence the adoption process and speed up the diffusion of the new product.
   d. Should Sony follow a penetration or a skimming policy in introducing the product? Why?

Exercises

1. Describe two situations in which you served as an opinion leader and two situations in which you sought consumption-related advice or information from an opinion leader. Indicate your relationship to the persons with whom you interacted. Are the circumstances during which you engaged in word-of-mouth communications consistent with those in the text's material? Explain.

2. a. Find ads that simulate and ads that stimulate opinion leadership and present them in class.
   b. Can you think of negative rumors that you have heard recently about a company or a product? If so, present them in class.

3. Identify a product, service, or style that recently was adopted by you or some of your friends.

Identify what type of innovation it is and describe its diffusion process up to this point in time. What are the characteristics of people who adopted it first? What types of people did not adopt it? What features of the product, service, or style are likely to determine its eventual success or failure?

4. With the advancement of digital technology, some companies plan to introduce interactive TV systems that will allow viewers to select films from video libraries and view them on demand. Among people you know, identify two who are likely to be the innovators for such a new service and construct consumer profiles using the characteristics of consumer innovators discussed in the text.

Key Terms

- Adopter categories
- Adoption process
- Consumer innovators
- Continuous innovation
- Diffusion of innovations
- Diffusion process
- Discontinuous innovation

- Dynamically continuous innovation
- Innovation
- Market maven
- Multistep flow of communication theory
- Opinion leader

- Opinion leadership
- Opinion receiver
- Opinion seekers
- Stages in the adoption process
- Two-step flow of communication theory

Notes

1. Chip Walker, "Word of Mouth," *American Demographics,* July 1995, 40.
2. Ibid., 42.
3. Dale F. Duhan, Scott D. Johnson, James B. Wilcox, and Gilbert D. Harrell, "Influences on Consumer Use of Word-of-Mouth Recommendation Sources," *Journal of the Academy of Marketing Science,* 25, 4, 1997, 283–295.
4. Eric Chi-Chung Shiu and John A. Dawson, "Cross-National Consumer Segmentation of Internet Shopping for Britain and Taiwan," *The Service Industries Journal (London),* 22, 1, January 2002, 147–166.
5. James Brooke, "Youth Let Their Thumbs Do the Talking in Japan," *New York Times,* April 30, 2002, A14.
6. Ibid.
7. Ralph F. Wilson, "The Six Simple Principles of Viral Marketing," *Web Marketing Today,* 70, February 1, 2000, accessed at www.wilsonweb.com/wmt5/viral-principles.htm; and searchcrm.techtarget.com/sDefinition/0,sid11_gci213514,00.html.
8. Marc Weingarten, "The Medium Is the Instant Message," *Business 2.0,* February 2002, 98–99.
9. "Virtual Viral Marketing Virus," *Wired,* November 2000, 116; Renée Dye, "How to Create Explosive Self-Generating Demand," *Advertising Age,* November 8, 1999, S20; Thomas E. Weber, "The Web's Newest Ploy May Not Make You a Very Popular Friend," *Wall Street Journal,* September 13, 1999, B1; Beth Snyder Bulik, "Upping the Cool Quotient," *Business 2.0,* August 22, 2000, 94–96; and John Gaffney, "The Cool Kids Are Doing It. Should You?" *Business 2.0,* November 2001, 140–141.
10. Jack Neff, "P&G Goes Viral with Test of Innovation Locations," *Advertising Age,* September 4, 2000, 4.
11. George Silverman, "The Power of Word of Mouth," *Direct Marketing,* 64, 5, September 2001, 47–52.

12. Geok Theng Lau and Sophia Ng, "Individual and Situational Factors Influencing Negative Word-of-Mouth Behaviour," *Revue Canadienne des Sciences de l'Administration (Montreal),* 18, 3, September 2001, 163–178.
13. Silverman, "The Power of Word of Mouth."
14. S. Ramesh Kumar, "The Might of the Word," *Businessline,* September 2, 1999, 1–2.
15. Pamala L. Alreck and Robert B. Settle, "The Importance of Word-of-Mouth Communications to Service Buyers," in *1995 AMA Winter Educators' Proceedings,* eds. David W. Stewart and Naufel J. Vilcassim (Chicago: American Marketing Association, 1995), 188–193.
16. Cathy L. Hartman and Pamela L. Kiecker, "Marketplace Influencers at the Point of Purchase: The Role of Purchase Pals in Consumer Decision Making," in *1991 AMA Educators' Proceedings,* eds. Mary C. Gilly and F. Robert Dwyer, et al. (Chicago: American Marketing Association, 1991), 461–467.
17. Pamela Kiecker and Cathy L. Hartman, "Predicting Buyers' Selection of Interpersonal Sources: The Role of Strong Ties and Weak Ties," in *Advances in Consumer Research,* 21, eds. Chris T. Allen and Deborah Roedder John (Provo, UT: Association for Consumer Research, 1994), 464–469.
18. Praveen Aggarwal and Taihoon Cha, "Surrogate Buyers and the New Product Adoption Process: A Conceptualization and Managerial Framework," *Journal of Consumer Marketing,* 14, 5, 1997, 391–400; and Stanley C. Hollander and Kathleen M. Rassuli, "Shopping with Other People's Money: The Marketing Management Implications of Surrogate-Mediated Consumer Decision Making," *Journal of Marketing,* 63, 2, April 1999, 102–118.
19. Leisa Reinecke Flynn, Ronald E. Goldsmith, and Jacqueline K. Eastman, "The King and Summers

Opinion Leadership Scale: Revision and Refinement," *Journal of Business Research,* 31, 1994, 55–64.

20. Mary C. Gilly, John L. Graham, Mary Finley Wolfinbarger, and Laura J. Yale, "A Dyadic Study of Interpersonal Information Search," *Journal of the Academy of Marketing Science,* 26, 2, 1998, 83–100.

21. Lawrence F. Feick and Linda L. Price, "The Market Maven: A Diffuser of Marketplace Information," *Journal of Marketing,* 51, January 1987, 85.

22. Michael T. Elliott and Anne E. Warfield, "Do Market Mavens Categorize Brands Differently?" in *Advances in Consumer Research,* 20, eds. Leigh McAlister and Michael L. Rothschild (Provo, UT: Association for Consumer Research 1993), 202–208; and Frank Alpert, "Consumer Market Beliefs and Their Managerial Implications: An Empirical Examination," *Journal of Consumer Marketing,* 10, 2, (1993), 56–70.

23. Brian T. Engelland, Christopher D. Hopkins, and Dee Anne Larson, "Market Mavenship as an Influencer of Service Quality Evaluation," *Journal of Marketing Theory and Practice,* 9, 4, Fall 2001, 15–26.

24. John Eighmey and Lola McCord, "Adding Value in the Information Age: Uses and Gratifications of Sites on the World Wide Web," *Journal of Business Research,* 41, 1998, 187–194.

25. Patricia Riedman, "Marketers Harvest Web Communities' Concealed Treasure," *Advertising Age,* February 14, 2000, 58.

26. Paul F. Lazarsfeld, Bernard Berelson, and Hazel Gaudet, *The People's Choice,* 2d ed. (New York: Columbia University Press, 1948), 151.

27. Thomas Petzinger, Jr. , "The Front Lines," *Wall Street Journal,* November 11, 1997, B9.

28. Joseph Pereira, "Toy Story: How Shrewd Marketing Made Elmo a Hit," *Wall Street Journal,* December 16, 1997, B1, B7.

29. Kate MacArthur, "Iced Coffee Market Gains Grounds," *Advertising Age,* September 4, 2000, 22; and David Goetzl, "Starwood's W Hotels Ads Display Interior Motives," *Advertising Age,* September 18, 2000, 13.

30. "In the News: Ploys," *New York Times Magazine,* February 13, 1994, 19.

31. Gaffney, "The Coil Kids are Doing It," 141.

32. Walker, "Starbucks' Word-of-Mouth Wonder," 40.

33. Roy Furchgott, "Surfing for Satisfaction: Consumer Complaints Go On-Line," *New York Times,* June 8, 1997, 8.

34. Ibid.

35. See, for example, Thomas W. Valente and Rebecca L. Davis, "Accelerating the Diffusion of Innovations Using Opinion Leaders," *Annals of the American Academy of Political and Social Science,* 566, November 1999, 55–67.

36. Joseph R. Mancuso, "Why Not Create Opinion Leaders for New Product Introduction?" *Journal of Marketing,* 33, July 1969, 20–25.

37. Barbara Bickart and Robert M. Schindler, "Internet Forums as Influential Sources of Consumer Information," *Journal of Interactive Marketing,* 15, 3, Summer 2001, 31–39.

38. Jan-Benedict E.M. Steenkamp, Frankel ter Hofstede, and Michael Wedel, "A Cross-National Investigation into the Individual and National Cultural Antecedents of Consumer Innovativeness," *Journal of Marketing,* 63, 2, April 1999, 55–69.

39. Diane Crane, "Diffusion Models and Fashion: A Reassessment," *Annals of the American Academy of Political and Social Sciences,* 566, November 1999, 13–24.

40. Thomas S. Robertson, "The Process of Innovation and the Diffusion of Innovation," *Journal of Marketing,* 31, January 1967, 14–19.

41. Everett M. Rogers, *Diffusion of Innovations,* 4th ed. (New York: Free Press, 1995); and Hubert Gatignon and Thomas S. Robertson, "Innovative Decision Processes," in *Handbook of Consumer Behavior,* eds. Thomas S. Robertson and Harold H. Kassarjian (Upper Saddle River, NJ: Prentice Hall, 1991), 316–348.

42. S. Ram and Hyung-Shik Jung, "Innovativeness in Product Usage: A Comparison of Early Adopters and Early Majority," *Psychology and Marketing,* 11, January–February 1994, 57–67; A. R. Petrosky, "Gender and Use Innovation: An Inquiry into the Socialization of Innovative Behavior," in *1995 AMA Educators' Proceedings,* eds. Barbara B. Stern and George M. Zinkan (Chicago: American Marketing Association, 1995), 299–307; Kyungae Park and Carl L. Dyer, "Consumer Use Innovative Behavior: An Approach Toward Its Causes," in *Advances in Consumer Research,* 22, eds. Frank R. Kardes and Mita Sujan (Provo, UT: Association for Consumer Research 1995), 566–572.

43. Earle Eldridge, "Pickups Get Women's Touch," *USA Today,* June 13, 2001, 1B, 2B.

44. Rogers, *Diffusion of Innovations,* 15–16.

45. Hsiang Chen and Kevin Crowston, "Comparative Diffusion of the Telephone and the World Wide Web: An Analysis of Rates of Adoption," in Suave Lobodzinski and Ivan Tomek (eds.), *Proceedings of WebNet '97—World Conference of the WWW, Internet and Intranet,* Toronto, Canada, 110–115.

46. Tina M. Lowrey, "The Use of Diffusion Theory in Marketing: A Qualitative Approach to Innovative Consumer Behavior," in *Advances in Consumer Research,* 18, eds. Rebecca H. Holman and Michael R. Solomon (Provo, UT: Association for Consumer Research, 1991), 644–650.

47. Quentin Hardy, "Will Miniature Phones Ring Up Bigger Sales?" *Wall Street Journal,* December 4, 1996, B1, B4.

48. Susan H. Higgins and William L. Shanklin, "Seeding Mass Market Acceptance for High Technology Consumer Products," *Journal of Consumer Marketing,* 9, Winter 1992, 5–14.

49. Richard Gibson, "Shelf Stable Foods Seek to Freshen Sales," *Wall Street Journal,* November 2, 1990, B1.

50. Paul A. Herbig and Hugh Kramer, "The Effect of Information Overload on the Innovation Choice Process," *Journal of Consumer Marketing,* 11, 2, 1994, 45–54.

51. Walter S. Mossberg, "Sony Again Attempts to Sell Its Mini-CD, Focusing on Recording," *Wall Street Journal,* May 28, 1998, B1.

52. Erin White, "Word of Mouth Makes Nike Slip-On Sneakers Take Off," *Wall Street Journal,* June 7, 2001, B1.

53. Everett M. Rogers and F. Floyd Shoemaker, *Communication of Innovations,* 2nd ed. (New York: Free Press, 1971), 32–33; see also Elizabeth C. Hirschman, "Consumer Modernity, Cognitive Complexity, Creativity and Innovativeness," in *Marketing in the 80's: Changes and Challenges,* ed. Richard P. Bagozzi et al. (Chicago: American Marketing Association, 1980), 135–139.

54. Hilary Chura, "Miller Breaks Ad Effort for Unbreakable Bottles," *Advertising Age,* September 4, 2000, 8; and Micheline Maynard, "When Hot Cars Go Cold," *New York Times,* August 31, 2001, F1.

55. Thomas W. Valente and Rebecca L. Davis, "Accelerating the Diffusion of Innovations Using Opinion Leaders," *Annals of the American Academy of Political and Social Sciences,* 566, November 1999, 55–67; and Ronald S. Burt, "The Social Capital of Opinion Leaders," *Annals of the American Academy of Political and Social Sciences,* 566, November 1999, 37–54.

56. Kenichi Ohmae, "Managing in a Borderless World," *Harvard Business Review,* May–June 1989, 152–161.

57. Jacob Goldenberg, Barak Libai, and Eitan Muller, "Riding the Saddle: How Cross-Market Communications Can Create a Major Slump in Sales," *Journal of Marketing,* 66, 2, April 2002, 1–16.

58. Dianne Neumark-Sztainer, et al., "Early Adopters of Olestra-Containing Foods: Who Are They?" *Journal of the American Dietetic Association,* 100, 2, February 2000, 198–204.

59. C. Page Moreau, Donald R. Lehmann, and Arthur B. Markman, "Entrenched Knowledge Structures and Consumer Response to New Products," *Journal of Marketing Research,* 38, 1, February 2001, 14–29.

60. David J. Burns and Robert F. Krampf, "A Semiotic Perspective on Innovative Behavior," in *Developments in Marketing Science,* ed. Robert L. King (Richmond, VA: Academy of Marketing Science, 1991), 32–35.

61. Wayne D. Hoyer and Nancy M. Ridgway, "Variety Seeking as an Explanation for Exploratory Purchase Behavior: A Theoretical Model," in *Advances in Consumer Research,* 11, ed. Thomas C. Kinnear (Provo, UT: Association for Consumer Research, 1984), 114–119.

62. Bruce MacEvoy, "Change Leaders and the New Media," *American Demographics,* January 1994, 42–48.

63. Susan Mitchell, "Technophiles and Technophobes," *American Demographics,* February 1994, 36–42.

REAL LOVE.

REAL SCIENCE.™

Hartz® Advanced Care™ Brand Plus kills fleas and ticks fast.

When compared with other leading brands, Hartz® Advanced Care™ Brand Plus couldn't be beat!

Real Love. Real Science.™ From Hartz.® And don't forget regular visits to your veterinarian to keep your pet healthy.

Zack was an only child... until Buster came along.

Here's the real story. Hartz® Advanced Care™ Brand Flea & Tick Drops Plus work fast to protect your pet against fleas and ticks. Nothing means more to us than helping you care for your pet.

HARTZ®
Every Pet's Best Friend®
www.hartz.com

HARTZ®
Every Pet's Best Friend®
www.hartz.com

Consumer Decision Making and Beyond

This chapter draws together many of the psychological, social, and cultural concepts developed throughout the book into an overview framework for understanding how consumers make decisions. Unlike the second part of Chapter 15, which examined the dynamics of *new*-product adoption, this chapter takes a broader perspective and examines **consumer decision making** in the context of all types of *consumption choices,* ranging from the consumption of new products to the use of old and established products. It also considers consumers' decisions not as the end point but rather as the beginning point of a **consumption process.**

What Is a Decision?

Every day, each of us makes numerous decisions concerning every aspect of our daily lives. However, we generally make these decisions without stopping to think about how we make them and what is involved in the particular decision-making process itself. In the most general terms, a decision is the selection of an option from two or more alternative choices. In other words, for a person to make a decision, a choice of alternatives must be available. When a person has a choice between making a purchase and not making a purchase, a choice between brand X and brand Y, or a choice of spending time doing A or B, that person is in a position to make a decision. On the other hand, if the consumer has no alternatives from which to choose and is literally *forced* to make a particular purchase or take a particular action (e.g., use a prescribed medication), then this single "no-choice" instance does not constitute a decision; such a no-choice decision is commonly referred to as a "Hobson's choice."

In actuality, no-choice purchase or consumption situations are fairly rare. You may recall from our discussion of core American cultural values (Chapter 12) that for consumers, *freedom* often is expressed in terms of a wide range of product choices. Thus, if there is almost always a choice, then there is almost always an opportunity for consumers to make decisions. Moreover, experimental research reveals that providing consumers with a choice when there was originally none can be a very good business strategy, one that can substantially increase sales.[1] For instance, when a direct-mail electrical appliance catalog displayed two coffeemakers instead of just one (the original coffeemaker at $149 and a "new" only slightly larger one at $229), the addition of the second *comparison* coffeemaker seemed to stimulate consumer evaluation that significantly increased the sales of the original coffeemaker.

Table 16-1 summarizes various types of consumption and purchase-related decisions. Although not exhaustive, this list does serve to demonstrate that the scope

TABLE 16-1 Types of Purchase or Consumption Decisions

DECISION CATEGORY	ALTERNATIVE A	ALTERNATIVE B
Basic Purchase or Consumption Decision	To purchase or consume a product (or service)	Not to purchase or consume a product (or service)
Brand Purchase or Consumption Decision	To purchase or consume a specific brand	To purchase or consume another brand
	To purchase or consume one's usual brand	To purchase or consume another established brand (possibly with special features)
	To purchase or consume a basic model	To purchase or consume a luxury or status model
	To purchase or consume a new brand	To purchase or consume one's usual brand or some other established brand
	To purchase or consume a standard quantity	To purchase or consume more or less than a standard quantity
	To purchase or consume an on-sale brand	To purchase or consume a nonsale brand
	To purchase or consume a national brand	To purchase or consume a store brand
Channel Purchase Decisions	To purchase from a specific type of store (e.g., a department store)	To purchase from some other type of store (e.g., a discount store)
	To purchase from one's usual store	To purchase from some other store
	To purchase in-home (by phone or catalog or Internet)	To purchase in-store merchandise
	To purchase from a local store	To purchase from a store requiring some travel (outshopping)
Payment Purchase Decisions	To pay for the purchase with cash	To pay for the purchase with a credit card
	To pay the bill in full when it arrives	To pay for the purchase in installments

of consumer decision making is far broader than the mere selection of one brand from a number of brands.

Levels of Consumer Decision Making

Not all consumer decision-making situations receive (or require) the same degree of information search. If all purchase decisions required extensive effort, then consumer decision making would be an exhausting process that left little time for anything else. On the other hand, if all purchases were routine, then they would tend to be monotonous and would provide little pleasure or novelty. On a continuum of effort ranging from very high to very low, we can distinguish three specific levels of consumer decision making: **extensive problem solving, limited problem solving,** and **routinized response behavior.**[2]

EXTENSIVE PROBLEM SOLVING

When consumers have no established criteria for evaluating a product category or specific brands in that category or have not narrowed the number of brands they will consider to a small, manageable subset, their decision-making efforts can be classified as *extensive problem solving.* At this level, the consumer needs a great deal of information to establish a set of criteria on which to judge specific brands and a correspondingly large amount of information concerning each of the brands to be considered.

LIMITED PROBLEM SOLVING

At this level of problem solving, consumers already have established the basic criteria for evaluating the product category and the various brands in the category. However, they have not fully established preferences concerning a select group of brands. Their search for additional information is more like "fine-tuning"; they must gather additional brand information to discriminate among the various brands.

ROUTINIZED RESPONSE BEHAVIOR

At this level, consumers have experience with the product category and a well-established set of criteria with which to evaluate the brands they are considering. In some situations, they may search for a small amount of additional information; in others, they simply review what they already know.

Just how extensive a consumer's problem-solving task is depends on how well established his or her criteria for selection are, how much information he or she has about each brand being considered, and how narrow the set of brands is from which the choice will be made. Clearly, extensive problem solving implies that the consumer must seek more information to make a choice, whereas routinized response behavior implies little need for additional information.

All decisions in our lives cannot be complex and require extensive search and consideration—we just cannot exert the level of effort required. Some decisions have to be "easy ones."

Models of Consumers: Four Views of Consumer Decision Making

Before presenting an overview model of how consumers make decisions, we will consider several schools of thought that depict consumer decision making in distinctly different ways. The term *models of consumers* refers to a general view or perspective as to how (and why) individuals behave as they do. Specifically, we will examine models of consumers in terms of the following four views: (1) an *economic view*, (2) a *passive view*, (3) a *cognitive view*, and (4) an *emotional view*.

AN ECONOMIC VIEW

In the field of theoretical economics, which portrays a world of perfect competition, the consumer has often been characterized as making rational decisions. This model, called the *economic man* theory, has been criticized by consumer researchers for a number of reasons. To behave rationally in the economic sense, a consumer would have to (1) be aware of all available product alternatives, (2) be capable of correctly ranking each alternative in terms of its benefits and disadvantages, and (3) be able to identify the one best alternative. Realistically, however, consumers rarely have all of the information or sufficiently accurate information or even an adequate degree of involvement or motivation to make the so-called "perfect" decision.

It has been argued that the classical economic model of an all-rational consumer is unrealistic for the following reasons: (a) People are limited by their existing skills, habits, and reflexes; (b) people are limited by their existing values and goals; and (c) people are limited by the extent of their knowledge.[3] Consumers operate in an imperfect world in which they do not maximize their decisions in terms of economic considerations, such as price–quantity relationships, marginal utility, or indifference curves. Indeed, the consumer generally is unwilling to engage in extensive decision-making activities and will settle, instead, for a "satisfactory" decision, one that is "good enough."[4] For this reason, the economic model is often rejected as too idealistic and simplistic. As an example, recent research has found that consumers' primary motivation for price haggling, which was long thought to be the desire to obtain a better price (i.e., better dollar value for the purchase), may instead be related to the need for achievement, affiliation, and dominance.[5]

A PASSIVE VIEW

Quite opposite to the rational economic view of consumers is the *passive* view that depicts the consumer as basically submissive to the self-serving interests and promotional efforts of marketers. In the passive view, consumers are perceived as impulsive and irrational purchasers, ready to yield to the aims and into the arms of marketers. At least to some degree, the passive model of the consumer was subscribed to by the hard-driving supersalespeople of old, who were trained to regard the consumer as an object to be manipulated.

The principal limitation of the passive model is that it fails to recognize that the consumer plays an equal, if not dominant, role in many buying situations—sometimes by seeking information about product alternatives and selecting the product that appears to offer the greatest satisfaction and at other times by impulsively selecting a product that satisfies the mood or emotion of the moment. All that we have studied about motivation (see Chapter 4), selective perception (Chapter 6), learning (Chapter 7), attitudes (Chapter 8), communication (Chapter 9), and opinion leadership (Chapter 15) serves to support the proposition that consumers are rarely objects of manipulation. Therefore, this simple and single-minded view should also be rejected as unrealistic.

A COGNITIVE VIEW

The third model portrays the consumer as a *thinking problem solver*. Within this framework, consumers frequently are pictured as either receptive to or actively searching for products and services that fulfill their needs and enrich their lives. The cognitive model focuses on the processes by which consumers seek and evaluate information about selected brands and retail outlets.

Within the context of the cognitive model, consumers are viewed as information processors. Information processing leads to the formation of preferences and, ultimately, to purchase intentions. The cognitive view also recognizes that the consumer is unlikely to even attempt to obtain all available information about every choice. Instead, consumers are likely to cease their information-seeking efforts when they perceive that they have sufficient information about some of the alternatives to make a "satisfactory" decision. As this information-processing viewpoint suggests, consumers often develop shortcut decision rules (called **heuristics**) to facilitate the decision-making process. They also use decision rules to cope with exposure to too much information (i.e., **information overload**).

The cognitive, or problem-solving, view describes a consumer who falls somewhere between the extremes of the economic and passive views, who does not (or cannot) have total knowledge about available product alternatives and, therefore, cannot make *perfect* decisions, but who nonetheless actively seeks information and attempts to make *satisfactory* decisions.

Consistent with the problem-solving view is the notion that a great deal of consumer behavior is goal directed. For example, a consumer might purchase a computer in order to manage finances or look for a laundry detergent that will be gentle on fabrics. Goal setting is especially important when it comes to the adoption of new products because the greater the degree of "newness," the more difficult it would be for the consumer to evaluate the product and relate it to his or her need (because of a lack of experience with the product).[6] Figure 16-1 diagrams goal setting and goal pursuit in consumer behavior.

AN EMOTIONAL VIEW

Although long aware of the *emotional* or *impulsive* model of consumer decision making, marketers frequently prefer to think of consumers in terms of either economic or passive models. In reality, however, each of us is likely to associate deep feelings or emotions, such as joy, fear, love, hope, sexuality, fantasy, and even a little "magic," with certain purchases or possessions. These feelings or emotions are likely to be highly involving. For instance, a person who misplaces a favorite fountain pen might go to great lengths to look for it, despite the fact that he or she has six others at hand.

Possessions also may serve to preserve a sense of the past and act as familiar transitional objects when one is confronted with an uncertain future. For example, members of the armed forces invariably carry photographs of "the girl (or guy) back home," their families, and their lives in earlier times. These memorabilia frequently serve as hopeful reminders that normal activities will someday resume.

If we were to reflect on the nature of our recent purchases, we might be surprised to realize just how impulsive some of them were. Rather than carefully searching, deliberating, and evaluating alternatives before buying, we are just as

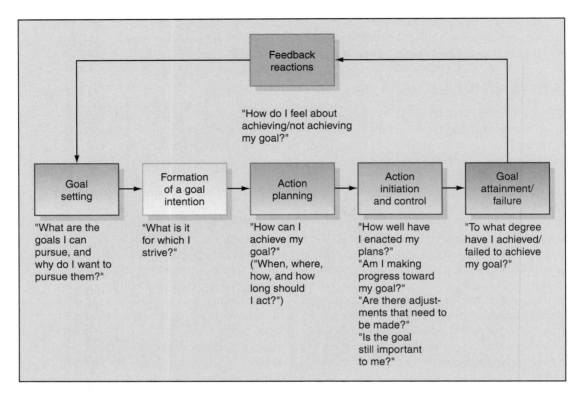

FIGURE 16-1

Goal Setting and Goal Pursuit in Consumer Behavior
Source: Richard P. Bagozzi and Utpal Dholakia, "Goal Setting and Goal Striving in Consumer Behavior," *Journal of Marketing*, 63, 1999, 21.

likely to have made many of these purchases on impulse, on a whim, or because we were emotionally driven.

When a consumer makes what is basically an emotional purchase decision, less emphasis is placed on the search for prepurchase information. Instead, more emphasis is placed on current mood and feelings ("Go for it!"). This is not to say that emotional decisions are not rational. As Chapter 4 pointed out, buying products that afford emotional satisfaction is a perfectly rational consumer decision. Some emotional decisions are expressions that "you deserve it" or "treat yourself." For instance, many consumers buy designer-label clothing, not because they look any better in it, but because status labels make them feel better. This is a rational decision. Of course, if a man with a wife and three children purchases a two-seater BMW Z3 (www.bmw.com) for himself, the neighbors might wonder about his level of rationality (although some might think it was deviously high). No such question would arise if the same man selected a box of Godiva chocolate (www.godiva.com), instead of a Whitman Sampler (www.whitmans.com), although in both instances, each might be an impulsive, emotional purchase decision.

Consumers' **moods** are also important to decision making. Mood can be defined as a "feeling state" or state of mind.[7] Unlike an emotion, which is a response to a particular environment, a mood is more typically an unfocused, preexisting state— already present at the time a consumer "experiences" an advertisement, a retail environment, a brand, or a product.[8] Compared to emotions, moods are generally lower in intensity and longer lasting and are not as directly coupled with action tendencies and explicit actions as emotions.[9]

Mood appears to be important to consumer decision making, because it impacts on *when* consumers shop, *where* they shop, and *whether* they shop alone or with others. It also is likely to influence *how* the consumer responds to actual shopping environments (i.e., at point of purchase). Some retailers attempt to create a mood for shoppers, even though shoppers enter the store with a preexisting mood. Research suggests that a store's image or atmosphere can affect shoppers' moods; in turn, shoppers' moods can influence how long they stay in the store, as well as other behavior that retailers wish to encourage.[10]

In general, individuals in a positive mood recall more information about a product than those in a negative mood. As the results of one study suggest, however, inducing a positive mood at the point-of-purchase decision (as through background music, point-of-purchase displays, etc.) is unlikely to have a meaningful impact on specific brand choice unless a previously stored brand evaluation already exists.[11] Additionally, consumers in a positive mood typically employ a mood maintenance strategy designed to avoid investing cognitive effort in any task unless it promises to maintain or enhance the positive mood.[12]

A Model of Consumer Decision Making

This section presents an overview model of consumer decision making (briefly introduced in Chapter 1) that reflects the *cognitive* (or *problem-solving*) consumer and, to some degree, the *emotional consumer*. The model is designed to tie together many of the ideas on consumer decision making and consumption behavior discussed throughout the book. It does not presume to provide an exhaustive picture of the complexities of consumer decision making. Rather, it is designed to synthesize and coordinate relevant concepts into a significant whole. The model, presented in Figure 16-2, has three major components: input, process, and output.

INPUT

The *input* component of our consumer decision-making model draws on external influences that serve as sources of information about a particular product and influence a consumer's product-related values, attitudes, and behavior. Chief among these input factors are the *marketing mix activities* of organizations that attempt to communicate the benefits of their products and services to potential consumers and the nonmarketing *sociocultural influences,* which, when internalized, affect the consumer's purchase decisions.

Marketing Inputs

The firm's marketing activities are a direct attempt to reach, inform, and persuade consumers to buy and use its products. These inputs to the consumer's decision-making process take the form of specific marketing mix strategies that consist of the product itself (including its package, size, and guarantees); mass-media advertising, direct marketing, personal selling, and other promotional efforts; pricing policy; and the selection of distribution channels to move the product from the manufacturer to the consumer.

FIGURE 16-2

A Simple Model of Consumer Decision Making

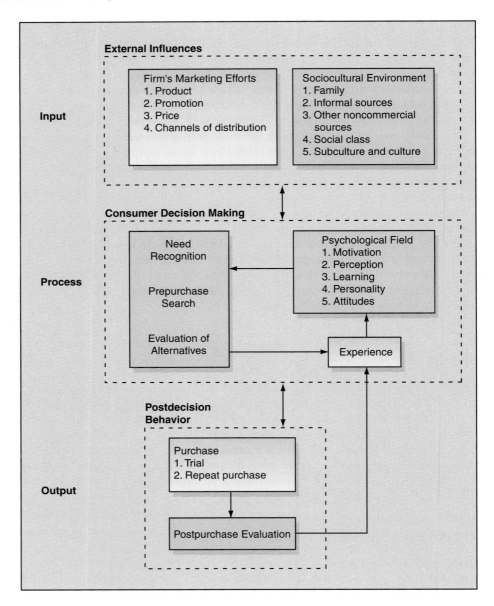

Ultimately, the impact of a firm's marketing efforts in large measure is governed by the consumer's perception of these efforts. Thus, marketers do well to remain diligently alert to consumer perceptions by sponsoring consumer research, rather than to rely on the *intended* impact of their marketing messages.

Sociocultural Inputs

The second type of input, the *sociocultural environment,* also exerts a major influence on the consumer. Sociocultural inputs (examined in Part III) consist of a wide range of noncommercial influences. For example, the comments of a friend, an editorial in the newspaper, usage by a family member, an article in *Consumer Reports,* or the views of experienced consumers participating in a special-interest discussion group on the Internet are all noncommercial sources of information. The influences of social class, culture, and subculture, although less tangible, are important input factors that are internalized and affect how consumers evaluate and ultimately adopt (or reject) products. The unwritten codes of conduct communicated by culture subtly indicate which consumption behavior should be considered "right" or "wrong" at a particular point in time. For example, Japanese mothers maintain much more control over their children's consumption than American mothers, because in the United States children are socialized to be individualistic (*to stand out*), whereas in Japan children are socialized to be integrated with others (*to stand in*).[13]

The cumulative impact of each firm's marketing efforts; the influence of family, friends, and neighbors; and society's existing code of behavior are all inputs that are likely to affect what consumers purchase and how they use what they buy. Because these influences may be directed to the individual or actively sought by the individual, a two-headed arrow is used to link the *input* and *process* segments of the model (Figure 16-2).

PROCESS

The *process* component of the model is concerned with how consumers make decisions. To understand this process, we must consider the influence of the psychological concepts examined in Part II. The *psychological field* represents the internal influences (motivation, perception, learning, personality, and attitudes) that affect consumers' decision-making processes (what they need or want, their awareness of various product choices, their information-gathering activities, and their evaluation of alternatives). As pictured in the *process* component of the overview decision model (Figure 16-2), the act of making a consumer decision consists of three stages: (1) **need recognition,** (2) **prepurchase search,** and (3) **evaluation of alternatives.**

Need Recognition

The *recognition of a need* is likely to occur when a consumer is faced with a "problem." For example, consider the case of Richard, a 35-year-old businessman working for a midsized marketing research firm in Los Angeles. Richard has developed into a first-class consumer researcher. As such, he is often out of town two or three days a week in order to moderate focus groups for his firm's clients (a focus group consists of 8 to 12 consumers sitting around a large table for about two hours discussing a particular product or service, and the discussion is led by a moderator—see Chapter 2). Because e-mail is now so important in the business world—it is the way that Richard can send messages to his clients and his colleagues at work (and vice versa)—he has begun traveling with his 3-year-old laptop computer. In the way of further background, Richard is a bit of a techno-geek, and by the time he got to college in 1983 he was one of the only students to have a computer in his dorm room; moreover, he was one of the few students who even knew, at that time how to use a personal computer. Today, Richard frequently visits Web site chat rooms to discuss high-tech, computer-related topics, such as new programs and new computers. He also knows a number of Web sites where highly specialized e-tailers are offering state-of-the-art computer equipment, some of it unavailable in brick-and-mortar stores such as CompUSA or mainstream e-tailers like Outpost and CDW. Richard enjoys unconventional, unique "WOW" technology. For example, he drives a Volkswagen Beetle and takes notes at meetings with his 40-year-old Parker fountain pen, which he purchased from a pen shop in Los Angeles that sells vintage fountain pens. He schedules his life, both professional and personal, via his Palm Pilot.

For Richard, the problem is that his current laptop (supplied by his employer), with its 15-inch screen, heavy battery, and built-in floppy disk and CD-ROM drives, weighs more than 8 pounds. When encased in its genuine leather carrying case there is another 2 pounds of weight, and when combined with his briefcase and his 21-inch carry-on piece of luggage, he has found that it is all just too much for him to comfortably handle through airplane aisles, airports, and taxis. Also because of its weight, he has found it very heavy to carry his laptop with him when he has to walk more than several blocks. Therefore, he normally leaves it on his desk when attending local business meetings outside his office. Maybe more than anything else, Richard does not feel that a large and bulky laptop fits his persona—which is to be thought of and known for using high-tech and eye-catching technology. Indeed, Richard feels that he is known by his family and friends to "love tech-toys." Moreover, reflecting on his current laptop, Richard realizes that he needs to leave it in the office and purchase an ultralight smaller laptop (about 2 to 3.5 pounds) to carry with him when he is fulfilling his role as a "road warrior." It is fair to say that he has *recognized the need* for a smaller, lighter-weight computer. And when he introduces the idea of a smaller computer to his boss, Richard is told he can go out and purchase whatever he feels will do the job, and the firm will pay for it.

Among consumers, there seem to be two different need or problem recognition styles. Some consumers are *actual state* types, who perceive that they have a problem when a product fails to perform satisfactorily (as a cordless telephone that develops constant static). In contrast, other consumers are *desired state* types, for whom the desire for something new may trigger the decision process.[14] Since Richard's current laptop can do the job, albeit painfully, he appears to be a desired state consumer.

Prepurchase Search

Prepurchase search begins when a consumer perceives a need that might be satisfied by the purchase and consumption of a product. The recollection of past experiences (drawn from storage in long-term memory) might provide the consumer with adequate information to make the present choice. On the other hand, when the consumer has had no prior experience, he or she may have to engage in an extensive search of the outside environment for useful information on which to base a choice.

The consumer usually searches his or her memory (the *psychological field* depicted in the model) before seeking external sources of information regarding a given consumption-related need. Past experience is considered an internal source of information. The greater the relevant past experience, the less external information the consumer is likely to need to reach a decision. Many consumer decisions are based on a combination of past experience (internal sources) and marketing and noncommercial information (external sources). The degree of perceived risk can also influence this stage of the decision process (see Chapter 6). In high-risk situations, consumers are likely to engage in complex and extensive information search and evaluation; in low-risk situations, they are likely to use very simple or limited search and evaluation tactics.

The act of shopping is an important form of external information. According to a recent consumer study, there is a big difference between men and women in terms of their response to shopping. Whereas most men do not like to shop, most women claim to like the experience of shopping; and although the majority of women found shopping to be relaxing and enjoyable, the majority of men did not have the same response.[15] In addition to gender differences, research reveals that price considerations can also play a role in determining the extent of the search process. For instance, consumers may engage in *smart shopping,* which indicates a willingness to invest a considerable amount of time and effort to seek and use promotion-related information in order to obtain a price savings. For such consumers, this search constitutes doing their "homework" prior to making a purchase.[16]

An examination of the external search effort associated with the purchase of different product categories (TVs, VCRs, or personal computers) found that, as the amount of total search effort increased, consumer attitudes toward shopping became more positive, and more time was made available for shopping. Not surprisingly, the external search effort was greatest for consumers who had the least amount of product category knowledge.[17] It follows that the less consumers know about a product category and the more important the purchase is to them, the more time they will make available and the more extensive their prepurchase search activity is likely to be. Conversely, research studies have indicated that consumers high in subjective knowledge (a self-assessment of how much they know about the product category) rely more on their own evaluations than on dealer recommendations.[18]

It is also important to point out that the Internet has had a great impact on prepurchase search. Rather than visiting a store to find out about a product or calling the manufacturer and asking for a brochure, manufacturers' Web sites can provide consumers with much of the information they need about the products and services they are considering. For example, many automobile Web sites provide product specifications, sticker prices and dealer cost information, reviews, and even comparisons with competing vehicles. Jaguar's Web site (www.jaguar.com), for example, lets you "build" your own Jaguar, and see how it would look, for example, in different colors. Some Web sites will even list a particular auto dealer's new and used car inventory. And then there are Web sites such as Reflect.com (www.reflect.com) that allow women to customize any number of cosmetic and beauty care products, and Customatix.com (www.customatix.com) that lets its customers design shoes.[19]

With respect to surfing the Internet for information, consider one consumer's comments drawn from a recent research study: "I like to use the Web because it's so easy to find information, and it's really easy to use. The information is at my fingertips and I don't have to search books in libraries."[20]

How much information a consumer will gather also depends on various situational factors. Getting back to Richard, while he works long hours in Los Angeles and some months spends more nights in hotel rooms than in his own bed due to business-related travel, he is willing to spend time researching his desired purchase. He starts by sitting at his office desk with his laptop connected to the firm's network broadband connection. He visits the Web sites of computer manufacturers such as Dell (www.dell.com), Toshiba (www.toshiba.com), Sony (www.sony.com), IBM (www.ibm.com) and Hewlett Packard/Compaq (www.thenew.hp.com), as well as e-tailer Web sites like CDW (www.cdw.com) and Outpost (www.outpost.com) to see if they offer lightweight machines. He finds several lightweight subnotebook computers that seem like possibilities. Richard also remembers reading about a company named Dynamism (www.dynamism.com) in both *PC Magazine* and *Wired,* which imports and adapts for English-speaking users some of the very smallest, ultralight laptop computers that are usually only available in Japan or a few other Asian markets.

Richard also talks to some of his friends and coworkers who are even more into tiny ("WOW") laptops than he is. One suggests that he try to find product reviews of any computer that he considers to be a possibility on such Web sites as CNET (www.cnet.com) and *PC Magazine* (www.pcmag.com). But Reid, the firm's resident computer geek, agrees with Richard that Dynamism is several years "ahead of the curve." According to Reid, Dynamism also provides warranty assistance (if the company can't fix it, it will provide free FedEx International Priority shipping to Japan to have the unit repaired by its manufacturer), support, and downloads for its customers. Richard is intrigued by the uniqueness of owning a subnotebook computer that few others in the United States have ever seen or heard of and by the fact that some of the subnotebooks offered by Dynamism are considerably smaller and possess more advanced and "futuristic" features than what is currently available in the United States.

As Table 16-2 indicates, a number of factors are likely to increase consumers' prepurchase search. For some products and services, the consumer may have ongoing experience on which to draw (such as a skier purchasing a "better" pair of skis),

---

TABLE 16-2 Factors That Are Likely to Increase Prepurchase Search

PRODUCT FACTORS

Long interpurchase time (a long-lasting or infrequently used product)
Frequent changes in product styling
Frequent price changes
Volume purchasing (large number of units)
High price
Many alternative brands
Much variation in features

SITUATIONAL FACTORS

Experience

First-time purchase
No past experience because the product is new
Unsatisfactory past experience within the product category

Social Acceptability

The purchase is for a gift
The product is socially visible

Value-Related Considerations

Purchase is discretionary rather than necessary
All alternatives have both desirable and undesirable consequences
Family members disagree on product requirements or evaluation of alternatives
Product usage deviates from important reference groups
The purchase involves ecological considerations
Many sources of conflicting information

PRODUCT FACTORS

Demographic Characteristics of Consumer

Well educated
High income
White-collar occupation
Under 35 years of age

Personality

Low dogmatic
Low-risk perceiver (broad categorizer)
Other personal factors such as high product involvement and enjoyment of shopping and search

or the purchase may essentially be discretionary in nature (rather than a necessity), so there is no rush to make a decision. In the case of Richard, our market researcher, while he is home in Los Angeles this week and looking ahead to a busy month of business travel he is, therefore, excited about the prospects of purchasing a new ultralight laptop before leaving on his trip.

Let's consider several of the prepurchase search alternatives open to a computer buyer. At the most fundamental level, search alternatives can be classified as either personal or impersonal. *Personal* search alternatives include more than a consumer's past experience with the product or service. They also include asking for information and advice from friends, relatives, coworkers and sales representatives. For instance, Richard spoke with a few friends and coworkers and asked them what they know about ultralightweight laptops. Richard also investigated whether PC-related publications, such as *PC Magazine* or *Laptops,* might have rated the various brands or types of laptops. Table 16-3 presents some of the sources of information that Richard might use as part of his prepurchase search. Any or all of these sources might be used as part of a consumer's search process.

Evaluation of Alternatives

When evaluating potential alternatives, consumers tend to use two types of information: (1) a "list" of brands (or models) from which they plan to make their selection (the evoked set) and (2) the criteria they will use to evaluate each brand (or model). Making a selection from a *sample* of all possible brands (or models) is a human characteristic that helps simplify the decision-making process.

Evoked Set Within the context of consumer decision making, the **evoked set** refers to the specific brands (or models) a consumer considers in making a purchase within a particular product category. (The evoked set is also called the *consideration set.*) A consumer's evoked set is distinguished from his or her **inept set,** which consists of brands (or models) the consumer excludes from purchase consideration because they are felt to be unacceptable (or they are seen as "inferior"), and from the **inert set,** which consists of brands (or models) the consumer is indifferent toward because they are perceived as not having any particular advantages. Regardless of the total number of brands (or models) in a product category, a consumer's evoked set tends to be quite small on average, often consisting of only three to five brands (or models). However, research indicates that a consumer's consideration set increases in size as experience with a product category grows.[21]

The evoked set consists of the small number of brands the consumer is familiar with, remembers, and finds acceptable. Figure 16-3 depicts the evoked set as a

TABLE 16-3   **Alternative Prepurchase Information Sources for an Ultralight Laptop**

PERSONAL	IMPERSONAL
Friends	Newspaper articles
Neighbors	Magazine articles
Relatives	*Consumer Reports*
Coworkers	Direct-mail brochures
Computer salespeople	Information from product advertisements
	Internal Web sites

FIGURE 16-3

The Evoked Set as a
Subset of All Brands in
a Product Class

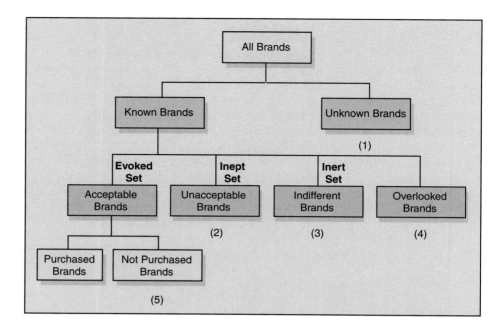

subset of all available brands in a product category. As the figure indicates, it is essential that a product be part of a consumer's evoked set if it is to be considered at all. The five terminal positions in the model that do not end in purchase would appear to have perceptual problems. For example, (1) brands (or models) may be *unknown* because of the consumer's selective exposure to advertising media and selective perception of advertising stimuli; (2) brands (or models) may be *unacceptable* because of poor qualities or attributes or inappropriate positioning in either advertising or product characteristics; (3) brands (or models) may be perceived as not having any special benefits and are regarded *indifferently* by the consumer; (4) brands (or models) may be *overlooked* because they have not been clearly positioned or sharply targeted at the consumer market segment under study; and (5) brands (or models) may not be selected because they are perceived by consumers as *unable to satisfy* perceived needs as fully as the brand that is chosen.

In each of these instances, the implication for marketers is that promotional techniques should be designed to impart a more favorable, perhaps more relevant, product image to the target consumer. This may also require a change in product features or attributes (more or better features). An alternative strategy is to invite consumers in a particular target segment to consider a specific offering and possibly put it in their evoked set.

It should also be pointed out that at times a consumer may feel as if he or she is being offered too many choices. For example, the brand proliferation on supermarket shelves may result in our trying a new brand, liking it, and then never being able to find it again.[22]

Criteria Used for Evaluating Brands The criteria consumers use to evaluate the alternative products that constitute their evoked sets usually are expressed in terms of important product attributes. Examples of product attributes that consumers have used as criteria in evaluating nine product categories are listed in Table 16-4.

When a company knows that consumers will be evaluating alternatives, it sometimes advertises in a way that recommends the criteria that consumers should use in

TABLE 16-4 Possible Product Attributes Used as Purchase Criteria for Nine Product Categories

PERSONAL COMPUTERS

Processing speed
Price
Type of display
Hard-disk size
Amount of memory
Laptop or desktop

VCRS

Ease of programming
Number of heads
Number of tape speeds
Slow-motion feature
Automatic tracking

35-MM CAMERAS

Autofocus
Built-in flash
Automatic film loading
Lens type
Size and weight

CD PLAYERS

Mega bass
Electronic shock protection
Length of play on batteries
Random play feature
Water resistant

COLOR TVS

Picture quality
Length of warranty
Cable ready
Price
Size of screen

FOUNTAIN PENS

Balance
Price
Gold nib
Smoothness
Ink reserve

WRISTWATCHES

Watchband
Alarm feature
Price
Water resistant
Quartz movement
Size of dial

FROZEN DINNERS

Taste
Type of main course
Type of side dishes
Price
Preparation requirements

COLOR INKJET PRINTERS

Output speed
Number of ink colors
Resolution (DPI)
Length of warranty
USB capability

assessing product or service options. For example, Figure 16-4 presents an ad for Hartz® Advanced Care™ Brand® that compares its product, in terms of selected benefits, to two competitive products. The comparison points to Hartz's advantages. Such information is designed to educate and assist potential consumers in their decision-making processes. Still further, research reveals, if evaluations are made online, information acquired later (the recency effect) is given more weight than information that had been acquired earlier (although this decreases with the amount of knowledge that consumers already possess).[23] In another study, the mere possession of a rebate coupon (whether it is used or not) for a product purchase enhances consumers' preference for that object.[24] There is also evidence to show that when making a "remote" purchase (i.e., the consumer is shopping from home or office rather than in the actual store), the leniency of the retailer's return policy can influence the decision process because it reduces consumer risk.[25]

We have probably all had the experience of comparing or evaluating different brands or models of a product and finding the one that just feels, looks, and/or performs "right." Interestingly, research shows that when consumers discuss such "right products," there is little or no mention of price; brand names are not often uppermost in consumers, minds; items often reflect personality characteristics or childhood experiences; and it is often "love at first sight." In one study, the products claimed by research participants to "just feel right" included Big Bertha golf clubs, old leather briefcases, Post-it notes, and the Honda Accord.[26]

Let's return for a moment to Richard and his search for an ultralightweight laptop. As part of his search process, he has acquired information about a number of

FIGURE 16-4

Ad Suggesting Criteria
for Decision Making
Courtesy of The Hartz
Mountain Corporation

relevant issues (or attributes) that could influence his final choice. For example, Richard has learned that the overall size of a notebook or laptop computer is very much a function of the size of its screen and that the weight of the machine is determined to a great extent by battery size/capacity (i.e., two hours or four hours of battery life), as well as what comes built into the machine itself (e.g., internal or external floppy disk drive, internal or external CD-ROM or CD-ROM/DVD, internal parallel, serial, and/or video ports; or just USB ports and anything else requiring a docking station).

As part of his search process, Richard has also acquired information about other relevant issues (or attributes) that could influence his final choice (see Table 16-5). For example, he has learned that some ultralight Japanese laptops have keyboards that do not have the "feel" of most laptops sold in the U.S. market and are, therefore, harder to type on.

On the basis of his information search, Richard realizes that he is going to have to make a decision regarding what he really wants from this new computer. Does he want just a lighter-weight version of his current laptop, or is he willing to sacrifice some features for a computer that is substantially smaller and lighter than the typical notebook machine? He comes to realize that on the road his main computer usage involves sending and receiving e-mails and making relatively minor changes

TABLE 16-5	Comparison of Selected Characteristics of Ultralight Laptop Computers		
FEATURE	**DELL LATITUDE C400**	**COMPAQ EVO N200**	**TOSHIBA LIBRETTO L**
Weight (pounds)	3.7	2.7	2.4
Dimensions (HWD, inches)	1 × 11.4 × 9.5	0.8 × 9.9 × 7.8	0.81 × 10.5 × 6.6
Processor	866MHz Pentium III	700MHz Pentium III	800MHz Crusoe
Display	12.1-inch TFT	10.4-inch TFT	10-inch TFT
RAM	256MB	192MB	256MB
Hard Drive	20GB	20GB	20GB
Battery Life	2.5 hours	2.5 hours	4 hours
Other Features	Built-in wireless and built-in Ethernet port	Needs PC card for wireless Has built-in Ethernet port	Built-in wireless and built-in Ethernet port
Price	$2,256	$2,238	$1,999

Source: Adapted from Jonathan Blackwood, "The Jet Set," *Computer Shopper,* 22, 3, March 2002, 144–147; Dan Costa, "The Lighter Side," *PC Magazine,* 21, 6, March 26, 2002, 94–106; and accessed from **www.dynamism.com.**

in focus group discussion guides. These uses involve no serious typing and no great length of time spent looking at the computer screen. Occasionally he is also asked to review a proposal that has to be sent to a client, but Richard learned years ago that to do this properly he has to print out the proposal, read it, make changes, and then e-mail the revised proposal back to his office. Thus, Richard realizes that he is willing to give up some functionality (such as a built-in floppy drive) in exchange for reduced size and weight.

Consumer Decision Rules Consumer decision rules, often referred to as *heuristics, decision strategies,* and *information-processing strategies,* are procedures used by consumers to facilitate brand (or other consumption-related) choices. These rules reduce the burden of making complex decisions by providing guidelines or routines that make the process less taxing.

Consumer decision rules have been broadly classified into two major categories: **compensatory** and **noncompensatory decision rules.** In following a compensatory decision rule, a consumer evaluates brand or model options in terms of each relevant attribute and computes a weighted or summated score for each brand. The computed score reflects the brand's relative merit as a potential purchase choice. The assumption is that the consumer will select the brand that scores highest among the alternatives evaluated. Referring to Table 16-6, it is clear that when using a compensatory decision rule, the Toshiba Libretto L scores highest.

A unique feature of a compensatory decision rule is that it allows a positive evaluation of a brand on one attribute to balance out a negative evaluation on some other attribute. For example, a positive assessment of the energy savings made possible by a particular brand or type of lightbulb may offset an unacceptable assessment in terms of the bulb's diminished light output.

In contrast, noncompensatory decision rules do not allow consumers to balance positive evaluations of a brand on one attribute against a negative evaluation on some other attribute. For instance, in the case of an energy-saving lightbulb, the product's negative (unacceptable) rating on its light output would not be offset by a positive evaluation of its energy savings. Instead, this particular lightbulb would be disqualified from further consideration. If Richard's choice of a laptop computer was based on the desire to have a built-in wireless capability (Wi-Fi) (refer again to

TABLE 16-6	Hypothetical Ratings for Ultralight Laptops		
FEATURE	**DELL LATITUDE C400**	**COMPAQ EVO N200**	**TOSHIBA LIBRETTO L**
Weight (pounds)	4	8	10
Dimensions	3	7	10
Processor	7	5	6
Display	10	7	6
RAM	10	8	10
Hard Drive	8	8	8
Battery Life	6	6	8
Other Features	8	5	8
Price	7	7	8
Total	63	61	74

Table 16-5), a noncompensatory decision rule would have eliminated the Compaq Evo N200.

Three noncompensatory rules are considered briefly here: the *conjunctive* rule, the *disjunctive* rule, and the *lexicographic* rule.

In following a **conjunctive decision rule,** the consumer establishes a separate, minimally acceptable level as a cutoff point for each attribute. If any particular brand or model falls below the cutoff point on any one attribute, the option is eliminated from further consideration. Because the conjunctive rule can result in several acceptable alternatives, it becomes necessary in such cases for the consumer to apply an additional decision rule to arrive at a final selection, for example, to accept the first satisfactory brand. The conjunctive rule is particularly useful in quickly reducing the number of alternatives to be considered. The consumer can then apply another more refined decision rule to arrive at a final choice.

The **disjunctive rule** is the "mirror image" of the conjunctive rule. In applying this decision rule, the consumer establishes a separate, minimally acceptable cutoff level for each attribute (which may be higher than the one normally established for a conjunctive rule). In this case, if an option meets or exceeds the cutoff established for any one attribute, it is accepted. Here again, a number of brands (or models) might exceed the cutoff point, producing a situation in which another decision rule is required. When this occurs, the consumer may accept the first satisfactory alternative as the final choice or apply another decision rule that is perhaps more suitable.

In following a **lexicographic decision rule,** the consumer first ranks the attributes in terms of perceived relevance or importance. The consumer then compares the various alternatives in terms of the single attribute that is considered most important. If one option scores sufficiently high on this top-ranked attribute (regardless of the score on any of the other attributes), it is selected and the process ends. When there are two or more surviving alternatives, the process is repeated with the second highest-ranked attribute (and so on), until reaching the point that one of the options is selected because it exceeds the others on a particular attribute.

With the lexicographic rule, the highest-ranked attribute (the one applied first) may reveal something about the individual's basic consumer (or shopping) orientation. For instance, a "buy the best" rule might indicate that the consumer is *quality oriented;* a "buy the most prestigious brand" rule might indicate that the consumer is *status oriented;* a "buy the least expensive" rule might reveal that the consumer is *economy minded.*

A variety of decision rules appear quite commonplace. According to a consumer survey, 9 out of 10 shoppers who go to the store for frequently purchased items possess a specific shopping strategy for saving money. The consumer segment and the specific shopping rules that these segments employ are:[27]

1. *Practical loyalists—those who look for ways to save on the brands and products they would buy anyway.*
2. *Bottom-line price shoppers—those who buy the lowest-priced item with little or no regard for brand.*
3. *Opportunistic switchers—those who use coupons or sales to decide among brands and products that fall within their evoked set.*
4. *Deal hunters—those who look for the best bargain and are not brand loyal.*

We have considered only the most basic of an almost infinite number of consumer decision rules. Most of the decision rules described here can be combined to form new variations, such as conjunctive-compensatory, conjunctive-disjunctive, and disjunctive-conjunctive rules. It is likely that for many purchase decisions, consumers maintain in long-term memory overall evaluations of the brands in their evoked sets. This would make assessment by individual attributes unnecessary. Instead, the consumer would simply select the brand with the highest perceived overall rating. This type of synthesized decision rule is known as the **affect referral decision rule** and may represent the simplest of all rules.

Table 16-7 summarizes the essence of many of the decision rules considered in this chapter in terms of the kind of mental statements that Richard might make in selecting a subnotebook computer.

Going Online to Secure Assistance in Decision Making For the past several years researchers have been examining how using the Internet has impacted the way consumers make decisions. It is often hypothesized that because consumers have limited information-processing capacity, they must develop a choice strategy based on both individual factors (e.g., knowledge, personality traits, demographics) and contextual factors (characteristics of the decision tasks). The three major contextual factors that have been researched are *task complexity* (number of alternatives and amount of information available for each alternative), *information organization*

TABLE 16-7	Hypothetical Use of Popular Decision Rules in Making a Decision to Purchase an Ultralight Laptop Computer
DECISION RULE	**MENTAL STATEMENT**
Compensatory rule	"I selected the computer that came out best when I balanced the good ratings against the bad ratings."
Conjunctive rule	"I selected the computer that had no bad features."
Disjunctive rule	"I picked the computer that excelled in at least one attribute."
Lexicographic rule	"I looked at the feature that was most important to me and chose the computer that ranked highest on that attribute."
Affect referral rule	"I bought the brand with the highest overall rating."

TABLE 16-8 Comparison of Electronic and Traditional Information Environment

		Electronic Environment	Traditional Environment
		CONSUMERS USE BOTH "HEADS" AND COMPUTERS TO MAKE DECISIONS. THE TOTAL CAPACITY IS EXTENDED.	**CONSUMERS USE "HEADS" TO MAKE DECISIONS. THEIR COGNITIVE CAPACITY IS FIXED.**
ASSUMPTION			
Contextual Factors	Task Complexity	More alternatives and more information for each alternative are available. Information is more accessible.	Information is scattered and information search is costly.
	Information Organization	Information presentation format is flexible. It can be reorganized and controlled by consumers. Product utilities can be calculated by computers without consumers' direct examination of the attributes.	Information presentation format and organization are fixed. They can only be "edited" by consumers manually (e.g., using pencil and paper).
	Time Constraint	Time is saved by using computers to execute the decision rules; extra time is needed to learn how to use the application.	Complex choice strategies require more time to formulate and execute.

Source: Lan Xia, "Consumer Choice Strategies and Choice Confidence in the Electronic Environment," *American Marketing Association Conference Proceedings,* American Marketing Association, 10, 1999, 272.

(presentation, format, and content), and *time constraint* (more or less time to decide).[28] Table 16-8 compares these contextual factors for both the electronic and traditional environments.

Lifestyles as a Consumer Decision Strategy An individual's or family's decisions to be committed to a particular lifestyle (e.g., devoted followers of a particular religion) impacts on a wide range of specific everyday consumer behavior. For instance, the Trends Research Institute has identified "voluntary simplicity" as one of the top 10 lifestyle trends.[29] Researchers there estimate that 15 percent of all "boomers" seek a simpler lifestyle with reduced emphasis on ownership and possessions. Voluntary simplifiers are making do with less clothing and fewer credit cards (with no outstanding balances) and moving to smaller, yet still adequate, homes or apartments in less populated communities. Most importantly, it is not that these consumers can no longer afford their affluence or "lifestyle of abundance"; rather, they are seeking new, "reduced," less extravagant lifestyles. As part of this new lifestyle commitment, some individuals are seeking less stressful and lower-salary careers or jobs. In a telephone survey, for example, 33 percent of those contacted claimed that they would be willing to take a 20 percent pay cut in return for working fewer hours.[30] Time pressure may also play a role in the consumer's decision process, as research has positively associated this factor with both sale proneness (i.e., respond positively to cents-off coupons or special offers) and display proneness (e.g., respond positively to in-store displays offering a special price).[31]

Incomplete Information and Noncomparable Alternatives In many choice situations, consumers face incomplete information on which to base decisions and must use alternative strategies to cope with the missing elements. Missing information may result from advertisements or packaging that mentions only certain attributes, the consumer's own imperfect memory of attributes for nonpresent alternatives, or because some attributes are experiential and can only be evaluated after product use.[32] There are at least four alternative strategies that consumers can adopt for coping with missing information:[33]

1. *Consumers may delay the decision until missing information is obtained. This strategy is likely to be used for high-risk decisions.*
2. *Consumers may ignore missing information and decide to continue with the current decision rule (e.g., compensatory or noncompensatory), using the available attribute information.*
3. *Consumers may change the customarily used decision strategy to one that better accommodates missing information.*
4. *Consumers may infer ("construct") the missing information.*

Recent research has demonstrated that consumers tend to deal with missing information by purchasing the option that is deemed to be superior on the common attribute (i.e., basing the decision on the information that is available for all of the options or brands being considered). For marketers, therefore, the decision as to what information to provide or not to provide can help determine the product's success or failure in the marketplace.[34]

In discussing consumer decision rules, we have assumed that a choice is made from among the brands (or models) evaluated. Of course, a consumer also may conclude that none of the alternatives offers sufficient benefits to warrant purchase. If this were to occur with a necessity, such as a refrigerator, the consumer would probably either lower his or her expectations and settle for the best of the available alternatives or seek information about additional brands, hoping to find one that more closely meets predetermined criteria. On the other hand, if the purchase is more discretionary (a second or third pair of sneakers), the consumer probably would postpone the purchase. In this case, information gained from the search up to that point would be transferred to long-term storage (in the psychological field) and retrieved and reintroduced as input if and when the consumer regains interest in making such a purchase.

It should be noted that, in applying decision rules, consumers may at times attempt to compare dissimilar (noncomparable) alternatives. For example, a consumer may be undecided about whether to buy a large-screen, high-definition television set or a new set of scuba gear, because the individual can afford one or the other but not both. Another example: A consumer may try to decide between buying a new sweater or a new raincoat. When there is great dissimilarity in the alternative ways of allocating available funds, consumers abstract the products to a level in which comparisons are possible. In the foregoing examples, a consumer might weigh the alternatives (TV versus scuba gear or sweater versus raincoat) in terms of which alternative would offer more pleasure or which, if either, is more of a "necessity."

A Series of Decisions Although we have discussed the purchase decision as if it were a single decision, in reality, a purchase can involve a number of decisions. For example, when purchasing an automobile, consumers are involved in multiple decisions such as choosing the make or country of origin of the car (foreign versus domestic), the dealer, the financing, and particular options. In the case of a replacement automobile, these decisions must be preceded by a decision as to whether or not to trade in one's current car. A study found that the attitudes and search behavior of consumers who replace their cars after only a few years (early replacement buyers) differ greatly from those who replace their cars after many years (late replacement buyers). In particular, early car replacement buyers were more concerned with the car's styling and image or status and were less concerned with cost. In contrast, late car replacement buyers undertook a greater amount of information and dealer search and were greatly influenced by friends.[35]

Since deciding how to pay for a purchase is one of the decisions facing consumers, it is of interest to point out that the use of debit cards has been gaining popularity in the United States as a payment option. Whereas in 1999, according to one study, 22 percent of purchases were made with credit cards and 21 percent with debit cards, by 2001 credit cards accounted for only 21 percent of purchases and debit card usage had risen to 26 percent. Online point-of-sale debit card transactions were expected to rise from 2.9 billion in 1999 to 13 billion in 2003. In contrast, the average American writes 21 checks monthly, about half of them at the time of purchase.[36]

Decision Rules and Marketing Strategy An understanding of which decision rules consumers apply in selecting a particular product or service is useful to marketers concerned with formulating a promotional program. A marketer familiar with the prevailing decision rule can prepare a promotional message in a format that would facilitate consumer information processing. The promotional message might even suggest how potential consumers should make a decision. For instance, a direct-mail piece for a desktop computer might tell potential consumers "what to look for in a new PC." This mail piece might specifically ask consumers to consider the attributes of hard disk size, amount of memory, processor speed, monitor size and maximum resolution, video card memory, and CD burner speed.

Consumption Vision Researchers have recently proposed "consumption vision" as a nonorthodox, but potentially accurate, portrayal of decision making for those situations in which the consumer has little experience and the problems are not well structured, as well as those in which there is a considerable amount of emotion. Under such circumstances, the consumer may turn to a consumption vision, a mental picture or visual image of specific usage outcomes and/or consumption consequences.[37] Such visions (e.g., a new college graduate envisioning working for a large corporation versus working for his Dad's small manufacturing firm, or a consumer visualizing lying on a beach in Hawaii) allow consumers to imagine or vicariously participate in the consumption of the product or service prior to making an actual decision. After "trying out" a number of different alternatives in one's mind, so to speak, the consumer then makes his or her decision.[38] In a recent study, consumers were more likely to construct consumption visions when they saw an advertisement presenting the product's attributes in concrete and detailed language or visually with pictures.[39] There is also research evidence to indicate that a consumer's preferences may change depending on the degree to which anticipated satisfaction is evoked. When anticipating satisfaction, the consumer forms mental images—consumption visions—of one or more of the options, and the final decision is very likely going to be based on this imagery. To illustrate, a real estate agent selling an expensive home might encourage clients to ask themselves (i.e., "envision") how satisfied they would likely be to live in such a home.[40]

OUTPUT

The output portion of the consumer decision-making model concerns two closely associated kinds of postdecision activity: **purchase behavior** and **postpurchase evaluation.** The objective of both activities is to increase the consumer's satisfaction with his or her purchase.

Purchase Behavior

Consumers make three types of purchases: *trial purchases, repeat purchases,* and *long-term commitment purchases.* When a consumer purchases a product (or brand) for the first time and buys a smaller quantity than usual, this purchase would be considered a trial. Thus, a trial is the exploratory phase of purchase behavior in which consumers attempt to evaluate a product through direct use. For instance, when consumers purchase a new brand of laundry detergent about which they may be uncertain, they are likely to purchase smaller trial quantities than if it were a familiar brand. Consumers can also be encouraged to try a new product through such promotional tactics as free samples, coupons, and/or sale prices.

When a new brand in an established product category (toothpaste, chewing gum, or cola) is found by trial to be more satisfactory or better than other brands, consumers are likely to repeat the purchase. Repeat purchase behavior is closely related to the concept of *brand loyalty,* which most firms try to encourage because it contributes to greater stability in the marketplace (see Chapter 7). Unlike trial, in which the consumer uses the product on a small scale and without any commitment, a repeat purchase usually signifies that the product meets with the consumer's approval and that he or she is willing to use it again and in larger quantities.

Trial, of course, is not always feasible. For example, with most durable goods (refrigerators, washing machines, or electric ranges), a consumer usually moves directly from evaluation to a long-term commitment (through purchase) without the opportunity for an actual trial. While purchasers of the new Volkswagen Beetle were awaiting delivery of their just purchased cars, they were kept "warm" by being sent a mailing that included a psychographic tool called "Total Visual Imagery" that was personalized to the point that it showed them the precise model and color they had ordered.[41]

It is also important that some observers believe that eventually there will be almost universal Internet access, at least in the United States. As a result, some authorities are forecasting that early in the twenty-first century consumers will be purchasing food and other basic household needs via in-home television computer systems. Choices will be made by the shopper after viewing brands and prices on the screen. So the purchasing process itself may change dramatically in the coming decades.[42]

Consider Richard and his decision concerning the selection of an ultralight laptop. There is really no way that he can try all three computers that he had been considering because the Toshiba Libretto L is not sold in traditional retail stores. So what does Richard do? First of all, a number of his coworkers use Dell laptops, and he knows that they are very good computers and come with a terrific warranty. However, he decides that at 3.7 pounds, the Dell Latitude C400 is just too heavy for his needs. Next, he calls several local computer retailers in the Los Angeles area and finds a store that carries the Compaq Evo N200 with one on display. On his lunch break, Richard visits this retailer and "plays" with the Compaq. He finds that, although the display is acceptable to him, the keyboard is too small for his hands. He also dislikes the fact that he would have to carry an external card for wireless Internet access (Wi-Fi).

Now Richard starts to seriously consider the Toshiba Libretto L, a computer that he found listed on the Dynamism.com Web site. Let's start with the fact that this Libretto laptop, at 2.4 pounds, admirably addresses the issue of weight and also offers a fairly speedy processor, a lot of memory, a good-sized hard drive, and more battery life than many other laptops (again, see Table 16-5). And Richard likes the idea that not very many people have ever heard of or seen the Libretto (it's unique and he is, therefore, unique). However, he also has to be practical because his firm is going to be paying for it. Dynamism.com is not a traditional retailer selling traditional products—it offers a range of subnotebooks available on the Japanese market and converts them for use by English-speaking consumers. These subnotebook computers are often available in Japan up to one or two years before they may be offered by their manufacturers for sale in the United States. And Dynamism.com is not the only place to purchase such computers. Richard visits the eBay Web sit (www.ebay.com) and finds a few listings for the lastest Toshiba Libretto L, some offering the machine at a price several hundred dollars less than what Dynamism.com is asking. So what should Richard do?

Richard next visits a Yahoo! chat room devoted to the Toshiba Libretto L computer (groups.yahoo.com/group/libretto-L1). The computer series started with the Libretto L1 and progressed through a series of Ls. There are hundred of postings on the Web site with some owners asking questions and other owners providing answers. Richard reads dozens of these "chats" and decides that the Libretto L will meet his need for an ultralight laptop. It also satisfies his desire to be unique. Users of the Libretto chat room are generally thrilled with the performance of the computer, and the keyboard was considered by a number of chat room participants to be outstanding. But now Richard must decide if he should save his firm a few hundred dollars by purchasing the computer on eBay or buy it through Dynamism.com. He posts this question to the chat room participants, and the overwhelming response is that the advantages of buying from Dynamism.com far outweigh the cost differential. Chat room participants praise Dynamism.com for the conversion job the firm does to make the computer usable to an English-speaking owner, provide stories of how the technical support staff at Dynamism.com helped them solve problems with this and other Japanese computers that they have owned, and how Dynamism.com's warranty is worth its weight in gold. Consequently, Richard decides to purchase the current Toshiba Libretto L from Dynamism.com, along with a spare battery and an external CD-RW drive. Three days after placing the order, the FedEx second-day air package from Dynamism.com is sitting on his office desk.

Postpurchase Evaluation

As consumers use a product, particularly during a trial purchase, they evaluate its performance in light of their own expectations. There are three possible outcomes of these evaluations: (1) actual performance matches expectations, leading to a neutral feeling; (2) performance exceeds expectations, causing what is known as *positive disconfirmation of expectations* (which leads to satisfaction); and (3) performance is below expectations, causing *negative disconfirmation of expectations* and dissatisfaction.[43] For each of these three outcomes, consumers' expectations and satisfaction are closely linked; that is, consumers tend to judge their experience against their expectations when performing a postpurchase evaluation.

An important component of postpurchase evaluation is the reduction of any uncertainty or doubt that the consumer might have had about the selection. As part of their postpurchase analyses, consumers try to reassure themselves that their choice was a wise one; that is, they attempt to reduce *postpurchase cognitive disso-*

nance. As Chapter 8 indicated, they do this by adopting one of the following strategies: They may rationalize the decision as being wise; they may seek advertisements that support their choice and avoid those of competitive brands; they may attempt to persuade friends or neighbors to buy the same brand (and, thus, confirm their own choice); or they may turn to other satisfied owners for reassurance.

The degree of postpurchase analysis that consumers undertake depends on the importance of the product decision and the experience acquired in using the product. When the product lives up to expectations, they probably will buy it again. When the product's performance is disappointing or does not meet expectations, however, they will search for more suitable alternatives. Thus, the consumer's postpurchase evaluation "feeds back" as *experience* to the consumer's psychological field and serves to influence future related decisions. Although it would be logical to assume that customer satisfaction is related to customer retention (i.e., if a consumer is satisfied with his Brooks Brothers suit he will buy other Brooks Brothers products), a recent study found no direct relationship between satisfaction and retention. The findings show that customer retention may be more a matter of the brand's reputation—especially for products consumers find difficult to evaluate.[44]

What is Richard's postpurchase evaluation of his new laptop? He absolutely loves it! First of all, because of his personality, the fact that nobody he knows has this same computer has done wonders for his ego. But from a practical standpoint, the computer has also been a huge success. It is so small and lightweight that he can carry it in his normal business briefcase rather than needing a separate piece of computer luggage. The screen, even though it is only 10 inches in size, is bright and clear and large enough for his needs when traveling, and the pointer, which is integrated into the keyboard, works so well that he sees no need to purchase a small mouse. Furthermore, when he first got the Libretto, he had a number of questions about it. He was able to get through to the technical support staff at Dynamism.com by telephone with no long waits, and all of his questions were answered and his concerns were resolved.

Consumer Gifting Behavior

In terms of both dollars spent each year and how they make givers and receivers feel, gifts are a particularly interesting part of consumer behavior. Products and services chosen as gifts represent more than ordinary "everyday" purchases. Because of their symbolic meaning, they are associated with such important events as Mother's Day, births and birthdays, engagements, weddings, graduations, and many other accomplishments and milestones.

Gifting behavior has been defined as "the process of *gift exchange* that takes place between a giver and a recipient."[45] The definition is broad in nature and embraces gifts given voluntarily ("Just to let you know I'm thinking of you"), as well as gifts that are an obligation ("I had to get him a gift").[46] It includes gifts given to (and received from) others and gifts to oneself, or **self-gifts.** Indeed, although 96 percent of Americans purchased at least one "gift" last year, the majority of products that we refer to as "gifts" are self-purchased (i.e., they are self-gifts).[47] Furthermore, gift purchases represent 10 percent of all retail purchases in North America, and over $100 billion is spent annually on gifts in the United States.[48]

Still further, gifting is an act of symbolic communication, with explicit and implicit meanings ranging from congratulations, love, and regret to obligation and dominance. The nature of the relationship between gift giver and gift receiver is an important consideration in choosing a gift. Indeed, gifting often

TABLE 16-9	Five Giver-Receiver Gifting Subdivisions		
		RECEIVERS	
GIVERS	**INDIVIDUAL**	**"OTHER" GROUP**	**SELF***
Individual	Interpersonal gifting	Intercategory gifting	Intrapersonal gifting
Group	Intercategory gifting	Intergroup gifting	Intragroup gifting

* This "SELF" is either singular self ("me") or plural ("us").
Source: Based on Deborah Y. Cohn and Leon G. Schiffman, "Gifting: A Taxonomy of Private Realm Giver and Recipient Relationships," Working Paper, City University of New York, Baruch College, 1996, 2–7.

impacts the relationship between the giver and the recipient.[49] Table 16-9 presents an enumeration of the relationships between various combinations of gift givers and gift receivers in the consumer gifting process. The model reveals the following five gifting subdivisions: (1) intergroup gifting, (2) intercategory gifting, (3) intragroup gifting, (4) interpersonal gifting, and (5) intrapersonal gifting.

Intergroup gifting behavior occurs whenever one group exchanges gifts with another group (such as one family and another). You will recall from Chapter 10 that the process and outcome of family decision making is different from individual decision making. Similarly, gifts given to families will be different than those given to individual family members. For example, a "common" wedding gift for a bride *and* a groom may include products for setting up a household rather than a gift that would personally be used by either the bride or the groom. When it comes to *inter-category gifting,* either an individual is giving a gift to a group (a single friend is giving a couple an anniversary gift) or a group is giving an individual a gift (friends chip in and give another friend a joint birthday gift). The gift selection strategies "buy for joint recipients" or "buy with someone" (creating intercategory gifting) are especially useful when it comes to a difficult recipient situation (when "nothing seems to satisfy her").[50] These strategies can also be applied to reduce some of the time pressure associated with shopping for the great number of gifts exchanged during the American Christmas season gift-giving ritual. For example, a consumer may choose to purchase five intercategory gifts for five aunt and uncle pairs (intercategory gifting), instead of buying 10 personal gifts for five aunts and five uncles (interpersonal gifting). In this way, less time, money, and effort may be expended.

An *intragroup gift* can be characterized by the sentiment "we gave this to ourselves"; that is, a group gives a gift to itself or its members. For example, a dual-income couple may find that their demanding work schedules limit leisure time spent together as husband and wife. Therefore, an anniversary gift ("to us") of a Caribbean vacation would be an example of an intragroup gift. It would also remedy the couple's problem of not spending enough time together. In contrast, *interpersonal gifting* occurs between just two individuals, a gift giver and gift receiver. By their very nature, interpersonal gifts are "intimate" because they provide an opportunity for a gift giver to reveal what he or she thinks of the gift receiver. Successful gifts are those that communicate that the giver knows and understands the receiver and their relationship. For example, a pair of earrings given to a friend in just the right shape and size can be viewed as "he really knows me." In contrast, a toaster oven given as a Valentine's Day gift, when the recipient is expecting a more "intimate" gift, can mean the deterioration of a relationship.[51] Still further, researchers who have explored the gender of gift givers and their feelings about same-sex gifting (female to female or male to male) and opposite-sex gifting (male to female or female to male) have found that both male and female gift givers feel more comfortable in giving gifts to the same sex; however, they also reported that they felt more intense feeling with respect to gifts given to members of the opposite sex.[52] Additionally, although females get more pleasure than males from giving gifts and generally play the dominant role in gift exchanges, both sexes are strongly motivated by feelings of obligation.[53] Still further, research has also found that interpersonal gifting can be the cause of "gifting anxiety" (which is related to social anxiety) on the part of the givers, the recipients, and the gifting situations themselves.[54] Knowledge of such gender differences are useful for marketers to know because it implies that additional support might be appreciated at the point of purchase (while in a store) when a consumer is considering a gift for an opposite-sex recipient. Table 16-10 presents a picture of the dynamics of the gift continuum in Hong Kong. Note how a number of issues associated with the gift, such as risk, emotional expectations, and the "why," vary across the four categories of gifts. For example, a gift given to a "romantic other" involves a high emotional expectation, but one given to a friend has a low emotional expectation.[55]

One study examined mothers giving gifts to their children (*interpersonal gifting*) across three different cultures: (1) Anglo-Celtic (mothers born in Australia), (2) Sino-Vietnamese (mothers born in Vietnam), and (3) Israeli (mothers born in Israel).[56] Whereas in all three of these cultures the mother plays a central role in family gift

---

TABLE 16-10 **The Dynamics of a Gift Continuum in Hong Kong**

WHO	ROMANTIC OTHER	CLOSE FRIENDS	JUST FRIENDS	HI/BYE FRIENDS
Chinese Terminology	*Sui Iáih maht*	*Yihhei*	*Renqing*	*Guanxi*
When (examples)	(1) Birthday Gift	(1) Birthday Gift	(1) Birthday Gift	(1) Birthday Gift
	(2) Special Occasions (e.g., Valentine's Day)	(2) Special Occasions (e.g., leaving on a trip)	(2) Maintenance Gift (e.g., souvenir from a trip)	
	(3) Spontaneous (e.g., small gifts)	(3) Spontaneous (e.g., special awards)		
	(4) Formal/Ceremonial (e.g., Mid-Autumn Festival)	(4) Formal/Ceremonial (e.g., New Year)		
Type of Gift	Expressive	Expressive	Expressive/Instrumental	Instrumental
Emotional Expectations	High	High	Medium	Low
Selection Criteria	Inexpensive (early) Expensive (later) No Gift (family)	Mostly Expensive	Somewhat Expensive	Inexpensive
Effort in Selection	Match Needs (e.g., jewelry)	Match Needs (e.g., desired clothing)	Typical Gift (e.g., having meal)	Typical Gift (e.g., birthday card)
Token Gift (Interim)	Often	Often	Occasionally	Occasionally
Why	Win Hearts	Care	Care/Build Network	Build Network
Face	Social (early) Moral (later)	Moral	Mostly Social	Social
Risks	Guilt/Shame	Guilt/Shame	Loss of Face	Loss of Face

Source: Annamma Joy, "Gift Giving in Hong Kong and the Continuum of Social Ties," *Journal of Consumer Research*, 28, September 2001, 244. Reprinted by permission of the publisher.

TABLE 16-11 Major Differences between Gift-Giving Behavior of Anglo-Celtic, Sino-Vietnamese, and Israeli Mothers

GIFT-GIVING ELEMENTS	ANGLO-CELTIC MOTHERS	SINO-VIETNAMESE MOTHERS	ISRAELI MOTHERS
1. Motivation			
Justification	Short-term goals	Long-term goals	Long-term/short-term goals
Significance	Prestige gifts	Practical gifts	Importance to recipient
	Birthday gifts	Lucky money	
Timing	Special occasions (e.g., birthdays, Christmas)	Chinese New Year and academic reward	Birthdays and general needs
2. Selection			
Involvement	High priority	Low priority	Low priority
	Social and psychological risks	Financial risks	
Family Influences	Children	Mother	Mother dominant with younger children and influenced by older children
Promotional Influences	Status symbols	Sale items	Sale items
Gift Attributes	Quality	Price	Price
	Money unsuitable	Money suitable	Money suitable
3. Presentation			
Presentation Messages	Immediate self-gratification	Delayed self-gratification	Immediate self-gratification
Allocation Messages	Multiple gifts	Single gifts	Single gifts
	Mothers favored	Eldest child favored	
Understanding of Messages	Always	Not always	Never
4. Reaction			
Achievement	Often	Most of the time	Never
Feedback	More expressive	Less expressive	Least expressive
Usage	Often private	Often shared	Never shared

Source: Constance Hill and Celia T. Romm, "The Role of Mothers as Gift Givers: A Comparison Across Three Cultures," in *Advances in Consumer Research,* 23, ed. Kim P. Corfman and John G. Lynch, Jr. (Provo, UT: Association for Consumer Research, 1996), 26. Reprinted by permission.

giving, Table 16-11 presents the major differences among these groups. For instance, when it comes to gift giving, Anglo-Celtic mothers were found to be motivated to select status or prestige gifts, whereas Sino-Vietnamese mothers were likely to pick practical gifts, and Israeli mothers tended to select gifts that they felt would be important to the recipient. Examine the table for other differences.

Intrapersonal gifting, or a self-gift (also called "monadic giving"), occurs when the giver and the receiver are the same individual.[57] To some extent a self-gift is a "state of mind." If a consumer sees a purchase as the "buying of something I need," then it is simply a purchase. On the other hand, if the same consumer sees the same purchase as a "self-gift," then it is something special, with special meaning. Consumers may treat themselves to self-gifts that are products (clothing, compact disks, or jewelry), services (hair styling, restaurant meals, spa membership), or expe-

TABLE 16-12 Reported Circumstances and Motivations for Self-Gift Behavior

CIRCUMSTANCES	MOTIVATIONS
Personal accomplishment	To reward oneself
Feeling down	To be nice to oneself
Holiday	To cheer oneself up
Feeling stressed	To fulfill a need
Have some extra money	To celebrate
Need	To relieve stress
Had not bought for self in a while	To maintain a good feeling
Attainment of a desired goal	To provide an incentive toward a goal
Others	Others

Source: David Glen Mick and Mitchelle DeMoss, "To Me from Me: A Descriptive Phenomenology of Self-Gifts," in *Advances in Consumer Research,* 23. Marvin E. Goldberg, Gerald Gorn, and Richard W. Pollay, ed. (Provo, UT: Association for Consumer Research, 1990), 677–682. Reprinted by permission.

riences (socializing with friends).[58] For example, while purchasing holiday gifts for others, some consumers find themselves in stores that they might not otherwise visit or find themselves looking at merchandise (such as a scarf) that they want but would not ordinarily buy.[59] Such intrapersonal gifts have their own special range of meaning and context. Table 16-12 illustrates specific circumstances and motivations that might lead a consumer to engage in self-gift behavior. Research focusing on college students' self-gifting behavior found that when they had the money to spend and when they either felt good or wished to cheer themselves up, they were particularly likely to purchase self-gifts.[60]

Finally, Table 16-13 summarizes the five gifting behavior subdivisions explored earlier.

TABLE 16-13 Gifting Relationship Categories: Definitions and Examples

GIFTING RELATIONSHIP	DEFINITION	EXAMPLE
Intergroup	A group giving a gift to another group	A Christmas gift from one family to another family
Intercategory	An individual giving a gift to a group or a group giving a gift to an individual	A group of friends chips in to buy a new mother a baby gift
Intragroup	A group giving a gift to itself or its members	A family buys a VCR for itself as a Christmas gift
Interpersonal	An individual giving a gift to another individual	Valentine's Day chocolates presented from a boyfriend to a girlfriend
Intrapersonal	Self-gift	A woman buys herself jewelry to cheer herself up

Source: Adapted from Deborah Y. Cohn and Leon G. Schiffman, "Gifting: A Taxonomy of Private Realm Giver and Recipient Relationships," Working Paper, City University of New York, Baruch College, 1996, 2.

Beyond the Decision: Consuming and Possessing

Historically, the emphasis in consumer behavior studies has been on product, service, and brand choice decisions. As shown throughout this book, however, there are many more facets to consumer behavior. The experience of using products and services, as well as the sense of pleasure derived from *possessing, collecting,* or *consuming* "things" and "experiences" (mechanical watches, old fountain pens, or a baseball card collection) contributes to consumer satisfaction and overall quality of life. These consumption outcomes or experiences, in turn, affect consumers' future decision processes.

Thus, given the importance of possessions and experiences, a broader perspective of consumer behavior might view consumer choices as the beginning of a **consumption process,** not merely the end of a consumer decision-making effort. In this context, the choice or purchase decision is an *input* into a process of consumption. The input stage includes the establishment of a *consumption set* (an assortment or portfolio of products and their attributes) and a *consuming style* (the "rules" by which the individual or household fulfills consumption requirements). The *process* stage of a simple model of consumption might include (from the consumer's perspective) the *using, possessing* (or having), *collecting,* and *disposing* of things and experiences. The output stage of this process would include changes in a wide range of feelings, moods, attitudes, and behavior, as well as reinforcement (positive or negative) of a particular lifestyle (e.g., a devotion to physical fitness), enhancement of a sense of self, and the level of consumer satisfaction and quality of life.[61] Figure 16-5 presents a simple *model of consumption* that reflects the ideas discussed here and throughout the book.

FIGURE 16-5

A Simple Model of Consumption

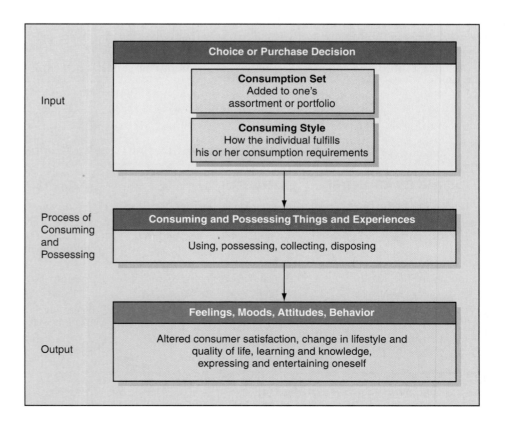

PRODUCTS HAVE SPECIAL MEANING AND MEMORIES

Consuming is a diverse and complex concept.[62] It includes the simple utility derived from the continued use of a superior toothpaste, the stress reduction of an island holiday, the stored memories of a video reflecting one's childhood, the "sacred" meaning or "magic" of a grandparent's wristwatch, the symbol of membership gained from wearing a school tie, the pleasure and sense of accomplishment that comes from building a model airplane, and the fun and even financial rewards that come from collecting almost anything (even jokers from decks of cards). In fact, one man's hobby of collecting old earthenware drain tiles has become the Mike Weaver Drain Tile Museum.[63] There are special possessions that consumers resist replacing, even with an exact replica, because the replica cannot possibly hold the same meaning as the orginal. Such possessions are often tied, in the consumer's mind, to a specific physical time or person.[64]

Consider how some consumers have a fascination with Swatch watches. For example, there is the story of how one woman hid in a department store for the lunch shift, so that the person filling in at the Swatch counter would sell her a second Swatch watch, or the man who paid someone $100 to stand in line overnight in front of a New York City food store where 999 special edition Swatch watches were to go on sale the next morning. Such collecting can be "both rational and irrational, deliberate and uncontrollable, cooperative and competitive, passive and aggressive, and tension producing and tension reducing."[65] In fact, with respect to Swatch watches, the company has changed its "limited-edition" strategy from offering 30,000 pieces worldwide to now offering certain designs in only a single outlet.[66]

Some possessions (such as photographs, souvenirs, trophies, and everyday objects) serve to assist consumers in their effort to create "personal meaning" and to maintain a sense of the past, which is essential to having a sense of self.[67] For instance, objects of the past are often acquired and retained intentionally (some become antiques or even heirlooms) to memorialize pleasant or momentous times and people in one's past.

Why are some consumers so interested in the past? It has been suggested that nostalgia permits people to maintain their identity after some major change in their life. This nostalgia can be based on family and friends; on objects such as toys, books, jewelry, and cars; or on special events, such as graduations, weddings, and holidays.[68] Providing the triple benefits of a sense of nostalgia, the fun of collecting, and the attraction of a potential return on investment, there is a strong interest in collecting Barbie® dolls. It is estimated that there are currently more than 100,000 Barbie doll collectors, who are dedicated to hunting down rare and valuable Barbie dolls to add to their collections.

And it appears that you're never too young to start collecting, as evidenced by the following story about a child that started collecting at the age of 2:[69]

> Cars have always interested Kevin LaLuzerne, a fifth-grader at Oakhurst Elementary in Largo. He has boxes and boxes of Hot Wheels, Micro Machines and other cars—more than 600! He started collecting them when he was just 2, and he still enjoys seeing all of the different cars and trucks he has collected over the years. He even has a "Weinermobile," the Oscar Meyer hot dog car. Kevin's newest addition to his collection is a limited-edition Chevron car that has a cartoon mouth, eyes and ears.

There is even a Web site devoted to kids who collect, which includes "An A to Z Guide to What Kids Can Collect" (**www.countrycollector.com/kids.html**).[70]

At the other end of the age continuum, older consumers are often faced with the issue of how they should dispose of such special possessions. Indeed, in the past several years, a number of researchers have examined this subject area. Sometimes it is some precipitating event, such as the death of a spouse, illness, or moving out of one's home (to a nursing home or retirement community), that gets the consumer thinking about the disposition of his or her possessions. Often the older person wants to pass a family legacy on to a child, ensure a good home for a cherished collection, and/or influence the lives of others. The aim is not to "sell" the items, because they could do that themselves.[71]

Relationship Marketing

Many firms have established **relationship marketing** programs (sometimes called *loyalty programs*) to foster usage loyalty and a commitment to their company's products and services. Relationship marketing is exceedingly logical when we realize credit card research has shown that "75 percent of college students keep their first card for 15 years, and 60 percent keep that card for life."[72] This kind of loyalty is enhanced by relationship marketing, which at its heart is all about building *trust* (between the firm and its customers) and keeping *promises* ("making promises," "enabling promises," and "keeping promises" on the part of the firm and, possibly, on the part of the customer).[73]

Indeed, it is the aim of relationship marketing to create strong, lasting relationships with a core group of customers. The emphasis is on developing long-term bonds with customers by making them feel good about how the company interacts (or does business) with them and by giving them some kind of personal connection to the business. A review of the composition of 66 consumer relationship marketing programs revealed three elements shared by more than 50 percent of the programs. They are (1) fostering ongoing communication with customers (73 percent of the programs); (2) furnishing loyalty by building in extras like upgrades and other perks (68 percent of the programs); and (3) stimulating a sense of belonging by providing a "club membership" format (50 percent of the programs).[74] A real relationship marketing program is more than the use of database marketing tactics to better target customers—the consumer must feel that he or she has received something for being a participant in the relationship.[75] In a positive vein, businesses have been finding that the Internet is an inexpensive, efficient, and more productive way to extend customer services.[76] This has resulted in the new phrase "permission marketing" to enter our vocabularies. It is the "art of asking consumers if they would like to receive a targeted e-mail ad, promotion, or message *before* it appears in their in-box." The opposite tact, sending a consumer spam and offering the option to "Click here to opt out," annoys consumers and is not permission marketing.[77]

An analogy can be drawn between two individuals who build an interpersonal relationship and the type of relationship marketers attempt to build between the company (or its products) and the consumer. Like personal relationships between individuals who are willing to do favors for each other, relationship marketers offer loyal customers special services, discounts, increased communications, and attention beyond the core product or service, *without* expecting an immediate payback (see Figure 16-6). However, they are hoping that, over time, they will reap the advantages of sustained and increasing transactions with a core group of loyal customers. Jaguar, for example, two years prior to opening its South Coast Jaguar dealership in the midst of the biggest luxury car market in the United States (Orange County, California), started underwriting fund-raising events for local charities and targeting about 500 leading philanthropists and business executives who live in the area. According to the head of the South Coast project for Jaguar, the marketing opportunity was seen as follows:[78]

> *It's not about bricks and mortar, or even about cars. It's about the overall experience. These are people who can afford to buy all the luxury goods they want. What we have set out to do is to create a retail experience that they cannot buy—one that shows them how important they are. Everything else will flow from that.*

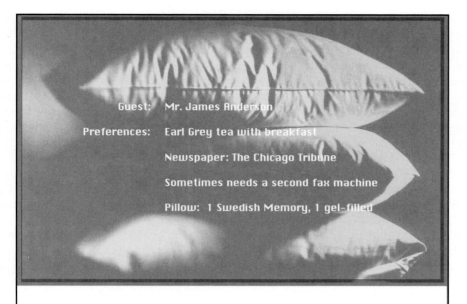

FIGURE 16-6

Ad Promoting a Firm's
Consumer Relationship
Program
Courtesy of Manhattan East
Suite Hotels.

WE DON'T JUST PUT CHOCOLATE ON THE PILLOW.
WE REMEMBER WHICH PILLOW TO PUT UNDER THE CHOCOLATE.

Imagine a hotel that offers 10 types of pillows, and remembers the one
you prefer. That's the kind of personal attention that makes staying at The Benjamin
so comfortable. In a classic building restored to its 1927 grandeur, this new
hotel offers you the perfect marriage of elegance and intimacy.

For conducting business, each spacious room or suite is equipped with all of
the state-of-the-art amenities that today's busy executive needs. And for pleasure,
An American Place restaurant beckons, as does a relaxing treatment from the
Woodstock Spa—both the perfect precursors to a night of restful comfort.

For reservations and information, call your travel counselor or 1-888-4-BENJAMIN.

INTRODUCING

THE BENJAMIN
AN EXECUTIVE SUITE HOTEL

125 East 50th Street, New York, New York 10022 ♦ 212.320.8002 ♦ Fax: 212.465.3697 ♦ www.thebenjamin.com
Manhattan East Suite Hotels

Although direct marketing, sales promotion, and general advertising may be
used as part of a relationship marketing strategy, relationship marketing stresses
long-term commitment to the individual customer. Advances in technology (such
as UPC scanning equipment, and relational databases) have provided techniques
that make tracking customers simpler, thus influencing the trend toward relationship marketing. Indeed, Wal-Mart's database is second in size only to the database
of the U.S. government.[79] Still further, a recent study suggests that relationship
marketing programs are more likely to succeed if the product or service is one that

buyers consider to be high involvement due to its association with financial, social, or physical risk.[80]

Relationship marketing programs have been used in a wide variety of product and service categories. Many companies call their relationship programs a club, and some even charge a fee to join. Membership in a club may serve as a means to convey to customers the notions of permanence and exclusivity inherent in a committed relationship. Additionally, those firms that charge a fee (such as the American Express Platinum card) increase customers' investment in the relationship that may, in turn, lead to greater commitment to the relationship and increased usage loyalty.

Airlines and major hotel chains, in particular, use relationship marketing techniques by awarding points to frequent customers that can be used to obtain additional goods or services from the company. This kind of point system may act as an exit barrier because starting a new relationship would mean giving up the potential future value of the points and starting from ground zero with a new service provider. Moreover, companies have recently been broadening the scope of such relationship programs. For example, Table 16-14 lists the many products and services offered to participants in the American Airlines AAdvantage Mileage Program.

Ultimately, it is to a firm's advantage to develop long-term relationships with existing customers because it is easier and less expensive to make an additional sale to an existing customer than to make a new sale to a new consumer.[81] This is why, for example, Lands' End tells consumers that if they are not 100 percent satisfied with their purchase, they can return it at any time, for any reason.[82] However, the effort involved in developing and maintaining a customer relationship must be weighed against the expected long-term benefits. Marketers must determine the lifetime value of a customer to ensure that the costs of obtaining, servicing, and communicating with the customer do not exceed the potential profits.[83] Recent research also suggests that a consumer's participation in a relationship marketing program is

TABLE 16-14 A Broad-Based Relationship Program

AIRLINES	**HOTELS** *continued*
Canadian Airlines International	Inter-Continental Hotels
Cathay Pacific Airlines	ITT Sheraton Hotels, Inns, Resorts, and All-Suites
Hawaiian Airlines	Marriott Hotels, Resorts, and Suites
Qantas Airways	Vista Hotels
Keno Air	Wyndham Hotels & Resorts
Singapore Airlines	
TWA	**CAR RENTAL**
US Airways	Avis Rent A Car
	Hertz
HOTELS	
Conrad Hotels	**OTHER**
Forte Hotels	Citibank AAdvantage Visa or MasterCard application
Forum Hotels	MCI Long-Distance
Hilton Hotels & Resorts	American AAdvantage Money Market Fund
Hilton International Hotels	The American Traveler Catalog
Holiday Inns	

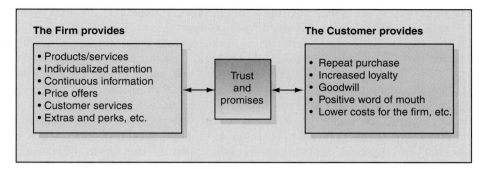

The Firm provides		The Customer provides
• Products/services • Individualized attention • Continuous information • Price offers • Customer services • Extras and perks, etc.	Trust and promises	• Repeat purchase • Increased loyalty • Goodwill • Positive word of mouth • Lower costs for the firm, etc.

FIGURE 16-7

A Portrayal of the Characteristics of Relationship Marketing

Source: In part, this portrayal was inspired by: Mary Long, Leon Schiffman, and Elaine Sherman, "Understanding the Relationships in Consumer Marketing Relationship Programs: A Content Analysis," in *Proceedings of the World Marketing Congress* VII-II, eds. K. Grant and Walker (Melbourne, Australia: Academy of Marketing Science, 1995), 10/27–10/26.

not only based on past and present experiences but also incorporates expected future usage and expected future satisfaction levels with the program.[84] Figure 16-7 portrays some of the characteristics of the relationship between the firm and the customer within the spirit of relationship marketing.

Why is relationship marketing so important? Research indicates that consumers today are less loyal than in the past, due to six major forces: (1) the abundance of choice, (2) availability of information, (3) entitlement (consumers repeatedly ask "What have you done for me lately?"), (4) commoditization (most products/services appear to be similar—nothing stands out), (5) insecurity (consumer financial problems reduce loyalty), and (6) time scarcity (not enough time to be loyal). These six forces result in consumer defections, complaints, cynicism, reduced affiliation, greater price sensitivity, and litigiousness.[85] Consequently, relationship programs that can retain customers are a vital part of a company's marketing program.

Summary

The consumer's decision to purchase or not to purchase a product or service is an important moment for most marketers. It can signify whether a marketing strategy has been wise, insightful, and effective, or whether it was poorly planned and missed the mark. Thus, marketers are particularly interested in the consumer's decision-making process. For a consumer to make a decision, more than one alternative must be available. (The decision not to buy is also an alternative.)

Theories of consumer decision making vary, depending on the researcher's assumptions about the nature of humankind. The various models of consumers (economic view, passive view, cognitive view, and emotional view) depict consumers and their decision-making processes in distinctly different ways.

An overview consumer decision-making model ties together the psychological, social, and cultural concepts examined in Parts II and III into an easily understood framework. This decision model has three sets of variables: input variables, process variables, and output variables.

Input variables that affect the decision-making process include commercial marketing efforts, as well as noncommercial influences from the consumer's sociocultural environment. The decision process variables are influenced by the consumer's psychological field, including the evoked set (or the brands in a particular product category considered in making a purchase choice). Taken as a whole, the psychological field influences the consumer's recognition of a need, prepurchase search for information, and evaluation of alternatives.

The output phase of the model includes the actual purchase (either trial or repeat purchase) and postpurchase evaluation. Both prepurchase and postpurchase evaluation feeds back in the form of experience into the consumer's psychological field and serves to influence future decision processing.

The process of gift exchange is an important part of consumer behavior. Various gift-giving and gift-receiving relationships are captured by the following five specific categories in the gifting classification scheme: (1) intergroup gifting (a group gives a gift to another group); (2) intercategory gifting (an individual gives a gift to a group or a group gives a gift to an individual); (3) intragroup gifting (a group gives a gift to itself or its members); (4) interpersonal gifting (an individual gives a gift to another individual); and (5) intrapersonal gifting (a self-gift).

Consumer behavior is not just making a purchase decision or the act of purchasing; it also includes the full range of experiences associated with using or consuming products and services. It also includes the sense of pleasure and satisfaction derived from possessing or collecting "things." The outputs of consumption are changes in feelings, moods, or attitudes; reinforcement of lifestyles; an enhanced sense of self; satisfaction of a consumer-related need; belonging to groups; and expressing and entertaining oneself.

Among other things, consuming includes the simple utility of using a superior product, the stress reduction of a vacation, the sense of having a "sacred" possession, and the pleasures of a hobby or a collection. Some possessions serve to assist consumers in their effort to create personal meaning and to maintain a sense of the past.

Relationship marketing impacts consumers' decisions and their consumption satisfaction. Firms establish relationship marketing programs (sometimes called loyalty programs) to foster usage loyalty and a commitment to their products and services. At its heart, relationship marketing is all about building trust (between the firm and its customers), and keeping promises made to consumers. Therefore, the emphasis in relationship marketing is almost always on developing long-term bonds with customers by making them feel special and by providing them with personalized services.

Discussion Questions

1. Compare and contrast the economic, passive, cognitive, and emotional models of consumer decision making.

2. What kinds of marketing and sociocultural inputs would influence the purchase of (a) a TV with a built-in VCR, (b) a concentrated liquid laundry detergent, and (c) fat-free ice cream? Explain your answers.

3. Define extensive problem solving, limited problem solving, and routinized response behavior. What are the differences among the three decision-making approaches? What type of decision process would you expect most consumers to follow in their first purchase of a new product or brand in each of the following areas: (a) chewing gum, (b) sugar, (c) men's after shave lotion, (d) carpeting, (e) paper towels, (f) a cellular telephone, and (g) a luxury car? Explain your answers.

4. a. Identify three different products that you believe require a reasonably intensive prepurchase search by a consumer. Then, using Table 16-2 as a guide, identify the specific characteristics of these products that make an intensive prepurchase search likely.

   b. For each of the products that you listed, identify the perceived risks that a consumer is likely to experience before a purchase. Discuss how the marketers of these products can reduce these perceived risks.

5. Let's assume that this coming summer you are planning to spend a month touring Europe and are, therefore, in need of a good 35-mm camera. (a) Develop a list of product attributes that you will use as the purchase criteria in evaluating various 35-mm cameras. (b) Distinguish the differences that would occur in your decision process if you were to use compensatory versus noncompensatory decision rules.

6. How can a marketer of very light, very powerful laptop computers use its knowledge of customers' expectations in designing a marketing strategy?

7. How do consumers reduce postpurchase dissonance? How can marketers provide positive reinforcement to consumers after the purchase to reduce their dissonance?

8. The Gillette Company, which produces the highly successful Sensor shaving blade, has recently introduced a clear gel antiperspirant and deodorant for men. Identify the perceived risks associated with the purchase of this new product and outline a strategy designed to reduce these perceived risks during the product's introduction.

9. Albert Einstein once wrote that "the whole of science is nothing more than a refinement of everyday thinking." Do you think that this quote applies to the development of the consumer decision-making model presented in Figure 16-2?

Exercises

1. Find two print advertisements, one that illustrates the cognitive model of consumer decision making and one that illustrates the emotional model. Explain your choices. In your view, why did the marketers choose the approaches depicted in the advertisements?

2. Describe the need recognition process that took place before you purchased your last can of soft drink. How did it differ from the process that preceded the purchase of a new pair of sneakers? What role, if any, did advertising play in your need recognition?

3. List the colleges that you considered when choosing which college or university to attend and the criteria that you used to evaluate them. Describe how you acquired information on the different colleges along the different attributes that were important to you and how you made your decision. Be sure to specify whether you used compensatory or noncompensatory decision rules.

4. Select one of the following product categories: (a) compact disk players, (b) fast-food restaurants, or (c) shampoo, and: (1) write down the brands that constitute your evoked set, (2) identify brands that are not part of your evoked set, and (3) discuss how the brands included in your evoked set differ from those that are not included in terms of important attributes.

5. Select a newspaper or magazine advertisement that attempts (a) to provide the consumer with a decision strategy to follow in making a purchase decision or (b) to reduce the perceived risk(s) associated with a purchase. Evaluate the effectiveness of the ad you selected.

Key Terms

- **Affect referral decision rule**
- **Compensatory decision rules**
- **Conjunctive decision rule**
- **Consumer decision making**
- **Consumption process**
- **Disjunctive rule**
- **Evaluation of alternatives**
- **Evoked set**
- **Extensive problem solving**

- **Gifting behavior**
- **Heuristics**
- **Inept set**
- **Inert set**
- **Information overload**
- **Lexicographic decision rule**
- **Limited problem solving**
- **Moods**
- **Need recognition**

- **Noncompensatory decision rules**
- **Postpurchase evaluation**
- **Prepurchase search**
- **Purchase behavior**
- **Relationship marketing**
- **Routinized response behavior**
- **Self-gifts**

Notes

1. Itamar Simonson, "Shoppers' Easily Influenced Choices," *New York Times,* November 6, 1994, 11.
2. John A. Howard and Jagdish N. Sheth, *The Theory of Buyer Behavior* (New York: Wiley, 1969), 46–47; see also John Howard, *Consumer Behavior in Marketing Strategy* (Upper Saddle River, NJ: Prentice Hall, 1989).
3. Herbert A. Simon, *Administrative Behavior,* 2nd ed. (New York: Free Press, 1965), 40.
4. James G. March and Herbert A. Simon, *Organizations* (New York: Wiley, 1958), 140–241.
5. Michael A. Jones, Philip J. Trocchia, and David L. Mothersbaugh, "Noneconomic Motivations for Price Haggling: An Exploratory Study," in *Advances in Consumer Research,* 24, eds. Merrie Brucks and Deborah J. MacInnis (Provo, UT: Association for Consumer Research, 1997), 388–391.
6. Richard P. Bagozzi and Utpal Dholakia, "Goal Setting and Goal Striving in Consumer Behavior," *Journal of Marketing,* 63, 1999, 19–32.
7. Meryl Paula Gardner, "Mood States and Consumer Behavior: A Critical Review," *Journal of Consumer Research,* 12, December 1985, 281–300; and Robert A. Peterson and Matthew Sauber, "A Mood Scale for Survey Research," in *1983 AMA Educators' Proceedings,* eds. Patrick E. Murphy, et al. (Chicago: American Marketing Association, 1983), 409–414.
8. Barry J. Babin, William R. Darden, and Mitch Griffin, "Some Comments on the Role of Emotions in Consumer Behavior," in *1992 AMA Educators' Proceedings,* ed. Robert P. Leone and V. Kumor et al. (Chicago: American Marketing Association, 1992), 30–39; and Patricia A. Knowles, Stephen J. Grove, and W. Jeffrey Burroughs, "An Experimental Examination of Mood Effects on Retrieval and Evaluation of Advertisement and Brand Information," *Journal of the Academy of Marketing Science,* 21, Spring 1993, 135–142.
9. Richard P. Bagozzi, Mahesh Gopinath, and Prashanth U. Nyer, "The Role of Emotions in Marketing," *Academy of Marketing Science Journal,* 27, 2, Spring 1999, 184–206; and Gardner, "Mood States and Consumer Behavior."
10. Ruth Belk Smith and Elaine Sherman, "Effects of Store Image and Mood on Consumer Behavior: A Theoretical and Empirical Analysis," in *Advances in Consumer Research,* 20, eds. Leigh McAlister and Michael L. Rothschild (Provo, UT: Association for Consumer Research, 1993), 631.
11. Knowles, Grove, and Burroughs, "An Experimental Examination."
12. Bagozzi et al., "The Role of Emotions in Marketing."
13. Gregory M. Rose, "Consumer Socialization, Parental Style, and Developmental Timetables in the United States and Japan," *Journal of Marketing,* 63, 3, July 1999, 105–119.
14. Gordon C. Bruner, II, "The Effect of Problem-Recognition Style on Information Seeking," *Journal of the Academy of Marketing Science,* 15, Winter 1987, 33–41.
15. Matthew Klein, "He Shops, She Shops," *American Demographics,* March 1998, 34–35.
16. Haim Mano and Michael T. Elliott, "Smart Shopping: The Origins and Consequences of Price Savings," in *Advances in Consumer Research,* eds. Brucks and MacInnis, 504–510.
17. Sharon E. Beatty and Scott M. Smith, "External Search Effort: An Investigation Across Several Product Categories," *Journal of Consumer Research,* 14, June 1987, 83–95.
18. Richard A. Spreng, Richard L. Divine, and Thomas J. Page, Jr., "An Empirical Examination of the Differential Effects of Objective and Subjective Knowledge on Information Processing," in *2001 AMA Educators' Proceedings,* 12, eds. Greg W. Marshall and Stephen J. Grove (Chicago: American Marketing Association, 2001), 329.
19. Ken Krizner, "Individuality Extends into Manufacturing," *Frontline Solutions,* 2, 3, March 2001, 1, 18.
20. Niranjan V. Raman, "A Qualitative Investigation of Web-Browsing Behavior," in *Advances in Consumer Research,* eds. Brucks and MacInnis, 511–516.
21. Michael D. Johnson and Donald R. Lehmann, "Consumer Experience and Consideration Sets for Brands and Product Categories," in *Advances in Consumer Research,* eds. Brucks and MacInnis, 295–300.
22. Thomas T. Semon, "Too Much Choice Not Ideal, but Not Enough Choice Likely Worse," *Marketing News,* November 5, 2001, 9.
23. Gita Venkataramani Johar, Kamel Jedidi, and Jacob Jacoby, "A Varying-Parameter Averaging Model on On-Line Brand Evaluations," *Journal of Consumer Research,* 24, September 1997, 232–247.
24. Sankar Sen and Eric J. Johnson, "Mere-Possession Effects without Possession in Consumer Choice," *Journal of Consumer Research,* 24, June 1997, 105–117.
25. Stacy L. Wood, "Remote Purchase Environments: The Influence of Return Policy Leniency on Two-Stage Decision Processes," *Journal of Marketing Research,* 38, 2, May 2001, 157–169.
26. Jeffrey F. Durgee, "Why Some Products 'Just Feel Right,' or, the Phenomenology of Product Right-

ness," in *Advances in Consumer Research,* 22, eds. Frank R. Kardes and Mita Sujan (Provo, UT: Association for Consumer Research, 1995), 650–652.

27. Laurie Peterson, "The Strategic Shopper," *Adweek's Marketing Week,* March 30, 1992, 18–20.

28. Lan Xia, "Consumer Choice Strategies and Choice Confidence in the Electronic Environment," in *1999 AMA Educators Proceedings,* 10, eds. Stephen P. Brown and D. Sudharshan (Chicago: American Marketing Association, 1999), 270–277.

29. Carey Goldberg, "Choosing the Joys of a Simplified Life," *New York Times,* September 21, 1995, C1, C9.

30. Ibid.

31. Nancy Spears, "The Time Pressured Consumer and Deal Proneness: Theoretical Framework and Empirical Evidence," in *2000 AMA Winter Educators' Conference,* 11, eds., John P. Workman and William D. Perreault (Chicago: American Marketing Association, 2000), 35–40.

32. Sandra J. Burke, "The Effects of Missing Information on Decision Strategy Selection," in *Advances in Consumer Research,* 17, eds. Marvin E. Goldberg, Gerald Gorn, and Richard W. Pollay (Provo, UT: Association for Consumer Research, 1990), 250–256.

33. Sarah Fisher Gardial and David W. Schumann, "In Search of the Elusive Consumer Inference," in *Advances in Consumer Research,* eds. Goldberg, Gorn, and Pollay, 283–287; see also Burke.

34. Ran Kivetz and Itamar Simonson, "The Effects of Incomplete Information on Consumer Choice," *Journal of Marketing Research,* 37, 4, November 2000, 427–448.

35. Barry L. Bayus, "The Consumer Durable Replacement Buyer," *Journal of Marketing,* 55, January 1991, 42–51.

36. Calmetta Coleman, "Debit Cards Look to Give Credit Cards a Run for Consumers' Money," *Wall Street Journal,* December 3, 2001, B1, B4; "Understanding Debit Cards," www.aarp.org/confacts/money/debitcards/html; and "Debit Cards," www.mcvisa.com/debi.html.

37. Diane M. Phillips, Jerry C. Olson, and Hans Baumgartner, "Consumption Visions in Consumer Decision Making," in *Advances in Consumer Research,* 22, eds. Frank R. Kardes and Mita Sujan (Provo, UT: Association for Consumer Research, 1995), 280.

38. Ibid., 280–284.

39. Diane M. Phillips, "Anticipating the Future: The Role of Consumption Visions in Consumer Behavior," in *Advances in Consumer Research,* vol. 23, eds. Kim P. Corfman and John G. Lynch, Jr. (Provo, UT: Association for Consumer Research, 1996), 70–75.

40. Baba Shiv and Joel Huber, "The Impact of Anticipating Satisfaction on Consumer Choice," *Journal of Consumer Research,* 27, 2, September 2000, 202–216.

41. Emily Booth, "Getting Inside a Shopper's Mind," *Marketing (U.K.),* June 3, 1999, 33.

42. Robert A. Peterson, Sridhar Balasubramanian, and Bart J. Bronnenberg, "Exploring the Implications of the Internet for Consumer Marketing," *Journal of the Academy of Marketing Sciences,* 25, 1997, 329–346.

43. Ernest R. Cadotte, Robert B. Woodruff, and Roger L. Jenkins, "Expectations and Norms in Models of Consumer Satisfaction," *Journal of Marketing Research,* 24, August 1987, 305–314.

44. Kare Sandvik, Kjell Gronhaug, and Frank Lindberg, "Routes to Customer Retention: The Importance of Customer Satisfaction, Performance Quality, Brand Reputation and Customer Knowledge," in *AMA Winter Conference,* eds. Debbie Thorne LeClair and Michael Hartline (Chicago: American Marketing Association, 1997), 211–217.

45. Deborah Y. Cohn and Leon G. Schiffman, "Gifting: A Taxonomy of Private Realm Giver and Recipient Relationships," Working Paper, City University of New York, Baruch College, 1996, 2.

46. Russell W. Belk and Gregory S. Coon, "Gift Giving as Agapic Love: An Alternative to the Exchange Paradigm Based on Dating Experiences," *Journal of Consumer Research,* 20, December 1993, 393–417.

47. "More Consumers Buy Gifts for Themselves Than to Give as Gifts; 'Gift Market' Is a Misnomer, Since Most Consumers Buy Gift Products for Personal Consumption," *Business Wire,* April 17, 2000, 1.

48. Michel Laroche, Gad Saad, Elizabeth Browne, Mark Cleveland, and Chankon Kim, "Determinants of In-Store Information Search Strategies Pertaining to a Christmas Gift Purchase," *Revue Canadienne des Sciences de l'Administration,* 17, 1, March 2000, 1–19.

49. Julie A. Ruth, Cele C. Otnes, and Frédéric F. Brunel, "Gift Receipt and the Reformulation of Interpersonal Relationships," *Journal of Consumer Research,* 25, March 1999, 385–402.

50. Cele Otnes, Tina M. Lowrey, and Young Chan Kim, "Gift Selection for Easy and Difficult Recipients: A Social Roles Interpretation," *Journal of Consumer Research,* 20, September 1993, 229–244.

51. John F. Sherry, "Reflections on Giftware and Giftcare: Whither Consumer Research?" in *Gift Giving: An Interdisciplinary Anthology,* eds. Cele Otnes and Richard F. Beltramini (Bowling Green, KY: Popular Press, 1996), 220.

52. Stephen J. Gould and Claudia E. Weil, "Gift-Giving and Gender Self-Concepts," *Gender Role,* 24, 1991, 617–637.

53. Cynthia Webster and Linda Nottingham, "Gender Differences in the Motivations for Gift Giving," in *2000 AMA Educators' Proceedings,* 11, eds. Gregory T. Gundlach and Patrick E. Murphy (Chicago: American Marketing Association, 2000), 272.

54. David B. Wooten, "Qualitative Steps Toward an Expanded Model of Anxiety in Gift-Giving," *Journal of Consumer Research,* 27, 1, June 2000, 84–95.

55. Annamma Joy, "Gift Giving in Hong Kong and the Continuum of Social Ties," *Journal of Consumer Research,* 28, 2, September 2001, 239–256.

56. Constance Hill and Celia T. Romm, "The Role of Mothers as Gift Givers: A Comparison Across Three Cultures," in *Advances in Consumer Research,* 23, eds. Kim P. Corfman and John G. Lynch, Jr., 21–27.

57. For a really interesting article on self-gifts, see John F. Sherry, Jr., Mary Ann McGrath, and Sidney J. Levy, "Monadic Gifting: Anatomy of Gifts Given to the Self," in *Contemporary Marketing and Consumer Behavior,* ed. John F. Sherry, Jr. (Thousand Oaks, CA: Sage, 1995), 399–432.

58. David Glen Mick and Mitchelle DeMoss, "To Me from Me: A Descriptive Phenomenology of Self-Gifts," in *Advances in Consumer Research,* ed., Goldberg, Gorn, and Pollay, 677–682; and Shay Sayre and David Horne, "I Shop, Therefore I Am: The Role of Possessions for Self-Definition," in *Advances in Consumer Research,* 23, eds. Kim P. Corfman and John G. Lynch, Jr., (Provo, UT: Association for Consumer Research, 1996), 323–328.

59. Cynthia Crossen, "'Merry Christmas to Moi,' Shoppers Say," *Wall Street Journal,* December 11, 1997, B1, B10.

60. Kim K. R. McKeage, Marsha L. Richins, and Kathleen Debevec, "Self-Gifts and the Manifestation of Material Values," in *Advances in Consumer Research,* 20, eds. Leigh McAlister and Michael L. Rothschild (Provo, UT: Association for Consumer Research, 1993), 359–364.

61. Kathleen M. Rassuli and Gilbert D. Harrell, "A New Perspective on Choice," in *Advances in Consumer Research,* eds. Goldberg, Gorn, and Pollay, 737–744.

62. For an interesting article on "consumption practices," see Douglas B. Holt, "How Consumers Consume: A Typology of Consumer Practices," *Journal of Consumer Research,* 22, June 1995, 1–16.

63. James M. Perry, "Mike Weaver Proves That Everything Can Be a Collection," *Wall Street Journal,* August 16, 1995, 1.

64. Kent Grayson and David Shulman, "Indexicality and the Verification of Irreplaceable Possessions: A Semiotic Analysis," *Journal of Consumer Research,* 27, 1, 17–30.

65. Mary M. Long and Leon G. Schiffman, "Swatch Fever: An Allegory for Understanding the Paradox of Collecting," *Psychology and Marketing,* 14, August 1997, 495–509.

66. "Nicholas Hayek Sees Affinities in Making Movies and Watches, David Evans Finds Swatch Head Stages Timely Job Switch," *The South China Morning Post (Hong Kong),* April 3, 2000, 10.

67. Russell W. Belk, "The Role of Possessions in Constructing and Maintaining a Sense of Past," in *Advances in Consumer Research,* eds. Goldberg, Gorn, and Pollay, 669–676.

68. Stacey Menzel Baker and Patricia F. Kennedy, "Death by Nostalgia: A Diagnosis of Context-Specific Cases," in *Advances in Consumer Research,* 21, eds. Chris T. Allen and Deborah Roedder John (Provo, UT: Association for Consumer Research, 1994), 169–174.

69. Andy Wright, "Oh, the Stuff We Collect Series: XPRESS," *The St. Petersburg Times,* August 30, 1999, 3D.

70. Ibid.

71. Linda L. Price, Eric J. Arnould, and Carolyn Folkman Curasi, "Older Consumers' Disposition of Special Possessions," *Journal of Consumer Research,* 27, September 2001, 2, 179–201.

72. Robert Bryce, "Here's a Course in Personal Finance 101, the Hard Way," *New York Times,* April 30, 1995, F11.

73. Susan M. Lloyd, "Toward Understanding Relationship Marketing from the Consumer's Perspective: What Relationships Are and Why Consumers Choose to Enter Them," in *2000 AMA Educators' Proceedings,* 11, eds. Gregory T. Gundlach and Patrick E. Murphy (Chicago: American Marketing Association, 2000), 12–20; Leonard L. Berry, "Relationship Marketing of Services—Growing Interest, Emerging Perspectives," *Journal of the Academy of Marketing Science* 23 (Fall 1995): 236–245; and Mary Jo Bitner, "Building Service Relationships: It's All About Promises," *Journal of the Academy of Marketing Science* 23 (Fall 1995): 246–251.

74. Mary Long, Leon Schiffman, and Elaine Sherman, "Understanding the Relationships in Consumer Marketing Relationship Programs: A Content Analysis," in *Proceedings of the World Marketing Congress VII-II,* eds. K. Grant and Walker (Melbourne, Australia: Academy of Marketing Science, 1995), 10/27–10/32.

75. Patricia A. Norberg, "Relationship Issues in Business-to-Consumer Markets," in *2001 AMA Educators' Proceedings,* 12, eds. Greg W. Marshall and Stephen J. Grove (Chicago: American Marketing Association, 2001), 381–390.

76. Marc E. Duncan, "The Internet and Relationship Marketing: A Framework for Application," in *2000 AMA Winter Educators' Conference,* 11, eds. John P. Workman and William D. Perreault (Chicago: American Marketing Association, 2000), 72–82.

77. Lauren Barack, "Pretty, Pretty, Please," *Business 2.0,* April 2000, 176–180.

78. John O'Dell, "Advertising & Marketing; Jaguar Is Talking Relationships; Luxury Car Maker Is Wooing

South O.C.'s Elite Before New Dealership Is Built," *The Los Angeles Times,* June 10, 1999, 1.

79. Emily Nelson, "Why Wal-Mart Sings, 'Yes, We Have Bananas,' " *Wall Street Journal,* October 6, 1998, B1, B4.

80. Mary Ellen Gordon and Kim McKeage, "Relationship Marketing Effectiveness: Differences between Women in New Zealand and the United States," in *1997 AMA Educators' Proceedings,* eds. William M. Pride and G. Tomas M. Hult (Chicago: American Marketing Association, 1997), 117–122.

81. Jagdish N. Sheth and Atul Parvatiyar, "Relationship Marketing in Consumer Marketing: Antecedents and Consequences," *Journal of the Academy of Marketing Science,* 23, Fall 1995, 255–271.

82. Barbara B. Stern, "Advertising Intimacy: Relationship Marketing and the Services Consumer," *Journal of Advertising,* 26, Winter 1997, 7–19.

83. Robert F. Dwyer, "Customer Lifetime Valuation to Support Marketing Decision Making," *Journal of Direct Marketing,* 3, 1989, 8–15; Jonathan R. Copulsky and Michael J. Wolf, "Relationship Marketing: Positioning for the Future," *The Journal of Business Strategy,* July–August 1990, 16–20; and Philip Kotler, "Marketing's New Paradigm: What's Really Happening Out There," *Planning Review,* September–October 1992, 50–52.

84. Katherine N. Lemon, Tiffany Barnett White, and Russell S. Winer, "Dynamic Customer Relationship Management; Incorporating Future Considerations into the Service Retention Decision," *Journal of Marketing,* 66, 1, January 2002, 1–14.

85. Steve Schriver, "Customer Loyalty: Going, Going. . . ," *American Demographics,* September 1997, 20–23.

1

Introduction

Case One: Digitization = Customization

The marketing concept states that companies must focus on consumer needs and develop products and services that meet these needs. Market segmentation and targeting—the strategic approaches that originate in the marketing concept—enable marketers to subdivide large markets into distinct consumer segments with relatively homogeneous needs and to select one or more of these groups as the target market(s) for the companies' offerings.

Broadly speaking, the premise of the marketing concept is the delivery of products geared to individual needs, a strategy seemingly congruent with such promotional slogans as "Have It Your Way" and "You're the Boss." In reality, however, the products offered by companies that moved from mass production (i.e., a single version of the product for all consumers) to market-focused strategies were not truly personalized products. Marketing-oriented companies offered consumers numerous versions and models of their products, each designed to meet the needs of a distinct, but still rather large, group of individual consumers.

Now, for the first time ever, digital technologies enable marketers to truly customize many products to the specific and individual needs of customers. For example:

1. *Dell Computer Corporation offers build-to-order computer systems at* www.dell.com *where consumers can design their own notebook or desktop PCs.*
2. *Based on a nutritional analysis at* www.acumins.com, *the company offers customers "Custom Packaged Nutritional Supplements" that can be quickly priced and shipped.*
3. *At* www.nikeid.com *buyers can choose among many models of sneakers in different price ranges, customize their chosen shoes from among several colors and features, have a personal ID applied to each shoe, pay for the product, and have it shipped directly to them.*
4. *The Wall Street Journal (*www.wsj.com*), as well as many other newspapers, offers readers customized, online editions of feature articles arranged according to the interests of individual readers.*

Questions

1. Will the marketing concept (as discussed in Chapter 1) become an obsolete concept as more and more companies adopt the kind of customization strategies illustrated in this case? Explain your answer.

2. Select a product or industry (other than the ones featured here) for which, in your view, product customization is impractical but market segmentation and targeting are advisable. Explain your answer.

Case Two: The Growth of "Personal TV"

The digital revolution has had a profound impact on consumer behavior and on marketing. One area in which technology is rapidly changing long-established behavior is TV viewing. For example, the TiVo digital recorder and service allow viewers to control what they watch on TV, when they watch it, and whether or not to watch the commercials for which marketers spend billions of dollars per year. The TiVo recorder downloads programming information and allows users to record many hours of TV programming onto a hard drive. Users can program the recorder by topic or a keyword and easily play back selected segments. In addition, users of the product can "pause live TV" when they want to take a short break from watching a live broadcast and then resume watching at the same place where they had stopped watching and use "thumbs up" and "thumbs down" buttons to indicate how much they liked or disliked what they were watching. TiVo records these preferences and then suggests programs that these viewers may want to watch. Users can hit a single button for preprogrammed quick skips of strings of TV commercials.

ReplayTV 4000 is similar to TiVo. Like TiVo, the product allows viewers to skip commercials when viewing recorded programs. It has no "thumbs up/down" buttons but its "quick skip" feature is a bit more advanced than TiVo's. Unlike TiVo, ReplayTV 4000 also allows viewers to share programs with others over the Internet. However, sending a high-quality video via the Internet, even over a high-speed connection, takes a very long time and is currently impractical for most consumers. ReplayTV 4000 also allows a recorded program to be stored on a VHS tape that can be shared with others, which is similar to any program recorded on a standard VCR. At present, SonicBlue—the manufacturer of ReplayTV 4000—is in the middle of a lawsuit. The legal action, brought by numerous media companies representing TV networks and movie studios, alleges that ReplayTV contributes to copyright infringement.

Questions

1. Because TiVo and ReplayTV are shifting the power over viewing behavior from the broadcaster to the viewer, should broadcasters develop their own TiVo-like systems?

2. Should broadcasters try to block the sales of such devices legally on the grounds that they contribute to copyright infringement? Or should they develop business models centered on viewers paying for content? In your answer, be sure to describe the threats and opportunities that the new recording devices and services represent for the TV networks and advertisers.

2

Consumer Research

Case One: Using Secondary Data in Targeting Consumers

The importance and strategic value of secondary data are discussed in the text. Today, thanks to technology, high-quality secondary marketing data are readily available to marketing students and educators. For example, Mediamark Research Inc. is a well-known provider of specialized, syndicated secondary data describing the audiences of selected media. The company also provides online access to some of its data through its MRI+ service.

In this hands-on case, we would like you to use some of Mediamark's secondary data. First, in order to use the data, you must register for free with Mediamark at **www.mriplus.com**.

After you register and your user status is activated, sign in and go to "Create Reports." Then, under "Pocketpieces," select "MRI—Magazine Pocketpiece." Check all of the data categories in the "Select Data to Display" window. Then select up to five magazines that you read or are familiar with and generate Pocketpiece Reports for them. You can then download these reports as Excel files.

Then obtain recent copies of the magazines for which you selected the MRI reports and make a list of all the products and brands featured in full-page ads in these publications. You now have the two sets of data needed to complete this case study.

Questions

1. In general, are the products prominently advertised in each magazine consistent or inconsistent with the magazine's MRI audience profile? Explain your answers.

2. Rather than relying on MRI's data, should the marketers of the products you selected collect their own data about the audiences of magazines in which they

want to advertise their offerings? Why or why not? In your answer, be sure to describe the advantages and limitations of relying on secondary research data in making strategic marketing decisions.

Case Two: Privacy Issues in Consumer Research

Sales and marketing teams have more access to consumer data than any other organizational units. Furthermore, as more and more consumers purchase products online and fill out the virtual registration forms needed to gain access to additional information about products and services, marketers collect increasingly more data about consumers more easily and inexpensively than ever before. Thus, protecting consumers' privacy is a key issue today in doing business.

Undoubtedly, more federal laws protecting consumers' privacy are yet to come. Recently, the Federal Trade Commission (FTC) has used existing laws to pursue companies that violate consumers' rights. For example, DoubleClick.com sells services to advertisers. After it bought an off-line seller of consumer data, DoubleClick was in a position to offer its clients 100,000 unique profiles of customers, including real-world identities and contact information. Then advertisers who use DoubleClick's targeting software in their Web sites could track the behavior of consumers whom they can also identify through the profiles they purchased from DoubleClick. DoubleClick was not forthcoming in announcing its plans to provide tools for merging online and off-line consumer data to its clients; it also maintained that it was a business-to-business company that did not interact with consumers. In early 2000, the FTC began investigating DoubleClick's deceptive data-handling practices, causing a major decline in the price of the company's stock.

GeoCities.com provides personalized Web sites for individuals (it is now part of Yahoo!). Several years ago, although its policy statement declared that the company would not share information about its consumers without their permission, the company released customers' responses to the virtual registration forms, including key customers' demographics and interests, to business partners and advertisers. The FTC charged the company with engaging in deceptive practices. Luckily for the company, GeoCities escaped penalties by simply changing its policy to reflect its practices.

Questions

1. Visit three Web sites where you were asked to provide some sort of personal data in order to gain access to information or to purchase products online. Do these sites have clearly stated and believable consumer privacy policies? Why or why not?

2. Do you believe that most consumers are ready to sacrifice some of their privacy for the convenience of shopping online? Explain your answer. Also, how can companies balance online consumers' desire to maintain privacy while also utilizing online buying and gaining access to product information?

Source: Mark McMaster, "Too Close for Comfort," *Sales & Marketing Management,* July 2001, 42–48.

3

Market Segmentation

Case One: A Muscle Car for Middle Age

Although many young adults may mourn the death of the Chevrolet Camaro, many middle-aged drivers would like to own a vehicle with Camaro-type power but are unwilling to put up with a harsh ride and the difficulty associated with getting in and out of such a low-slung vehicle. For the Mercury division of Ford Motor Company (www.mercuryvehicles.com), cars bearing its brand typically are about as far from a Camaro as you can get. The average age of a Mercury buyer is 62, with buyers of the Mercury Grand Marquis sedan averaging 69 years of age.

In an attempt to woo younger buyers, in 2003 Mercury plans to offer a version of its Grand Marquis sedan called the Marauder. The car, available only in black (with a charcoal interior), comes equipped with a 302-horsepower V8 engine, four-speed automatic transmission, antilock brakes, rear wheel drive, 18-inch wheels with speed-rated tires, and a performance handling suspension. To provide a high level of interior comfort, the vehicle also has power adjustable pedals and both front passenger seats are equipped with eight-way power adjustments, including power lumbar support.

Question

1. Considering all of the different bases for segmenting a market, which base is being addressed by Mercury with the introduction of the Grand Marquis Marauder sedan?

Source: Jean Halliday, "Muscle Car for Mercury," *Advertising Age,* July 8, 2002, 3, 40; and www.mercuryvehicles.com.

Case Two: Is There Such a Thing as Women's Toothpaste?

Crest, which for many years was the Procter & Gamble (P&G) market share leader in toothpaste, was recently overtaken by Colgate-Palmolive. In an effort to regain its leadership position in this important personal care product category, Procter & Gamble has recently introduced Crest Rejuvenating Effects toothpaste and has spent about $50 million for this new-product rollout.

What makes Crest Rejuvenating Effects toothpaste unique? Well, even P&G will admit that the product does not functionally do anything particularly new or different. However, it is the first toothpaste that is specifically targeted to women. Other personal care product companies have for many years offered brands for women, such as Secret deodorant and the Venus women's razor. But this is the first time that a toothpaste has been marketed to only women.

The primary target for this product is the 30- to 44-year-old woman. In order to reach this group, the teal-toned toothpaste is marketed in a teal tube, inside a "glimmering pearlescent box." The taste of the toothpaste includes hints of vanilla and cinnamon, and in the mouth the product produces a mild tingling sensation that P&G hopes users will associate with fresh breath and healthy gums.

Question

1. Which VALs segments, if any, do you feel would be most likely to purchase Crest Rejuvenating Effects toothpaste?

Source: Jack Neff, "Crest Spinoff Targets Women," *Advertising Age,* June 3, 2002, 1, 53.

CHAPTER FOUR

4

Consumer Motivation

Case One: The Product Collection at New Product Works

The essence of the marketing concept is understanding consumer needs and developing products that meet these needs effectively. And yet, every year scores of new products are withdrawn from the market after being introduced; many other products also "fail" when their sales fall short of the revenues needed to cover their development costs and also generate profits. Clearly, understanding consumer needs is a complex issue.

Most of the new products introduced, including failed products, fall within the product categories sold in supermarkets—including food, beverage, household maintenance, personal care, baby care, and other categories. In an effort to pinpoint causes of product failures in these areas, an organization named New Product Works maintains a vast collection of food, beverage, household, and personal care products that were introduced and subsequently withdrawn from the marketplace at **www.newproductworks.com**.

The objective of New Product Works is to provide grounded-in-the-marketplace assistance to companies developing new products. The organization's product collection also provides insights regarding how misunderstanding consumer needs can lead to the development and introduction of costly but unsuccessful products.

Questions

1. Visit the online product collection at New Product Works. Go to the "Poll: Hits or Misses?" link. Rate three of the new products featured on this link, compare your ratings to those of previous respondents, and explain your ratings in the context of the chapter's discussion of consumer needs and motivation.

2. Now go to the "Hits & Misses" section (located within the "Poll" section). Scroll down to "Favorite Failures." Select three of the products featured there and explain why they failed in the context of consumer needs and motivation.

Case Two: Need-Focused Definition of Business

As illustrated in Table 4-1, savvy companies define their missions and business domains in terms of the needs that they satisfy rather than the products that they create. Doing so enables such companies to be in the forefront of searching for new products and solutions that satisfy consumers' needs more effectively than older products.

Here are several additional companies whose philosophies illustrate need-focused definitions of business:

1. *Merck—at* **www.merck.com** *go to "About Merck" and then "Mission Statement."*
2. *Panasonic—at* **www.panasonic.com** *go to "Our Company" and then "Overview."*
3. *Johnson & Johnson—at* **www.jnj.com** *go to "Our Company," and then "Our Credo" and "Our Credo History."*

Questions

1. Go to the sites listed here and prepare a short summary of each company's vision and definition of its business.

2. How does each of the three business definitions reflect the material covered in this chapter?

3. Based on their Web sites, list the major product lines of each of the three companies. Then describe how each company's products stem from its definition of the business in which it operates.

5

Personality and Consumer Behavior

Case One: Four-on-the-Floor

At one time, the typical purchaser of an automobile with a manual transmission was an individual who wanted to save money on his car (an automatic transmission can sometimes add more than $1,000 to the price of a car) or wanted better gasoline mileage (manual transmissions usually offer slightly better gas mileage). Today, though, the buyer of a manual-transmission vehicle is most likely to be an affluent, college-educated male at least 45 years of age. It has been written that "driving a stick shift reflects a preoccupation with authenticity and the unrefined . . . that provides its own cachet in our plastic, materialistic society." The driver of a manual-transmission car is also saying to the world "I would rather drive the car than have the car drive me."

Research results also reveal that owners of cars with manual transmissions are more likely than the average U.S. consumer to cook from scratch, do their own financial planning, and engage in "solo" leisure activities, such as jogging and skiing. They also like to make their own bread and pasta and prefer buying foods that require more work (e.g., they brew coffee rather than spoon out instant coffee).

Question

1. Considering the discussion of trait theory in Chapter 5, which traits do you believe owners of manual-transmission vehicles might score higher or lower on than the general U.S. population?

Source: Michael J. Weiss, "Feel of the Road," *American Demographics,* March 2001, 72–73.

Case Two: Product Testing on the Internet

Procter & Gamble (P&G) is offering a number of different products and/or product versions over the Internet that you can't buy at your local retail store. But a consumer can go to the Procter & Gamble Web site (**www.pg.com**) and under "Services and Offers" a consumer can click on "Try and Buy." Then, for a number of products, P&G will offer you a free sample, a cents-off coupon, or the ability to purchase the actual product online. If the purchasers of a new item offered on the Web site give it great reviews, then P&G will consider making the product available in retail stores.

Although P&G only began testing products online in 1998, the company already is doing 40 percent of its 6,000 product tests and related research projects online. One successful new product that was launched as a result of online testing is Crest Whitestrips, a home tooth-bleaching kit. Despite its $44 retail price, P&G was able to sell 144,000 whitening kits online over an eight-month period, thereby providing evidence that the public would not balk at the product's rather steep price. When the product was finally introduced nationally into retail stores, consumers spent almost $50 million on kits in the first three months.

Question

1. What personality traits (see Chapter 5) do you believe many of the consumers who buy and try products found on the Procter & Gamble Web site might share in common?

Source: John Gaffney, "How Do You Feel About a $44 Tooth-Bleaching Kit?" *Business 2.0,* October 2001, 126–130; and **www.pg.com**.

6

Consumer Perception

Case One: Purchasing Medicines Online

Some U.S. consumers claim that they have been saving as much as 50 percent a month by purchasing their prescription drugs online from a Canadian mail-order pharmacy. The prescriptions, written by physicians in the United States, are generally mailed to a Canadian pharmacy, where they are cosigned by a Canadian physician. This is done because it is illegal for a Canadian pharmacy to fill a prescription that is not written by a doctor licensed to practice medicine in Canada. After the prescription has been filled once, refills can thereafter be routinely obtained online.

Although appearing to be simple, buying prescription medicines from a Canadian pharmacy is not without controversy. Some studies have found that the savings are only as much as 25 percent, whereas other studies have determined that some medicines actually cost more on the Internet than they do at local retail pharmacies in the United States. Furthermore, there is the issue of how long the consumer might have to wait for the Canadian pharmacy to fill the prescription and how long it will take the postal system to deliver it. A few individuals, for example, have reported receiving bills for their medications 30 to 90 days before the prescriptions were actually shipped.

Questions

1. Perceived risk is a powerful consumer behavior concept discussed in Chapter 6. Explain how perceived risk and its various component risks are especially relevant in determining whether U.S. consumers would be willing to purchase prescription medications from an online Canadian pharmacy.

2. Is there anything that Canadian pharmacies could do to reduce the amount of perceived risk that U.S. consumers might experience in deciding whether to purchase their medicines online from a Canadian pharmacy?

Source: Sana Siwolop, "Buying Your Pills Online May Save You Money, But Who's Selling Them?" *The New York Times*, September 29, 2002, BU 10.

Case Two: Repositioning and Revitalizing Classic Brands

Regardless of how well a product is positioned, marketers must often reposition successful brands. Many established brands reach market maturity where the demand for them stabilizes and stops growing. At that point, these offerings become vulnerable to newer offerings positioned as more contemporary and exciting than the old brands. Successful repositioning, suggesting new uses or targeting new market segments, can revitalize old brands and significantly increase their life span.

For example:

1. *The Web site for Kellogg's Rice Krispies features numerous uses of the product, including recipes for special occasions (e.g., Thanksgiving) and "sweet tooth" snacks in which this product is a key ingredient.*

2. *Old Spice is a mature brand that is almost 70 years old. Older men, many of whom are highly loyal to this brand, associate it with the long-running. Old Spice logo—a burly mariner in sailor cap and peacoat with a seagoing burlap sack slung over his shoulder. A visit to the Old Spice Web site reveals that the brand name now covers three lines of men's grooming products, including deodorants and antiperspirants, colognes and aftershaves, and cleansers. In addition, the brand's items are positioned as contemporary and dynamic (e.g., two of the deodorants are named Old Spice "Red Zone" and "High Endurance").*

3. *Approximately 30 years ago, the sales of the classic Arm & Hammer brand were dropping due to the decline of home baking and the introduction of ready-to-bake packaged food products. The manufacturer responded by marketing the product as a deodorizer for refrigerators, freezers, and kitchen sink drains, and sales increased greatly. Today, the product's Web site includes an extensive list of suggested uses of the product for both personal hygiene and household care.*

Questions

1. In some of your marketing courses, you discussed a concept termed the "product life cycle." Do the marketing situations listed here confirm or contradict the concept and strategies of the product life cycle? Explain your answer.

2. Why must marketers of highly successful brands always be on the lookout for repositioning opportunities for their products?

7

Consumer Learning

Case One: Stimulus Generalization, Consumer Confusion, and the Law

Stimulus generalization explains why manufacturers of private-label brands try to make their packaging closely resemble the national brand leaders. They are hoping that consumers will confuse their packages with the leading brand and buy their product rather than the leading brand. Similarly, product names, slogans, or ads for less well-known brands that are similar to those of national brands may result in consumer confusion and benefit the less well-known brands at the expense of the national, well-positioned, and extensively advertised brands. The associations consumers make regarding familiar products and services lead directly to consumer choices and are the focus of billions of dollars of annual advertising. So valuable are these consumers' product associations that many laws, collectively called trademark laws, aim to "protect" ordinarily prudent consumers from confusion. Basically, trademark laws ensure that consumers get what they want; that is, they are not "tricked" into selecting a product they believe is associated with something with which it is not. This means not only that "knockoffs" are illegal but also that product packaging, color, size, names, slogans, and other descriptions of one product or brand cannot be confusingly similar to a competing product or unfairly "dilute" the potency of a "famous" mark.

Ringling Bros. and Barnum & Bailey Circus has continually used the trademark "The Greatest Show on Earth" since 1872 in conjunction with its circus performances. In one year alone Ringling spent about $19 million on advertisements bearing its mark. Ringling's mark also receives considerable free publicity because it is famous. In order to promote the ski industry in Utah, the State of Utah began using the slogan "The Greatest Snow on Earth." Ringling Bros. sued the State of Utah for trademark infringement.

Questions

1. What arguments support Ringling Bros.? What arguments support the State of Utah's right to use the slogan "The Greatest Snow on Earth" to promote its ski industry? Who do you think won this case and why?

2. Why do we care about enforcing trademark laws? Wouldn't consumers benefit more by completely unfettered competition among all suppliers of goods and services? Whom do you think trademark laws are designed primarily to protect: consumers or the trademark owners? How do each benefit from trademark laws?

Sources: *Mishawaka Ruber & Woolen Mfg. Co. v. SS Dresge Co.* 316 U.S. 23 (1942); *Ringling Bros.-Barnum & Bailey Combined Shows, Inc. v. Utah Division of Travel Development,* 170 F.3D 449, 50 U.S.P.Q. 2d 1065 (4th Cir. 1999).

Case Two: The Pitfalls of Reinforcement of Customer Behavior

Learning theory stresses that reinforcement is crucial in shaping future behavior. Today, thanks to technology, service marketers can track past behavior of customers more effectively than ever before and easily reward desirable behavior. Thus, the records of highly profitable customers are given special codes designed to provide them with faster and better service when they contact the company, move them ahead of other customers in service queues, and provide them with upgrades and special discounts unknown and unavailable to other customers. Furthermore, since many companies share data about customers' transactions, customers are often assigned to "reward tiers" before they even begin to do business with a given company because their buying potential has already been measured.

However, rewarding the best customers also means that "lesser" patrons receive inferior service. For example, the calls of selected customers calling a brokerage company are answered within 15 seconds while other customers wait 10 minutes or more. At the Web sites of some banks, highly profitable customers have access to special links directing them to service agents and special phone lines while other customers never even see these links. At many financial institutions, service agents are permitted to grant fee waivers to highly profitable customers while other patrons have no negotiating power. In addition, the special treatment of selected customers also means that other customers pay more service fees.

Questions

1. In the context of learning theory, what are the drawbacks of creating a reward system based entirely on measured past behavior?

2. How can marketers create more effective reward systems designed to shape the future behavior of less profitable customers?

Source: Diane Brady, "Why Service Stinks," *Business Week,* October 23, 2000, 118–122, 124.

8

Consumer Attitude Formation and Change

Case One: It's Raining, So I'll Order Soup

Over the course of our lives, we all develop attitudes toward different foods (e.g., those we *like* or those we *dislike*). While one person may love broccoli, another person might prefer going hungry in order to avoid eating broccoli. And there is one food category, known as "comfort foods," that includes the foods that we eat under specific situations (e.g., meat loaf, pizza, burgers and fries, french toast—really whatever we "love" and makes us feel "safe" and "secure") in order to obtain some measure of psychological comfort. So on a cold and rainy afternoon, a bowl of chicken soup or tomato soup might be "just what the doctor ordered." Interestingly, consumers are more likely to seek out comfort foods when they are happy (as a "reward" they give themselves) than when they are lonely, depressed, or bored.

According to a recent survey conducted by the Food and Brand Lab of the University of Illinois, the most popular comfort foods, in order of popularity, are (1) potato chips 24%, (2) ice cream 14%, (3) cookies 12%, (4) candy/candy bars 11%, (5) pizza and pasta 11%, (6) beef/steak burgers 9%, (7) fruits and vegetables 7%, (8) soup 4%, and (9) other 9%. Additionally, individuals in a "happy" mood are more likely to seek out selective foods like pizza or steak, whereas "sad" people are more likely to reach for ice cream and/or cookies. Bored people often opt for a bag of potato chips.

Question

1. What factors discussed in Chapter 8 might help account for our need for comfort foods?

Source: Brian Wansink and Cynthia Sangerman, "The Taste of Comfort," *American Demographics,* July 2000, 66–67.

Case Two: Domino's for Pizza—Not Exactly!

When you think of Domino's, you think about a chain of 4,800 stores that sells a variety of different pizzas. But now Domino's has added Buffalo Chicken Kickers™ to its menu. This newest menu item—breaded, baked, white-meat chicken fillets—comes packaged in a "grab 'n go" box with two types of sauce and is designed to appeal to both men and women.

Why should a chain known for pizza suddenly start selling chicken? During the past few years, all of the fast-food hamburger chains have begun offering chicken in one form or another, with great success. Domino's expects that the success of Buffalo Chicken Kickers™ will allow the firm to also sell whole breast chicken and thereby increase both sales and profitability. It has been estimated that Domino's may put as much as $40 million of its $115 million annual advertising budget behind this new product.

Whether Domino's needs to enter the chicken business is an interesting question. While its main rivals, Pizza Hut and Papa John's International, have experienced flat or negative store sales, Domino's same-store sales were up 4 percent in 2001 and rose even higher during the first half of 2002.

Question

1. How does the preceding case relate to the foot-in-the-door technique discussed in Chapter 8?

Source: Kate MacArthur, "Domino's Serves Up Chicken Fillets," *Advertising Age,* August 19, 2002, 4, 33.

Communication and Consumer Behavior

Case One: The Growing Interactivity of Standard Television

American television producers have broadcast what has traditionally been impersonal, mass, commercially driven programming for over 60 years. Much like a book or a movie, such programming arose without significant input from the audience — the receivers of the communication. Only after a one-way electronic dissemination did others analyze, critique, rate and review the programming. Generally, Nielsen ratings have been used to gauge the "success" of TV programs and determine the advertising rates for various broadcasts. Moreover, although a proliferation of new channels has somewhat sharpened the formerly blunt impersonal focus of programming, now there are shows tailored to specific demographic and psychographic groups within a more general audience. Until the arrival of the Internet, the unidirectional nature of television remained pretty much unchanged. Viewers may have always talked back to their televisions, but the producers never heard them. Now they do, and they listen with increased attentiveness.

Internet Web sites such as Televisionwithoutpity.com ("TWop") closely track, discuss, summarize, grade, criticize, and occasionally compliment approximately 35 television shows. Although such discussions may have taken place informally for decades, TWoP offers a centralized location where vast numbers of people can virtually visit immediately after or even during a broadcast to discuss their views about a particular show. Because the viewers who post their comments about such shows represent those viewers who care about them, the producers of such shows in turn care about these viewers' comments and they now monitor them to get a sense of what the viewers are thinking. Because television production generally occurs several weeks prior to a broadcast, television producers can and have changed yet-to-be-broadcast programming to address concerns expressed by viewers' TWop postings. Not only can programmers now receive an enormous amount of feedback but also much of this feedback is nearly instantaneous. Indeed, Aaron Sorkin, producer of *The West Wing,* was so incensed by TWop criticism concerning a particular episode of *The West Wing* that he took revenge by writing a later episode that depicted TWop users as "obese shut-ins who lounge around in muumuus and chain-smoke Parliaments."

Questions

1. How is the feedback received through Web sites such as TWop different from that received by conventional fan mail? Do you believe it is in the interest of television programmers to accept and use the criticisms of TWop reviewers and posters? Why or why not?

2. Compare and contrast the Nielsen rating process with the concept of posting messages on Web sites such as TWop about a particular show. How are they similar? How are they different?

Source: Marshall Stella, "The Remote Controllers," *The New York Times Magazine* (Section 6), October 20, 2002, 68.

Case Two: Target Audience

Effective media strategy is the placement of ads in specific media viewed, heard, or read by selected target markets. And yet, in reality, this appears to be untrue regarding TV programs. For example, in an effort to capture younger consumers, advertisers routinely pay significantly more to advertise on television programs with vastly lower ratings than other shows if those lower-rated programs nevertheless include marginally better or improving numbers with respect to the 18- to 34-year-old demographic viewing group. Also, although people over age 50 watch more TV and generally have more disposable income than younger individuals, the key factor in defining a network's success (and the ability to charge higher advertising rates) is its ability to deliver more programs that attract 18- to 49-year-olds than other networks.

Whether the definition of "younger" adult viewer is 18 to 34 or 18 to 49, pursuing younger adults on TV and paying much more to reach them than the older consumers who watch more TV appears on the surface to be an unwise strategy. From their perspective, TV executives are in the market of delivering a vehicle to reach the audiences that advertisers want to reach. Therefore, if advertisers are willing to pay $23.54 to reach 1,000 viewers ages 18 to 34 versus $9.57 to reach 1,000 consumers over age 35, the TV networks will continue to focus on this segment regardless of who actually watches more TV.

Thus, TV networks have pursued younger viewers because advertisers have done so. And advertisers have done so because they believe that, as consumers, these individuals purchase more of the products advertised on TV. Also they believe that by "hooking" these consumers when they are young, they will make them brand loyal for their offerings and keep them as consumers as they mature.

Questions

1. Do you think TV producers should continue pursuing younger viewers even though market research findings suggest that older viewers watch more TV? Explain your answer.

2. Watch a popular 30-minute TV sitcom targeting 18- to 34-year-old viewers and make a list of the products and brands advertised on the program. Go to the U.S. Census Bureau Web site (www.census.gov) and find the link to population projections. Looking at the projections for the age distribution in the United States, discuss whether the marketers of the products and brands that you listed earlier should continue to advertise for the next five years on the type of sitcom that you watched earlier. How about the next 10 years?

Source: Jonathan Dee, "The Myth of '18 to 34'," *The New York Times Magazine,* Section 6, October 13, 2002, 58–61.

10

Reference Groups and Family Influences

Case One: Child-Free, Not Childless

In a recent *Current Population Survey,* the U.S. Census Bureau reported that about 18 percent of married women of childbearing age (15 to 44 years old) were childless, with a subgroup of these women calling themselves "voluntarily childless." This subgroup has risen from 2.4 percent in 1982 to 6.6 percent in the mid-1990s (the most recently available statistic), with all available data indicating that this percentage figure is going to climb higher. The trend toward a desire to be child-free appears to cover all the age ranges within the 15- to 44-year-old group for females. For example, the 25- to 29-year-old bracket has gone from 16 percent childless in 1976 to 28 percent childless in 1998, whereas the 40- to 44-year-old segment was 10 percent childless in 1976 and 19 percent childless in 1998. It is also of interest to note that child-free married couples, in the manner similar to married couples with children, consider themselves to be a family.

Other data indicate that 30 percent of child-free couples are composed of two college graduates (for couples with children, it's 17 percent) and that they are more likely to have professional or managerial jobs. Furthermore, child-free couples appear to be a group that marketers tend to pay little attention to, with most of their advertising targeted to 30- to 40-year-olds who are or wish to be parents.

Questions

1. How do child-free couples fit into the family life cycle discussion in Chapter 10?

2. How would you imagine that their consumption of products and services might differ from couples with children?

Source: Pamela Paul, "Childless by Choice," *American Demographics,* November 2001, 45–50.

Case Two: Who Is Harley Earl?

Recently, Harley Earl, a deceased General Motors executive, played by an actor, became a new TV pitchman for the Buick Motor Division of General Motors. You may be thinking, "Who is Harley Earl?" After Henry Ford and Alfred Sloan, Jr. (who helped create General Motors), Harley Earl is considered to be the third most influential person in the history of the U.S. automobile business. Mr. Earl joined General Motors in 1927 and became GM's head of styling; he was the man who for decades dominated the styling of American automobiles and helped create our love affair with cars. His efforts ranged from the curves of the Buick La Salle in the late 1920s to convincing GM that it needed a sports car with the result being the 1953 Corvette.

Although Mr. Earl died in 1969, the notion of a U.S. consumer falling in love with a piece of Detroit iron has never ended. However, it is generally believed that it is currently the non-U.S. manufacturers that are selling cars that make us want to fall in love. For example, have you seen the new Nissan 350Z or the Mini Cooper?

Questions

1. How does Harley Earl relate to the discussion of reference groups in Chapter 10?

2. Are there differences between Harley Earl and Tiger Woods when it comes to reference group influence?

Source: Randall Rothenberg, "In Praise of Harley Earl, Architect of Automotive Eroticism," *Advertising Age,* September 30, 2002, 22; Kate Fitzgerald, "Buick Rides the Tiger," *Advertising Age,* April 15, 2002, 41; and **www.idavette.net/HistFact/earl.htm**.

11

Social Class and Consumer Behavior

Case One: Make Mine Top Loading

Americans do a lot of washes. Indeed, according to some experts, it is a uniquely American phenomena to consider an article of clothing dirty after only one wearing. Because of this, Americans tend to subject their clothing to more frequent washing and drying, which, in turn, results in more wear and tear on their clothes.

To make matters worse, Americans also prefer top-loading washing machines rather than front loaders. The reason for this seems to be their reluctance to bend over in order to load or remove clothes from the machine. Top-loading washing machines also tend to be larger in capacity than front loaders, so it allows Americans to wash larger loads.

However, top loading washing machines tend to damage clothes more than front loaders because garments are beaten by an agitator to get them clean. In contrast, front loaders are easier on clothing because they merely tumble clothing inside their rotating tub. Procter & Gamble chemists experimented by washing one-half of a white dress shirt collar in a typical American top-loading washing machine and the other half in a European front-loading machine. The half washed in the top loader ended up looking more worn and yellower.

So why haven't a substantial number of Americans switched to front-loading washing machines if they are so much better? Perhaps a major barrier to purchase is the fact that a typical top loader may be priced at $450, whereas a typical front loader costs $1,300, which is almost three times as much. Clearly, at such a price, it is probably safe to assume that only affluent households would consider such a purchase.

Question

1. Assume that you work for an advertising agency whose client, an appliance manufacturer, has introduced a line of front-loading washing machines (to complement its line of top loaders). Considering the discussion of the affluent

in Chapter 11, what types of magazines would you suggest be used to promote these front loading washing machines to American consumers?

Source: Emily Nelson, "In Doing Laundry, Americans Cling to Outmoded Ways," *The Wall Street Journal,* May 16, 2002, A1, A10.

Case Two: Do They Still Make Plastic Slipcovers?

Although most of you probably did not grow up with plastic slipcovers over the living room couch and/or the dining room chairs, many Americans did. Plastic slipcovers, which first appeared in Chicago in the mid-1950s and spread quickly to New York, are designed to protect the fabric of a chair or sofa while still permitting consumers to see the cloth and its design. With plastic slipcovers, someone's head leaning on the back of a fabric chair will not stain the fabric, nor will the color of someone's new jeans come off on the couch. And although many people who grew up with plastic slipcovers in their homes like to make fun of this fact, these same individuals were glad that the couch or chair had plastic slipcovers when they, in their youth, spilled milk or soda on the furniture.

Over the years, plastic slipcovers have undergone a number of product improvements. The use of thinner-gauge plastic has made the material more supple, cloth bindings have been replaced with clear bindings, and nylon thread has been substituted for cotton thread.

Question

1. Which social class, or classes, would you expect to be the primary purchasers of plastic slipcovers?

Source: Barry Newman, "It Seems Quite Clear That Plastic Slipcovers Just Won't Fade Away," *The Wall Street Journal,* August 2, 2001, A1, A4.

12

The Influence of Culture on Consumer Behavior

Case One: Eat and Run

Recently, a number of major food marketers have developed versions of their products for Americans "on the go." For example, General Mills introduced Nouriche, which turns its Yoplait yogurt into a nonfat yogurt smoothie bolstered with 20 vitamins and minerals. And Campbell Soup Company has launched four different flavors of its "Soup at Hand," microwavable containers from which the single-serving size of soup can be sipped. Still further, Hersheys offers its portable puddings in tubes, and a number of food companies now market meals specifically designed to fit into an automobile's cup holder.

One might imagine that the American culture is changing and that it is no longer necessary or desirable to sit down at a table for a meal or, in many cases, to even require utensils in order to eat a meal. Just put your breakfast or lunch in your car's cup holder and drive off.

Question

1. Do you feel that the introduction of these "meals on the go" constitutes a fundamental change in American core values, or do they "fit in" with the core values examined in Chapter 12?

Source: Stephanie Thompson, "'To Go' Becoming the Way to Go," *Advertising Age,* May 13, 2002, 73.

Case Two: Make My Rent-A-Car "Personal"

In recent years, Enterprise Rent-A-Car has benefited by focusing on the ultimate or household consumer rather than the business renter. The company, long known for its willingness to pick customers up at their homes or offices and transport them to the Enterprise branch, has traditionally located its offices in towns rather than at airports. From just 40 rental locations in 1980, Enterprise today operates more than 4,000 company-owned offices in the United States (and several hundred more outside of the United States).

Research conducted by Enterprise has found that the market for consumers renting cars and/or trucks where they live (as opposed to rentals related to business travel) in order to accommodate special needs (e.g., picking up a load of lumber for building a tree house) has been growing recently by more than 10 percent a year.

To satisfy the desires of its customers, current Enterprise television commercials make the point that the company rents a wide variety of vehicles. So the renter is offered the flexibility to choose a pickup truck, minivan, standard passenger sedan, SUV, or even a sporty convertible.

Question

1. How does the Enterprise Rent-A-Car business model fit in with the American core value of freedom of choice?

Source: Jean Halliday, "Enterprising Angle," *Advertising Age,* September 10, 2001, 4.

13

Subcultures and Consumer Behavior

Case One: Subculture by Satellite

Paterson, New Jersey, is situated about 20 minutes from New York City and has a large and diverse immigrant population. Some observers have suggested that if you want to know which houses are occupied by immigrants and which are occupied by nonimmigrants, all you have to do is look at the home's satellite dish. If the dish is aimed to the southeast, it is picking up programming from satellites broadcasting primarily mainstream American programming. But if the satellite dish seems to be pointed toward Texas, then it is most likely capturing Latino, Asian, or Arabic programming.

Direct broadcast satellite (DBS) services have more than 14 million subscribers and are growing at about 25 percent a year. By 2005, DBS is expected to have 25 million subscribers. DISH Network, from EchoStar, offers a number of packages for immigrants, including 15 Spanish-language channels, a six-channel Arabic package, and a four-channel South Asian package. Its competitor, DirectTV, offers a Para Todos package with over 40 Spanish-language channels.

Question

1. What opportunities does the growth of direct broadcast satellite services offer marketers?

Source: Hassan Fattah, "Direct Access," *American Demographics,* February 2001, 30–33.

Case Two: Avon's Anew Ultimate

Avon (www.avon.com) is presently one of the largest direct sellers of beauty-related products (with sales of more than $6 billion), including skin care, hair care, and makeup products. As a marketing company, Avon is well recognized for selling its products via more than 3 million independent sales representatives residing in more than 140 countries.

One of its emerging skin care products is Anew Ultimate Skin Transforming Cream. This product is an outgrowth of some of the latest advances in skin care technology. Anew Ultimate Skin Transforming Cream promises to fight skin aging.

Avon's Anew Ultimate Skin Transforming Cream promises to release powerful anti-aging ingredients—including an amalgam of pure gold, copper, and magnesium—to create a cream that plays an important role in "the growth, development, and maintenance of young skin."

In terms of consumer benefits, Anew Ultimate Skin Transforming Cream promises to (1) restore the skin's suppleness, (2) lift and firm skin, (3) smooth deep lines and wrinkles, and (4) enhance a natural skin brilliance.

Avon indicates that its testing reveals that after one week of using Anew Ultimate Skin Transforming Cream more than 90 percent of the women had improved skin texture and clarity, and 80 percent had improved skin tone. Still further, after one month, consumers experienced a positive shift in the look and feel of their skin (e.g., a more sculpted or contoured look and a smoothing out of skin creases and folds).

The product price of $30 for a 1.7 fl. oz. jar moves Avon and Anew further upscale in terms of a target market.

Questions

1. Cognitive age and the New-Age Elderly are two interrelated concepts explored in Chapter 13. How are these two concepts relevant to Avon in marketing this new product?

2. Do you feel that the $30 price of the product makes it an upscale product?

Source: **www.avon.com**; and Christine Bitter, "Avon's Anti-Aging Ultimate Gets a New Launch," *Brandweek,* vol. 43, 34, September 23, 2002, 4.

14

Cross-Cultural Consumer Behavior

Case One: Starbucks

About 15 years ago, Starbucks consisted of 17 coffee shops in Seattle, Washington. Today, there are 5,689 outlets, spread across 28 countries, with the world's busiest Starbucks located in the Shibuya district of Tokyo. There are even Starbucks stores in Vienna, a city long known for its coffee houses. Over the past few years, Starbucks has realized that a major portion of its growth will have to come from outlets outside of the United States. For example, although there were 281 overseas stores in 1999, today there are more than 1,200. Within the past year, Starbucks has added outlets in Berlin, Jakarta, Zurich, and Madrid and shortly will be moving into Mexico and Puerto Rico. Still further, Starbucks has announced that it will soon be offering high-speed wireless Internet access (Wi-Fi) in over 1,000 locations both in the United States and Europe.

Starbucks does vary its menu according to local tastes. In Asia, you can walk into a Starbucks and order a Green Tea Cream Frappuccino, which *Business Week* has described as "a blend of green tea powder, nonfat milk, ice cubes, and 1,000 years of Zen Buddhist tradition." But in other parts of the world, Starbucks may face stiff competition from coffee vendors who operate differently. In Italy, for example, coffee bars offer food as well as coffee, and Starbucks has had problems over the years with its food offerings.

Question

1. Which of the cross-cultural consumer behavior factors discussed in Chapter 14 might have a direct impact on Starbucks' continued effort to expand overseas?

Source: Stanley Holmes et al., "Planet Starbucks," *Business Week,* September 9, 2002, 99–110; and Chester Dawson, "Starbucks' Asian Tea Party," *Business Week,* September 23, 2002, 14.

Case Two: Baby-Sitting by Cell Phone

If you live in Hong Kong, there is a new way that you can keep tabs on your children and their nanny while you're out of the house. New World Mobility, a cellular telephone provider in that city, has a new service for working parents. Home Care Mobile Viewing Service allows the subscriber to view real-time video through a cell phone. A high-speed Internet connection links a home computer's Webcam to a cell phone that is capable of showing video clips of footage of the home's interior space. Over 75 percent of Hong Kong's population have cell phones, and about 30 percent of all households have broadband connections.

The service is being targeted to working women living in Hong Kong, many of whom have domestic helpers to take care of their children during working hours (most middle-class families in Hong Kong are two-income families). Although the service intends to provide parents with peace of mind, it could work equally well for pet owners.

Questions

1.   Could this service be equally successful in Paris, New York, and/or Sydney?

2.   Would it be more or less difficult for different cultures to accept a new food product or New World Mobility's Home Care Mobile Viewing Service?

Source: Normandy Madden, "Hong Kong Phones Help Keep an Eye on Nanny," *Advertising Age,* December 9, 2002, 4.

15

Consumer Influence and the Diffusion of Innovations

Case One: Let the Robot Pick It Up

Although currently available in Europe and Japan, robot vacuums are just starting to be sold in the United States. Dyson's DC06 vacuum, sold in the United Kingdom, has been called "the first fully autonomous household appliance." In Sweden, AB Electrolux (which owns Eureka, a U.S. brand) sells its Trilobite vacuum robot, a red, disk-shaped appliance, for approximately $1,300. The Trilobite's price is well below the $3,800 robot vacuum that Matsushita sells in Japan. In the United States, The Sharper Image offers the Roomba Floor Vac Robot for $199.95.

Typically, a robot vacuum is cordless (it uses rechargeable batteries to avoid problems with tangled or snared power cords) and has some type of sensor (often infrared) that allows it to avoid bumping into furniture and walls. Alternatively, several manufacturers have developed robots that offer a vacuum feature or that are capable of operating a standard household vacuum cleaner (although the power cord can still present a problem). These more robot-like devices are often programmed by their owners via a standard personal computer; the consumer uses the computer's mouse and appropriate software to "teach" the robot the location of doorways, furniture, and walls.

Question

1. Chapter 15 notes that researchers have identified five product characteristics that appear to influence consumer acceptance of new products—relative advantage, compatibility, complexity, trialability, and observability. How would you relate each of these five characteristics to the acceptance of a robot vacuum cleaner by American consumers?

Source: Jack Neff, "Race for the Robot Intensifies in U.S.," *Advertising Age,* April 22, 2002, 59; **www.sharperimage.com/us/en/catalog/productview.jhtml**?pid= 40660800; and **www. personalrobots.com/inthenews/online/zdnet.html**.

Case Two: Selling Movie Tickets

Although about 22 percent of the U.S. population consists of 12- to 24-year-olds, this age group accounts for 41 percent of movie theater attendance. As a result of such heavy movie attendance by this age segment, every movie studio today has developed Web sites as a way to reach this important segment of their target market. More than half of those between the ages of 12 and 17 claim that they go to the movies at least once a month, compared to only 28 percent of those 18 years of age or older.

A Web site for a movie is nothing new—such sites have been around for a number of years. But ever since *The Blair Witch Project* was transformed from a teenage horror movie into a megahit, movie studios have viewed such Web sites as an important part of a film's promotional program rather than as just an afterthought. New Line Cinema, for example, is reported to be spending millions of dollars on its online campaign for its *Lord of the Rings* film trilogy and will be presenting new online content every week through 2004.

Question

1. Relate the notion of a movie having its own Web site to the discussion of opinion leadership and viral marketing in Chapter 15.

Source: Hassan Fattah, "Hollywood, The Internet, & Kids," *American Demographics,* May 2001, 51–55.

16

Consumer Decision Making and Beyond

Case One: Making Paper Obsolete

One of the latest devices vying for our consumer dollars is the tablet PC (hint: search "tablet PC" in www.google.com or some other search engine for the most-up-to-date information). Although these computers allow the user to write directly onto the screen (with a stylist or "pen"), most versions of the product do include a keyboard. Compared with previous efforts to digitize handwriting, this new breed of writing tablet does not try to convert handwritten documents into text; instead, it stores and retrieves these files as handwritten notes, using a new Microsoft note-taking utility called Journal. With this software, for example, any handwritten word that you cross out on the screen is automatically erased.

Several versions of the tablet PC are on sale for about $2,000 to $2,500. The Compaq Evo Tablet PC is the size of a piece of paper and allows both pen and keyboard input, the Fujitsu Stylistic Tablet PC turns into a desktop PC when placed on its docking station, and the Viewsonic Tablet PC has a built-in Wi-Fi card and a wireless keyboard. For about $2,500, the Acer Travelmate, which resembles a standard notebook computer, has a rotating screen that a user can write on with a stylist.

Consider the typical "road warriors" (i.e., frequent business travelers). In addition to taking their laptops on business trips, their briefcases also include a lot of handwritten notes on legal pads and printouts that have been marked up with a highlighter. It is believed that the tablet PC can reduce and perhaps even eliminate the need to carry these papers.

Question

1. If you were considering the purchase of a tablet PC, which possible product attributes (discussed in Chapter 16) might you use as purchase criteria for this product category?

Source: Chris Taylor, "The Pen as Mighty as the Keyboard," *Business 2.0*, August 2002, 104.

Case Two: A Really Big Zippo

Since it introduced its first lighter in 1932, the name Zippo has been synonymous with reliable cigarette lighters. Indeed, the company's standard flip-top windproof lighter has achieved cult collector status. Now the company has a new product, known as the Zippo Multi-Purpose Lighter. It is 8 inches long, comes with a black or silver barrel, includes a window to let the user know how much fuel is left, has a childproof feature, and its flame is adjustable. The product can be used for lighting a barbeque grill, candles, or to start a fire in a fireplace. The black barrel version has a list price of $14.95, whereas the deluxe version, in silver, is $19.95 (and comes with a pouch and gift box).

A number of other manufacturers offer products that perform the same function, with many being disposable, and selling in stores like Kmart for under $5. However, as with Zipper cigarette lighters, Zippo guarantees to fix its refillable Multi-Purpose Lighter if it should ever break (i.e., a lifetime guarantee).

Question

1. Considering the Chapter 16 discussion on "gifting," do you think that the Zippo Multi-Purpose Lighter is likely to be a commercial success?

Source: Cara B. DiPasquale, "Zippo: Rebel Has New Cause," *Advertising Age,* July 15, 2002, 3, 40.

Glossary

Absolute Threshold. The lowest level at which an individual can experience a sensation.

Acculturation. The learning of a new or "foreign" culture.

Acquired Needs. Needs that are learned in response to one's culture or environment (such as the need for esteem, prestige, affection, or power). Also known as *psychogenic* or *secondary needs*.

Acquisition-Transaction Utility. This theory suggests that there are two types of utilitites that are associated with consumer purchases: Acquisition utility, which represents the consumer's perceived economic gain or loss associated with a purchase, and Transaction utility, which concerns the perceived pleasure or displeasure associated with the financial aspect of the purchase.

Actor. A celebrity that is employed to promote a product or service.

Actual Self-Image. The image that an individual has of himself or herself as a certain kind of person, with certain characteristic traits, habits, possessions, relationships, and behavior.

Adopter Categories. A sequence of categories that describes how early (or late) a consumer adopts a new product in relation to other adopters. The five typical adopter categories are innovators, early adopters, early majority, late majority, and laggards.

Adoption Process. The stages through which an individual consumer passes in arriving at a decision to try (or not to try), to continue using (or discontinue using) a new product. The five stages of the traditional adoption process are awareness, interest, evaluation, trial, and adoption.

Advertising Resonance. Wordplay, often used to create a double meaning, used in combination with a relevant picture.

Advertising Wearout. Overexposure to repetitive advertising that causes individuals to become satiated and their attention and retention to decline.

Affect Referral Decision Rule. A simplified decision rule by which consumers make a product choice on the basis of their previously established overall ratings of the brands considered, rather than on specific attributes.

Affluent Market. Upscale market segment that consists of only 25 percent of all households and 62 percent are employed in either a professional or managerial capacity.

African American Consumers. About 36 million Americans that represent about 13 percent of the U.S. population and constitute the largest racial minority.

Age Subcultures. Age subgroupings of the population.

AIOs. Psychographic variables that focus on activities, interests, and opinions. Also referred to as Lifestyle.

Approach Object. A positive goal toward which behavior is directed.

Asian American Consumers. The fastest-growing American minority with a population of about 12 million in size made up of Chinese, Filipinos, Indian, Vietnamese, Korean, and Japanese.

Attitude. A learned predisposition to behave in a consistently favorable or unfavorable manner with respect to a given object.

Attitude Scales. Instument used most frequently to capture evaluative data.

Attitude-Toward-Behavior Model. A model that proposes that a consumer's attitude toward a specific behavior is a function of how strongly he or she believes that the action will lead to a specific outcome (either favorable or unfavorable).

Attitude-Toward-Object Model. A model that proposes that a consumer's attitude toward a product or brand is a function of the presence of certain attributes and the consumer's evaluation of those attributes.

Attitude-Toward-the-Ad Model. A model that proposes that a consumer forms various feelings (affects) and judgments (cognitions) as the result of exposure to an advertisement, which, in turn, affect the consumer's *attitude toward the ad* and *beliefs and attitudes toward the brand*.

Attitudinal Measures. Meaures concerned with consumers' overall feelings (i.e., evaluation) about the product and the brand and their purchase intentions.

Attribution Theory. A theory concerned with how people assign causality to events and form or alter their attitudes as an outcome of assessing their own or other people's behavior.

Attributions towards Others. Consumers feel that another person is responsible for either positive or negative product performance.

Attributions towards Things. Consumers judge a product's performance and attribute its success or failure to the product itself.

Audience Profile. Psychographic/demographic profile of the audience of a specific medium.

Autonomic (Unilateral) Decision. A purchase decision in which either the husband or the wife makes the final decision.

Avoidance Object. A negative goal from which behavior is directed away.

Baby Boomers. Individuals born between 1946 and 1964 (approximately 45% of the adult population).

Behavioral Learning Theories. Theories based on the premise that learning takes place as the result of observable responses to external stimuli. Also known as *stimulus response theory*.

Behavioral Measures. Measures based on observable responses to promotional stimuli.

Benefit Segmentation. Segmentation based on the kinds of benefits consumers seek in a product.

Brand Equity. The value inherent in a well-known brand name.

Brand Loyalty. Consumers' consistent preference and/or purchase of the same brand in a specific product or service category.

Brand Personification. Specific "personality-type" traits or characteristics ascribed by consumers to different brands.

Broad versus Narrow Categorizers. Broad categorizers are uninvolved consumers that are likely to be receptive to a greater number of advertising messages regarding the purchase and will consider more brands. Narrow categorizers are highly involved consumers that find fewer brands acceptable.

Celebrity Credibility. The audience's perception of both the celebrity's expertise and trustworthiness.

Central and Peripheral Routes to Persuasion. A promotional theory that proposes that highly involved consumers are best reached through ads that focus on the specific attributes of the product (the central route) while uninvolved consumers can be attracted through peripheral advertising cues such as the model or the setting (the peripheral route).

Chapin's Social Status Scale. A social class rating scheme that focuses on the presence or absence of certain items of furniture and accessories in the home.

Class Consciousness. A feeling of social-group membership that reflects an individual's sense of belonging or identification with others.

Classical Conditioning. (See Conditioned Learning.)

Closure. A principle of Gestalt psychology that stresses the individual's need for completion. This need is reflected in the individual's subconscious reorganization and perception of incomplete stimuli as complete or whole pictures.

Co-Branding. When two brand names are featured on a single product.

Cognitive Age. An individual's perceived age (usually 10 to 15 years younger than his or her chronological age).

Cognitive Associative Learning. The learning of associations among events through classical conditioning that allows the organism to anticipate and represent its environment.

Cognitive Dissonance. The discomfort or dissonance that consumers experience as a result of conflicting information. (See Balance Theory.)

Cognitive Dissonance Theory. The consumer feels discomfort when having conflicting thoughts about a belief or an attitude object.

Cognitive Learning. The acquisition of new knowledge about the world.

Cognitive Learning Theory. A theory of learning based on mental information processing, often in response to problem solving.

Cognitive Personality. *Need for cognition* and *visualizers versus verbalizers* are two cognitive personality traits that influence consumer behavior.

Communication. The transmission of a message from a sender to a receiver by means of a signal of some sort sent through a channel of some sort.

Comparative Advertising. Advertising that explicitly names or otherwise identifies one or more competitors of the advertised brand for the purpose of claiming superiority, either on an overall basis or in selected product attributes.

Comparative Reference Group. A group whose norms serve as a benchmark for highly specific or narrowly defined types of behavior. (See also Normative Reference Group.)

Compensatory Decision Rule. A type of decision rule in which a consumer evaluates each brand in terms of each relevant attribute and then selects the brand with the highest weighted score.

Composite-Variable Index. An index that combines a number of socioeconomic variables (such as education, income, occupation) to form one overall measure of social class standing. (See also Single-Variable Index.)

Comprehension. A function of the message characteristics, the consumer's opportunity and ability to process the information, and the consumer's motivation (or level of involvement).

Compulsive Consumption. Consumers who are compulsive buyers have an addiction; in some respects, they are out of control and their actions may have damaging consequences to them and to those around them.

Concentrated Marketing. Targeting a product or service to a single market segment with a unique marketing mix (price, product, promotion, method of distribution).

Conditioned Learning. According to Pavlovian theory, conditioned learning results when a stimulus paired with another stimulus that elicits a known response serves to produce the same response by itself.

Conditioned Stimuli. When new products bear a well-known symbol on the belief that it embodies the same attributes with a name it is associated with.

Conjunctive Decision Rule. A noncompensatory decision rule in which consumers establish a minimally acceptable cutoff point for each attribute evaluated. Brands that fall below the cutoff point on any one attribute are eliminated from further consideration.

Consumer-Action Group. Groups that are dedicated to providing consumers with assistance in their efforts to make the right purchase decisions, consume products and services in a healthy and responsible manner, and to generally add to the overall quality of their lives.

Consumer Behavior. The behavior that consumers display in searching for, purchasing, using, evaluating, and disposing of products, services, and ideas.

Consumer Conformity. The willingness of consumers to adopt the norms, attitudes and behavior of reference groups.

Consumer Decision Making. Cognitive and emotional aspects such as impulse, family, friends, advertisers, role models, moods, and situations that influence a purchase.

Consumer Decision Rules. Procedures adopted by consumers to reduce the complexity of making product and brand decisions.

Consumer Ethnocentrism. A consumer's predisposition to accept or reject foreign-made products.

Consumer Fieldwork. Observational research by anthropologists of the behaviors of a small sample of people from a particular society.

Consumer Imagery. Products and brands have symbolic value for individuals, who evaluate them on the basis of their consistency with their personal pictures of themselves.

Consumer Innovativeness. The degree to which consumers are receptive to new products, new services, or new practices.

Consumer Innovators. Those who are among the first to purchase a new product.

Consumer Materialism. A personality-like trait of individuals who regard possessions as particularly essential to their identities and lives. (See also Materialistic Consumers.)

Consumer Profile. Psychographic/demographic profile of actual or proposed consumers for a specific product or service.

Consumer Research. Methodology used to study consumer behavior.

Consumer Socialization. The process, started in childhood, by which an individual first learns the skills and attitudes relevant to consumer purchase behavior.

Consumption Process. A process consisting of three stages: the *input stage* establishes the consumption set and consuming style; the *process* of consuming and possessing, which includes using, possessing, collecting, and disposing of things and experiences; and the *output stage*, which includes changes in feelings, moods, attitudes, and behavior toward the product or service.

Content Analysis. A method for systematically analyzing the content of verbal and/or pictorial communication. The method is frequently used to determine prevailing social values of a society in a particular era under study.

Continuous Innovation. A new product entry that is an improved or modified version of an existing product rather than a totally new product. A continuous innovation has the least disruptive influence on established consumption patterns.

Copy Pretest. A test of an advertisement before the ad is run to determine which, if any, elements of the advertising message should be revised before major media expenses are incurred.

Copy Posttest. A posttest is used to evaluate the effectiveness of an advertisement that has already appeared and to see which elements, if any, should be revised to improve the impact of future advertisements.

Core Values. Criteria that both affects and reflects the character of American society.

Countersegmentation Strategy. A strategy in which a company combines two or more segments into a single segment to be targeted with an individually tailored product or promotion campaign.

Cross-Cultural Consumer Analysis. Research to determine the extent to which consumers of two or more nations are similar in relation to specific consumption behavior.

Cross-Cultural Consumer Research. Research methods designed to find the similarities and differences among consumers in a marketer's domestic market and those it wants to target in a foreign country.

Cross-Cultural Psychographic Segmentation. Tailoring marketing strategies to the needs (psychological, social, cultural, and functional) of specific foreign segments.

Cues. Stimuli that give direction to consumer motives (i.e., that suggest a specific way to satisfy a salient motive).

Culture. The sum total of learned beliefs, values, and customs that serve to regulate the consumer behavior of members of a particular society.

Customer Lifetime Value. Profiles based on the collection and analysis of internal secondary data.

Customer Retention. Providing value to customers continuously so they will stay with the company rather than switch to another firm.

Customer Satisfaction. An individual's perception of the performance of the product or service in relation to his or her expectations.

Customer Satisfaction Measurement. Quantitative and qualitative measures that gauge the level of customer satisfaction and its determinants.

Customer Value. The ratio between the customer's perceived benefits and the resources used to obtain those benefits.

Defense Mechanisms. Methods by which people mentally redefine frustrating situations to protect their self-images and their self-esteem.

Defensive Attribution. A theory that suggests consumers are likely to accept credit for successful outcomes (internal attribution) and to blame other persons or products for failure (external attribution).

Demographic Characteristics. Objective characteristics of a population (such as age, sex, marital status, income, occupation, and education) which are often used as the basis for market segmentation.

Demographic Segmentation. The division of a total market into smaller subgroups on the basis of such objective characteristics as age, sex, marital status, income, occupation, or education.

Depth Interview. A lengthy and relatively unstructured interview designed to uncover a consumer's underlying attitudes and/or motivations.

Differential Threshold. The minimal difference that can be detected between two stimuli. Also known as the *j.n.d. (just noticeable difference)*. (See also Weber's Law.)

Differentiated Marketing. Targeting a product or service to two or more segments, using a specifically tailored product, promotional appeal, price, and/or method of distribution for each.

Diffusion of Innovations. The framework for exploring the spread of consumer acceptance of new products throughout the social system.

Diffusion Process. The process by which the acceptance of an innovation is spread by communication to members of a social system over a period of time.

Direct Mail. Advertising that is sent directly to the mailing address of a target consumer.

Direct Marketing. A marketing technique that uses various media (mail, print, broadcast, telephone interview) to solicit a direct response from a consumer. Also known as database marketing.

Discontinuous Innovation. A dramatically new product entry that requires the establishment of new consumption practices.

Disjunctive Rule. A noncompensatory decision rule in which consumers establish a minimally acceptable cutoff point for each relevant product attribute; any brand meeting or surpassing the cutoff point for any one attribute is considered an acceptable choice.

Distributed Learning. Learning spaced over a period of time to increase consumer retention. (See also Massed Learning.)

Dogmatism. A personality trait that reflects the degree of rigidity a person displays toward the unfamiliar and toward information that is contrary to his or her own established beliefs.

Downscale Consumers. Frequently defined as consumers with annual household incomes of $30,000 or less.

Downward Mobility. Consumers who have a lower social class level than their parents in terms of the jobs they hold, their residences, level of disposable income, and savings.

Dynamically Continuous Innovation. A new product entry that is sufficiently innovative to have some disruptive effects on established consumption practices.

Ego-Defensive Function. A component of the functional approach to attitude-change that suggests that consumers want to protect their self-concepts from inner feelings of doubt.

Elaboration Likelihood Model (ELM). A theory that suggests that a person's level of involvement during message processing is a critical factor in determining which route to persuasion is likely to be effective. (See also Central and Peripheral Routes to Persuasion.)

Emotional Motives. The selection of goals according to personal or subjective criteria (e.g., the desire for individuality, pride, fear, affection, status).

Encoding. The process by which individuals select and assign a word or visual image to represent a perceived object or idea.

Enculturation. The learning of the culture of one's own society.

Endorsements. Celebrities who may or may not be users of a particular product or service may lend their names to advertisements for such products or services for a fee.

European Union. A union of fifteen independent states based on the European Communities and founded to enhance political, economic and social co-operation.

Evaluation of Alternatives. A stage in the consumer *decision-making process* in which the consumer appraises the benefits to be derived from each of the product alternatives being considered.

Evoked Set. The specific brands a consumer considers in making a purchase choice in a particular product category.

Expectations. What people expect to see based on familiarity or previous experience.

Expected Self. How individuals expect to see themselves at some specified future time.

Exploratory Study. A small scale study that identifies critical issues to include in data collection.

Extended Family. A household consisting of a husband, wife, offspring, and at least one other blood relative.

Extended Self. Modification or changing of one's self by which a consumer uses self-altering products or services to conform to or take on the appearance of a particular type of person (e.g., a biker, a physician, a lawyer, a college professor).

Extensive Problem Solving. Decision-making efforts by consumers that have no established criteria for evaluating a product category or specific brands in that category or have not narrowed the brands to a manageable subset.

External Attribution. A theory that suggests that consumers are likely to credit their success to outside sources.

Extrinsic Cues. Cues external to the product (such as price, store image, or brand image) that serve to influence the consumer's perception of a product's quality.

Family. Two or more persons related by blood, marriage, or adoption who reside together.

Family Branding. The practice of marketing several company products under the same brand name.

Family Life Cycle. Classification of families into significant stages. The five traditional *FLC* stages are Bachelorhood, Honeymooners, Parenthood, Postparenthood, and Dissolution.

Feedback. Communication—either verbal or nonverbal (body language)—that is communicated back to the sender of a message by the receiver.

Field Observation. A cultural measurement technique that focuses on observing behavior within a natural environment (sometimes without the subjects' awareness).

Figure and Ground. A Gestalt principle of perceptual organization that focuses on contrast. Figure is usually perceived clearly because, in contrast to (back) ground, it appears to be well defined, solid, and in the forefront, while the ground is usually perceived as indefinite, hazy, and continuous. Music can be figure or (back) ground.

Focus Group. A qualitative research method in which about eight to ten persons participate in an unstructured group interview focused on a product or service concept.

Foot-in-the-Door Technique. A theory of attitude change that suggests individuals form attitudes that are consistent with their own prior behavior.

Formal Communications Sources. A source that speaks on behalf of an organization—either a for-profit (commercial) or a not-for-profit organization.

Freudian Theory. A theory of personality and motivation developed by the psychoanalyst Sigmund Freud. (See Psychoanalytic Theory.)

Functional Approach. An attitude-change theory that classifies attitudes in terms of four functions: *utilitarian*, *ego-defensive*, *value-expressive*, and *knowledge* functions.

Gender Subcultures. Sex roles are an imporant cultural component and require products that are either exclusively or strongly associated with the members of one sex.

Generation X. The 18- to 29-year-old post baby-boomer segment (also referred to as *Xers* or *busters*).

Generation Y. Approximately 71 million Americans that were born between the years 1977 and 1994.

Generic Goals. The general classes or categories of goals that individuals select to fulfill their needs. (See also Product-Specific Goals.)

Geodemographic Clusters. A composite segmentation strategy that uses both geographic variables (zip codes, neighborhoods, or blocks) and demographic variables (e.g., income, occupation, value of residence) to identify target markets.

Geographic Segmentation. The division of a total potential market into smaller subgroups on the basis of geographic variables (e.g., region, state, or city).

Gestalt. A German term meaning "pattern" or "configuration" that has come to represent various principles of perceptual organization. (See also Perceptual Organization.)

Gifting Behavior. The process of gift exchange that takes place between a giver and a recipient.

Global Strategy. Standardizing both product and communications programs when conducting business on a global basis.

Group. Two or more individuals who interact to accomplish either individual or mutual goals.

Grouping. A Gestalt theory of perceptual organization that proposes that individuals tend to group stimuli automatically so that they form a unified picture or impression. The perception of stimuli as groups or chunks of information, rather than as discrete bits of information, facilitates their memory and recall.

Hemispheral Lateralization. Learning theory in which the basic premise is that the right and left hemispheres of the brain "specialize" in the kinds of information that they process. Also called Split Brain theory.

Heuristics. (See Consumer Decision Rules.)

Hispanic American Subculture. About 35.3 million Americans that represent about 12 percent of the U.S. population. The three largest groups are Mexican Americans, Puerto Ricans, and Cubans.

Hybrid Segmentation. The use of several segmentation variables to more accurately define or "fine tune" consumer segments.

Ideal Self-Image. How individuals would *like* to perceive themselves (as opposed to Actual Self-Image—the way they *do* perceive themselves).

Ideal Social Self-Image. How consumers would like others to see them.

Imagery. The ability to form mental images.

Impersonal Communication. Communication directed to a large and diffuse audience, with no direct communication between source and receiver. Also known as *mass communication*.

Index of Status Characteristics (ISC). A composite measure of social class that combines occupation, source of income (not amount), house type, and dwelling area into a single weighted index of social class standing. Also known as *Warner's ISC*.

Indirect Reference Groups. Individuals or groups with whom a person identifies but does not have direct face-to-face contact, such as movie stars, sports heroes, political leaders, or TV personalities.

Inept Set. Brands that a consumer excludes from purchase consideration.

Inert Set. Brands that a consumer is indifferent towards because they are perceived as having no particular advantage.

Informal Group. A group of people who see each other frequently on an informal basis, such as weekly poker players or social acquaintances.

Information Overload. A situation in which the consumer is presented with too much product- or brand-related information.

Information Processing. A cognitive theory of human learning patterned after computer information processing that focuses on how information is stored in human memory and how it is retrieved.

Innate Needs. Physiological needs for food, water, air, clothing, shelter, and sex. Also known as *biogenic* or *primary needs*.

Inner-Directedness. Consumers who tend to rely on their own "inner" values or standards when evaluating new products and who are likely to be consumer innovators.

Innovation. A totally new product, new service, new idea, or new practice.

Institutional Advertising. Advertising designed to promote a favorable company image rather than specific products.

Instrumental Conditioning. A behavioral theory of learning based on a trial-and-error process, with habits formed as the result of positive experiences (reinforcement) resulting from specific behaviors. (See also Conditioned Learning.)

Intention-to-Buy Scales. A method of assessing the likelihood of a consumer purchasing a product or behaving in a certain way.

Interference Effects. The greater the number of competitive ads in a product category, the lower the recall of brand claims in a specific ad.

Internal Attributions. Consumers attribute their success in using a product or source to their own skill.

Interpersonal Communication. Communication that occurs directly between two or more people by mail, by telephone, or in person.

Interpretivism. A postmodernist approach to the study of consumer behavior that focuses on the act of consuming rather than on the act of buying.

Intrinsic Cues. Physical characteristics of the product (such as size, color, flavor, or aroma) that serve to influence the consumer's perceptions of product quality.

Involvement Theory. A theory of consumer learning which postulates that consumers engage in a range of information processing activity, from extensive to limited problem solving, depending on the relevance of the purchase.

Joint Decisions. Family purchase decisions in which the husband and wife are equally influential. Also known as *syncratic decisions*.

Just Noticeable Difference (j.n.d.). The minimal difference that can be detected between two stimuli. (See also Differential Threshold and Weber's Law.)

Knowledge Function. A component of the functional approach to attitude-change theory that suggests that consumers have a strong need to know and understand the people and things with which they come into contact.

Learning. The process by which individuals acquire the knowledge and experience they apply to future purchase and consumption behavior.

Level of Aspiration. New and higher goals that individuals set for themselves.

Lexicographic Decision Rule. A noncompensatory decision rule in which consumers first rank product attributes in terms of their importance, then compare brands in terms of the attribute considered most important. If one brand scores higher than the other brands, it is selected; if not, the process is continued with the second ranked attribute, and so on.

Licensing. The use by manufacturers and retailers of well-known celebrity or designer names (for a fee) to acquire instant recognition and status for their products.

Limited Problem Solving. A limited search by a consumer for a product that will satisfy his or her basic criteria from among a selected group of brands.

Local Strategy. Customizing both product and communications programs when conducting business on a global basis.

Long-Term Store. In information-processing theory, the stage of real memory where information is organized, reorganized and retained for relatively extended periods of time.

Market Mavens. Individuals whose influence stems from a general knowledge and market expertise that lead to an early awareness of new products and services.

Market Segmentation. The process of dividing a potential market into distinct subsets of consumers and selecting one or more segments as a target market to be reached with a distinct marketing mix.

Marketing Concept. A consumer-oriented philosophy that suggests that satisfaction of consumer needs provides the focus for product development and marketing strategy to enable the firm to meet its own organizational goals.

Marketing Ethics. Designing, packaging, pricing, advertising, and distributing products in such a way that negative consequences to consumers, employees, and society in general are avoided.

Marketing Mix. The unique configuration of the four basic marketing variables (product, promotion, price, and channels of distribution) that a marketing organization controls.

Maslow's Need Hierarchy. A theory of motivation that postulates that individuals strive to satisfy their needs according to a basic hierarchical structure, starting with physiological needs, then moving to safety needs, social needs, egoistic needs, and finally self-actualization needs.

Mass Marketing. Offering the same product and marketing mix to all consumers.

Massed Learning. Compressing the learning schedule into a short time span to accelerate consumer learning. (See also Distributed Learning.)

Megabrands. Well-known brand names.

Message Framing. Positively framed messages (those that specify benefits to be *gained* by using a product) are more persuasive than negatively framed messages (that specify benefits *lost* by not using a product).

Micromarketing. Highly regionalized marketing strategies that use advertising and promotional campaigns specifically geared to local market needs and conditions.

Modeling. (See Observational Learning.)

Mood. An individual's subjectively perceived "feeling state."

Motivation. The driving force within individuals that impels them to action.

Motivational Research. Qualitative research designed to uncover consumers' subconscious or hidden motivations. The basic premise of motivational research is that consumers are not always aware of, or may not wish to reveal, the basic reasons underlying their actions.

Multiattribute Attitude Models. Attitude models that examine the composition of consumer attitudes in terms of selected product attributes or beliefs.

Multinational Strategies. Decisions that marketers make on how to reach all potential consumers of their products in countries throughout the world.

Multiple Self or Selves. Consumers have different images of themselves in response to different situations and are quite likely to act differently with different people and in different situations.

Multistep Flow of Communication Theory. A revision of the traditional two-step theory that shows multiple communication flows: from the mass media simultaneously to opinion leaders, opinion receivers, and information receivers (who neither influence nor are influenced by others); from opinion leaders to opinion receivers; and from opinion receivers to opinion leaders.

National Subcultures. Nationality subcultures in a larger society in which members often retain a sense of identification and pride in the language and customs of their ancestors.

Need for Cognition. The personality trait that measures a person's craving for or enjoyment of thinking.

Need Recognition. The realization by the consumer that there is a difference between "what is" and "what should be."

Negative Motivation. A driving force away from some object or condition.

Negative Reinforcement. An unpleasant or negative outcome that serves to encourage a specific behavior. (Not to be confused with punishment, which discourages repetition of a specific behavior.)

Neo-Freudian Personality Theory. A school of psychology that stresses the fundamental role of social relationships in the formation and development of personality.

Neo-Pavlovian Conditioning. The creation of a strong association between the conditioned stimulus (CS) and the unconditioned stimulus (US)—requires (1) forward conditioning; (2) repeated pairings of the CS and the US; (3) a CS and US that logically belong together; (4) a CS that is novel and unfamiliar; and (5) a US that is biologically or symbolically salient.

Noncompensatory Decision Rule. A type of consumer decision rule by which positive evaluation of a brand attribute does not compensate for (i.e., is not balanced against) a negative evaluation of the same brand on some other attribute.

Nonprobability Sample. Findings are representable of the population.

Normative Reference Group. A group that influences the general values or behavior of an individual. (See Comparative Reference Group.)

North American Free Trade Agreement. Provides free-market access to 400 million consumers from the United States, Canada, and Mexico.

Nuclear Family. A household consisting of a husband and wife and at least one offspring.

Objective Price Claims. Specific phrases that are used to promote a single discount level for a product line, an entire department, or sometimes an entire store.

Objectives. Reasons for why a study is to take place that will help determine the type and level of information that is needed.

Observational Learning. A process by which individuals observe the behavior of others, remember it, and imitate it. Also known as *modeling*.

Observational Research. A form of consumer research that relies on observation of consumers in the process of buying and using products.

One-Sided Versus Two-Sided Messages. A one-sided message tells only the benefits of a product or service; a two-sided message also includes some negatives, thereby enhancing the credibility of the marketer.

Opinion Leader. A person who informally gives product information and advice to others.

Opinion Leadership. The process by which one person (the *opinion leader*) informally influences the consumption actions or attitudes of others, who may be *opinion seekers* or *opinion recipients*.

Opinion Receiver (Recipient). An individual who either actively seeks product information from others or receives unsolicited information.

Opinion Seeker. Individuals who actively seek information and advice about products from others.

Optimum Stimulation Level (OSL). A personality trait that measures the level or amount of novelty or complexity that individuals seek in their personal experiences. High OSL consumers tend to accept risky and novel products more readily than low OSL consumers.

Organizational Consumer. A business, government agency, or other institution (profit or nonprofit) that buys the goods, services, and/or equipment necessary for the organization to function.

Other-Directedness. Consumers who tend to look to others for direction and for approval.

"Ought-To" Self. Consists of traits or characteristics that an individual believes it is his or her duty or obligation to possess.

Participant-Observers. Researchers who participate in the environment that they are studying without notifying those who are being observed.

Passive Learning. Without active involvement individuals process and store right-brain (nonverbal, pictorial) information.

Perceived Price. How a consumer perceives a price—as high, as low, or as fair.

Perceived Quality. Consumers often judge the quality of a product or service on the basis of a variety of informational cues that they associate with the product; some of these cues are intrinsic to the product or service; others are extrinsic, such as price, store image, service environment, brand image, and promotional messages.

Perceived Risk. The degree of uncertainty perceived by the consumer as to the consequences (outcome) of a specific purchase decision.

Perception. The process by which an individual selects, organizes, and interprets stimuli into a meaningful and coherent picture of the world.

Perceptual Blocking. The subconscious "screening out" of stimuli that are threatening or inconsistent with one's needs, values, beliefs, or attitudes.

Perceptual Distortion. The influences on an individual that separate that person's perception of a stimulus from reality.

Perceptual Mapping. A research technique that enables marketers to plot graphically consumers' perceptions concerning product attributes of specific brands.

Personal Consumer. The individual who buys goods and services for his or her own use, for household use, for the use of a family member, or for a friend. (Also referred to as the Ultimate Consumer or End User.)

Personality. The inner psychological characteristics that both determine and reflect how a person responds to his or her environment.

Positioning. Establishing a specific image for a brand in relation to competing brands. (See also Product Positioning.)

Positive Motivation. A driving force toward some object or condition.

Positive Reinforcement. A favorable outcome to a specific behavior that strengthens the likelihood that the behavior will be repeated.

Positivism. A consumer behavior research approach that regards the consumer behavior discipline as an applied marketing science. Its main focus is on consumer decision making.

Postpurchase Evaluation. An assessment of a product based on actual trial after purchase.

Prepotent Need. An overriding need, from among several needs, that serves to initiate goal-directed behavior.

Prepurchase Search. A stage in the consumer decision-making process in which the consumer perceives a need and actively seeks out information concerning products that will help satisfy that need.

Price-Quality Relationship. The perception of price as an indicator of product quality (e.g., the higher the price, the higher the perceived quality of the product).

Primary Needs. (See Innate Needs.)

Primary Research. Original research undertaken by individual researchers or organizations to meet specific objectives. Collected information is called Primary Data.

PRIZM (Potential Rating Index by Zip Market). A composite index of geographic and socioeconomic factors expressed in residential zip-code neighborhoods from which geodemographic consumer segments are formed.

Probability Sample. Findings are projectable to the total population.

Product Benefits. Benefits featured in a product's positioning reflect attributes that are important to and congruent with the perceptions of the targeted consumer segment.

Product Conspicuousness. The degree to which a product stands out and is noticed.

Product Line Extension. A marketing strategy of adding related products to an already established brand based on the Stimulus Generalization Theory).

Product Positioning. A marketing strategy designed to project a specific image for a product.

Product-Specific Goals. The specifically branded or labeled products that consumers select to fulfill their needs. (See also Generic Goals.)

Product Standardization. An orientation for assessing whether to use a global versus local marketing strategy concentrating on a high-tech to high-touch continuum.

Psychoanalytic Theory. A theory of motivation and personality that postulates that unconscious needs and drives, particularly sexual and other biological drives, are the basis of human motivation and personality.

Psychographic Inventory. A series of written statements designed to capture relevant aspects of a consumer's personality, buying motives, interests, attitudes, beliefs, and values.

Psychographic Segmentation. Identifying segments of consumers based on their responses to statements about their activities, interests, and opinions.

Psychological Noise. A barrier to message reception (i.e., competing advertising messages or distracting thoughts).

Psychological Reactance. A state where people become motivationally aroused by a threat to or elimination of a behavioral freedom.

Psychological Segmentation. The division of a total potential market into smaller subgroups on the basis of intrinsic characteristics of the individual, such as personality, buying motives, lifestyle, attitudes, or interests.

Publicity. When messages appear in space or time usually reserved for editorial messages.

Purchase Behavior. Behavior that involves two types of purchases: *trial purchases* (the exploratory phase in which consumers attempt to evaluate a product through direct use) and *repeat purchases*, which usually signify that the product meets with consumer's approval and that the consumer is willing to use it again.

Qualitative Research. Research methods (interviews, focus groups, metaphor analysis, collage research, and projective techniques) that are primarily used to obtain new ideas for promotional campaigns and products.

Quantitative Research. Research methods (experiments, survey techniques, and observations) that enables researchers to understand the effects of various promotional inputs on the consumer, thus enabling marketers to predict consumer behavior

Racial Subcultures. The major racial subcultures in the United States are Caucasian, African American, Asian American, and American Indian.

Rational Motives. Motives or goals based on economic or objective criteria, such as price, size, weight, or miles-per-gallon.

Receivers. Targeted prospects.

Recognition and Recall Tests. Tests conducted to determine whether consumers remember seeing an ad, the extent to which they have read it or seen it and can recall its content, their resulting attitudes toward the product and the brand, and their purchase intentions.

Reference Group. A person or group that serves as a point of comparison (or reference) for an individual in the formation of either general or specific values, attitudes, or behavior.

Reference Prices. External or internal prices that a consumer uses as a basis for comparison in judging another price.

Regional Subcultures. Groups who identify with the regional or geographical areas in which they live.

Rehearsal. The silent, mental repetition of material. Also, the relating of new data to old data to make the former more meaningful.

Reinforcement. A positive or negative outcome that influences the likelihood that a specific behavior will be repeated in the future in response to a particular cue or stimulus.

Relationship Marketing. Marketing aimed at creating strong, lasting relationships with a core group of customers by making them feel good about the company and by giving them some kind of personal connection to the business.

Reliability. The degree to which a measurement instrument is consistent in what it measures.

Religious Subcultures. Groups classified by religious affiliation that may be targeted by marketers because they at times make purchase decisions that are influenced by their religious identity.

Repetition. A basic concept that increases the strength of the association between a conditioned stimulus and an unconditioned stimulus and slows the process of forgetting.

Repositioning. Changing the way a product is perceived by consumers in relation to other brands or product uses.

Response. How individuals react to a drive or cue.

Retention. The ability to retain information in the memory.

Retrieval. The stage of information processing in which individuals recover information from long-term storage.

Ritual. A type of symbolic activity consisting of a series of steps (multiple behaviors) occurring in a fixed sequence and repeated over time.

Rokeach Value Survey. A self-administered inventory consisting of eighteen "terminal" values (i.e., personal goals) and eighteen "instrumental" values (i.e., ways of reaching personal goals).

Role. A pattern of behavior expected of an individual in a specific social position, such as mother, daughter, teacher, lawyer. One person may have a number of different roles, each of which is relevant in the context of a specific social situation.

Routinized Response Behavior. A habitual purchase response based on predetermined criteria.

Secondary Data. Data that has been collected for reasons other than the specific research project at hand.

Secondary Needs. (See Acquired Needs.)

Secondary Research. Research conducted for reasons other than the specific problem under study. Resulting data are called Secondary Data.

Selective Perception. (See Selective Attention.)

Self-Gifts. Gifts to oneself.

Self-Perception Theory. A theory that suggests that consumers develop attitudes by reflecting on their own behavior.

Seniors. Individuals from 65 years of age and older.

Sensation. The immediate and direct response of the sensory organs to simple stimuli (e.g., color, brightness, loudness, smoothness).

Sensation Seeking. A trait characterized by the need for varied, novel, and complex sensations and experience, and the willingness to take physical and social risks for the sake of such experience.

Sensory Adaptation. "Getting used to" certain sensations; becoming accommodated to a certain level of stimulation.

Sensory Receptors. The human organs (eyes, ears, nose, mouth, skin) that receive sensory inputs.

Sensory Store. The place in which all sensory inputs are housed very briefly before passing into the short-term store.

Sex Roles. The gender that a product assigns certain traits to.

Shaping. Reinforcement performed before the desired consumer behavior actually takes place.

Shopping Group. Two or more people who shop together.

Short-Term Store. The stage of real memory in which information received from the sensory store for processing is retained briefly before passing into the long-term store or forgotten.

Single-Parent Family. Households consisting of one parent and at least one child.

Single-Variable Index. The use of a single socioeconomic variable (such as income) to estimate an individual's relative social class. (See also Composite Variable Index.)

Sleeper Effect. The tendency for persuasive communication to lose the impact of source credibility over time (i.e., the influence of a message from a high credibility source tends to *decrease* over time; the influence of a message from a low credibility source tends to *increase* over time).

Social Class. The division of members of a society into a hierarchy of distinct status classes, so that members of each class have either higher or lower status than members of other classes.

Social Marketing Concept. Satisfing the needs and wants of target markets in ways that perserve and enhance the well-being of customers and society as a whole.

Social Self-Image. How consumers feel others see them.

Social Status. The amount of status those members of one social class have in comparison with members of other social classes.

Socialization of Family Members. A process that includes imparting to children and other family members the basic values and modes of behavior consistent with the culture.

Societal Marketing Concept. A revision of the traditional marketing concept that suggests that marketers adhere to principles of social responsibility in the marketing of their goods and services; that is, they must endeavor to satisfy the needs and wants of their target markets in ways that preserve and enhance the well-being of consumers and society as a whole.

Sociocultural Variables. Sociological and anthropological variables that provide further bases for market segmentation.

Socioeconomic Status Scores (SES). A multivariable social class measure used by the United States Bureau of the Census that combines occupational status, family income, and educational attainment into a single measure of social class standing.

Source. The initiator of a message.

Source Credibility. The perceived honesty and objectivity of the source of the communication.

Spokesperson. A celebrity or company executive who represents a product, brand, or company over an extended period of time, often in print, on television, and in personal appearances.

Stages in the Adoption Process. (See Adoption Process.)

Stimulus Discrimination. The ability to select a specific stimulus from among similar stimuli because of perceived differences.

Stimulus Generalization. The inability to perceive differences between slightly dissimilar stimuli.

Stimulus Response Theories. The premise is that observable responses to specific external stimuli signal that learning has taken place.

Subcultural Interaction. Because consumers are simultaneously members of several subcultural groups, marketers must determine how consumer's specific subcultural memberships interact to influence the consumer's purchase decisions.

Subculture. A distinct cultural group that exists as an identifiable segment within a larger, more complex society.

Subliminal Perception. Perception of stimuli received *below* the level of conscious awareness.

Substitute Goal. A goal that replaces an individual's primary goal when that goal cannot be achieved or acquired.

Symbol. Anything that stands for something else.

Symbolic Group. A group with which an individual identifies by adopting its values, attitudes, or behavior despite the unlikelihood of future membership.

Targeting. The selection of a distinct market segment at which to direct a marketing strategy.

Tensile Price Claims. Specific phrases that are used to promote a range of price discounts for a product line, an entire department, or sometimes an entire store.

Testimonial. A promotional technique in which a celebrity that has used a product or service speaks highly of its benefits in order to influence consumers to buy.

Theory of Reasoned Action. A comprehensive theory of the interrelationship among attitudes, intentions, and behavior.

Theory of Trying to Consume. Recasts the theory-of-reasoned-action model by replacing *behavior* with *trying to behave* (i.e., consume) as the variable to be explained and/or predicted.

Traditional Family Life Cycle. A progression of stages through which many families pass.

Trait Theory. A theory of personality that focuses on the measurement of specific psychological characteristics.

Tricomponent Attitude Model. An attitude model consisting of three parts: a cognitive (knowledge) component, an affective (feeling) component, and a conative (doing) component.

Two-Step Flow of Communication Theory. A communication model that portrays opinion leaders as direct receivers of information from mass media sources who, in turn, interpret and transmit this information to the general public.

Upward Mobility. Movement upward in social-class standing from the class position held by a consumer's parents.

Use-Related Segmentation. Popular and effective form of segmentation that categorizes consumers in terms of product, service, or brand–usage characteristics, such as usage rate, awareness status, and degree of brand loyalty.

Usage-Situation Segmentation. Segmentation that is based on the idea that the occasion or situation often determines what consumers will purchase or consume (i.e., certain products for certain situations, special usage occasions).

Utilitarian Function. A component of the functional approach to attitude-change theory that suggests consumers hold certain attitudes partly because of the brand's utility.

Validity. The degree to which a measurement instrument accurately reflects what it is designed to measure.

VALS. (See SRI Values and Lifestyle Program [VALS/&II].)

Value-Expressive Function. A component of the functional approach to attitude-change theory that suggests that attitudes express consumers' general values, lifestyles, and outlook.

Variety-Novelty Seeking. A personality trait similar to *OSL*, which measures a consumer's degree of variety seeking.

Verbalizers. Consumers who prefer verbal or written information and products, such as membership in book clubs or audiotape clubs. (See also Visualizers.)

Virtual Personality or Self. A notion that provides an individual with the opportunity to "try on" different personalities or different identities, such as creating a fictitious personality in an on-line chatroom.

Visualizers. Consumers who prefer visual information and products that stress the visual, such as membership in a videotape cassette club. (See also Verbalizers.)

Weber's Law. A theory concerning the perceived differentiation between similar stimuli of varying intensities (i.e., the stronger the initial stimulus, the greater the additional intensity needed for the second stimulus to be perceived as different).

Word-of-Mouth Communication. Informal conversations concerning products or services.

World Brands. Products that are manufactured, packaged, and positioned the same way regardless of the country in which they are sold.

Company Index

Name Index

Subject Index